At the time of its "discovery," the American continent was identified as the Fourth World of our planet. Today the term has been taken up again by its "Indian," or native, peoples to describe their own world – both its threatened present condition and its political history, which stretches back thousands of years before Columbus. Using indigenous sources as primary sources, *Book of the Fourth World* explores the landscapes and chronologies of this world as they have been seen and interpreted from the inside. Mapping the continent by this literary means, it pays particular attention to the well-documented traditions of the Nahuatl (Aztec) and Maya to the north of the isthmus, and the Quechua-speaking Inca to the south. According to both the literary evidence and the testimony of Native Americans themselves, notably at the Quito conference of July 1990, an underlying coherence is to be found in the creation story told in the "bible of America," the *Popol vuh* of the Quiché Maya. A classic of world literature, this sixteenth-century work sets out a story of evolution understood only hundreds of years later by Europe; its natural philosophy is now being defended, as a way of life critical to that of the planet itself, in the tropical forests of the Amazon.

Taking a skeptical view of the 1992 quincentenary and respecting the testimony of the Indians themselves, this study brings together a wide range of evidence from what is now Latin and Anglo America. In doing so, it offers detailed analyses of texts that range far back into the centuries of civilized life that antedated Columbus.

D0913474

BOOK OF THE FOURTH WORLD

BOOK OF THE FOURTH WORLD

READING THE NATIVE AMERICAS
THROUGH THEIR LITERATURE

GORDON BROTHERSTON
Indiana University at Bloomington
University of Essex, England

CAMBRIDGE
UNIVERSITY PRESS

For Ana

PUBLISHED BY THE PRESS SYNDICATE OF THE UNIVERSITY OF CAMBRIDGE
The Pitt Building, Trumpington Street, Cambridge CB2 1RP, United Kingdom

CAMBRIDGE UNIVERSITY PRESS
The Edinburgh Building, Cambridge CB2 2RU, United Kingdom
40 West 20th Street, New York, NY 10011-4211, USA
10 Stamford Road, Oakleigh, Melbourne 3166, Australia

First published 1992
First paperback edition 1995
Reprinted 1997

Printed in the United States of America

Typeset in Bembo

A catalogue record for this book is available from the British Library

Library of Congess Cataloguing-in-Publication Data is available

ISBN 0-521-30760-0 hardback
ISBN 0-521-31493-3 paperback

Contents

Illustrations

COLOR PLATES

All color plates appear on twenty-four unnumbered pages between pages xiv and 1.

FIGURES

MAPS

TABLES

Prefatory Notes

The beginnings of this book go back to the mid-1960s, when "American Indian literature" gained some currency in English as a term relevant not just to the USA and Canada but to the continent as a whole. As journals like Jerome Rothenberg and Dennis Tedlock's *Alcheringa* confirmed, this was the time of pioneer literary translation, "reworking," as it was called, of American-language texts. Direct involvement with native texts of this kind led in turn to curiosity about their verbal and visual language and continuities they establish over time and the memory they defend. Moreover, they could be seen to have been drawn upon, as palimpsest, by Western authors from Michel Montaigne to Miguel Angel Asturias; conversely, the traditions they represent have incorporated Western texts from the days of the Aztec Aesop. Some results of my inquiries were published in articles in the 1970s and in *Image of the New World: The American Continent Portrayed in Native Texts* in 1979.

In bringing together and discussing over a hundred native texts, *Image of the New World* raised more questions than it resolved. Among the key issues that emerged were script and how to define it, modes of embodying and mapping space, calendars as the reckoning of tribute in kind or labor, the pastoralism peculiar to the Andes, and the links between food production and the shape of cosmogony. Over the 1980s, when native America began to loom larger as the "Fourth World," these largely technical problems fed more and more into awareness of that world's global significance. Offered here, this "book" of and about it does not claim to do full justice to all or any of these issues. It does, however, at least correlate them, in terms suggested in the first and last instance by the testimony of Native Americans themselves, in a time and space their very texts imply and affirm. It attends to that native coherence ceaselessly splintered by Western politics and philosophy.

ON SPELLING AND OTHER CONVENTIONS

Where possible, spellings of native names and terms are those of manuscript sources, though a certain standardization has been made in the interests of consistency; for example, the older form "Tahuantinsuyu" is adhered to throughout, *cua-* covers *qua-,* and the Latin *i* is preferred to the English *e* (as in *tipi,* not *tepee*). Set titles of native works have also been used, and these are listed in the first section of the Bibliography. Dating years B.C. is done according to the astronomers' count, which includes a year 0, rather than to that of the historians, which does not.

Normally, stress has not been marked on native words, especially when to do so would reflect a European rather than a local pronunciation (for example, Tenochtitlán). For convenience, Mesoamerican "number-names" are with a digit when they identify days or years (for example, 1 Reed) and are written out when they refer to other concepts (for example, the person Eight Deer or the world age Four Wind).

Unless otherwise stated, translations into English are the author's.

Acknowledgments

A list of acknowledgments of sources quoted and reproduced appears at the end of the Bibliography.

If the present study is seen to succeed in its stated aim, the thanks must go first to Native Americans who have subtly shown a way, in a phrase, story, or academic response, among them Cuthbert Simon, Simon Ortiz, Roger Echo-Hawk, Roberto Cruz, Salvador Palomino, Luis Reyes García, Pedro Bello, and many others whose names I never knew. I have also gained immeasurably from discussion at various forums over the years, among them the Essex MA group, whose meetings in the Museum of Mankind were kindly hosted by Elizabeth Carmichael; the American Indian Workshop of the early 1980s (Christian Feest, Nelcya Delanoe); Olivia Harris's Jornadas andinas (Tristan Platt, Rosaleen Howard); the "Oxford" Archeoastronomy group (Tony Aveni, William Breen Murray, Anna Sofaer); several symposia on Latin American culture organized by William Rowe in London; and Johanna Broda's informed and delightful seminar at the Escuela Nacional de Arqueología in Mexico City. Other events that have left a mark include the International Congresses of Americanists at Manchester (1982) and Amsterdam (1988), the highly memorable World Archaeological Congress at Southampton (1986), and the II Coloquio Mauricio Swadesh in Mexico City (1990), as well as smaller occasions like "The Mexican Cultural Renaissance" (Warwick; Alistair Hennessey), "Amerindian Cosmology" (Edinburgh; Emily Lyle), and "Textual Authenticity" (Berlin; Peter Masson).

In general, I owe much advice, encouragement, and correction to friends and colleagues too many to name, among them Miguel León-Portilla, Raymond DeMallie, Munro Edmonson, John Bierhorst, Norman Hammond, David Kelley, David Piper, Linda Newson, Antonio Olinto, Warwick Bray,

Robert Pring-Mill, Stanley Diamond, Gayatri Spivak, Felicity Nock, Sister Mary Meneses, Denis Williams, Eduardo Merlo, Ramón Arzápalo, Constanza Vega, Ed Dorn, Alice Notley, Jean Franco, Frank Lipp, Peter Gerhard, Ann Fink, Christopher Peebles, Anabel Torres, Ruth Moya, Juan de los Santos, Michael Dürr, Günter Vollmer, Thomas Barthel, Hanns Prem, Gesa Mackentun, Jacqueline Durand-Forest, Peter Worsley, Tony Shelton, Elizabeth Baquedano, Francisco Rivas, Roberto Ventura; and others now deceased: Gerdt Kutscher, Günter Zimmermann, Sir Eric Thompson, William Fellowes, Alfredo Barrera Vásquez, Peter Bennett, and Jesús Lara. Above all, at the University of Essex I have gained more than I can easily express from friendship and a long-standing readiness to listen and share on the part of Peter Hulme, Francis Barker, Dawn Ades, Val Fraser, Philip Stokes, Tim Laughton, and Colin Taylor.

For practical help and copies of unpublished documents, I am indebted to the staff of the British Museum and the Museum of Mankind (London), the Iberoamerikanisches Institut and the Dahlem Museum (Berlin), the Bibliothèque National (Paris), the Bodleian Library (Oxford), the Ulster Museum (Belfast, in particular Winifred Glover), Glasgow University Library, and the Archivo General de la Nación (México). Jorge Eduardo Navarrete, Ignacio Durán, Margo Glantz, Daniel Dultzin, Raúl Ortiz y Ortiz, Elena Uribe, and other former and present colleagues attached to the Mexican Embassy in London have been persistently generous, as were Richard Watkins, Jonathan Greenwood, and the staff at the British Council in Mexico City.

For research and travel throughout the Americas, financial help has come and been gratefully received from several sources: Essex University Research Endowment Fund, British Academy, Nuffield Foundation, Alexander von Humboldt Stiftung, American Philosophical Society Penrose Fund, British Council. The inclusion of color plates was made possible by a grant from Indiana University; certain of the black-and-white drawings were done by Tony Young, and some of the photographs were taken by Barry Woodcock. Jaime and Alfonso gave support of all kinds.

The expert and patient advice offered by Michael Gnat has been invaluable, and I thank him warmly, as I do Jane Van Tassel for going through the typescript so carefully.

Finally I thank my wife Ana for participating, so that in part the book is really hers.

a

b

c

Plate 1. Text. (a) Deer icon (*Borgia,* p. 53). Among the Twenty Signs, Deer (VII) is drawn on deerskin, on the deerskin of the page itself. (b) Nine Wind Quetzalcoatl teaching the arts of rhetoric and writing at the start of the Era (*Tepexic Annals,* p. 5). (c) Bird messenger on ear adornment (gold inset with spondylus and other shell; Moche, Peru). (d) Birth in the *Mu ikala* (read right to left, left to right, right to left).

d

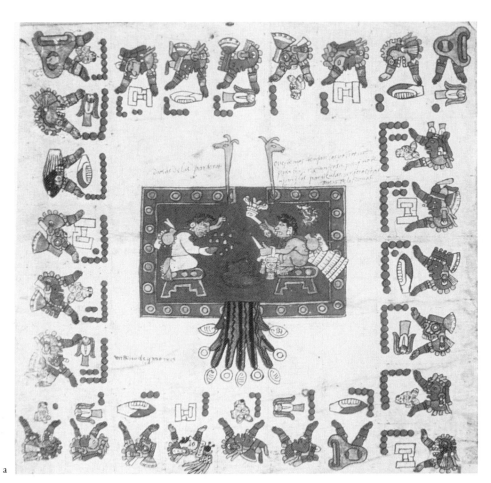

a

Plate 2. The Night Lords. (a) Night Lords as guardians of the years, around Oxomoco and Cipactonal (*Borbonicus,* p. 21). (b) Night Lord no. 3, Piltzin-tecutli, riding a jaguar that has caiman features and whose tail blossoms as a tree (*Laud,* Night Lords chapter, p. 33).

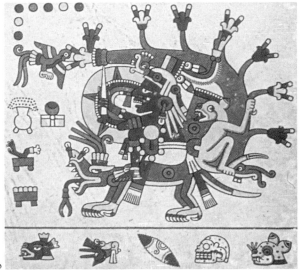

b

Plate 3. Odd-numbered teeth. (a) Bear Mother, Tlingit totem pole. (b) Urn, Arkansas River. (c) Mixtec gold pendant (note the years Wind and House below). (d) Urn, Napo River, upper Amazon. (e) Stone carving, San Agustín. (All have seven teeth except Bear Mother, who has nine.)

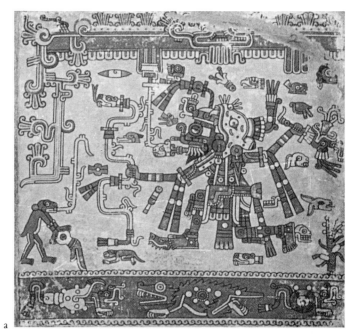

Plate 4. Icons with the Twenty Signs. (a) Tlaloc (*Laud*, p. 45). (b) Tezcatlipoca (*Borgia*, p. 17).

a

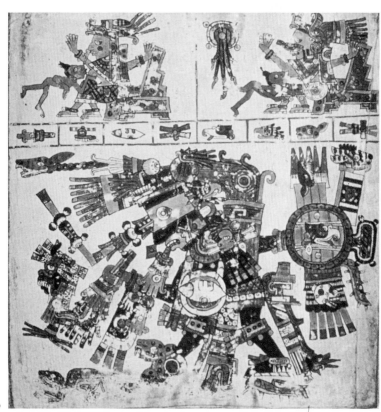

b

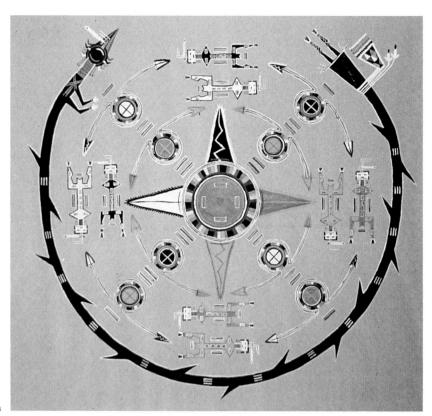

a

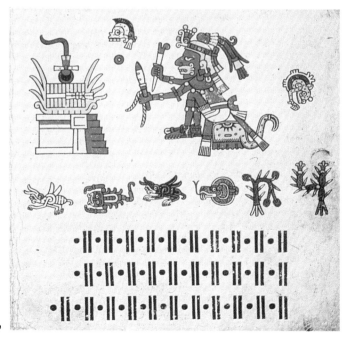

b

Plate 5. Elevens. (a) Star with eleven division (Big Star dry painting, Hand-trembling Evil Way). (b) The opening of the Zodiac Eleven chapter (*Féjérváry*, p. 5).

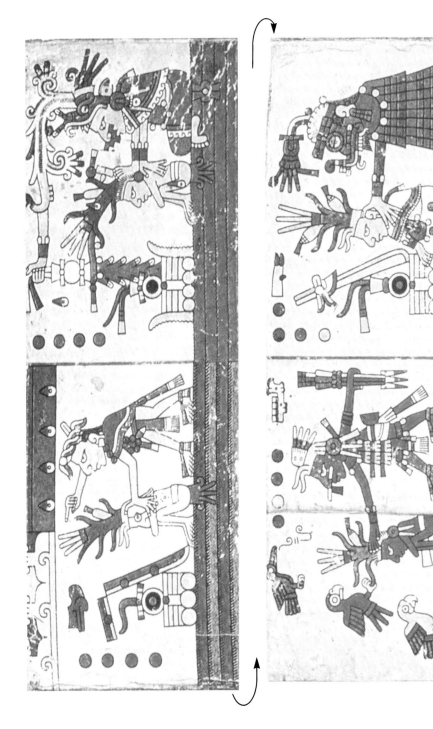

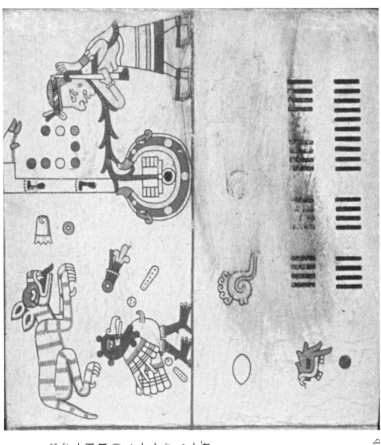

Plate 6. Planting and burial. (a) (Planting chapter, *Fejérváry*, pp. 33–4.) Fates of the newly planted maize, according to guardian, weather, behavior of animals and birds, and the year Signs of Series II (right to left: XVII II VII XII). (b) Miccailhuitl (Feasts chapter, *Laud*, p. 21). Burial in hollow depicted as the seven orifices of an ophidian head (ears, eyes, nostrils, mouth); domestic Dog and Turkey (who shakes the seeds of maize, beans, and squashes from under her wings); footprint path of the traveling soul (the hoof and dots indicate Eight Deer).

Plate 7. Birth. (Birth chapter, *Laud,* pp. 1–8.)

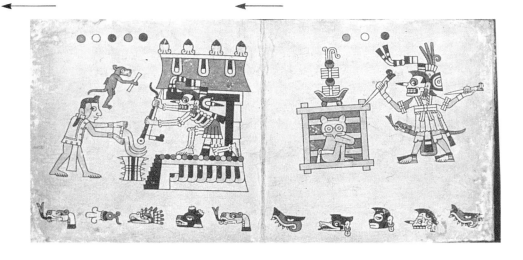

Plate 7 (cont.)

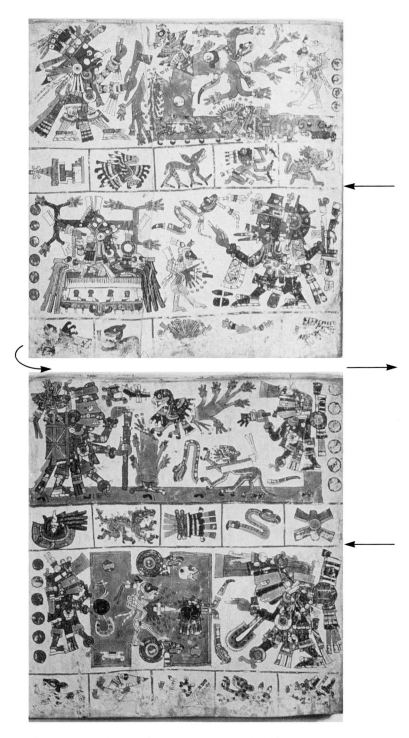

Plate 8. Mores. (Mores chapter, *Borgia*, pp. 18–21.)

Plate 8 (cont.)

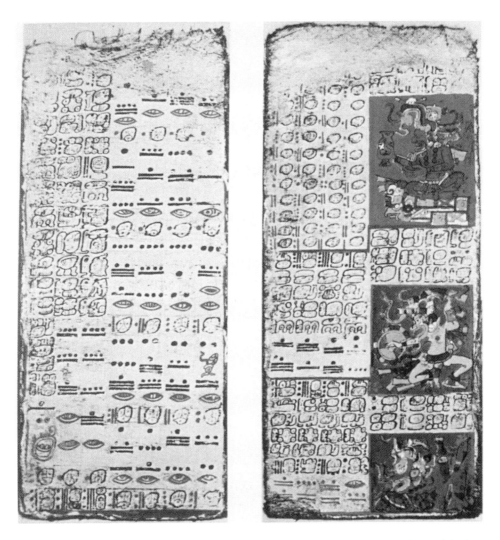

Plate 9. The planet Venus. (Venus tables, *Dresden*, pp. 24, 46.) Initial Series dates in the Era (left), and the first of the five Venus years in the *octaeteris*, the planet being shown in its aggressive heliacal aspect (right).

Plate 10. Huichol Creation. "Womb of the World," Yucauye Cucame yarn painting. Shaped from Tatei Yurianaka's gourd bowl matrix, with wild plants at center (mushroom, onion, tomato, chili, guaje, nopal), Fire God Tatewari to left, Sun God Taweviekame to right; at the corners four eagles rise from the encircling sea foam.

Plate 11. Quincunx 1. Coixtlahuaca (center), Tepexic and Teotlillan (upper left and right), Nexapa and Mictlan (lower left and right); correlated with fifths of the *tonalamatl* (5 IV, 5 XVI, 5 VIII, 5 XX, 5 XII with intervening dots). (*Coixtlahuaca Map.*)

a

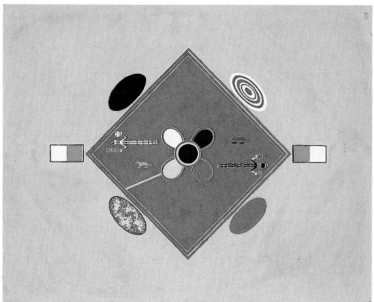

b

Plate 12. Quincunx 2 and 3. (a) Tenochtitlan, the lake city, under siege; Tecpatepec and Xochimilco above, Tlacopan and Coyoacan below. (*Tlaxcala Lienzo.*) (b) *Place of Emergence* dry painting, Blessing Way. Site of emergence and emblem of four world ages at center, Dibentsah and Tsisnadjini upper left and right, Dokoslid and Tsodzil lower left and right.

a

Plate 13. Quatrefoil 1 and 2. (a) Quarters with trees, birds, and pairs of Night Lords correlated with the quarters of the *tonalamatl,* shown as the Twenty Signs that begin the Trecenas; at the diagonals, Reed and Rabbit (above), Flint and House (below) as year Signs. (*Féjérváry,* p. 1.) (b) Quarters marked by Maya hieroglyphs for direction (west – *chikin* – at top) and correlated with quarters of the *tonalamatl.* (*Madrid,* pp. 75–6)

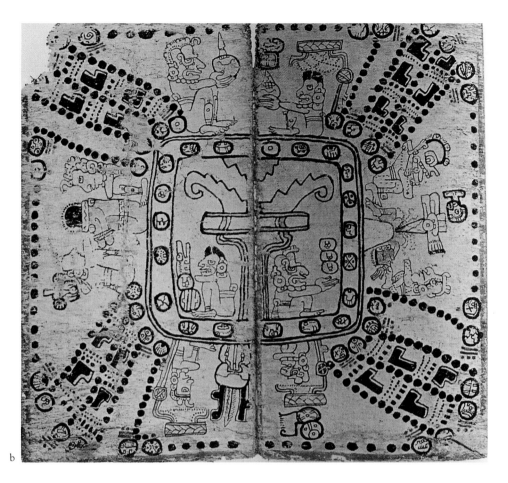

b

Plate 13 (cont.)

a

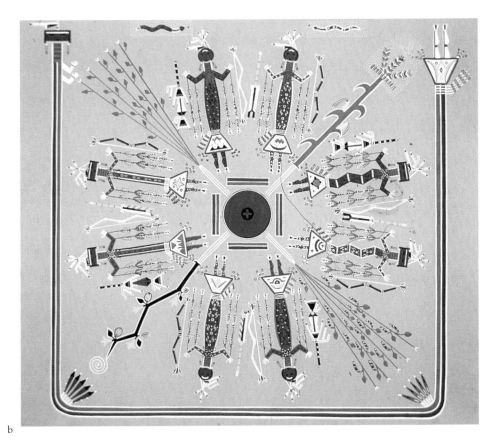

b

Plate 14. Quatrefoil 3 and 4. (a) Tribute quarters of Tenochtitlan correlated with year Signs, shown as House (above, west) and Reed (below, east); fire kindling at 2 Reed 1351 in the outer year frame (*Mendoza,* p. 1). (b) "Red Mountain" dry painting, Male Shooting Chant.

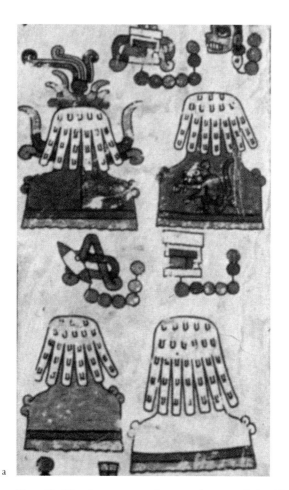

a

Plate 15. The four snow volcanoes that guard the Cholula Plain: Matlal-cueye ("blue skirt," Malinche) and Poyauhecatl ("the white one," Orizaba) below; Popocatepetl ("smoke mountain") and Iztaccihuatl above. (a) *Te-pexic Annals,* p. 14; (b) *Cuauhtinchan Map 2.*

b

Plate 15 (cont.)

a

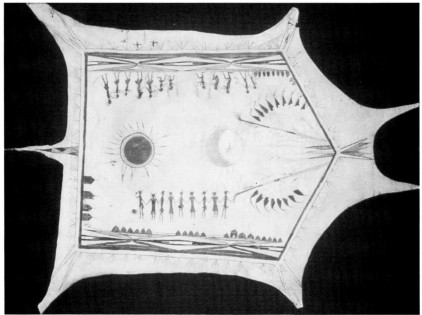

b

Plate 16. Patterned towns. (a) Tepexic as tribute center (right to left): Tepexic (split mountain), Tliltepexic (black Tepexic, checkers), the "old-people" place Huehuetlan and allied towns, on their raised metropolitan base (*Tepexic Annals,* p. 32). (b) Quapaw Embassy. Glosses on Quapaw

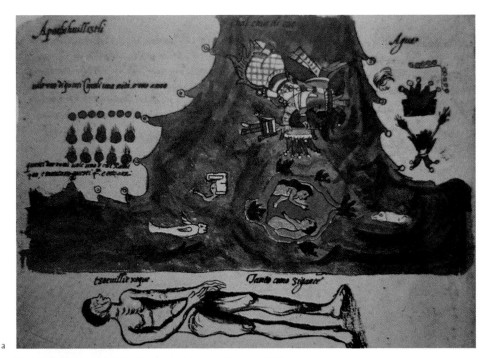

a

b

Plate 17. World ages. (a) The Flood and the giants (*Ríos*, p. 5). (b) Tamoanchan (*Telleriano Codex*, Trecenas chapter).

Caption to Plate 16 (cont.)
towns between the Mississippi and Arkansas rivers accompany the buildings along the lower and left-hand edges (?17th-century painted skin, Musée de l'Homme, Paris, 34.33.7).

Plate 18. Cultural antecedents. (a) Early artifacts (*High Hawk Winter Count*, p. 1). (b) *Boraro*, or forest spirits (drawing by the Barasana Paulino).

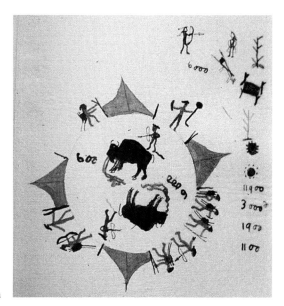

a

b

Prologue: America as the Fourth World

How many worlds define this planet? Where is the heart of each, and its frontier? According to the *mappamundi* invented by the Babylonians and later adopted by the Romans and medieval Europe, there were once three worlds. Within the surrounding ocean, Asia, the first and greatest, occupied the upper eastern half-circle; below to the west lay the Second and Third Worlds Europe and Africa. Numerically, in this Old World scheme, America then came to occupy the fourth and final place, as the *quarta orbis pars* of post-Columbian cartography.

This fact has the advantage of establishing for the Fourth World an identity analogous to those of the other three. It has the disadvantage of the numerical series as such: When translated into time, it militates in principle against the notion of "New World" antiquity.

On being labeled the New World, America entered into a story of depredation for which the planet has no parallel. Despite shifting boundaries and massive displacements in language and custom, the three worlds of the Babylonian *mappamundi* are recognizable today; indeed, they even come to find fresh modes of self-assertion. Hence the rhetoric of black Africa and of a Europe that is making of 1992 the moment to recover the epic self-definition to east and south established by the *Iliad, Niebelungenlied,* and *Poema de Mío Cid.* But what of America?

As a result of invasion from beyond its shores it has suffered uniquely. In the course of a just a few centuries its original inhabitants, though settled there for millennia and countable in many millions, have come to be perceived as a marginal if not entirely dispensable factor in the continent's destiny. In not one of its nation-states is the dominant or official language effectively an indigenous one. Rare are the educational systems that consistently relate surviving indigenous peoples to the deeper past of America, insofar as this can be known through literature and archaeology. Rarer still is the historiography that seeks to excavate its premise locally rather than blindly corroborate imported versions of this planet's story. In short, America is the only one of the four worlds to have undergone through dispossession.[1]

It will be said: History cannot be undone. However criminal it may be deemed, the initial European assault on America happened, and in any case it has been succeeded by another more complex reality, that constituted today by the various republics of Latin America, the United States, and Canada.

A response is this: Of course, but history is not yet over and will become what we choose to make it. At the brute and military level, native territories are still being invaded, most notoriously now in Amazonia. Then, in the populace of certain nation-states Native Americans still constitute a majority and struggle to have that fact respected. Again, thanks largely to revolutionary change sustained to a greater or lesser extent in the Andes, Mexico, Cuba, Chile, and Nicaragua, Native Americans have found at least some redress through law and ideology.[2] At the same time, from within the citadel of what is now called First World capitalism, certain voices ask whether the end of the peoples Columbus began to exterminate might not mean an irrevocable loss of identity and the end of all our selves.

It is true that in archaeology, and according to the norms currently respected by Western science, America's deeper identity is gradually being revealed in terms of language, physiological features like blood group, and techniques of curing, weaving, metallurgy, ceramics, mummification, mathematics, and above all agriculture, which made of it the garden of the planet, the source of all our best food. Then, thanks to improved dating methods, we can now better trace back the memory of the Fourth World's great emplacements, the urban splendor of Chan Chan, Tikal, and Teotihuacan, in its day probably the largest city in the world.

Indeed, American horizons are being pushed back so far as to threaten the once unquestioned priority of the Old World,[3] upsetting that traditional bias of diffusionism which Lévi-Strauss scathingly exposed as early as the 1950s:

> The example of America shows convincingly enough that this cumulative history is not the exclusive privilege of one civilization or one period of history. This immense continent doubtlessly saw men arrive in small groups of nomads moving over the Bering Strait in the course of the last ice age, at a date which modern archaeological knowledge tentatively sets around the twentieth millennium B.C. During this period, these men achieved one of the world's most astonishing demonstrations of cumulative history. They explored thoroughly the resources of a new natural environment. Besides the domestication of some animal species, they cultivated the most diverse vegetable forms for their food, their remedies, and their poisons. And – something unequalled anywhere else – they adapted

such poisonous substances as cassava plants to the role of basic food; they used other plants as stimulants or anaesthetics; they collected certain poisons or narcotics according to the way they affected certain animal species; finally, they perfected to the highest degree certain industries such as weaving, ceramics, and the working of precious metals. In order to appreciate this immense accomplishment, it is enough to measure the contribution of America against the civilizations of the Old World. In the first place, there are potatoes, rubber, tobacco, and coca (the basis of modern anaesthetics) which, in various ways, constitute four pillars of Western culture; there are corn and ground nuts, which were to completely transform the African economy before becoming widespread in the alimentary diet of Europe; then cocoa, vanilla, tomatoes, pineapples, pimentos [chilis], several types of beans, cotton, and gourds. Finally, the zero, basis of arithmetic (and, indirectly, of modern mathematics), was known and used by the Maya at least half a millennium before being discovered by Indian scholars, from whom Europe received it through the Arabs. For this reason perhaps, their calendar was then more accurate than that of the Old World. Much ink has been spilled about the question whether the political regime of the Inca was socialist or totalitarian. In any case it fell within the most modern formulae and was many centuries ahead of European phenomena of the same type. The recent revival of interest in curare should call to mind, if necessary, that the scientific knowledge of the native Americans, applied to so many vegetable substances unused in the rest of the world, can still provide the latter with important contributions.

Indispensable as they are for placing America in historical perspective, these "scientific" data have so far seldom been integrated into the urgent political and environmental concern, new in its turn, that is being felt for the very survival of America's native peoples. For his part, Lévi-Strauss went on in *Mythologiques* (1964–71) to deal with native America just in the timeless realm of structuralism, washing his hands, as it were, of the actual fate of its human subjects. Conversely, many of those who champion the resistance fighters in Amazonia or highland Guatemala do not invoke the deeper history of these people even as a means of arguing title to land.

The medium that offers optimally to represent the Fourth World in these diverse respects is its book, that is, the texts through which over time its peoples have represented themselves, most often despite and against accounts of them offered by Western science. Such an approach is not unprecedented. Among many other works, Nunes Pereira's *Moronguetá: Um decameron indigena* (1967) and Hugo Niño's adhesion to the same Amazonian charter (1976), Eduardo Galeano's *Genesis* (1982; the first in his trilogy *Memoria del fuego*), Juan Negrín's presentation of Huichol paintings (1985), Hugh Brody's *Maps and Dreams* (1986), Angel Rama's superb analysis of "transculturation" in Latin America (1982): All argue precisely against the slippage between archaeology and anthropology on the one hand and politics on the other, that is, the destitution of "the fourth world inside the first world." Refining modern economic definitions of the Fourth World as the one that lies even lower or more at the margins than the Third, Brody announces, "I feel my own need to be clamorous on behalf of Indians – indeed, of all the peoples of what the great Indian leader George Manuel called the Fourth World."[4]

With no lessening of political charge, the approach to the Fourth World made here inquires further into properties of its texts. For respecting the Fourth World model secures a community for works authored and authorized by Native Americans that otherwise they have lacked: In the Library of Congress systems, for instance, the categories Native America and Fourth World literature are simply absent. After all, if the prime function of classic texts is to construct political space and anchor historical continuity, it becomes easier to focus on those of the Fourth World on the understanding that such a world may actually exist. This is truer still when these classics are understood also to consecrate belief, say in our origins as humans or our debt to the earth, which in some way implicitly opposes the whole authoritative and prescriptive weight of Old World biblical dogma (as the Aztecs fully realized when answering the Franciscans in 1524) or the blithe universalism of Western science.

The concept of the Fourth World text and literature in general has been especially fragmented as a result of having had imposed upon it imported notions of literary medium. For a start, jejune Western pronouncements on what does and does not constitute script, and the categorical binary that separates oral from written, have proved especially inept when applied to the wealth of literary media in native America: for instance, the scrolls of the Algonkin, the knotted strings (*quipus*) of the Inca, Navajo dry paintings, and the encyclopedic pages of Mesoamerica's screenfold books. Whole modes of representation have as a result been simply ignored, along with the configuring of space and time whose reason is assumed in the placement and enumeration of every native detail. For using these languages, visual and verbal, the text in this sense may construct the world as it constructs itself, so that its self-definition or ontology corroborates political self-determination. Though technical, these grammatological questions carry a heavy ideological charge, have stifled in their way the voice of the Fourth World, and need therefore to be clarified right from the start. This is what the chapters in Part I, "Text," attempt to do, opposing Lévi-Strauss's and Derrida's respective notions of language and building on the only theoretical analysis published to date of the Mesoamerican books, Nowotny's *Tlacuilolli* (1961).

In July 1990, representatives of nations from all over the Fourth World met in Quito to review their experience of the past five centuries.[5] The sheer number of participating nations, some 120, is more than can be conveniently listed here, yet agreement was reached on eight points, which are prefaced by a declaration that begins: "[We] have never abandoned our constant struggle against the condition of oppression, discrimination and exploitation which were imposed upon us as a result of the European invasion of our ancestral territories." This continental conference on "500 years of Indian resistance" was prompted by "1992" triumphalism, even within American "Third World" states, whose "national juridical structures . . . are the result of . . . neocolonization" (Article 8). The participants brought together political memory, definitively subordinating all local differences in the face of the threat that began with Columbus and has grown ever since. Moreover, going deeper than political alliance, their unanimity was founded on notions not just of Indian dispossession but of human survival. Articles 3 and 6 refer to communally held faith in the earth matrix and to the life and philosophy that explicitly conserve nature's resources, unlike the international capitalism that to date has been responsible for such abuse.

A guide to the chapters grouped as Parts II and III ("Political Memory" and "Genesis"), this Declaration implies a historiography of native America that has admittedly seen internal conquest and oppression and divisive loyalties identified by, say, a type of script or the name of a city. Yet over and above all this, it recognizes in European and Western intrusion a larger threat and order of destruction. This simple but decisive point exposes the ploy that has sustained generations of popular accounts and even academic studies of American civilization; written in this sense from the outside and in a third-party interest, these enforce the divide between diabolically bad and helplessly good Indians, barbaric Carib, Aztec, and Sioux to one side, helpless Arawak, Maya, and Pawnee to the other, denying strategy and memory to all. Hence we begin to recover the "unwritten" history of American resistance that begins with the loyalty of Cuauhtemoc in Tenochtitlan (1520), Tecun Uman in Quiché (1524), and Manco Capac in Tahuantinsuyu (1540) and later includes Pontiac's defense of the Ohio in 1761 and the truly international campaign of his Algonkin successor Tecumseh in 1812; Canek's 1761 "rebellion" in Yucatan, which, carrying forward the Itza cause from the previous century, heralded the Caste War that began in 1847; the great Andean uprising of 1780–1 of the Comuneros, Tupac Catari, and Tupac Amaru II, who, named after his direct forebear Tupac Amaru I (murdered in Cuzco in 1572), inspired the *tupamaros* of the Independence Wars and this century's urban guerrilla; and, in Mexico, the so-called corn riot of 1692, in fact a planned campaign to "recover the kingdom" from eclipse (the largest solar eclipse there for centuries gave the signal). Remembering the rout of Cortes in 1520, adepts in the ancient cult of *pulque* and the women fighters for this cause generated the cry taken up over two centuries later by Zapata in the Mexican Revolution: "Is this land not ours?"[6]

In this way, the Quito forum establishes the decisive principle of continuity before and after 1492, of known histories whose beginnings long antedate Columbus, affirming them against the insistent Western urge to curtail and sever. In the Fourth World it has been a case not so much of the "poverty of history" as of its deliberate scholarly impoverishment. In U.S. discourse, the apocopation has been so severe as to produce the categorical distinction between historic and prehistoric Indians, one now covertly exported to Latin America in the cause of intellectual and physical genocide.

Native American tenacity and resilience in the face of such assault ("the harms caused us"), and against all technological odds, argue for belief that is both practicable and renewable. As the Quito Declaration indicates, its source lies in cosmogony, ancient yet modern accounts of how the earth was and is still being formed and of how we as a species have come to inhabit it. Hinging on the agricultural act, this American story has been told alphabetically from the sixteenth to the twentieth centuries in master narratives like *Ayvu rapyta, Watunna, Runa yndio niscap Machoncuna* (or *Huarochiri Manuscript*), *Inomaca tonatiuh* (as *Legend of the Suns* names its protagonist in Nahuatl), *Dine bahane,* and, the least exhaustible and most comprehensive of all, the *Popol vuh,* the Bible of the continent and a major achievement in world literature.[7]

Pre-European in origin, this literary tradition has been inscribed from the start in the verbal and visual languages of the Fourth World. Updated over the centuries, it continues to be a mainspring of Native American society today, a reason for health and survival. In particular, absorbing the facts of post-Columbian life, it has shaped translation "Into the Language of America" (Part IV), that is, the adapting of imported texts to local priorities. The opposite of what Malinowski understood as "acculturation," this capacity for renovation from within is at last, five hundred years on, beginning to receive some recognition from governmental and international bodies. It is palpably modifying policies in education, where the wholesale drive to integrate is being displaced by a new awareness of Fourth World language and memory.[8]

I

Text

teysokku kwaple narmakkar nait e
    kartakine

ie henikekoni iesaai abina henohenorite
    bikino komuitate kai ari atidiekino
    rafuema

çan ca tlacuilolpan nemia moyollo
    amoxpetlatl ypan toncuicaya

uooh cibin u nuc than

indeed it was all written down in his
    notebook
                – Olowitinappi's report

then at the foot of the sky Rafuema
    thought hard about the story told
    here
                – Witoto Genesis

in this painted space your heart lives
    in this woven book you sing
                – Cantares mexicanos

the word-glyph shall give us the
    answer
                – Ritual of the Bacabs

1

Provenance

CIRCUM-CARIBBEAN

What's in a place name? In the opinion of the Aymara leader Takir Mamani, "calling our cities, towns and continents by a foreign name means subjecting ourselves to the will of our invaders and their descendants."[1] In fact, though European nomenclature abounds on today's maps of Latin America, the United States, and Canada, so does that of its substratum. These native names are, of course, filtered through the languages of the Spanish, French, Portuguese, and English invaders; and they sometimes indicate displacement rather than origin, like Potosi, transposed from the mines of the Andes to those of Mexico; Miami, the Algonkin nation of the Ohio who were removed to and named a town in Florida; or Copacabana, the Aymara shrine on Lake Titicaca that now also identifies the beach at Rio de Janeiro. Similarly, the native name will often be the only memorial to people exterminated or removed entirely from their territory. Yet, easily accessible and little used, this cartographic evidence has its value as a means of orienting us in the first instance. Through their native syllables, clusters of towns plot the great polities of the past, and toponyms more generally reveal the shapes of cultures distorted and dismembered by invasion but alive still in native thought, language, and custom (Map 1).

In turn, this exercise becomes a means for approaching native texts, since the data that survive on today's maps often provide clues to the very different geography that these texts record and defend. This is especially so with the great charter texts of the Fourth World nations, which from given centers and arenas of provenance establish patterns and lines of coherence, paradigms of territory, and ancient paths over the seas and lands of North and South America.

Bright with coral, the American sea first plundered by Europe is its Mediterranean, the Caribbean that takes its name from the Caribs. An emporium and focus of migrations over thousands of years, this sea in fact conjoins the three cultures that principally shared its shores, Carib, Maya, and Chibcha, and through them their hinterland and the continent more generally. Its eastern arc, which admitted Columbus and fellow voyagers from the Atlantic, was dominated by the Carib and the Arawak, whose common history had grown out from the rainforest of the tropical South American lowlands. Together these people have in fact supplied names not just for the sea once plied by their great canoes (also their word) but for the archipelago to the east and the mainland to the south: Tobago, Haiti, Cuba, Jamaica, Aruba, Maracaibo, Caracas, and Guyana. After resisting militarily for over three centuries, the island Carib succumbed to sugar capitalism, though now on Dominica and elsewhere survivors are regaining their history.[2] On the mainland they and the Arawak have held onto their strongholds, defended by the rainforest and the rapids of north–flowing rivers. A model case is that of the Makiritare, or Soto Carib, who live near the headwaters of the Orinoco at the western end of the Pacaraima ridge that runs from Roraima to Marahuaka; their great narrative *Watunna* surveys the Caribbean Sea (*dama*) and the mainland peoples from the Orinoco estuary across to the present borders of Venezuela with Guyana, Brazil, and Colombia. Exemplified in *Watunna* and its companion piece *Medatia,* as well as *Tauron panton* of the Pemon and *Makunaima* of the Taulipang and Arekuna, this highly coherent tradition recounts the cosmic beginnings of highland Carib territory and diagnose in Columbus a cause of the homicidal madness known as *kanaima.*

Beyond the western tip of Cuba and extending into the Gulf of Mexico, the Caribbean washes a further arc of shore recognized as the "land of the Maya" by Columbus when he intercepted a large trading canoe off the Honduran coast in 1502. The Maya are still there today, in the lowland area that comprises the Motagua estuary, Peten, Belize, and the Yucatan peninsula, and in the highlands centered on the uppermost Motagua and mountainous Quiché in southern Guatemala. In the extensive literature of the Maya, notably the lowland *Books of Chilam Balam* and the highland *Popol vuh,* the Caribbean features as an eastern source of life and light strangely contraverted by European invaders.[3] The *Books of Chilam Balam* also record the names of over a hundred Yucatec towns that are still Maya, not least those from which surviving examples of these texts stem, like Chumayel, Tizimin, Mani, Oxcutzcab, and Kaua. Culturally the Maya belong to Mesoamerica, a region defined precisely by its wealth of literature, scripts, and calendars, and which also includes Nahuatl, the language of the Aztecs, as well as older Otomanguan and Mixe–Zoque tongues whose history goes back to the beginning of urban development, before 1000 B.C. The remarkable consistency of life in Mesoamerica is, incidentally, reflected in the fact

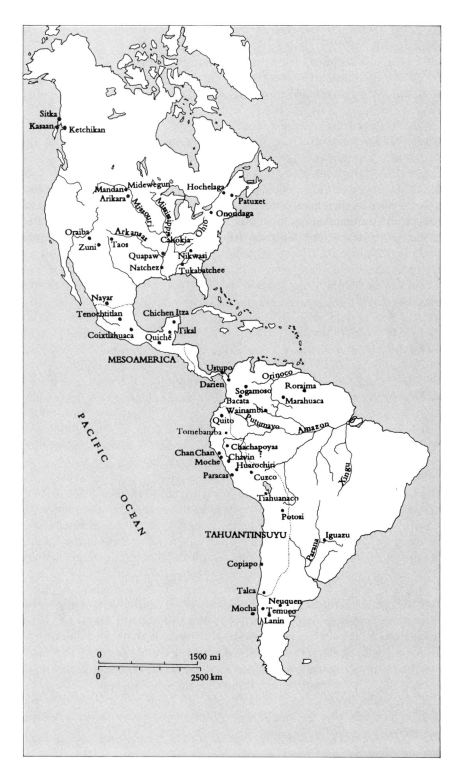

Sitka
Kasaan Ketchikan

Mandan Midewegun Hochelaga
Arikara Patuxet
Missouri Mississippi Ohio Onondaga
Oraiba Arkansas Cahokia
Zuni Taos
Quapaw Nikwasi
Natchez Tukabatchee

Nayar
Tenochtitlan Chichen Itza
Coixtlahuaca Quiche Tikal

MESOAMERICA

PACIFIC

Ustupo Orinoco
Darien Roraima
Sogamoso
Bacata Marahuaca
Wainambi
Quito Putumayo Amazon
Tomebamba
Chan Chan Chachapoyas
Moche Chavin
Huarochiri
Paracas Cuzco
Xingu
Tiahuanaco

OCEAN Potosi

TAHUANTINSUYU Parana Iguazu

Copiapo

Talca Neuquen
Mocha Temuco
Lanin

0   1500 mi

0   2500 km

Map 1. Native settlements in America.

that the canoe cargo inventoried by Columbus – maize and other food-stuffs, cotton garments, copper axes, and cacao beans – reads like a page from the tribute books kept by Moctezuma in the Aztec capital Tenochtitlan far away at the western end of Mesoamerica.

Running between Maracaibo and Nicaragua, the remaining arc of the Caribbean hinges on the Gulf of Darien and the isthmus of Panama, the "place of fishermen" that served as a gateway to the Pacific and the empires of Peru long before the days of Balboa and Pizarro. It belonged primarily to the Chibcha goldworkers, varieties of whose language were then spoken all over the territory that became New Granada and Greater Colombia. Responsible for an exquisite lexicon in gold, in Tairona and Sinu, this culture has offspring today among Chibcha-speakers who live along or near the coast, like the Kogi on the slopes of snow-capped Santa Marta, the Cuna at Ustupo, Mulatupo, and other island towns (*tup*) in Panama, and the Talamanca in Costa Rica, as well as the Paez at the very head of the Magdalena and Cauca rivers at the grand watershed marked by the tombs of Tierradentro and the stelae of San Agustín. The major history of the Cuna, *Tatkan ikala,* starts with creation and the deeds of epic heroes (*nele*s) borne in on golden plates, of the kind produced in quantity in Panama and exported as far as the Maya city of Chichen Itza in northern Yucatan. Subsequently we hear how the gold-hungry Spaniards tortured Iguab, and of French "sea birds" who consume voraciously and foul their resting places; forts built like Cartagena in the sixteenth century are said to threaten the souls of the Cuna ancestors.[4] Invoking this history has been an important factor in Cuna relations with the Panamanian government, especially when in 1925 under Nele Kantule they declared an independent republic.

Beginning in 1502, the upriver assault, so violent as to erase the "lost kingdom" of Dabeiba from the map, reverberated to the dense network of towns in the valley of Bacata (Bogotá), suddenly ending the construction of Chacha's palace at Ramiriqui and leaving its pillars as mute horizontal testimony to change. The great concentration of Chibcha towns in the Bacata basin, fief to the deity Chibchachun, is still there in name, and elaborate goldwork depicts the raft ceremony of El Dorado, the kernel of the legend, in which offerings were made to Lake Guatavita. From the eastern plains and *Watunna*'s rainforest, the source of excellent hardwoods, a causeway reaches up to Sogamoso, the shrine of Bochica and the Rome of these towns. Their inherited rights, for example, to the salt mines at Zipaquira, played a part in the Comuneros uprising of 1781, yet the language had long vanished and with it most record and memory. This loss becomes the more acute given the centrality of Bacata within the Chibcha realm and of the Chibcha realm within the Fourth World, mediating as it does between rainforest and Pacific, the Inca and the Aztec empires, and Carib and Maya neighbors along the Caribbean shore.

As the Fourth World's Mediterranean, the Caribbean has long conjoined the two great halves of the continent in a tropical amalgam characteristic of its shores and hinterland. Accordingly, *Watunna,* the *Popol vuh,* the *Chilam Balam Books, Tatkan ikala,* and other texts remind us that this is the place of the cotton hammock that cradles dreams under palm thatch; the tropical food garden – *milpa* of maize, *conuco* of lowland manioc (bitter in Guyana, sweet in Panama and Yucatan) – that is respected as a sacred space; poisons that stun fish, tip blowgun darts, and cure infection; rubber-tree sap from which the ballplayer extracts a game; quartz crystal held by the diviner to be the semen of lightning; the eerie "double-ego" stelae (with a feline or ophidian head surmounting that of a human) that face each other across the miles that separate Nicaragua from Tierradentro; the mighty one-legged Storm revered as an effigy (*zemi*) in Jamaica and as Hurucan (whence "hurricane") in Quiché; the prehistoric caiman, and the jaguar with its star-inscribed pelt; the troupe of thirteen bird-dancers that at the solstice commemorates the moons of the year at festivals of the Carib in Essequibo and Surinam and of the Chibcha at Sogamoso, and which appears as the set of Thirteen Quecholli, or "fliers," on the pages of Mesoamerican books; the monkey, tailed half-brother, and the human who is defined numerically in Carib, Maya, and Chibcha alike as the true owner of twenty agile digits that count works and days.[5]

MESOAMERICA

A community over millennia, Mesoamerica extends from Nicaragua in the east to Michoacan in the west, finding its coherence in economy, agriculture, town planning, language, calendars, and the use of books of paper and skin, folded characteristically as a screen. In their own right and as the palimpsest of alphabetic texts written in the main literary languages of the area – Nahuatl and lowland and highland Maya – these screenfold books authoritatively map Mesoamerica, whose contours underlie those of New Spain, Europe's major acquisition in the Fourth World (Map 2).[6]

Thanks partly to Aztec hegemony and to the ambitions of its opponents, the Tlaxcalan allies of Cortes, Nahuatl was the most widespread Mesoamerican language in the early sixteenth century, and it names the three main nation-states found there today: Nicaragua (*Nican-nahua,* where the Nahua are), Guatemala (*Cuauhtemallan,* place of fine wood, equivalent in meaning to the Maya *Qui-ché*), and Mexico. It also names non-Nahuatl peoples like the Otomanguan Mazatec (deer people), Popoloca (destroyers), Mixtec (cloud people), Zapotec and Otomi, and the Maya Chontal (of another language), provinces like Cozcatlan (necklace place, later El Salvador), Chiapas (Chiapan, *chia*-river), Oaxaca (Huaxyacac, *guaje*-fruit promontory), and Michoacan (fish place), as well as literally thousands of local

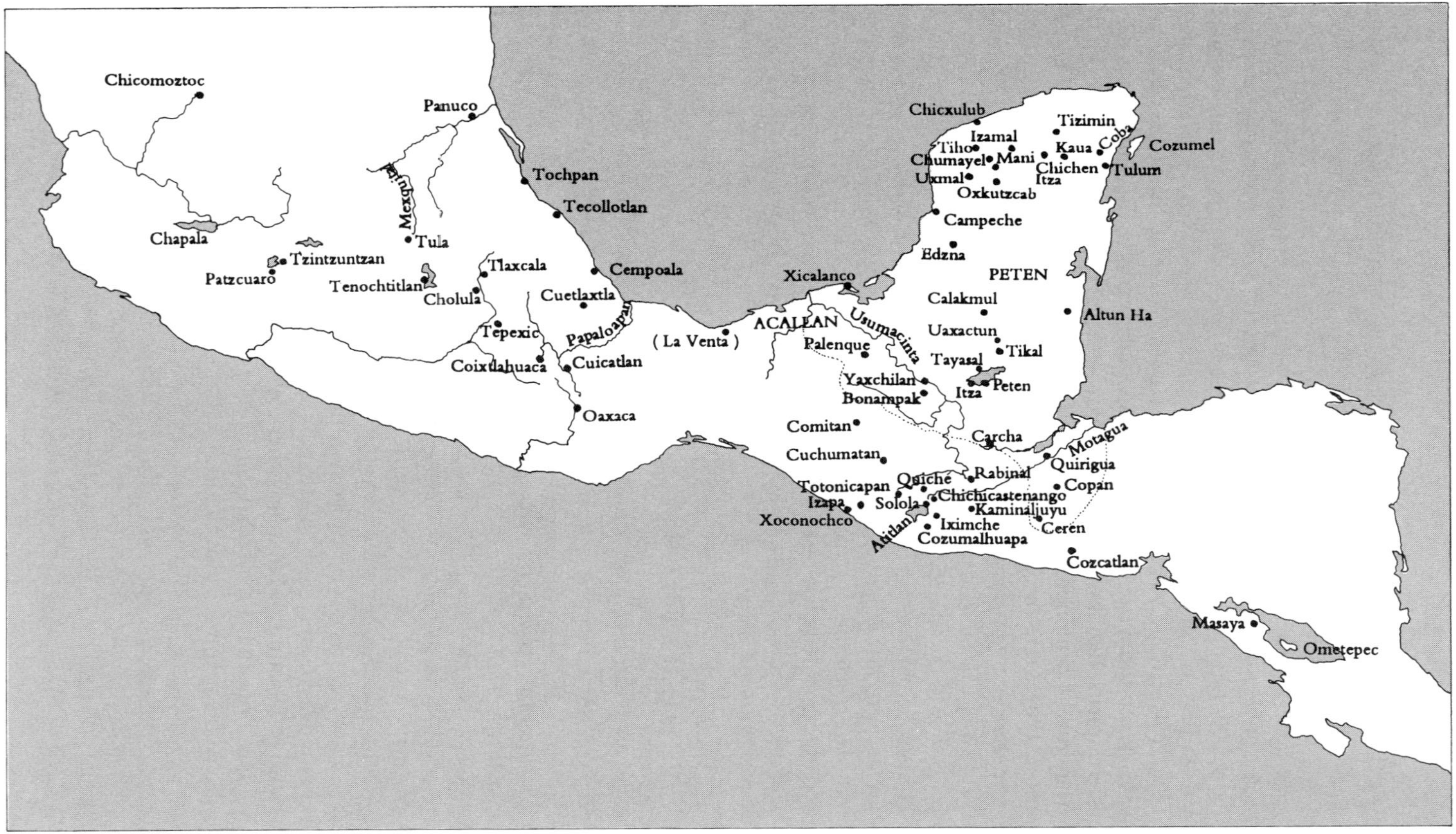

Map 2. Mesoamerica.

toponyms that dot the whole area with such characteristic endings as -*tlan* (tooth or simply place), -*tepec* (pyramid or mountain), -*apan* (river), -*tenanco* (fort), -*milco* (field shrine), and -*calco* (house shrine).

Beneath its geographical and linguistic diversity, Mesoamerica found its surest agreement in how to define and measure time, especially the seasonal year with its eighteen Feasts of twenty days, and human pregnancy with its nine moons and 260 nights. Everywhere acknowledged as fundamental, these cycles decidedly modified the imposed rhythms of the Christian calendar and even today are felt and calculated in daily life, along with vestiges of ancient spirits, like the *gloriosus huehuentzin* seen at carnaval from Tlaxcala to Nicaragua.[7] Combined and used in different ways according to region and period, they were integrated into the two main types of Mesoamerican script, the hieroglyphics of the Maya lowlands and the iconic script used outside that area.

A panoramic view of Mesoamerica is afforded us by the highland Maya who occupy its middle ground and who have staked their rights to it in sixteenth-century "titles" that range far in time and space, notably the *Cakchiquel Annals* of Sololá and the Quiché *Popol vuh,* which explicitly claims to have been transcribed from an original in native script. An important supplement to these Maya sources is the *Tlaxcala Lienzo,* which in iconic script records the campaigns of conquest waged through Mesoamerica from 1519 onward (Fig. 1).[8] On this evidence, Mesoamerica falls in the first instance into three parts, determined respectively by the groups of settlers said to have emerged from the east, or sunrise. In the middle, the principal groups of highland Maya converge, Quiché, Cakchiquel, and Zutuhil, who share a history as they continue to share the shores of the crystalline oval Lake Atitlan (also Nahachel or Chi-aa; Fig. 1c), and the cult of Maximon. North of here, between the arms of the Motagua and Usumacinta, lie Peten and the territory of the lowland Maya, studded with such ancient cities as Palenque, Yaxchilan, Tikal, Quirigua, and Copan. Inscribed in the hieroglyphic script of the lowland Maya, monuments in these cities precisely date Mesoamerica's Classic period (A.D. 300–900) and map its densely urban geography and network of *zac-be* (paved roads); they stand as the antecedent for the three or four surviving hieroglyphic books from the post-Classic and, in turn, for the alphabetic *Chilam Balam Books* of Chumayel, Tizimin, Mani, and other towns in Yucatan. They also feed into what has been called the Lacandon *Book of Chan Kin.*[9]

From their capital Cumaracaah (Utatlan), near present-day Quiché Santa Cruz, the Quiché dominated the north, yet only as far as the boundary with the lowland hieroglyphic zone; they name as their outposts such towns as Carchah and Rabinal – the provenance of *Rabinal Achi,* a four-act tragedy about a captive Quiché knight.[10] For their part, the Cakchiquel pressed south toward the lush Pacific piedmont, the site of such ancient cities as

Figure 1. Places between Nicaragua and California: (a) Cholula; (b) Tonatiuh Ihuecotian (California); (c) Tecpan Atitlan (Guatemala); (d) Cozcatlan (El Salvador); (e) Cozamaloapan; (f) Atlpopocayan (Masaya, Nicaragua). (*Tlaxcala Codex,* Scenes 36, 100, 105, 121, 134, and 139.)

Cozumalhuapa, the "rainbow" town (Fig. 1e) that in their geography formed part of the nether region generally known as Xibalba, the counterpart of the "place where God is," or north. From their middle position in Mesoamerica, the *Popol vuh* and the *Cakchiquel Annals* refer principally, however, to the territories to either side, east and west. In the *Popol vuh* the easterners are those who "stayed at sunrise," the "fish keepers" (Chahkar) and "rubber people" (Oliman, like Olmec, from the Nahuatl *ollin:* "rubber, movement, or earthquake"); salient along the eastern settlements depicted in the *Lienzo* is Masaya, a volcano of active flames and a local center of worship[11] (Fig. 1f). To the west and "what is called Mexico today" are assigned the Nahuatl-speakers, who include the Aztecs, or Mexica, who founded Tenochtitlan close to Mesoamerica's western frontier, and the Yaqui, who as "travelers" passed beyond it. From their western stronghold, the Mexica connected their name with the new moon (*meztli*), the actual emblem of the western frontier state of Metztitlan in the *Lienzo* and later the heraldic device of the most Mexican Virgin of Guadalupe.

The logic of the east–west axis, confirmed in the Quiché and Cakchiquel texts by explicit reference to the rising of both sun and Venus, has often been overlooked in our scholarship, though it was clearly enough perceived by the first European arrivals in Mesoamerica, who placed the seas of those

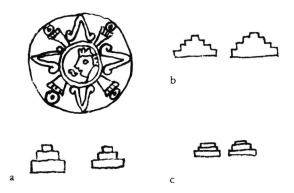

Figure 2. Pyramids of sun and moon at Teotihuacan: (a) *Huamantla Codex,* (b) *Xolotl Map 1,* (c) *Tlatelolco Map.*

latitudes (Atlantic and Pacific) north and south, above and below, as in the heaven–hell binary of the Cakchiquel. Moreover, the east–west alignment amounts to a statement in time that takes us from the sunrise of the Olmec mother culture through the Maya Classic to the Mexican empire of the *Popol vuh*'s day.

The home of almost all the four hundred or so surviving texts in iconic script, and of inscribed monuments that long antedate those of the Classic Maya cities, western Mesoamerica has a highly complex political geography. Through its own sources we may piece together a story of successive empires that began in the Olmec lowlands before 1000 B.C. and culminated in the Aztec capital Tenochtitlan, where Cortes was received as a guest in 1519. Significant moments along the way include those of Papaloapan, the Popolocan domain on the upper reaches of that river of the "butterfly" (*papalo-*), celebrated for its very early agriculture, ceramics, and irrigation; the cities of Oaxaca with their wealth of year dates, which were later disputed by Zapotecs and Mixtecs; and further Olmec extensions westward like Chalcatzingo; Cacaxtla, whose murals highlight the trader's carrying frame (*cacaxtli*); and Cholula, with its vast adobe pyramid, designated in the *Tlaxcala Lienzo* by the Feather-Snake (Fig. 1a), the deity whose cult was centered there, guaranteeing the power to confer authority on rulers from all over Mesoamerica. In its more immediate surroundings in and around the Highland Basin, Tenochtitlan counted on Teotihuacan, partner to Maya cities like Tikal and Copan and possibly the largest city in the world in its day, the metropolis whose stepped pyramids to Moon and Sun are meticulously portrayed in later texts (Fig. 2); the Tula that lies near the uppermost Mexquital valley; and Texcoco, an ally on the eastern bank of the main lake of the basin and the home of the poet-king Nezahualcoyotl.

In continuing this story, the Aztecs gave it new shapes and emphases, just as they adapted the ancient paradigm of the center surrounded by four quarters to the economic facts of their tribute empire. These quarters are clearly set out on the title page of the *Mendoza Codex,* which was prepared as a gift for the first viceroy of New Spain and which details the commodity tribute due from them (this information is also given in the earlier native-paper document known as *Matrícula de tributos*). Though clearly ritualized, the geography in question corresponds to actual landscapes and climates and even underlies state boundaries in modern Mexico;[12] for present purposes, it provides a useful means of locating and grouping texts.

At the heart of things lies Tenochtitlan (Map 3), the place of the stone (*tetl*) and cactus (*noch-tli*), which, set strategically in the Highland Basin's system of three lakes, was linked by causeways to its west bank. Thickly studded with towns that, like Coyoacan, Churubusco (once Huitzilopochco), and Xochimilco, today form suburbs of the megalopolis Mexico City, the central tribute area reached south over the mountains to Cuauhnahuac (Cuernavaca) and Oaxtepec, which now constitute the state of Morelos, and north through Cuauhtitlan toward the Mexquital valley. Superb overviews of the three lakes and their surroundings are given in the map of Tenochtitlan's twin city Tlatelolco, which is likewise oriented to the west, and in the *Xolotl Maps* of Texcoco on the east bank, which are oriented to the east.[13] Too vast even to summarize here, the literary legacy of this metropolitan area includes annals and histories and the more poetic "cosmic" accounts known as *teoamoxtli,* which after Cortes were in many cases transcribed into Nahuatl and Spanish.[14]

From this heartland the *Mendoza Codex* then takes us out to the provinces, beginning with the western quarter that is uppermost in the title-page map. Heavily wooded and largely Otomi-speaking, the "wild west" ran toward the frontier with Michoacan and provided the capital with massive beams of timber. With its provincial capital in the ball-court town Tlachco (Tasco), the south stands as the blueprint for the modern state of Guerrero; among its tribute goods are crimson spondylus shells from Acapulco and the Pacific. Still strongly Nahuatl-speaking, it tells the history of its relations with Mixtecs and Aztecs in a remarkable pair of deerskin screenfolds from Tlapa-Tlachinollan, and in *lienzos* from Chiepetlan and other nearby towns.[15] Opposite stood the cotton-growing north washed by the other ocean, also a Nahuatl stronghold, with a wealth of early inscriptions but very few later texts. The only quarter not contiguous with the capital and hard to control because of the intervening presence of Tlaxcala, it became Cortes's bridgehead and the site of the true cross (Veracruz).

By far the richest source of tribute, the east stretched from Chalco, on the lake of its name within the basin, to the far-flung enclave of Xoconochco on the Quiché border (now that of Mexico with Guatemala), the source of

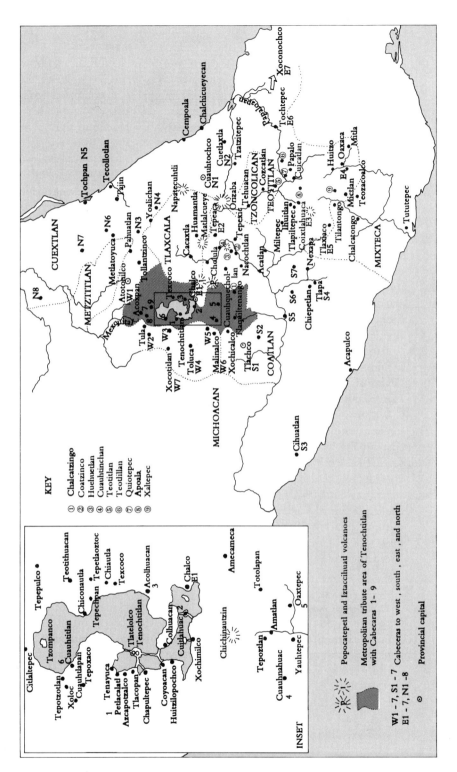

Map 3. Tenochtitlan and surroundings.

KEY

① Chalcatzingo
② Coatzinco
③ Huehuetlan
④ Cuauhtinchan
⑤ Teotitlan
⑥ Teotitlan
⑦ Quiotepec
⑧ Apoala
⑨ Xaltepec

⊙̇́ Popocatepetl and Iztaccihuatl volcanoes

▨ Metropolitan tribute area of Tenochtitlan with Cabeceras 1- 9

W1 - 7, S1 - 7   Cabeceras to west , south , east , and north
E1 - 7, N1 - 8

⊚   Provincial capital

CUEXTLAN
METZTITLAN
TLAXCALA
TZONCOLICAN
TEOTITLAN
MIXTECA
MICHOACAN
COATLAN

Tochpan N5
Tecollotlan
Tajin
N7
N6
Metlatoyuca
Atotonilco
Mexquititlan
N8
Tula W2
Xocotitlan W7
Toluca W4
Malinalco W6
Xochicalco W5
Tlachco S1
Pahuatlan N3
Yoalichan N4
Napatecuhtli
Cacaxtla
Huamanda
Tepeaca
Matalcueye
Acapan W1
Tollantzinco
Texcoco E1
Chalco E1
Cuauhquechol- lan
Tlaquiltenango
S2
Acapulco
Cihuatlan S3
Tlapa S4
Chiepetlan
S6
S5
S7
Nexapa
Tlaxiaco E5
Tilantongo
Chalcatongo
Teozacoalco
Tututepec
Mitla
Oaxaca E4
Mictlan
Huitzo
Coixtlahuaca ⑧
Tilpiltepec ⑦
Ihuitlan
Miltepec
Acatlan
Nayochtlan
Tepexi Tehuacan E2
Cozcatlan
Papalo ⑨
Ucicatlan
Tochtepec E6
Xoconochco E7
Chalchicueyecan
Cempoala
Cuauhtochco
Cuetlaxtla N2
Orizaba
Tzatzitepec
Cuahtochco N1
Chol- ula
Pahuatlan

INSET

Citlaltepec
Tepepulco
Teotihuacan
Tzompanco 6
Chiconautla
Tepotzotlan
Xoloc
Cuauhtlapan
Tepoxaco
Tenayuca
Petlacatl
Azcapotzalco
Tlacopan
Chapultepec
Coyoacan
Huitzilopochco
Xochimilco
Tlatelolco Tenochtitlan 8
Colhuacan
Cuitlahuac 2
Chalco E1
Acolhuacan 3
Texcoco
Chiauhtla
Tepetlaoztoc
Amecameca
Totolapan
Oaxtepec 5
Tepoztlan
Amatlan
Cuauhnahuac 4
Yauhtepec
Chichinautzin

exotic jaguar pelts and *quetzal* feathers and of screenfold books burned by the Christians as late as 1691–2. Along the way travelers passed through the Cholula Plain guarded by its four snow-capped volcanoes; Papaloapan, inherited now by Coixtlahuaca and Cuicatlan; the northern tip of the Mixteca and Oaxaca; and Tochtepec. This eastern quarter came into its own in 1467, when by taking Coixtlahuaca the Mexica gained access to its arterial tribute road that passed down the Papaloapan River to the great *pochteca,* or trading center, of Tochtepec – a lure for Cortes after only days in Tenochtitlan and renowned as a source of cacao, rubber, and exquisitely wrought blankets, jade necklaces, and gold tiaras. Of the thirty or so texts on native paper and skin that have survived from pre-Cortesian times, a high proportion stem from this eastern area: annals from Papaloapan towns like Cuicatlan and Quiotepec; and *teoamoxtli* like the glorious *Coixtlahuaca Map,* with its quincunx of landmarks, and the closely related *Cuicatlan* screenfold (Fig. 3).[16] In the *Coixtlahuaca Map,* a privileged place is given to Tepexic, the citadel to the northwest that emerged toward the end of the Classic and once had the highest masonry walls in Mesoamerica. Politically it retained such power that, even under the Aztecs, its ruler Moctezuma Mazatzin had the authority to bargain with Cortes in October 1520 in the name of all Papaloapan, also including Tehuacan, Cozcatlan, and Teotitlan.[17] It is still a focus of native devotion, and its annals, of inestimable significance, preserve the longest native count of years known in the Fourth World.

Within western Mesoamerica, the territory of Tenochtitlan's empire was never a whole. Independent domains intervened between the quarters and sustained political traditions of their own, like Metztitlan; Coatlan, the heir to Xochicalco;[18] Tilantongo, the dynastic seat of the Mixteca and focus for a considerable body of annals; and Teotitlan. And the north was kept entirely separate, thanks in the first place to Tlaxcala, then a little larger than the modern state of that name.[19] Yet it was given coherence through the paradigm of quarters that has left its mark on Mexico today and that, like the quincunx of Coixtlahuaca, gave shape to other polities within and beyond Mesoamerica.[20]

GREATER MEXICO AND TURTLE ISLAND

Besides detailing the internal geography of Tenochtitlan's empire and the eastern campaigns in Nicaragua, the *Tlaxcala Lienzo* takes us over the western frontier to "unknown Mexico."[21] Deeply affected over the centuries by the culture of Mesoamerica and at times politically incorporated in it, this area includes such modern Mexican states as Michoacan, whose ancient towns and pyramids (*yacata*) plot the maps of the Purepecha or Tarascans; Zacatecas, the site of the huge fortified hill Chicomoztoc ("Seven Caves"),

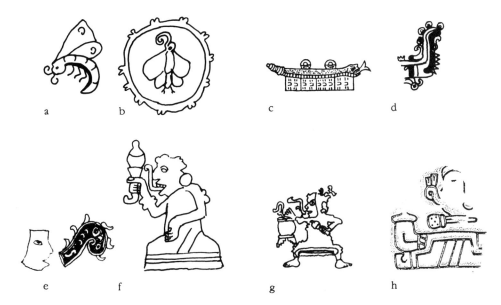

Figure 3. Towns of the Papaloapan domain: (a,b) "butterfly" places Papalotlan (*Tlapiltepec Lienzo*) and Papalo (*Quiotepec Annals*); (c,d) "snake-plain" Coixtlahuaca (*Mendoza,* p. 43; *Coixtlahuaca Map*); (e–h) "singer" place Cuicatlan (*Mendoza,* p. 43; *Tepexic Annals,* p. 8; *Eight Deer* [*Nuttall* verso], p. 32; inscription at Monte Alban, after Marcus 1980:55).

claimed as a tribal birthplace by the resilient Otomi-speaking and other northern desert dwellers collectively known as Chichimecs, or dog people;[22] and Xalisco, Colima, and Nayarit, where Nahua-speakers had preceded the Spanish in driving their linguistic kin, the Huichol and Cora, into the sierra. In painting the world claimed by the ancestors, the Huichol focus on Nayar Mesa as the center between the highlands of the peyote cactus to the east and the lush Pacific lowlands to the west; to the south, images of Lakes Chapala and Patzcuaro overlap with those of the Purepecha texts. From there we are then taken up out of the tropics, beyond Mesoamerica's farthest-flung former frontiers, to the rest of greater Mexico, following "a Nahuan toponymy as far as Arizona and New Mexico" and encountering further linguistic kin of the Mexica, like the Tarahumara, Yaqui,[23] and Pima-Papago, who are linked in turn with the Hopi, Ute (whence Utah), and Shoshoneans of the Great Basin far to the north. At its extremes the *Tlaxcala Lienzo* shows us the setting sun of Tonatiuh Ihuecotzian, the Californian Far West; and to the north, the image of Cibola and its seven city gates, usually identified with Zuni, with which the text ends (Figs. 1b, 4).

Close to the continental divide, in their Emergence narrative the Zuni map their own space in the image of a water skater, head to east, whose diagonal legs are the rivers that flow, as the Rio Grande and Colorado in fact do, to the oceans of the Atlantic and Pacific, firmly identified now at these latitudes with east and west. Zuni lies in fact near the middle of that millennial complex of ball courts, *kivas*, or underground temples, six-storey buildings, irrigation systems, and tribute roads and other urban architecture archaeologically now identified by the Navajo word Anasazi (Map 4).[24] Like those of the Hopi and other pueblo-dwellers in this area, the Zuni narratives spell out reciprocal traffic with Mesoamerica and the "Coral Sea" long before the Spaniards arrived, the source of Nahuatl place names and ritual terms in Hopi texts and of twentieth-century revivalism identified with the Mexican emperor Moctezuma (and in the Chicano case with the first Aztec homeland, Aztlan).[25] Running up through west and north Mexico, bordered by the maizeless sands of Tamaulipas and Texas that all but engulfed Cabeza de Vaca, Anasazi culture shows continuity with Mesoamerica not just materially but in modes of expression. The screenfold annals are echoed in Pima Year Counts, which similarly carry forward an older story of settlement in ancient Hohokan towns like Civanoqi (Casa Grande); the page maps of the *teoamoxtli* find striking counterparts in the Huichol gourd designs recently developed as yarn paintings and in the Anasazi corpus of murals and dry paintings.

In all likelihood once part of Mesoamerican ceremonial, dry painting[26] involves making intricate framed designs by means of colored sand, pollen, and other materials for purposes of curing, and the practice remains vigorous among the Navajo, who as later Athapaskan arrivals to Anasazi (their word for "ancient ones") say they learned this literary art from Hopi and established Pueblos and, going farther back, from scribe masters who owned deerskin books. Functioning as maps, dry paintings situate Anasazi between the east and west oceans and, like Tenochtitlan's tribute map and the Zuni water skater, establish its quarters, east opening to the sun like the doors of their hogans; they also materially set up the four mountains that in the quincunx pattern traditionally guard their old homeland Dinetai and its center on the continental divide near the ancient walled towns of Gran Chaco. These remarkable texts even feature toponyms and settlements like the yellow-and-white-banded Kininaeki, the House of Dawn in Canyon de Chelly. Overall they brilliantly complement the Navajo story of creation and settlement, recently published under the title *Dine bahane* and readily comparable with the Maya *Popol vuh*.

Following trade routes through Pima territory that they themselves mark, dry paintings extended to California on the continent's Pacific rim, whose people have been all but obliterated even as names on the map. Farther up this coast, which has certain maritime traits of its own, like the whale songs sung by the Seri, invading Europe met itself in the eighteenth century, Spain from

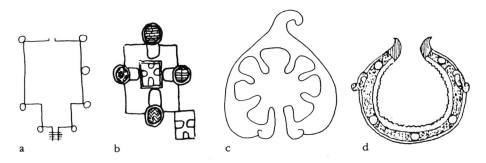

a   b   c   d

Figure 4. Places of Seven: (a) mountains in Road of Emergence dry paintings; (b) gates at Cibola, or Zuni (*Tlaxcala Codex,* Scene 156); (c) Chicomoztoc Seven Caves (*Cuauhtinchan Annals,* fol. 16r); (d) grave with eyes
and the other head orifices (*Laud,* p. 21; see Plate 6b).

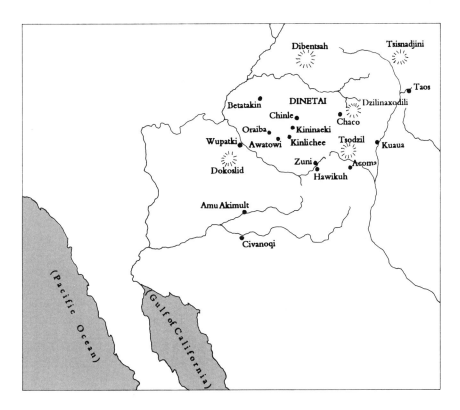

Map 4. Anasazi.

the east, Russia from the west. The latter trailed, albeit thousands of years later, the last immigrants from Asia, that is, the distinctive peoples of the Northwest. These are predominantly Athapaskan, living bearers of America's archaic hunting culture, authors of their own "maps and dreams" and Na-dene kin of the Navajo (Dine) and Apache and more locally of the Tlingit and Haida, among the seven main groups found along the "conifer coast" from Alaska to Oregon. As "the world's most elaborate non-agricultural society,"[27] sedentary, enjoying an abundance of salmon and red cedar, trading in vast canoes and via potlatch ceremonies held until 1951, the coast dwellers, who also include the Tsimshian, Kwakiutl, and Salish, built substantial houses and towns of wood, like Ketchikan, Tongass, Sitka, Kasaan, and Ninstints; and they plotted their territory of islands and inlets by means of their celebrated totem poles, which, like the older corpus of petroglyphs, link the seat and precedence of family dynasties to a history that runs from creation to missioneering by Russian Orthodox priests (Fig. 5).

As for Anasazi's northeast frontier, also that of Greater Mexico, it is signaled in the dry paintings by the *tipis* of the buffalo people, whose territory was viewed as alien and dangerous by the ancestors (Fig. 6), as indeed it was by the adventurous Coronado, who in 1540 rode up from Mexico to Anasazi and then on across to Kansas. In native geography, by crossing this boundary we enter another part of North America, Turtle Island, that great theater of the Mississippi and, beyond the Appalachians, the Atlantic Coast, which resisted onslaught from the east for three hundred years, only in the end to be all but emptied of its original inhabitants.

At the time Europeans first reached America, this great area still acknowledged a focal point in Cahokia, the metropolis that dominated the Missouri–Mississippi confluence, as its urban successor St. Louis does today, and that had reached the height of its power around A.D. 1300. It boasted a great array of earthworks, plazas, and public buildings, among them the largest platform pyramid of the continent, built in successive layers of earth. Drawing on the earlier mound cultures of Ohio and enriched by Mexican maize and agriculture, Cahokia cast a network of trade and skill that reached to the confines of Turtle Island: obsidian and pipestone from the Rockies, exquisitely engraved shell and sophisticated pottery from the Gulf of Mexico, copper from the Great Lakes. This "Mississippian Mound Culture" celebrated its agriculture in anatomical motifs evocative of Mexico, created ceramic *vases communicants,* and propagated the ballgame known in English as chunkey. As the epitome of this culture, Cahokia informed the life of many nations encountered by Europeans in Turtle Island from the sixteenth century onward.

The continuity is clearest in the case of the "civilized tribes" of the lower Mississippi and the chiefdoms of the rich south that spread, as it were, from the stairway of the great pyramid: Natchez, Choctaw, Muskogee (Creek), and Seminole, whose mounds extended round to the "ten thousand islands"

Figure 5. Totem-pole figures: (a) bear biting on ceremonial copper shield (Kwakiutl); (b) Russian Orthodox priest (Haida, Kasaan; after Barbeau 1950:406).   b

a   b

Figure 6. Anasazi images of the Great Plains: (a) *tipi;* (b) buffalo. (Home of
the Buffalo, Shooting Chant dry painting.)

of the Florida peninsula and who bore the brunt of the invasion mounted by
De Soto in 1542 (yet again with Tlaxcalan help). The basis of a trade language
that has provided English with considerable vocabulary, Muskogee named
Alabama, Mobile, Tuscaloosa, and the Appalachian Mountains, as well as the
refuge territory Oklahoma. Long-standing neighbors of the Creek, the Iro-
quoian-speaking Cherokee laid claim to their fourfold set of guardian mountains at the southwestern end of the Appalachians that form the other rim of
Turtle Island (Map 5); and they set their council fires and seven-sided houses
atop Mississippian pyramids at Hiwassee, Setsi, Nikwasi, and other hallowed
places. While holding fast to this landscape that still bears their names (Tennessee, Echota, Tellico, Citico), the Cherokee went so far as to print newspapers
in the syllabary of their language before being brutally forced west in 1838.[28]
At the northeastern end of the Appalachians, their Iroquois cousins, that is,
the Oneida, Onondaga, Mohawk, and other nations of the Iroquois League,[29]
visualized their union as a great tree whose branches spread in four directions;
despite violent assault, they continue to occupy this area. In the past, through
the alliance consecrated in their Ritual of Condolence, they long controlled
access to the waters they named as Ontario, Huron, Erie, Ohio, Scioto, and

Map 5. Appalachia.

Niagara. The earliest stages of this Appalachian story are preserved in such works as the manuscripts of Ayunini (Swimmer), some of them written in the Cherokee syllabary, and David Cusick's *Sketches of . . . the Six Nations.*

Upstream from Cahokia ran the great river roads of the Mississippi and the Missouri, trade routes to areas settled by mound builders, Oneota to the north and Kansas (Coronado's city of Quivira) to the west. Much of this territory, like Iowa, Minnesota, Kansas, and the Dakotas, bears Siouan names, and archaeologists have long suspected Siouan involvement in Mississippian culture. Cahokia itself features on a skin painted by the Quapaw,[30] Siouans of the lower Missouri, a text of considerable importance because of its early date and because it foreshadows the use of painted deer and buffalo skins by those Siouan-speakers who, their economy transformed by the horse, later took possession of the Plains. A clear analogue of the screenfold books typical of Mesoamerica and recalled in Anasazi, this tradition of skin painting appears once to have been known in Cahokia and east of the Mississippi; in the hands of the seven bands of Plains Sioux and their neighbors to north and south, Siksika and Kiowa, it served to record battle exploits, censuses, and above all calendar histories known as Winter Counts,[31] which by the toponyms they employ and by their sheer provenance map the western part of Turtle Island that spreads between Anasazi and Canada.

The actual name by which we know Cahokia belongs to the remaining great language family of Turtle Island, that of the Algonkin. So widespread by the time of European arrival that their language was referred to as "the language of America,"[32] these people stretched in a great northern band from the Atlantic to the Rockies and divided their territory into three parts that today are densely populated with Algonkin names: the Atlantic seaboard – Massachusetts, Connecticut, Manhattan, Chesapeake; the Ohio valley and the Great Lakes – Ottawa, Michigan, the original Miami, Illinois, Chicago (the western goal in the Menomini gods' game of lacrosse); and the West – Wisconsin and the great Mississippi–Missouri river, along whose upper reaches the Siksika, Arapaho, and Cheyenne pressed as far as the Rockies.[33] For their part, as the original people of the north (Ashinaubeg), the Ojibwa Algonkin hold still to their homeland on the multiple watershed that feeds the Mississippi, the Great Lakes, and the Arctic Ocean and defend it to this day from attempts to alter its hydrography. This focus is consecrated in the remarkable corpus of scrolls, a hundred or so in all fashioned from the bark of the northern birch, that belongs to the Midewiwin society of the Ojibwa.[34] Following a characteristic pattern, the Origin and Migration scrolls identify four moments in an ancestral journey from the Atlantic and the east that culminates in the "Great Temple" (Midewegun) of Lake Superior and, via portage, Red and Leech lakes (Fig. 7). Through the mediation of the Ottawa, Lenape, and Shawnee, Mide texts came to validate Pontiac's Ohio campaigns of 1761 and hence Tecumseh's grand defense of the whole east in 1812.

Vividly reported in the battle images and spoken biographies of the Sioux, the heroic military resistance of Turtle Island was ended only at the turn of the twentieth century, by which time the machine gun had decisively improved the U.S. rate of kill. Driven to the Rockies from towns and territories they had inhabited for centuries, the Sioux, Algonkins, and Iroquoians exchanged songs as tokens of value and mutual support and recalled the ancient charter of peace-pipe diplomacy they revered in common. From this Ghost Dance[35] was born a new pan-Indian consciousness of America.

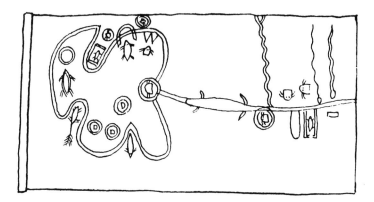

Figure 7. Mide map of the sacred watershed. Reached from the east (right), Leech Lake is shown with its promontories and islands. (*Eshkwaykeezhik Migration Chart,* and section; after Dewdney 1975.)

TAHUANTINSUYU

The Inca empire, Tenochtitlan's South American counterpart, was easily the largest polity encountered by Europeans in the Fourth World; it is also the one that has had the most profound effect on political thought everywhere. Meaning "four districts" in Quechua, or Runasimi, the Inca language spoken today by ten million Andeans, Tahuantinsuyu extended along the Andes from the border with the Chibcha kingdoms in the north to Tucuman and Talca in what is now Argentina and Chile. Recognizable by such typical components as *pampa* (plain), *mayu* (river), and *cocha* (lake), Quechua place names abound over this whole area and stand out especially among the snow peaks of the cordillera.

The shape of Tahuantinsuyu is discussed in several of the native texts in Quechua and Spanish that were prompted by Pizarro's invasion; and it still informs Quechua narrative and song, imaged as the great body that has its brow in Quito (Ecuador), its navel in Cuzco – the meaning of that word in Quechua – (Peru), and its sex in Titicaca (Bolivia). The most systematic early account is given by the native author Guaman Poma in a 1,179-page letter sent to Philip III of Spain under the title *Nueva corónica y buen gobierno;* the "good government" is the Inca practice he wished to restore and reinforce in the viceroyalty of Peru, which he saw being ravaged by Pizarro's heirs. Like the *Mendoza Codex* of Tenochtitlan, Guaman Poma's text gives a comprehensive account of empire; it is complemented by the most important early document in Quechua to have survived, the sixteenth-century *Runa yndio* manuscript from Huarochiri that describes Tahuantinsuyu's geography in terms of its *huaca*s, that is, pyramids and mountains and other

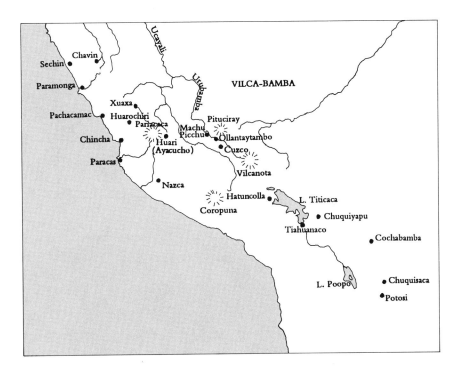

Map 6. Cuzco and surroundings.

landscape features worshiped as shrines.[36] Guaman Poma's work, regularly
enhanced with page illustrations throughout, contains a remarkable two-
page "mapamundi de las Indias" (pp. 983–4; Fig. 8) that epitomizes his
argument in geographical terms. In it we see Tahuantinsuyu physically
expanding to include most of Spanish South America along just the lines of
enterprise followed by the Inca; in so doing it formally combines the ritualized model of the four *suyu* with a Western cartography that includes the
areas beyond.

At the center of his map Guaman Poma places Cuzco, the highland
valley chosen by the Inca as the site for Tahuantinsuyu's capital (Map 6).
This arrangement announces a preference that is both particular, in demot-
ing the coastal European capital Lima, and general, in promoting the
central-highland location that was respected by the invaders in the case of
Tenochtitlan/Mexico City and Bacata/Bogotá. From the position selected
for it, Cuzco ably connected the three very different types of terrain
known in Tahuantinsuyu, which appear as three bands on the map: the
coastal desert; the cordillera – a crumpled starched shirt, in Guaman

Figure 8. Tahuantinsuyu. Cuzco is shown at the center of the four *suyu.*
(Guaman Poma, *Nueva corónica,* pp. 983–4.)

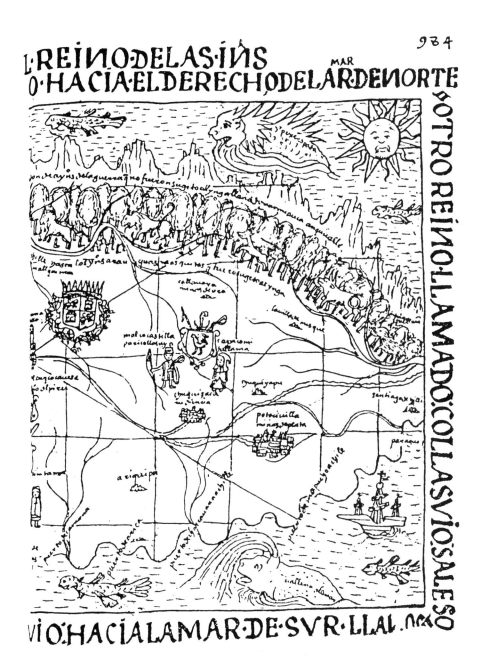

Figure 8 (cont.)

Poma's words – the main area of Inca activity and expansion; and the Atlantic drainage of the Andes that issues into the vast rainforest of the tropical lowlands. This threefold terrain is imaged very early on the Caiman stela at Chavin[37] where spondylus from the Pacific shore on the one hand combine on the other with domesticated plants growing from the caiman earth beast of the Amazon. The particular reciprocity between coast and highlands is brought out in the text from Huarochiri, which lies between the two, in a dialogue between two foxes, one from "above" and one from "below."

As Tahuantinsuyu's political focus, Cuzco is shown on the map as the place where the boundaries of its "four districts" converge: Chincha to west, Anti (whence Andes) to north, Colla to east, and Conde to south. Just like Tenochtitlan, at the center of its tribute quarters Cuzco surveyed and prized its *suyus* for the goods they supplied and as epithets for style in general. In so doing it placed particular emphasis on the west–east axis of Chincha and Colla, which historically had generated previous *tahuantinsuyus*, or quartered polities, of their own and which were extended farthest by the Inca and then by their Spanish successors.

Named after a coastal town due west of Cuzco, Chincha had as its major shrine the *huaca* mountain Pariacaca, close to Huarochiri and the major concern of the *Runa yndio* text. Paired with the Pachacamac pyramid on the coast, this sacred peak also lies to the west of the Huamanga, or Ayacucho, area upon which the ancient Huari culture was centered. Himself from there, Guaman Poma refers to the queen (*coya*) of local dynasties older and more august than Cuzco's and heavily underlines his own links with them; similarly, *Runa yndio* recalls local precedence by revealing how recently Cuzco had imposed its practices and by suggesting that it was in the Ayacucho area that the very first *tahuantinsuyu* was set up. Then, as it expanded northwestward, Chincha came to amalgamate the immense wealth of coastal and highland kingdoms renowned in archaeology, drawing particularly on the brilliant legacy of Moche,[38] contemporary with Teotihuacan and unsurpassed in metallurgy (even electroplating was practiced) and ceramics, which provide a vivid encyclopedia of its world. From its coastal valley, the site of the vast *huaca*s, or adobe-brick pyramids, of Sun and Moon, Moche reached to Chile for lapis lazuli, to the equator for spondylus, and across to the rainforest for the fauna of snake, monkey, and parrot so salient in the iconography of its ceramics. These pots depict Moche's landscape of coastal sand dunes and the runners who pass through it carrying incised beans that are then read by the officials of its communication system (Plate 1c). In this and much else Moche prefigured its imperial successor in these parts, Chimu, or Chimor, which ruled from the nine adobe labyrinths of its capital Chan Chan and in turn profoundly affected the Inca. This upper part of Chinchasuyu is also the home of Pañamarca with its murals, Sechin with its ancient bas-reliefs, Chavin with its Caiman and other primordial stelae on the uppermost Amazon, Chachapoyas[39] with its vast ellipse of fortifications – ever "rebellious," according to Guaman Poma – and Manta on the equatorial coast, which communicated with Mesoamerica and received Pizarro arriving from Panama. Supplier of the spondylus depicted at Moche and Chavin and savored by Pariacaca, *huaca* of the whole *suyu,* the equatorial coast claims some of the continent's oldest ceramics (4000 B.C.) and catches the currents that reputedly bore Kon Tiki westward; above it, there rises the dazzling avenue of snow volcanoes whose Quechua names read like a poem: Carihuairazo Chimborazo Illiniza Cotacachi to west, Ayapungo Sancay Cotopaxi Antisana Cayambe to east. Seduced by this northernmost part of Chinchasuyu, after Huayna Capac's death Huascar placed his capital there, in Tomebamba, thus precipitating the civil war against his half-brother Atahuallpa in Cuzco and remotely anticipating the notion of Ecuador.

Approached through precipitous valleys whose turbulent rivers are alive with caimans and snakes, Anti features as a *suyu* both admired and feared. On the one hand, its naked denizens are viewed as savage and beyond sexual taboo: The men, playing their panpipes, dance like transvestites, and the women dally with monkeys. On the other hand, they are as fierce as the jaguar emulated by the Inca; they are not idolatrous and are ingenious in their knowledge of agriculture and poison. In *Runa yndio* it is precisely when the boundaries are set against the wild beyond Antisuyu that the federation of quarters is established. Anti's guardian *huaca* is Huanayaco in the Huarochiri text, and in Guaman Poma's Cuzco-based system it becomes the twin-peaked Pituciray, just north of Ollantaytambo and the Urubamba, paired in turn with Sauaciray[40] (see Fig. 50c). Under Apu Ollantay, Anti recurs as an emblem of danger and rebellion in the Inca cycle of kingship plays. It was to Antisuyu, Machu Picchu, and Vilcabamba that the Inca themselves repaired after Pizarro's murder of Atahuallpa (a story told by his nephew Titu Cusi, which ended in the further assassination in 1572 of the last emperor, Tupac Amaru I, a lad of fifteen).

As Cuzco's political predecessor, Collasuyu received special deference in ceremonies that hallowed the royal eastern road from Vilcanota, the watershed guardian *huaca* of this quarter, and that even revered in Lake Titicaca the womb of the first Inca rulers. The offerings made accordingly to the lake mother recall those that tie the El Dorado legend to the Chibcha Lake Guatavita while locally they stimulated the cult of the Virgin of Copacabana. Economically there was a direct link in pastoralism – Cuzco was said to have stolen llama herds from the Colla in order to constitute its own first capital – and in the metals that flowed from the provinces of what is now Bolivia, like Chuquiayapu (La Paz) and Chuquisaca (Sucre). In language, the Quechua of the Incas appears to have taken key terms from the Aymara of the Colla, unique in Tahuantinsuyu in having to this day survived the propagation of that imperial successor; and, part of the same legacy, the script of the Inca, the knotted-string device known as the *quipu,* has clear antecedents in Tiahuanaco. In 1781 the intimacy between the center and this *suyu* was reinforced when Tupac Amaru II's great uprising in Cuzco was matched by Tupac Catari's in Collasuyu; defeated, each leader was then pulled apart by horses straining in four directions in a gruesome would-be dismemberment of the *tahuantinsuyu* ideal itself.

Completing the set of four *suyu* and dedicated to the *huaca* peak Coropuna, Conde was ever contained by its ocean and desert. Strong in the fisher cult of Mamacocha, this quarter is also the home of cotton and the finest weaving tradition: Adorned with parrot feathers from the Amazon, textiles from Paracas date to 800 B.C. Shared by the now vanished peoples whose language named Antofagasta (salt town), its ultradry climate has likewise preserved the oldest known mummies in the world.

Finally, at the center of its Four Districts, Cuzco had as a metropolitan *huaca* Pacari Tampu, the Three-Doored House of Dawn where sun, moon, and Venus illuminate the Inca, his queen, and their child (see Fig. 50a). Adorned with the Coricancha sacred to Viracocha and other great temples and palaces whose foundations continue to resist earthquake and utter destruction, the city provided the model for and of its empire, for the layout of its wards and metropolitan area anticipated the four *suyu*s beyond. A system of roads so paved as to be still serviceable today spanned chasms on hanging bridges and entered Cuzco from the end of every *suyu;* and along them chains of *tampu* (staging posts) sustained the armies of conquest and teams of *chasqui* (runners) who carried goods or information knotted into *quipu*s, the Inca books of knotted strings. Known as *ceque*s and seen as coordinates in Guaman Poma's map, four lines radiated from the city, creating the frame for celestial arithmograms of the kind also found in Tenochtitlan's map of tribute towns. Since just this patterning of data is known to have been recorded in the *quipu*s, these lines and *huaca*s, which are still visible in the landscape, may be construed as the strings and knots of a giant *quipu* radiating from the capital.[41] Encoded and deciphered by a bureaucracy of *amauta* scribes, the *quipu* became the palimpsest of the *Nueva corónica* and many other Andean texts in Quechua and Spanish. It merits separate attention as a script form that defies received Western notions of writing.[42]

BEYOND TAHUANTINSUYU

Politically dominant in South America, Tahuantinsuyu impinged on the other main cultures of the subcontinent, those of the Chibcha and Mapuche at the northern and southern extensions of the Andes and of the rainforest of the lowlands. The territory that belongs to the Araucanians, as

Guaman Poma calls them, or Mapu-che ("people of the land," as they call themselves), lay beyond Collasuyu's southern edge and was repeatedly attacked by the Inca. According to narratives collected over the last few decades, the Mapuche world traditionally straddled the Andean watershed that now divides Argentina from Chile (in his nineteenth-century testimony *Kuifike,* Pascual Coña looks to Santiago and Buenos Aires alike), and it has long coincided with the area designated by Mapuche place names on today's map from Pacific to Atlantic, like "town" (*cara*), "mountain" (*huinkul*), "shrine" or *huaca* (*chelcura*), "plain" or pampa (*leflun*), and "water" (*co*), and the places of many kinds of trees and plants, each with its own leaf and story, and of fauna that range from choike to coypu, luan (*huanaco*), and a hundred birds.

According to the *Huinkulche Narrative,*[43] the snow cordillera Pire Mahuida represents the "mother" and matrix of this world. Its once giant peak Threng-threng provided refuge from the great flood and hence stood as the place of Mapuche emergence. The *Huinkulche* text concords with other creation stories in identifying this place with the fossil-rich massif from which five finger lakes spread as if imprinted on the cordillera by a giant hand: Lacar, the fabulous necropolis of the ancestors and the creatures of past ages, Lolog, Huechu-Paimun, the heart of the sunken Threng-threng, Tromen, and Quillen, "also a Threng-threng." Towering still above the lakes stands the volcano Lanin, supported by its four lesser mountains, or feet, the Melihuinkul; it guards the hidden workshop of creation and will protect the ancestral treasure until the world ends. The legendary passages reaching out from the cave under Lanin also function as the node between the two sides of the cordillera, the dry pampa of Argentina to the east beyond Neuquen, and the rich forests of Chile to the west. A continuation of Huahum, a notably low Andean pass, Lake Lacar similarly communicates between the two Andean slopes.

The houses (*ruka*) of the traditional Mapuche community, like the steps and face carved into the *rehue,* or sacred tree, which gives it its center, always face east. In the eighteenth and nineteenth centuries, riding out from Neuquen onto the pampa as expert horsemen, the Puelche, or eastern Mapuche, pressed to the very gates of Buenos Aires and knew their apogee under Calfucura.[44] Only the machine gun, changing the rate of death as it did for the Sioux, forced from them treaties that reduced their land to those telltale lines of white geometric projection. Moving in the same easterly direction in much earlier times, emissaries from the Melihuinkul are credited with having helped to civilize the older inhabitants of the pampa, the Leflunche, whose Patagonian life was so criminally ended in the 1920s.

The other horizon of the sun's daily course is everywhere named as the great ocean, Fucha Lafken, in particular the offshore island Mocha. Here at sunset, or Conhue Antu, the spirits of the dead are transported on the backs of female ancestors who have become whales. Mocha is also distinguished as the home of the first tree, which once connected the upper and lower worlds and from which stem the many varieties commemorated all along the western mainland in names like Radal, Temuco, Lumaco, Maiten, and Copihue.[45] The vast lowland counterpart to Lake Lacar in the Threng-threng story and the source of the terrifying *tripalafken*, tidal waves, the ocean is the object of offering and penance; it is also the home of the merman Shumpall who steals his bride from the shore.

Just as the east and west of the Mapuche invoke the sun's day, so their north and south match the halves of its year in a mirror image of Mide geography. The *Shaihueke Narrative* recalls the summer of Inca times when all was warmth, gold, palaces, llamas, maize. The marks of that contact are clear in such matters as arithmetic ("hundred" and "thousand" are Quechua terms), the use of *quipus* to count days and plot places, the concept of llama wealth, the thirty-day month, and the military levy. The Inca are even credited with having had a palace and a tribute center on Lake Paimun, though to the west of the cordillera the traditional frontier was farther north, on the river Maule. In any case, far less sunny a view is taken of subsequent pressure from that direction, in the story of "Cristo Colón," who is diagnosed as the instigator of unprecedented greed and cruelty. Ever defending a northern frontier that did not crack until the concessionary treaties with the Argentine and Chilean governments in the 1880s, the Mapuche are then said to have been driven back to an ancestral winter, to a south dark as if in chronic eclipse, yet white with snow and the "frost" of the *huinka*s (invaders) and everywhere prey to the sea that covers old valleys and roads. To find a way back from here is to hold onto the story itself, the hanging bridge (*cuicui*) in time and space. In the epic part of this story, Patagonia and the South figure as the last refuge of Ollal, who taught its people, the Huilliche, to make their skin coracles and keep fire (in them) and taught such tropical-forest arts as anesthesia, blending tobacco, and stunning fish with poison in rivers like the Calle Calle (Valdivia).

With its federal organization of Aillirehue (the ninefold community) and its groupings of local heads (*lonco*), the overall Mapuche territory, or Ftah Mapu, had no single concentric capital. Yet larger territorial schemes are visible or implied in such models as the Melihuinkul of Lanin; the "great" and "small" lakes, *fucha* and *pichi lafken,* of the Pacific below and the Lacar above; and the clearly marked paths of the winds, funneled north and south (*picun, huilli*) by the corridors of the cordillera, steady from the western sea and hot and violent as the Puelche that bursts across from the pampa.

In Guaman Poma's map of Tahuantinsuyu, Ftah Mapu extends the Andean course of Collasuyu, just as, diagonally opposite, the Chibcha kingdoms extend that of Chinchasuyu. Both are known worlds. Not so, however, the lowland rainforest that constitutes the rest of South America. For in Guaman Poma's map, Antisuyu extends into fantasy (this frontier was oddly reinforced by the Treaty of Tordesillas that in 1494 divided Spanish and Portuguese interest in America and anticipated the western border of Brazil). Beyond the thick wall of trees that protects a mixed fauna of giant snakes, monkeys, jaguars, and "naked savages," towering mountains reach into an ocean of fish and stars. The last huge domain of America to have resisted invasion, the actual rainforest has survived precisely because of sophisticated human solidarity with its green habitat, which was developed by the riverine ancestors of the Arawak and Tupi at least as early as 3000 B.C. and which now, five thousand years later, is threatened by genocidal fires. Devoid of masonry, annals, and empires, this huge tropical territory is renowned for the plurality of its speech – Carib, Arawak, Tucano, Shuar, Pano, Ge-Bororo and Tupi-Guarani. It has the shape of its river systems, Orinoco, Amazon, and Parana, the first two linked by the improbable Casiaquiare, the second two by the inland sea produced in the pantanal by seasonal rains.

The larger patterns of landscape and communication here emerge from texts edited and translated in this century, of which a remarkable synthesis is made in Nunes Pereira's "indigenous decameron," *Morongueta*.[46] Constant motifs are the rivers and the conversations they hold, the uplands from which they are born and which separate their lower paths, their manifold tributaries, waterfalls that send out a primal mist of rainbow and iridescent life, deep eddies and rapids (*cocheiras*) inhabited by siren brides and their fearsome fathers, reaches that lead to estuaries and distant trade and contact with non-Indians of unlikely shape, skin, and language, and the ever-present likelihood of overflow and flood that spare only the highest palms and recall the river births that once rerouted archaic paths. Hence, along the Pacaraima ridge that separates the Orinoco from the Amazon, *Watunna* traces the ancestral journey of the planters who preceded the first Soto Carib, from the eastern peak of the "food mountain" Roraima to the great "felled tree" Marahuaka, from which last the rivers first flowed; this is the east–west path followed by Koch-Grünberg in *Vom Roroima [sic] zum Orinoco* (1924) and traced in the Arekuna narrative *Makunaima* published in that pioneer study. More widely, *Watunna* inscribes a territory that extends from Dama, Caracas, and the Caribbean Sea (where we began) to Maraca Island in the Amazon, and from Rupununi and Essequibo in Guyana to the Andean foothills, to the Piaroa and the Matuto, the Colombian butterfly people of the Vaupes. *Watunna* and other Carib and Arawak texts from this area distinguish Orinoco and Amazon as northern and southern catchments and pay special attention to the Casiaquiare bond between the two, unique in world hydrography. Rapids and other significant points along these water roads from Essequibo to Vaupes, and even the one-time passage along them of Spanish galleons, are marked by rock inscriptions, attributed by the Carib to Makunaima and generally known by the Carib term *timehri*. Such markers correlate the first emergence at Wainambi, or Panure, the navel eddy in the lower Vaupes, and the drive upstream to the Papuri, Pira-parana, and allied rivers, in a whole succession of Desana, Barasana, and other Tukano narratives[47] that culminate in Umusin Panlon's *Antes o mundo não existia* (1980). Thanks to the mediation of Koch-Grünberg's contemporary K. T. Preuss, whose journey also led him to contemplate the double-ego statues at San Agustín, the myriad world of the Amazonian headwaters was made known through the narrative of the Witoto shaman Rigasedyue (K. T. Preuss 1921); in the Canimani story a successor vividly describes the birth of the Amazon and its tributaries (not least the Canimani, or Putumayo) as literal branches of the great tree that, like Marahuaka, gave birth to the rivers when it was felled. (The Witoto language is distantly akin to Carib.) For their part, Arawak groups like the Machiguenga and Campa on the Ucayali, and the Shipibo and other Pano-speaking neighbors, relate today's downward drive of Andean colonists to Inca campaigns waged four centuries ago in the name of Pachacamac and Viracocha;[48] on the Napo tributary, as the old Inca frontier continues to move downstream, Quechua reciprocally absorbs lowland stories like that of the incestuous male moon and the intrepid rainforest women who earned for the Amazon its Old World name.

To the south, the names of waterfalls, rivers, and whole countries – Iguazu, Izozog, Parana, Paraguay, Uruguay – belong to the Tupi-Guarani language, once the "lingua geral" of Brazil and still more widely spoken than Spanish in Paraguay: Through its classic *Ayvu rapyta,* first published in 1944 by an anthropologist who became a Guarani (Kurt Onkel/Nimuendajú), the rainforest is established as the mid earth from whose trees language flows (*wyra neery*). Matching the Arawak memory of Pachacuti, the westernmost of these Guarani traditions recall Tahuantinsuyu, specifically through Tupac Yupanqui's campaigns in the Chaco (Quechua for "hunting ground"); down the Parana, others concentrate on the centuries-long war fought against the Jesuits and the slaver *bandeirantes*. Along the coast and far back into the Amazonian system, skirting the uplands of Ge-Shavante that today house Brazil's capital, the Urubu, Wayapi, Tenetehara, Mundurucu, and other Tupi kin of the Guarani continue to recite creation stories first intuited by the French and Portuguese in the sixteenth century. Historically, these people's search for the paradisacal "first earth" (*yvy tenonde*) has led east to the coast, or alternatively west far up the Amazon, where they reached the city of Chachapoyas in 1549.[49] Since 1964, in the upper Xingu, a new focal point has been found for the whole rainforest for citizens of these and many other nations who continue to defend their millennial settlement of the Amazonian cosmos.[50]

This preliminary excursus into the Fourth World has regarded its landscapes, the shore of the Carib sea, the convergences of great river systems, the western backbone of Rockies and Andes with its inset sacred Andean lakes – Lacar, Titicaca, Guatavita, Atitlan – and the Pacific rim with its whale lore, ceremonial poles, spondylus delights, and westbound voyagers. It has also indicated how before Columbus the place occupied by Mesoamerica within the northern part of the continent resembled that occupied by Tahuantinsuyu to the south. Throughout, the Fourth World emerges as a continent well mapped before Europe arrived. At every isomorph of rock and water we detect a pre-Columbian palimpsest, town names that echo former or present native settlements, roads and frontiers that follow older ways. Taking notice of this evidence helps us to envisage native polities that live in body and in memory, and to compensate for the erasure and balkanization that Native American geography has undergone.

Even this topographic evidence gives the first hints of the deeper coherence explored in detail in following chapters. For example, nine and seven, ciphers of the night and moon, are widely respected as principles of social organization, the former in the Mapuche Airillehue, Chan Chan, and Chiconautla, the latter in the "seven caves" of tribal origin Chicomoztoc and in the clans, towns, and tombs of Sioux, Cherokee, Zuni, and Paez. Tribute was ideally levied from four quarters, and the set of mountains guarding the center, or place of emergence, corresponds to a quincunx in cases as distant as the Mapuche Melihuinkulche, the *huacas* that surrounded Cuzco's Pacari Tampu, the *Coixtlahuaca Map,* and the Navajo Dzilinaxodili.

Most important, our chief source in all this has been literary texts, classics, and charter statements in native languages, like *Watunna, Popol vuh, Dine bahane, Runa yndio,* and *Ayvu rapyta,* that are prime guides to their own provenance, as are accounts written, like the *Mendoza Codex,* in native script. These works have served to define and defend territory, even in law where necessary, and especially as responses to the invasion begun by Columbus. The account offered here is not nor could ever be a survey of every known native focus; rather, relying on bodies of texts both distinguished and comparable with each other as native testimony, a series of arenas and the multiple interfaces between them are defined, from Patagonia to the Ojibway Midewegun.

2

Language and its instances

SCRIPT AND TEXT

In "The Effectiveness of Symbols," one of the essays in *Structural Anthropology,*[1] Lévi-Strauss shows how the *Mu ikala,* a therapeutic epic of the Panamanian Cuna, represents the "way" (*ikala*) of countering the dark and dangerous forces of Mu during a difficult childbirth. In his analysis he draws out the multiple meanings of "way," as psychic procedure and actual uterine road, and precisely diagnoses the contest between the mobile shaman and the retentive Mu. He is particularly adept at revealing the ploys and rhythms of the text as sung rhetoric, allowing us too to feel the powers of its persuasion and the "effectiveness" of its symbols.

Going back to the source used by Lévi-Strauss, we find an alphabetic text in the Cuna language (plus an English translation), which had been transcribed from a 956-character text in Cuna script (Plate 1d). Yet nowhere does Lévi-Strauss even allude to the fact of Cuna script, whose characters were specially developed to record their *ikala* and other canonical literature, each of them corresponding to a line or phrase of speech. In fact, ranged in their boustrophedon lines, certain of these characters register, visually and graphically, just those qualities in the text that Lévi-Strauss, by referring only to the song, has to argue the harder for. For example, the slow pace of the preliminaries is physically evident in the ponderous four-square paragraphing of the opening lines, whereas the excitement of the conflict with Mu's beasts can actually be seen in the rapid repetition and postures of the animal images in question. Also the details of certain of the written characters make explicit such factors as the angles of the shaman's approaches, the entire coverage of the iron nets used to seal the uterus against reentry, and the direction in choreography and geography from which power is sum-

40

moned (e.g., "east," Plate 1d). In addition, the sheer boustrophedon progress of the reading itself is designed to match the shifts in the shaman's
position as at the start of successive lines he faces one way and then the
other, weaving his therapeutic web.

This commentary by Lévi-Strauss on a work of Cuna literature conveniently raises a whole set of questions about the nature of language – verbal,
visual, tactile, and so on – that are of immediate consequence for any sustained approach to Fourth World texts. For his part, Lévi-Strauss took to
further extremes his preference for verbal over visual language when preparing his great American oeuvre, the four-volume *Mythologiques* (1964–71),
which assembles texts and traditions from southern and northern parts of
the continent. In this wide-ranging work, Lévi-Strauss contrives to build
for us a frame for the mythology of all native America. Moving out from
the rainforest, the area of his own anthropological fieldwork, he extends his
comparisons up through the isthmus to Turtle Island and the Pacific Northwest (also the main setting for *La voie des masques*, 1975–9). In so doing he
constructs the boldest of parallels over the widest of spaces, bringing order
and clarity to what before him had been an unsignposted morass for stu-
dents of myth. In its own terms, and based as it is on "myth units" that
consist of his summaries of the widest variety of "oral" sources, *Mythologiques* vindicates that homogeneity of American experience argued for
elsewhere by Lévi-Strauss, and on decidedly more material and historical
grounds, in the encomium of the New World quoted above.

In defining the sources used in *Mythologiques*, Lévi-Strauss appeals above
all to the notion of primitive and scriptless societies, whose "traditions lend
themselves to an experimental research which requires a relative stability in
its object." The "myths" through which he constructs America interest him
precisely because they stem from people untroubled and unspoilt by the
practice of writing, a point he clarified when changing the title of his lecture
series at the École Practique des Hautes Études from "Religions des peuples
non-civilisés" to "Religions comparées des peuples sans écriture." The point
could hardly be clearer: Nothing acts like the letter as a destabilizing factor,
one that promotes the lapse from grace. Philosophically he here continues a
long-standing aversion to the idea of script that is traceable back to Plato
and that in French found telling expression in Montaigne's remarks on the
same tropical-forest dweller studied by Lévi-Strauss, the denizen of a world
"so new and infantine, that he is yet to learn his ABC."

This policy of his has meant in practice that in surveying the Fourth
World Lévi-Strauss has not just concentrated on the rainforest but positively
avoided those "high cultures" that, like Tahuantinsuyu and Mesoamerica,
articulated society through scriptlike media: *quipus* and books. On just this
point he has been challenged even on anthropological grounds: Zuidema,
for example, has pointed out an impressive array of sociostructural parallels

between Inca texts like the *Zithuwa Hymns* and the *Runa yndio* on the one hand and, on the other, texts authored by the Ge, Bororo, and rainforest peoples upon whom Lévi-Strauss has principally based his own analyses.[2] Similarly, he has been taken to task for the depoliticizing effect that his method necessarily produces, taking his subjects out of time and landscape and depriving them explicitly of material reference. Stressing how critical script has been to the Cuna's political idea of themselves in connecting their first experiences of European invasion with the founding of their republic in 1925, Kramer trenchantly concludes: "The assumption that tribal peoples are 'writingless cultures' is one of the most persistent errors of ethnology" (1970: 12).

As an enthusiast of pure speech, and on the whole subject "What is writing?," Lévi-Strauss has met his most incisive critic in Jacques Derrida, who was provoked by the first volume of *Mythologiques* and its antecedents to produce his remarkable *De la grammatologie* in 1967. Of Lévi-Strauss's Rousseauesque, script-free societies he says: "The ideal profoundly underlying this philosophy of writing is therefore the image of a community immediately present to itself, without difference, a community of speech where all the members are within earshot. . . . Writing is here defined as the condition of social inauthenticity" (1976:136). For Derrida, "writing" is in fact present everywhere, in gesture and speech itself, in the traces and paths of landscape: Orality and script do not therefore constitute a mutually exclusive binary; still less are they moral opposites. Again Lévi-Strauss's binary is undermined by the fact that degrees of phoneticism vary between scripts, and even alphabets can never register sound entirely, while even the most rudimentary-seeming pictography will always imply a kind of language. Lévi-Strauss's position is characterized as "phonologism," which "is undoubtedly the exclusion or abasement of writing" (p. 102) as well as "a profound ethnocentricism" that in fact privileges the model of phonetic writing, "a model that makes the exclusion of the graphie easier and more legitimate." In this reading, contrary to first appearances, Lévi-Strauss's characterization of the New World as some preferable other turns out itself to be exploitative in its way, yet another chapter in the long history of an imperialism for and within which alphabetic script has in practice been a main agent of dogma and repression.

Derrida's great strength is that he highlights the idea of script and its power, for "reflection on the essence of mathematics, politics, economics, religion, technology, law, etc. communicates most intimately with the reflection upon and information surrounding the history of writing" (p. 88). At the same time, through the very term "grammatology" he enables us the better to conceptualize script in the most various forms it can take, technically on the page, in other visual and tactile media, and in lining and encoding within "purely" verbal language. Yet in practice he does not have very much to say about the Fourth World or the American media neglected and misrepresented (according to him) by Lévi-Strauss. Whatever the reasons for this (and they surely have to do with his fascination with "le peuple écrit," the Jews chosen by God in the Old World), his clarity of argument may encourage us here to draw out, locally in the Fourth World, the implications of his general grammatology.

First, in texts that are apparently "just oral," the very phrases of human breath affect the all-important concept of line (literally *gramma* in Greek), as for example Sherzer has shown in relation once again to the same Cuna tradition to which the *Mu ikala* belongs.[3] Line patterning, with its implicit spatial and number logic, stands as the major criterion for Dell Hymes and others in their "recovery" of other Anasazi and Turtle Island texts from amorphous prose transcriptions made up to a century ago for the Bureau of American Ethnology; Tedlock's transcription of Zuni discourse even introduces typographical refinement. Beyond this, the encoding process synonymous with script and visual language may in Derrida's terms operate within speech, that is, an encoding into time-resistant, condensed, and poetic forms that stand at the opposite pole to the linguistic "norms" of Saussure and that lend themselves the more readily to systemic analogy with visual language. Evidence of this type of oral language can be found throughout the South American lowlands whence Lévi-Strauss set out. A telling case comes in *Watunna*, whose editor, the French anthropologist Civrieux, offers in this text a complex specimen of oral language capable of just this order of self-inscription (1980, pp. 16–7):

> The *Watunna* is in its essence a secret teaching restricted to the circle of men who undergo the initiations of the *Wanwanna* festivals. But there is another, popular *Watunna* which belongs to everyone regardless of sex or age, and this is the *Watunna* which is told daily outside the ritual dance circle. It is an exoteric *Watunna* told in everyday language, a profane reflection of that of the sacred space. . . . These variations, altered and abbreviated, subject to personal interpretations and the teller's level of knowledge and memory, still fulfill the *Watunna*'s essential role of teaching the tribe's history and spreading its ethical and social ideals. More concerned with the anecdotal aspects of the *ademi* however, these popular versions are unable to preserve the symbolic structure created by their secret language. The phonetic games and mental associations which are such an important part of the sacred dance cannot be translated into profane language.

Passing then to visual language in the Fourth World, Derrida reveals how Lévi-Strauss actually suppressed evidence of it in order to further his phonologism. He starts with the much-cited Amazonian story about a Nambikwara Indian who comes to exploit his fellows simply as a result of undergoing a "writing lesson" and appearing to know the alphabet. Comparing Lévi-Strauss's different versions of what happened, Derrida reveals a whole range of ambiguities in the author as both narrator and participant and shows how in *Tristes tropiques* he forgot the notes he had dedicated in *La vie familiale et sociale des Indiens Nambikwara* (1948) to the graphic designs incised by these Pano-speaking people on their gourds and other objects. Known by the term *ierkariukedjutu,* these designs are specifically credited with a script function and therefore importantly anticipate the alphabetic practice "suddenly and disastrously" grasped by one of their number. As others have shown, American literary traditions, among them that of *Watunna* itself, typically display full awareness of the problems of script and have explicitly resisted the impoverishment brought about by phonetic and alphabetic writing.[4] Derrida also omits to comment on a yet more notorious inconsistency in *Mythologiques* in which writing is linked to ideas of human perception (vol. 1, p. 331). Here we learn of the iridescent snake Muyusu, also the rainbow, who brought script to the Tupi-speaking Mundurucu ("désireux d'enseigner l'écriture aux hommes, [il] les attira en imitant la voix de toutes sortes d'animaux"). So plausibly is this put that we could be forgiven for forgetting that, like their neighbors the Nambikwara, the Mandurucu were supposed to be integrally innocent and ignorant of script. One might retort that the types of script in question differ substantially, yet Lévi-Strauss himself only ever talks of scripts as such, and in any case the script consciousness implied is in principle the same. We have here a further example of particular evidence being neutralized in order not to disrupt the overall model of an oral America.

Widespread in the rainforest, these graphic conventions of the Nambikwara and the Tupi find ready analogues in the *timehri* of the Carib and more remotely in Cuna and Chibcha iconography. As examples of visual language, these rainforest signs are typically said to have been fetched or acquired long ago, together with corresponding examples of oral language like the nation's store of songs and narratives, according to a dual grammatological model that inheres in the all-encompassing medium of rite and performance – also left undeveloped by Derrida. In North America, too, the same reciprocity exists between the chants and the dry paintings of the Navajo, for example, or the songs and incised birchbark scrolls of the Midewiwin, which each fall into tetradic stanzas equivalent in number to the stages of initiation and degrees of knowledge. Systemic in their own way, these signs can palpably affect our interpretation of the corresponding verbal texts. This is certainly so in the case of the *Mu ikala* with which we started. Helbig, for example, has appealed to the original in native script when amplifying Lévi-Strauss's psychological and physiological reading of this text; he invokes the corresponding pictographs (semicircle of "halbgerundete Erde," houses with lines of approach, etc.) precisely when arguing that the body guarded by Mu refers also to an exterior location of earth and sea, just as the shaman's road follows terrestrial directions in time and space in the attack on "forts," which historically recall those of the Spanish.[5] In other words, respecting Cuna script helps us to understand how the *ikala* invokes both inner and outer space, and hence individual and collective experience over time of a particular part of the world whose northern coast is the Caribbean Sea. Finally, in those cultures avoided by Lévi-Strauss precisely because they were so script-saturated in pre-Columbian times, and by Derrida out of apparent lack of interest in New World civilization, the function of nonverbal language is so complex, in the screenfold books of Mesoamerica and the *quipu* of Tahuantinsuyu, as to demand discussion below. Derrida's neglect of the *quipu,* historically transcribed into the alphabet by Quechua *amautas,* is the more surprising because as a medium it excellently exemplifies his claim for the functional equivalence of script in society above and beyond particular media.

From all this we may confirm that the Fourth World indeed has its own complex grammatology. Deciphering it means entering the history of both its internal relations and its five-hundred-year encounter with the West. It also means becoming aware of how the Fourth World has fared in supposedly universal histories of humankind's efforts to write, most of them characterized by that crass evolutionism that celebrates the Semitic–Greek alphabet, like the wheel, as a turning point in human achievement to which America was unfortunately not party. (The Totonacs used wheels for their children's toys, and, as we have seen, the impoverishment implicit in the phonetic alphabet was well understood in the Fourth World.) Hence, America makes only brief, fragmented appearances in I. J. Gelb's *A Study of Writing* (1963) and David Diringer's *The Alphabet: A Key to the History of Mankind* (1968); in the latter the quotation from a Maya hieroglyphic text is upside down.

In approaching Fourth World literature in its great diversity of origin and form, we need to settle the matter not just of grammatology but of text. Traditional in literary criticism and recently resurrected in linguistics, text is no more (or less) than a particular or framed instance of language. Indeed, as a privileged example of discourse and the space in which meaning happens, a text may actually frame and define itself, reflexively, whether it consists of words or some visual sign system. As a result it may propose analogies between media, notably the verbal and the visual, that override the differences between them and thereby become an artifact or entity that is specifically and consciously literary. Invoked within a textual frame and possibly centered on an explicit title, breathed words in this way become the exact analogue of painted signs, and their respective sources acquire the same authorial identity. It is true that Derrida and other theorists have wished to dispense with these old literary preferences entirely, in equating *graphie* with "traces" in whatever process of perception; but they do so ignoring the (for us) all-important concepts of frame and analogy between media, which sustain "the-text-itself," its announced ontology.

Hence, in *Watunna* we find internal reference to how this narrative was first composed from secret songs and signs brought by the Carib ancestors; and this motif is widely repeated elsewhere, for example in the Navajo *Shooting Chant* narrative where the hero twins win its constituent sets of chants and dry paintings from more ancient occupants of their territory Anasazi; or the *Tatkan ikala,* which tells how the *nele*s, or teachers, who feature in this epic invented Cuna script. In turn, the visual texts in question will characteristically provide an encompassing frame for more particular forms of representation. Hence, Cuna script incorporates details of the *mola*s, or embroidered cloths, used by the shaman (and now commercially developed as images in their own right); Huichol yarn paintings include within their frame ceremonial objects like incised gourds whence they historically derive, the elaborate round *nierika,* mosaic mirrors, and shieldlike designs themselves of colored yarn. In ending in 1879, Wapoctanxi's Sicangu Winter Count displays the image of a pen,[6] indicating the missionary school that threatened to usurp older methods of representing Dakota chronology.

In Mesoamerica, home of the pre-Columbian screenfold books, play is characteristically made not just with the act of writing – as in the *Tepexic Annals'* dual image of Quetzalcoatl's writing and singing lesson or the tongue-pen of the Maya scribe – but with the surface written upon, of paper or skin. The *teoamoxtli,* or cosmic books, specialize in images of a deerskin drawn upon the deerskin of which they are made (Plate 1a,b); this is a literary trope that recurs thousands of miles to the north in the deer on Powhatan's deerskin mantle and in the painted Illinois deerskin, which specifies as its frame such a deerskin, drawn symmetrically within the physical margin. Invoking the literal "text-ile" analogy, one especially germane to the strings of the *quipu,* the Aztec poet identifies the threads of his song with the fibers of the screenfold paper page, and a Maya inscription at Copan brilliantly contrives to weave its hieroglyphic thread into stone.[7] The resulting mat, or *pop,* is the emblem of political authority that, referring to its palimpsest, the highland Maya *Popol vuh* uses to entitle itself.

In these examples we see text as a framed composition, with its own integrity, an "author-ized" example of discourse, which has its own inner structure and capacity to reflect upon itself while forming part of a larger literary system. At the most basic level, respecting text in this sense means inquiring into source and provenance. As critics have often pointed out, the myth "units" out of which Lévi-Strauss constructs his *Mythologiques* consist of no more than summaries and extracts, seamlessly translated into French and taken from a wide variety of originals. In the process, very different orders of source are homogenized, from direct dictation in a native language to remote report transmitted by European missionaries centuries ago; furthermore, we lose all sense of authorial motive and practice in disseminating a text, it being the case that in most traditions, and in the dry-painting code, strong taboos prevent the total reproduction of an original for profane purposes or profit. A story in themselves, the lines along which Fourth World texts have in fact been transmitted to produce versions available to and legible by us can often seriously affect how we interpret them. Similarly, provenance can be a key factor in assessing the status or centrality of a text, which indeed may itself be a principal guide to the native geography of its part of America. Among the many dozen winter counts extant it is possible to distinguish no more than ten or so master counts that define schools, each with its own historical perspective and emphasis.[8] In the rainforest, as an authorized and central statement of Orinoco Carib creation, *Watunna* had its form and detail agreed in repeated discussion between Civrieux and the Soto themselves; likewise Umusin Panlon allowed his son and Bertha Ribeiro to translate and publish the Tukano cosmogony precisely because it was felt that it had been traduced and misrepresented in previously published versions.

Hence, only by acknowledging the native text as an entity in itself can we properly open the question of its structure and internal sequence of episodes. Scholars working, for example, on Carib, Barasana, Guarani, and other rainforest texts, as well as those of the Mapuche, have highlighted the need to identify successive cycles of myths, and what has been called their "matrix-sequence," within a range of versions and variants. Recognizing this dimension in Siksika narrative would have helped Grinnell, for one, to reconcile "contradictions" in the ancestral story that in fact are different time phases of it.[9] On this understanding, texts both written and spoken employ, for example, the subtle technique of matching one passage with another widely separate from it in the narrative, so that their respective meanings reinforce each other through a whole range of positive and negative definitions. Cases in point are the iconic script account of Eight Deer's life, notably his two maritime campaigns, one successful, the other not; the *Popol vuh* story of the descent to Xibalba first of the father and much later of the sons; or again the *Dine bahane* account of how the Holy People and then humans emerged from maize in deerskin ceremonies that are parallel but remote from each other in time. Clearly, only by appreciating a text in its length and entirety can we hope to make sense of such literary finesse or begin to respect its assay into diachronic time (the concept so inimical to Lévi-Strauss and his method). The question of structure is made the more crucial by the fact that certain classics have been denied their integrity and dismembered by critics; in the cases of *Rabinal Achi,* the *Tlaxcala Lienzo,* and even the *Popol vuh,* Europeans have been credited with assembling fragments, bestowing on them a coherence they otherwise would have lacked.[10] In fact, the first and second parts of the *Popol vuh* finely complement each other as cosmogony and history, and the episodes of the first are fitted together with the ingenuity of a Chinese puzzle, making the more perceptive reader aware of how the text creates itself in analogy with the world-making it describes or narrates.

Again, only when texts are perceived as entities can they be effectively related to each other within a literary corpus and specifically within a taxonomy of genres. For in most native traditions complex sets of terms are used to refer to different types and orders of composition, each of which, once announced, carries with it its own expectancies (and hence chance of parody). Indeed, genre is the more critical as a concept in the absence of any author cult, "ownership" of texts by individual scribes sometimes being positively guarded against. As Kramer has shown, the *Mu ikala* of the Cuna represents the first of three main types of epic, concerned respectively with therapy, initiation, and the realm of the dead; such epics are actually included in the more comprehensive text of *Tatkan ikala,* which covers time from the beginning of the world to the European invasion. Again, thanks to the recent census compiled by Selwyn Dewdney, Mide texts may now similarly be allocated to genres, from the grand cosmic maps to the migration and initiation scrolls with their characteristic stanzas of 4 + 4 images.[11] As for the major literary languages of Mesoamerica and Tahuantinsuyu (Nahuatl, Maya, Quechua), they are rich in alphabetic texts dating from the sixteenth century to the present day, which to a greater or lesser degree respect norms and genres that derive from indigenous script systems; notable cases are the continuation of the screenfold *xiuhtlapoualli* as Nahuatl annals, and the hieroglyphic and then alphabetic Katun Count of the lowland Maya.

Beyond this valency within its own literary system, a given text may also invite comparison with texts in other systems that are similar in scope or narrative mode. Based technically on the serial count of years and copiously represented in iconic script, annals from all over North America demand to be compared (see Table 4), though the main lineaments of the American "epic" have been laid out by Paul Radin, for one. The captive's challenge prominent in rainforest rhetoric and called *carbet* by the French provides the focus of the Quiché play *Rabinal Achi* and underlies the Inca drama *Apu Ollantay,* whereas elaborate hymns of worship characterize the imperial capitals of Tahuantinsuyu and Mesoamerica. Like the *Mu ikala,* formulaic cures in Maya, Nahuatl, Otomi, Carib, and Cherokee conflate inner and outer space in diagnosing the body's ill in the story of the world ages and, again like the Cuna text (as *Olowitinappi's Report* specifically confirms), appeal to or actually use forms of native writing as their prescription. Riddles, whose pre-European existence in the Fourth World was flatly denied by Boas, form part of a dialogue from Arapaho to Mapuche and constitute an important chapter in the Maya *Chilam Balam Books;* they find their roots in shamanic ways of hearing words and, more critical, seeing their meaning through the eyes of, say, a jaguar or a snake.[12]

One important effect of this exercise is to highlight those texts that within a given tradition stand as classics or charters, central points of reference for literary production. These are the great cosmogonies of America that, largely ignored as such from the outside, have sustained generations of life and thought from within, marking time–space coordinates and generating the energy of politics. Those known or available to us represent only the smallest part of a possible total, yet among them they offer an authoritative version of the Fourth World – above all the magnificent *Popol vuh,* which in every respect deserves its epithet "the Bible of America."

As its palimpsest the *Popol vuh* specifies a text of the same name that belongs to the Mesoamerican corpus written in native script, whose surviving examples offer the most precious resource of all. A Fourth World testimony is legible still in these pre-Cortesian texts, and though imperfectly understood, their script nonetheless offers a more direct reading than is ever possible with visual or verbal language that has been transcribed, translated, and edited. Superb facsimiles now recreate at least the principles of the libraries to which their originals once belonged, and in so doing offer unrivaled access to the intellectual traditions of the Fourth World, especially in matters of chronology and genesis.

Precisely because they recognized their challenge to the biblical version of the planet's history, the first Christian missionaries burned whole libraries of these Mesoamerican texts (Fig. 9), sending a few specimens back to Europe in the vain hope that their code might be cracked. For the same reason they burned libraries of *quipus* in Tahuantinsuyu, another token of the effective power of these string texts. Later, in northern Turtle Island, they confiscated "pagan libraries" of Mide scrolls. Indeed, throughout America the Christians' proselytizing on the sole basis of their particular scripture provoked surprise, even consternation, wherever it was announced, and formed the core of debates with prospective converts. Typically these last would respond that the concept of scriptures was not entirely new to them, for they already had their own authoritative texts. This was the argument put forward by the Aztecs to the Franciscans in 1524, by the Tupi to the Capuchins in 1612, and by the Algonkin to the Puritans in 1642. The speech of the Aztecs in particular, *Totecuyoane,* is worth quoting from as an apologia for the continent:

> Where is it you come from,
> how is it that your gods have been scattered
> from their municipal centres?
> Out of the clouds, out of the mist,
> out of ocean's midst you have appeared.
> The Omneity takes form in you,

in your eye, in your ear, in your lips.
So, as we stand here,
we see, we address,
the one through whom everything lives,
the night, the Wind,
whose representatives you are.

And we have felt the breath, the word
of our lord the Omneity,
which you have brought with you.
The speaker of the world sent you because of us.
Here we are, amazed by this.
You brought his book with you, his script,
heaven's word, the word of god.

. . .

You say
that we don't know
the Omneity of heaven and earth.
You say that our gods are not original.
That's news to us
and it drives us crazy.
It's a shock and it's a scandal,
for our ancestors came to earth
and they spoke quite differently.[13]

TLACUILOLLI

The most ingenious visual language of the Fourth World, Meso-american iconic script, is designated by the Nahuatl term *tlacuilolli*,[14] that which is produced with a brush-pen by the painter-scribe (*tlacuilo*). Among the scripts of the world it is the one that has perhaps most defied definition and analysis. Nonphonetic, it may register sound-concepts and does so in Nahuatl, Mixtec, and other Mesoamerican languages. Highly flexible in layout, it may conform by turns to a chronicled narrative, an icon or map, or a mathematical table. Indeed, integrating into one holistic statement what for us are the separate concepts of letter, picture, and arithmetic, it positively flouts received Western notions of writing: Round fruits on a tree count out units of time (Fig. 10); the sign for a place also denotes a date in the Era; a bird serves to characterize and date the space through which it flies.

Appropriately, the finest texts in this script are preeminently "painted" in this sense of *tlacuilolli* on the pages of Mesoamerican screenfold books. Thanks to Christian incendiarism and the ravages of time, the once copious libraries of these books are now represented by no more than thirty or so texts, which for that reason alone merit the description classic. Stemming from within a two-hundred-mile radius of Tepexic, they have been scattered

Figure 9. Book burning. (*Tlaxcala Codex,* Scene 13 ["in nican quin tlahtiqui tlatlatecollo teopixque"].)

from their original places of manufacture and use and are typically identified today by the alien names of collectors (Bodley, Laud, Selden, Aubin, Borgia, Cospi, Féjérváry) or of cities and institutions that have come to house them (Vienna, Vaticanus). Formed from different materials (paper, skin), cut to different page sizes, and written in different regional styles, these pre-Cortesian texts nonetheless constitute a clearly defined corpus and for that reason provide a principal guide and reference point in any discussion of *tlacuilolli.*

According to the reading principle they observe, these books may be classified either as annals (*xiuhtlapoualli*), which proceed by years, or as cosmic books (*teoamoxtli*), which intricately combine the Number and Sign sets of the yearly seasons and the *tonalamatl* of human pregnancy. Dating

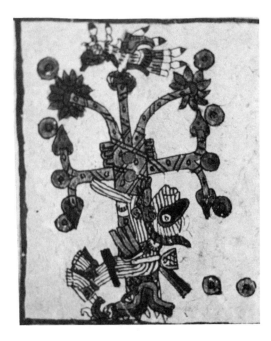

Figure 10. Round fruits on a tree as calendar units (*Vaticanus,* p. 17). The ten combine with the two free-floating units to produce an interval of twelve days.

from the thirteenth to the sixteenth century A.D. they stand as a precedent for works composed in native script after the invasion that are more or less affected by European norms, and for many others transcribed into the alphabet, albeit with enormous semantic loss. Materially they are complemented by murals on plaster and by the corpus of inscriptions in stone and wood, notably the bas-reliefs of Tenochtitlan, which likewise were once colored.

The Mesoamerican roots of *tlacuilolli* may be traced back at least to the first millennium B.C.; features of the script are already superbly exemplified in Olmec rock carvings at Chalcatzingo, the elaborate framed designs at Izapa, and the slim year-date stelae at Monte Alban.[15] And the tradition is still alive, despite the demise of professional scribes. In rituals performed today we find configurations that may explain and be explained by those in the screenfold books. The Otomi of Pahuatlan, for example, use figures of native paper that directly appeal to the logic of the *tonalamatl* (*Historia de la curación de antigua*), and in the Tlapa area altars are constructed in patterns reminiscent of *Féjérváry.*[16]

Part of a tradition that runs from the first millennium B.C. to the present

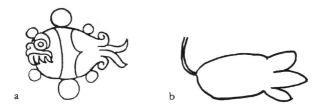

a   b

Figure 11. Doubled images of the heart (*yolotl*): (a) fish (*Magliabechiano,* fol. 3v); (b) flower (*yolloxochitl*) (*Libellus,* fol. 53v).

day, *tlacuilolli* is also extensive in space. Many of its diagnostics, of detail and specific convention, recur in a wide range of media and contexts, even beyond the borders of Mesoamerica. Indeed, it is instructive to examine how its lexis of images and signs corresponds to visual vocabulary from farther afield. On the one hand, wider comparison brings out significance underlying the more recondite or now arcane visual statements in the pre-Cortesian books; on the other, with these books as a constant and summum, otherwise remote or discrete images suggest forgotten threads of Fourth World coherence.

The maize plant whose cobs bear the face of a young man; swimming fish that look like human hearts that look like flowers (*yollo-xochitl*); the feline caiman whose tail grows into a tree that bears different fruits; rushes that double as a bird head and beak: These puns on vegetal and animal life-forms (Plate 2b, Figs. 11–13; see also Fig. 42d) take us deep into the philosophy of American plant genetics and evolution testified to in the oldest known iconography, on stelae at Chavin and Izapa. The Caiman Stela at Chavin anticipates not just the growth of plants from the reptilian body (manioc, peanuts, gourd; Fig. 61) but the place of this body between its fish tail and the bird above its head: At its joints are the faces and eyes that typify the earth figures of Aztec sculpture. On pottery, the same trope of the domesticated plant educed from a reptilian body surfaces far to the north in Cahokia, in this case a gourd whose vine is also the tail of a snake that is also the earth tilled by a woman; a Chimu depiction of the bean-runner shows sprouts growing into the arms and legs of a messenger. Quick and ingenious, this multiple punning not only evokes an agricultural story but explores the idea of transformation itself, a process encoded elsewhere in *Féjérváry* (p. 1: plant, insect, vertebrate; see Fig. 62). It also privileges a certain nonessentialism, equating full face with double profiles (Fig. 14), a visual play made throughout the continent, not least in the statue of Coatlicue, the great earth goddess of Tenochtitlan.[17]

Within this discourse of life-forms, a special place is accorded human anatomy and its component parts. Most literally deconstructed in victory scenes already announced at Sechin, these feature organs and limbs (head everywhere signifying capital trophy), while as the standard set of torso, head, arm, and leg they are assigned to the corners of a building or the quarters of empire. Moreover, each of these four principal structures, owned and embodied by the skeletal lord of hell, has its own internal impulse and numeracy. The counters of the torso, vertebrae, and ribs may run to monstrous serpentine lengths or locally confirm their human time and value; the head orifices prefigure the seven caves of tribal origin and stand in a 7:9 ratio to the skin orifices of the whole body. The digits of hand and foot feed most directly into numeracy in providing the categories of base 20, the complement of the whole human being preferred in Mesoamerican and Caribbean arithmetic; base 10, also a linguistic unit even with Mesoamerica; and base 5, a bar in Papaloapan, Oaxaca, and lowland texts and also a widespread linguistic unit. As actual digits or the prints they make, hands and feet serve particularly to highlight variation from the norm: in excess, as six fingers on Cahokia and Panama pottery and Sechin carving, or in default, as in the the sets of three- and four-toed prints in *Borgia* that make an arithmetical statement while recalling humanity's lesser-toed reptilian antecedents.[18] A similarly adjustable numeracy operates with regard to the principal orifice of the head, the mouth whose teeth everywhere affirm binary addition and the powers of 2: Teeth in the open-jaw emblem at Xochicalco signal the sets of tooth-total tribute towns arranged around the main pyramid (16 + 16). Yet the most striking example of dental numeracy is the deliberate denial of the binary it epitomizes through frontal representation of odd-numbered sets that hinge on an "impossible" central unit. A true American paradigm, the spirit mask with its eerie odd-numbered teeth has been sewn onto mummies in Paracas, incised in head pieces of pottery urns from the Amazon to the Arkansas rivers, carved in stone in the circum-Caribbean double-ego statues and in cedarwood in the Tlingit Bear Mother totem pole, painted in Zapotec murals at Huitzo and on Classic Maya vases, worked into Huichol yarn paintings, and cast in gold by the Quitocara in Ecuador, by the Chibcha, and by the Mixtecs (Plate 3). In the screenfolds such teeth are a common attribute of the rain god that, as an upper being, in this particularly resembles the Chimu mountain god Ai Apec.[19]

In all, like the general life-form lexis to which it belongs, this particular body paradigm of itself argues powerfully for the coherence of American culture. Unequivocal in all the examples cited, and others that might be, it appears over vast areas of time and space, marked in many different materials. More narrowly, within North America the screenfolds find clusters of yet more precise analogues in cultures that similarly acknowledge skin of deer (or buffalo) as a prime surface of and for representation. Here we find not just the reflection of that fact on the page in question but whole vocabu-

Figure 12. Bean-runner. Chimu vase (after Kutscher 1954:pl. 29).

Figure 13. Caiman-tree. A bird perches on the tree that grows from the caiman, whose head is downmost. (Izapa Stela 25; after V. G. Smith 1988:fig. 56c.)

Figure 14. Eagles in profile and Owl full-face: (a) *Tilantongo Annals*, p. 16; (b) *Historia de la curación*, p. 1.

laries dedicated to gesture or sign language, the measurement of time periods and their multiples, the establishing of the key ciphers of ritual life, and the naming of people tribally or through individual masks or souls, say in battle scenes or rosters (Fig. 15; see also Fig. 44), and above all of places, in toponyms that typify features of landscape and architecture[20] (Fig. 16; see also Figs. 1–4).

For their part, fiercely resistant to intrusion into ways of life they have developed in Greater Mexico and Anasazi, the Huichol and the Navajo use modes of representation in their paintings that are clearly analogous to screenfold pages and that moreover have been the object of detailed commentaries by author-scribes. Like the screenfolds, the Huichol *Creation* series painted by Tutukila and Yucauye Cucame highlight types of message and address distinguished by a repertoire of speech scrolls and even the image of writing on the page; numeracy embedded in such elements as attire and landscape, ingenious metamorphoses of plant and animal forms, inset dreams, the incised-gourd bowl of the sky and rain (*xucuri;* cf. Nahuatl *xicalli*), temples ("god houses" in both languages) that contain mosaic mirrors and other paraphernalia, and conquest as an arrow shot into a toponym. Indeed, affinity in language extends to the arrow-pierced heart, or valentine, that denotes the capture of the life force (*iyari;* cf. Nahuatl *iyolli*) and hence a literal "concept"[21] (Fig. 17). Carefully measured spatial compositions within a frame that imitates the hogan floor, Navajo dry paintings correspond predominantly to *teoamoxtli* page maps like the quincunx of Coixtlahuaca and the quatrefoil of *Féjérváry.* At the same time, like the yarn paintings, they offer clues to encoded cosmogony and openly explain such Greater Mexican paradigms as the lightning that descends as a snake from the thunder clouds, which also occurs in the screenfold books; or the function of sacred mountains like Popocatepetl and Matlalcueye, profiled on the page as well as molded in ritual from edible or therapeutic materials. As we have seen, the Navajo identify deerskin books as the true originals of the dry paintings, a tradition confirmed by Anasazi mural art and by the Kiowa, whose migration history closely parallels that of the Navajo and who prepared their deerskins with the same cactus-juice mixture as the Mesoamericans. Indeed, precisely those dry paintings that most closely resemble the screenfold books are customarily prepared on a deerskin surface.[22]

Within this framework, *tlacuilolli* emerges as a highly specialized form of more general practices of representation. This is true in the first instance in regard to the page frame itself; after all, screenfold pagination is known nowhere else in America. In the *tlacuilolli* classics the very dimensions of the page and the page totals and subtotals of a text are everywhere significant. Within the page frame, design in plan interchanges with design in profile: Shifts in horizontal register or 90° angle correspond to changes in category or order, all of which allows for (or better, demands) the principle of multi-

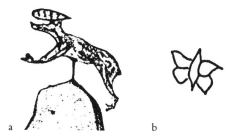

Figure 15. Personal names: (a) Mato Wamni-yomni, or "Bear whirlwind," the latter element being shown as the cocoon of transformation (*Oglala Roster:* Mallery 1893:604; (b) Xicotencatl, or Honeybee (*Tlaxcala Lienzo*).

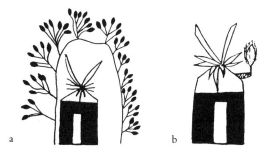

Figure 16. Locations of the Kiowa Sun Dance (Kado): (a) Ado-byuni, or Timber Circle; (b) Ahin-doha, or Cedar Bluff. (*Settan Year Count,* 1858, 1859.)

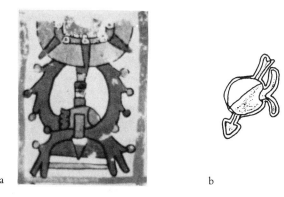

Figure 17. Arrow-pierced hearts: (a) *Cospi*, p. 2; (b) Yucauye Cucame painting "Kauyamarie and the Second World."

ple reading. Such are the holistic resources of *tlacuilolli* in this respect that even the requirements of a plan, ledger, or calculating table need not preclude the view of a profiled landscape. Complex in the classic texts, many of these procedures are best appreciated in the first instance in the copious body of post-Cortesian documents elicited by the viceregal courts of New Spain, where, in cases of limited and defined argument, alphabetic glosses and copies explain the meaning of the native original. A superb example of such a text has recently come to light in Belfast: Written on amate paper and datable to 1556, it concerns a suit brought by the towns of Xoloc, Cuauhtlapan, and Tepoxaco against Tepotzotlan, the *cabecera* just to the north of Tenochtitlan promoted by the Spanish (Fig. 18).[23]

In this *Tepotzotlan Codex,* ten columns detail the goods paid to representatives of that town by the *tlaxilacalli,* or wards, of Xoloc (four), Cuauhtlapan (four), and Tepoxaco (two). In the horizontal register, these columns distinguish between daily *comida* and less frequent transactions; and through the 90° angle they distinguish between commodity items (turkeys, tortillas, firewood, pottery, etc.) and labor, female and male. Quantities of items are shown by the usual signs and include the possibility of incompletion (e.g., 15 as three-quarters of a flag [*pantli,* or 20]); infixes denote quality and type of item and in turn display a subsidiary numeracy (e.g., sticks of firewood in a bundle).

Forming a row at the top of the ten columns, the place signs draw fully on the resources of *tlacuilolli,* first evident in this mode in inscriptions carved at Monte Alban one and a half millennia before (see Fig. 3h). Indicating type of terrain and soil, they state a logic of their own, not just as sets of wards (4 + 4 + 2) but as a series that alternates the natural with the man-made, interweaving as it were the notion of a united front (5 + 5): While odd numbers feature hill and river, even numbers feature house and altar shrine. Moreover, two of the even-numbered man-made toponyms that appear in plan – the "old market" Tianquizçolco (6) and the perfectly formed fields of Coamilco (10) – show a complex internal logic that reflects the very structure of the page and the text. At Tianquizçolco, the 5 × 5 calculation infixed into the market circle recalls the frequency of the old five-day market cycle and the fivefold horizontal registers of the page, the first and uppermost of which is occupied by the toponyms (for good measure, the sigma count of 5, [i.e., 1 + 2 + 3 + 4 + 5] is stated in the dots that indicate porosity in soils of the place names, as at Tepoxaco). At Coamilco, the tenth and last toponym, the proportions of the two fields are spelled out by ten dots arranged so as to determine the field area according to native convention. Carefully measured, the proportions and area of these two fields prove to be the exact model for the two vertically divided halves of the text itself.[24]

What is more, while succinctly conveying all these practical and theoreti-

a   b   c   d

Figure 18. Place signs in the *Tepotzotlan Codex:* (a) Xoloc; (b) Tianquiz-çolco; (c) Tepoxaco; (d) Coamilco. (Numbers 1, 6, 9, and 10, respectively, in the horizon of ten toponyms.)

cal data, the row of toponyms sets out the profile of the actual landscape they occupy. Running north–south from Xoloc (left) to Coamilco (right), this profile implicitly corresponds to the eastern horizon, exactly like that of the toponyms along the upper edge of *Xolotl Map 1* of Texcoco. Moreover, in representing landscape in this maplike way, the toponyms that begin here with Xoloc and "hill of Xolotl" (known in Spanish as La Columna, the hill is still a clear marker in the landscape) encode the history of that Chichimec leader who in establishing the political order of this whole area in the eleventh century preferred Xoloc, Cuauhtlapan, and Tepoxaco to Tepotzo-tlan, the object of the text's complaint. In all these details and within its frame, the extreme sophistication of this page as a legal and literary state-ment is further confirmed by negative definition when it is compared with the "copy" on European paper that exists in the Archivo General de la Nación in Mexico, whose format is reduced simply to that of the European ledger.[25] Such radical loss is true of Europeanized native texts generally, which fragment iconic script into the separate modes of narratives, say of acquired rights, arithmetical bookkeeping, and two-dimensional maps of the *lienzo* type. By contrast, the iconic-script original intimates history, settles accounts, and theorizes and pictures geography, all within one holis-tic and reflexive design, in the best tradition of *tlacuilolli* and the screenfold books.

In the pre-Cortesian screenfolds, these capacities of *tlacuilolli* are percepti-bly greater still, thanks to a finer calligraphy of line and dot, lexis of color, and appeal to embedded data and multiple reading. Indeed, the very diagnos-tic of these texts is the system of Signs and Numbers generated by the *tonalamatl* and the seasons of the year; these may be set into a design in profile or plan, adding a further dimension to the reading of it. The complex-ity of the statement that is made as a result, especially in works of a certain length, like the *Tepexic Annals* (fifty-two pages) or the *Borgia teoamoxtli*

Table 1. *The* tonalamatl

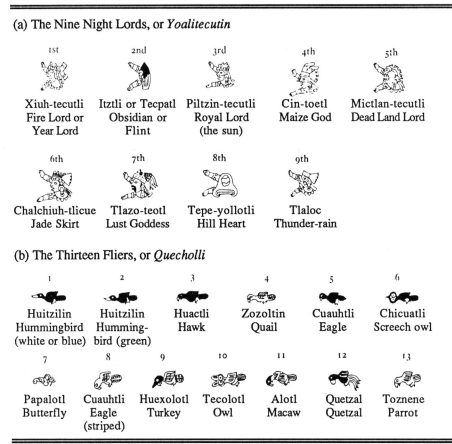

(a) The Nine Night Lords, or *Yoalitecutin*

1st	2nd	3rd	4th	5th
Xiuh-tecutli Fire Lord or Year Lord	Itztli or Tecpatl Obsidian or Flint	Piltzin-tecutli Royal Lord (the sun)	Cin-toetl Maize God	Mictlan-tecutli Dead Land Lord

6th	7th	8th	9th
Chalchiuh-tlicue Jade Skirt	Tlazo-teotl Lust Goddess	Tepe-yollotli Hill Heart	Tlaloc Thunder-rain

(b) The Thirteen Fliers, or *Quecholli*

1	2	3	4	5	6
Huitzilin Hummingbird (white or blue)	Huitzilin Humming-bird (green)	Huactli Hawk	Zozoltin Quail	Cuauhtli Eagle	Chicuatli Screech owl

7	8	9	10	11	12	13
Papalotl Butterfly	Cuauhtli Eagle (striped)	Huexolotl Turkey	Tecolotl Owl	Alotl Macaw	Quetzal Quetzal	Toznene Parrot

Note: In the count of nights, the Nine are articulated as nine moons ($9 \times 29 - 1 = 260$);

(seventy-six pages), so far exceeds the limits of verbal language as to render transcription an unending task. Basic equipment for any approach is some prior familiarity with the *tonalamatl* (Table 1) and seasonal sets and their semantic resonance. Imparting or invoking just this knowledge appears to have been one of the functions of the genre of *teoamoxtli*, which for that reason deserve consideration in their own right.

TEOAMOXTLI

In his *Sumaria relación*, the Texcocan historian Ixtlilxochitl describes how in the seventh century A.D. the Toltec Huematzin authored a text

Table 1. (*cont.*)

(c) The Twenty Signs, or *Tonalli*

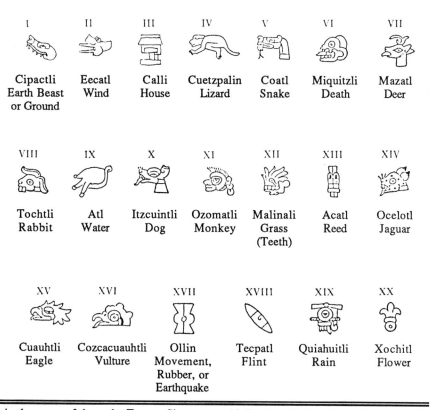

I	II	III	IV	V	VI	VII
Cipactli Earth Beast or Ground	Eecatl Wind	Calli House	Cuetzpalin Lizard	Coatl Snake	Miquitzli Death	Mazatl Deer

VIII	IX	X	XI	XII	XIII	XIV
Tochtli Rabbit	Atl Water	Itzcuintli Dog	Ozomatli Monkey	Malinali Grass (Teeth)	Acatl Reed	Ocelotl Jaguar

XV	XVI	XVII	XVIII	XIX	XX
Cuauhtli Eagle	Cozcacuauhtli Vulture	Ollin Movement, Rubber, or Earthquake	Tecpatl Flint	Quiahuitli Rain	Xochitl Flower

in the count of days, the Twenty Signs are multiplied by 13 ($20 \times 13 = 260$).

known as *teoamoxtli,* a divine or cosmic book. It was said to contain "all the stories that the Toltecs had from the creation of the world to that time . . . their sufferings and fortune, rulers, laws, good government and examples, temples, idols and rites . . . ; astronomy, philosophy, architecture and other arts, a compendium of science and knowledge."[26] This encyclopedic range matches that of the nine pre-Cortesian texts commonly referred to as "ritual," for which a fitting term is therefore *teoamoxtli.* They are *Borbonicus* and *Tonalamatl Aubin* from the highland Basin and Tlaxcala; *Borgia* and the closely related *Cospi* and *Vaticanus,* probably from Cholula; and three works distinguished by the toponyms of the Papaloapan area, *Laud, Cuicatlan,* and the *Coixtlahuaca Map,* plus the closely related *Féjérváry.* Formally, rather

Table 2. Teoamoxtli: *Pagination and chaptering*

A. *Pagination*

Borbonicus*ᵃ* (Bb)	44ff	> pp. 1–40 I (reverse blank)
Tonalamatl Aubin (Ta)	20ff	< pp. 1–20 I (reverse blank)
Borgia*ᵇ* (Bg)	38ff	< pp. 1–28 v pp. 29–38 I v 39–46 < pp. 47–76
Vaticanus*ᶜ* (Vt)	48ff	> pp. 1–48 I < pp. 49–96
Cospi (Cs)	20ff	> pp. 1–13 (pp. 14–20 blank) I < pp. 21–31
		(pp. 32–40 blank)
Féjérváry (Fj)	22ff	< pp. 1–22 I pp. 23–44
Laud*ᵈ* (Ld)	22ff + 2 pp.	< pp. 1–22 I pp. 23–46
Cuicatlan*ᵈ* (Cc)	21ff	< pp. 1–10 (pp. 11–42 blank or annals)
Coixtlahuaca Map (Cx)	1f	p. 1 I (reverse blank)

Symbols: >, <, v = reading direction; I = turn from obverse to reverse of screenfold.
*ᵃ*Initial and end pages are now missing.
*ᵇ*Pages 29–46, a single chapter, form the middle section of the text.
*ᶜ*Repetition of chapters between the two sides of the screenfold ("Twenty Signs," "Burial": see "Chapter topics" below) suggests that they represent two texts.
*ᵈ*Nowotny (1961), in line with most scholars, keeps to the old pagination, which corresponds to a reversed reading order.

B. *Chapter topics*

	1		2																											
	a	b	a	b	c	d	e	f	g	h	i	j	k	l	m	n	o	p	q	r	s	t	u	v	w	x	aa	bb	cc
Bb	*		*	*			*																						
Ta			*	*			*																						
Bg	*		*	*	*	*	*	*	*	*	*		*		*	*		*		*		*	*	*	*			*	*
Vt			*	*	*	*	*		*	*			*	*			*	*	*		*	*	*					*	*
Cs		*	*	*																		*							*
Fj	*	*	*					*				*	*		*	*	*	*	*			*	*				*	*	
Ld	*	*	*		*			*	*					*			*	*				*	*				*	*	
Cc			*					*				*						*									*		
Cx								*														*	*						

than narrate events year by year, like the *xiuhtlapoualli,* or genre of annals, these *teoamoxtli* gather a great wealth of information into highly condensed thematic chapters (Table 2).

In a continuous stream, linear or boustrophedon, annals typically proceed by years that are named by the *tonalamatl* over 52-year cycles, produced by the Thirteen Numbers and four of its Twenty Signs. By contrast, the chapters into which the *teoamoxtli* are divided draw on the full resources of the

Table 2. (*cont.*)

1	Cycles of the year (20–2)			
a	Feasts	Bb 23–40	Bg 29–46	Fj 5–22 Ld 21–2
b	Eleven	Cs 21–31	Fj 5–14	Ld 39–44

2 *Tonalamatl* (1–19)

a	Night Lords (9)	Bb 21–2 Bg 14	Vt 13–16 Fj 2–4 Ld 31–8 Cc 1–2
	[in Trecenas Bb Ta, Grid Cs, Map Fj]		
b	Quecholli (7)	Bg 71 Vt 13–16	Cs 12–13 [in Trecena Bb Ta]
c	Number Pairs (8)	Bg 58–60 Vt 33–42 Ld 9–14	
d	Twenty Signs (1)	Bg 9–13 Vt 28–32 Vt 87–94	
e	Trecenas (11a)	Bb 1–20 Ta 1–20 Bg 61–70 Vt 49–68	
f	Amazons (16b–c)	Bg 47–8 Ld 15–18	
g	Birth (2c)	Bg 15–17 Vt 33–42 Fj 23–9 Ld 1–8 Cc 3	
h	Burial	Bg 25–6 Vt 12(3c) Vt 71	
i	Copal Offering (16f)	Bg 75–6	
j	Drinkers (3h)	Vt 72	
k	Hazards	Vt 24–7 Fj 41–2 Cc 9	Cx 1 [in Tribute Trees Bg]
l	Judges	Fj 33–4 [linked with Quecholli augurs]	
m	Kindling (3g)	Ld 23–30 [in Tribute trees Bg]	
n	Marriage (16i)	Bg 57 Fj 35–7	
o	Martial Arts (16l)	Fj 38–43	
p	Mores	Bg 18–21 (16h) Fj 26–9 (16m) Ld 15–20	
q	Partners (3d)	Vt 9–11 Fj 23–5 Cc 4–8 ?Ld 19–20	
r	Planting	Bg 27–8 Vt 69 Fj 33–4	
s	Rain Gods (16k)	Vt 43–8	
t	Roofbeams (3i)	Vt 9–11 Fj 30–2	
u	Travel (3a)	Bg 55 Fj 30–2, 35–40	
v	Tribute Trees	Bg 49–53 Vt 17–18 [in Map Fj]	
w	Venus (18)	Bg 53–4 Vt 80–4 Cs 9–11	
x	Workers (16c)	Bg 47–8 Vt 77–9 Cx 1	
aa	Map Fj 1 (quatrefoil)	Ld 46 Cc 10 Cx 1 (quincunx)	
bb	Icon as Tezcatlipoca	Bg 17 Fj 44 Tlaloc Ld 45 Deerskin Bg 53 Vt 96	
	Dog and Monkey	Vt 85–6 Snakes Bg 73 Vt 75 Scorpions Vt 95	
	Male and Female	Bg 74 Vt 74 Life and Death Bg 56 Vt 76	
cc	Grid with 52 columns (16a)	Bg 1–8 Vt 1–8 Cs 1–8	

Note: Numbers in parentheses refer to the "Katalog" of *teoamoxtli* chapters in Nowotny (1961:193–285), which is based on the formal criterion of Number of Sign set; they are omitted when imprecise by that criterion, or when misleading here (also, in that source the Sign sets of the Night Lords and Quecholli are in several cases not recognized as topics). Duplicated page numbers result from double registers. Except for two or three enigmatic pages, the listing covers surviving *teoamoxtli* chapters.

tonalamatl, with its 13 × 20 days and 9 × 29 nights, or the year, with its 18 Feasts of 20 days and 11 sky phases, systems that regulated all aspects of life in ancient Mesoamerica and relate respectively to pregnancy and the seasons. Among them, these sign systems numerically determine the reading order of every single page and chapter of every *teoamoxtli* extant, a fact that places enormous weight upon them as classifiers of reality, and a fact underappreciated even in Nowotny's indispensable catalogue.[27] In some cases they become the topics of the *teoamoxtli* chapters in their own right and in a fashion that helps us to see how they relate to each other and to the society that formulated them while again inviting comparison beyond Mesoamerica.

Fundamental to the *tonalamatl,* the ninefold Yoalitecutin count out and preside over its 260 nights from conception to birth (see Table 1). Embodying the power of the night, they bestow fates by threes, good, bad, and indifferent, and their ultimate identities coincide with the nine moons of pregnancy according to an ancient paradigm of trimesters evident in Olmec figurines from Chalcatzingo (where for instance the third trimester is marked by the *linea gris*).[28] Ranged in four pairs around the first of their number, Xiuhtecutli, the Fire Lord literally of kindling, they tell the story of gestation: the hard Obsidian of possible miscarriage or the budding Precious Child (Royal Lord) of the visible embryo (2, 3), Maize God who fattens the flesh and Hell Lord who builds the skeleton (4, 5), the females Jade Skirt and Weaving Woman (Lust Goddess) who may determine the earliest possible births (6, 7), and Hill Heart's wild breech baby and the rain god's amniotic waters (8, 9). Prominent in the ancient calendars of the Mixe and the southern Zapotec, the Night Lords are celebrated in every one of the *teoamoxtli* and, like the 3,000-year-old Olmec mosaic pendant from Las Bocas, accord prime significance to the nights and moons of the *tonalmatl.*[29] Their force is still felt today, not just in native calendars but in customs like the "soothing of the child" (*arrullar al niño*) over nine nights that symbolically rehearse the nine-moon gestation and birth of Christ, that is, Huitzilopochtli, at midwinter. Beyond Mesoamerica they find ready analogues in the nine-night rituals of Anasazi and the nine mothers of Kogi creation, which further sustain the link with the night and the womb.

While the Yoalitecutin count and allot the night fates of the *tonalamatl,* its days are so allotted by the Thirteen Numbers and Twenty Signs. Though elsewhere linked with the sidereal moon, the set of Thirteen corresponds chiefly to diurnal time and may comprise no more than straightforward arithmetical units, like dots and bars. As an element in a person's birthday name, these numbers may be paired in what is effectively the prototype of the Marriage chapter (twenty-five pairs, 2–26). At the same time, the set is frequently correlated with that of the Heroes who helped create the Mesoamerican world, and above all with the Quecholli. Related above (Chapter 1, n. 5) to the feathered solstice dancers of the Chibcha and Carib kin, these fliers well vindicate the general notion of America as "the continent of the bird." Behaviorally they are defined by such concepts as habitat, diet, song, type and time of flight, plumage, whether edible or not, and whether domestic or not.

Very early examples of the three precious-feathered members of the set, Macaw (11), Quetzal (12), and Parrot (13), occur with a human flier (*volador*) at Chalcatzingo, apparently in the paradigm applied a millennium later to One Reed of Tula, whose *quetzal* heart, between the iridescence of Macaw and Parrot, became the planet Venus. They epitomize the tropical plumage that was traded far to south and north even as currency, like the Mesoamerican Feather (*tzontli*) that stands for 400. High-flying Eagle (5) is everywhere the paragon of military virtue, just as his double, Owl (10), is the night seizer with second sight who bodes ill: In *tlacuilolli* the numerical relation between the two birds is caught in the visual pun that equates two facing Eagle profiles with the full face of Owl (see Fig. 14). With its amazing metabolism, Hummingbird (1), the first of the set, emerges "supreme" in Amazonian narrative, Chimu pottery, and the Nazca lines, names the first queens in the *Popol vuh* and the emperors Huitzilopochtli and Huascar in Mexico and Peru, is the "first bird" of the Mide scrolls,[30] and with Butterfly (7) best exemplifies the principle of transformation through flight, displayed on stelae at Teotenango and Teotihuacan and analyzed at length by Eva Hunt with reference to a Tzotzil poem. Wing-borne messengers of the augur, in the *teoamoxtli* the Thirteen impinge especially on the subject's own later coupling and reproduction, and may bear the sign for *tilmatli,* or cloth, which according to Luis Reyes denotes "burden," that is, their charge as augurs; elsewhere four of them speak from four temples, plain and eared Owls of ill omen (6, 10) plus the edible Quail and Turkey (4, 9; in Nahuatl, "eats" are *tla-qualli* and "good" is *qualli*). Initially domesticated in Mexico, Turkey is the companion who when abused or forgotten recovers its own voice and the military quality celebrated on Mississippi shell and in the very name of Huascar's rival, the Inca emperor Atahuallpa. In *Borgia* (p. 71), framed by all Thirteen Quecholli in their magnificence, Quail, the Sun's bird of sacrifice, provides the focus of the augury for Four Movement, the name of this Sun or Era.

Determined by the digits of human hands and feet and the vigesimal count also used by the Chibcha and Carib, the Twenty Signs stand as the property of the scribe and appeal more narrowly to the Mesoamerican scriptural tradition as such. Having amongst them the face masks, or personae, of Night Lords and Quecholli, they denote ingenuity as much as fate, like musical and other skills. Distributed over the body like the twenty *megis* shells of the Midewiwin, they indicate nodes and moments of significance, Signs on the deerskin painted on the deerskin, and as the attribute of deities in the page icons typical of *teoamoxtli,* the complete set defines complete power (Plate 4). Hence, they articulate the figure of the warlike Tezcatlipoca in *Borgia:* Deer (VIII) and Wind (II) placed at his extremities suggest speed, and his single foot makes the reptilian Earth beast (I) tremble. In the *Laud* icon of the rain god Tlaloc, Jaguar roar and Snake scepter suggest his thunder and lightning; indeed, in explaining the esoteric "jaguar-snake" phraseology (*ocelo-coatl*) in the Sacred Hymn (*Inin icuic*) to Tlaloc,[31] the Signs here also construct that god arithmetically, since his Rain mask (Sign XIX) is the sum of Jaguar-thunder (Sign XIV) and Snake-lightning (Sign V). In the *tonalamatl,* these Signs combine with the Thirteen Numbers to count out 260 days and its twenty "Trecenas."

As for the *teoamoxtli* chapters dedicated to the yearly seasons rather than the *tonalamatl,* these all derive their topics from their meters, elaborating on either the eighteen 20-day Feasts or the corresponding nocturnal set of eleven zodiac figures. Though the items of commodity tribute, paraphernalia, and choreography specified for the Feasts show marked regional variation, we may detect the recurrence of key symbols like Tonantzin's spindle and thread and her broom at Ochpaniztli (September), Xipe's cap and stripped-off skin at Tlacaxipehualiztli (March), Huitzilopochtli's flag (*pantli*) in Panquetzaliztli (December), and Tlaloc's boiling pot that marks the onset of the rains in Etzalqualiztli (June). Other notable feasts include Quecholli (November), when Cortes first came to Tenochtitlan and when the migrating birds flock to the highland lakes; and Micailhuitl (August), the feast of the dead, when the Aztecs decided on surrender and when the journeying soul is offered four seeds of comfort (maize, bean, two types of squash) by the domestic companion Turkey. Though exclusive to Mesoamerica, these Feasts find echoes farther afield, both in detail – for example, Turkey's seeds of Micailhuitl appear in Navajo ceremonials today – and structurally, in their placement at and between the equinoxes and solstices.

The zodiac Eleven have escaped general recognition as a set, though it is present for example in the Bonampak murals and possibly forms part of the Lunar Series in hieroglyphic dates in the Classic period. Bearing axes (*tepuztli*), adepts of the *maguey* plant and *pulque,* and adorned with crescent moons, the Eleven relate thematically to the pioneer house builders in the *Popol vuh* who, drunk on *pulque,* rose into the night sky to become the Pleiades and first signposted the zodiac road of the year. The *maguey,* which possesses its own fermenting agents, matures over eleven years (also the sunspot cycle), and eleven is the number of days in the yearly epact of the moon, whose phases affect the amount of liquid carried in the *maguey* plant. As "the place of the axe" surrounded by eleven hill shrines, Tepoztlan is home of Tepuztecatl, president of eleven axe bearers from the Chichinautzin–Popocatepetl ridge, who include the *maguey* and *pulque* goddess Mayauel and her consort Patecatl, expert in herbs. (The Nahua story supplies the names of the ancient Olmec who drank at the foaming mouth of the nearby volcano Chichinautzin, the Olympus of Tamoanchan and Mesoamerica.) The astronomical nature of the Eleven is further confirmed by the fact that, as with the hieroglyphic zodiac, they preside over formulas relevant to the synodic and sidereal cycles of the sun, the moon, and the wasp-star Venus, an arrangement epitomized in the Cempoala murals, where these three, the brightest bodies in the sky, are numerically correlated and where the sun has inset into it the elevenfold hallmark of the zodiac. In both *Cospi* and *Féjérváry,* under the aegis of the eleven zodiac figures, these formulas are in turn calculated in units whose optimal base number itself is eleven. As axe-bearing pioneers, the Eleven also prefigure totals of conquests and garrisons in *Mendoza* and the chronicles of Texcoco and on the giant round altar now again displayed in Mexico/Tenochtitlan.[32]

Though scarcely recognized by scholars, as a celestial and nocturnal cipher eleven has currency far beyond Mesoamerica. Telling in *Dine bahane* how the first eleven constellations were made, as 4 + 7 (i.e., the center and six directions), the Navajo place eleven radii in their Big Star dry painting (Plate 5a); the Huichol tell of and depict the metamorphosis of drunken bees into eleven flower-stars; the Kogi have a zodiac of eleven stations that double back between the Pleiades (Uha) and Scorpio (Ahu); and the Mapuche count with a meteorological cycle of $5\frac{1}{2} + 5\frac{1}{2}$ years. Eleven is also the number of speeches and marked deerskins offered to the Night Spirits at the Wagigo, or Winter Feast, of the Winnebago, one of their principal ceremonies. In all, they appear to be inseparable from what Lévi-Strauss identified as one of his key myths: the origin of the Pleiades, the prime marker of the zodiac.

Having this clear resonance throughout the Fourth World, the Number and Sign sets of the *tonalamatl* (9/13/20) and the seasons (18/11) were at the same time elaborated according to exclusively Mesoamerican norms as measures of tribute time and as main ingredients of *tlacuilolli* and the pre-Cortesian books. Conceptually, the yearly seasons stand to commodity tribute as the *tonalamatl* does to labor. Defined by the seasons of the sun and the night sky, the year relates to quantities and types of items "offered" or due over its eighteen Feasts, as well as to the less obvious periodicities of planets contemplated by the eleven *pulque* drinkers. The measure of the nine moons that separate conception from birth, the *tonalamatl* relates rather to human gestation, body, and skill, and by extension to the construction of society, its mores and callings. As such, the opposition between the two types of service and value is neatly confirmed by the *Féjérváry* screenfold, whose sides are respectively devoted to the one and then the other; moreover, in this, and in the title-page map they share, *Féjérváry* exactly anticipates the *Mendoza Codex,* which deals first with the conquest and levying of tribute items and then with the birth, growth, and duties of the citizens of Tenochtitlan.

The "labor" chapters of the *tonalamatl* and pregnancy, whose prototypes date back to the Olmec and Zapotec inscriptions,[33] receive the most elaboration in surviving texts. They develop clear thematic concepts out of the very Sign sets according to which they are read, celebrating their intrinsic powers or weaving them into patterns of human experience. Of these, the most highly articulated and eloquent are the following:

Planting – anthropomorphic maize is set into the caiman earth, and its yield is announced over the four-year harvest span (Plate 6a).

Travel – the *pochteca* and other bearers of goods and information, with their *tameme* backpack and frame (*cacaxtli*), staff and fan, move along the footprint trail on land or the water route of the canoe, or emulate sun, moon, and planets along the zodiac road.

Venus – appearing heliacally (just before the sun) in the east, five times over eight years and ninety-nine moons the planet hurls its arrows into respective victims, like potentates or water sources.

Burial – objects that the soul needs on the journey beyond death accompany patterned mummy bundles (Plate 6b).

Hazards – bat, caiman, eagle, and jaguar ambush the roads of the would-be conqueror.

Kindling – the new calendrical cycle, typically of fifty-two years, is begun when flame is engendered by the fire drill and carried to the quarters.

Tribute Trees – the four quarters of tribute that surround the capital are typified by the trees and vegetation and birds that respectively thrive in them.

Drinkers – flaunting the privilege of the aristocrat and the aged, occupants of thrones and power have brought to them cups of foaming *pulque* or *cacao*.

The gamut of these topics, which in a given chapter may appear alone or in combination, includes such other matters as Martial Arts, Judges, Partners, Marriage, Amazons, the fivefold male and female Workers, and Roofbeams. Especially brilliant and instructive are those topic-chapters that, like Birth and Mores, dispose of whole subsets of acts and events (see Table 2; Plates 7, 8; Figs. 19–21).

The Birth chapter covers the longer story of gestation that corresponds to the very logic of the *tonalamatl*, thematically highlighting two paired acts and states. After impregnation or creation, coded as the bone gimlet that pierces an eye or cell, the child is carried, literally on the palm of a hand; after the severing of the umbilical cord, which reaches down from the sky, the baby suckles on the breast and its ideally black nipple, as thirsty as a fish or in vain. The opening chapter in *Laud* (pp. 1–8) presents two versions of the sequence, one bad and one good. The bad sequence is dominated by Mictlantecutli, whose power, necessary for the formation of good bones and blood, can be deadly in excess: The impregnating bone fails to feel its way through to the dark cell in which the unborn child sits, owllike, and the fetus is a mere miscarriage, equipped with the paper passport of the unborn; the cutting of the umbilicus is watched by a gray bird of bad omen, and the would-be suckling mother is as dry as a stick. In the good sequence, Mictlantecutli's

Figure 19. Snake as sexual indicator. (*Borgia,* p. 59 [24 in the Number Pairs chapter].)

power is tempered by that of Weaving Woman, who holds the thread of life (respectively numbers 5 and 7 of the Night Lords, these two are both invoked in the *Florentine Codex* account of birth). Here the woman comes instantly to bear the child and, her belly round, is kissed by the golden bird; the placenta is properly buried, and her suckling does not prelude sexual excitement (a red-tipped penis) on the part of her husband. In these details, there is a hint of natal practices still observed in rural Mesoamerica: for example, the choice of the mother's food as "hot" or "cold," the wicker mat that keeps her from touching the ground, and the proper burial of the placenta.[34] In *Féjérváry,* this chapter opens side two of the screenfold, which is devoted to the "labor" chapters of the *tonalamatl,* just as its derivative opens the section of the *Mendoza Codex* that is devoted to Tenochtitlan's citizens; both link birth rites with the 80-day period. Highly defined, the images of these paired acts plus states – beget and bear, sever and suckle – are also recognizable in *xiuhtlapoualli* narratives, as in the *Tepexic Annals* account of Nine Wind's earthly gestation and his sky umbilicus;[35] they also encode practices and beliefs that extend to South America, for example the birth, in *Watunna,* of the monstrous Odosha from an improperly buried placenta.

Once born and suckled, the subject faces service, contract, and rank in precisely the labor discourse that defines the *tonalamatl* in the first place and whose images and Nahuatl phraseology have been extensively preserved in the *Florentine Codex* and the *Huehuetlatolli* texts of the sixteenth century. The

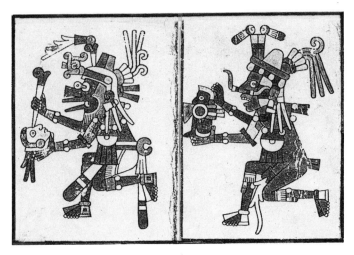

a   b

c   d

Figure 20. The four acts and events of the Birth chapter: (a) impregnation (pierced eye); (b) "bearing" the child; (c) cutting the umbilicus; (d) suckling. (*Féjérváry,* pp. 23–9.)

topics in question are legible in the subsequent chapters in *Féjérváry* and the corresponding section of *Mendoza,* which overtly deals with birth, marriage, labor tribute, warrior rank, and *pochteca* cults among Tenochtitlan's citizenry ("from the grave of the womb to the womb of the grave," as

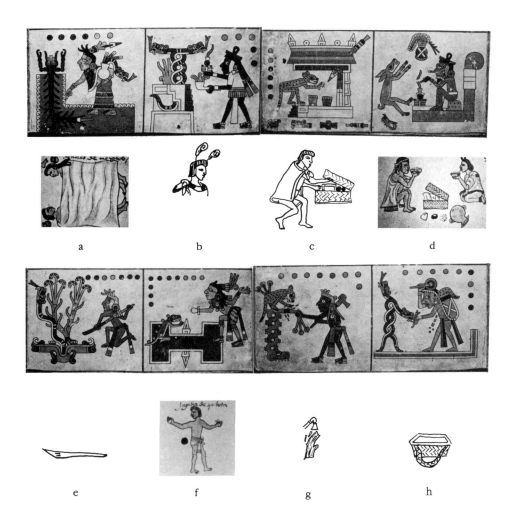

Figure 21. Concepts in the Mores chapter: (a) drunkenness; (b) theft; (c) two-tongued gossip; (d) lust; (e) backpack; (f) axe; (g) gaming; (h) handplow, or *coa*. (*Féjérváry*, pp. 26–9, correlated with *Mendoza*, pp. 70–1.)

Purchas put it).[36] The particular parallel between *Féjérváry* and *Mendoza* extends to their respective title-page maps and helps us to interpret the remarkable Mores chapter about work in general that is common to both texts and to other *teoamoxtli* like *Borgia* and *Laud*. It is legible thanks mainly to the *Mendoza* version of it (pp. 70–1), which, devoid of the *tonalamatl*, has Spanish glosses that go some way to explaining the ingenious logic and metaphor of the iconic-script original.

Generalizing the question of work and training, this Mores chapter rests basically on a contrast between the useful citizenry who carry the hod (*huacal*) and the hoe (*coa*) of the public worker, and their useless counterparts who loiter, gamble on the ballgame, thieve, gossip, drink *pulque*, and fornicate. With its tumpline, the *huacal* indicates all forms of transport and travel; the *coa,* or planting stick, together with its twin tool, the woodcutter's axe, denotes sedentary agriculture (whence the binary Nahuatl expression *ti milla chiazque / ti cuahcuahuizque:* "we'll prepare the milpa / we'll clear the trees"). On the negative side, theft means lifting the lid of the "treasured casket," the gossip is double in tongue and in its listening ears, and the fornication of the snakelike penis occurs "under the blanket."[37]

In the *Borgia* version (pp. 18–21), these notions of civic duty and misdemeanor are established first through the four basic urban, or masonic, forms of temple, pyramid, waterway, and ballcourt together with the cults proper to them, plus the four social conditions defined by backpack, hoe, axe, and *pulque* pot. Privileged role models, representatives of the Thirteen Heroes, preside over each so that, for example, the Sun guards the temple against theft, Jade Skirt (phallic snake in her water jar)[38] (see Fig. 19) epitomizes lust, Tezcatlipoca indulges in the ballgame yet also bears his *pochteca* load, Tlaloc wields the *coa* as Tlahuizcalpantecutli (Lord of the House of Dawn) wields the axe, and the Hell Lords exult in the waste occasioned by *pulque*. The scenes of felled forests and blooming *milpa*s of maize are especially graphic.

Like *Borgia,* yet concentrating on only a few multivalent Signs (Snake, V; Jaguar, XIV; Deer, VII; Lizard, IV). *Féjérváry* also proposes an internal structure of 4 + 4 moments or images, chapter halves that reflect each other in terms of bad and good. In the first half,

    a. the drinker thirsty as a deer for foaming *pulque* is admonished by Tlaloc;

    b. the thief idle like the jaguar steals food from the temple;

    c. the hissing, two-tongued gossip becomes a two-headed snake that sets ablaze, with the fire offering made to it, the temple it inhabits; and

    d. the adulterer's companion, on her bent waterway, shows her complicity by carrying a phallic snake in her water jar.

Then, thanks to work,

    e. the two-headed snake becomes two snakes, one of which tamely licks the carrier's hand as he sweats blood under his load;

    f. the jaguar is driven back to the forest, which it endeavors to defend from the woodcutter's axe;

    g. little excitement is generated in the ball court by players that are, respectively, one-handed and a lizard; and

    h. through the hoe, the phallic snake (*coa-tl*) becomes the community work (*coa-*) that produces maize.

Mendoza	*Féjérváry*

Introductory

pp.		pp.	
1	Quatrefoil title-page map	1	Quatrefoil title-page map
2–16	Conquests over nine imperial reigns	2–4	Nine Night Lords as conquerors

Commodity tribute and cycles of the year

| 17–18 | Sets of eleven garrisons within and beyond the Basin of Mexico | 5–14 | Eleven armed figures |
| 19–55 | Quantities of tribute due from 9 + 29 districts, according to the Feasts of the year | 15–22 | Feasts of the year with quantities of offerings |

Labor tribute and the *tonalamatl*

[change of format and style]	[reverse of the screenfold]
57–22 topics include: birth (re 80-day period), *pochteca,* ranks of judges, marriage, martial arts, mores of the citizenry	23–44 chapters include: Birth (re 80-day period), Travel (*pochteca*), Judges, Marriage, Martial Arts, Mores

Figure 22. Mendoza and *Féjérváry:* parallels of structure and detail. (Cf. Plates 4b, 5c; Table 2; Figs. 20, 21.)

Finally, in patterning experience in this way for purposes of social control and "divination," the *teoamoxtli* appeal nonetheless to specific historical experience, just as Ixtlilxochitl indicated. *Borbonicus* alludes repeatedly to Aztec origins in the nearer and more distant past, and the very three-part structure of *Borgia* corresponds to that of the Toltec Chichimec history of the Cholula area, Nowotny (1961) having detected actual coincidences of detail. In *Féjérváry,* the historical subtext is best understood through the overall structural similarity to *Mendoza,* which in setting out its complete account of conquest and commodity tribute on the one hand, and the life story of labor on the other, draws on the particular experience of Tenochtitlan (Fig. 22).

In all, these books, articulating politics and cosmos, epitomize the dazzling capacities of iconic script; they explicate the Sign sets that calendrically sustained political memory, and they map patterns of human experience. Consummate in expression, they await fuller decipherment.

MAYA HIEROGLYPHS

Self-dating inscriptions in Maya hieroglyphs begin to make their appearance in the Maya lowlands toward the end of the third century A.D. Thereafter this script is inscribed, molded, and painted, with and without color, on stone, wood, bone, shell, jade, onyx, alabaster, obsidian, paper, ceramics, plaster, wet adobe, and rock walls; and it is fitted to panels broad as the sides of buildings, narrow stelae many meters high, bulbous zoomorphs, and chaptered pages. In and beyond the lowland area, within the broader and older iconic tradition of the Olmec, Mixe–Zoque, and Zapotec, some of its characteristics are announced by the tendency to arrange ideas of information in columns that read from top to bottom and left to right. Yet its appearance as such is unmistakable, thanks to its diagnostics. Chief among these is a perfect grid patterning of the squares within which the hieroglyphs are placed and that supposes they will be read in double columns from left to right and top to bottom. In principle this grid is adhered to regardless of the surface the text is inscribed on or whether it is flat or not. Second, elements within each glyph space, classified by scholars as main signs and affixes, in turn follow their own regular reading order. There is now no doubt that a majority of these elements register the sounds of lowland Maya speech (Fig. 23).[39]

As the Soviet scholar Knorozov showed in the 1950s, the typical hieroglyphic text proceeds by syllables, that is, groups of consonants plus vowels; these are predominantly paired so that the vowel of the second consonant both harmonizes with that of the first and is redundant, in accordance with the fact that most Maya noun-verbs are consonant-vowel-consonant monosyllables. Legible statements on the monuments of the Classic period stick to the third person and concern themselves with the lives and ambitions of royalty. They tell of the names and deeds of cities, dynasties, and individuals, the birth and "seating" of rulers (this last having an Olmec antecedent), success in war and at the ballgame. Through these texts, buildings name and date themselves, and sculptors and scribes add their signatures (*u tzib*).[40]

Though systemic, this script left its rules of syllabic spelling open to great inventiveness and play.[41] And though phonetic, it remained mixed in the sense of retaining iconic elements to supplement or reinforce meaning, especially when naming people or places or when invoking the Number and Sign sets of the *tonalamatl* and the year. For all that, Maya hieroglyphic writing came to exult in its attachment to speech, the specifically Maya glyph (*uoh*) being constantly invoked as a token even in shaman curing chants. In this self-imaging there is an exemplary contrast with the iconic tradition. Poems recited at the Aztec court make continuous play with the tones of the singer, which match the colors of the scribe, just as images in the books counterpoint the acts of speaking and writing. In the Maya texts, the tongue *is* the pen. Consistent with this is the fact that unlike iconic script, which merged gradually with Western representation over centuries, Maya hieroglyphic either continued to be used, as at Tayasal until the eve of the eighteenth century, or was transcribed into and replaced by the imported alphabet, as in the *Chilam Balam Books*.

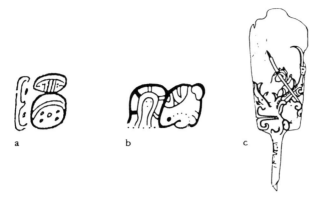

Figure 23. Maya hieroglyphs: (a) *u tzi-b[i]* 'its script'; (b) *ho-ch[o]* (fire drill); (c) tongue as pen.

In practice, the phoneticism and grid layout diagnostic of hieroglyphic went hand in hand with a further order of standardization: the integration of the *tonalamatl,* the year cycles, and yet other Number and Sign sets into a single system in which the 360-day *tun*/year served as the central cog. Everything was made rigorously to mesh with it: the Feasts of the year, which as a result no longer correspond to the seasons; and the nine Yoallitecutin of the *tonalamatl,* which as a result lose their particular link with the nights of pregnancy, becoming a mere fortieth of the *tun*'s 360 days. Implicit in this standardization is the equation of labor with commodity tribute, which in turn points to a very high degree of political and economic control in the limited arena of the Maya lowlands. Mathematically it involved place-value notation, a principle consistent with the hieroglyphic grid itself, and led to an accuracy, unrivaled on the planet, in the measurement of both astronomical and historical time, so that events were pinpointed to the day over hundreds of millions of years.[42]

In the Classic inscriptions the sheer capacity to locate the subject in time becomes an exercise in itself. Whole texts may be devoted to synchronizing the *tun*/year with other cycles relevant to sun, moon, sky, tribute, and politics, while measuring the period that had elapsed since the first day of the Era, 4 Ahau (customarily read as 10 August 3113 B.C.), in what are known as "Initial Series" texts. Indeed, early success by Ernst Förstemann in analyzing these calendrics led for a while to an emphasis on time counting and astronomy as such and to the notion that the ancient Maya were seriously interested in little else.

Compared with the corpus of inscriptions, which spans the Classic between A.D. 300 and 900, that of the hieroglyphic books is meager. All post-

Classic, the four books that have survived come from Yucatan (*Dresden, Paris, Madrid,* and the recently discovered *Grolier*); remains of much earlier examples are known at such sites as Altun-ha in Belize and Ceren in El Salvador, the latter under several feet of volcanic ash.[43] Though obviously part of the same Mesoamerican tradition of making screenfold books, they differ instructively from their counterparts in iconic script. For a start, they are more uniform physically. Although the iconic books generally have a squarish format, broader than tall, they vary greatly in material (paper or skin), absolute size, reading direction (right to left, left to right, bottom to top, top to bottom), style, and use of color. By contrast, all the Maya books are of native paper, are taller than broad, and follow the standard reading order of hieroglyphic script.

On the hieroglyphic pages many chapter topics are familiar from the iconic books – marriage, water-borne trading in heavily laden canoes, the five heliacal risings of Venus – and others are analogous: hunting deer with trap and poison, pot making, beekeeping. The historical dimension of the annals genre is generated here in the count of *tuns* and *katuns* (20 *tuns*) over thirteenfold cycles (about 256 years), a system that largely displaces the Initial Series of the Classic inscriptions. Yet, in line with the standardization of the Classic, everything is technically reduced, chapter by chapter, to multiples of thirteen and twenty days.

Above all, what appears as a holistic design in the iconic books is separated out, according to hieroglyphic norms, into phonetic script complemented by arithmetic and pictures. The Venus chapter common to both traditions excellently illustrates how they come to differ in this respect. Introduced by highly complex mathematical tables based on the Era date, the Maya version consists of vivid pictures of Venus's heliacal risings as an armed warrior, for which the hieroglyphs serve as captions describing the action and placing the planet successively to east, zenith (superior conjunction), west, and nadir (inferior conjunction; Plate 9). In other words, on the typical page of a Maya book there is hieroglyphic writing; there is arithmetic, unembedded, pure and abstract, with its vigesimal place value and its clear specification of such astronomical periods as the Venus cycle and lunar and solar eclipses; and there are pictures, illustrations just like those in an alphabet text.[44]

Despite certain lexical and other shifts, the hieroglyphic script encountered by Europeans was basically the same as that elaborated by the Classic Maya well over a thousand years previously, at the start of this peculiarly lowland Maya line of literacy. As a medium of continuity, hieroglyphic script came to be seen to embody characteristics of Maya civilization itself, not least in its phonetics that directly render lowland Maya speech and its mathematically unsurpassed calculation of time. How then are we to account for Jack Goody's dismissive references to the Maya in his *Literacy in*

Traditional Societies, where, for example, we read, "It is not clear who was ever literate in that language"?[45]

THE CASE OF THE *QUIPU*

"With pieces of string, the Inca developed a form of recording that forces a reconsideration of writing as we generally understand that term." Such is the opinion of the Aschers, authors of the first census of surviving *quipu*s and sharply logical analysts of their "code." To cite this authority is necessary, since the prejudice still survives that these bits of string were no more than mnemonics, which for example is what Bronowski says in *The Ascent of Man.* Even so great an Andeanist as Murra has referred to Inca society as "pre-literate."[46]

There is of course nothing odd about using knotted strings to tally, say, material objects, phrases of prayer, or units of time, and *quipu*s in this sense have been used widely in the Fourth World, especially its southern half.[47] Yet even within these functions, matters change when we introduce the semantic variables that define the *quipu* proper, that is, type of knot and its position on the string, color of string and its position on the main cord, and the code or program of the main cord. First diagnosed thanks to the Inca practice of double entry,[48] knot position involves place-value notation on the decimal base and in this recalls the grid of Maya hieroglyphic script. Its prime function appears to have been to tally llama flocks, and hence it forms an integral part of the economically complex pastoralism of Tahuantinsuyu.

In principle such a resource easily covers the requirements of mathematics, calendar, liturgy, narrative, and even spatial mapping. That it did so in practice, in the form of the Inca *quipu,* is clear from direct and indirect testimony and from the fact that the enormous empire of Tahuantinsuyu was minutely regulated and described by this medium. By means of the *quipu,* messages were sent to and from the capital (Fig. 24) specifying date and address (also a feature of the Mapuche *quipu*), and a continuous check was kept on such tiny details as individual absences from work, the offspring of a llama, and the last stick of firewood. The native historian Pachacuti Yamqui refers to Cuzco as the archive where the "chapters" of the *quipu* were put together. Although to become literate in this *quipu* system of the Incas required four years' training at the university (*yacha huasi*) in Cuzco, messages for more general consumption could be "printed out" in graphic designs typically found together with *quipu*s in burials;[49] the scribe responsible for transcription between media was known as the *quillcacamayoc.*

After the Spanish invasion, *quipu*s, like Mesoamerican books, were proscribed and burned precisely as "soguillas" that preserved the memory of pagan ritual and dogma.[50] At the same time, the *quipu* medium actually went on being used in several of its former functions, recording the thousands of pesos spent in the upkeep of monasteries, the niceties of legal practice and of *mita* service in the mines, public and private supplies for the *corregidor,* liturgy, and the "whole Roman calendar with its Saints and festivals" (Murúa 1962–4, 2:59). That *quipus* could indeed record and therefore transcribe not just mathematics but also discourse is affirmed by several sources, the most explicit being Garcilaso, "El Inca." In his *Comentarios reales* (book 2, chap. 27), this author tells how he came by a hymn authored by an *amauta* and designed to foster belief in Viracocha and his power over lightning and thunder: "The fable and verses, Padre Valera says he found in the knots and beads of some ancient annals in threads of different colours: the Indian accountant in charge of the historical knots and beads told him the tradition of the verses and the fable and, surprised that the amautas should have achieved so much, he copied down the verses and memorized them" (1966:88). The Quechua original, plus Latin and English translation, runs as follows:

Súmac ñusta	Pulchra Nimpha	Fair maiden,
Toralláiquin	Frater tuus	Thy brother
Puiñuyquita	Urnam tuam	Thine urn
Paquir cayan	Nunc infringit	Is now breaking.
Hina mantara	Cuius ictus	And for this cause
Cunuñunun	Tonat fulget	It thunders and lightens
Illapántac	Fulminatque	And thunderbolts fall,
Camri ñusta	Sed tu nympha	But thou, royal maiden
Unuiquita	Tuam limpham	Their clean waters
Para munqui	Fundens pluis	Shalt give us in rain;
Mai ñimpiri	Interdunque	And sometimes too
Chichi munqui	Grandinem, seu	Shalt give hail
Riti munqui	Nivem mittis	And shall give snow.
Pacharúrac	Mundi factor	The world's Creator,
Pachacámac	Pacha cámac	Pachacámac,
Viracocha	Viracocha	Viracocha,
Cai hinápac	Ad hoc munus	For this office
Churasunqui	Te sufficit	Has appointed thee,
Camasunqui	Ac praefecit	And has created thee.

Given this evident capacity, it is easier to accept the *quipu* as a literary medium that was widely transcribed into alphabetic Quechua and Spanish and became the source of particular kinds or even genres of text analogous in their way to the annals and *teoamoxtli* of Mesoamerica. For example, noting Pizarro's murder of Atahuallpa in Caxamarca in 1533, Garcilaso says he took the fact from the *quipu* annals of that place. Year events of Inca reigns generally, like accession and conquest, are widely ascribed to the same *quipu* source, and the presence of *quipus* in burials, along with framed and coded images of the deceased, suggests that they could also tell the

Figure 24. Hatun chasqui, or Inca messenger: (a) with shell trumpet and *quipu* message; (b) with posthorn and letter. (Guaman Poma, *Nueva corónica,* pp. 350, 811.)

biographies of lesser persons. That these *quipu* annals could in principle reach back into ages prior to the Inca, patterned by Guaman Poma and others according to the four prior ages of the world, is affirmed by Murúa (see "Andean Ascent" in Chapter 10), who notes that the world-age system represented in gold in the Coricancha of Cuzco was calculated in the *quipu*s up to the year A.D. 1554. In turn, these Inca chronicles are elaborated in the series of kingship dramas that, in the case of *Apu Ollantay,* explicitly invoke the *quipu.*

Besides annals, the *quipu* demonstrably underlies texts that deal with ceremonial cycles, notably the seasonal year, the twelve calendar months which, hinging on Capac Inti Raymi (December, the summer solstice) and subdivided into half-months, each required its tribute, penance, and hymns of worship. The Viracocha hymn recorded by Garcilaso belongs to the type performed at the Zithuwa festival in Coya Raymi (the spring equinox, September); Guaman Poma details the grand settling up of *quipu* accounts in the month of Hatun Cusqui Aymoray (May). Like *Runa yndio,* Guaman

Poma also brings out the significance in these matters of the *tahuantinsuyu* structure as such, otherwise visible in the *huacas* and queens that characterize each of the four *suyu* and in the *quipu* scribe Suyuyoc, who oversaw the four quarters.

The possibilities of the *quipu* as a literary medium are in fact admirably summed up in Guaman Poma's *Nueva corónica,* which makes up the first part of his long letter to Philip III of Spain. As a complete account of empire based on native-script records and submitted as advice to Spanish authority, this work finds a strong functional parallel in *Mendoza.* Formally it consists of an alphabetic narrative, in Spanish plus some Quechua, which is interspersed between sets of full-page framed line drawings. Though undoubtedly affected by motifs and techniques from Europe, these page illustrations also betray native elements and logic reminiscent of the *quipu* "print-outs"; indeed, in this respect some have gone so far as to consider the *Corónica* the work of a *quillcacamayoc.*[51] Similarly, though Guaman Poma was indebted to imported alphabetic literacy, particularly Spanish chronicles, he nonetheless drew directly on the *quipu.* In fact, when discussing his sources at the end of Part I, Guaman Poma specifically mentions the *quipu* and depicts himself amidst ancient *quipu* readers from all parts of Tahuantinsuyu who "declare" to him the account he passes on to his reader, assuring its correct shape and structure. Christian authorities, he says, were only a subsidiary source.

In the text, support for this claim comes principally from the chapter sets of framed page drawings, which, corroborated as they are by the author's use of the term "primer capítulo" and his index (*tabla*), correspond to the *Corónica*'s ten main chapters. Introduced by the Christian prologue and rounded off with the author's self-portrait, the plan of chapters looks like this (with number of illustrations):

1. The American world ages (4)
2. Incas (12; plus 2 Christian scenes), queens (12), captains (15), and ladies (4); laws
3. Census, by gender, usefulness, and age (10 + 10)
4. Months of the year (12)
5. Huacas and sorcery (2 + 4; 4)
6. Funeral rites (1 + 4)
7. Aclla Huasi (royal convent; 1)
8. Punishments (5)
9. Fiestas (2 + 4)
10. Government and administration (4; 12 + 1)

Now, not only does this total of chapters invoke the decimal base number used in the *quipu,* but the internal divisions of each likewise obey ciphers known to have characterized that medium. This is most obvious in the Census chapter, where the male and female populations of Tahuantinsuyu are each divided into a set of ten categories that respect the concepts of both usefulness and age. Guaman Poma's respective subsets of drawings show tasks appropriate to these categories, like soldiering or spinning, plus indicators of age, like the cradled baby and the bent crone, setting all within a notion of the total human life span (another echo of *Mendoza*). Another clear case is the Calendar chapter, which details the ceremonies characteristic of the twelve 30-day months of the Inca year. Keeping accounts of service at these ceremonies and dues of commodity tribute according to the mechanism of these months and their corresponding 15-day half-months is known to have been one of the prime functions of the *quipu*. So here again it is reasonable to assume a direct connection between *quipu* taxonomy and Guaman Poma's chaptering. The calendar cipher twelve also governs the total of pre-Hispanic emperors it was seen fit to record in chapter 2, a sequence that, moreover, displays a decimal subset of the first ten emperors, whose reigns (unlike those of the last two, Tupac Yupanqui and Huayna Capac) exceed normal human spans and esoterically link the world ages with modern history. For their part, the *auqui,* or captains, number fifteen, the total of days in the Inca half-month; and the remaining chapters and parts of chapters all follow the *suyuyoc* paradigms of the four provinces that surround Cuzco. In fact, none of the picture-page sets in any of the chapters fails to conform in one way or another with ciphers known to have been used in the *quipu* and the administration of Tahuantinsuyu. For good measure, echoing both the *quipu* and the Mesoamerican books, the overall page total equals the days in the year (with Guaman Poma appearing as author on the final leap-day page, 366).

Guaman Poma himself has the last word on the subject: Praising the clarity and concision of his *quipu* sources (pp. 260, 359), he remarks on the difficulty of transcribing them in the *Corónica:* "Since so much was known in the strings I was hard put in the alphabet" ("pues que en los cordeles supo tanto que me hiciera a fuerza en letra").

3

Configurations of space

MAPS

Lifeless and atemporal, the post-Renaissance grid map deals in two-dimensional space, geometrically determining its orientation and scale through abstract coordinates.[1] As in Europe, before Columbus maps of this kind were quite unknown in the Fourth World. Confined mainly to North America, mapmaking there had priorities more in tune with those of the medieval *mappamundi*. Fourth World maps sooner trace process and formation, like histories, setting politics into cosmogony. Formally they may register space according to the sequence of encounter: for example, the four moments of east–west migration on the Mide scrolls, or the houses of Chichimec initiation ranged north to south in the *Borgia* Feasts chapter. Or they may take their view from above, seeing the earth's living face in plan from the high moment of Carib or Navajo trance. As for scale, it ranges from the smallest to the largest; in Mesoamerica, with its tribute hierarchies and urban stratification, seven successive levels are spelled out, from local plot (*tlalli/predio*), ward or parish (*tlaxilacalli/barrio*), borough or town (*altepetl/pueblo*), head town (*tlatoyotl/cabecera*),[2] provincial capital (*?huetlatoyotl/gobernador*), and imperial capital to the world itself (*cemana-huac*). Throughout, nothing is left random or discrete; everything rather adheres to an intelligible and memorable scheme, to the extent, indeed, that many Fourth World maps have long gone unrecognized as such.

By far the most elaborate Fourth World maps extant are those found in the *teoamoxtli*, typically as title pages. Of the nine examples of this genre that have survived, those in the Papaloapan group (to which for these purposes *Féjérváry* is added) are distinguished by their maps (*Coixtlahuaca Map, Cuicatlan, Laud*), which in detail and design cross-reference with each other and with the sets of toponyms in the *Tepexic Annals* from slightly to the west[3] (Table 3). They make full use of the resources of iconic script and exhibit all the graphic precision within the page frame that was revealed above in the *Tepotzotlan Codex*. In plan, with impeccably traced lines, they are able to employ and make finer measurement, demarcating areas of relative significance and appealing to the logic of exact proportions also operative in timetables like the opening chapter of *Borgia*. What is more, though legible in plan, they simultaneously present views in profile, as it were inviting the reader into their landscapes, an effect also achieved in the Tepotzotlan text and well understood and reproduced in the recent Mexican film *Tlacuilo* about the title-page map in *Mendoza* that is modeled on *Féjérváry*.

After Cortes, *teoamoxtli* maps such as these provided the precedent for what in New Spain became a distinct geographical mode of *lienzo*s, cadastral plans, and the like. Not least, several of these texts have defended territory from capitalist invasion even into this century, cases in point being local maps of the Tlapa area and the Anenecuilco maps (Oaxtepec district) drawn upon by Emiliano Zapata, the great champion of the native cause in the Mexican Revolution.[4] Originally the work of municipal as well as metropolitan scribes, they embody a communal reason for existence.

Besides providing a visual precedent in this way for New Spain, the Papaloapan group of texts finds spectacular parallels throughout the rest of North America, above all in the dry paintings of Anasazi and the Navajo. Indeed, the worldview common to these two visual languages is nowhere more pronounced than in their respective configurations of space, their mappings of human experience. In both bodies of texts, natural and man-made landscape features fall into or are contained within the same patterns, paradigms that prove to obey the same underlying American philosophy.

Perhaps the most radical map boundary is that which separates inner from outer, water source from desert, life from chaos. The gourd that holds the world of the rainforest defines it by its rim in section, the outermost concentric circle in Huichol painting[5] (Plate 10). In the dry paintings the slim body of the guardian curves to form a wall set inside that of the hogan in which the map is made, its entrance aligning with the hogan door to face the rising sun; in the *Borgia* screenfold (p. 27) the wall is the monster body that encloses ceremonial space. Opening onto the earth's surface, the central source then extends in four directions, as in the four arms of the swastika[6] that are steadied in the "Whirling Logs" dry painting (Plume Chant), the Mississippi gorget, and the sky-snakes *teoamoxtli* icon. Everywhere the horizons reached are in turn celebrated in their own right when political time begins, fourfold and each rich with color and promise: skies that herald years in High Hawk's Winter Count, plants and birds in the dry paintings and the screenfolds, trees atop the pre-Classic Maya pyramid at Cerros and

Table 3. *Landmarks of Papaloapan in texts from that area*

Source	Mictlan	Teotillan	Tepexic	Nexapa	
	I	II	III	IV	IV(bis)
(a) *Coixtlahuaca Map*					
(b) *Selden Roll*					
(c) *Tlapiltepec Lienzo*					
(d) *Tequiztepec Lienzo*					

(p. 38)

(p. 36)

(p. 32)

(p. 42)

(p. 33)

(p. 46)

(e) *Cuicatlan teoamoxtli* (p. 10)

(f) *Gomez de Orozco Fragment*

(g) *Laud* (p. 46)

(h) *Tepexic Annals* (p. 34)

(i) *Mendoza*  (p. 43)

See notes on following page.

85

Notes to Table 3

Landmarks (see also map at right):

I Mictlan (Santiago Mictlantongo): place of the dead (*mic*), denoted by bones, skull, mummy.

II Teotlillan (Teutila): place of divine blackness (*teo-tlil-*), denoted by a sun or solar ray, with black house (i), or under threat of eclipse (a,d,g,h).

III Tepexic (Tepeji de Rodríguez): mountain with chasm (*tepe-xic*), also with checker for twin town Tlil-tepexic (a,c,d,e,f,h), or strands of lineage (b); joined to "old-people" place Huehuetlan and Tentzon ridge emblems (a,e,h).

IV Nexapa (San Mateo Nejapa): river (a,b,e, f,h) with ash (*nex-tli*) (a,h); broken chevron warpath only in (c) (part of scene to west in [b] and the *Baranda Codex* [Caso, in Acuña 1989:40]). IV(bis)?: bird sipping celestial blood (d,g,h).

Sources:

(a–f) are from the central area: (a–d) represent the federated towns of the Coixtlahuaca Valley on the NW branch of the Upper Papaloapan; (e,f) stem from Cuicatlan (cross-referenced in [b,c]), (e) framing the annals common to that town and Quiotepec on the SE branch. (Each group has its respective *papalo*, or butterfly, town.)

As maps, (a–c) and (e) all pattern I–IV to the SE, NE, NW, and SW, and in (a–c) chevron roads lead to these positions (from, in [II]a]; in [b], I and II invert). In (a), I–IV (+ center) correspond to fifths of the *tonalamatl*; in (e), they correspond to the Signs XX, V, X, XV.

As genealogies, (d,f) identify I–IV(bis) and I–II with Eagle and Owl (5 and 10 of the Quecholli), equivalent in (f) to upper and lower western towns.

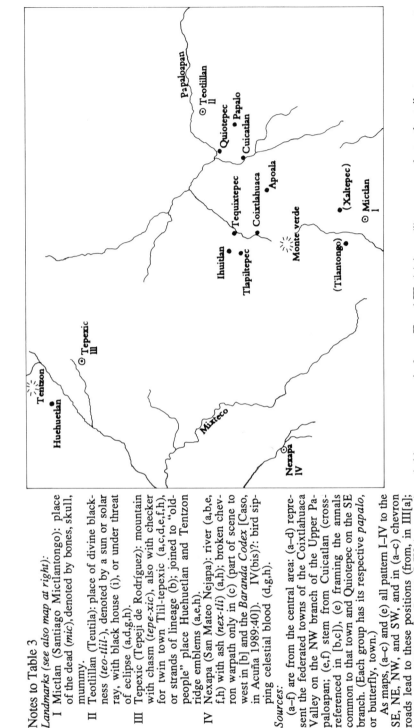

(g,h) center respectively on II and III: (g) is an end-page title map, set vertically between east and west horizons, with II as center, I below, and IV(bis) above; in (h), III lies at the center of the tribute quarters, with I south and II east (IV is in an intermediary position; IV[bis] is also east).

(i) corresponds to the tribute arrangement imposed by Tenochtitlan, which allotted I to Coixtlahuaca (as it did Cuicatlan), II to Tochtepec, and III to Tepeaca.

at the start of the *Book of Chumayel*'s history of the Maya. And fourfold sets of city emblems are inscribed on the hieroglyphic stelae.

Highly defined in this repertoire of boundary and horizon are those maps, again common to Anasazi and Mesoamerica, that configure center and periphery in particular ways. Salient here are the quincunx, where the center (typically a geological base) is attended by pairs of subsidiary places set in northern and southern registers; and the quatrefoil, where the center is surrounded by four quarters, the flowering fields of tribute separated by diagonal streams or arms and dominated by the east and west horizons. Superbly exemplified in the quincunx of the *Coixtlahuaca Map* and the quatrefoil of the *Féjérváry* title page, these models have widespread currency and signify in their own right. Using the quatrefoil of *Féjérváry*, the *Mendoza* title-page map predicates the arrangement that follows in the text, of metropolitan plus four provincial tribute areas; in setting out the tribute quarters that Tepexic dominated from its own raised base, the *Tepexic Annals* appeal to just the same model in the course of its narrative. In Guaman Poma's *mappamundi* of Tahuantinsuyu (*Nueva corónica,* pp. 983–4 – in fact, all of South America from Chile to Panama; see Fig. 8) we see an ingenious amalgam of both models plus the imposition of a European-style grid. At the center stands Cuzco, a city whose streets and squares themselves were a model for the empire: Through the quincunx it relates to its *huaca* mountain supports, north above and south below; through the radiating diagonals of the quatrefoil it relates to its four tributary *suyu,* Colla and Chincha being elongated horizontally to the east and west of sun and moon.

Recognizing these paradigms or set apportionings of space, the map reader moves between scales or levels of significance even within the same text. In Anasazi this principle is established by concentrating larger territory into the world of the hogan, while the mechanism that makes it work is well illustrated by the paradigm and cipher seven that organize the successive levels of Siouan life from the micro clan to the macro nation. As a result, in the grand reading the flat local domain is integrated into larger space, precisely that of the seven Siouan directions that places the center not just between the four horizons but also between above and below. Widely rehearsed in North American ritual and graphically shown in the Cuna *ikala* (Fig. 25), this unfolding of the two-dimensional surface appeals to north and south, "sides" of the east–west planetary path, as upper and lower moments along the same path in the three-dimensional model; that is, zenith and nadir.[7] Phenomenologically, this accords well with the apparent movement of the sky and its travelers in tropical latitudes: a wholesale passage from eastern to western horizon night and day, the poles remaining invisible or close to the ground on either side. A double reading in these terms is offered in a great range of Mesoamerican texts: Transcribing the direction glyphs of the *Dresden* Venus table, the *Chilam Balam Books* equate north (*xaman*) with zenith and south (*nohol*) with nadir. The *Tepexic Annals* set out tribute quarters on the page so that Tlaloc the Rain God of Perote (Napatecutli) rises "high" in the north, and the underworld skull of Mictlantongo sinks "low" in the south (Fig. 26; see also Table 3). *Féjérváry* concurs with this arrangement, through the Night Lords Tlaloc and Mictlantecutli and emblems that respectively reflect the sky and open the maw of hell; between the horizons of east and west, *Laud* opposes to hell the high-flying eagle. The convention recurs in Guaman Poma's *mappamundi* insofar as stars shine from the northern ocean beyond Antisuyu. In Classic Maya architecture it is actually built into ceremonial space at such sites as Copan (Temple 11), Palenque, and Izamal, where the height of the pyramid placed on the north side points explicitly to the zenith of the sun's circuit.[8]

Constant as they are as layouts on the page, these map paradigms create a framework for astronomical space, laying it in this way over geography; in turn, this framework coordinates details of terrestrial and celestial experience. An astounding yet unequivocal fact about Tenochtitlan's tribute system is that the total of *cabeceras* in each of the four provinces was made to correspond with the nights of the moon (29), just as the total of towns subjected to the metropolis and the provincial capitals could be counted as days of the year (365). Yet other combinations reflect the phases of the sidereal moon, a factor that has been authoritatively detected in the total of *huacas* subjected to Cuzco in the *ceque*-line map of Tahuantinsuyu. The synodic lunar total (29) is likewise respected in the *Tepexic Annals* in the enumeration of toponyms in its tribute quarters (Fig. 27); and in the quatrefoil map of *Féjérváry,* as in the *Borgia* Tribute chapter, this same total recurs, now brilliantly encoded in the birds, or Quecholli, that perch on the trees of the quarters, imbuing them with their respective number values. Essential to the success of this imperial ideology of number is the actual or implied quatrefoil map that in the first place integrates and sets out the corresponding sectors of earth and sky.

Besides grouping totals of toponyms, these map frames serve to underpin their symbolism, furthering the discourse of the "heaven" and "hell" towns that lie, for example, on either side of Tepexic. While places in the Winter Counts intimate the registers of the northern climate in alternating between the *tipi* of the Sun Dance and the timbered snow-covered house, Mesoamerican texts typically highlight "sun" towns like Teotitlan and Teotlillan as eastern. And they go further in invoking the apparatus of the *tonalamatl.* Hence, the five areas defined by the quincunx in the *Coixtlahuaca Map* correspond to fifths of the *tonalamatl,* and the quarters of the quatrefoil in *Féjérváry* correspond to its quarters and to the set of four year Signs that arithmetically derives from them. Here, Rabbit and Reed belong to east as Flint and House do to west, a standard arrangement repeated in texts like

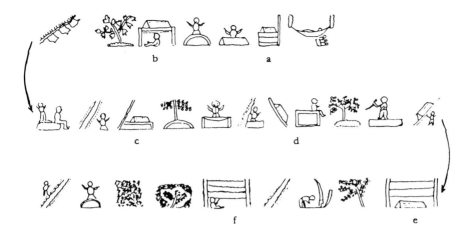

Figure 25. The six time–space moments (*neka*) of the Cuna world: (a) sunrise; (b) sunset; (c) north (*mu-pili* 'big sea'); (d) "opposite north"; (e) above; (f) below. (*Serkan ikala,* ending. Note patient in hammock, the different plants – nettle and types of chili pepper (incarnations of the "Nele" epic heroes and helpers) – and the *mola*s or shaman pages that accompany the nettle at sunset.

Figure 26. North and west quarters of Tepexic: (a) Napatecutli, or Rain god (*Tepexic Annals,* p. 43; *Cuauhtinchan Map 2*); (b) Nacochtla, or earplug place (*Tepexic Annals,* p. 48; *Mendoza,* p. 42).

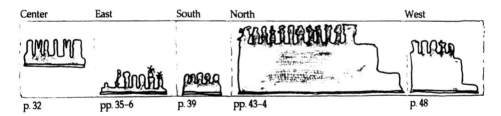

Figure 27. Profile of places at and around Tepexic. The center and the quarters are represented as blocks of towns (*Tepexic Annals*). Note the total of six in the center (see Plate 16a) and twenty-nine (i.e., 7 + 5 + 12 + 5) in the quarters.

Mendoza and the *Coetzala Codex* as well as in numerous post-Cortesian diagrams of the 52-year Round.

Just like the *Tepotzotlan Codex,* which through Xoloc recalled how the Chichimecs arrived in the Highland Basin along the very horizon of the text, *Mendoza* and the *Coetzala Codex* imbue their designations of place with historical memory, complementing the ritual logic of the *tonalamatl.* According to the norm, *Mendoza* assigns House to west and Reed to east: Of the pair of horizons over which sun, moon, and planets pass, west is the House where these bodies repose or set; east is where they hurl reed arrows as heliacal rays. With its rough thatch, the House in *Mendoza* additionally suggests the "wild" western frontier of Mesoamerica that, uppermost on the map, the Mexica dominated and made into the first of the tribute quarters; the Reed-arrow plus shield emblemizes the warfare they prosecuted chiefly toward the east. In the Coetzala text, the year Signs are again paired on the horizons, Flint and House to west, Rabbit and Reed to east. Exactly like the Navajo mountains with their "inner forms" that recall moments of the past, the "Flint" mountain contains at its core a memory of the Chichimec tribal home Chicomoztoc, or Seven Caves, that lies beneath its horizon in time and space. An identical memory of Seven Caves is embedded in the toponym of Tepexic itself in its annals and in the Toltec–Chichimec maps from Coixtlahuaca and Cuauhtinchan that, beginning with the migration from that tribal home, open out spatially to set the boundaries of their respective arenas in Upper Papaloapan and the Cholula Plain. Post-Cortesian, these remarkable time maps reveal the concise historical logic that inheres in native cartography.

In all, following principles of their own, these Fourth World maps define space and fix the relative positions of places identifiable in the landscape today. Produced as political statements to defend land and home, they appeal to a deeper notion of geography that does not exclude the cosmic movements of the sky, history, or even therapy. For, responding to endemic human need, the Anasazi maps serve in the first place to cure, affirming the ground through sand physically brought from the guardian mountains and quickening through the flower pollen of the horizons.

QUINCUNX

The *Coixtlahuaca Map,* classic example of the quincunx, once displayed its town of provenance at its center, but the toponym in question is now mostly obliterated (Plate 11). It can be reconstructed thanks to remaining traces and with the help of a copy made before the damage was done. It shows the snake (*coa-*) adorned with star-eyes (*-ix-*) stretched out as on a plain (*tla-huaca*): exactly the image given in *Mendoza.* Moreover, through its jaws and other details, the snake acquires the feather-caiman aspect that character-

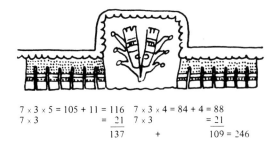

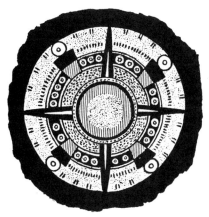

$7 \times 3 \times 5 = 105 + 11 = 116 \quad 7 \times 3 \times 4 = 84 + 4 = 88$
$7 \times 3 \qquad\qquad\quad = \underline{21} \quad 7 \times 3 \qquad\qquad = \underline{21}$
$\qquad\qquad\qquad\quad 137 \qquad + \qquad\qquad 109 = 246$

116 = one synodic Mercury cycle; 88 = one sidereal Mercury cycle; 137 = five sidereal moons; 109 = four sidereal moons; 246 = nine sidereal moons.

Figure 28. Astronomical data: (a) dots on maguey paper (*Coixtlahuaca Map,* under Tepexic; see Plate 11); (b) sun with 11 + 11 markers inset (mural in Structure 8 ["El Pimiento"], Cempoala).

izes Coixtlahuaca in *lienzos* later produced by the town. The great strategic significance enjoyed by Coixtlahuaca at the center of Papaloapan is widely acknowledged in texts from the Cholula Plain to the north and the Mixteca to the south; its erstwhile power is also testified to in enormous platforms and other architectural remains. *Lienzos* from neighboring towns, as well as the *Selden Roll* and other histories linked with the *Tepexic Annals,* entwine its snake into a heraldic device that suggests a Coixtlahuaca Valley federation, supreme in Upper Papaloapan in the days of the eleventh-century ruler Four Jaguar.[9]

From its large central circle, Coixtlahuaca dominates pairs of towns above and below, registers that correspond to the northern and southern regions commanded by the town from its position near the continental divide. The upper towns feature suns to the right, or east, and mountains to the left, or west, and the lower towns both lie on rivers: Overall, the configuration is that of the landmarks of Papaloapan, which Tepexic and Teotlillan adjust according to their own geographical priorities (see Table 3). Placed here to the northwest of Coixtlahuaca, the mountains in fact denote Tepexic itself, with its characteristic cliff and cleft and with the inset black checker that denotes its twin settlement Tlil-tepexic; as in the *Tepexic Annals,* we also see the "old people" suffix of Huehuetlan, and the *maguey* of the Tentzon ridge (here also a page surface showing astronomical data; Fig. 28). To the northeast, the sun glyph is set into a blood-red field, a serried row of flint knives and images of daytime stars and Venus as the "stinging" planet; another sun occurs in a subsidiary role, together with a trail of footprints. The knives are possibly mementos of the *tzitzimine,* who as stars monstrously revealed in daytime descend to excoriate during the solar eclipse, which is caused by stings from Venus;[10] together, these indicate Teotlillan, the town of divine or solar darkness to the northeast. (The sun with feet may indicate Teotitlan del Camino on the old tribute road that passed down this same river valley.) Below to the southeast (lower right) we see the bones of the dead (*mic*) that denote the underworld, Mictlan, shown as Coixtlahuaca's tributary in *Mendoza* (p. 43) and revered as the ancestral shrine Mictlantongo in the annals of Xaltepec, Tilantongo, and other Mixtec centers. Then, completing the set, to the southwest (lower left) lies Nexapa, the ash of whose name (*nex-tli*) is produced by a volcano rising from under the water: Along the chevron road to it there is an image of Eight Deer complete with his byname "Jaguar Claw," he being the Mixtec ruler of Tilantongo who met a superior power in Coixtlahuaca's Four Jaguar and whose hill is here shot through with arrows.

At the first level of reading, the design commemorates the domain of Papaloapan, whose landmarks are so clearly set out in several texts from the upper reaches of that river, the Coixtlahuaca Valley to the northwest and Cuicatlan to the southeast (see Table 3). In this *Coixtlahuaca Map,* as in the *Cuicatlan* screenfold (p. 10), the territorial arrangement as such acts as a frame and mediates in time between ancient Popolocan settlement and annals of more recent history. In Coixtlahuaca's case, these concern political power enjoyed under Four Jaguar (portrayed in the *Tlapiltepec Map*) and again in the twelfth century, with Tepexic as an ally; indeed, the patterning and style of the toponyms strongly recall those in the *Tepexic Annals.* Whereas at Mictlan(tongo), Teotlillan, and Nexapa the impulse of Coixtlahuaca's victory is shown by warpath chevrons that lead past temples ablaze and pierced by arrows, at Tepexic the warpath runs out from, not into, the town, and a decapitated pair of Jaguar and Eagle warriors suggest a match that led to alliance. In all, within its quincunx Coixtlahuaca rests on a support system of four bastions in the upper and lower landscape.

Lending ritual stability and "rightness" to the whole, the scribe correlated each of the five territorial areas with a 52-day fifth of the *tonalamatl,* introducing the reading principle diagnostic of the *teoamoxtli* genre; and in each fifth stands the pair Ciuateteo and Tonaleque, the female and male Workers who occupy the fifth position in the set of Thirteen Heroes. Their heads thrown far back in the arrogant (*aquetza*)[11] posture at the center and their hands holding impressive round shields, they represent the victors in Coixtlahuaca's joint enterprise with Tepexic.

This geohistorical dimension of the *Coixtlahuaca Map* is echoed in quincunxes that quite specifically coordinate battles and conquests in later documents. A clear-cut example comes in the *Tlaxcala Lienzo,* in the scene that shows Tenochtitlan under siege in the summer of 1521 (Toxcatl to Miccailhuitl). After an arduous series of eleven battles, at this key moment we switch to a view in plan that is based on the quincunx (Plate 12a). Surrounded by its lake and defended by four war canoes, the Great Pyramid of the Aztec capital is threatened strategically from four corners by towns already in the possession of the Tlaxcalan–Spanish allies after the campaigns of the preceding months. As a pair and inverting the geography of the *Coixtlahuaca Map,* Tepactepec and Xochimilco face each other above toward the southern mountain rim of the Basin, as do Coyoacan and Tlacopan below on the causeways that linked Tenochtitlan to the mainland. The battles that had been waged at these four places are shown by the usual arrow of conquest and by the severed heads and trunks, arms, and legs of the defeated. Affirming the prior victories in theme and number as well as space within the fixed areas of the quincunx design, these anatomical units (themselves part of a ritual foursome) cross-match each other arithmetically, as do the four groups of victors; themselves subdivided as ten shield-bearing Tlaxcalans and five mounted Spaniards, these last fifteen anticipate the encounter with Tenochtitlan, marking already the fifteen occupants of the Aztec war canoes. In other words, this later text draws not only on the *teoamoxtli* quincunx as such but as well on its complex arithmetic of fives. It does so, however, inverting both the upper–lower registers and the victory, whose impulse comes here from without, not within. Hence, it better urges its argument that the support Tenochtitlan had relied upon in its quincunx of towns was now militarily denied, leaving the center itself open to defeat.

The geographical reading of Coixtlahuaca's quincunx is further supported in principle by the very close resemblance it bears to the dry paintings that represent the center and four guardian mountains of Navajo territory, notably in the Night Chant and the Blessing Way (Plate 12b; see Map 4). Focused on the original homeland Dinetai, the Navajo quincunx places at its center the Place of Emergence, Spruce Hill, or the Moving Mountain Dzilinaxodili, these last two corresponding to the Gobernador and Huerfano peaks at the very head of the San Juan River. Above and below this center and the sun's east–west path that runs through it, there are again two pairs of toponyms: Dibentsah and Tsisnadjini, Tsodzil and Dokoslid. Though schematized in this way, this arrangement respects the geography of the area, so that these places may be located on a grid map in positions that do not contradict the ritual scheme of north above and south below and that even point to ancient trade patterns. On the jet-black peak of Dibentsah (Hesperus) to the northwest, mountain sheep have their home; the white shell of Tsisnadjini to the northeast is echoed in the subsequent Spanish name Sierra Blanca. To the southeast, the turquoise mountain Tsodzil (Mount Taylor) lies on the route to the Pueblo mine of that stone just beyond the Rio Grande; to the southwest the abalone mountain Dokoslid (Humphreys Peak) guards the Colorado River route to the Pacific, the source of that shell. Moreover, deeply rooted in Anasazi cosmogony, this quincunx continues to exert a strong political charge, keeping alive among the Navajo the concept of the larger homeland that now lies mostly outside their reservation.

Upon moving west at the close of Emergence, Changing Woman (Nayenezgani's mother) re-created this home landscape precisely through this painting, its model. Among the Huichol, a similar placement is made in the first of Tutukila's Creation paintings, where ritual heroes begin to create the space of their territory: Between upper and lower worlds and again to a total of five they establish the center in Nayar Mesa by engraving there their respective *nierika* symbols. Within the same Upper Papaloapan drainage that contains Coixtlahuaca, the Cuicatec at Papalo to this day construct their cosmos through their own "quincunx of mountains," as Eva Hunt calls them (Fig. 29). Yet again in South America the House of Dawn of Inca Emergence lies at the center of Cuzco's quincunx of *huaca* mountains (see Map 6).

Undeniable at the geopolitical level, the analogy between the Coixtla-huaca and Navajo designs extends deeper into time, since both appeal via a quincunx to the system of world ages or suns distinctive in Fourth World cosmogony (see Part III). In the Navajo design, enhanced with "inner forms" each mountain commemorates an earlier stage of Emergence and the very strata of creation, the Flood being alluded to through the image of the ladder up which people climbed so as not to be drowned. As a fivefold spatial statement, then, that demands a multiple reading exactly akin to that demanded by the toponyms of the *Coixtlahuaca Map,* it finds a temporal base at the deepest levels of memory. Indeed, in the map the arrangement and detail of the toponyms directly recall the magnificent *Sunstone* that once adorned Tenochtitlan. For this major artifact displays the same pattern at its center: There, shaped like a quincunx, the Sign of this Era, Ollin, incorporates the Signs of the previous ages as upper and lower pairs. The catastrophes that ended each are partly indicated by supplementary symbols; they may be known more fully through such texts as the *Cuauhtitlan Annals* and the *Popol vuh.* Between the *Sunstone* and the *Coixtlahuaca Map* there are consistent and detailed parallels within the quincunx frame that argue closely for the kind of cosmic depth inherent in the quincunx of Anasazi territory.[12]

A full account of these Creations, or Suns, is entered into in Chapter 10. Here we may note that in the case of Four Jaguar, upper right, and Four Rain, lower left, the catastrophes may be read out of the main toponymic image. For the daytime stars and serried flint knives that oppress the sun of Teotlillan invoke the solar eclipse of Four Jaguar, when the *tzitzimine* and jaguars descended with their murderous knives, and exactly this flint knife is likewise featured on the *Sunstone.* (All this adds weight to the reading

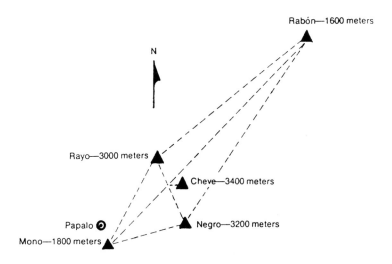

Figure 29. The Papalo quincunx: (After Hunt 1977:98.)

"Teotlillan" and relates in turn to the solar-eclipse image that dominates the title-page map of *Laud,* suggesting this town as its provenance.) Then the rising volcanic ash of Nexapa is just what was precipitated by the fire-rain of Four Rain, and it is approached by one of the saurians that characterized that world age. As for the remaining catastrophes Four Water (lower right) and Four Wind (upper left), they are matched in the Coixtlahuaca text by details affixed to the toponyms in those positions that otherwise would lack obvious point. The red river beside Mictlantongo's pyramid, where heart-fish swim, is shown rising up the steps at its edge, recalling the Flood that ended the age Four Water when vertebrate life reverted to the fish swimming in it. Affixed to the edge of Tepexic's cliffs, howling wind intimates the hurricane of Four Wind, which is also shown in the same image on the *Sunstone.* Finally, at the center the good flat earth of Coixtlahuaca matches the visage of the Earth Lord Tlaltecutli, our whole terrestrial space: Thus configured, the text comes to measure its power in terms of the Era named Four Ollin and the prior world ages that inhere in it.

Refining this cosmic argument, yet further sets of data are legible in the Coixtlahuaca text that ingeniously distinguish between types of arithmetic in counters embedded in the lower and upper toponyms. On the left-hand side of the map (west), growing up in Nexapa's pyramid of ash, we see arrangements of dots that, as in Tepoxaco's glyph in the *Tepotzotlan Codex,* denote porous volcanic rock or matter, within a large and sophisticated repertoire of signs for soil types. The larger dots present a perfect calculation in "pyramid," or sigma, arithmetic, whereby with each emergent row or stratum a unit is added, so that, as here, four equals the combined units of the rows to have emerged altogether, that is, ten $(1 + 2 + 3 + 4 = 10)$. In the sets of the *tonalamatl* this sigma principle connects the Eagle of the Quecholli, 5, with the Eagle of the Twenty Signs, XV (i.e., $1 + 2 + 3 + 4 + 5 = 15$), and exactly the same type of calculation is presented in Tepoxaco and other soil signs in the Tepotzotlan text, where, building on the "natural versus artificial" opposition, they allude to the transformation of raw matter into workable or knowable form. Contrasting with this lower logic of base, quite a different celestial order of calculation is made above at Tepexic, in dots written on *maguey* paper. Here, modifying a model of twice seven by three, units are so arranged as to present the kind of astronomical formula discussed earlier in relation to *Féjérváry*'s Zodiac chapter and the eleven who drink *pulque,* the product of *maguey,* and correlate the moon with Mercury (see Fig. 28a). This thematic contrast between the "base" and defeated Nexapa below and the celestial and triumphant Tepexic above is recapitulated in the center, as is a possible corresponding contrast between the lower and upper towns on the right-hand side of the map (east), specifically between the numerate heart fish at Mictlantongo and a year-calendar reading of Teotlillan's solar flints.

In sum, just as comparison with the *Tlaxcala Lienzo* sharpens the politicomilitary message of the *Coixtlahuaca Map,* so comparison with known cosmogonical texts like the *Sunstone* and the Emergence dry painting brings out its geological depths. Through the paradigm of the quincunx itself, siege and mountain pillars, we move from imperial surface down into the earth's crust, a vaster claim in time and space.

QUATREFOIL

The quatrefoil title-page map of *Féjérváry,* perhaps the Fourth World's most celebrated page, similarly brings together whole dimensions of space by means of a well-established paradigm (Plate 13a). In its simplest outline form, of four outfolding lobes, or quarters, the quatrefoil is ubiquitous: Seen in the Teotihuacan murals, Maya hieroglyphic panels, and the "Morning Star" skins of the Siksika, it corresponds to a fundamental Nahuatl term for empire, Nacxit Xochitl, the tetrarchy, fourfold flower. Reaching to east and west horizons, its inset diagonals have been compared by astronomers to the yearly pattern of sunrise and sunset positions and may be read as the four ways commemorated at the winter-solstice Feast (*Borbonicus,* p. 34); as insect legs, the diagonals hold the center between these horizons, like the Zuni waterskater or the spider of the Mississippian shell disk, which moreover carries on its back the fire that is the center of the *Féjérváry* page. The priority of the east–west axis is shown by the fact that the corresponding quarters above and below are joined to the central area, whereas those to either side are not.[13]

Diagnostic of the *Féjérváry* design is the flow of life and value through the diagonals and the priority of the east–west axis, which determines the days and nights of sun, moon, Venus, and other epic travelers along the zodiac. It has a curious counterpart in the Maya hieroglyphic tradition, in a map in the *Madrid* screenfold (p. 74) that, like *Féjérváry,* correlates the tribute quarters with the 65-day quarters of the *tonalamatl;* the corresponding geography is clearly specified in the set of four direction glyphs, west here being upper-most (Plate 13b). Textually its most significant analogues are, first, the title page of *Mendoza,* the tribute book concerned with politics and economics, and, second, the dry paintings of Anasazi, which here again draw in cosmogony. The parallel between *Féjérváry* and the Red Mountain map design of the Navajo Shooting Chant[14] is strikingly close.

Precisely because its subject matter has been so widely understood, the *Mendoza* title page makes a good starting point (Plate 14a). It centers on an imposing image of Tenochtitlan as the place (*-tlan*) where an eagle perches on a stone cactus (*te-noch-*). Around it spread quarters planted with rushes and reeds, separated by four turquoise streams and occupied by the council of nine principals who backed the protoemperor whose name prefigures that of the city: Tenoch. At the most local level the streams evoke the canals cut to drain Tenochtitlan's marshy ground; on a grander scale they suggest inflow from the four provinces of the tribute empire. By means of the same spatial shift, the skull rack (*tzompantli*) shown opposite Tenoch could denote the northerly architectural feature of the Templo Mayor precinct or the town Tzompanco (i.e., Zumpango) due north of Tenochtitlan on the farther shore of the northern lake.

Below are the first events in the story of empire, the conquests of Colhuacan and Tenayuca, towns that had dominated the southeastern and northwestern sides of the lake now encroached upon by Tenochtitlan and that in profile can be seen standing as if in the landscape to south and north of the capital. Around the edge of the page run the year dates of Tenoch's reign, when Tenochtitlan was founded and conducted its first fire kindling, here attached to the year 2 Reed 1351. It begins with a House year of the west (2 House 1325), ends with a Reed year of the east (13 Reed 1375), and runs on subsequent pages through the reigns of nine Aztec emperors, from the first year of Acamapichtli's reign, 1 Flint (1376), to the last of Moctezuma II's.

Similarly, the four fields enclosed by the years, west above and east below, anticipate the later listings of the conquered towns and the commodity tribute due from them. After the nine metropolitan *cabecera*s come those of the provinces, Atotonilco and the west with seven, Tlachco and the south

with seven, Chalco and the road east to Xoconochco with seven, and finally
Cuauhtochco and the north with eight, making up the lunar twenty-nine in
all (see Map 3). As we have seen, the privileging of west historically corresponds to Tenochtitlan's perception of itself as a bastion of Mesoamerica's
western frontier and the city of the Mexica, immigrants from the west who
punned their name with the crescent new moon, later Guadalupe's emblem.
The original Aztec house, or home, in Aztlan lay to the west; once established, Tenochtitlan relied on conquests to the east for the bulk of its tribute.
The map of the highland lake authored by Tenochtitlan's twin city Tlatelolco similarly places west at the top;[15] the geographical alignment in itself is
confirmed by such other indicators as the northerly Tzompanco in the right-
hand quarter and the landscape position of Colhuacan and Tenayuca.

As the title page of *Mendoza,* this map anticipates through its quarters and
years the commodity tribute to which the first part of the text is devoted;
through the human figures who occupy the quarters, it anticipates the labor
tribute to which its final part is devoted. In turn and as a set, these figures
propose their own logic of symbol and number. For example, with his finer
tilmatli, or cape, his *icpalli,* or wicker throne, his sandals, and the dark skin
paint evident on his face, the emperor Tenoch differs from the nine principals, or judges, who accompany him; and their relative status may in turn be
gauged by the subsidiary ("underseat") number of layers that make up their
lesser reed-mat thrones (a graphic lexis of layers was also used to mark the
severity of earthquakes).[16] Their combined name signs suggest an analogy
for the whole in a double human anatomy, five to left and four to right, the
banners of jaguar and eagle above, head, trunk, and leg between, and the
sandal and the severed bird head below. In the plan of the book as a whole,
these elements point to the later account of the life and labor of Tenochtitlan's male and female citizens, their birth and growth, their calling as
jaguar or eagle knights, judges or *pochteca,* and their ranks and employment
generally within the authority of the emperor. In the *teoamoxtli* these are all
topics that relate to the *tonalamatl* (here absent perhaps out of political considerations) as commodity tribute does to the cycles of the year.

Because of its date, the 1530s, the *Mendoza* text can hardly be considered a
classic of the iconic script tradition, and it is written on European and not
native paper. Yet it makes good use of the formal capacities of *tlacuilolli* in
elaborating this title-page map, integrating into it historical allusion (Tenoch)
and a count of years, views in profile (Colhuacan, Tenayuca), shifts in level or
scale (Tzompanco; streams as local canals or imperial inflow), and interplay
between design in profile (like the patriarchs, rushes, and reeds) and in plan
(like the land they are set in). Just because there can be no doubt about the
irreducible geopolitical dimension of this tribute-book title page, its overtly
ritual patterning of space and time is of the greatest interest. The patent
harmony of the quatrefoil declares Tenochtitlan's nascent power.

On the *Féjérváry* title page, we find the same overall design as in *Mendoza,* with the same interplay between design in plan and in profile. Toward the central city emblem or area, here a plaza placed between a stepped pyramid and a temple platform, flow four diagonal streams, of blood rather than water, separating four quarters that sustain plant growth, now trees rather than rushes and reeds, and occupied by nine figures, here the midwives' Night Powers rather than Tenoch's patriarchal judges. Within the set of four quarters there is the same east–west preference or time axis, though here east, the sun rising over the pyramid steps, is placed at the top, and west, the crescent moon hanging from the temple platform, below – an alignment in the iconic script area appropriate to a possible provenance along the eastern tribute road.

The dominant element in the quarters is the set of four trees, in flora the equivalent of *Mendoza*'s rushes and reeds. Standing one per quarter and each a different variety, these trees are surmounted by representatives of the Thirteen Quecholli: Quetzal (east), Parrot (south), Hummingbird (west), and Hawk (north). The direct relevance of this tree imagery to tribute is confirmed in other *teoamoxtli,* like *Borgia* and *Laud,* which have their own sequences of attendant Night Lords, perching Quecholli, and tribute "offerings." The same motif occurs in Maya hieroglyphic in *Dresden.* Certain alphabetic texts, in Nahuatl and in Maya, explicitly decode the birds as collectors and feeders on provincial produce. *Tudela* typifies variety in geography and even human types by means of these tribute-tree quarters, in a fashion that reinforces our earlier reading of *Mendoza.*[17]

Besides, the Quecholli in *Féjérváry* display an exact numerical correspondence with the actual totals of towns listed as sources of tribute in *Mendoza.* Each of them has its unvarying number value, so that the four can be simultaneously read as arithmetic: Quetzal, 12, to east; Hawk, 3, to north; Hummingbird, 1, to west; Parrot, 13, to south. The total is clearly 29, the same lunar cipher we encountered earlier in *Mendoza* as the sum of the *cabeceras* allotted to the four provincial quarters around Tenochtitlan. Through the symbolic visual language of the Quecholli, the *Féjérváry* map adheres, then, to a pattern proper to tribute: Perched on their trees, the Quecholli symbolize the input from each of their quarters according to the topic developed in the *teoamoxtli* Tribute Trees chapter, where again they exhibit their inherent number value (*Borgia,* pp. 49–53; *Laud,* pp. 31–8). The fact that both *Féjérváry* and *Mendoza* respect this cipher here confirms that ritual–astronomical logic applies to a text unquestionably devoted to the tribute and economic system of a known city, Tenochtitlan (*Mendoza*), while conversely bringing out the material underpinning of what otherwise might be considered a purely mantic *teoamoxtli* (*Féjérváry*).

Following this line of comparison, we come to the question of the year dates, which in *Mendoza* constitute an outer frame running from 2 House

(1325) to 13 Reed (1375), that is, Tenoch's reign of one year less than the full 52-year cycle. As we saw above, in *Féjérváry* four year Signs are clearly marked, two at each horizon; but at first sight they lack qualifying Numbers and therefore cannot signify as dates. Yet by virtue of being borne on the backs of a further set of Quecholli they acquire Numbers, respectively Parrot (13) Rabbit and Quetzal (12) Reed to east, Macaw (11) Flint and Eagle (5) House to west, and so form year dates that imply a span of twice 52 years over intervals of 25 + 25 + 33 + 21 years. How these dates might correlate with the Christian calendar remains an open question, since we are ignorant of the time depth and lack the 1 Reed = A.D. 1519 formula with which the *Mendoza* sequence culminates. The main point here is that such dates could exist at all, as, for that matter, they patently do in the Feasts chapter in *Borbonicus* (pp. 23–40) and the Tribute Trees chapter in *Borgia* (pp. 49–53), providing counterparts to those in *Mendoza* and adding material history to the material geography already deciphered in the *Féjérváry* map. In short, they are an added token of how *teoamoxtli* may be implicated in the basically historical business of levying tribute.

In the *Féjérváry* quarters each of the trees is flanked by a pair of Night Powers in an arrangement whereby the first of their number, Xiuhtecutli "Fire Lord," stands alone in the central plaza (i.e., 1 + 4 × 2; other arrangements of these nine include having three in one quarter and pairs in the rest, i.e., 3 + 3 × 2, as in *Laud* and in *Mendoza* – Tenoch's principals). Here in *Féjérváry* the nine spiral out from the center, tracing gestation along the retrograde path of the lunar phases and opening out the four directions to six by double-reading north and south like the *Coixtlahuaca Map.* Shod males and females are placed to east and west, unshod males to south (also the nadir of maize and bones) and to north (also the zenith of mountain and thunder-rain). Between these pairs of figures, the gestation theme is developed in two sets of emblems placed at the diagonals: One concerns human anatomy, the head, hand, leg, and trunk that severed serve as the source of the blood streams; the other, a more complex model of growth that culminates in the maize plant, the human substance and analogue according to the *Popol vuh.*

As in the *Coixtlahuaca Map,* this opening out of the directions is accompanied by an argument through embedded or subsidiary numeracy, here biological and botanical rather than geological. Hence, we find that the flowering trees of south and north constitute a pair: The former triples the twice double three of the eastern tree (i.e., twice 3 × 3 × 3 = 54 leaves); the latter modifies this in the name of calendrics, reducing the 54 to the 52 year leaves of the Round (i.e., twice 3 × 3 × 3 less 2 = 52 leaves). Put another way, the relentless base arithmetic of the underworld with its squares and cubes is fitted to the more idiosyncratic phases of the sky as these are registered in the lunar *tonalamatl* and the solar year Signs (4) and Numbers (13; 4 × 13 =

52). Like the subsidiary numeracy that defines the height of the judges' thrones in *Mendoza,* this persistent distinction in the *Coixtlahuaca Map* and *Féjérváry* between upper and lower arithmetical modes may possibly have specific social and class resonance. In any case, the constant echoes of *Mendoza* in detail and layout can leave little doubt about the economic parameters of the *Féjérváry* page – its valency as a map of tribute territory.

Moreover, as a quatrefoil title page, the *Féjérváry* map introduces a text whose overall structure and logic remarkably foreshadow that of *Mendoza,* its respective screenfold sides being dedicated first to the conquest and organization of yearly commodity *tribute* and then to the labor tribute of the *tonalamatl.* As we saw in Figure 22, there are even exact coincidences of detail, for example in the eleven armed figures, or garrisons, that guard the empire, the attention to the *pochteca* who carried the goods, and the topics of Birth, Marriage, Combat, and Mores, *Mendoza* serving here as the key to the more enigmatic *teoamoxtli.*

A corollary for all that underlies the political surface of the *Féjérváry* map, its evolutionary subtext, may be found in dry paintings, notably among the five designs won from the Snakes by the Navajo Twins in the Shooting Chant. The last of these recapitulates the Twins' expedition among the earth people and serves in particular to restore to Holy Man the senses he lost when tricked by Red Coyote, a rival for Big Snake's daughter. To effect the cure he first passes through four hoops that strip his body of coyote skin; then representatives appear from places where Holy Man had been given paintings, Sky-reaching Rock, Coiled Mountain, and Striped Mountain, and they successively restore his speech, hearing, and sight. This leaves the fourth and final painting from and of Red Mountain to restore his senses and health entirely and to set the premise for the humans who will inherit the present age (Plate 14b). In *Dine bahane* this story is matched by that of Coyote and his Bear lover and the series of four annihilations they inflict on each other before truly human sensibility can emerge.

The map image that registers and relates to all this, a quatrefoil, intercalates the four diagonal plants with pairs of figures in four quarters, and centers on fire, the crossed fire sticks that denote the Red Mountain hearth, exactly as the *Féjérváry* map does. Indeed, the maize and squash plants occupy identical positions in both texts, to southeast and northwest, and the pairs of figures match east–west and north–south surrounding the fire represented in *Féjérváry* by the first of the Night Powers, Fire Lord (Xiuhtecuhtli). In the dry painting their lunar nature is intimated by crescent phase markings on body and dress. Even in the leaf totals of the intercalated plants there are precise echoes of the calendrical data in *Féjérváry.*[18] The advantage of the dry paintings is that generations of Navajo scribes have commented upon them and explained their significance as images of both territory and genesis, and their precise function in curing and therapy. In

Figure 30. Four sense emblems. (Xiuhtecutli's head, *Féjérváry,* p. 1; see Plate 13a.)

refining our general perception of *Féjérváry*'s deeper message in these terms, the Anasazi story could also help to translate the curious set of emblems that attaches to Fire Lord's head as he dominates the central plaza. Placed above the eye, the first is a small bird; the second, atop the cerebellum, a basket of copal incense; the third, the soft fur of a jaguar's ear; and fourth, above the ear, a schematic hand: in all an adequate indication of sight, smell, touch, and hearing (Fig. 30). Just these human senses are achieved by Holy Man at Red Mountain and are similarly shown in the dry paintings, for example, as marking on Nayenezgani's cheek.[19] In addition, in thus qualifying the central figure of the *Féjérváry* map, they just possibly denote its now forgotten provenance.

Within the Fourth World the dry paintings of Anasazi and the Mesoamerican books, among other texts, develop their own representation of space and contrive to combine nearer and deeper levels of time and experience. In the case of the quincunx and the quatrefoil maps, the successive coincidences of detail and layout can only be attributed to a common source, despite the distance that separates the two kinds of text in space and time.

4

Configurations of time

YEAR COUNTS

Who entered whose history? This is a question urgently asked by the
authors of the *Chilam Balam Books,* Chimalpahin and a whole school of
Nahuatl historians, Guaman Poma – indeed, chroniclers and annalists from
all over America. The most effective means of resisting the imperial sum
through which the Fourth World is "discovered" and simply added to the
other three is to recognize its local historiography, how its chronicles relate to
each other, their length, and the rhythms and phases of time they propose.

Of the records intelligible to us, that of Maya hieroglyphic is the most
celebrated. Demanding greater chronometric sophistication than the West
was at first capable of, it is a system unrivaled in accuracy and range that
minutely established the dates of a civilization over more than a thousand
years. Comparable with the now illegible Inca *quipu* on mathematical
grounds, it represents a special development of and within the calendrics of
Mesoamerica, its standardized year of 360 days comparing in this respect
with the even more schematic Cakchiquel year of 400 days.[1] In particular, in
achieving its mathematical perfection the Maya hieroglyphic calendar severed its immediate connection with the seasonal year, which serves as the
basic unit of chronology almost everywhere else.

American annals extant in fact stem almost entirely from the northern half
of the continent (Table 4). This difference from the south is due in part to
medium. Whereas the painted skins and page surfaces of Greater Mexico and
Turtle Island have in practice readily lent themselves to reading and alphabetic
transcription by native and outside historians, such has not at all been the case
for the *quipu* and other South American recording systems. As a result, apart
from partial transcriptions by Guaman Poma and others, the archives of

Table 4. *Annals in North America*

Provenance					Title
TURTLE ISLAND	Algonkin	Siksika			*Bull Plume*
	Siouan	Mandan and Hidatsa			*Butterfly*
		Sioux	Teton	Hunkpapa	*High Dog*
				Itazipico	*The Flame*
				Oohenupa	
				Miniconjou	*Lone Dog*
				Oglala	*Cloud Shield*
				Sicangu	*Wapoctanxi*
					High Hawk
			Yankonai		*Blue Thunder*
					John K. Bear
	Kiowa				*Anko*
					Settan
					Poolaw
ANASAZI	Pima	Pima	Kamatuk Wutca		*Kaema A*
			Amu Akimult		*Tcotub Nak*
		Papago	San Javier del Bac		*Santos*
MEXICO	Basin of Mexico				*Tula*
					Cuauhtitlan
					Chiautla
					Xolotl Maps
					Aztlan
					Tlatelolco
	Cholula Plain				*Cuauhtinchan*
					Tlaxcala
	Papaloapan				*Coixtlahuaca Valley Lienzos*
					Tepexic
					Selden Roll
					Cuicatlan
					Baranda
					Quiotepec
	Mixteca				*Tilantongo*
					Eight Deer
					Eight Deer and Four Wind
					Xaltepec
	Tlachinollan				*Tlapa*

Note: Restricted to titles listed in the present volume's native text bibliography, this table represents only a fraction of texts extant, and by no means all those cited. Geographical assignment is to general area and surroundings.

Tahuantinsuyu remain a closed book, and the case of the Chibcha kingdoms is similar. At the same time, the societies of the rainforest and of the Mapuche have traditionally shown extreme caution in the production and ownership of annals, alleging the oppressive use to which the genre may be put in the interests of class and empire.

In North America a clear distinction emerges between the annals of Meso-america and those from beyond. Whereas the *xiuhtlapoualli* name years according to a calendrical system that exists in its own right, this is not the case for annals elsewhere. Like the corresponding corpus (large and un-dercataloged) of iconic inscriptions, the *xiuhtlapoualli* name years according to the 52-year Round (*xiuhmolpilli*), this total being produced by the two parts of the year name: its Number in the series of the Thirteen Numbers; and its Sign, one in a set of four "bearers" taken from the Twenty Signs. Regionally and over time, sets of bearers varied, Series III (House, Rabbit, Reed, Flint – Signs III, VIII, XIII, XVIII) being the commonest.[2] The norm in Tenochtitlan, Cuauhtinchan, Tepexic, and Tilantongo, Series III was used right across to Nicaragua, while Wind, Deer, Tooth, Ollin (Series II) occur in early Monte Alban, Tlapa, Cuicatlan, Quiotepec, and Quiché; a Series IV was also known. Moreover, not only could the series bearer vary, but the qualifying Number as well, so that the year of Cortes's arrival, 1519, was 1 Reed in Tenochtitlan, 13 Reed in Tilantongo, and probably 4 Reed in Coixtlahuaca and Tepexic. Yet these were mere variations within a single system that, moreover, offers its own internal correlations, a celebrated example being the Mixtec gold pendant that shows a year respectively named 10 (or 12) Wind and 11 House as a pair of lungs breathing in time with each other (Plate 3c). Highly technical, these correlations help us to define political rivalry in and between the Basin of Mexico, the Cholula Plain, Papaloapan, the Mixteca, and other arenas of western Mesoamerica.

Once named, these years are distinguished from other *tonalamatl* Num-bers plus Signs by a special marker (Fig. 31). In most highland *xiuhtlapoualli* from Tenochtitlan and its surroundings, this consists of a square, diamond, or circular box colored turquoise or red (in Nahuatl, *xiuh* means "year," "turquoise," and "fire"). Other designs include a knot; storm clouds and deities of annual rains; the circle with inner quartering to show the equi-noxes and solstices of the year; and the A-shaped solar ray that is standard in the major bodies of annals from Coixtlahuaca and the Mixteca. A tra-pezelike design found, for example, at Xochicalco has been linked by some scholars to clocks capable of measuring the complex solar-shadow variables of the tropics.[3] Convention further varied on whether or not to note the passage of every year (boxed years usually do this) or divisions within the year, like the 20-day Feasts, days (usually given in A-type texts), or even the time of day. Again, textual format could differ, being linear or boustro-phedon, as could reading direction (left to right, right to left, bottom to top,

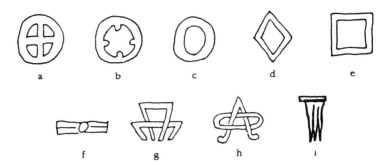

Figure 31. Year markers: (a) Monte Alban; (b) *Metlatoyuca Lienzo* (Census 199; Brotherston 1982:85); (c) *Tepechpan Annals* (Census 317), *Féjérváry;* (d) *Tepetlaoztoc Codex* (Census 181); (e) *Aztlan Annals, Mendoza Codex;* (f) *Baranda Scroll;* (g) Xochicalco; (h) *Selden Roll, Tepexic Annals;* (i) *Chiepetlan Lienzo* (Galarza 1972).

top to bottom) and focus (individual biography, municipal history). The genre encompasses them all.

The potential of the genre may be usefully brought out by comparing two of its score or so classic texts, one from the Highland Basin, the other from the Mixteca. Principal account of Mexica migration into the Basin of Mexico, the *Aztlan Annals* occupy one side of the *amatl*-paper screenfold named after Boturini, and run over twenty-one pages from 1 Flint to 6 Reed, A.D. 1116–1303 according to the Tenochtitlan correlation. It is a key text that tells of the Mexica before they founded Tenochtitlan in 2 House 1325, the start of the imperial reigns in *Mendoza*. Reading from left to right, we begin in the island homeland of Aztlan whence, heeding Huitzilopochtli, the war god who speaks to them from a cave in Colhuacan in 1 Flint, the migrants set off along a trail marked by footprints through an open landscape (Fig. 32). This takes them to the felled tree Tamoanchan, where they separate into their future calling as planter or hunter towns,[4] and then to Coatepec. Only now (p. 6) are further dates given: Enclosed in their square boxes, they are ranged in five boustrophedon rows (read from the bottom, left to right, right to left) that fill the page and issue into the fire kindling of 2 Reed (1142). Thereafter the footprint trail resumes, taking us to Tula, the first in a series of places that lead to Colhuacan in the Basin of Mexico. Here the further installments of years are arranged now in columns rather than rows but still read in boustrophedon; they typically provide a left-hand margin for place events that are linked by loops of a footprint trail.

Having twice the numbers of pages that the *Aztlan Annals* have, the biography of the Mixtec conqueror Eight Deer occupies the reverse of the *Zouche–Nuttall* screenfold and runs from 6 Flint (A.D. 992), the date of his

Figure 32. Aztlan Annals (p. 18): foot trail of migration over years 1 Flint–4 Reed (1272–5) and 5 Flint–8 Reed (1276–9), and arrival at Chapultepec (grasshopper mountain) with its water source.

father's first marriage in Tilantongo, whose correlation is used, to 12 Rabbit (1050), the eve of his own. From the start we are made aware of a very different narrative manner. Color illuminates persons and places, to which attaches a rich lexis of gesture, dress, and architectural and natural forms, all being intricately arranged within a regularly channeled boustrophedon that starts at the bottom column of the first page and runs from right to left. Only on very special occasions, like Eight Deer's famous waterborne attacks, does this reading stream open into a larger page area. Then, rather than form self-defining blocks unit by unit, years are immersed in the flow of events, being indicated by the solar ray and named only when necessary; moreover, days within years are noted that readily interchange with the day names of the characters. Again, the finer texture of the page, of skin rather than *amatl* paper, allows for a line so precise as to suggest the imbalance in Eight Deer's supposedly triumphal fire kindling in 9 Reed (1047). In addition, much amplifying the effect that the *Aztlan Annals* achieve by placing Colhuacan toponyms at the start and end of the text, the pairing of events reciprocally enhances their meaning: the two waterborne attacks, for example, the one by night successful, and the other, by day, not (pp. 32, 40); the father's first and second marriages at the opening; and the sacrificial acts performed by Eight Deer first with his older half-brother, when his reddened ear receives a message from the sky, and then with his younger brother, when his psychic disarray becomes apparent (pp. 3, 28).

In short, the two annals differ as much as they can in year markers, correlation, reading direction, color, style, and even the stuff they are made of, and make quite different uses of the resources of *tlacuilolli*. Nonetheless, they are identical by virtue of being *xiuhtlapoualli*, of belonging to a genre that is homogeneous and always involves the same year unit and narrative principle. Compatible with European annals, *xiuhtlapoualli* flourished for many decades after Cortes in native script and in varying degrees of alphabetic transcription. As year narratives they contributed directly to the grander alphabetic histories of New Spain produced by Chimalpahin, Tezozomoc, Castillo, Ixtlilxochitl, and other writers in the Nahuatl tradition.

In the annals of Turtle Island, the passage of a year is marked not through a system of calendar Signs but simply by the image of an event that occurred during it. This convention is amply exemplified in the Winter Counts of the Dakota (*waniyetu yawapi*);[5] these characterize years by such events as battles, epidemics, and major ceremonies, for which appropriate pictographs are found and drawn out on skin or paper. Agreed upon by local committees, the actual events chosen to represent years vary overall, though the counts tend to group themselves politically according to the elaborate sevenfold structure of Dakota council fires, for example as Teton or Yanktonai, and, more narrowly, the sevenfold divisions within those fires, for example as Oglala- or Sicangu-Teton. The style of the pictographs used may vary according to the individual author, but they adhere nonetheless to the norms of Plains pictography. Scripturally, they stand as the antecedent to counts and glosses on counts written in syllabic and in alphabetic script in Dakota or English. Correlations between them and with the Christian calendar can usually be made via certain "universal" events, mainly astronomical, like eclipses and meteor showers. Their earliest starting date is before 1700; some are still being kept up to date.

The several dozen Dakota *waniyetu* constitute the bulk of the genre, but examples are also known from other Siouans like the Mandan as well as from other political and linguistic groups, like the Siksika Algonkin to the northwest. As for eastern Turtle Island, no original is extant or now legible, though evidence abounds of what must once have been a vigorous tradition. A prime use of the wampum belt of diplomacy was to enumerate years, according to Iroquoian and Algonkin histories based on that medium. The Pamunkey Algonkin in seventeenth-century Virginia, like the Sioux in nineteenth-century Dakota, recorded the passage of years by placing picto-

Figure 33. Anko's Year and Moon count.

graphs on skins, and the particular count seen by John Lederer two centuries previously noted the arrival of European ships in the image of a white swan shooting flame from its mouth.[6] Though largely indirect, this testimony means that the annal convention surely existed in the east.

Certain counts that stem from the area between Turtle Island and Mesoamerica represent a practice that is intermediary between the *waniyetu* and the *xiuhtlapoualli*. These people customarily register year units as such independent of the event images that may or may not attach to them. The case of the Kiowa[7] is very clear, for the year units in question are qualified by pictographs for both winter and summer halves of the year. One count, by Anko, further registers a sequence of thirty-seven moons that runs over three years between the Sun Dance ceremonies of 1889 and 1892, correlating the respective lunar and year units (Fig. 33). (Similar concern with the moon, both synodic and sidereal, appears in skins and mantles painted by the neighboring Apache in the same period.)

Yet more revealing are the counts of the Pima, whose year begins with the summer rains. Like the Sioux and Kiowa counts, these employ pictographs, and certain of the events recorded are actually identical with those in the more northern sources, like the meteor showers of 1833. (This astronomical event marks the start of the two main Pima counts, by Kaema A and Tcokut Nak, being approximated in that of Dohasan and Settan's Kiowa counts, and in that of the Mandan Butterfly.) Yet the Pima pictographs are extremely schematic: They are inscribed in the first instance in the concise medium of the notched stick. Calendar sticks painted and incised with abstract designs economically convey considerable spans of time in this culture; and the practice as such serves to affirm its links with the Plains, where similar sticks complement the pictographic Winter Counts, and with southern Appalachia, where their use is also attested. A much-quoted example seen by Clark among the Santee Sioux covered a thousand-year span. The primary role of Plains calendar sticks in relation to pictographs, as among the Pima, is brought out in the initial stages of the Sicangu count of Wapoctanxi (Brown Hat), who depicts a collection of them, remarking: "From time immemorial they have kept large number of sticks, each one about as thick and as long as a lead-pencil, for the purpose of counting and keeping record of numbers, and they cut notches in larger sticks for the same purpose."[8]

In other words, this Pima practice, like that of the Kiowa, alerts us to principles of numeracy that underlie the mere characterization of years; and these recur in identical form in Mesoamerica. Reproducing the story of migration from Aztlan, the *Sigüenza Map* notes the passage of years in unnamed circles, as do other texts in the Mexica and Chichimec tradition; for the same purpose other texts use year markers alone without the system of year Numbers plus Signs. Moreover, the very term for the 52-year Round, *xiuhmolpilli*, or year bundling, distantly evokes the gathering of years like sticks, of the kind sculpted in Aztec year bundles of stone.

In its ready legibility, the annals tradition to the north generally makes an instructive point of comparison for the *xiuhtlapoualli* of Mesoamerica itself, revealing features of the latter that have sometimes been obscured for scholars by the sheer complexity of the calendrical system there. In this perspective we get a clearer sense of the year unit as such, and its seasonal nature, the annal snows of the *waniyetu* corresponding experientially to the monsoon rains depicted in certain of the *xiuhtlapoualli* year markers. Clocks or quartered circles, these last also point to the year's equinoctial and solstitial moments, the "hinges" measured by the superbly crafted shaft to the underground temple at Xochicalco, as they were by the ingenious spirals incised on the portals of Gran Chaco and the "woodhenge" alignment with the great pyramid at Cahokia.[9]

Although exclusive to Mesoamerica, the system of eighteen yearly Feasts of twenty days, plus five (or six) "useless," or epagomenal, days, was and is

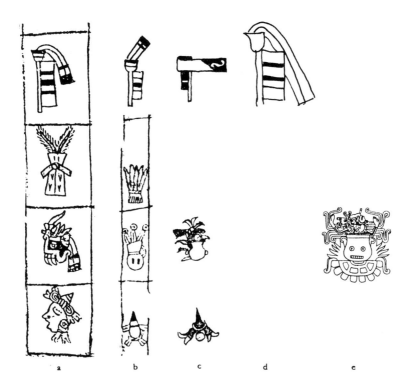

Figure 34. Quarterly Feasts of the year – Tlacaxipehualiztli–Etzalqualiztli–Ochpaniztli–Panquetzaliztli (March–June–September–December). (a) *Tlapa Annals 2* verso; (b) *Tlaquiltenango Fragment* (Census 343); (c) *Ríos* (years 1519–21); (d) *Borbonicus,* pp. 23–40; (e) *Borgia,* pp. 29–46.

operated to accord with this broader pattern of seasons, the equinoxes corresponding to the Feasts of Tlacaxipehualiztli and Ochpaniztli (Fig. 34) and the solstices to those of Etzalcualiztli and Panquetzaliztli. Although all four Feasts could feature as tribute points, for example in *Tlapa Annals 2* and in *Mendoza* (for metals), the equinoctial pair mark the primary division of the year as the terms for the basic six-monthly cloth tribute, and incidentally for all the tribute due from distant Xoconochco; indeed, the structural halves of the eighteen-feast cycle – that is, each as the equinox plus four double Feasts – confirm this emphasis. In the special case of the lowland Maya, where the standardizing effect of the *tun*/year decoupled the Feasts from the seasons, evidence exists that the slippage between the two, hinged on the equinoxes, in itself became a focus of attention, for example in Teeple's "Determinant" dates.[10] North of the tropics, where these halves of the year become more identifiable with cold winter and warm summer, exactly the same preference governs the March new-year ceremonies of the Mide and the Winter Counts, which oppose the summer of the Sun Dance to the winter of darkness.

In acknowledging a common term in the seasonal year in narrative and administration, annals throughout North America likewise concur in grouping years in larger periods. In Mesoamerica it is true that such periods are principally determined by the vigesimal arithmetic of tribute – flag for twenty, feather for four hundred, and so on – and by the 52-year Round itself. Within and beneath all this, however, other rhythms make themselves felt that are geographically far more widespread. Spans of four and of seven years are salient. Coincident with the leap-day period and commemorated in Mesoamerica in the series of bearer Signs, the four-year span ("nauhxiuh-tica," to quote *Inin cuic*)[11] determined the learning periods of the Navajo Twins, membership in the tribal societies of the Siksika, and travel to the windswept netherworld among almost all North American nations.

Synonymous with the night-guardian sequence in Mesoamerica (see *Borbonicus,* pp. 21–2), seven relates more pointedly to body growth, exemplarily in the seventy-year lifetimes spelled out in the *waniyetu* and presented as typical of Tenochtitlan's subjects in *Mendoza*. Echoed far to the south in Chibcha calendrics, the seventy-year lifetime is numerically underpinned in the counting-stick tradition, where finishing off one stick and beginning another means the completion of seventy years. In Santos's Pima/Papago count this event takes place in 1911 and is anticipated by the completion of forty- and fifty-year cycles in 1881 and 1891, while Kaema A's count runs to just over seventy years. On the Plains, the same seventy-year period is attributed to the counting sticks in the Sicangu counts of Wapoctanxi, where both before and after 1700 time is measured out in lots of seventy years. Seventy years also functions as an ideal span in the spiraling Winter Count of Lone Dog and other Miniconjou and Hunkpapa texts (Bush, Mata Sapa, The Swan, Old Bull, Charging Thunder). The norm in Turtle Island, the inherent decimal here proves through this and other examples to be a recognizable number base in Mesoamerica within the vigesimal system.

With their more elaborate calendrics, Mesoamerican annals draw the finest distinctions between these ciphers in making an overall argument. A clear example comes in the screenfold pair of *Tlapa Annals 1* and *2,* each of which covers more or less the same period of Tlachinollan's history. *Annals 1,* which emphasizes the genealogy dealt with more fully on its verso side, groups years seven per page, the ritual span of the midwives' year guardians appropriate to notions of birth and lineage; *Annals 2,* whose concern is rather conquest and tribute, groups years 4 + 4 per page, the tetradic pattern that recurs on the verso in the quarterly Feasts of the tribute levy.

Acknowledging the existence of these ciphers and year multiples means

a   b   c

Figure 35. Place and year multiples: (a) Challcatl, at 80-year interval (*Cuauhtinchan Annals,* fols. 39–40); (b) Cuauhquecholtecatl, at 40-year interval (*Cuauhtinchan Annals,* fols. 39–40; (c) Cuauhquechollan (*Mendoza,* p. 42).

inquiring into how they are visually represented in the text, a fraught question in which the more legible *waniyetu* may again serve as a guide. There the lifetime is typically imaged as a spiral or *tipi* circle, to which High Hawk puts the unambiguous gloss "seventy years."[12] Black Elk equated the years of this Era with the hairs on a buffalo's leg, whereas the four-year period corresponded to the horizons. For their part, the Mide scrolls confirm the tree as an emblem of the thousand years inscribed on the Santee calendar stick, and in the Huichol paintings years can be read from inset disks. In *tlacuilolli* texts, this order of visual language is developed according to local needs, in the annual fenceposts that enclose a field in Tlacotepec in time and space (1519–65), the millennial tree with boulders of the *Tlapiltepec Map,* the flame-Rounds of the 52-year New Fire ceremony that sum up years along the *Sigüenza* migration route, and the ages buried like Seven Caves in the Flint mountain of Coetzala.[13] These examples in fact belong to a complex repertoire of embedded numeracy that remains to be explored and that includes the Round not only as flame, but also as smoke, cloud, and the scroll set before or interchangeable with the mouth and lip, or the star-eye set into an actual sky. The four-year span could be denoted by a stone or flint, reminiscent of the fourth of the Series III bearer Signs (Flint), while in the annals of Cuauhtinchan and Cuauhtitlan the "cross-eagles" sign that denotes the place Cuauhquechollan coincides with defeats that are set exactly forty years apart; the jade of Chalco similarly correlates with the 80-year period[14] (Fig. 35).

Even more striking than the agreement on ciphers that govern significant multiples of years is the convention, again ubiquitous in North America, whereby these serve not just to delimit year spans but to bring about shifts between years and other levels or dimensions of time. Quite obvious in the case of the *tonalamatl*'s Night Lords, who determine both the nine-night count and the nine moons of pregnancy, this time-shift principle derives from shamanist techniques of psychotropy, which with or without hallucinogens modify received norms and expectations of duration; it is just as evident in the case of the seven that governs both year guardians and the seven-night quarters of the moon, each of which has its distinct Mide and Winnebago symbol and is the catamenial norm of Turtle Island (Cherokee, Lenape). In truth, this principle of moving from nights to years underlies the whole notion of the Winter Count, in that the winter at those latitudes *is* the night of the year, the hibernation of beasts, people, and gods, who stir in their sleep at the midnight solstice. A Lenape account of their people's journey east specifies "each night's encampment" as "a halt of a year in a place," and Lafitau noted the same "manner of counting" among the Iroquois ("Les Iroquois et les Hurons ont une manière de compter, laquelle est du style de conseil, où les nuits supposent pour des années").[15] For its part, the *Anko Winter Count,* with great visual ingenuity, identifies twenty-nine years of Kiowa life (1863–92) with the nights of the moon while attaching a subsidiary count of moons to the years 1889–92 (when a thirteenth moon is intercalated).

Yet more prevalent is the formula that equates *utas* with *octaeteris,* that is, the 4 + 4 span of days and years whose primary definition is given by the three brightest bodies in the sky. The Venus chapter in the *teoamoxtli* and the hieroglyphic *Dresden* screenfold make quite explicit the analogy between the 4 + 4 years (2,920 days) that coordinate the sun with moon and Venus, and the 4 + 4 days taken by Venus to descend to and reemerge from the underworld (inferior conjunction). In the zodiac sequence in *Féjérváry* (pp. 5–14), the same shift between utas and octaeteris forms part of an especially ingenious formula that specifies the minute actual slippage between the cycles of these bodies in terms of the time-shift principle:

$$
\begin{aligned}
2{,}914 &= \quad 8 \text{ solar years} \quad \text{less 8 days at} \quad 365.24 \text{ d. per year} \\
&= \quad 5 \text{ Venus years} \quad \text{less 5 days at} \quad 583.92 \text{ d. per year} \\
&= \quad 99 \text{ moons} \quad\quad\ \text{less 9 days at} \quad\ 29.53 \text{ d. per moon}
\end{aligned}
$$

Indeed, the tetradic sequences of the Venus journey, along with the time shift between days and years, recurs everywhere in North America: At the wake of Aztec, Sioux, and Algonkin, the four days spent by the mourners are experienced as four years by the deceased traveling to the underworld, and each lot of four days spent on the path through life by Anasazi heroes equals four years for normal beings. In a narrative by the Muskogee chief Chekilli, the four (plus four) days of the annual maize festival *pushkita* (whence *busk*) ritually appear as years of an ancestral journey.[16] Inscribed in the very stanza structure of Mide script, for example in the *Kweweziashish Song Scroll,* the 4 + 4 pattern corresponds to degree days, and years, along the path of Mide initiation. Moreover, the Mide accounts of Venus's journey well exemplify how the double tetradic pattern can be applied to yet other dimensions of time, for instance the minuter phases within the sun's day and its journey through the sky in stages marked by "rests." The same is true of the set of four years embedded in the Huichol texts, only here, in the Creation series, the shift is in the other direction: to years that experientially stand for far greater spans of time.

Readily recognizable throughout North America, the shamanic time shift is taken to enormous lengths in Mesoamerican calendrics, with its wealth of Number and Sign sets. The Thirteen Numbers alone take us from the *trecenas,* or thirteen days, of the *tonalamatl,* a main chapter topic in the *teoamoxtli,* to the thirteen years or quarters of the 52-year Round, which are ranged as arms of the swastika in the *Chiautla Annals;* and in the hieroglyphic system we move similarly to the thirteen *katun*s (20 *tun*s; 7,200 days) of the Katun Round (a purely mathematical progression here because of the standardized nature of the *tun* calendar and its detachment from naturally determined time units – other, that is, than the sun's day).

Bringing together the *waniyetu* and *xiuhtlapoualli* traditions is mutually illuminating. It points up the principles according to which Fourth World annals actually work and how they construct their current time, held as this is in the larger spans of the Era and cosmogony.

THE ERA

The earliest surviving evidence of Era dating in Mesoamerica can be found in Olmec inscriptions, which place themselves at about the time of Christ by counting out time units from the year 3113 B.C. Subsequently the lowland Maya used this base date in their hieroglyphic inscriptions during the Classic period and identified it with the day and *katun*-ending "4 Ahau" (Sign XX), generally read as 10 (or 12) August of that year; hence, an Initial Series inscription registers A.D. 675, for example, as "Maya Era (= M.E.) 9.12.3"; that is, 3 *tun*s (360 days), 12 *katun*s (20 *tun*s), and 9 *baktun*s (20 *katun*s) from that base date. By its very structure, this lowland *tun* calendar generates an Era span of thirteen *baktun*s, prompting some scholars to announce an end date in A.D. 2012, M.E. 13.0.0, 5,200 (or 13 × 400) *tun*s from 3113 B.C. Especially interesting is the evidence of the *Chilam Balam Book of Tizimin,* which reports on the eighteenth-century calendar reform that led to a general approximation between the *tun* and the seasonal year of the Christians. The end date calculated here is A.D. 2088,[17] 5,200 seasonal years rather than 5,200 *tun*s from 3113 B.C.

This same span of 5,200 years is attributed to the present Sun, or Era, in the iconic tradition, being calculated as either thirteen 400-year *tzontli* ("feathers") or a hundred 52-year Rounds. As one hundred Rounds it is depicted on the *Sunstone* of Tenochtitlan and is transcribed in the Nahuatl histories of Cuauhtitlan and Chalco (Chimalpahin's source, and later Boturini's), while the *Pinturas Manuscript* speaks of a half-Sun measured as approximately fifty Rounds (2,600 years) in that source[18] and *Inomaca tonatiuh*. In the opening chapter of *Ríos,* it is depicted as thirteen feathered turquoise units that for good measure are glossed as "quattrocenti anni" by the Vatican copyist (see Fig. 64b). In matching in years the hieroglyphic span of 5,200 *tuns,* the iconic texts also appeal to the same base date, gestured toward in Chimalpahin's cluster of near-3000 B.C. dates (Seventh Relation) and precisely stated on the *Sunstone* and in the *Tepexic Annals* as the year 13 Reed 3113 B.C. Within this year, while the hieroglyphic 4 Ahau (Sign XX) equals 10 August, the name of this Sun emblazoned on many iconic pages and monuments, 4 Ollin (Sign XVII), announces the spring equinox, 21 March, a seasonal moment appropriate to the year calendar.

On the *Sunstone,* directly above and uppermost, stands the year name 13 Reed. This possibly alludes to the contemporary Aztec date A.D. 1479; but it also corresponds nominally to 3113 B.C. in the more august correlation of Tepexic and Coixtlahuaca. The same casting back occurs in the *Cuauhtitlan Annals,* which recount events in the Basin of Mexico up to the time of Cortes, moving year by year from the seventh-century Chichimec base, Round 72 of the Era, acknowledged widely in Basin of Mexico texts and just possibly encoded in the very name of the Chichimec goddess Itzpapalotl: Obsidian Butterfly.[19] Over the first two Rounds, culminating in the year 13 Reed A.D. 751, the Cuauhtitlan text switches right back to the beginnings of the Era Four Ollin, telling how it emerged from the previous world ages in the year of that same name, millennia ago. In doing so it translates into roman numerals the cloud-snake Rounds (*mimixcoa*) that, ranged on the back of the *Sunstone*'s encircling celestial dragon, allot 5,200 years (10 × 10 × 52) to this Era, the fifth in the scheme of Suns and a fifth of the precessional cycle of 26,000 years (see Chapter 12, especially Fig. 54).

Detailed accounts of the Era, its intricate mechanisms and grand perspectives, are given in several year-calendar texts. Here three are taken as examples: the *Mexicanus Codex* of Tenochtitlan and Eight Deer's biography, both of which use meshed-wheel devices (Fig. 36), and the *Tepexic Annals,* which carry us all the way from the beginnings of the Era in an unbroken narrative of years.

Mexicanus is a post-Cortesian text whose eleven-page opening chapter is overtly calendrical in dealing with Christian saints' days, dominical letters, and the Old World zodiac and in seeking to reconcile the Mesoamerican and Christian calendars. The dual-wheel design on page 9 juxtaposes Christian with Mesoamerican years. Of the former, there are 28, or a solar cycle, identified by the 4 × 7 Sunday, or dominical, letters a–g; of the latter, there are 52 of a Round, identified by the thirteen Numbers and four Signs of a Series III Round. In the position shown, the b year of the Christian wheel,

a

b

Figure 36. Calendar wheels: (a) *Mexicanus,* p. 9; (b) *Eight Deer* (*Nuttall* verso), p. 35.

seventeen years before the b year 1575 (glossed as such in Arabic numerals),[20] is just touching the first of the Rabbit years on the Mesoamerican wheel, under the rabbit's nose: in the Tenochtitlan convention, 1558 was in fact the year 1 Rabbit, the last of the Aztec fire-kindling Rounds completed before the *Mexicanus* was written. Hence, the wheels not only are juxtaposed but mesh and may carry us forward or backward in time in correct calendrical sequence. In the center of the Christian wheel Saint Peter holds a triple-pronged key in his right hand and in his left an open book displaying four dots on each of two pages, five of which have been revealed; above his head a cross occupies an extra division of the solar-cycle wheel, raising from 28 to 29 the total of the divisions that will mesh with the 52 Mesoamerican years should the wheels be turned farther in either direction.

In the position given, to alter or break the Christian cycle in this way seems to point to the major calendrical event that occurred just four years (the leap-day span) after the last letter was recorded: e, or 1578 (that is, the Gregorian reform of 1582), otherwise alluded to in *Mexicanus,* which did effectively cause a break in the 28-year Sunday-letter sequence. At the same time, in the Mesoamerican system this alteration ingeniously points to the reasons behind the reform in question: that is, the imperfect Julian measurement of the seasonal year and hence of the need for leapyear days, insofar as this last had long been calculated in Mesoamerica according to a superior formula involving the number 29 rather than 28. This formula, also found in the *tun* calendar, specifies that over 29 Rounds, or 1,508 years, the difference between the metric year of 365 days (i.e., without leap days) and the slightly longer seasonal year (365.242 days) itself amounts to a year;[21] and this is exactly the total of years produced by the operation of the two wheels in question, since 1,508 is the lowest common multiple of 29 and 52. Complex enough in itself, this still leaves unexplained the remaining numerical data in the design, to wit, the three prongs of Saint Peter's key and five dots on his book.

In Christian calendrics the 28-year solar cycle has been commonly used to produce larger spans, either in conjunction with, for example, the Metonic or indiction period, which produces the Julian cycle that begins in 4713 b.c., or alone, to postulate Usher's creation date of around 4004 b.c. Here in *Mexicanus,* taking into account Saint Peter's numerical clues, the emended 29-year cycle can be seen to produce the distance between the start of the first Round of the Mesoamerican Era in 1 Flint 3112 b.c. (Tepexic correlation) and the end of the last Aztec Round in 1 Rabbit a.d. 1558 (Tenochtitlan correlation), thus linking and confirming the two separate decodings of date and cycle made so far. For fully turned thrice through all combinations, as the lock imagery of the key suggests they should be, the wheels produce 4,524, or 3 × 1,508, years and the date a.d. 1412, to which may then be added five turns of the Christian wheel, or 145 years, the interval to the goal of a.d. 1558. In other words, in matching their calendar with that of the Christian invaders, the Tenochtitlan authors of this page contrived to appeal alike to a year significant in their own local annals (1 Rabbit a.d. 1558)[22] and the grander scheme of the Mesoamerican Era.

The life of Eight Deer furnishes us with a similar correlation, this time one that is pre-Cortesian. In the biographies dedicated to him, Eight Deer is shown to have exerted high privilege in personally conducting, at the age of thirty-six, the New Fire kindling of 9 Reed, the Mixtec year that Alfonso

Caso has identified with 1047 A.D. In the Colombino–Becker version, *Eight Deer and Four Wind,* this is shown as a glorious culminating moment, and although in the Zouche–Nuttall version, which generally takes a poorer view of its subject, Eight Deer's fire drill is slightly crooked, the calendrical significance of the year as such is brought out no less (pp. 35–6). For a special toponym emblem anticipates the year name 9 Reed; it consists of a sun into which are set two concentric wheels, and is glossed with the words *nauh ollin,* that is, the Sun, or Era, name Four Ollin. The outer circle registers the 52 divisions of the Round; the inner one is of jade, the element identifiable with the 80-year period.[23] (Tichy has suggested, moreover, that the standard Mesoamerican division of the circle itself was into 80 parts.) The product of the two would, then, be 52 × 80, or 4,160 years, which is exactly the distance from 3113 B.C. to the date in question, A.D. 1047. Appropriated, as it were, by Eight Deer, this date has a particular resonance in the Era, for it marks the ratio of four-fifths to one-fifth that determines the Era itself within the Great Year. As the Colombino version shows in the twenty star-eyes that overlook the event, it is also twenty Rounds, or one-fifth of the Era, from the base date of Round 60 observed in several Mixtec histories and defined as such in the *Xaltepec Annals* (see Fig. 38).[24]

In all, this hypothesis about Eight Deer's kindling in A.D. 1047 and its significance within the Era is prompted by the numerical detail of the toponym glossed *nauh ollin* in one biography of this hero and by the wealth of solar imagery that attaches to it in another. It relies on the notion that calendrical meshed-wheel devices of the kind seen in *Mexicanus* were also pre-Cortesian, and that Caso's Mixtec datings, disputed by some, are correct. Further support comes from the Era span measured out in the *Tepexic Annals.*

Equipped with the facsimile of the *Vindobonensis* screenfold (1963), we may now enjoy the unparalleled sensation of reading through the *Tepexic Annals,* which are written on the fifty-two pages of its obverse over the physical length of about forty feet. Moving along the winding boustrophedon stream, pausing in larger page areas, or "pools" of time, we are carried through thousands of years from year date to year date, Round to Round, page to page, and chapter to chapter, each of these last culminating in a fire-kindling ceremony (Table 5). As we go forward in time, chapter length diminishes: After the marathon twenty-two pages of chapter 1, chapter 2 takes up only ten pages, and the remaining eight are bunched in the final twenty pages of the screenfold. At the same time we notice a preference for particular year names over others, like 7 Reed and 1 Reed, the twentieth and the fortieth years of the Round that begins in 1 Flint, while particular year-plus-day names recur exclusively at particular intervals, as if to cross-check the progress of the text. Hence, the 2 Reed/2 Reed first seen in Round 27 upon a star-mountain (see Fig. 63) later establishes a nine-

Round rhythm in the text at Rounds 39, 48, and 57 that numerically harmonizes with the appearances of the patron deity of the whole story, Quetzalcoatl Nine Wind, ninth of the Thirteen Heroes. Again, the face symbol of the rain god known as Napatecutli, "four-times lord," appears four times in the text over a span of exactly 4,004 years. At the end, looking back over the huge distance that has been covered, we realize that the average interval between the 180 year dates recorded is twenty-five years and that the span between the first, 5 Flint, and the last, 8 Flint, amounts to precisely 4,800 years. Readily legible in Mesoamerican calendrics as twelve lots of 400 years, this period also stands to the Era's 5,200 years in the lunar–solar proportion of twelve to thirteen, Quetzal to Parrot.

From the technical point of view, the course of these magnificent annals follows just the conventions and format used in the Mixtec annals that Caso, for one, has translated into more than a Christian millennium. Moreover, it quite unambiguously crosschecks itself by highlighting significant intervals and by other means. Yet so far no one has chosen to admit publicly that the text covers so long a time span, and some have positively rejected the idea. Faced with the 3,000-year span proposed in the first chapter alone (pp. 1–22), Nowotny decommissioned most of it by separating off pages 5–16 as a subsection ("Unterabschnitt"), deeming it a mere summary of previous and subsequent parts of the text ("Rekapitulation der ganzen Bilderfolge . . . vor und nach"). According to him, the year names recorded on these pages are just symbolic, synchronic clusters devoid of any linear connection. On formal and all other grounds there is no justification for treating the narrative in this way: The pages in question are wholly continuous with the general reading stream and are not separated off at all, so that the very use of the term "Unterabschnitt" (which implies a cut or section) is technically incorrect. After all, if these dates do not at all denote sequential time, why bother to place them in the sequential reading stream characteristic of the *xiuhtlapoualli?* Indeed, it is all the more important to hold onto the formal sequence, for, as the Cuauhtitlan example showed us, *xiuhtlapoualli* habitually invoke distant events, exactly like the Maya Initial Series texts, casting backward and forward in time within and between years in the progressive count. Subsequently, Nowotny's diffidence has been echoed by Melgarejo, Furst, Jansen, and others, who feel that reading the annals straight would yield an "impossible" time depth, and who propose that the dates recorded are merely symbolic and quite unrelated to the linear chronology of the *xiuhtlapoualli* genre.[25]

Derived as they are from the *tonalamatl,* Mesoamerican year-bearer names are of course imbued with symbolism. An obvious case is the Aztec fire-kindling year, which was moved from 1 Rabbit to the next year, 2 Reed, because of an association between Rabbit years and drought. In the *Tepexic*

Table 5. *Year in the Era* (Tepexic Annals)

(page)	1	2	3	4	5	6	7	8	9	10	11	12	13
(2)	1 VII	1 VII	1 II	7 II		12 II	13 II	4 V		7 V	4 I	11 II	
	(30 MARCH — 3113)												
(3)	7 XIX	7 XV	5 XVIII			0.5 / −3108	0.42 / 3071	1.39 / 3022	(4)	1.40 / 3021	2.18 / 2991	3.10 / 2947	4.10 / 2895
(5)	2.19 / 2990	3.19 / 2938	}						{	5.21 / 2832			}
(6)			(6)			4.19 / 2886	5.10 / 2843		{	5.49 / 2804	6.5 / 2796	6.20 / 2781	7.5 / 2744
(7)	8.18 / 2679	8.20 / 2677	8.35 / 2662	8.40 / 2657	9.18 / 2627	9.35 / 2610	9.37 / 2608	9.43 / 2602		10.17 / 2576	10.20 / 2573		
(8)	10.39 / 2554	11.40 / 2503	11.39 / 2502	12.34 / 2455	13.16 / 2450	14.16 / 2421	14.40 / 2369	15.35 / 2345	2298	16.27 / 2254	16.42 / 2239	17.20 / 2209	
(9)	18.25 / 2152	19.10 / 2115	19.41 / 2084	20.16 / 2057	20.32 / 2041	20.44 / 2029	21.36 / 1985	22.20 / 1949	22.25 / 1944	23.20 / 1897	23.40 / 1877	24.40 / 1825	
(10)	25.40 / 1773	25.42 / 1771	26.40 / 1721	27.4 / 1705	27.20 / 1689	27.28 / 1681	28.20 / 1637	29.18 / 1587	29.39 / 1566	30.5 / 1548	30.18 / 1535	30.40 / 1513	
(11)	32.11 / 1438	32.20 / 1429	32.27 / 1422	33.4 / 1393	33.27 / 1370	33.33 / 1364	34.27 / 1318	35.10 / 1283	35.20 / 1273	36.10 / 1231	36.47 / 1194	37.47 / 1142	
(12)	38.8 / 1129	38.19 / 1118	39.6 / 1079	39.28 / 1057	40.25 / 1008	40.33 / 1000	40.40 / 993	41.11 / 970	41.43 / 938	42.6 / 923	42.8 / 921	42.40 / 889	
(13)	43.20 / 857	44.20 / 805	44.39 / 786	45.8 / 765	45.34 / 739	46.8 / 713	46.20 / 701	46.43 / 678	47.34 / 635	47.40 / 629	48.8 / 609	48.17 / 600	
(14)	49.20 / 545	49.45 / 520	49.46 / 519	50.21 / 492	51.8 / 453	51.20 / 441	51.40 / 421	52.40 / 369	53.20 / 337	54.5 / 300	55.5 / 248	55.40 / 213	
(15)	57.18 / 131	57.28 / 121	57.35 / 114	58.20 / 77	58.21 / 76	59.21 / 24	59.39 / 6	AD	60.39 / 46	(18)	61.39 / 98	62.21 / 132	
(20)	63.10 / 173	63.39 / 202	64.20 / 235	64.39 / 254	(21)	65.39 / 306	66.19 / 338	(23)	66.35 / 354	66.39 / 358	66.44 / 363		
(26)	67.42 / 413	68.35 / 458	68.39 / 462	68.44 / 467	(28)	69.35 / 510	(29)	70.8 / 535	71.5 / 584	72.5 / 636	(30)	73.5 / 688	
(31)	74.39 / 774	(32)	75.18 / 805	(33)	75.34 / 821	(34)	75.39 / 826	(35)	76.16 / 855	76.33 / 872	(36)	76.49 / 888	
(37)	77.18 / 909	(38)	77.35 / 926	(39)	77.40 / 931	(40)	78.20 / 963	(41)	79.20 / 1015	80.5 / 1052	(42)	81.5 / 1104	
(43)	81.20 / 1119	82.20 / 1171	82.40 / 1191	(48)	83.18 / 1221	84.18 / 1273	(49)	84.32 / 1287	85.32 / 1339	85.36 / 1343	85.40 / 1347		
(50)	86.2 / 1361	86.40 / 1399	87.10 / 1421	87.40 / 1451	(51)	88.33 / 1496	89.18 / 1534	89.27 / 1543	90.4 / 1572				
(52)	90.27 / 1595	90.47 / 1615	91.39 / 1659	92.21 / 1692									

Notes: (2)–(52): page numbers in the Tepexic Annals

1 VII–5 XVIII: opening sequence of days, pp. 2–3 (= $7 \times 260 = 5 \times 365 - 5$ days)

0.5 etc.: Round in the Era, and year in the Round that has 1 Flint as its first year

−3113: equivalent to 3113 B.C.; years from −3113 to −6 (pp. 2–15) are years B.C.

Annals a similar logic underlies the avoidance of twenty of the fifty-two year names in the Round and, among the thirty-two that are used, a preference for Reed and Flint years (which each provide nine out of possible thirteen names) over House and Rabbit (which each provide only seven). Moreover, reflected in the very pagination of the chapters, this whole scheme appeals to the body ciphers of teeth (32), digits (20), and orifice (the 9:7 ratio). Then, just as the total of pages equals the years of the Round, so the overall total of dates equals the days between the equinoxes Tlacaxipehualiztli to Ochpaniztli (9 × 20), while the maximum on any one page is the lunar–solar 12:13. Other ritually significant data include the fact that besides ten chapters and kindlings it has ten characters named Two Dog (Sign X).

Again, events are repeatedly imaged in the cyclic terms of the *teoamoxtli,* notably the topic chapters Birth, Mores, Drinkers, and Kindlings. Indeed, five of the ten kindlings and chapters, distinguished by conjoint toponyms set into blocks with a single base, conform exactly to the synchronic tribute paradigm of metropolis surrounded by four quarters, to east, south, north, and west. At the center, the metropolitan block of Tepexic itself is privileged with a raised base,[26] unlike the lower-based four provincial blocks, where, for good measure, the total of *cabeceras* adds up to the lunar 29 (see Fig. 27). Respecting even the numeracy of the quatrefoil tribute paradigm as it is found in *Mendoza* and *Féjérváry,* this detail further confirms metropolitan Tepexic as the provenance of the text.

So ingenious is the construction of the *Tepexic Annals* that yet other examples of such patterning of time and experience could be found that would support a synchronic or symbolic reading of the text and the corresponding denial of an unbroken linear sequence from start to finish. Yet to do so would be to undermine the very definition of the *xiuhtlapoualli.* For all its ritual and cyclic propensities, this genre must be held, at least at a minimal level, to record successive dates, for if this principle is flouted, even in a single case, then the whole chronological–literary system is called into question. What we have is rather the shaping of time into significant and intelligible patterns of the kind preferred with such insistence in Christian decades and centuries: The *xiuhtlapoualli* typically aim at constructing patterns out of the year dates that plot their linear flow. It is true that a local effect of this can be that the year sequence may appear to function in its own right, as it were detached from any accompanying story; which is precisely the case, say, in the Tenochtitlan and Tlatelolco sections of the *Osuna Codex,* where year disks for the period 1556–64 are embedded in successive pages of the text, so that, regardless of the detail on any one page, they constitute a self-defining ninefold series of their own. But that in no way alters the fact that, as in the *Tepexic Annals,* the years are sequential and relate to a particular time period overall. In the case of the Tepexic text, the beginning of this period appears, on all available evidence, to coincide with the beginning of the Era, 13 Reed in the correlation of that town.

Hence, from the spring equinox of 3113 B.C., the opening day count leads us through seven *tonalamatl*s to the first named year, 5 Flint 3108 B.C., with its emphatic marker; and just 4,800 years later the final date, 8 Flint, becomes A.D. 1692. The 1692 projected end date serves to round off the narrative and give it calendrical significance – a convention found in many iconic and hieroglyphic texts; and in fact this very same year appears as a projected finish in annals from the Cholula Plain (Acatzinco) and Tlaxcala. Besides commemorating twelve-thirteenths of the Era, it foretells the ("corn riot") revolution caused by the largest solar eclipse seen in Mexico for centuries before and after, as well as the decision of Quetzalcoatl-Uotan's scribe-priests in Xoconochco finally to surrender their ancient screenfold books.

In the long opening chapter, Quetzalcoatl Nine Wind's birth and the migrations that follow demand to be set into the Era frame of Toltec history, whose material base is discussed below. It is further significant that precisely those texts that most share Tepexic's Papaloapan perspective likewise overtly begin their history with the Era itself. Like the Tepexic text, the *Selden Roll* places this beginning in the sky, the realm of Quetzalcoatl and the primordial pair Lord and Lady One Deer, and counts the way down to Chicomoztoc through rows of star-eyes, of the kind that also open the Gómez de Orozco, or Cuicatlan, fragment. At Chicomoztoc, the *Tlapiltepec Map* amasses four boulders marked by a millennial tree to indicate the time that had elapsed since the Era began (Fig. 37).[27]

Further cross-reference becomes possible, this time with the Mixtec texts, when we reach the tree birth at Apoala. Dating to the time of Christ, the Apoala event features as the inaugural term for several annals of Mixtec genealogy (Fig. 38), together with just the characters registered here by Tepexic: the distinctive bald- and egg-head pair; Ten Death, colored gray and black; Seven Flower; Eleven Caiman; the lady Eight Monkey, blue in the face; and last in the list, Eight Wind with his eagle headdress, to whom the *Tilantongo Annals* devote a brief biography.[28]

The second chapter, whose span of A.D. 338–805 echoes that of the Classic period originally defined by the hieroglyphic inscriptions, then ends in a kindling that lands us firmly in Tepexic. Just as in the *Coixtlahuaca Map*, its split mountain pairs with the checkerboard of Tlil-tepexic, its twin town that is now just an unexcavated ruin opposite the main site, plus the images for nearby Huehuetlan, the town of the old people, male and female, and the maguey indicative of the Tentzon ridge to the northwest. Inset in this conjoint toponym is a memory of Chicomoztoc, the Chichimec secondary base in Round 72. As at other kindlings, cut stone is brought in (on feet) for the construction of buildings and great eight-level walls carefully engraved by

Dupaix in 1807 and still remarkable to the view. A specialty of the area, the otate canework depicted as tribute was later supplied to Tenochtitlan, according to *Mendoza*. The rise of Tepexic as an urban center during the Classic is vouchsafed for by very recent excavation at the site.

Performed by Quetzalcoatl Nine Wind with Two Dog as officiator, this second kindling fundamentally affirms Tepexic's political power, a statement corroborated in texts from Coixtlahuaca, Tequiztepec, Cuicatlan, and the other Papaloapan towns in whose name, centuries later, Moctezuma Mazatzin[29] bargained with Cortes, and a fact that today makes it the home of a government center for the study of "Nahua, Chocho, and Mixtec" cultures. To the south, the Mixtec annals acknowledge Tepexic's literally cardinal importance as the power on their northern frontier at the time when their local dynasties were establishing themselves, two centuries before Eight Deer.

Over the remaining kindlings we move in stately fashion through the quarters. East, with its cacao tribute, reaches to the tree of Apoala and the "sun" (eclipsed) of Teotlillan. In the Mixtec South, at A.D. 909 the kindling is entrusted to the skeletal matron deity Nine Tooth and Nine Monkey, mentioned at this date in the *Tilantongo Annals* (p. 23), and enlists a low group of only five *cabeceras*, among them the skull town Mictlantongo and two places near Tilantongo later taken by Eight Deer – in all, a meager tribute source. The spectacular range of the twelve northern toponyms rises to the full height of the page, intimating the actual view north from Tepexic. Masked as the rain god, the first of them is the mountain Napatecuhtli, which here makes the last of its four appearances; in the *Xolotl* and *Cuauhtinchan* maps it occupies the same key position in the northwestern corner of the Chichimeca-tlalli.[30] At the other end of the block stands Zoltepec, the Quail Mountain also prominent in the Cholula Plain sources and the *Huamantla Codex* from Tlaxcala, along with such intervening features as the nose of Tepeaca, the jaguar of Ocelotepec, and coal of Tecolcuauhtlan, the star of Citlaltepec, and (for Burland) the jade face of Tlaxcala. A literal high point in the *Tepexic Annals,* this northern kindling in A.D. 1171 is presided over by the last of the Two Dogs and performed by Nine Wind. Politically it corresponds to the twelfth-century drive north shown in several *lienzos* of the Coixtlahuaca federation, which include in their boundaries Cuauhtinchan and Tepeaca on the Cholula Plain, towns whose annals reciprocally allude to these events, attaching great significance to the ancestral memory of Tepexic.

Finally, the west, again a limited quarter, includes the "ear-plug" town Nacochtlan (Necochtla today) and Coatzinco. This last kindling is, however, distinguished from all the others in the fact that it has not yet been performed. Lying reading on its block, the fire drill indicates the likely date of the text's composition, 5 House A.D. 1273. From here on, projecting to

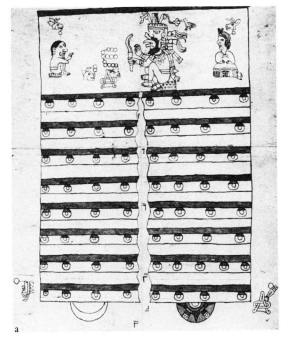

Figure 37. Era counts to Seven Caves: (a) sixty-five star-eyes arranged in eight layers (*Selden Roll*); (b) four boulders qualified by the "millennial" tree affix (*Tlapiltepec Map*).

Figure 38. Era count to Round 66. Bar-and-dot total of 66 (i.e., 21 + 45), correlated with six star-eyes (*Xaltepec Annals*, p. 1).

the 1692 close, the text sets its dates in toponyms four per page over four pages in the sixteenfold pattern of federation found alike in *Coixtlahuaca Lienzo 2* (where Tepexic is included, with a ruler named after the Era "nauh ollin") and on the Quetzalcoatl pyramid at Xochicalco.

In sum, as the longest annals extant in native script, the *Tepexic Annals* technically provide a common term of reference for the other groups of annals, with their various correlation and base dates, that stem from areas around that town, from Cuicatlan to the Basin of Mexico, and from the Mixteca to Cholula and Tlaxcala. At the same time, as a year-calendar text it demands to be considered fully commensurate with the *tun*-calendar texts of the lowland Maya, which unquestionably narrate events over the full span of the Era that begins in 3113 B.C. In this, it adds to the growing archaeological evidence at Teotihuacan, Cacaxtla, Tikal, and elsewhere of the strong political and economic interdependency throughout Mesoamerica that was the legacy of the Olmec, the mother culture of Mesoamerica in whose inscriptions Era dates first appear. As a history, it even offers to take us back to these beginnings, assigning dates to the legendary story of the Toltecs and Mesoamerican civilization; and finally it helps to fit this Era, for which Tahuantinsuyu and other polities have their counterparts, in the larger cosmogonical story of the Fourth World.

CORRELATION

In some measure, correlating the Christian and Fourth World calendars is a technical matter. It is also a philosophical and ideological one. For the Christian system of reckoning time tends automatically to be taken as standard and universal, so that when tested against it native texts have more often been taken in isolation than they have been reintegrated into their own traditions of chronology within the arena, say, of Turtle Island or Mesoamerica. In Mesoamerica, defined as it is by its "patrimonium commune" of time-constructing Numbers and Signs, most work on hieroglyphic dating has in practice gone on with little reference to the *xiuhtlapoualli;* in turn, these have rarely received full respect as a genre that transcends local differences of convention and style. This balkanization adversely affects the chances of any one text being considered historical: Out of context and bereft of its own chronological frame, it stands more chance of seeming fanciful or plain wrong when held against the Christian norm.

As with maps, the critical problem is one of location, and in this a further factor has been the nature of the Christian calendar itself. From the B.C./A.D. base, the advance of its years is implacable and linear, and it simply adds on time units whose proportional significance in the list grows ever tinier. On the other hand, a single jejune concept – fingers – underpins the recurrence of its decades and centuries, quincenturies and millennia, and the general superstition, even in high intellectual theory, with regard to their significance as concepts or units of apocalypse. Moreover, in itself this calendar has put up little resistance to that categorical distinction, so trite and imperialist when applied to the Fourth World, between diachronic story and synchronic structure. How different the situation where the present sooner blooms in time, is the moment rooted via ciphers in successive temporal levels – years, lifetimes, ages – and is a name among those that unendingly recall the nights and days of the womb and shape and place this Era within the story of civilization and the Suns of the world.

In Mesoamerica, the cycles of the *tonalamatl* and the year, all-encompassing, have become the subject of a certain scholarly polemic, since the dates registered, not just in the millennia of the *Tepexic Annals* but elsewhere in the *xiuhtlapoualli,* have been cavalierly dismissed as not really dates at all, but just symbolic. Charged with significance in their own right, erecting self-validating structures, they are said to have nothing to do with "real" time, that is, the direct experience on earth of the human beings who over enormous periods and with enormous effort built the cities and landscapes of Mesoamerica and created its civilization. One such recent account of the *xiuhtlapoualli,* which openly espouses the synchronic principles of structuralism, has been acutely decoded in terms of political conquest in the phrase "Lévi-Strauss in Tenochtitlan."[31] To argue that the Mesoamerican chronological system defies translation is one thing: Its cycles and inner resonance, its ratios and counterpoint, far richer than it has been possible to demonstrate here,[32] indeed find no equivalent in the Christian calendrical apparatus. Yet to claim that it has no connection with material history is quite another. Saying this certainly removes the psychic discomfort of having to acknowledge time depth, continuity, and political memory in the Fourth World, a discomfort that, indicatively enough, afflicted Friedrich Engels[33] no less than Christian missionary or conquistador. It does so, however, by removing texts, their authors, and their descendants from their landscapes; it furthers intellectually the murderous territorial dispossession that began with Columbus.

II

Political memory

ᏣᎳᎩ ᏔᎷᏅ ᎢᏐᎦᎥᎥᎥᎥ Ꮁ Ꮪ
elayeli iyuta skwalewistataniga

on mid earth you placed me
— *Gatigwanasti Manuscript*

auch cuix ie teoantin
toconitlacozque in ueue tlamanitiliztli

and now, should we
break the tradition?
— *Totecuyoane*

inca uanacauri maytam rinqui

Inca Huanacauri, where are you going?
— Guaman Poma, *Nueva corónica*

5

Peten

PRELIMINARIES

The Fourth World historiography offered in this and succeeding chapters relies predominantly on native sources; and it attends to only four among many more possible traditions. In each case, a body of native texts is identified and serves as a constant term of reference. Such political memories as emerge are ones that these texts themselves construct in the major arenas of Mesoamerica, Turtle Island, and the Andes.

In the first instance, the problem is the formal one of recognizing in native texts the norms that govern the representation and placing of time, its periodicities and depths. Internally consistent to greater and lesser degrees, these textual patterns may then be matched with data from other sources, above all archaeology. Cross-referenced, all this information in turn sets up ideas of perspective and continuity. Heightened moments make their mark at the beginning of a story or at the hinge between epochs.

In these terms, a privileged position is enjoyed by the body of hieroglyphic texts from Peten and the Maya lowlands. Since Förstemann and others began to decipher *tun* calendar dates a century or so ago, there has been no doubt in principle about their range: According to the Initial Series convention used in the Classic inscriptions and echoed even in the *Chilam Balam Books,* such dates are customarily fixed by counting out units of time from the 3113 B.C. Era base. By contrast, the less-centralized year calendar of Mesoamerica has still to be acknowledged by scholars as a coherent and wholly competent system in its own right; this reluctance is in part due to the nature of iconic script itself and its capacity to embed time units in complex designs or landscapes. For this reason pains were taken to emphasize that *xiuhtlapoualli* texts written in this script constitute a genre that has its set rules and procedures, its internal correlations, and a time span commensurate with that of the Maya *tun* calendar.

When we go beyond Mesoamerica and the calendrical systems that define that area, identifying potentially chronological statements becomes of itself a primary concern. In Turtle Island, whose calendars have yet to be comprehensively surveyed, the problem is one of fragmentation; besides, several indispensable texts, the *High Hawk Winter Count,* for example, have never been properly edited. In Tahuantinsuyu, the difficulty stems in part from the fact that we cannot read *quipus* and in part from how the imperial Inca chose to define and measure the past.

Now that carbon-14 and other dating methods have pushed back the horizons of ancient America, establishing ever-earlier dates for agriculture and urban settlement, we may hope to gauge more adequately the millennia of pre-Classic Mesoamerica and the Mound Builder phases of Turtle Island. In these circumstances, our reading of native texts needs constantly to be revised: What once might have seemed to be an impossible or mythical back projection may now be seen to concur with the archaeological record. In the case of Peten, where the dynastic and material history of the Classic is now being confidently read from the hieroglyphic inscriptions, text and archaeology ask to be cross-referenced at earlier horizons. Working back from Alfonso Caso's correlations, a similar argument can be made for the year-calendar texts of Mesoamerica.

Having this approach in common, these four studies of "political memory" in the Fourth World trace particular paths. Each, guided by a body of native texts, goes in its own direction and highlights its own issues. Calendrically unambiguous and evidenced in texts that themselves span more than a millennium, lowland Maya chronology involves us in the issue of continuity, the conscious furthering or rejection of particular loyalties within the world of lowland Peten and – a critical point – Mesoamerica generally. For, among other factors, the very mathematical perfection of the lowland Maya calendar in the Classic period has sometimes encouraged a view of its authors as exceptional, quasi-divine architects of "lost cities," superior to the Maya-speakers who politically succeeded them, and separate from the Mesoamerican matrix. With the *xiuhtlapoualli,* the more urgent question is rather one of beginnings, especially insofar as these are tied up with the fabled Tula, the "first city" of Mesoamerica and home of the Toltecs, with whom civilization itself is said to have started. Theater that in practice has been staged in successive epochs, the story of Tula proves to be inseparable from that of the Era itself. In the Andes, on the other hand, official Inca history is largely inscrutable on the subject of its beginnings. Indeed, all political time in Tahuantinsuyu appears rather to hinge on the reigns of the ninth and tenth emperors in the late fifteenth century. This is when the Inca state becomes fully recognizable as such and when Andean pastoralism emerges as a major ideological force.

Brutally dispossessed over the past five centuries, Turtle Island presents the starkest case. For here most scholars have refused to apply the term "history" at all to the time that elapsed before contact with Europe. Hence, the "historic" Indians of this territory owe their very existence to the invaders who displaced them, to their capacity to be reflected in the white mirror. They are thereby deprived of even notional connection with their "prehistoric" ancestors, people who in fact remembered the gifts of tobacco and maize and built towns and roads long before the "founding fathers" reached America.

As lines of inquiry, these chapters can in no way claim fully to reconstruct the historical landscapes of Peten, Tula, Turtle Island, and Tahuantinsuyu, let alone that of America as a whole. This is notably true of the Andes, where so much remains encoded in language and custom, in Cuzco-centric memories of Inkarri, or in more widespread belief in the *tahuantinsuyu* ideal as a guarantee against savagery. Within this strict limitation, however, the different bodies of texts examined can be seen to have a further feature in common as expressions of political memory, literal rememberings of past polities. In just this capacity they mediate in their various ways between the two terms set out in the Quito Declaration. These are, on the one hand, the yet deeper time of Fourth World cosmogony that first shaped land and sky and, on the other, the continuing defense of native territory within and beyond law.

CITIES OF WORDS

Applicable in the first instance to the northern Yucatecan peninsula, where it is invoked in the *Chilam Balam Books,* the term "Peten" (Maya for "land") may readily be extended to include the whole lowland Maya domain. It accurately denominates the zone where hieroglyphic writing, the antecedent of the *Chilam Balam Books,* once flourished and that found its geopolitical center in the northern department of Guatemala appropriately known today as Peten. In America and over time, Peten is unrivaled in cultural coherence: Nowhere else do we find such consistency of culture and language, such an absence of enclave and checkerwork. Arrivals to this area, be they Carib castaways or Mexicans invading from west and south, have long been clearly distinguished as foreigners (*dzulob*), a term likewise applied to Europeans.

Over the continent Peten is unrivaled not just in length and consistency of occupation but in memory and record of it. In detailing Maya settlement there, the opening chapter of the *Chilam Balam Book of Chumayel* recalls the thousands of pyramids built by the ancient Maya. The first principle of continuity is found in the Maya builder himself, the creator and namer of an enduring landscape (p. 16):

> Hele tin tz'ibtah uchci yutzcin nabal nucuch muullob tumen ch'iballob yetel he cen baal u mentah ahauuob. . . . he ix u chun mul yutzcinnah ob e holhun baak u kaalal u mullil catac lahu y oxkal u much' cuentail mul y utzcinnah ob tu yuklah cabil peten bay ti kaknab tac tu chun cab u patah ix u kaba ob xan yetel u ch'eenil

> On this day I have written how the great pyramids came to be built by the lineages and all the deeds of the lords. . . . This was the origin of the pyramids they built, some six thousand plus fifty more to make the total, all over the land. From the [Caribbean] sea to Campeche they made names for them and for the wells.

The same chapter also offers to date this activity, by means of the 360-day *tun* of the lowland calendar, whose use is traced back to the first settling and naming of over a hundred towns in Yucatan and the start of service (*patan*) at Chichen Itza. Within what may be understood to be the Era frame, periods of more than three or four *baktun*s are said to have elapsed before the end of major construction, that is, the end of the Classic in *baktun* 10 (ca. A.D. 900). This puts its beginning early in the first millennium, a moment in the so-called Formative, when many lowland Maya sites underwent considerable growth and when neighboring Olmec cities on the Gulf Coast began to organize their wide-ranging economic empire. Out of all this, toward the end of *baktun* 8, emerged the splendor of the Maya Classic, whose urban architecture everywhere displays the hieroglyphic word, texts that so firmly established the Classic span A.D. 300–600 in the first place and that provide the scriptural antecedent for the Chumayel author.

As a result of recent phonetic decipherment, a fuller reading of these texts is now possible. There emerges a vivid fabric that on the grand scale tells of the Classic rise and fall, punctuated by the sixth-century hiatus that many scholars read economically as a rehearsal for the collapse and by the complex trade and other relationships that bound Peten to cities like Kaminaljuyu in highland Guatemala and the great Teotihuacan in the Basin of Mexico. Read through their own texts, the supposedly lost cities of Peten reacquire their status within the tight urban network plotted by their emblem glyphs, a network now made visible archaeologically in the NASA photography that suggests very high population densities throughout the area in Classic times.

Distinguished by the oldest provenanced Initial Series stela recovered to date (M.E. 8.12.14; A.D. 292), Tikal dominated the center under two main dynasties, safeguarding its power through satellites like Río Azul and Uaxactun. At the east and west frontiers lay Copan and Palenque, each boasting texts of great length; the bond between them in these positions was affirmed in the seventh century by intermarriage with the daughter of Pacal, the renowned king of Palenque who with his son Chan Bahlum designed much of the architecture that survives there today. At Copan a four-sided altar once believed to represent a conference of astronomers commemorates a line of sixteen kings that stretches over 350 years from Mah Kina Yax Kuk Mu's reign at the start of *batkun* 9 (A.D. 435) to the monarch of the day, Yax Pac (A.D. 763), the position of the kings in the series being marked by an "S" symbol also indicative of planetary phases; with its 1,250 glyphs, the stairway that leads to the tomb of a royal scribe presents the longest known hieroglyphic text in stone. On the stelae at Quirigua, which dominated the lower Motagua River just to the north, we read of warfare with Copan and the capture of that city's Eighteen Rabbit by Two-Leg Sky in 763; of sandstone and the tallest known, these stelae are remarkable on the one hand for celebrating Quirigua's rulers as individuals, finding cosmic antecedents for their persons millions of years in the past, and on the other for rigorously following the sheerly calendrical pattern of five-*tun* and *katun* endings. A similar testimony to conflict occurs in Yaxchilan, Piedras Negras, and Bonampak, cities that cluster along the Usumacinta, the other river of mesopotamian Peten. Yaxchilan, whose dynastic story can now be read over ten generations inscribed in a set of four superb lintels, celebrates especially the prowess of Shield Jaguar and Bird Jaguar III in the mid eighth century. Recent analyses of what had been termed the Primary Standard Sequence of glyphs on ceramics from this western region suggest that toward the end of the Classic the cult of the individual was taken so far as to demand the signature of the painter or scribe. Like the royal scribe's hieroglyphic stairway at Copan, this detail indicates the esteem in which writing was held.[1]

This material–historical reading of hieroglyphic texts has been corroborated by archaeology in other ways. When the span of the Classic was first agreed upon as a result of correlating hieroglyphic dates in the inscriptions with years A.D., it was largely assumed that its beginning coincided with the beginning of Maya urban culture more generally as this had emerged from the preceding Formative period. Hence, the many events dated in the inscriptions to earlier stages of the Era, from the third to the first millennium B.C., were automatically assigned to the realm of myth when not to astronomy. Now, with the excavation of enormous pre-Classic sites like Tikal's predecessor El Mirador, full-scale urbanism can be seen to antedate the Classic by many centuries. Settlement at Tikal goes back to at least 600 B.C., and burials at Copan date from the very start of the first millennium B.C., illuminating the complex eastern frontier between Mesoamerica and South American cultures like the Lenca. On the basis of radio-carbon dating, Maya settlement near the Caribbean coast has been traced far back into the second millennium B.C., providing a quite different context for events placed early in the 3113 B.C. Era[2] and suggesting a particularly Maya experience within what is otherwise known as the Olmec horizon.

Defying any notional opposition between calendrical–astronomical and historical schools of decipherment, hieroglyphic texts themselves offer both possibilities in their articulation of time. Salient cases are those texts at Palenque and Bonampak examined by Lounsbury that show how Classic rulers timed their military campaigns to coincide with the phases of Venus; at Bonampak the murals in question unfold below an eleven-station zodiac roof design. In any case, as in the *katun*-ending stelae at Quirigua, the very mechanisms of the calendar never ceased to shape the terms of political life.

Because it is geographically and phonetically so specific, the phenomenon of hieroglyphic writing has of itself tended to encourage a view of the Maya as *sui generis;* and a feature of recent scholarship has been intense concentration on it as the expression of a quite particular worldview. Given the idiosyncrasy of court life in the Classic period, its charismas, sexual tastes, and royal blood penance, this is readily understandable. Indeed, there can be no doubt that the principle of royal succession here was taken to greater length and celebrated in more lavish detail than anywhere else in Mesoamerica. Yet for all that, Peten even then did not cease to function as part of Mesoamerica, and the task of decipherment can be helped by respecting paradigms common to the region as a whole. Though applying their own emphasis, the Maya inscriptions fully shared the heritage of the *tonalamatl* and the year cycles that underlie both the *tun* and the year calendars of the region, and they acknowledge the same divine masks and insignia: Maize Cob, Skull, annual Rain, and Mirror-smoke (Tezcatlipoca). Arrangements of the four direction glyphs, as on the four walls at Río Azul, represent the quarters and anticipate the full quatrefoil model of geography found in the *Madrid* screenfold and transcribed in the *Book of Chumayel* with its detail of colors, trees, and birds. Architecture was modeled according to the same spatial paradigms, steep east–west stairways denoting the path of the sun and northside pyramids marking its zenith. An excellent illustration of this common vocabulary is provided by the trio of temples at Palenque known by the names Cross, Sun, and Foliated Cross, which among them house a major three-part text (Fig. 39).

The text in question consists of three panels set in three temples atop pyramids that stand, in descending order of height, to north, east, and west of a plaza in the city. Each of the panels has the same format: a picture flanked by columns of hieroglyphics, the greater standing of the northern Cross panel here being reflected in the fact that it has an extra column to left and right. Calendrically, all three follow a pattern whereby the left-hand

Figure 39 (facing). Tree, Maize, and Shield. *Palenque Foundation Trilogy.* (Maudslay 1889–1902, 4: pls. 75, 81, 88.)

columns record events early in the Era and the right-hand ones deal with history nearer to the probable date of composition, A.D. 692. Each starts with an exemplary Initial Series date with magnificent baroque body numbers and a full complement of data, not just about the distance in days and *tuns* from the Era date but also about the *tonalamatl* and Nine-night cycle, the day in the 365-day year, the moon age, and zodiac series.

Keys to these Palenque panels have been suggested ever since they were reproduced in John Stephen's *Incidents of Travel in Central America, Chiapas and Yucatan* (1841). Maudslay[3] provided the terminology Cross (north), Foliated Cross (east), and Sun (west), labels that have stuck, not always to the advantage of iconographical analysis. Attending more to calendrical data, Eric Thompson rearranged the reading sequence of the panels, retaining the priority of the Cross panel but switching the order of the other two on the ground that the first date in the Sun panel falls fourteen days earlier in the year 2358 B.C. than does its equivalent in the Foliated Cross panel.

In the wake of the dynastic readings established by Peter Mathews and Linda Schele,[4] recent decades have seen an overwhelming emphasis on the textual role, in this and other Palenque inscriptions, of the seventh-century monarch Pacal and his successor, Chan Bahlum, who is now credited with having erected the temples with their trilogy of panels in order to commemorate the ascension of his father. Rather than anonymous officiating priests, the paired figures on each panel, who bear the manikin that symbolizes royal authority already on Tikal's earliest stelae, are to be read as Pacal, who died in 683, and his son Chan Bahlum, who succeeded him in the following year. That the former existed beyond the grave when the trilogy was composed is indicated by braids and knots typical of funeral attire.

This new dynastic reading of a text long famous among Mesoamerican scholars carries much conviction. Yet it should not blind us to other levels of significance, for which we need a broader frame of reference than the Classic Maya Debrett. Following the descending reading order of the panels and respecting the visual design no less than the verbal text, we can see that the biographical message is in fact set into a triple paradigm characteristic not just of the Classic Maya but of Mesoamerica as a whole. For the set of three illustrated panels corresponds more widely to a social model that identifies the aristocracy and priesthood as the estate that mediates above and between the two other – opposing – estates: farmers and warriors. This model may be detected with remarkable clarity all over Mesoamerica from earliest times, consecrated in local deity figures. It is an "ideal" all-male structure that undoubtedly excludes other groups and classes that in practice are known to have exercised key social roles, like Oxomoco's midwives or the *pochteca* traders. It finds its clearest expression a millennium later in *Totecuyoane*, the 1524 Aztec address to the Franciscan missionaries,[5] where the three estates are cast as the three gifts of their gods, each being allotted a stanza that begins with the words "They gave" or "give" (*yehuan-maca-*) and ends with the question "Where?" (*in canin*).

We begin with the priests, who draw their power from self-denial and penitence, a shamanist way that goes back to the Paleolithic and the eldest darkness (*inoc yoayan*), the time when humans were first distinguished from animals by their capacity in principle to worship "heart of the sky" with the copal incense identified as the "brains of the sky."

> They gave us
> their law
> and they believed,
> they served, and they taught the honor among gods;
> they taught the whole service.
> That's why we eat earth before them;
> that's why we draw our blood and do penance;
> and that's why we burn copal and kill the living.
> They were the Lifelord
> and they became our only subject.
> When and where? – In the eldest Darkness.

Then come the farmers, the American agriculturalists who after their economic success with gourds, manioc, chilis, and other millennial crops surpassed themselves with the invention of maize, the staple highly adaptable to altitude and soil type whose protein value is much increased when paired with beans. Maize and beans with their respective flours amaranth and sage are the primary agricultural produce shown to be due annually in *Mendoza*, while the staple maize becomes the very substance of humankind in the *Popul vuh*. The space–time of this invention is the rain god's lush abode Tlalocan: In his role as the ninth of the Night Lords, the rain god Tlaloc is also the most propitious protector of the annual maize crop.

> They gave us
> our supper and our breakfast,
> all things to drink and eat,
> maize and beans, amaranth and sage.
> And we beg them
> for thunder–Rain and Water
> on which the earth thrives.
> They are the rich ones
> and they have more than simply what it takes;
> they are the ones with the stuff,
> all ways and all means, forever,
> the greenness of growth.
> Where and how? – In Tlalocan
> hunger is not their experience
> nor sickness, and not poverty.

Third come the hunter-warriors, the founders of empire, whose first impulse is to acquire and enhance the urban center with luxury goods of clothing, incense, and jewelry, likewise listed in the tribute books, in the same sequence. Indeed, this third group initiates political history and the "long tradition" of six major cities that begins with Tula, Mesoamerica's first named city:

> They gave also
> the inner manliness, kingly valor
> and the acquisitions of the hunt:
> the insignia of the lip, the knotting of the mantle,
> the loincloth, the mantle itself;
> Flower and aromatic leaf, jade,
> quetzal plumes, and the godshit you call gold.
> When and where? – It is a long tradition.
> Do you know
> when the emplacement of Tula was, of Uapalcalco,
> of Xuchatlappan, of Tamoanchan,
> of Yoalli ichan, of Teotihuacan?
> They were the world makers who founded
> the mat of power, the seat of rule.
> They gave
> authority and entity,
> fame and honor.
> And should we now destroy the old law,
> the Toltec law
> the Chichimec law,
> the Colhua law,
> the Tepanec law,
> on which the heart of being flows,
> from which we animate ourselves,
> through which we pass to adulthood,
> from which flows our cosmology
> and the manner of our prayer?

Of considerable interest in its own right and distinguished by initial verb tense in the speech, the typal opposition between planter and hunter-warrior occurs throughout Native American societies from which pastoralism is absent. In Mesoamerica it is seen in such other sources as the *Popol vuh* and the *Cantares mexicanos* manuscript, which distinguishes the *xopancuicatl,* or "burgeoning song," of the planter from the *yaocuicatl,* or war song, of the warrior. Similarly, when depicting the Aztec migration into the Valley of Mexico, the *Aztlan Annals* appeal to the same division in order to characterize the separation of the eastern agriculturalists of Huexotzinco with their *milpa*s from the western hunters of Malinalco with their arrows and nets (p. 4; Fig. 40). In architecture, it was emblemized in the twin temples atop

Figure 40. Planter and Hunter place emblems. From bottom to top: Huexotzingo, Chalco, Xochimilco, Acolhuacan, Malinalco, Tlahuica, Tepanec, and Matlatzinca. (*Aztlan Annals,* p. 2.)

Tenochtitlan's main pyramid, the one dedicated to the rain god Tlaloc, the other to the war god Huitzilopochtli. As for the complete three-part model that places the first-born priest-aristocrats above the farmers and warriors, it too is widely manifest in books and architecture. A key example from Classic times is the trilogy of stelae from Xochicalco, with their respective allusions to the priestly Quetzalcoatl, here also patron of lineage; the rain god; and the military conquest which establishes the palace of tribute, enslaves captives and initiates the year dates of political history.[6] In sum, the paradigm opposes the warrior to the sedentary farmer under the initial and primary aegis of the priesthood, representatives of which were, after all, delivering the speech of 1524.

In the Palenque text, there can be little doubt about the priority of the first priestly panel, given its extra physical height, conventionally synonymous with a northern placing, and its extra columns of hieroglyphs, which on no fewer than three occasions invoke the name-date Nine Wind, indicative par excellence of the priestly Quetzalcoatl, the Feather-snake or Plumed Serpent, after whom the Aztec priests named themselves. Moreover, it pictures not so much a cross as a tree, specifically the ceiba, or *yax che,* that on Pacal's sarcophagus lid issues from the royal navel as the source of lineage. As we have seen, in the iconic screenfolds a tree similarly bears lineage at Apoala under the supervision of none other than Quetzalcoatl Nine Wind. This reading accords with the fact that here the manikin of lineage is cradled like a child that lies and then sits.

As for the other two panels, facing each other east and west, they demand to be read as tokens of Palenque's farmers and warriors, complementary to each other and with their respective horizons beneath the northern zenith. The farmers' "foliated cross" is in fact not a cross either, but their consummate genetic achievement, the maize plant, its cobs and tassels intimating human faces and hair and hence the *Popol vuh* doctrine of how this Era's people were formed from maize. The jade skirt worn by the left-hand officiating figure, which has been cited as evidence of Pacal's desire to own all qualities, male and female, finds a deeper echo in Mesoamerican culture in the skirted Tlaloc that guards the maize plant, also human in aspect, in the *Féjérváry* Planting chapter.

Diametrically opposite, to the west, stands the Sun panel, which is architecturally designed so as to relate to a solstitial motif also elaborated in the Temple of the Inscriptions and the shaft of Pacal's tomb below. At its most obvious, however, the actual centerpiece of the panel includes the shield and crossed spears of the warrior, below which crouch captives in the uniforms of Eagle and Jaguar knights; the diagonal cross of the spears, moreover, schematically recalls the quatrefoil of tribute. As for the recently detected Jupiter relevance of the Chan Bahlum dates on this panel,[7] it also supports rather than contradicts this military reading. Most important, the placing of the warriors' shrine to the west perfectly fits Palenque's own view of itself as the western bulwark of Mayadom.

Viewed in this perspective, the three Palenque panels conform in their most basic iconography and logic to just the triple paradigm proposed by the priests of Tenochtitlan, though of course such a reading could never pretend to exhaust the wealth of detail, royal and astronomical, found in them.[8] Besides pointing to a major cultural resonance for the paradigm as such in Mesoamerica, this analogy serves locally to balance our reading of this particular trilogy at Palenque and so to distinguish it in mode from that in the Temple of the Inscriptions, where three unillustrated panels indeed focus chiefly on Pacal's biography, extending it into cosmic time. Bound more to the history of this Era and to sociological practice, albeit under the ubiquitous eyes of its rulers, the threefold set of high-birth, maize, and shield panels might more properly be thought to constitute the *Foundation Trilogy* of the city. Last, insofar as they can be translated from architecture into linear sequence – this process as such clearly being unnecessary to the general argument – these three panels are best read in the order Maudslay originally gave them, which conforms to the Tenochtitlan model and respects such inherent factors as descending height, priority of east over west, alternating balance between the left- and right-hand officiating figures, and the incremental position and number of the manikins they hold (one lying, one sitting, two sitting).

With its close attention to Pacal and Chan Bahlum, Palenque's *Foundation Trilogy* without question deals with the politics of late-seventh-century Peten, the ambitions and strategies of ruling families that are now being detailed in the new wave of decipherment. Yet here, as in comparable texts from the other lowland Maya cities, the hieroglyphic scribes relied on paradigms that belong not just to them but to all Mesoamerica. Recognizing this helps to restore the Maya Classic to its true Mesoamerican – indeed, Native American – matrix.

U KAHLAY KATUNOB

After the collapse that marked the end of the Classic and its spectacular corpus of inscriptions, the principal medium for Maya hieroglyphic script became paper screenfold books. The four surviving examples, those currently housed in Dresden, Paris, Madrid, and Mexico City (Grolier), are customarily assigned to Yucatan – *Paris* to the Caribbean coast and *Madrid* to Campeche – and dated to two or three centuries before the Spanish seizure of Tihoo. To the south at Tayasal (near Tikal), the Itza were still reading books of this kind right up to the end of the seventeenth century, before surrendering them at the *katun* date 10 Ahau (12.4.0; 1697 – a *tun* date comparable in the Era to the 1692 of the year calendar).

As almanacs of daily life and astronomy, these books are in principle well understood, though only *Dresden* has undergone detailed analysis. Whereas the humbler tasks regulated by the *tonalamatl* introduce themes apparently absent from the inscriptions – the *milpa*-plus-seed, venison, deer-haunch, cooked-iguana, and turkey glyphs appear here for the first time, for example – all that touches on astronomy offers a direct line of continuity from the Classic. Well-established cases are the *octaeteris* table in *Dresden,* which in proposing exact measurements of Venus's synodic cycle (583.92 days) takes as its base seventh-century Initial Series dates consecrated in Pacal's biographies; and the lunar-eclipse table also in *Dresden,* which, like the zodiac in *Paris,* draws on Classic distinctions between synodic and sidereal time. Going beyond the Era, *Madrid* offers a set of cosmic calculations that runs into the millions of years previously inscribed in stone at Quirigua and Palenque.

In other words, we are presented with the same intellectual apparatus, only this time without the dynastic rider. Like their counterparts in the *teoamoxtli* (*Borgia, Vaticanus, Cospi*), the *Dresden* Venus tables focus primarily on the planet itself, its movement between east zenith west and nadir, and its aspects at each of the five heliacal risings that it makes over the octaeteris. In this example there is indeed a high degree of correspondence between the heliacal aspects and prognoses detailed in *Dresden* and in Mexican sources like the *teoamoxtli* and the Nahuatl of the *Cuauhtitlan Annals*. The Mexican parallel adds edge to what is a general exclusion of Maya dynastic history in the post-Classic hieroglyphic books, to the extent of suggesting that ideologically it has become an undesirable topic. Moreover, the Initial Series system typically used for dynastic dates in the inscriptions is itself largely displaced in the books by the cycle known as *u kahlay katunob,* the *katun* count, which certainly has an ideological charge in the larger perspective of Maya history.

In post-Classic times generally, the main calendrical usage becomes the *katun* count. In a sequence determined by their end dates, always the twentieth Sign, Ahau (XX), combined with the Thirteen Numbers in the sequence 13, 11, 9, 7, 5, 3, 1, 12, 10, 8, 6, 4, 2, the *katuns* of this count form a cycle of thirteen, that is, 260 or 13 × 20 *tuns* (about 256 years); this features prominently in the hieroglyphic books, giving rise to the longest continuous texts, and literally provides the core of the *Chilam Balam* tradition. Now, though in the inscriptions this count never appears with its post-Classic autonomy or untrammeled by the totalizing apparatus of Initial Series dating, interest in *katun* endings does surface, often in situations that are politically suggestive, where they are given prominence in the Initial Series count. An early case is the 3 Ahau date (8.16.0.; A.D. 356) at Uaxactun associated with a Mexican-looking ruler; just this link recurs at Tikal in the stelae erected to a pair of rulers, successors to the renowned Stormy Sky, in 2 Ahau (9.3.0.; A.D. 495), where the one has Maya pedigree and a full Initial Series date and the other has neither, only the *katun* ending and the unusual attribution of a wife, possibly the daughter of a Maya ruler. Tikal is further remarkable for the shift in calendrical taste that occurred near the hiatus, in 3 Ahau (9.9.0; A.D. 613), that involved celebrating *katun* endings in specially built enclosures – read by some as a demagogic gesture on the part of the old aristocracy – and that achieved great prominence under Ah Cacao, the first of the Jaguar dynasty, who commemorated the 8 Ahau of his reign (9.13.0; A.D. 692) as a full *katun* count in time from the 8 Ahau of Stormy Sky's reign (9.0.0.; A.D. 436).[9]

The idea underlying all this is that the *katun* Round was politically less identified with hereditary Maya aristocrats than was the Initial Series and was therefore more accessible to newcomers, typically powerful merchants and those with Mexican connections. Toward the end of the post-Classic this hypothesis finds strong support in the mural painting of eastern Yucatan, at Tulum and Santa Rita,[10] which is clearly Mexican in style and which calendrically favors the cycles of the *katun* and of the *tun*. The Santa Rita mural finds an exact analogy in the *Paris* screenfold (assigned to the east for this reason), not just in style but in the single and paired figures who accompany the sequences of *tun* and *katun* dates that run along one side of the screenfold. In *Dresden,* owing to missing pages the count breaks off just as it starts (11 Ahau, p. 60), but in the alphabetic *Chilam Balam Books* it emerges in full flower, providing not just most of the content but the main principle of literary organization, which may be said to be federal in the full sense of the term.

From all this evidence it appears that the chief political charge of the *katun* count is not so much the Maya–Mexican opposition as such – rather the contrary – but the fact that it corresponds to federal and meritocratic government rather than to the dynastic privilege celebrated in the Initial Series inscriptions, and that it represents a less-totalizing calendar and economy.[11] This is not to say that dynasties did not remain an important factor in post-Classic Yucatecan politics: Following the rule of Fiery Shield at Chichen Itza in 880 (M.E. 10.2.11), the legendary struggles between the Itza and Xiuh to east and west of the peninsula undoubtedly shaped the course of history; and the Itza at Peten in 1697 acknowledged Canek as royalty. But they did so formally through the *katun* system, via arguments about calendrical precedent, all of which reemphasizes the signifiance of *u kahlay katunob* itself.

On the larger scale, the *katun* count served to regulate political power in post-Classic Yucatan, being the means by which it was rotated among the towns of the region. The *Book of Chumayel* contains a wheel showing the league of thirteen that participated in this system, among them Chichen Itza, Zaci, Mani, and Tihoo. (As "the place of 5," Tihoo is a "number" town like Tikal [20], Uaxactun [8], and Uxmal [3].) Like its constituent *tun*s, the *katun* period was ceremonially installed to music and dance, vividly shown at Santa Rita, and with perorations about its character, which amount to what we might term a speculative history that interweaves forecast with the recollection of identically named *katun*s from the past. It is the cycles of these perorations that are recorded in *Paris* and in the *Chilam Balam Books*.

In 1697, the fateful *katun* 10 Ahau (12.4.0) that saw the Itza surrendering their hieroglyphic books, the missionary Avedaño offered the following commentary. "These katuns are thirteen in number; each has its separate idol and its priest, with a separate prophecy of its events. These thirteen katuns correspond to the thirteen parts into which this kingdom of Yucatan is divided."[12] This description helps us to understand the structure of the *Paris katun* count even if the glyphs themselves remain largely illegible. Below the *tun* count in the upper register, we detect three blocks of paragraphs to left and above and below the main picture, which shows the *katun* names placed between pairs of seated figures. This arrangement matches Avendaño's description insofar as it distinguishes first the place and ruler of the *katun,* then its general qualities, and last its specific events.

This general structure is further confirmed by the alphabetic transcriptions of the *katun* count found in the *Chilam Balam Books;* the text for *katun* 13 Ahau 1539 in the *Book of Oxcutzcab* is an example:

> Katun 2 Ahau ends so that Katun 13 Ahau may be set up. Katun 13 Ahau ends in the sixth *tun* of Katun 9 Ahau: it will keep company with 11 Ahau in the Katun Round. This is its word, Kinchil Coba is the seat of Katun 13 Ahau; and Mayapan. Itzamna, Itzam tzab is its face during its reign.
>
> The ramon nut will be its food. For five *tun*s nuts and fruits will fall from the ramon tree. Three *tun*s will be locust *tun*s, ten generations of them. Bread and water will be unobtainable. The fan shall be displayed, the bouquet shall be displayed, held by Yaxaal Chac in the heavens; Ixma Chucbeni shall arrive to eat sun and moon.
>
> The charge of the *katun* is doubly heavy. The Batab, impotent and lost, the Ah Kin, impotent and lost, because of Ixma Chucbeni. Perdition of the Halach Uinic, of the Ah Bobat and the Ah Naat; drunkenness of the Ah Bobat and the Ah Kin, because of Ix Dziban Yol Nicte. Derangement through lewdness and adultery begins with the Batab, who are corrupt at the start of the reign of Ah Bacocol, who wants devotion and reverence only for himself; the Halach Uinic are scorned in the communities, in the bush and rocky places, by the offspring of the lewd and the perverse, those who despise their elders and forget their maker, the sons of Ah Bacocol. The bread of this *katun* is not whole because its people are also under Ah Bolon Yocte, those of the two-day mat, the two-day throne, the motherless and the fatherless, the offspring of mad and lewd schemers. The face of the sun and of the moon will be eaten and Balam, the Jaguar, will speak and Ceh, the Deer, will speak, and suffer the stick with groans and make payment to the world by their sudden deaths and their pointless deaths. The charge of sudden and violent deaths will not be over when the great hunger has ceased. This is what the charge of Katun 13 Ahau brings. (Barrera Vásquez and Rendón 1963:65–6)

The first paragraph deals with the town Kinchil Coba, in which the *katun,* commemorated by a stela, is "set up" with its ruler and its president, or "face," the deity Itzamna; and it traces the elaborate interweaving of the *katun*'s influence backward and forward in time, from 2 Ahau before it to 11 and even 9 Ahau after it. The second paragraph treats of its "food," or general substance. The third, which includes allusions to particular events and personages, recounts its political charge in terms of relationships between officials: the Halach Uinic, the supreme authority or "real man"; Batab, his local agents; Ah Kin, the priests; Nacom, the military; Ah Bobat, the prophets or planners; and Ah Naat, the adviser-scholars.

Here intimating the Spanish invasion that culminated in 1542, this *katun* 13 Ahau was characterized by strife: One cycle previously, in 1283, it had followed the Itza invasion of northern Yucatan, and one cycle later, adjusted by calendar reforms, it anticipated the caste war of the nineteenth century,

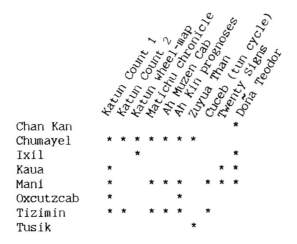

Figure 41. *Chilam Balam* chapters.

when the Maya drove foreigners out of much of their territory. Rhetorically, the peroration as such achieves its power through play between full and half repetition ("impotent and lost," "impotent and lost"; "Balam will speak," "Ceh will speak") and a sustained development of root concepts like the hunger that the bread of the *katun* will not satisfy. Though adapted to the more overtly communal terms of the *katun* count, we find too the constant play between sky and earth, the phases of celestial and human life, for which the Classic inscriptions are notable.

In the *Chilam Balam Books,* the all-important *katun* count is shown to be the organizing principle for a whole range of related texts (Fig. 41): historical chronicles based like the Matichu on elapsed *katun* counts, personal prophecies for future *katuns,* like those of Chilam Balam himself, and two sets of twenty riddles in "Zuyuathan" (Zuyua langauge), with which candidates for office under the *katun* system were examined. These take the form of cryptic requests that the examinee must know how to hear. They include syllabic play of the kind that characterizes hieroglyphic script; in the *Ritual of the Bacabs* Zuyua language cures disease.[13] In this they defend "Maya men" from imposters and outsiders, like a national password. At the same time they make play with the notion of visual language as such, along lines evident elsewhere in Mesoamerica, not least in the Metaphor chapter of the book of Nahuatl rhetoric (*Florentine Codex,* book 6, chap. 43). Indeed, the very term "Zuyua" appears to be more Nahuatl than Maya and for these reasons belongs to a larger Mesoamerican interest in riddle images of language, whether this be phonetic or not, hieroglyph or *tlacuilolli.* Through the *Book of Chumayel*'s dazzling inaugural set of seven riddles (pp. 29–31),

Zuyuathan even finds distant parallels in Turtle Island and the rainforest in shamanic dialogues of initiation and power transfer. Like the *Foundation Trilogy* at Palenque, it represents a broader paradigm fitted to specific practices in the Maya lowlands, in this case the count of twenty *tun*-years.

A CIPHERED HERITAGE

> U kahlay cab tu kinil, lay tumen dziban lae, tumen ma kuchuc tu kin u meyah lay hunob lae, picil thanob lae, utial katabal u chi Maya uinicob uay yohelob bix zihanilob edzlic cab uay ti peten lae

> The account of the world in those days, because it is written down, because the day is not past for making these books, these many words: so that Maya men may be asked whether they know about how they were born here in this country when the land was founded. (*Book of Chumayel,* p. 42)

As the diagnostic of the *Chilam Balam Books,* chapters relating to the *katun* count appear in all the main surviving examples, from Chumayel, Tizimin, Kaua, Tusik, Mani, Ixil, and Oxcutzcab. This resulted from the fact that after contact with Europe, which began several decades before Francisco de Montejo's seizure of Tihoo (Mérida) in 1542, hieroglyphics were gradually transcribed into the Maya version of the Roman alphabet, most notably in the corpus of *Chilam Balam Books,* which were understood to further specifically Maya literacy.[14] This is made clear in several ways, like internal textual references to the screenfold (*u uich u uohil* "the face of the book") from which they were being copied and parallels in structure and phraseology in almanac chapters that prognose days or in the perorations proper to *u kahlay katunob.* Glyphlike designs representing the faces of the *katuns* in the count are actually included in the Mani and Chumayel texts.

In the *Chilam Balam Books,* the *katun* perorations occur in two main cycles[15] that cover the half-millennium between the thirteenth and the eighteenth century and that reach forward and back by means of additions and comparisons between like-named *katuns* in a fashion reminiscent of the 52-year *xiuhtlapoualli* Round. For its part, the lean historical list of *katuns* known as the Matichu Chronicle reaches back to the Classic period (to 13 Ahau 9.4.0.; A.D. 514), though without naming its spectacular cities and rulers, while elsewhere we are moved forward to the Era ending in A.D. 2087–8 via individual *katun* prophecies and through calendar adjustments whereby new-style *katuns* were designed to mesh with the Mexican and Christian years. The books of Chumayel, Tusik, and Mani contain the sets of the riddles asked of prospective candidates for office under the *katun* system, while the Cuceb, or "year wheel," in the books of Mani and Tizimin correlates the *tun* cycle with twenty years of the 52-year Round.

Besides this *katun* literature, the *Chilam Balam Books* transcribe other chapters of the hieroglyphic heritage, like those devoted to the New Year ceremonies of the 52-year cycle, which were part of the Initial Series apparatus in the inscriptions and which, like the *katun* count, achieved a degree of autonomy after the collapse. We find here the same language of quarters, with their respective trees and year bearers, as in the iconic tradition. Medical chapters also appear that have analogies in the well-known *Ritual of the Bacabs* manuscript and that find antecedents in hieroglyphic curing almanacs.

While continuing these Maya and Mesoamerican traditions, the *Chilam Balam Books* responded from the start to the new conditions brought about by the Spanish invasion. As in the post-Cortesian literature of highland Mexico, we find chapters devoted to correlating the native and imported calendars, comparative historiography that critically examines the biblical version of world events, and numerous adaptations and translations of Old World texts. In particular, the *katun* count lent itself to devastating commentaries on the Spanish invasion, in which Maya value and phrase undercut the imported rhetoric of the Christian books. Here is the *Book of Chumayel's* version of *katun* 11 Ahau (1539–59):

> . . . the true God, the true *Dios,* came, but this was the origin too of affliction for us. The origin of tax, of our giving them alms, of trial through the grabbing of petty cacao money, of trial by blowgun, stomping the people, violent removal, forced debt, debt created by false testimony, petty litigation, harassment, violent removal, the collaboration with the Spaniards on the part of the priests, the local chiefs, the choirmasters, public prosecutors through the agency of the children and the youths of the town, and all the while the mistreated were further maltreated. There were the people who had been reduced to want but who did not depart even when they were so squeezed. It was through Antichrist on earth, the kinkajous of the towns, the vixen of the towns, blood-sucking bugs of the town, those who suck dry the common people. But it will happen that tears will come to the eyes of God the father. The *justicia* of God the father will settle on the whole world, it surely will come from God upon Ah Kantenal, Ix Pucyola, the opportunists of the world.

A *Chilam Balam* chapter that gains especially from being put in this perspective is the one that opens the *Book of Chumayel,* the only book in the corpus to invoke Era dating, to reflect at length on Maya history, and to elaborate a Maya philosophy of time. Early translators like A. Médiz Bolio (1973 [1930]) and Ralph Roys (1933) recognized its special qualities. Yet they were working at a time when ignorance of Maya literature was even greater than it is now and when few suspected the high degree of continuity implicit, for example, in the *katun* count. Though masterly in its calendrical analyses, Munro Edmonson's more recent version (1986) militates against this continuity by fragmenting the text and fitting the pieces into a chronology of Christian centuries.

Over its twenty-one pages (arranged as three chapters by Roys and two by Médiz Bolio), the opening chapter of the *Chumayel* book takes us from the setting up of the world quarters, with their trees and birds, through the settlement of Yucatan and the institution of the *katun* calendar and labor tribute at Chichen Itza, right up to the entry of the Spanish into Tihoo. Particularly telling are the explicit references, quoted above, to the pyramid building carried out by the lineages of the past, which lasted more than three *baktuns*, or 1,500 years, and ended in a catastrophe compared to the biblical destruction of Egypt. In the final pages (pp. 19–21), prompted by the Spanish arrival in the sixteenth century, the authors reflect on this long historical experience and take stock of the political and military options open to them, in lines that read as follows:

	Mat yoltahob u paktob dzulob	They didn't want to join the foreigners;
	ma u kat cristianoilob	Christianity was not their desire;
	ma yoltahob u bot patan	they didn't want another tax –
	Ah uayom chichob	Those with their sign in the bird,
5	ah uayom tunob, ah ziniltunob	those with their sign in the stone, flat worked stone,
	ah uayom balamob-ox uayohob	those with their sign in the jaguar – three emblems –
	can bak hab u xul u cuxtalob	four times four hundred years was the period of their lives
	catac holhun kal hab yan cataci u xul cuxtalob	plus fifteen score years before that period ended
	tumen yohelob u ppiz kinob tubaob	because they knew the rhythm of the days in themselves.
10	tuliz U tuliz hab	Whole the moon, whole the year,
	tuliz kin tuliz akab	whole the day, whole the night,
	tuliz ik cu ximbal xan tuliz kik xan	whole the breath when it moved too, whole the blood too
	tu kuchul tu uayob tu poopoob tu dzamob	when they came to their beds, their mats, their thrones;
	ppiz u canticob yutzil oraob	rhythm in their reading of the good hours,
15	ppiz u caxanticob yutzil kin	rhythm in their search for the good days,
	la tu ppiz yilicob yocolob utzul ekob tu yahaulil	as they observed the good stars enter their reign,
	tan u ppix ich ticob yocolob yahaulil utzul ekob.	as they watched the reign of the good stars begin.
	Utz tun tulacal	Everything was good.

	Catun u takbez yalob tu cuxolalob yan
20	manan tun keban tu santo okolalob yan u cuxtalob
	manan tun chapabal manan tun chibil bac tiob
	manan tun dzam chacuil tiob minan tun xpomkakil tiob
	minan tun elel tzemil tiob minan tun ya nakil tiob
	minan tun tzemtzem cimil tiob minan chibil pol tiob.
25	Tzolombil tun u bin uinicilob.
	Ma bay tun u mentah dzulob ti uliob lae
	zubtzilil tal zahob ca talob
	ca cuxhi yol nicte cuxhi tun yol tu nicteob Nacxit Xuchit tu nicte u lakob
	minan tun yutz kinob yetzahob toon
30	lay u chun cakin xec cakin ahaulil
	lay ix u chun cimil toon xan
	manan yutz kin ton xan minan cuxolal toon
	tu xul ca zatmail ilil y zubtalil etlahom tulacal
	minan nohoch can minan yahau than minan ahau can
35	til lay u hel ahauoob ti uliob lae
	tzuc cep ah kinil cu talel u mentabal ti telae dzulob
	catun tu ppatahob yal u menehob uay Tancah lae
	Lay tun kamicob u numyailob uchci u chibil lae dzulob lae he bin ah Itzaobe

For they kept sound reason;

there was no sin in the holy faith of their lives, there was no sickness, they had no aching bones, they had no high fever, they had no smallpox,

they had no burning chest, they had no bellyache,

they had no chest disease, they had no headache.

The course of mankind was ciphered clearly.

Not what the foreigners arranged when they came here:

then shame and terror were preferred,

carnal sophistication in the flowers of Nacxit Xuchit and his circle;

no more good days were shown to us;

this was the start of the two-day chair, the two-day rule;

this was the start of our sickness also;

there were no good days for us, no more sound reason.

At the end of the loss of our vision and of our shame everything will be revealed.

There was no great priest, no lord speaker, no lord priest with the change of rulers when the foreigners came.

The priests they set down here were lewd;

they left their sons here at Mayapan.

These in turn received their affliction from the foreigners called the Itza.

oxtenhii bin uchci dzulob	The saying is: since the foreigners came three times
40 lay tun tumen oxkal haab yan toon lukzicob ca patan	threescore years is the age to get us exempted from tax.
tumen uchci u chibilob tumen uinicob ah Itzaob lae	The trouble was the aggression of those men the Itza;
ma toon ti mentei toon botic hele lae	we didn't do it; we pay for it today.
Heuac consierto yanil yan u xul ca yanac hum olal ton y dzulob	But there is an agreement at last to make us and the foreigners unanimous.
Uamae bin yanac toon noh katun	Failing that we have no alternative to war.

The complexity of this passage no doubt reflects that of the historical situation the Maya found themselves in; but it is also due to the wit and allusiveness with which they describe it, and their anger at the treachery of fellow Maya (p. 14). Yet two main parties may at once be distinguished: the Maya and foreigners. The former comprise the author himself (who sometimes uses the first person singular), his contemporaries (referred to as "we"), and his ancestors in the land Peten. On the other side, foreigners include the Christian Spanish, of course, but also the Itza, who fought unsuccessfully against the Spanish, and the shadowy predecessors of the Itza, whose language was not Maya when they arrived in Yucatan, according to the Matichu chronicle. They fall, then, into three groups, Toltec(?), Itza, and Christian; and from the Maya point of view the impression of three invasions is so clear that a joke is made of it (lines 39–40). Roys supplies the further information you need to get the point: The third group, the Spaniards, exempted old men, the "over sixties," from tax or tribute.[16] In the vigesimal arithmetic of the Maya, it is like saying, "Next time, the fourth invasion, we'll have to be eighty (four-score years) to get exempted."

Allusiveness of this order presupposes a highly developed historical consciousness. True, we are faced with a radical contrast between Maya and foreign ways in the negative in line 26, the turning point of the passage. But the foreigners are not all condemned out of hand, or for the same reason; and they are dealt with separately in chronological order. In the comment "We didn't do it; we pay for it today" (line 42) there is an ironic reminder that the non-Maya military powers in Yucatan (the Itza "captains") failed to defend themselves and their subjects against the Spanish. A word of Spanish origin, *santo* (line 20), is used as a term against which the lewdness of the Toltecs (line 36) may be contrasted. And so on. Confident in their own tradition, the Maya see this or that culture as they find fitting.[17] Things first go wrong with Nacxit Xuchit: As in the personal prophecy by Chilam Balam that closes the book, this Nahuatl name (Nacxit Xochitl) is bad news.

Generally it has been assumed to represent the intrusion from highland Mexico that became more and more marked after the collapse and that was institutionalized when Tutul Xiuh installed himself in Uxmal in 4 Ahau 987, beginning what has been described as the New Empire in Yucatan. This reading is probably the fairest, since the name, hard to identify with any one character, can be read in Nahuatl texts as a title, whereas its etymology (four-foot flower) suggests tetrarchy, the quatrefoil of tribute. The surest things here are the nature and the approximate date of the change it represents. We hear insistently of a deterioration diagnosed in the first instance as calendrical: a loss of sovereignty in time once enjoyed by the lowland Maya calendar and script.

Throughout, whole phrases are recognizable as rhetoric proper to the *katun* peroration, especially from the older of the two complete surviving *katun* Rounds, like so many hieroglyphic formulas: "the loss of vision and shame"; "the start of sickness"; "there were no good days for us"; and so on. The lewdness of Xuchit (lines 28–9) and the deathly sickness he brings (*cimil*) are rejected in terms characteristic of the 11 Ahau *nicte,* or "flower," *katun,* while the good coursing and wholeness (*tuliz*) of both moon and blood (lines 10–12) recall the text for a *katun* 13 Ahau (*Chumayel,* p. 100): "tu lobil kik tu hokol U; tuliz iuil U u chac cuchie tuliz kik." The particular complaints negatively deducible from lines 20–4 are less interesting for themselves, medically, than as symptoms of disease in the body politic as a whole, this body being federal, like the cities of the *katun* count, and not subject to a single head town or capital. The same close association of *katun* politics and medicine recurs unambiguously as late as the nineteenth century in the prefatory note to the medicinal section (pp. 30ff.) of the *Book of Chilam Balam of Nah.* With its explicit reference to the caste war (*tu haabil katun*), this note also invokes the remedy foreseen in the *Chumayel* in the absence of an agreement: expulsion of the foreign body. Further, just as the health of society depended not just on internal politics but on the sky, and the coursing of breath and blood corresponded to astronomical movement, so the good days of the past were assured by the correct calendrical reading of the reign (*ahaulil*) of good stars. What had been sound and whole was afflicted and eclipsed, *chibil* serving for both meanings in *katun* rhetoric.

The particular image of eclipse evokes the salient achievement of the lowland Maya *tun* calendar itself, so well equipped to predict this phenomenon, thanks to its rigorous insistence on the formula "one day = one unit," the use of place-value notation that anticipates the grid pattern of hieroglyphic script, and the consequent capacity to calculate tens of thousands to millions of days, always with precision to the day. Hence, when we read that in the past "the course of mankind was ciphered clearly" (line 25), we see that the main term, *tzolombil,* is charged with connotation. *Tzol* means "to set in order" or "count" or "make clear" and describes exactly the mental processes formulated in the arithmetical logic of hieroglyphic writing. The usual translation of *tzolombil* has been "orderly," which is not incorrect. But it does not alert us sufficiently to the principle of this ordering.

Putting things in this perspective affects in turn our reading of the words *ppiz* and *tuliz,* which carry such weight in the account of the days when "everything was good." Roys translates *ppiz* as "in due measure" when in fact rhythm is a key part of the meaning; then to have *tuliz* as "complete" goes little of the way toward the notion of a "whole, sound thing, not broken or divided or begun" ("entera cosa sana, no quebrada ni partida ni comensada," as the Vienna dictionary puts it). In Maya numerical logic, completion is better expressed as wholeness of the basic day unit and its sums and multiples: lunar, menstrual, solar, planetary, moral, political, and so on. Ratio is of things in time, measured from moment to moment, from rest to rest (bed, mat, throne – line 13). Maya astronomy and the script that conveyed it may in turn be held responsible for the remarkable concept *cuxolalob* (line 19): a sound or living knowledge, a science that is rational yet animate ("whole" means "hale" or "healthy").

In the Golden Age that preceded foreign invasion, pulses and cycles of time were, then, stabilized and "seated." That is, by standardizing units of labor and commodity tribute, the hieroglyphic *tun* calendar serves ideologically as the guarantee against excessive excitement, sickness, fever, and sloth. While the ancient rulers knew "the rhythm of the days in themselves" (line 9), the foreigners, led by Nacxit Xuchit, introduced a "two-day chair" and a "two-day rule." Roys took the phrase *ca-kin* 'two-day' to mean temporary or short-lived, which it might do. It could more purposefully refer to the leap-year or double-day system of the Mexican calendar and by extension the sadly inept leap year of the Julian calendar. This highly determined placing of moral value on the mechanics of hieroglyphic calendar and script is likewise evident in the curing texts of the *Ritual of the Bacabs,* which directly identify the health of the patient with the proper ordering of time, specifically according to the *tun* and *katun* dates that name this and previous Eras, and with the very notion of the Maya hieroglyph (*uoh*), the ultimate "pre-scription."[18]

Finally, the "great priests and speakers" who presided over the time when "everything was good" are identified only by their emblems and their antiquity. The paragraphing introduced by Roys makes them identical with those contemporaries of the Maya author who did not want Christianity or "another tax" (lines 1–3). But they are much more necessary as the subject of lines 4–9, which otherwise are deprived of one. The three signs they bore – bird, stone, and jaguar – remain opaque, though they do recall the triple-emblem pattern inscribed in the Classic cities; and going farther back, to the dates stated in the text, they also coincide strikingly with the three glyphs represented on Monument 13 from the Olmec city at La Venta, usually dated to 900 B.C.[19] In supplying the date, the text follows the formula used earlier with reference to the pyramid building carried out by the dynasties of the pre-Classic and Classic; that is, we are given a sum of *baktun*s and *katun*s, in this case a total of 1,900 Maya years, 400 more than before. Again taking the collapse and the start of Xuchit's New Empire as the necessary end point, we move back this time to the very start of the first millennium B.C.

In establishing the historical perspective peculiar to them within Meso-america and the Fourth World, the lowland Maya authors of the *Book of Chumayel,* and by extension the authors of the other *Chilam Balam Books,* had recourse to the great literary system of the *katun* count, which has its hieroglyphic roots deep in the Classic. The opening chapter of the *Chumayel* book reaches back farther still to notions of urban architecture and, above all, of arithmetical clarity typified in the Olmec and Maya calendrical inscriptions of the first millennium B.C., to which the text chronologically refers us. This political and philosophic view supports faith in Maya culture more effectively than any explicit named appeal to the dynasties who used the hieroglyphic calendar, especially with Initial Series dating, in order to glorify themselves and their caste. In assuring political continuity,[20] these Maya books reach deep into society, its rhythms, and its cure. At the same time they open into the future: Following twenty numbered lines that match the *tun*s of the *katun* and renew themselves halfway, the *Book of Chumayel* ends with the question "Who the sage, who the sun-priest that shall read the word of this book?"

6

Tollan

TOLTEC SKILL

Originally a Nahuatl toponymic that meant simply someone from Tollan or Tula, the place of rushes (Fig. 42), the term "Toltec" came throughout Mesoamerica to designate craftsman, artist, intellectual. According to native texts, Toltec accomplishment was encyclopedic: These people excelled as architects and masons, scribes and painters, carpenters and sculptors, lapidaries and experts in jade and turquoise, miners and workers of gold, silver, copper, tin, and other metals, makers of mosaics and feather tapestries, potters, spinners and weavers, musicians and composers, medical doctors, experts in astronomy, chronology, and calendrics, and true readers of dreams. Of someone adroit and learned it was said "He is a true Toltec," just as blockheads and loud dressers were equated with the rough Otomi. In the *Popol vuh* the very list of creator gods includes the artisan Tultecat; the *Florentine Codex* and other Nahuatl manuscripts gathered by Fray Bernardino de Sahagún report the overall concept of skill and artistry as *toltecayotl* 'Toltec-ness'.

Of all Toltecs, the most renowned was the figure referred to variously as Topiltzin ("our lord") and Quetzalcoatl (the plumed serpent) as well as by other names and epithets. It is he who first brings all the social skills, notably writing, to his people and to Mesoamerica as a whole. His role as leader always equivocal and his paternity unsure, he is challenged by an archopponent identified with Tezcatlipoca, who mocks him and tricks him into incest; evils befall the town that include the presence of a stinking corpse of unbelievable weight. (Such details recall the story of Oedipus in Thebes.) Finally Quetzalcoatl leaves, or is driven from, Tula on a journey that takes him to the eastern frontier of earth and sky, where he burns himself; other versions say that he set sail on a raft of intertwined snakes,

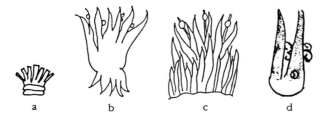

Figure 42. Tollan, place of rushes: (a) *Tepexic Annals,* p. 7; (b) *Ríos,* p. 11; (c) *Cuauhtinchan Annals,* p. 1; (d) *Tudela* Zodiac chapter.

that his life force returned in the burgeoning maize, or that he died in battle and his ashes were brought to Cholula.

For its part, Tula itself is celebrated as is no other city: its architecture, splendor, and power. Its name evokes the aquatic plants that since early times have supplied riverine and lacustrian settlements with shelter, mats, thrones, and, in the remarkable case of Titicaca, even boats and food. As the first settlement named in a very wide variety of texts, this place can denote the idea of people gathered together, like rushes, or "a group of craftsmen or officials."[1] Indeed, it stands for the very idea of the civilized, to the extent of serving as the model of urban wealth. Its citizens possessed plentiful agricultural produce, a common currency of exquisite jade and gold, and gorgeous songbirds:

> the Toltecs were certainly rich
> food was not scarce enough to sell
> their vegetables were large
> gourds for example mostly too fat to get your arms round
> maize ears millstone size
> and they actually *climbed*
> their amaranth plants
> cotton came ready dyed
> in colors like crimson saffron pink violet leaf-green azure
> verdigris orange umbra grey rose-red and coyote yellow
> it all just grew that way
> they had all kinds of valuable birds
> blue cotingas quetzals turpials red-spoonbills
> which could talk and sang in tune
> jade and gold were low-priced popular possessions
> they had chocolate too, fine cocoa flowers everywhere
>
> the Toltecs did not in fact lack anything
> no one was poor or had a shabby house
> and the smaller maize ears they used as fuel
> to heat their steam baths with

At the same time, we are treated to the more plebeian view of those who came to the city from outside and found themselves supporting this luxury from below. The Nahuatl *Tratado de las supersticiones* (1629) includes a shamanic chant of the kind used still for hunting. It urges the deer into capture as people were once brought to the gates of Tula, their servitude there appealing to the echo between *mazatl* (deer) and *mazehual* (pleb).[2] The Old World parallel here is Babylon sooner than Thebes, a parallel that indeed is explicitly made in more than one text, where the fate of Tula's early populations parallels that of the biblical Israelites. Further, insofar as abuse by Tula's overlords could no longer be borne, the city became in turn the topic of exodus and dispersal in the "Toltec lament" found alike in the *Cantares mexicanos* and the *Popol vuh*.[3] From the evidence of maps, the toponym as such, along with allied forms like "Tulapan" and the diminutive "Tollantzinco," was carried all over Mesoamerica and served to name not just minor towns but wards of those towns and the smallest plots of land. It also functioned as an epithet attached to towns of another name, the best example being Quetzalcoatl's shrine at Cholula, Tollan-Chollollan.

By the time Europeans arrived in Mexico, no one city or principality could be recognized as this preeminent Tula, although the Aztecs and others confidently linked themselves to the Toltec tradition. The city itself was definitely a thing of the past. A brilliant image of its ruined architecture and its permanence of meaning, comparable to and contemporary with Joachim du Bellay's meditation on Rome, comes in the *Cantares mexicanos* manuscript, which gathers the poem-songs recited at the Aztec court. From its imperial position, this collection combines the styles of the regions with a set of modes derived from specific social activities: mourning the dead, whence the *icno-cuicatl* "orphan song"; planting the fields, whence the *xopan-cuicatl* "burgeon song" as well as *xochi-cuicatl* "flower song," or poetry itself; and war, whence *yao-cuicatl* "battle song." Concentrating first on the ruins of Tula and the general sorrow at the loss of Topiltzin, and then on his transformation into a resplendent maize plant, the poem in question, "Tollanaya huapalcalli," falls into two parts, respectively in the orphan and burgeon modes.[4]

The stanzas and refrains of the first part make play between the ruin of the city and the loss of Topiltzin, the architect of its columns and palaces and the scribe of its inscriptions, and trace his route to destruction past Cholula and Orizaba (Poyauhtecatitlan) eastward to Xicalanco, Zacanco, and Tlapallan:

> At Tula stood the beamed sanctuary,
> only the snake columns still stand,
> our prince Nacxitl has gone, has moved away.
>> Our vanguard is wept for with conches;
> 5   he is going to his destruction in Tlapallan.

He was there in Cholula,
made an end at Mount Poyauhtecatitlan,
crossed the water at Acallan.
    Our vanguard is wept for with conches;
10   he is going to his destruction in Tlapallan.

I come to the frontier with winged finery,
the lord who pierces and the victim.
    My fine-plumed lord has gone away
    has left me, Ten Flower, an orphan.

15   The pyramid burst apart hence my tears
the sacred sand whirled up hence my desolation.
    My fine-plumed lord has gone away
    has left me, Ten Flower, an orphan.

Tlapallan is where you are expected
20   is where you are destined to rest;
you are moving on, my fine-plumed lord,
destined for Xicalanco and perhaps Zacanco.
        . . .

You wept endlessly, great lord;
    your house will always be there, your gates
    your palace will always be there.
30   You left them orphaned here at the Tula frontier.

Stone and wood, you painted them
in the city of Tula.
    Where you ruled, our prince Nacxitl,
    your name will never be destroyed;
35   your people will always cry for you.

The turquoise house and the snake house, you built them
in the city of Tula.
    Where you ruled, our prince Nacxitl,
    your name will never be destroyed;
40   your people will always cry for you.
               —*Cantares mexicanos,* fols. 26v–27r

Then in the sequel the poet or first-person speaker is reborn, made of maize like the first people of this Era. The godlike skill in genetics that historically made possible the production of maize and the people's food is identified as that of the Toltec artist who, likewise singer and scribe, authors the counterpoint between the "uttered flower" and the "painted song." The "royal fibers" of his screenfold book are the woven mat of authority; the textile text that yet is transcended in the finely expressed vision, the complete heart. Awareness of his power gives the poet hope for survival and continuity through its being transplanted in others, like the prince and cacao and peyote flowers, fellow poets who surround him in the Aztec court with perceptions heightened like his own.

As white and yellow maize I am born,
The many-colored flower of living flesh rises up
and opens its glistening seeds before the face of our mother.
In the moisture of Tlalocan, the quetzal water-plants open their corollas.
45   I am the work of the only god, his creation.

Your heart lives in the painted page,
you sing the royal fibers of the book,
you make the princes dance,
there you command by the water's discourse.
50   He created you,
he uttered you like a flower,
he painted you like a song:
a Toltec artist.
The book has come to the end:
55   your heart is now complete.

Here through art I shall live forever.
Who will take me, who will go with me?
Here I stand, my friends.
A singer, from my heart I strew my songs,
60   my fragrant songs before the face of others.
I carve a great stone, I paint thick wood
my song is in them.

    –Cantares mexicanos, fol. 27r–27v

As a whole, the poem turns on the idea of Tula, by now a city of the mind elaborately woven between the two modes in the tense structure. The sanctuary once "stood": the snake columns that bore its beams "still stand," like flowers upright in the rain. The sand pictures have gone, the pyramid has cracked, yet Topiltzin's sacred houses "will always be there," like the word implanted. Abandoned, the painted "stone and wood" of Tula now, as it were, organically speak for themselves, and through memory the heart will come back.

Apart from testifying to the sophistication of Nahuatl poetry, "Tollanaya huapalcalli" neatly intimates the factors that to date have made so difficult a historical reading of Tula, this elusive amalgam of the Old World's Babylon, Thebes, and Rome. Few major Mesoamerican texts fail to refer to Tula at some point or other and to do so from the most diverse provenance, from the Maya highlands and lowlands in the east to the Michoacan frontier in the west. Equally we are faced by a variety of genres, from highly charged poems and incantations to annals and chronicles that chart a mosaic of dates and locations. Deciphering the script of Tula, to use the *Popol vuh* phrase ("u tzibal Tulan," line 7,315), may indeed be said to recognize Mesoamerica's idea of itself, especially as an image in time.

From the time they arrived in Mesoamerica and began to interest themselves in its history, European chroniclers found this complex legacy hard to synthesize. Working from Highland Basin texts, however, they recognized that the Tula nearest and most immediate to the Aztecs and their neighbors was the town and archaeological site of that name that exists in Hidalgo, just to the north of the Basin of Mexico, close to the Mexquital drainage. This location was confirmed for the scholarly world by Wigberto Jiménez Moreno and his colleagues at a seminar held in Mexico City in 1941. Names given to towns and mountains around Tula and to its river were convincingly plotted on the map, pottery sequences were invoked, and, most important, on-site identifications were made of the distinctive architectural features of the city mentioned in the *Cantares mexicanos* and other sources, like its famous snake columns, the beam-bearing pillars each of whose bodies is a snake, its head thrust to the ground.

Nonetheless, the Tula question has remained a fraught one. Some continue to intimate locations elsewhere or remain content simply to assign the city to the realm of myth; that is, basically to exclude it from the process of material history.

MEXQUITAL TULA

Few doubt that the Tula referred to in texts from the Basin of Mexico is normally the Mexquital town plus its immediate extensions to north and south. These texts include the annals of Cuauhtitlan, midway between Tula and Tenochtitlan, the *Xolotl Maps* of Texcoco to the east of the main lake, and the alphabetic histories transcribed from them by Ixtlilxochitl, migration histories and other documents from Tenochtitlan, and a native-paper scroll of annals from the town itself. Among them, they construct a history whose details may conflict but whose overall shape is clear.

Pride of place belongs to the *Cuauhtitlan Annals.* An unbroken Nahuatl narrative that extends year-for-year from the emergence of the Chichimecs in the seventh century to the arrival of Cortes, this text takes pains to reconcile anomalies in dates and events that arose in the native-script *xiuhtlapoualli* from Cuauhtitlan and other towns from which it was transcribed. Some of its datings have been challenged, notably by Nigel Davies[5] in his painstaking reconstruction of events between the fall of Tula and the rise of Tenochtitlan. Yet it is remarkably consistent internally, and it tallies exactly with prime sources from other schools like the *Aztlan Annals,* the histories of the Chalco historian Chimalpahin, and the *Cuauhtinchan Annals,* or *Historia tolteca–chichimeca.* In any case, no one has yet come up with a better single sequence of year dates; and even if error in the Cuauhtitlan text were conceded, it would amount only to a Round or two at most, too little to affect the present argument.

The *Cuauhtitlan Annals* open with the Chichimecs celebrating their prowess as desert dwellers who have forced their way southeast into Mesoamerica proper. Their goddess Itzpapolotl, Obsidian Butterfly, eats the four hundred Mixcoa (Cloud Snakes) – a metaphor for the Chichimec calendar base in Round 72 of the Era – and enables the year count proper to begin, so that in 1 Reed A.D. 635 the Chichimec are said to have emerged from Chicomoztoc, the Seven Caves of tribal origin and a city with a grand lifestyle whose majestic remains are found in Zacatecas.[6] From the year 1 Flint 864, under Mixcoatl and other kings these Chichimec then spread into the Basin of Mexico and beyond, west to Michoacan, east to Cuextlan, and southeast to Tlaxcala and the approaches to Cholula. Meanwhile the year count of the Toltecs begins in A.D. 726, with explicit references back to the system of world ages and this Era's place in it, and leads to a line of rulers that includes One Reed, named after his birth year, 1 Reed 843, and honored by the epithets "Topiltzin," "Our Prince," and "Quetzalcoatl," the Feather-Snake or Plumed Serpent.

One Reed's life story unfolds over the ensuing pages. When nine years old he searched for his father's bones and carried them to the royal house; at twenty-eight he traveled to Tollantzinco and Cuextlan, where he built a bridge of stone and mortar; at thirty he was invited to become king of Tula; and then at forty (2 Reed 885) he became a recluse and, according to the "false" Texcoco version cited in the text, actually died. Here the last years of his life are cast in terms of the archetypal struggle, depicted in *Borbonicus* and other screenfolds, between himself in the role of Quetzalcoatl and his relentless opponent the war god Tezcatlipoca. He loses and ruins himself: Made drunk on the proverbial fifth draught of *pulque,* he sleeps with his sister. His overwhelming shame led him to abandon the city and undertake the long journey to Tlapallan and the eastern sea alluded to in the *Cantares mexicanos* poem, where, in the year 1 Reed 895, one Round of fifty-two years on from the year 1 Reed of his birth, he burned himself and became the planet Venus. From all this we then switch quite abruptly back to the annals and learn how Ten Flower, Huemac, and others succeeded One Reed as kings of Tula. Amid omens and violence typified by the human sacrifice abhorred by One Reed, the city begins to deteriorate and finally collapses in 1 Flint 1064; soon after, Huemac commits suicide, and the Toltecs utterly disperse, spreading this time to Cholula, Coixtlahuaca, Tehuacan, Cozcatlan, Nonoualco, Teotlillan, along the Papaloapan road to Acallan. The span of Toltec power, poised equally to either side of One Reed's death, is precisely stated as 339 years, which in years A.D. means from 731 to 1070.

On the matter of One Reed's life, the *Cuauhtitlan Annals* are supplemented by a host of texts, notably *Inomaca tonatiuh,* like the *Annals* physically part of the *Chimalpopoca Codex,* and the *Pinturas Manuscript. Inomaca tonatiuh,* more episodic, includes a map of One Reed's origins, before which the text reaches back to the start of the first millennium B.C. (955 B.C., or 2,513 years before the date of composition, A.D. 1558) and deals with Teotihuacan in the context of Era history. Thereafter, we learn about One Reed Topiltzin, who this time appears as the son of Mixcoatl (elsewhere Camaxtli) and Chimalman, a woman encountered during a campaign in Huitznahuac, generally taken to mean Morelos. Mixcoatl and Chimalman appear in the drawing with One Reed's cradle, so represented as to suggest the crags named after them and the river that runs between. The *Pinturas Manuscript* says One Reed's father turned into a rock, and names his birthplace as the river Michtlauhco. This cluster of names in fact exists in Amatlan, the "place of books" close to Tepoztlan that has energetically claimed the honor, on these and other grounds, of being the place of One Reed's conception, if not birth.[7]

Strong support for the case comes in the *pulque* chapter of the *Magliabechiano* group of manuscripts, which internally indicate their provenance to be Tepoztlan and that eastern half of Morelos settled by the Xochimilca and allotted to Huaxtepec in *Mendoza* (as opposed to the western half of the Tlahuica, whose *cabecera* was Cuernavaca).[8] Here eleven zodiac shrines spread eastward from Tepoztlan and Yauhtepec toward Totolapan and the slopes of Popocatepetl, traditionally the heart of the *maguey-* and *pulque-* making area identified by Kirchhoff with Tamoanchan. The list includes Tula, possibly a ward of Amatlan, and leads to the image of Topiltzin Quetzalcoatl, for whom *pulque* had such drastic consequences. In one text, the place glyph for Tula visually puns its rushes (*tol-*) with the open beak of a bird (*totol-*), which phonetically could suggest "our Tula here" (*to-tol-*), as opposed to the city of Mexquital (see Fig. 42d).

Inomaca tonatiuh also explains that One Reed at first accompanied his father on his campaigns and that only when the latter was assassinated by One Reed's uncles did he search for his bones to give them proper burial. Omitting the *pulque* and incest story and the struggle against the warlike Tezcatlipoca, this source also accounts for the journey eastward in terms of outright military endeavor on the part of One Reed himself, and it adds the important detail that having reached Acallan he crossed the river to Tlapallan. Geographically this can refer only to the Usumacinta that separates Campeche and Yucatan from Mexico; the military intent ties in better with the *Chilam Balam* version of events at this date and with the fact that Maya temples at Chichen and Tulum replicate the snake columns and other features of Mexquital Tula's architecture. The general term for the invader used in the *Chilam Balam Books,* Nacxit Xuchit, strongly recalls the Topiltzin Nacxitl of the *Cantares mexicanos* and finds an echo in the deference made to this figure at this same stage by the highland Maya authors of the *Popol vuh* and the *Cakchiquel Annals*. Finally, we are told that One Reed died not after a perfect Round of years but at the age of fifty-six, and that rather than burning himself and becoming Venus he simply died of disease and that as a result his body was burned. Neither is he graced here with the name Quetzalcoatl. In fact, comparing *Inomaca tonatiuh* with the *Cuauhtitlan Annals,* we can sense the raw facts of the hero's life that were then ritualized according to ancient Mesoamerican paradigms.

With the end of One Reed and the fall of Tula, the story becomes one of rival would-be successors. The obligatory visit to Tula's ruins, in homage or assertion, appears in several texts. The stones lie spread there for us to see in the first of the *Xolotl Maps,* which are dedicated to the twelfth-century Chichimec ruler of that name, ancestor of both Acolhua and Tepanec, and his descendants in Texcoco, notably the poet-king Nezahualcoyotl (1402–72). Recounting their own subsequent arrival on the scene, the Aztecs placed Tula on the road that brought them from their legendary homeland Aztlan; geographically Tula heralds their all-important entry into the Highland Basin. Their twenty years there, during which the *Pinturas Manuscript* says they extirpated all remaining inhabitants, are clearly marked in the *Aztlan Annals* (p. 12); the Tula episode is also registered in the *Aubin* group of manuscripts[9] and in one case actually starts the narrative off.

Also linked with this story of highland Tula is the corpus of documents from Cholula and its surroundings, in particular Cuauhtinchan with its maps and its annals, or "Toltec–Chichimec History." These have as a common theme how the Cuauhtinchan Chichimecs journeyed from Seven Caves (Chicomoztoc) to Cholula before establishing political power locally in the thirteenth and fourteenth centuries A.D. Placing the great pyramid and temples of Cholula at the center, Map 2 traces the routes taken from Seven Caves, far to the northwest, and clearly shows Tula as a stage along the way. In defining its own political arena, Cuauhtinchan clarifies the further inroads of the Chichimec into the southern border area that included Huehuetlan, Tepexic, and Coixtlahuaca, an important source of documents that in turn feature the tribal womb Seven Caves as well as the Chichimec character Two Dog who plays so prominent a role in the *Tepexic Annals*. In this context, Coixtlahuaca was reported to have a "Toltec" ruler, Atonal, in 1446.[10]

In turning finally to the one native-script history to have survived from Mexquital Tula itself, we have confirmed for us chiefly the fact that the place did indeed experience collapse. Running from 1361 to Cortes, the narrative does not once allude to former greatness. Rather, counterpointing its own sad story of vacant thrones and rulers who continued to desert the city, it concentrates on the deeds of the Triple Alliance of Tenochtitlan, Texcoco, and Tlacopan, taking a particular interest in the distant capture of Tepexic's ally Huehuetlan and of Coixtlahuaca, which opened the Aztec tribute road to the east.

In all these texts from the Basin of Mexico and farther afield, the place identified with Mexquital Tula is always contained within the greater Chichimec story of invasion from beyond Mesoamerica's northwestern frontier. In some cases One Reed's drive east is posed as the result of his humiliation at the hands of Tezcatlipoca; in others, as a military thrust in its own right. In some cases the ruins are visited reverentially by the newcomers, keen on enhancing their pedigree and cultural status; in others, the remaining inhabitants are assaulted. These and other conundrums remain, yet here they signify less than the city's overall time frame. Nowhere do we find a foundation date that precedes the seventh-century emergence from Chicomoztoc or an apogee that antedates the ninth-century specified by the *Cuauhtitlan Annals*.

THE GREAT TULA

Although the Tula of Mexquital certainly fits most Mesoamerican textual references to a town of that name, it just as certainly fails to fit the rest. As a highland center that had its apogee no earlier than the ninth century, it is badly placed in time and space to qualify as the Tula invoked in these other cases; and as others have remarked, the quality of its artifacts and inscriptions scarcely qualifies it as the first home of Mesoamerican art and script.

In the matter of sheer sequence, the extensive *Historia tolteca–chichimeca,* or *Cuauhtinchan Annals,* places Tula not after but *before* the Chichimec emergence from Chicomoztoc. Just as the first chapter tells the story of the inaugural city of Tula and of Toltec arrival in Cholula, so the second tells how the Toltecs then journeyed to Chicomoztoc in search of allies and how they returned with the Chichimecs over a sequence of thirteen plus ten "days" (which on grounds of distance alone they cannot be: Calendrically they demand to be read as Rounds); in the third and final chapter, the political power of Cuauhtinchan is established in 1 Flint A.D. 1176. The *Relación* of nearby Cholula proposes a similar plot: In this text, from the inaugural Tula, the exact memory of which is said to be lost in the mists of time, émigrés again arrive in Cholula (which counted Tula among its names) as well as in the highland Tollantzinco and Mexquital Tula, leaving no doubt at all about the primacy and priority of the original great Tula after which later cities named themselves. Pipil accounts of their migration from Cholula to Nicaragua, 700 or 800 years before Cortes, also fit well into this time frame.[11]

Yet more indicative, the very texts that we have seen dealing with Mexquital Tula sometimes refer earlier on to the existence and practices of another Tula. Before dealing with the Chichimec migrations from Seven Caves and the Toltec progress from Tollantzinco to Tollan, the *Florentine* version of Mesoamerican history (book 10, chap. 29: Mexica) also reports how the grandparents Oxomoco and Cipactonal invented the *tonalamatl* and the year calendar of the Toltecs. This is said to have happened in Tamoanchan prior to the building of the pyramids of the Sun and the Moon at Teotihuacan. Before giving its version of the life of One Reed, *Inomaca tonatiuh* narrates the heroic deeds performed millennia ago at Tula, Tamoanchan, and Teotihuacan, making a pointed contrast between the Quetzalcoatl of this older city and the One Reed of the more recent one. Here Tula belongs to another order of time in the urban sequence neatly summarized in *Totecuyoane,* where the roll call of ancient emplacements that Europeans could be expected to know nothing about begins with Tula, passes through Tamoanchan, and ends with Teotihuacan. Here Tula again stands as a calendrical source, being named as the first of four calendrical usages (the others being the Chichimec, the Colhua, and the Tepanec).

Elsewhere Tula stands unequivocally as the place where many key things first happened in the economy and politics of Mesoamerica. *Ríos* associates the Tula of the older Quetzalcoatl with the very first production of maize, as does the *Popol vuh,* which, ages prior to Nacxit Xochitl, names Tullan as Mesoamerica's first city and the place where the pioneers of this Era exchanged the life of the family (*chinamit*) for that of the town (*tinamit*) (lines 5080, 5247). The annals of Cuauhtinchan and of Tepexic both place Tula well before Seven Caves, and the latter show it to be the city of the Quetzalcoatl Nine Wind who gave human beings their first writing lesson. Centuries before Nacxit Xuchit, Tulapan initiates the Matichu chronicle of the lowland Maya *Chilam Balam Books.* Like the Cholulans, the Cakchiquel obtain from there their agricultural deity, Nine Rain. And so on.

According to this evidence, before the Tula of Mexquital other places of that name flourished in Mesoamerica. The time depths in question may vary or be hard to estimate, but the precedence is clear. To the discrepancy in time we should add that of environment and geographical position. Mexquital is known for its high, bare plains and extremes of temperature best endured by the hardy, slow-growing mesquite plant after which the area in named, and for frost and snow that, according to Tula's own annals, could fall knee deep. By contrast, the earlier Tula abounded in vegetal wealth, growing massive maize crops and the cotton, cacao, and rubber peculiar to the tropical lowlands, likewise the habitat of its splendid-feathered and sweet-singing birds. Again, Mexquital Tula lies very much at the western end of Mesoamerica and conceived itself to be a frontier town and bulwark against Chichimec invasion. With reference to this western frontier, the general position of the lowland site, when indicated, is easterly, the binary opposite in Mesoamerican astronomical terms.

At this stage it could seem attractive to resolve the anomaly as many have done before simply by assigning this earlier lowland Tula or Tulas to the realm of myth, and thereby to account for this seam of Toltec memory in terms of ancient paradigms, which by definition shun specific location. After all, on the subject of location the *Cakchiquel Annals* speak of the first city of the Era not as one but as a ritually patterned four, to east and west, north and south. Support for this approach comes in highly wrought literary products like "Tollanaya huapalcalli," where the whole notion of Topiltzin and his city appeals overtly to the mind's play. This poem indeed would then be the most succinct statement of the more general process we noted when comparing the *Cuauhtitlan Annals* version of One Reed's life with that given in *Inomaca tonatiuh.* That is, the Toltec hero Topiltzin is gradually assimilated into an archetypal identity that belongs to no specific place. The years of his life, actually fifty-six, are made exactly to match those of the fifty-two-year Round; the path of his exodus intimates that of Venus between west and east horizons, to the extent that he may be said to rise as the planet on the *tonalamatl* days of its heliacal risings, and with ritually appropriate postures and intent (see Chapter 11, "Quetzalcoatl"). As for his parentage, One Reed's mother, Chimalman, from being a local woman encountered during his father's campaigning near Amatlan, conceives him in the manner of the divine mother, parthenogenically, by swallowing a jade while sweeping. Then after his father's death, what initially was just the desire to honor a fellow warrior becomes the deeper psychic search for the paternal bones, which in Mesoamerican cosmogony drove the divinely conceived Quetzalcoatl down to Mictlan to gather the bones from which this Era's people were fashioned. Similarly, political conditions in the town are imaged in terms of an older, more general story: Corruption becomes the stinking corpse that in fact One Reed dreams into existence and into a substance so heavy that removing it is a nightmare. And neatly completing this cycle and order of explanation, upon leaving Tula he exiles its magic birds and switches its vegetation from the tropical lushness of fantasy to the mesquite scrub actually found near Mexquital Tula today.

Yet this cannot be the whole story. For, though no doubt hyperbolic and allegorical in part, this mass of contrasting detail points to a specific moment in time and place for this other Toltec home. In this reading, the eastern lowlands are not just a back projection from western Mexquital,[12] the virtual image of a poetic mirror or binary intellect; they exist substantially and in their own right. The birds and the vegetable and mineral wealth attributed to Tula in the *Florentine Codex,* for example, correspond in the first instance to the material commodities actually produced in the Tochtepec and adjoining areas on the Gulf Coast, according to the precise lists given in *Mendoza.* The product also of the *Tepexic Annals'* eastern quarter, the cacao bean provided the link and currency farther east to the markets of Tikal, for instance, and its value was later measured as a fraction of the Spanish peso. Cotton, the stuff of civilized Toltec dress, as opposed to Chichimec leathers and skins, grew in a variety of colors, a claim that would indeed seem hyperbolic were it not for the fact that naturally colored cotton soberly features in the *Mendoza* lists of lowland tribute (e.g., p. 38).

The wealth of lowland flora and fauna attributed to the Toltecs in the *Florentine Codex* is closely paralleled in another passage in that same text, where there can be no doubt that the location is the Olmec territory that stretches east from the lower Papaloapan. Its parts are referred to variously to Anahuac, Acallan, Tlapallan, and Nonoualco; the eastern counterpart to the Nonoalco of highland Tula, the last definitely has its own geographical base. The hairstyle of these Toltecs is that of this Nonoualco, Quetzalcoatl's hat is typical of the same area, and the local inhabitants who enjoy its wealth are known as "ipilhoa Quetzalcoatl": sons of Quetzalcoatl. Indeed, we are told that in their way the Olmec here may be thought of as Toltec, a remnant of Tula's line; just this connection is made in the highland Maya sources, where the Oliman are located in or near Tabasco.

Further clues are provided by the dense narrative of the *Cuauhtinchan Annals,* which situate Nonoualco on the lower Papaloapan and in so doing include in its boundaries the "speaking hill" known as Tzatzitepec. *Ríos* and the *Florentine Codex* (book 3, chap. 3) report how Tula's patron deities, urging people to work the fields, would issue commands from this place that belongs to Zongolica and for which this time there appears to be no obvious highland counterpart. Also, in tracing the Toltec from Seven Caves in the company of their new allies the Chichimecs, along a route that differs from both of those given in the *Cuauhtinchan Maps* and that excludes Mexquital Tula, the *Cuauhtinchan Annals* (fol. 24r) situate a town named Tula between Cuetlaxtlan (Cotaxtla) in the lower Papaloapan vicinity and the towns on its upper reaches, like Teotitlan, Cozcatlan, and Tehuacan.

Above all, on its opening page the Cuauhtinchan text represents the "fingers and toes" of Tula, that is, its confederates, which as four groups of five spread west to east along the Gulf Coast, from the Pantepec Valley and Tochpan (Tuxpan) to Nonoualco (Tabasco) and Campeche:

Pantecatli	Nonoualca
Ytzcuitzoncatli	Cuitlapiltzinca
Tlematepeua	Aztateca
Tlequaztepeua	Tzanatepeua
Tezcatepeua	Tetetzincatli
Tecollotepeua	Teuhxilcatli
Tochpaneca	Zacanca
Cenpoualteca	Cuixcoca
Cuetlaxteca	Quauhchichinolca
Cozcateca	Chiuhnauhteca

All but one of the ten places to the west (left column) can be firmly identified as ports on the coast (Tochpan, Tecollotlan, Cempoala) or as towns on
the rivers that drain toward it (Pantepec, Itzcuintepec, Tlemaco, Tezcatepec,
all on the Pantepec–Tuxpan drainage, plus Cuetlaxtlan, the unequivocal
place of innards, and Cozcatlan, far up the Papaloapan). To the east (right
column) Zacanco stood as the furthest term of Quetzalcoatl's exodus to the
east in the *Cantares mexicanos* poem, and Cuixco is placed in Tabasco by the
Tlaxcala Lienzo and *Inomaca tonatiuh*. Like Nonoualco (also known as a
highland name), Chiconautla appears with Tulapan at the start of the
Yucatecan Matichu chronicle.

In his day, anxious not to dissociate these names from the one Tula that
had been accorded a geography, Paul Kirchhoff found ways of attaching
them to Mexquital. Doing so meant scouring the landscape at parish level
and actually defying the anatomy of the text in order to reconstruct a
notional set of five lots of four names instead of the four lots of five "fingers" actually listed. Acknowledging the difficulties involved, Kirchhoff
also changed his mind about some of his proposed locations.[13] Given that
the set serves as the prologue to the "Historia tolteca–chichimeca" told in
these annals, which is epic and wide-ranging and certainly focuses on the
Papaloapan and on Cholula more than it does on Mexquital, the Gulf Coast
seems preferable on grounds of the status and geographical grouping of the
towns in question even if it is the case that the textual statement also involves some allegorical translation up to Mexquital.

Just as Mexquital generally accommodates post–Seven Caves highland
references to Tula, so the Gulf Coast, especially the lower Papaloapan,
emerges as its lowland forerunner. Topiltzin approaches the east because he
is expected and because "his house is already there"; or, as Nigel Davies
acutely put it after reviewing native texts and a host of Spanish chronicles,
"Such reports reinforce the tentative suggestion that some kind of Toltec
colony had existed on that [Gulf] Coast, which could later have become a
receiving area for Toltec fugitives [from Mexquital], though archaeological
confirmation is scanty."[14] Bearing in mind such archaeological evidence as
does exist, which firmly points to this area as the home of urbanism at least
by 1000 B.C. long, long before Mexquital, and which situates here initial
achievements in script and calendrics, Davies (p. 52) also follows the *Florentine Codex* in suggesting the Olmec as "the true Toltec," when it is a question of the larger Mesoamerican framework. Again, this Gulf Coast siting
better suits as the first city named in histories originating on either side of it,
in Mexico to the west and in the Maya realm to the east.

In attempting to locate lowland Tula precisely in time and space, it is hard
to go further than this, for several reasons. We generally lack the run of
dates that, out of a more recent past, pertains to Mexquital. Some texts
propose an order of time, like the two and a half millennia mentioned in

Inomaca tonatiuh, the *Pinturas Manuscript* and Muñoz Camargo, and the five millennia of *Ríos;* but no straightforward linear chronology has so far been agreed upon.[15] Referring to the beginnings of the Toltec calendar in the early days of Tamoanchan, prior to Teotihuacan, the *Florentine Codex* reports that "the history of it was saved but was burnt when Itzcoatl ruled in Mexico. A council of rulers . . . said, 'There is no need for all the common people to know of the writings; government will be defamed and this will bring unrest to the land.' "[16]

To this incendiarism we may add the fact that, as foundation history, accounts of Tula appear typically to have been integrated into the scheme of world ages out of which this Era emerged, through the device of multilevel reading best exemplified in the *teoamoxtli;* and it is just these dimensions of native script and literature that are hardest to transcribe into the Western alphabet and consciousness. Such is undoubtedly the case with *Ríos,* for example, where in the interplay between the world ages and the life episodes of Quetzalcoatl and Tula we are explicitly told that some images have been transcribed inadequately and others not at all. Similarly, it is the cyclic resonance of the year names of the *xiuhmolpilli* that in the *Cuauhtitlan Annals* permits the dramatic flashback to the start of the Era at the moment in the seventh century A.D. when Mexquital Tula was founded. Thanks to allusions to the Era name Four Ollin and its year 13 Reed, the same sort of effect is achieved in *Inomaca tonatiuh,* where Quetzalcoatl and One Reed mirror each other on either side of the central image of the latter's birth; the case of the more dilapidated Spanish text of *Pinturas* is parallel.

A further factor is the likelihood that in any case, just as with Mexquital, discrepancies existed among the histories of lowland Tula according to the political interest they served and the geography they defended. It is with this in mind that we may best approach the *Tepexic Annals,* the text among all those extant that offers, in native script, the longest-known continuous narrative, serving in this respect as the yardstick for lowland Tula that the *Cuauhtitlan Annals* are for Mexquital. For this text does not represent its sequence of 4,800 years out of calendrical bravura: It tells the story of a particular place and landscape. Widely respected for its link with the Toltec kings, in this way the town of Tepexic defended its particular version of that dynastic tradition. It is a narrative integral with an actual landscape that deals with the lives of cities and people; and this fact forms the other part of the validation of its span, for as a result its story can be related to other historical texts and to the archaeology of Mesoamerica.[17] This much was recognized already in the eighteenth century by Robertson,[18] who correctly read the kindlings as tribute periods. After all, when the year 3113 B.C. was first proposed as the base date for the hieroglyphic corpus, it was assumed to lie in a remote prehistorical or "mythic" past; today a continuous material record is being established for that past, especially in matters of settlement, ceramics, and maize agriculture.

Recounting the terrestrial and celestial birth of Quetzalcoatl Nine Wind, the Tepexic narrative shows the four temples he built at Tula, at the very start of the Era, adding calendrical detail to the general Toltec claim that it was Mesoamerica's first city. Here at this inaugural moment he teaches the arts, not least that of the *tlacuilo* who wrote the text. Anticipating the long Toltec diaspora otherwise all but lost in the mists of time, Quetzalcoatl then literally precipitates the story into continuous geography by raising the sky so that its waters run to the sea on either side of the continental divide. Here, due north of Apoala, the original watershed of the text (p. 3), he stands atop Napatecutli, the "four-times lord," which makes the first of its four appearances, its square, or boxlike, summit (also depicted in the *Cuauhtinchan Maps*) being picked out in its Spanish name Cofre de Perote. The great majority of the initial place names (pp. 6–8) in fact relate to rivers, and on the Gulf Coast drainage their courses, tributaries, and marshes and the settlements near them may in some cases be guessed at: for example, the flint-bearing caiman named Oxichan in *Mendoza,* the place of innards Cuetaxtlan, and the pair of islands placed off Veracruz–Chalchicueyan by Melgarejo Vivanco. The concern with hydrography and the depiction of man-made water courses find a particular echo in texts from the upper Papaloapan, the scene of Mesoamerica's earliest irrigation. We also see the landmarks of the *Ríos* migration from Tula to Cholula (for example, Tzatzitepec, Nonoualco's speaking mountain in Tzoncolican [Zongolica], and the *symplegades,* or crusher, mountain) in the same general area (Fig. 43). Over the vast span of this early period, the narrative generally centers on Papaloapan (the Cuicatlan and Coixtlahuaca federations of towns), touching on the Mixteca to the south and what became its own tribute quarters to the north (Napatecutli, Cuauhtinchan and its four snow peaks) and west (Nacochtlan, Coatzinco) (Plate 15; Table 3; Figs. 26, 27). In broad terms, the concentration on Papaloapan, corroborated by toponymy in the Cuicatlan and Coixtlahuaca texts (Fig. 37) – which, moreover, themselves typically invoke an Era time depth – corresponds archaeologically with the remarkably early Popolocan evidence of culture and civilization in this part of Mesoamerica: specifically, cultivated plants, pottery (including the fine orangeware exported to Teotihuacan), and irrigation.[19]

Out of this wealth of toponymy we are brought back to the continental divide, this time to Apoala, from whose trees the remote ancestors of Coixtlahuaca and Mixtec dynasties also emerged, as we saw. The prominence of the name-date Nine Wind at this epochal moment vindicates it as an ancient and august designation of the Quetzalcoatl figure of Mesoamerica; found in certain early Olmec inscriptions, it has great prominence in the

Figure 43. Toponyms in the early story of Tula: (a) Tzatzitepec; (b) *symplegades;* (c) Cuetlaxtlan "place of innards." (Left, *Tepexic Annals,* pp. 8, 9, 13; right, *Ríos,* pp. 10, 12, and *Mendoza,* p. 49.)

Classic, at Cholula, Xochicalco, and Cacaxtla (as Nine Serpent-eye) in various Palenque texts as well as the Mixtec annals. Some of these last differ from the Tepexic text, however, in showing this figure to have been imposed upon native-born Mixtec families, according to just the model cited in Reyes's account of Apoala, the central watershed from which the "lawgivers" like Nine Wind spread out in four directions.[20] After further details of these forebears, their marriages, children, and nursery toys, this extensive first chapter ends when Quetzalcoatl Nine Wind goes on to perform the first kindling in the Tepexic text (A.D. 338).

The second chapter focuses more closely on aristocratic urban life: granting insignia, arts of rhetoric, supplies of luxury goods, symposia of *pulque* drinkers, consumers of hallucinogenic mushrooms. Among the principals we see one named after the Era itself, Nauh Ollin, like the later monarch of Tepexic shown in the *Coixtlahuaca Lienzo.* Like that of the *Tilantongo Annals,* and consistent with the very occurrence of the hieroglyphic inscriptions, the span of this second chapter coincides with that of the Classic, a concept further defined by its absence from the highland Chichimec tradition. Halfway through, at the time of the hieroglyphic hiatus, a moment marked by the unique repetition of a 5 Flint date, the revolution of a wheel overturns a ruler: His power is then, however, restored in a brilliant display of solar imagery. The interest that Tepexic and the Mixteca show in Quetzalcoatl specifically as a dynastic patron is matched by their common chronological attention to the very idea of the Classic. That period culminates here in the second kindling at Tepexic and the story of its tribute quarters.

Finally, in details of the second kindling, held at Tepexic in A.D. 805, and of the ninth, which in 1171 saw its power extended to Cuauhtinchan, the Cholula plain, and the range that runs west from the Chichimec "corner-stone" Napatecutli, there are clear signs of that Chichimec involvement in Toltec affairs so fully told in the *Cuauhtinchan Annals*. The president of these kindlings, Two Dog, evokes the doglike Chichimec by his very name (as indeed does the Xolotl of the Basin of Mexico), and in A.D. 805 in the toponym of Tepexic seven inset orifices recall their tribal home Chicomoztoc (Plate 16). Above all, as in Cuauhtinchan's *Historia tolteca–chichimeca* (and possibly in the Cholulan *teoamoxtli Borgia*), we are presented with a whole phase of Chichimec history that mediates between Toltec beginnings and modern politics.

In this reading, the *Tepexic Annals* flesh out the suggestion made in *Ríos* that in the iconic script tradition of Mesoamerica the history of Tula is that of the 5,200-year Era. In defending local political interests, this text casts back to the beginning of the Era, proposing sequences of actual dates and places for that history; central to Mesoamerica's self-imaging in time, it helps to give broader shape to its main historical periods and perspectives. Unique among surviving texts, it lends material substance to the great Toltec vision appealed to subsequently by cities like Mexquital Tula, which has by no means vanished from Mesoamerican consciousness.

7

Turtle Island

HISTORY AND PREHISTORY

If dispossession has defined recent centuries of Turtle Island history, then this fact has been well accommodated in official U.S. discourse. Consulting the scholarship fostered by the Bureau of American Ethnology, we rapidly become aware of a hallowed binary that separates that area's original inhabitants into two types: prehistoric and historic. The former settled and created its landscapes, yet are knowable only through mute material evidence of the kind archaeologists piece together. The latter exist only insofar as they come into contact with the white invader, being in this sense a pure extention of Western historiography.

Whereas this prehistoric–historic distinction may have had a certain practical use, it more surely carries an ideological charge that is both powerful and inimical to native interest. For it necessarily deprives natives of this part of America of their own history: They emerge, as it were, solely in order to be dispossessed, cut off from roots and political memory. At its height, this ideology was even applied to Anasazi, that densely and continuously populated extension of Mesoamerica that lies beyond Turtle Island's southwestern frontiers. Like "Hohokan" and other local archaeological labels, the very name Anasazi was allowed to denote not the "ancient people" whom present dwellers in the area, Pueblo and Athapaskan, recognize as ancestors, but rather a former civilization quite separate in its being. As a result, mysterious lost creatures who might as well have visited from outer space, the creators of the Anasazi landscape no longer related effectively to those who were now living in it.

Today the situation has begun to change, thanks in part to conscious native resistance to this imposed scheme. Histories authored by the Hopi,

Navajo, and others have provided the framework into which recent archaeo-logical findings may more reasonably be fitted. Beginning, like *Watunna* and the *Popol vuh,* in cosmic time, *Dine bahane* introduces us to precisely the territory the Navajo still occupy and claim, naming the guardian mountains that make up the quincunx of the dry painting *Place of Emergence,* detailing visits to the settlements in Chaco and Chelly canyons – all over a series of 102-year lifetimes and lesser year periods that begins the twelfth century. Fully confirming the far longer Pueblo occupation of the area, the Book of the Hopi recorded by Frank Waters (1963) also indicates its actual links with pre-Hispanic Mexico.

If a similar shift may now be discerned in views of Turtle Island, it stems from attempts by the few scattered survivors in the area likewise to have its archaeology recognized as part of their inheritance. This archaeology as such has steadily refined its account of the two main phases of mound building in Turtle Island, centered respectively on the Ohio and Mississippi rivers. Referred to by the fortuitous labels "Hopewell" and "Adena," the beginnings of the earlier phase coincide with the transition from Archaic to "Woodland" culture around 1000 B.C. and may now be seen to have spread right down the Ohio, across the Mississippi, and up the Missouri; hence, a huge and distinctive egg-swallowing Serpent Mound in Ohio finds its coun-terpart in Kansas.[1] At the end of the first millennium, a complex of struc-tures was built on the Scioto and other rivers that flow south into the Ohio: Guarded to east and west by the tall sentinels of Grave Creek and Miamis-burg, and linked to Kentucky by the lines of causeways, these settlements produced exquisite artifacts in mica, copper, and shell as well as incised stone tablets and a whole repertoire of carved pipes. This Ohio culture was in part carried forward by those who began building the flat-topped Missis-sippian pyramids toward the end of the first millennium A.D.: We find the same copper adornments and carved pipes and the same attention to the bird-man who represents the thunderers of the highest heavens. At the same time, new elements appear: a far richer lexicon of incised shell – typically cameo gorgets in round frames, the cult of the sacred fire in its temple atop the pyramid, more lavish burials, and above all a much improved agricul-ture that included maize and other cultigens brought from Mexico. This culture reached its epitome in the mid Mississippi, between the confluences with the Missouri and the Ohio, the former being marked by a huge rock painting of the Piasa, or horned serpent;[2] the latter, by its own set of mounds. Here lay the great pyramid and city of Cahokia, reaching from east to west bank, now brought back to life in its new and richly appointed museum.

Complementing this archaeological knowledge are bodies of native texts whose authority is now being more generally deferred to. The return of the sacred Cherokee fire from Oklahoma to its homeland in southern Appalachia has helped create a more appropriate perspective for the earlier history of that nation and its particular connections with that of the Iroquois, linguistic cousins, to the north. Now more respected as the historic and geographic documents or titles of a once great confederacy, the painted skins of the Siouans forward the line of native iconography; together with versions written in the alphabet, they tell a story commensurate with that of the Mound Builders. The actual count year by year begins in 1682, that is, before the massacre of surviving Mound Builders at, say, Natchez or Hiwassee. Similarly, collated stage by stage with native alphabetic histories, the incised migration scrolls of the Mide involve the northern Algonkin in the same story. In short, respecting these sources and their common testimony helps to redress the damage done by the prehistoric–historic divide and brings back the native memory of Turtle Island.

APPALACHIA

The Cherokee are facing the onslaught of a superior enemy coming from the southeast. Driven back, they retreat to their strongholds in the upper Tennessee drainage, on the other side of the southern Appalachian divide. When all seems lost, help suddenly comes: From out of the pyramid on which their council house stands at Nikwasi, powerful allies appear who look and talk like the Cherokee themselves, specifically the western Overhill division from farther downstream into Tennessee. They put the enemy to flight, restore the peace, and then disappear back into the pyramid. So goes one of the narratives given to James Mooney in the late nineteenth century by Ayunini, Swimmer, a Cherokee who spoke no English and who had evaded the forced removal of his nation to Oklahoma in 1838.

Normally invisible, these helpers belong to an ancient race. Siting their council houses inside pyramids like Nikwasi, they rarely show themselves; they can more often be heard making music with drums and dancing in their hidden houses. Called Nunnehi, they well illustrate the Cherokees' relationship to their Appalachian landscape, its mountains and rivers and above all its pyramids and other earthworks.

Emerging from the heart of the pyramid, the Nunnehi historically represent the society of Mound Builders who had earlier occupied Cherokee territory; they come from farther down the river route that led to Cahokia, the Overhill area where, for example, the Hiwassee Island pyramid continued to operate according to the old rules until at least 1700. Between these predecessors and themselves the Cherokee set no bound, and so consciously placed themselves with the Mound Builder tradition.[3] Furthering Mississippian culture, they kept up the distinction between sacred and profane fire; they smoked the pipe of peace and war, played the ballgame chunkey (which had once given birth to the moon), and recited their national history at the annual new-fire and green-maize ceremony (*busk,* a Muskogee term). The central image in another of Ayunini's narratives, about the first bringing of fire, is exactly predicated in the Mississippian shell cameo that shows crossed sticks (fire) carried on the back of a spider. Yet another explains the iconography found, for example, in Cahokia ceramics, of the woman who provides and shows how to multiply maize.

In fact, as well as adapting older structures the Cherokee too constructed mounds in Mississippian fashion, placing a sevenfold burial at the center, shaping the shaft for the sacred unquenched fire, and leveling the platform for their temples and council houses. Besides Nikwasi, a political center until 1819 and known today as Franklin, such landmarks included Kituhwa, held to be the most ancient of all; Setsi; and others now in part drowned, like Cherokee memory, under reservoir water. In thus bridging the gap between "prehistoric" and postcontact America, the Cherokee readily compare with other southern societies, for instance the Yuchi, whose town squares, even after removal to Oklahoma, represent a Mound Builder cosmic model; the Natchez of the southern Mississippi, who sustained the line of their Great Suns (reputedly forty-five or fifty in all) well into the eighteenth century and before being massacred by the French refused to contemplate removal precisely because they had occupied their territory so long; the Muskogee, who occupied Tukabatchee Mound through three archaeological phases from 1400 to 1837; or again the Choctaw, who still today cling to the Emergence Mound Nanih Waiya in Alabama from which they claim to have emerged.[4]

Besides mounds, the Nunnehi inhabit other features of the Cherokee landscape, notably the bald peaks that define the multiple watershed of the Cherokee rivers Cheowa, Hiwassee, Tennessee, Tugaloo, Tomassee, and Naduli (Nottely). In this perspective they fit into the larger scheme whereby Cherokee territory opens out of cosmogony itself, as in the Navajo and Mesoamerican cases. The buzzard beating its wings on a still-soft earth shaped the Appalachian valleys in the first place. Under the set of four Cherokee peaks, the bears, though assigned a subhuman rank in evolution, retain their own council fires and in winter dance around them, like the Nunnehi; the names of the four peaks – Tsistuyi, Kuwahi, Uyaye, and Gatekwa – consolidate the shaman cures or songs written out in the Cherokee syllabary by Ayunini.[5] Kanata, the keeper of game and husband of the maize woman Selu, occupies Black Mountain, and the giant Tsulkula, stealer of a human bride, occupies Tsuneguhyi at the very head of the Tennessee drainage and made the inscriptions found on the rock named after him. Ridding the earth of monsters, the epic hero Agan-unitsi pursues the giant serpent Uktena over a ritual seven locations from the Smoky Mountains down to Cohutta in Georgia, prefiguring the line that now divides Tennessee from North Carolina. Moreover, in finishing off Uktena he establishes the serpentine stone fortress still visible at Cohutta that, like other such features, marks an ancestral Cherokee boundary. In other words, at this level the story of the Nunnehi who emerged from Nikwasi belongs to a general territorial affirmation, echoes of which survive in narrative stories told in Cherokee even today in distant Oklahoma.

This affirmation must appear the more striking when we recall that although they certainly continued Mississippian culture in southern Appalachia, the Cherokee fully acknowledged that their territory had long been settled before them: After all, the difference between the Nunnehi and them derives precisely from the fact that the former, more ancient, emerge from the true heart of the pyramid. Moreover, in their annual new-fire narrative they recounted a journey from a former homeland situated rather at the northern end of Appalachia, where their Iroquois kin were and still are concentrated. At this earlier time they had constructed mounds there too (though now acknowledging no counterpart to the Nunnehi). The Lenape knew they had built forts on the southern shore of Lake Erie; Jefferson observed them paying their respects to a mound he later excavated near Monticello; and when Grave Creek Mound on the upper Ohio was opened by whites in 1840, it was a Cherokee who denounced the desecration of the national heritage.[6] All these structures originate in the earlier Ohio phase of mound building.

The history that conjoins the Ani Yunwiya (Cherokee) with the Onwi honwe (Iroquois) and both with the Mound Builders is still being written.[7] The clear linguistic affinity is matched in literature, in Cusick's *Sketches of Ancient History* (1823) of the Iroquois and other texts that offer to explain the origins of the famous League of Five Nations. Starting again from cosmic beginnings, the earth itself emerges thanks to the Turtle, according to the *Cherokee Phoenix* (the bilingual Cherokee newspaper of the late 1820s) on the one hand and Cusick on the other. In both traditions maize is given by and embodied in a woman from the sky who with her sisters, squash and beans, belongs to the three graces;[8] the giant who keeps the game animals steals a human bride; huge serpents represent military siege and remain as earthwork mementos; and Ayunini and Cusick give similar specifications for the construction of temple mounds. The Seneca account of how the Five Nations sent an embassy to the Cherokee seeking political cooperation invokes the same ritual acts – burying of weapons, hanging up the wampum belt – that had previously led to the establishment of the Iroquois League.

Cusick's perspective in these matters is of interest, for he belonged to the Tuscarora, who became the sixth nation of the Iroquois in 1723 and who had hitherto lived not far from Cherokee territory. He sets events on a grand stage and carries his reader not just through Appalachia but from one end of Turtle Island to the other in showing how Iroquoian-speakers migrated and divided up. We learn how one party went west as far as the Rockies, crossing the

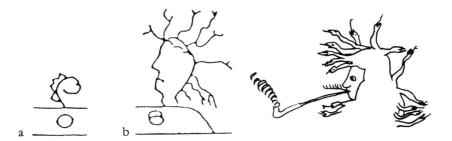

Figure 44. Founders of the Iroquois League: (a) Hiawatha; (b) Atorarho. (Roll-call glyphs in Fenton 1950; Cusick 1825.)

Mississippi by means of a vine bridge (also a Cherokee motif), while others went south by various routes toward what is stated to be the more urban and civilized part of Turtle Island. Even so, firm purchase is kept on the original homeland and subsequent territory of the Five Nations in northern Appalachia. In part by means of illustrations, Cusick shows how major events from the wider past are rehearsed in the masks and choreography of Five Nations ritual: the flying head of the hurricane, for example, or the stony giants encountered far out in the wild West. As in other native sources, the foundation of the League itself is emblemized in the presentation of wampum, the principle of threaded order, and the combing out of Atotarho's snake hair; at the same time the Okayondongheera Yondennase ritual, through which member nations console each other in bereavement, is elaborated, the stately rhetoric being systematically matched with visual patterns and name glyphs incised on the chief's cane (Fig. 44).[9] In recording this historical pact among the five – Mohawk and Seneca to east and west, Onondaga the great central tree, Oneida and Cayuga as the "lesser" two – Cusick anticipates the later incorporation of the Tuscarora by casting them as a sixth family and nation that went south.

A notable feature of Cusick's narrative is its chronology. Hinging on the year of Columbus's arrival – that, is ca. A.D. 1500 – it casts back over the previous two and a half millennia, exactly the "half Sun" of *Inomaca tonatiuh* and comparable Nahuatl texts. It is unashamedly schematic; using the decimal arithmetic common to the Iroquoian and Christian calendars, it proceeds at first by fractions of millennia and centuries, and then, once Atotarho I appears, in A.D. 500, by the reigns of rulers of that name, thirteen in all, each of a half-century or its multiple in length. The Five Nations concept is first mentioned as early as A.D. 0; the Ottawa, Shawnee, and other Algonkin nations intrude into Appalachia by the eighth century. These two dates would find little general acceptance; moreover, an attack by a legendary bear in 1250 fits uneasily between accounts of the league formed by the

Tuscarora the century before when still in their mid-Appalachian home and of Five Nations military engagements with the Muskogee to the south and the Mohican to the east the century after. Nonetheless, precisely because of the longer perspective now offered by archaeology, the span in principle need not seem as unlikely as it once might have done, nor indeed need some of the accompanying details.

When Cusick starts specifying dates toward the end of chapter 2, we are emerging from cosmogony and epic into a landscape still thick with danger-ous beasts. We learn how, in the first millennium B.C., "2200 years before Columbus," the "northern nations" who occupied Lake Erie and Kanawage (the St. Lawrence River) made their first confederacies and how they "re-paired to the south and visited the great Emperor who resided at the Golden City, a capital of the vast empire." Later war destroys them all, leaving the way open for the emergence of the Iroquoians in the first centuries A.D. The identity of this Golden City remains quite obscure, but it is significant that Turtle Island is already credited with a degree of civilization at this early stage. Moreover, the dates given correspond to those of the first Mound Builders, who, as we have seen, were focused on the Ohio.

Chapter 3, beginning at the time of Christ, deals with the Iroquoians proper, heirs to the first civilization. Released from Oswego Mountain, they travel down the Mohawk and Hudson rivers and arrive on the shores of the Atlantic. Then "some of the people went to the banks of the great water towards the midday sun," while "the main company returned as they came" and set up the Goneaseabneh, the league, or Long House, of five families, or nations. Another division then occurs when the sixth nation, the Tuscarora, go to the mouth of the Neuse River in North Carolina. In context, the first division, which linguistically preceded that of the Tuscarora, could well refer to the Cherokee and hence cross-reference the Cherokees' own narra-tive of migration from the north.

Among the many events that mark the reigns of the Atotarhos, from A.D. 500 on, one in particular stands out. Under Atotarho VII, in A.D. 900, a Five Nations embassy reaches the Mississippi, where it is met and lavishly enter-tained: "A duke of Twakanah had collected the people from several towns, came out to meet them the people around them, singing, beating their little drums; after danced the ceremony was performed the band of warriors was invited into the national house" (the idiosyncratic English is a result of Cusick's translating from the Iroquois).[10] This is precisely the moment when Mississippian culture began to flourish in Cahokia. Its impact, mas-sive in the case of the Cherokee in southern Appalachia (as we have seen), was also felt by the Iroquois, not least in their cult of the "three sisters": domesticated plants of ultimately Mexican origin.

At the very least, Cusick's narrative accords with what is independently known about Iroquoian occupation of Appalachia: the Five Nations in the original homeland to the north, the Cherokee migrant in the south. More-over, it offers a chronology of the earlier stages of native culture that for all its obvious idiosyncrasies does not flout what is now known about the Ohio and Mississippi Mound Builder horizons. Above all, as a text it finds impor-tant corroboration in other native histories of Turtle Island.

THE SIOUAN PIPE AND ITS HORIZONS

Among their opponents at the ballgame, a common synonym for battle, the Cherokee counted the Manahoac, Siouan-speakers who lived near them toward the Atlantic shore. When driven from this territory by whites, the Tutelo, other members of the same Manakan division of the Siouans, went to live with the Five Nations as the Tuscarora did, and they added to those of the Onondaga their own choreography and dances (which Speck posited had had Mound architecture as their original setting).[11] At the same time, far to the west toward the Rockies, it was Siouans who claimed the Black Hills and the middle reaches of the Missouri. The story that joins these extremes is generally one of movement from east to west that, through its very extent, finds its hinge in the Mississippian heart of Turtle Island.

The geographically most detailed and precise version of the Siouan east–west story belongs to the Omaha and Quapaw, "upstream" and "down-stream" people respectively (approximated as "U-maha" and "U-qapa"), whose very names point to separation at that key Cahokian stretch of the Mississippi between the Missouri and Ohio confluences. The account dic-tated by a chief of the Poncas, an Omaha division, at Christmas-time 1928 tells how their forebears once lived in the east before journeying down the Ohio to the Mississippi, where they occupied both sides of the river.[12] From there they moved upstream and farther west, seeing and leaving a trail of petroglyphs; having touched the middle reaches of the Missouri, where their sacred pipe was fashioned at Pipestone in A.D. 1300 or so, they established their earthwork forts (*nasa*) toward what became their south-western frontier with the Apache and Comanche, outriders from Anasazi and the Great Basin.

For their part, the Quapaw, or downstream people, also known as Arkan-sa, likewise recalled descending the Ohio and the sojourn on the Cahokian stretch of the Mississippi. Their own journey from this point of separation was in fact much shorter than that of the Omaha; when encountered by the French in the late seventeenth century between Cahokia and the mouth of the Arkansas River, they still had the custom of returning annually to Caho-kia, which by that time was occupied by the Algonkins, who gave that place its present name. Judging again from their own traditions and from details of De Soto's brief encounter with them in 1540, movement farther south had long been effectively blocked for the Quapaw by the considerable power of Natchez, at first also an obstacle for the French. What is more, just this situation is graphically recorded in the three Quapaw skins brought back to France early in the eighteenth century.[13] The oldest surviving texts of their kind from Turtle Island, these painted skins portray the pipe ceremonies central to Mound Builder culture, dances of the Buffalo Society later encountered widely over the Plains, and the exploits of armed warriors or traders, all three being linked to the sky and astronomy. In the last case, adorned with devices that correspond numerically to the internal divisions of Quapaw society, lunar and solar circles mediate between the warriors on the one hand and, on the other, dancers from places represented by groups of domed houses that are joined by a line to a possible fort in which two people are smoking pipes (Plate 16b). Happily for us, these places are glossed alphabetically, the houses corresponding to Quapaw towns placed by French maps on and between the Mississippi and Arkansas rivers: Quapaw itself, which also has a sweat lodge, Toriman, and Ackansas-Osotonoy. Larger in size, the other structure reads "Cahokia," confirming not just the political link of the day but its underpinning in earlier Siouan history.

Echoes of this same story persist among others of the seven grand divisions of the Siouans who occupied the west, like the Mandan; the Wahpeton, who recall once living "south of New York"; and other Dakota or "allies," usually referred to as the Sioux proper. In turn, the Dakota themselves formed a confederacy of seven council-fire places (*Otceti cakowi*), each defined by the widespread Siouan term for dwelling place, *tonwan,* plus such qualifiers as "Mdewakan" (spirit lake), "Wanqpe" (woods), "Ihank" (end), and "Ti-nta" (plains); as the Teton, historically masters of the Plains, these last divided yet again into seven,[14] this time according to a logic of the body and human activity, hence Sihasapa ("black feet"), Sicangu ("burnt thighs"), and Oglala ("scatters one's own"). The social consciousness presupposed by this successive sevenfold layering of society is made explicit in the histories of these Sioux, especially the Teton, which in Fourth World fashion typically concentrate cosmogony into local time and space, moving from great visions of the world's birth to annals or Winter Counts of more recent times.

Certain histories of the southern Teton, Sicangu, and Oglala, that are written in or transcribed from pictographs actually articulate these different levels of time by means of intervening or medieval cycles of seventy-year lifetimes, imaged as a *tipi* circle like that on the Quapaw skin; they therefore impinge critically on any general idea of Siouan and Turtle Island history. The decisive first event in these histories is the visit of the mysterious white buffalo woman who with her gift of the pipe and maize makes civilized life possible. Before this, Left Heron (Oglala) reports that there was no social

organization, while in the visionary tradition[15] best known through the
narratives of Black Elk, Wapoctanxi (Sicangu) reports how, in the ancestral
Black Hills, the prior visit of Eagle Woman revealed to him the need to
respect the fourfold constituency of the world. Wapoctanxi's son High
Hawk puts more emphasis on social development as such: knives and hoes
of seashell, bows of inferior wood, travois pulled by coyote-dogs, fire drills
of yucca and elm, and hides stretched over hollows in which hot stones
were placed in order to boil meat.

In bestowing the pipe, Buffalo Woman affirms its key role in human
affairs, offering the smoke to the four directions and colors of clouds: the
blue east whence she had come; the uncertain south; the west, where the
horse would eventually transform the hunt; and the north, whose breath
would blow the buffalo down into range. Like the pipe, the maize too is
fourfold, coming in kernels of four colors: "squaw-maize," it is literally her
milk, the agricultural product of the hunted animal. For like the Iroquoian
maize-woman, she embodies that plant, just as the snake braids of sage on
her ankles signify green growth.

Inaugural in every sense, the appearance of Buffalo Woman initiates no less
the measured count of time by means of the annalist's year sticks. With her
order established, we move into the series of seventy-year lifetime cycles that
lead up to the start of the annals proper in the year 1700. (In certain Winter
Counts this span is apocopated by having an analogue of Buffalo Woman
stand as the marker for the first year, 1785 in the case of the Yanktonai *Blue
Thunder Count*). Wapoctanxi places more of these lifetime cycles between
Buffalo Woman and the start of the annals than does Left Heron, and High
Hawk adds still more. Yet they concur on main events, like the first Sun
Dance, the first vision of the horse, an enemy concealed among a buffalo
herd, the first horseborne buffalo hunt; they all also provide a list, analogous
to the Iroquois roll call of chiefs, of "bearers" of the pipe bestowed by Buffalo
Woman. Most notably, both Wapoctanxi and High Hawk effectively date her
appearance around A.D. 900. This precise inauguration is interestingly corroborated by the east Dakota (Santee) Winter Count seen by Lewis and Clark,
which, intricately carved on a long pole, covered the thousand years that
preceded their nineteenth-century visit.

Not much scholarly credence has been given to this dating, High Hawk's
editor Curtis having completely distorted it by reducing it tenfold. Particular exception has been taken to the fact that horses appear before Columbus
(shown disembarking by High Hawk); yet if we read Left Heron closely we
see that the horse is the shape of a cloud. Rather, like apprenticeships, the
lifetimes gauge the social tension between planting and hunting, in which
the dream of the horse implanted by Buffalo Woman becomes ever stronger:
Only in the last cycle (1631–1700) is the horse finally mounted and used.

Given what is now known about the Mississippian culture that flourished from A.D. 900 or so, these Sioux histories demand more serious attention. Not only do they provide a wholly appropriate date for the "gift" of the superior four-colored maize that, introduced from Mexico, had disseminated from Cahokia at that time, they also indicate the right setting, at the center that lies between south and north, "downstream" and "upstream," as it does between eastern ocean and western mountains. (For his part, High Hawk unambiguously links the beginnings of the ancestral east–west journey with the ocean – "the Great Water beside which they lived" – when discussing the origins of the first Sioux tools and their mussel-shell hoes.) Indeed, Blue Thunder's Yanktonai count specifically associates Buffalo Woman with the mouth of the Missouri, the Cahokian center of the four-part diplomacy emblemized by those elaborate Mound Builder pipes. Josephy usefully summarizes our current scholarly version of events:

> It is not known definitely how the Mississippian Culture arose; presumably it began locally with ideas and systems derived from the Hopewell Culture, then about A.D. 900 received a strong agricultural base, together with an infusion of new cultural traits, that came from the Huastec area of Mexico. . . . An intensified agriculture, based on new and more productive strains of corn and new implements, supported the growth of the Mississippian Culture, which was marked, also, by . . . more tightly knit social systems organized around new religious beliefs and ceremonies.
> . . . The new stage appears to have extended westward on to the plains all along the front. . . . In the north, Woodland Siouan-speakers with strong Mississippian influences moved to the middle Missouri Valley.[16]

On this basis we may take a further step back and note the fact that in the Sicangu histories year spans are also given for the cultural beginnings that characterize the period before Buffalo Woman. Both Wapoctanxi and High Hawk assign to it the two millennia that, exactly as in Cusick's Iroquoian history, return us to the 1000 B.C. turning point out of the Archaic into the Woodland and Mound Builder cultures identified with the Ohio. Archaeologically there is every reason to link the Siouans likewise with this earlier Mound Builder phase, even if in this remoter case their texts, through images of nascent society and the petroglyphs of ancestral trails, offer no focus comparable with the Mississippian vision of A.D. 900.

Whether or not the Iroquoian cross-references in these Siouan histories are held to be anything more than chance, and whether or not they are believed to relate at all to archaeologically established phases of Mound Builder culture, the fact remains that they represent a time–space that corresponds with what is independently known about Siouan history in Turtle Island. What is more, the first of the histories to be published, Wapoctanxi's, in 1893 (recorded in 1888–9), did so well before such knowledge could have been gleaned from anywhere but Siouan tradition itself. Along the lines of the *Popol vuh* and the Mesoamerican model, these histories begin by estab-

Figure 45. Tipi beside earth lodge. (The Flame Winter Count, 1793.)

lishing a broad frame within which more local and recent experience may then make its sense, this literary effect being matched socially by the successive levels governed by the cipher seven. Establishing a first base even broader than that of the Siouans and defending it ideologically against white invaders, Left Heron here makes reference to the seven council fires that "included all the North American Indians."

Hence, these records of charter visions of pipe and maize, brilliantly elaborated in the Oglala narrative of Black Elk, serve as touchstones for later experience, not just with the Dakota but their southern neighbors, for instance the Ponca, who have their own version of the buffalo "gift" of maize; the Osage, with their fourfold origin chant; and the Omaha, with their Wahta tradition. A similar case might be argued for the Hako ceremony of the (non-Siouan) Pawnee, which possibly draws on the Arkansas mound culture of their Caddoan kin and which enabled Alice Fletcher, for one, better to understand the time depth and rhythms of Plains history.[17] In the Sicangu annals that follow in Wapoctanxi's and High Hawk's texts and that exist separately in other Sioux divisions, events fall into patterns that go beyond local hostility and ambition when referred back to these grander beginnings.

Herself one of the sky people whom Black Elk describes as being "like stars," the white Buffalo Woman anticipates other beings who "fall from the sky," saliently in the meteor showers of 1833, at the same time as she prefigures the albino buffalo who bring good luck and issue timely warnings. The westerly direction she assigns to the Dakota is coincident with the great artery of the Missouri, whose behavior when iced over or in flood is caught in strikingly dramatic year images. Her gift of maize affects social relations within and beyond the tribe, in the dialectic between planters and hunters now horseborne, between sedentary Mound Builder earth lodges (*ti tanka*) and mobile tents (*ti pi;* Fig. 45). Offered in four directions, the pipe anticipates missions of war and diplomacy that reach to bands and nations at the bounds of Turtle Island. The emblems of these people, who in many cases offer reciprocal accounts, appear from the start of the earliest counts (John K. Bear's Yanktonai count begins in 1682) and include emblems for fellow Siouans like the Hidatsa, their hair streaked with red clay; the Mandans in their earth lodges; the cropped-head Omaha; the Ponca with their roach; the "loud-voice" Assiniboin and the Winnebago, Algonkins like the Siksika; the Cheyenne; the stockadad Ojibwa; Caddoans like the maize-growing Pawnee and Arikara; and the Kiowa and Ute neighbors of Anasazi and the Great Basin. And Buffalo Woman's allocation of this part of Turtle Island to Native Americans sustains keen awareness of intrusion by foreigners likewise distinguished by nationality, like the French trader of 1684, Villasur's defeated Spanish platoon of 1720, and English-speaking missionaries after 1800. Accompanying shifts in technology, markets, and health are also vividly registered; hence kettles (1780), umbrellas (1785), horseshoes (1802), whiskey (1821), the dollar coin (1833), the school pen (1879), and a litany of disease (cramp, smallpox, whooping cough, puerperal fever; 1845 saw the fourth plague of measles).[18]

These various threads are concisely interwoven in a very widely reported event of 1823: the first major military attack made by the United States west of the Mississippi, in which certain of the Dakota divisions played a part and which provides the first event of Jaw's Hunkpapa count. The objects of the attack were the towns of the Arikara, horticulturalists who, like the Pawnee, are designated by a maize cob; after their defeat, great quantities of maize were in fact looted from their caches, or silos. Uneasiness about the whole exercise is shown in the different perspectives on it given in north and south Teton and in Yanktonai counts (Fig. 46). The Miniconjou counts of Lone Dog and the Swan depict a U.S. soldier firing directly into the pallisaded earth-lodge town of the Arikara and hence indict General Leavenworth and his men as the instigators of the attack. The Sicangu Wapoctanxi divides the blame, showing the maize cob that denotes the Arikara threatened by both a U.S. gun and a Sioux arrow, while the Oglala Cloud Shield features these two weapons, held respectively by a white man (hat) and a Sioux (long hair) in a heraldic device indicative of alliance. More complex is the case of the Yankton and Yanktonai, who in fact provided no fewer than five hundred of the seven hundred Dakota allies, for their counts tend to ignore the military attack as such and name the winter after just its "maize." In Blue Thunder's count we simply see the cache of dried maize that provided food in abundance that winter, no mention being made of the looted source. The Hunkpapa count of High Dog goes even further, attributing the maize to a "harvest" favored by the Great Spirit; that of Swift Dog even suggests that the maize in question was looted by whites (not Dakota) from Dakota fields (not Arikara silos). In all this, the common reference point of these annals is to be presupposed precisely through their differences of view.

Finally, through the figure who begins the Winter Count and year-stick chronology in the first place, also a consequence of Buffalo Woman's charter, the larger arena is confirmed reflexively by the sheer provenance and cohesion of these texts. Technically the practice may have been connected

a   b   c   d   e

Figure 46. The attack on Arikara in the year 1823: versions of the event in the Sioux Winter Counts. (a) "White soldiers made their first appearance here." U.S. soldier with gun fires into the pallisaded Arikara town. (*Lone Dog,* Miniconjou-Teton.) (b) "General Leavenworth first appeared and the Dakotas aided in an attack on the Arikara." U.S. gun above Sioux arrow fires into maize cob, the Arikara emblem. (*Wapoctanxi,* Sicangu-Teton.) (c) "The Dakotas joined the whites in an expedition up the Missouri river against the Rees." A line physically joins the allies, armed with their respective weapons. (*Cloud Shield,* Oglala-Teton.) (d) "Cache of dried maize." Maize that has been dried and stored is looted. (*British Museum Count* [Howard 1979], Yanktonai.) (e) "The year the corn crop was plenty, the Great Spirit blessed the tribe." A maize stalk growing in the open. (*Swift Dog* and *High Dog,* Hunkpapa-Teton.)

with Mexico, as Pima and Aztec analogues suggest – Mexico was, after all, the source of Cahokian maize. Nonetheless, shared by Siouans and many neighbors in Turtle Island, this cult of chronology has decided qualities of its own, a perspective that alternates between summer Sun Dance and frozen winter night and that had illuminated a vision no less than a thousand years old by the time its adherents came to relive it in the Ghost Dance of 1890.[19]

NORTHERN MIGRATIONS

Linguistically, Siouan and Iroquoian belong to the same phylum, as does Caddoan, for that matter. Not so Algonquian, as the people themselves suggest. The term applied by the Ojibwa to their western neighbors the Dakota, "enemies" or "snakes" (*Naudawa-sewug,* whence "Sioux"), equally included the eastern Iroquois, yet not fellow Algonkin like the Ottawa. Reciprocally, on the Plains, the Ponca distinguished the Algonkin from fellow Siouans by referring to them as "not us."[20] At the same time, while Siouan and Iroquoian histories claim Mound Builder origins, those of the Algonkin do not. The homeland recalled by peoples of this language family lies rather in the frozen north beyond the Mound Builders arena. In more southerly latitudes their experience has typically been of incessant migration from sea to sea, east to west and west to east. For the Shawnee, at one moment intermediary between the Atlantic and the Cherokee (the Swimmer had Shawnee blood) and at the next migrant to "the remotest West," this journeying has had overtly cosmic significance; for their ancient intimates the Kickapoo, it has meant an eventual homeland in Coahuila, Mexico.

So well established on the eastern seaboard that through French and English they named much of both it and the interior, at the time of mid-seventeenth-century European incursion the Algonkin claimed to have been settled there for not more than 350 years or so.[21] No earlier than the start of the fourteenth century had they forced a way eastward from Ohio through the Appalachians, between Iroquois and Cherokee, and laid claim to the mouths of the four great rivers Potomac, Susquehanna, Lenapewhittuck (Delaware), and Mohicanittuck (Hudson). According to such sources as the *Mohican Narrative* of Aupumut, there they cultivated the three sisters – maize, beans, squash – of their Iroquoian neighbors and formed the Wapanachki, or Eastern, Confederacy, the "ancient convenant of our ancestors" the Unami (Turtle), Unalachtgo (Turkey), and Minsi (Wolf) divisions of the Lenape, plus the Nanticoke and Kanawke, who proceeded south to Virginia, Powhatan's polity, and the further offshoot of the Mohican, who pressed on into Connecticut and Massachusetts.[22] Prominent among the settlers on the coast, where they acquired the name Delaware, the Lenape used beads of wampum to keep an exact count of their years there (370, in 1676) and were known for having first sighted Cartier's ships. According to the Wyandot, or Huron, historian Dooyentate, their image of them – "great dark animals with broad wings spitting out fire and uttering the voice of thunder" (p. 3) – was widely cited and finds echoes in the year glyph of the Pamunkey and the records of the Cherokee.

An earlier home of these Algonkin had been the Ohio valley, where they had resided for "many hundred years" and which country they had reached by pushing eastward from across the Mississippi. The main narrative of this epoch also belongs to the Lenape, who, though later concentrated on the Atlantic shore, never forgot the larger eastward movement. It was they who distinguished the three main Algonkin territories that resulted from it: on the coast, around the Ohio, and west of the Mississippi. Their particular attachment to the middle stage is apparent from more than their own accounts. For in acknowledging their central position, the Cherokee called them grandfather, as did the Wyandot, also Iroquoian in speech and long-standing allies to the north. When orchestrating his great Ohio campaign in the early 1760s, the Ottawa Pontiac appealed to the authority of none other than the Lenape – indeed, to that of an inscribed stick given to a member of that nation by the "Master of Life."[23] For their own part, when driven entirely from the coast they successfully reclaimed Ohio lands to live on from former Algonkin neighbors like the Miami and Potawatomi.

In order to gain their place in Ohio, the Lenape, crossing the Mississippi together with their Wyandot allies, had to overcome its previous inhabitants, "a very powerful nation who had many large towns built on the great rivers flowing through their land."[24] These can be none other than Mound Builders defended by impressive earthworks and fortifications. By their own account, only after protracted military effort did the Lenape succeed in gaining a foothold east of the Mississippi. However, having displaced these former inhabitants, who fled down the Mississippi, they adopted their towns and pyramids and were responsible for what is archaeologically known as intrusive activity, like burial, in older structures. As a matter of fact, along with Illini, Miami, and other neighbors, they also named these places in their language, from Chillicothe, with its shell portrait of the Algonkin epic hero Manabozho, to Cahokia, with its bird-snake Piasa;[25] Cahokia was also the site of Pontiac's death. Moreover, upon their return to Ohio from the coast, they occupied territories closely defined by mounds, on the Scioto, Muskingum, White, and other rivers that flow into the Ohio, and defended them legally from U.S. intrusion as ancient seats in their tradition.

Literally parallel to this story, in the sense of latitude, is that of the Anishinabe, the "original" Algonkin who lived and live farther to the north. Here a whole cluster of nations – Mississauga, Ottawa, Potawatomi, Ojibwa – shared not just a near-identical speech but the memory of northern beginnings where Turtle Island emerges specifically from ice water and where Nanabush contemplating the divisions of men actually sits atop the North Pole (thus the Mississauga historian Kahkewaquonaby, Peter Jones).[26] Running counter to that of the Lenape, east to west, their own migration story tells how their ancestors had moved upstream from the ocean and the St. Lawrence estuary to Moneaung (Hochelaga, or Montreal) and into the Great Lakes, passing in the case of the Ojibwa to their westernmost drainage, the grand continental watershed that also divides the Mississippi from the Arctic Ocean. Similar accounts are given by yet other northern Algonkin groups, like the Cree and the Sauk and Fox. At the same time, the Siksika, and the Plains Algonkin specifically, recall their own movement yet farther west from the Ojibwa watershed. In the Arapaho and Cheyenne Ghost Dance songs there are precise evocations of the Turtle Island (read by Mooney as Mackinaw on Lake Superior)[27] where they once dwelt; indeed, of the emergence of the earth as a turtle and its gift to them of the pipe.

In the birchbark scrolls of the Midewiwin, the cult that centered precisely on this Ojibwa watershed, the great migration is vividly recorded over four principal stages and coincides with the path of Mide teaching itself. These correspond on the one hand with the fourfold genesis of the origin scrolls (which similarly feature the turtle) and on the other with the four-degree east–west path depicted on the initiation scrolls. Despite their highly ritual nature, the Mide migration scrolls carry a fair amount of hydrographical detail – rapids, falls, promontories, portages – especially by the fourth and last stage of the journey, to the great temple and atlas of the world, Lake Superior (Midewegun) and the watershed.

Ojibwa sources, as well as giving a route, state how long ago the migration was undertaken, concurring in the claim that they reached their goal no fewer than three centuries before 1790, that is, at just the Columbian hinge used by Cusick in his history. A plate of virgin copper owned by Tugwauganay, great-uncle of the historian Warren, marked the passage of time since then by "eight deep indentations, denoting the number of his ancestors who had passed away."[28] A hat incised beside the third generation marked the first appearance of a European in that region (ca. 1610). Then, just as in comparable Iroquoian and Siouan texts, this chronological sequence is preceded by another that deals rather in millennia. Eshkwaykeezhik, nephew of the great scroll master Powassan, was told that periods on the origin scrolls referred not to "one day, one week or one month" but to 2,000 years (compare Wapoctanxi), "maybe 4000 years." These periods are matched graphically on his scroll by four trees, suggesting the kind of embedded numeracy present in Cusick's account of how the Onandaga tree flourished between A.D. 500 and 1500.

How, then, should these two ancestral Algonkin traditions, with their common lexis of Turtle and Manabozho, be interrelated, running as they do in contrary directions over the half-millennium or so that preceded Cartier? In his account of the drive eastward to the Atlantic, Aupumut states that its starting point beyond the Mississippi had been from a place "west by north"; the Turtle, preeminent in the north of Turtle Island, named the pipe-bearer division of the Lenape, and it gave the Arapaho their pipe. In any case, linguistic evidence alone attributes the oldest form of the language to the "Shield Algonkin" who are supposed long to have been inhabitants of the northern forests.

Then, from their more northern position, the Anishinabe complement Lenape accounts of the Ohio and Mississippi Mound Builders. For while Anishinabe texts as authoritative as the Mide scrolls record movement from east to west in the northern realm, others point southward beyond it to an origin, if not of migration, then of culture. One Mide scribe, Everwind, identified the ocean of origin not with the barren shores of the North Atlantic but with the Gulf of Mexico, into which the Mississippi flows. One material support for this horizon is the moneta shell central to Mide ritual: This creature flourishes not in the cold Atlantic assigned to it by Warren but in tropical water, whence it more immediately reached the mounds of Alabama. Similarly, while the more recent history of the Siksika acknowledges the east–west road, a tradition from "very long ago" points again to origins in the south that have everything to do with culture and "fixing up the world as we see it today" by a patron hero called Old Man.[29]

Another indirect strand of evidence links Ojibwa ritual and that of their Siouan neighbors in Wisconsin, the Winnebago, as it does these in turn with Oneota, the northern offshoot of Cahokia that lay en route to the copper mines on Lake Superior. The turtle, bear, and other figures in the Mide scrolls exactly reproduce the clan-effigy mounds in Winnebago territory; the Winnebago epic combines features that point on the one hand to the ballgame insignia of the Mound Builders and on the other to the time shifts and choreography of the Mide trance journey. A similar case has been made for the calendar sticks once owned by the Winnebago chief Tshizunhaukau, with its moon-phase symbols and solar–lunar correlation.[30]

Many key features of Algonkin involvement in Turtle Island history are sharply focused by the *Walum Olum,* the Lenape text in native and alphabetic script published by Rafinesque in his *American Nations* (1836). Indeed, were its authenticity more assured,[31] this work would constitute not just the "Hoosier Iliad" dreamt of by Eli Lilly but one of the Fourth World's major classics. In Fourth World fashion, it works its way from cosmos to politics, beginning with the emergence of Turtle Island itself and the epic of Nanabush. The fourfold patterning of the glyphs here, and indeed throughout the texts, adheres to that of the scrolls and especially the songboards of the Mide, as Brinton, Mooney, and others have remarked. Pointing to an original homeland in the "freezing north," the long migrations that ensue follow the course from west to east reported by the Lenape to Beatty, Heckewelder, and others later in the nineteenth century. The narrative here includes a sequence of sachems or chiefs, forty plus forty in all, whose names and deeds are depicted by just the type of name-and-head glyph found all over Turtle Island since Mound Builder days and seen in the celebrated roll call of the Iroquois League, the rosters of the Dakota, and Mississauga and other Algonkin treaty signatures. The name glyph of the scribe, Olumapi, even typifies the standard fourfold stanza of the text, while those of Taguachi and Huminiend ("Maize Grinder"), who went south for maize, propose a direct link between the Lenape and Cahokian agriculture.

As scholars have noted, even if shaped into a single text by Rafinesque (as, say, the *Kalevala* was by Lönnrot), the script of the *Walum Olum* – fourfold stanzas, sachem names – and its story gainsay nothing that has been discovered independently about the Lenape and Turtle Island, in some cases well after Rafinesque's time. Lenape elders themselves have, after all, accepted it as a version of their history. That it is an unwelcome text is clear. But that could also have to do with its political memory. Like Algonkin texts assuredly genuine, in defending the Ohio as a prime focus in ancient and modern Turtle Island it has upset yet again the official U.S. doctrine of "American" prehistory and history, touching the particularly raw nerve of the Ohio. By expropriating this region and flouting its own notions of legality, the United States converted itself from a coastal to a continental power; and its defense was a main objective of the campaign orchestrated by the Ottawa Pontiac in 1762–3, in which the Lenape were much involved, and of the last-ditch and truly international crusade of the Shawnee Tecumseh in 1812, which also embraced the Muskogee Mound Builder heirs of the south.

8

Tahuantinsuyu

LOCATING INCA POWER

Throughout Tahuantinsuyu there is only one known historical record, that of the Inca. According to the partial transcription in Guaman Poma's chronicle, it begins with the four ages of the American world, here the *suyu* of time; these then lead directly into the succession of Inca emperors – their official characters and their pattern of conquests, wives, and captains – from the first, Manco Capac, to the twelfth, Huascar, Atahuallpa's half-brother and Pizarro's victim. *Runa yndio* and other documents from the *suyu*s offer only hints of alternative or contradictory traditions. Moreover, in its singular purpose this Cuzco-based account has little to say about the several millennia enjoyed by civilization in Tahuantinsuyu prior to the Inca: We look in vain for more than mention of even immediate predecessors like the Chimu, let alone the prelude of incised stone at Chavin and Sechin. This absence may well stem from the fact that documents in native script, the now unintelligible *quipu*s discussed in Chapter 2, were so little transcribed, a situation that contrasts completely with that of Mesoamerica. At the same time, like production in the Inca state generally, the past appears to have been centralized and incorporated into one system as nowhere else in the Fourth World.

In Guaman Poma's text, the imperial succession crosses a threshold in the reign of the ninth emperor, Pachacuti (1438–71). Before him, Inca reigns and conquests are extended back in decimal time cycles over one and a half millennia, further emphasizing their preeminence: Even Christ and Saint Bartholomew are intercalated between the second and third Incas. With and after him, there is a count of actual years that ends in his great-grandson Huascar's death and the subsequent story of resistance from Vilcabamba, known also through accounts by Titu Cusi Yupanqui and others,[1] being taken up to Tupac Amaru I's execution in Cuzco in 1572. Also, starting with Pachacuti's predecessor Viracocha, the geographical detail of conquest becomes far more precise as Chincha and the coast are reached and Collasuyu is extended to Chile.

Historically the shift indicated by Pachacuti's reign[2] corresponds to the fact that he and his son Tupac Yupanqui (1471–93) consolidated the Inca *tahuantinsuyu,* reconstructing Cuzco as a suitable capital (Fig. 47). Other *tahuantinsuyu*s had certainly preceded this one. Guaman Poma himself touches on the precedent of his own Chincha city Ayacucho/Huamanaga, and Garcilaso notes that of Colla Tiahuanaco (I xviii), both of which had ruled *tahuantinsuyu*s in their day. Yet Cuzco eclipsed them both in organization and scale, not just in the Andean area but in the whole Fourth World. In particular, the Inca empire was distinguished by the creation of a *quipu* bureaucracy that Guaman Poma assures us was capable of dealing with every organizational detail, as well as the privileging of a pastoral discourse whose economic origins were inseparable from those of the *quipu,* the tally of flocks.

Unique in the ancient Fourth World precisely because of its pastoral tradition, the Andes provided a habitat for four types of camelid: the llama and the alpaca, the huanaco, and the vicuña. These animals differ somewhat in size, the llama being the largest; in quality and color of wool, the vicuña having the finest and the alpaca the most; and in range, the huanaco extending down onto the Argentine pampa. Most important, only the first two have been successfully domesticated, the llama possibly deriving from the huanaco.

Economically the llama (the term used here for both domesticates) served as a multiple resource for the predecessors of the Inca[3] and combined features that elsewhere America provided not at all or separately, for example through such other mammals as the large edible buffalo; the bighorn sheep, whose long hair was woven in Anasazi; the fine-skinned deer; and the travaux-tugging dog. For the Andeans ate its low-cholesterol flesh, fresh or as *charqui;* wore its skin as sandals or cut it into thongs to secure the foot plough (*taclla*) or into bottles to carry water across the desert; turned its fat into tallow; spread its dung as manure or gathered it for fuel; made its tendons into slings for the scarecrow, the herder, and the soldier; shaped its bones into weaving instruments; and spun and wove its wool into cloth both coarse (*auasca*) and fine (*cunbe*) and into the threads and main cord of the *quipu* (though surviving examples are generally of cotton). As well as singly providing these organic and commodity resources, and in the absence of any analogue except the human being itself, the llama was also widely exploited for transport; and through breeding it compounded its value. Guaman Poma places the beginning of domestication in his world ages;

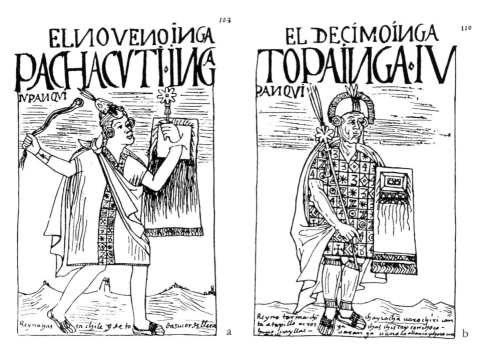

Figure 47. (a) Pachacuti and (b) Tupac Yupanqui. (Guaman Poma, *Nueva corónica*, pp. 108, 110.)

archaeologically it goes back to about 4000 B.C. at centers like Lake Titicaca, where llamas served mainly as suppliers of wool and for transport (to the Pacific coast) and Ayacucho and Junin farther north in Chinchasuyu, where they were used mainly for meat. However, Moche ceramics from the time of Christ supply cameos of load-bearing llamas; one looks back over its shoulder.[4]

By all accounts, Tiahuanaco in Collasuyu was whence the Inca drew support when they came to establish their own center of power at Cuzco. It was the Aymara-speakers, or Colla, who claimed that the Inca made off with Colla animals in order to build up herds of their own.[5] From the Inca side, it was more a question of deference to the llama typical of the Collao during royal initiation and other ceremonies. That the Inca, from the time of Manco Capac, acknowledged their origin to have been in Titicaca is made quite clear by Guaman Poma (pp. 84, 265); they favored the white llama that the Collas themselves had gone so far as to revere as a tribal ancestor, and they would deck out such llamas, known as *napa*s, with red shirts and necklaces and gold earrings. In the chapter of his *Nueva corónica* that he devotes to the festivals typical respectively of the Inca and of the four *suyu*s of the empire, Guaman Poma also shows how pastoral songs of the Colla and Collasuyu were held in particular esteem at the royal court of Cuzco, to the extent of being sung in Aymara, the Colla language (pp. 319, 129).

At the hinge in Inca history, under Pachacuti, conqueror and acquirer of territory especially at the expense of the Colla, and Tupac Yupanqui, the great consolidator under whom herd units ran into many millions, the pastoral reached its apotheosis. Impossible to detect in the Kalisasaya carvings at Tiahuanaco, where power is celebrated in more ancient predatory feline and ophidian motifs,[6] the llama image begins to impose itself, especially in stone, metal, and woven artifacts. The territory becomes the pasture and the Inca its divine herder whom only "outlaws" disobey.

PASTURE WITHIN ITS FENCE

A prime Incaic use of the llama was military. By mobilizing troops and ranks of llamas for both transport and food on the hoof little affected by season and harvest, the Inca disposed a state army unparalleled in America whose campaigns related less to ritual than to policies of permanent territorial gain and which in its day proved largely irresistible. In his chapter on the world ages that preceded the Inca (pp. 48–78), Guaman Poma makes much of the military potential that went with the llama breeding characteristic of the latter two ages: the Purun and the Auca (whose name means "warlike") (see Fig. 56). Then after military conquest and as part of Inca policies of pacification and colonization, the llama had no less critical a role. In the case of people already in possession of herds, these and all their reproductive goods, in Murra's words, "became the property of the Inca crown, which then reissued some of it back to the inhabitants and set public boundaries"; again, after conquest "all llama were defined at least in theory as state property."[7] In practice, no other interest group was permitted to keep herds that might in any way rival those of the Inca, the former being linguistically distinguished from the latter by the respective terms *huaccha* ("poor") and *capac* ("mighty").

For all these and yet other purposes, the Inca instituted a program of breeding, distinguishing and counting types and ages of beast down to the minutest detail by means of the *quipu* and conducting a thorough census in the month Aya Marcay (November: Guaman Poma, p. 256). Also, through running and other athletic trials (which conjoin the two meanings of "race"), they prized the strongest and fittest beasts. *Runa yndio* further tells us (chap. 10) that the prowess revealed by such trials was associated with the enhanced penis displayed by golden and silver llama statuettes that have survived from Inca times. By means of controlled reproduction, the llama came to acquire another order of value, one of permanency more like that of the precious metals with which it was equated and into which it was cast ceremonially, while through multiplication and increase it became literally capital (whence "cattle"), perhaps its most distinctive role of all in the plan of the Inca *tahuantinsuyu*.

For, according to Inca policy, llamas were granted as capital to settlers in conquered territory where previously there had been few or none; known as *mitima,* these grantees were further encouraged to migrate by being made exempt from labor tribute and other state obligations. Through the device of the llama grant, the Inca secured their hold on the coastal valleys, filling in and completing Condesuyu as an imperial quarter; and between the larger and repeatedly extended Colla and Chinchasuyu they removed populations over thousands of miles – no fewer than four thousand *mitima* families were seen journeying up to occupy former Canari lands in Ecuador and Chinchasuyu when Pizarro was already at Caxamarca. Herding was speci-fied as the first of the skills required of a *mitima.* The head shepherds among them and the longest-standing came from the Collao. In return for their official generosity, the Inca expected to gain from the multiplication of their grantees' animals, taking, as it were, interest from capital. They also ex-pected cloth woven from llama and alpaca wool to be supplied – universally recognized as "one of the main bonds and symbols of citizenship."[8] They might even be seen to have created a market demand for the *mitima* and for llama producers generally in the strict laws they instituted, which, accord-ing to Guaman Poma (pp. 272–3), obliged every community, however small, regularly to sacrifice these animals in order to consume their blood and meat.

Above all, through the *mitima*s (those who "leave" their first homes, having an interest [in both senses] in being displaced), the Inca achieved stability for Tahuantinsuyu as a continuous territory within its frontier, or outer fence of pasture. In this respect, it is highly significant that of the four *suyu* the one that most resisted conquest, the Antisuyu of the *montaña* and valleys of the upper Amazon, was also the one known to be least adaptable to llama herding.

In all these respects, at the time of the European invasion nothing like Tahuantinsuyu existed elsewhere in America, the difference being directly attributable to the resource inherited by the Inca as Andeans and heirs to Tiahuanaco and exploited by them as architects of their *tahuantinsuyu:* the domesticated camelid. This key economic difference doubtless relates in turn to the different ways in which the four-quarter model of tribute was developed in Mesoamerica and Tahuantinsuyu. The former yielded only commodity tribute, which was collected along routes that often ran through neutral or hostile territory within and between quarters. In the latter, despite an even less tractable terrain, the four quarters (*tahuantin-suyu*) were territori-ally more compact, with no unintegrated slices at the diagonals; the internal packaging of land down to the last *ayllu* was more standardized; only one language was spoken over far greater areas; and the degree of metropolitan control was much firmer over all aspects of commodity and labor tribute. The empire was consolidated entirely, like pasture inside its fence. Even the sky became pasture, allotted to Yacana, the celestial llama at its center.[9]

These characteristics of Tahuantinsuyu were surely identified by those who lived near its borders. The Amazonians saw more difference between themselves and the Inca than between them and the similarly pastoral Europeans, and the Chibcha identified an *amauta* who visited Sogamoso by referring to the llama he brought with him. Above all, the Mapuche, who to the south record paying tribute in llamas to the Inca and regularly raiding the empire to get them back, had a persistent dream of wealth valued primarily in llamas and women (the pastoral equation of the Semitic Tenth Commandment). In one story about an old man desiring a young bride, we even see llama wealth inverting the morality traditional to South America outside Tahuantinsuyu whereby the prospective husband, by working for and lending service to her father, earns his partner; thanks to Inca influence, in this Mapuche case the old man simply buys his, paying his *quempu* (father-in-law) in metal and cloth and above all in live bearers of meat and wool.[10]

HERDERS AND FLOCKS

So fundamental was herding to the Inca enterprise that in Tahuantinsuyu the social relations it implies as an activity were transformed ideologically to become a model for the state itself; indeed, it arguably provided the enabling concept of state in the first place. This is so for the two dominant social models of the Inca state: that which relates ruler to ruled, and that which relates ruler to authority. For both, a wealth of evidence is provided by the native sources used so far; in addition we have the eleven hymns, or prayers, recorded in the sixteenth century in Quechua by Molina, that make up the liturgy of the Zithuwa, a ceremony of cleansing and purgation held in the month Coya Raimi (September).[11]

First, the *Zithuwa Hymns* repeatedly equate flock with folk, as subjects, both, of the Inca "who founded Cuzco." Requests are made, in the same terms and the same phrase, that under the Inca both people and animals (*runa llama*) should enjoy peace and safety, should increase and multiply, and should not fall into enemy hands or stray into sin.

> O dew of the world
> Viracocha
> inner dew
> Viracocha
> you who dispose by saying
> "Let there be greater and lesser gods"

great Lord
dispose that here
men do multiply
fortunately.

. . .

Let me live in peace and in
safety,
Father Viracocha,
with food and sustenance,
with maize and llamas,
with all manner
of skills.
Abandon me not,
Remove me
from my enemies
from danger
from all threat
of being cursed, ungrateful
or repudiated.

– J. H. Rowe 1953:92

The parallels here with Semitic liturgy and the logic of, say, "The Lord is my Shepherd" (Psalm 23) are so strong that an influence via the Spanish Christian mission might be suspected were it not for numerous independent testimonies to the nature of the Zithuwa. What is more, while obviously a piece of spiritual rhetoric, the flock–folk equation proves to have a firm material and economic basis in Tahuantinsuyu. For the sheer tally of the two orders of unit in question, animal and human, was consigned to the recording device used initially for the former: the *quipu*. This prime piece of the herder's equipment (Guaman Poma, p. 351) registered animal units with decimal place-value notation; displayed colors as semantic variables that corresponded in the first instance to those of and to actual llama wool; and had a structure of cord and dependent thread that even replicated the main-cord custom of llama tethering.

The competence of the *quipu* as a human as opposed to a merely animal tally in Tahuantinsuyu can be judged not least from the fact, recorded in the *Nueva corónica,* that the llama census of the month Aya Marcay (November) was also a human census; Guaman Poma even makes an implicit comparison between the selection of males and of females from both species for particular purposes: for instance, male troops for warfare, and chosen virgins for wool production (p. 257). In another chapter (pp. 193–234), the *Nueva corónica* details the categories of age and usefulness, ten for male and ten for female, according to which the human census, or "visit," was conducted. Extended to the minutest element of value in the state, reliably and retrospectively over the years the *quipu* accounting system in fact had as a major feature the noting of absence and nonperformance. The Quechua term for this failure in conduct, *hucha,* was noted on the *quipu* as greater (*hatun*) or lesser (*huchuy:* p. 361). For its part, à propos ceremonies that accompanied irrigation work, *Runa yndio* (chap. 31) notes darkly how absences of goods and of personnel were recorded on official *quipus.* By these means and through a matching apparatus of police, whose initially pastoral function is patent from the official title (*llama michic; michic*), the state was able precisely to gauge quantities not just of commodity but also of labor tribute rendered.

Outraged by Spanish lawlessness and lamenting the demise of Tahuantinsuyu, Guaman Poma in his day significantly appealed to the notion of the *michic* as a last means of preventing disaster and of restoring order to society. At the same time he underpinned the traditional flock–folk equation of Tahuantinsuyu most succinctly when complaining to Philip III that in viceregal Peru the Indians bore the burden of tax payments like domesticated animals while mestizos and other mixed-bloods exempt from tax were allowed to remain wild like the vicuña (pp. 890, 1153, 215).

From the nonperformance and noncompliance monitored by the *quipu* it was but a step to the rhetoric of disobedience, crime, and sin and corresponding retribution in the name of the state. One of Guaman Poma's chapters is devoted precisely to orders and types of official punishment (*Nueva corónica,* pp. 301–14); one such was reserved for those who simply moved without permission from their allotted place in the realm. In other words, the subjects of Tahuantinsuyu, like their flocks, could be considered contained and penned, pastured elements of the great Pax Incaica, safe as such from the threat of enemies and the barbaric wild beyond its rim.

When it comes to relations not so much between ruler and ruled as between ruler and authority, the *Zithuwa Hymns* further highlight the pastoral model. For here, in what emerges as a truly monotheistic impulse, monarchy is endorsed by the supreme spiritual principle known as Viracocha and as the "creator" (*camac*) of earth and people, and so on. Invoked in most of the hymns, this figure is asked to guard the Inca just as the Inca guards his flocks. Throughout Tahuantinsuyu the rites of this supreme herder can be shown to have been imposed over local deities and *huacas* (*Nueva corónica,* pp. 261–73). Irreverence beneath the Inca imposition is shown up in *Runa yndio,* which basically remains loyal to the lightning god Pariacaca and other shamanist *huacas* of the region that had been subordinated to Viracocha; this source also tells how the priests imported and appointed by the Inca left their posts on hearing about Pizarro's advance (chap. 18). This last detail is significant also because it indicates how far religion, or "the church," as it is often called, had become subject to and regulated by the state, exposing the universally imposed Viracocha or divine herder to have been in practice a back projection of and from the secular power of the Inca themselves. Similarly, though formally distinct and guarded by special herders, who possibly included the *aclla,* or chosen virgins of the sun (another exclusively Inca institution), the church herds relied on the state for allocations of pasture, just as ritual llama sacrifice imposed by the Inca served *mitima* and state-herding interests.

On the same subject of Inca-appointed priests, *Runa yndio* in passing specifies their period of service as fifteen days, the *chicta quilla,* or official half-month. This indicates in turn how the appropriation of divine authority coincided in practice with the institution of a state year calendar, one that could encompass in a single standardized system the various rhythms of agricultural, curing, and the myriad other rituals of society as well as the demands of material tribute. According to Guaman Poma's chapter on the subject (pp. 236–60), between the solstitial and equinoctial celebrations in honor of the divinely sanctioned Inca and his queen, this calendar deferred thematically to the tasks of the pastoral year with its llama census in Aya Marcay (November) and an intervening one in Aimoray (May), and with its regular sacrifices of llamas and alpacas throughout, like that actually depicted for Pacha Pucuy (March).

From these further sets of evidence, Tahuantinsuyu appears to have been as distinctive ideologically within native America as it was economically. The sort of entreaty made in the *Zithuwa Hymns* – to a single god who can guarantee monarchic power and guide its course like a shepherd – goes beyond anything that can be found in comparable Native American religious texts, in particular *Inin cuic* of Tenochtitlan, which likewise are entirely devoid of equations in principle between human and animal herds that are faithful to their keeper. In these lines from another prayer to Viracocha, learning obedience to state and church is directly equated with animal domestication:

purun wikuna	the vicuña of the wilds
qaqa wiskacha	the viscacha of the rocks
uywaman tukun	become domesticated
paypaj qayllanpi	in his presence
sunqoypas kikin	so too my heart
sapa paqarin	with each dawn
anayniskuni	renders you its praise
yayay kamaqey	my father and creator[12]

Within the Fourth World the enormous significance of the pastoral model so thoroughly developed by the Inca can be judged from how far it entered not just political discourse but cosmogony too. Endowed with apparently human solidarity, the llama warns of the Flood that ends the first world age and is the other party to the domestic contract that goes wrong in the second, in the Eclipse. In the rival epic of Huarochiri, power is typified in the teams of llamas that oppose the few wild vicuña sympathetic to the poor local hero Huatyacuri (*Runa yndio,* chaps. 4–5). Indeed, patently reshaping images of power along with their extension into the divine, it altogether modified codes of interaction between humans and animals generally shared by Fourth World societies, notably cults of propitiation that go back to the Paleolithic hunter, and the concept of the *nahual,* or animal alter ego.

How the tamed llama is perceived as the ritual ally and even social companion of the Inca is well illustrated in Guaman Poma's report of the ceremonies proper to the month Uma Raimi (October) (p. 254), in which suppliants for rain included not just human children and dogs, whose tears and howls were elicited as sympathetic magic, as in Mexico, for example, but a black llama as well. Indeed, as a general rule in sacrifice the llama came actually to substitute for humans, a key displacement vouchsafed in the *Runa yndio* account of the very foundation of Tahuantinsuyu. There, in the Andean version of Abraham and Isaac, the ogre Huallallo with his appetite for human victims is replaced by Pariacaca, who prefers llamas.

The Inca doubtless continued to share a Native American recognition of the moral problem raised by the use and exploitation of animals, and of the need to regulate and ritualize it; and in practice they would refrain from eating llama meat at certain periods out of that contractual respect that in Mexico extended even to maize, doctrinally the source of human flesh. Yet as objects of Tahuantinsuyu's pastoral economy, llamas were nonetheless bound to be treated in ways that could not be contained within these traditional contractual limits. For they were obliged to function as mere units of value, items of exchange devoid of particular status or rights, and were transacted on the grand decimal scale of the *quipu* as the indispensable capital-plus-interest of the state. This is certainly the role they are assigned in Guaman Poma's account of the world ages, which lies closer to official Inca thinking than does the more shamanist *Runa yndio* of Huarochiri and emphasizes the material and statistical value of llamas and their wool as the factor that distinguished the age of the Purun and the beginnings of state power.

One response to this discrepancy or moral dilemma appears to have been the selection of individuals on which to bestow, in a sacred-cow logic of compensation, as it were, the regard that could not practically be accorded to the species generally. In this respect the single black llama who sang at Uma Raimi while hundreds of his lesser brethren were slaughtered and consumed by state order resembles the royally chosen and lavishly attired *napa* of the Colla ceremonies, or the red llama that the emperor himself took as a singing companion and musical guide in court performances of the Quechua *yaravi* (Fig. 48). Indeed, only in terms of such privileging could individual llamas have come to serve humans as their representatives in their deeper spiritual needs, which is what they undoubtedly did as bearers of guilt, a paradoxical and terminal privilege. In the Zithuwa ceremony, human sins and failings

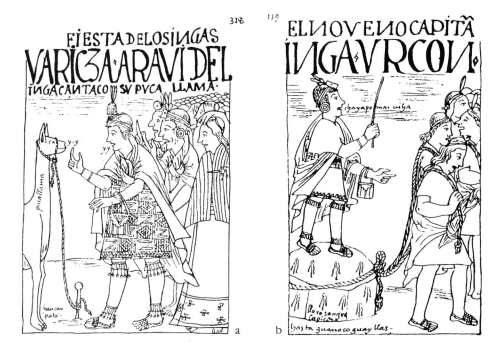

Figure 48. Cuzco life: (a) llama singing with the emperor; (b) stone dragged from the capital weeping blood. (Guaman Poma, *Nueva corónica,* pp. 318, 159.)

were transferred to eviscerated llamas, which were washed out of the capital via its river. Once again, no other American religion offers anything like this parallel to the well-known scapegoat and sacrificial-lamb practices developed in the Old World by the Semitic pastoralists.

THE OUTLAW FROM
OLLANTAYTAMBO

Besides modifying cosmogonical and other paradigms found widely in native America, Inca herding led to a literary pastoralism, in mode and genre, that was otherwise quite absent from the continent. While the courts at Tenochtitlan and Cuzco alike cultivated poetry in modes that derived from social practice – planting songs from the farmer, battle songs from the warrior, funeral songs from the mourner, and so on – only in the Inca case were the pastoral songs of the herder also heard, for reasons that by now will be obvious. Themes characteristic of this pastoral mode included the nameless yearning inspired in the keepers of flocks by the landscape of the high *puna,* lonely and sublime (unruly sons of royal families were customarily exiled to pastoral life on the *puna*); love between male and female herders, in which the desired one is compared with the elusive, untamed vicuña or is revealed as the inaccessible princess of the *aclla* who guarded the church's flocks; and the herders' flutes, whose plaintive sound could presage the suicide of one or both victims of an impossible love. Pituciray and Sauaciray, Antisuyu's twin *huaca* rocks near Ollantaytambo, are such pastoral lovers turned to stone, princess and local lover.[13]

So strong are these Andean pastoral conventions that they survive even today in Quechua poetry, despite the influence of their more sexist European analogues. They likewise inform a whole series of legends ("Hirten-märchen," as Kelm calls them) and even dramas, which, however, tend to allude more directly to the social conditions and constraints under which herders actually worked. A pastoral love story recounted by Murúa in this way reveals the pastures beyond the edge of town and agriculture as the place of transformation and fantasy: The metamorphosis of shamanism is here made to serve the particular needs of a lonely or alienated individual, who changes into a staff, a snake, a bear, in the cause of sexual fulfillment.[14]

The drama *Apu Ollantay,* where the rebellious Antisuyu hero strays from the right path like a disobedient llama lamb, foregrounds the *aclla* and the caste breeding policies of the Inca. An illustrious *auqui,* or warrior earl, from Antisuyu, Ollantay is refused the hand of Cusi Coyllor, Pachacuti's daughter, though he has served the Inca well and she is pregnant by him.[15] Rejected, he rebels and proclaims himself Inca in his ancestral domains. At first he prospers but is then outwitted by the loyal *auqui* Rumi Naui, a former comrade in arms who stems from Collasuyu. Ultimately Ollantay is pardoned by Pachacuti's successor, Tupac Yupanqui, who also releases Cusi from prison and restores her to Ollantay along with their daughter Sumac (Fig. 49).

Customarily thought of as a love story, *Apu Ollantay* undoubtedly is that. At the same time it is a powerful piece of political propaganda that belongs generically to the cycle of Inca kingship dramas. Performed in Cuzco by courtiers and guests of the Inca for their own and public entertainment on public holidays, these works celebrated Inca battles against heathen and rebel and extended from the legendary Manco Capac and Mama Occlo through Viracocha, Pachacuti, Tupac Yupanqui, and Huayna Capac (the eighth to eleventh Incas) to the last, Atahuallpa. The strength of their survival is indicated by the fact that in 1781, after the great uprising of Tupac Amaru II, a direct descendant of the namesake murdered in 1572, the performance of *Apu Ollantay* and the other royal dramas was specifically forbidden by the Spanish crown; even today, in the play dedicated to him, Atahuallpa's tragic end at the hands of Pizarro is commemorated annually in Collasuyu. More than that of Mesoamerica, Inca history came to be domi-

	Locations (4)		
Antisuyu:	Cuzco:		
Ollantaytambo	Inca palace	Coya palace	Aclla Huasi
	Scenes (15)		
6, 7	3, 4*, 5, 9*, 10, 14	1*, 2	8, 11*, 12, 13*, 15*
* Takes place outside.			
	Named characters: (12–13)		
	Male		Female
	Pachacuti	Anahuarqui	
Ollantay		↓	Mama Ccacca
	Tupac Yupanqui	Cusi Coyllur	
		↓	
		Ima Sumac	Pitu Salla
Hanco Huallu	Villca Uma		
Urco Huaranca	Rumi Naui		
	Piki Chaki		

Figure 49. Structure of *Apu Ollantay.*

nated by its line of monarchs, the lives and deeds of the "herders," a fact eloquently reflected in Guaman Poma's *Nueva corónica* (with its pun on *corona*) and Garcilaso's *Comentarios reales* as well as the dynastic paintings of the Cuzco school. Even the plays written in and adapted to Quechua, allegedly to spread the Christian word, continued this royal bias, as evidenced by the eponymous Faustian heroes of *Yauri Titu Inca* and *Usca Paucar,* who sell their souls to regain that huge lost power; and it has survived the uprising of Tupac Amaru II in the modern doctrine of the Inkarri.[16]

In *Apu Ollantay,* whether manifest in the severity of Pachacuti or in the clemency of his son Tupac Yupanqui, Inca power is the pivot on which all turns and by which characters are located and defined. Even at the height of his insubordination, Ollantay appears only a puny counterfeit Inca; the walls he builds are said to be tiny compared with those of Cuzco, and his cadre of aides and administrators, military and religious, though modeled exactly on that of the Inca, lacks efficiency. (The high priest who advises him – as Villca Uma, or Head Speaker, advises the Inca – is called Hanco Huayllo, which means something like half-baked and bland.) We are shown that against Cuzco and Inca power, Ollantay never really had a chance from the start, this message being further confirmed by dramatic irony at Ollantay's expense. Guaman Poma (p. 159) tells how during the surveying and construction work carried out under Pachacuti a block of stone cried out and wept blood at the prospect of being removed from Cuzco to the provinces. Hence, when in Scene 11 Rumi Naui arrives from Cuzco and enters Ollantay's camp in disguise, describing himself as the stone (*rumi*) that wept blood (*chaymi yawarta hichany*), his allusion escapes Ollantay as a character on stage but can only have delighted a knowing Cuzco audience[17] (see Fig. 49). Like the actual streets and squares of the city, which intimated the shape of the empire, the physical locations of scenes in the play – its very structure – were made to correspond to the designs of Inca power. At the center, dominating all, stand the royal palaces of the Incas, including the rooms of Pachacuti's queen, Anahuarqui; to either hand lie Ollantay's fortress in Antisuyu and Rumi Naui's home Collasuyu (the Aclla Huasi, or House of Chosen Women, belonging to the city quarter equivalent to the last). A metropolitan product, the play similarly enforces its message through its very frame, as when Ollantay is warned to keep away from Cusi by the song "Don't eat now, little bird, dove, dove of mine, in the lady's field." A well-known Quechua song in its own right, this warning is then doubly framed: Performed before Pachacuti at his court, it constitutes a small play within the play.[18]

Concentrating on Inca power, the play touches specifically on Pachacuti's large-scale expansion of Inca territory. Popular discontent with the hardships caused by his campaigns, not just against the Anti but also in the coastal deserts, is voiced in the play and exploited by Ollantay in his bid for power, yet to no avail because of Pachacuti's care in consolidating the empire internally by means of *quipu* bureaucracy, land surveys, road networks, *mitima* programs, censuses, and the code of law. He also standardized the calendar year, "binding" time into twelve thirty-day months named according to their produce, with royal festivals (*raymi*) in five special months, which in Guaman Poma culminate in "the great solemn festival of the sun" (p. 258) at the summer solstice in December, the Inti Capac Raymi. In *Apu Ollantay* much is made of this solstitial new year of the "sun king" Pachacuti (the *Inti huatana punchaupas*), which is prepared for and referred to with the utmost solemnity by the priest Villca Uma in the opening scene. Since Ollantay later chooses precisely this date to declare himself emperor, he even acquires a certain heretical air: Who but a false "second sun" like himself would choose to contravene so minute an organization of time and space? According to the same duodecimal logic, deities worshiped locally in the *suyu* were subjected to Viracocha, being formed into a council of twelve representatives (*ranti*), tame oracles to be consulted by the Inca on demand (Guaman Poma, p. 261). Tupac Yupanqui's successor, Huayna Capac, treated this council quite bloodily, killing off representatives who failed to give him the answers he wanted to hear.

By all accounts, the most signal demonstration of royal hegemony at this period of Tahuantinsuyu history was Pachacuti's pronouncement that his family was celestial to such a degree that it would not procreate with ordinary mortals. In future the royal prince was to be allowed to wed only his own sister, which is precisely what happened in Tupac Yupanqui's case. And although he and his brothers were not otherwise to be restrained sexually, the unmarried royal daughters were to be confined to the House of Chosen Women, an institution founded in Cuzco by Pachacuti for this very purpose. It is of course just this pronouncement that triggers the action in *Apu Ollantay*. Quite apart from the matter of Ollantay's loyal service to the emperor Pachacuti, the two were related in other ways, since Pachacuti had Anti blood. The son of an Anti princess, he denies his daughter to an Anti prince, treating the request as outrageous, even sacrilegious. This rebuff is the first cause of Ollantay's rebellion. And after Pachacuti's death the continuing disharmony in the state is left as a problem to his successor, Tupac Yupanqui, who resolves it by emending his father's decision, though only de facto, not de jure.

In focusing on the rebellious Ollantay, the play tests the Inca claim to divinity and uses it as a yardstick to measure other discontents: the resentment of the once independent peoples formed into the *suyu*s and of the men conscripted to fight in the Inca's imperial wars. Yet though Ollantay, as a widely acclaimed champion of the oppressed, comes to embody so much of political consequence in the *tahuantinsuyu*, his concerns remain basically erotic: He fights to regain a love denied, the Venusian "shining star" Cusi Coyllur. This is confirmed in the happy end, where the emperor Tupac Yupanqui, sidestepping the issue of political unrest, is seen to settle everything by simply returning Cusi (by now, ten years on, admittedly somewhat wrinkled) to Ollantay and by appointing him to a post that, historically, he created: that of *ranti*, with responsibility for Antisuyu. Tupac Yupanqui is thus shown to be more statesmanlike than his father, in a play that is itself statesmanlike in successfully avoiding the very issues it appears to explore (though the fact that such issues were raised at all says a lot about the social consciousness of Tahuantinsuyu). However clement Tupac Yupanqui may seem after Pachacuti, nowhere is it asked what gives either the right and authority in the first place to reject and imprison or to pardon and instate.[19] In this sense, the fact that he is made *ranti* compromises and thwarts Ollantay more than ever: He becomes obliged to the Inca for what had been his lifeblood, his true territorial constituency. In this he differs exemplarily from the Quiché hero of *Rabinal Achi*, the other major example of Fourth World drama, whose entire plot stems from the bravery and defiance of the captive, who here meets an end not of accommodation but of ritual sacrifice, actively despising the very thought of "pardon."[20]

This view of the character Ollantay is enhanced by the fact that he is from Anti rather than another *suyu* – the quarter of the Amazonian "savages" who bewildered Inca armies. He delights precisely because he is untamed and yet contained in the play. Probably non-Quechua in origin, the very syllables of his name in that language (*ullu* = penis) confirm him as a character vigorous and willful in failing to heed his master's voice; and his speeches of defiance belong to the type of rhetoric, the *carbet*, used by the Amazonian captive (and performed to amuse the sixteenth-century French court). After Pizarro's seizure of Cuzco, the Inca repaired to Machu Picchu and Vilcabamba; themselves resisting from the Anti quarter, Manco Inca and the Tahuantinsuyu loyalists built higher the walls of the fortress that bears the hero's name, Ollantaytambo.[21]

As one of the cycle of kingship plays, at the end of which all the actors ranked in order of social importance, sat before their audience on a flight of steps, *Apu Ollantay* can only have served as propaganda for the Inca and the system they controlled. It focuses on a moment in their rise to power, the special difficulties of which may be perceived in other works of Tahuantin-suyu literature. In the state created by Pachacuti and refined by Tupac Yupanqui, old reciprocities like those between Pachacuti's and Ollantay's families were replaced by ideas of law as defined first of all in the Ten Maxims of Pachacuti (noted by Garcilaso) and then in the far more sophisticated Legal Code of Tupac Yupanqui (noted by Guaman Poma). To enforce this law and keep the peace, a vast police and civil service was constructed, involving twelve principal posts, with the *ranti* above and, below, the shepherds or judges (*michic*) and the notorious "binders" (*uatacamayoc*) who brought straying objects to justice and prison. The pastoral idiom here is also made explicit in the play, where Ollantay is said to be a "straying lamb" bound by love to Cusi Coyllur as he should be by duty to her father. Also included in this civil service were those who handled the instrument that made the whole exercise possible, the *quipu,* duly mentioned and displayed in *Apu Ollantay.*

There are two occasions in the play (Scenes 5 and 14) when a *quipu* is actually produced and handled on stage as a prop. According to Tahuantin-suyu practice, these *quipu*s are carried in by a *chasqui* (messenger; see Fig. 24) and then are read by an expert in the royal palace, the first one by Rumi Naui to Pachacuti and the second by Villca Uma to Tupac Yupanqui. Both messages concern Ollantay, his initial success and then his downfall as a rebel; and they have the same format. On ethnographic grounds alone these passages in the play deserve attention, since they reveal how significant elements of the *quipu* – position of strings on the main cord; types and positions of knots on the strings; color – were translated into Quechua. The messages read:

cayca llauta	As to the main cord,
nam kahuahua cay umanpi huatascana	so the skeins that are bound to his head;
cay rurucanari runam tucuy payman	as kernel-knots the men all united with
tinkiscana.	him.

– Scene 5

cay kipupim can killimsa	As the *quipu* is carbon-black,
nam Ollantay rupascana	so Ollantay is burnt;
cay kipupakmi kimsa piscucuna	as the *quipu* is bound with three
huatascana	quintuple knots,
nam Antisuyu hapiscu	so the Antisuyu is taken
nam Inca makeykipina:	so it is in the Inca's hand:
chaymi huatacuncaypiscu	here the quintuple knots,
kinsa piscu tucuypinas.	three fives altogether.

– Scene 14

A telegraph essential to the very mechanics of the plot, the *quipu* is twice displayed, flaunted for its technological efficacy, not unlike the metal chains, another Inca specialty, used to imprison Cusi Coyllur. Just enough is said for the audience to realize that the *quipu* works systematically, yet in terms they can only partly understand, given the technical difficulty of the medium. A term like "kernel-knot" may suggest more rudimentary earlier uses of the *quipu,* but is also highly technical, making the explanation sound like a riddle in its turn. Note too the riddle analogies between the head of the *quipu* and of Ollantay in the first reading, and between the fingers of the quintuple knot and of the Inca's hand in the second. The senior *quipu* reader and adviser to the Inca, Villca Uma, is in fact referred to as one who deals in riddles, or "*quipu* text" (*cay kipusca caytucta,* Scene 1); he is recognized as having the power to unravel Ollantay's thoughts and to foreknow "the thread of his destiny." There could be no better example of how ancient shamanist techniques of persuasion were adapted for use by Inca officialdom and the *quipu* system.

In the general gratitude shown to Tupac Yupanqui in the finale, Cusi Coyllur hopes that her brother "will count" for many years to come. Like Guaman Poma, she here alludes to the etymology of his name (*yupanqui* = count) and to his refinement of the numerical *quipu* as an instrument of power. In fact, placed tenth in the line of emperors, Tupac Yupanqui arithmetically affirms the decimal-place value of the *quipu,* just as, historically, he extended its use as the tally of subject wealth: flocks and folk. As for "the years to come," they remind us that we have now crossed the threshold into Inca annals proper.

Finally, just as Guaman Poma's chronicle reveals its *quipu* origins in its very structure, so too does *Apu Ollantay,* the official frame that contains the outlaw. For the number of dialogues (30) matches the days of the Inca month as that of the scenes does those of the half-month (15); the centers of the action are balanced between "male" and "female" (2 : 2), like the census of the *Nueva corónica,* and within this same scheme we may note a geographical preponderance in frequency of the center over the *suyu* (3 : 1) in the proportions of the Cuzco council. Above all, the total of the characters (12) conforms to just the duodecimal paradigm found in Guaman Poma, with the thirteenth character, Tupac Yupanqui, by appearing only after the death of the twelfth, replacing his father, Pachacuti. Guaman Poma can also help us to relate the total of scenes (15) to the number that defines the category of *auqui,* or earls, to which Ollantay belongs; and to interpret the fivefold knots of the second *quipu* in terms of the five royal punishments and corrections (see Chapter 2: "The case of the *quipu*").

With stunning finesse, the play actually comments on this number logic, in the lines appended to the reading of the second *quipu:* "Here the quintuple knots, three fives altogether." Expressed as 3 × 5, this total of fifteen points to the sigma count, already noted elsewhere in the Fourth World, whereby a given number equals all the numbers up to and including itself (viz., $1 + 2 + 3 + 4 + 5 = 15$); here it suggests that, since the rebellious hero is in the "hand," or five digits, of the Inca, the play with its fifteen scenes is as good as over. In other words, read aloud in the penultimate scene, the sets of *quipu* knots prepare the audience for the resolution of the play, or, to use a term particularly appropriate to this form of literacy, the dénouement.

Shaped by *quipu* literacy and pastoral ideology, these Inca and Quechua texts offer a distinctive version of history and construct time in their own way. Their overriding emphasis is on the rightness and necessity of the state in its current order, in territory, hierarchy, and law. As a result, whereas political memory follows various graphic threads in the northern half of the Fourth World, in the south, in Tahuantinsuyu's vast domain, it is concentrated or has survived in only one main story, that of the Inca herders themselves, the creators of the most recent *tahuantinsuyu* before Pizarro. Ideologically of enormous consequence, this *tahuantinsuyu* was above all perceived to work, to represent a society cohesive within its capacious frontiers, and unquestionably more just than the chaos installed by Spanish greed. Still today it sustains beliefs about the destiny of the *puka llacta* (red people), how the presocial ogre that devours its own children must be banished beyond the pale, and how Inkarri will revive. An amalgam of several former emperors, Inkarri competes with the Colla king at Vilcanota, like Manco Capac, in order to establish Cuzco in the first place; at the baths in Caxamarca, like Atahuallpa he is murdered by Pizarro, after which his severed head is taken to Cuzco; like Tupac Amaru II in Cuzco's main square, he has his limbs pulled off and taken to the four parts of Tahuantinsuyu. When head and body grow together, Tahuantinsuyu can again be properly constituted, as it was in Inca geography.

Distinctive as it is, the Inca political tradition[22] emerges nonetheless from space–time paradigms common to the Fourth World. Privileging the east–west axis of Colla and Chincha and studding the upper northern space with stars, the four (*tahua*) *suyu* recall the quatrefoil of Anasazi and Mesoamerica, and likewise match totals of constituent towns to celestial rhythms. Supports

Figure 50. The *huaca* mountains of Tahuantinsuyu arranged as a quincunx: (a) Cuzco and the *suyu*s of (b) Chincha, (c) Anti, (d) Colla, and (e) Conde. (Guaman Poma, *Nueva corónica,* pp. 264–72.)

for the metropolitan House of Dawn and *huaca* of emergence, Pacari Tampu, are provided in the quincunx by the surrounding four mountains, or *huaca*s, Pariacaca, Pitusiray, Vilcanota, and Coropuna (Fig. 50). And political annals are similarly integrated into the all-encompassing story of genesis that, though modified by pastoralism, continues to adhere to and signify within the general pattern of world ages. Appalled by news of Pizarro's behavior at Caxamarca and his treatment of Atahuallpa, the priests at Huarochiri suggested that society was about to regress to the former and more barbaric world age of the Purun. Here as elsewhere the ultimate appeal is to a model of human evolution and possibility whose roots are entirely American.

III

Genesis

x kizk etamah ronohel   x ki muquh   they understood everything   they saw
                                                it

kah tzuq   kah xukut   the four creations   the four
                                                destructions

– Popol vuh

9

Popol vuh

STRUCTURE AND STORY

Any competent account of American genesis is bound to center on the *Popol vuh,* the Quiché Maya text aptly referred to as the Bible of America. The reasons for this are several but quite simple. The *Popol vuh* tells the Fourth World story of creation legibly and at length and in a fashion that draws ingeniously on the native-script tradition from which it claims to have been transcribed. Stemming as it does from the middle of Mesoamerica, it serves as an unrivaled point of reference for cosmogonical texts from cultures to west and east, and beyond that, from North and South America. Its qualities as both record and construct make of it, without question, a major work not just of New World but of world literature. Offering a critique of the *Popol vuh* means searching for the heart of native America, which in turn means raising philosophical questions that have appeared fundamental over millennia.

The oldest surviving manuscript of the *Popol vuh* is the Rabinal copy of the Chichicastenango copy of the sixteenth-century Quiché original written alphabetically in Maya Quiché. Its title is justified by internal references in the text (lines 49 and 8,149) to its pre-Hispanic source, also called by that name. In Quiché, and in Maya languages generally, the element *pop* means woven mat, seat of authority, and counsel; it is also a year-Feast name for which the lowland Maya hieroglyph is woven threads (Fig. 51). *Vuh* simply means book, in both highland and lowland Maya. The first direct translation into English was made by Munro Edmonson in 1971; a second, by Dennis Tedlock, followed in 1985. The great virtues of Edmonson's edition are that it reproduces the Quiché text (in a standardized spelling) and scrutinizes the eleven major translations previously made direct from Quiché into

Spanish, French, German, and Russian. It also attends seriously to the question of line structure, a factor generally ignored hitherto. Following his view that native Mesoamerican literature as a whole is characterized by the couplet, Edmonson arranges the whole text in pairs of numbered lines, which if nothing else is a great aid to critical commentary and has the added advantage of drawing out exact proportions of length between episodes and parts that had previously remained hidden or obscure. For its part, Tedlock's edition, though devoid of the Quiché original, brings in a valuable new element insofar as his reading is informed by time spent among the Quiché who live in Guatemala today. In particular, Tedlock was alerted to the ritual logic in the text through study and conversation with Quiché shamans, who in many respects may fairly be considered the intellectual heirs of those who wrote the *Popol vuh*. Announcing itself to be definitive (as Borges remarked in "The Homeric Versions," "the concept of the definitive text belongs only to religion or to exhaustion"), Tedlock's version spurns Edmonson's repeatedly, yet for the most part in small details. He also rejects Edmonson's binary line structure, which is, however, retained for what are sensed to be heightened moments in the narrative.

In terms of literary genre, as Edmonson has shown, the *Popol vuh* is best thought of in the first instance as a title, *título* in Spanish. That is, like a host of other native documents from sixteenth-century Mesoamerica, it was composed by a local community or even part of a community, in this case the Kavek faction of the town Santa Cruz Quiché, in order to defend under Spanish colonial rule an interest or privilege dating from before the invasion. The text opens and closes by clearly acknowledging the current power of Christendom and of the invaders who were led into Quiché by Cortes's lieutenant Pedro de Alvarado in 1524. Contained by these two moments, the narrative starts at the very beginning of time, gives an account of the four world ages, and then concentrates on Quiché history as such and the particular events on which the Kavek based their legal claim. Hence, volcanoes thrust up early in creation are later identified as the landmark guardians of Quiché territory. Far from diminishing the text, having the practical function of the *título* sooner enhances it and alerts us to how different levels of time and purpose are conjoined in the narrative overall.

Much has rightly been made of the fact that the *Popol vuh* refers to itself as a derivative of a prior text also called the *Popol vuh,* from which readers are said now to "hide their faces." There is no reason to disbelieve this claim, since it is soberly stated and matches similar claims in many other texts in the Maya and Nahuatl languages that draw in one way or another on the script traditions of Mesoamerica. True, certain passages in the text have a strong speechlike quality, for example, the onomatopoeic end of the second world age and the supple and ironic dialogues between the Twins and their animal antagonists; and to this extent it seems unlikely that the Maya alpha-

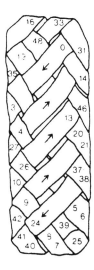

Figure 51. Woven text of Maya hieroglyphs. (Stela J. Copan.)

betic version was composed over its entire length as a direct transcription from a nonalphabetic original. Other features, however, like the overall structuring of world-age episodes and the political detail of later Quiché history, find significant analogues in the native-script tradition.

Where there has been scholarly disagreement is over which particular native script is meant; the *Popol vuh* is not specific on the matter. Basing themselves on no more than the fact that Quiché belongs to the Maya language group, several critics, including both Edmonson and Tedlock, have automatically assumed that the native script in question must have been Maya hieroglyphic. There are good reasons for thinking otherwise.

First, Maya hieroglyphic script is exclusively dedicated to the phonetics of lowland Maya (Chol–Yucatec) and its particular formations of consonants and vowels; though also Maya, Quiché is a highland language whose phonetics differ significantly (*r* for *l*, *a* for *i*, for example). Second, Quiché occupies an area outside the hieroglyphic zone as this is defined by surviving monuments and inscriptions. Again, in all known cases of its use, Maya hieroglyphic script is bound up with the 360-day *tun* calendar privileged by the lowland as opposed to the highland Maya; by contrast, the seasonal-year calendar, bound up historically with the nonhieroglyphic or iconic script of Mesoamerica, was and is used by the Quiché and is mentioned in the *Popol vuh*. Fuentes y Guzmán even records the iconic signs and markers used by them in conjunction with their year calendar. Yet again, on one occasion when writing is mentioned in the text – that is, when the forefathers of the Quiché go to the great city of Tula to receive the insignia and gifts of Quetzalcoatl – the script they take back with them is defined as *u tzibal Tollan,* the script of Tula, or Toltec script. Like the use of the year calendar, this definition corresponds less readily to the Maya hieroglyphic tradition, in which Toltec is typically something alien and inferior, than to the iconic tradition, in which Tula and Quetzalcoatl are repeatedly celebrated as the keystones of Mesoamerican political history. Again, rather than invoke the phonetic tongue-pen of Maya hieroglyphic, the texts make play with the *tlacuilolli* binary between verbal and visual language, *tzih* and *tzib* in Quiché.

Besides, the fact remains that though the *Popol vuh* is undoubtedly in Quiché, the text incorporates a large number of words of Nahuatl origin, which langauge has historically always been bound up with iconic rather than hieroglyphic script. Further, although it was once fashionable to attribute the Nahuatl element in Quiché to Aztec or Tlaxcalan influence and hence to view it as late and inconsequential in literary terms, scholarly opinion is now beginning to concede much earlier horizons. This longer perspective fits better with the primary role that Nahuatl has in the *Popol vuh:* It provides the names of founder gods like the grandmother Xmucane who casts the maize kernels, and her consort, Xpiacoc – a pair corresponding to the Oxomoco and Cipactonal of the *teoamoxtli*. Right at the start, the epithet applied to the great Feathered Snake (*tepeu,* or "majesty") comes from the same Nahuatl source.

Not relegating the *Popol vuh* entire to the Maya hieroglyphic corner has important consequences for the reading of the text, particularly in the matter of perceiving how its structure relates to orders of spatial logic typical more of iconic than of hieroglyphic script. Within its Christian frame – that is, between the prologue that situates the text in Christendom and Pedro de Alvarado's intrusion at the end of the narrative – the *Popol vuh* falls into two clearly defined parts of about equal length. The first concerns the origins of the world itself and, culminating as it does in the Twins' victory over the Lords of Hell, prepares us for the creation from maize of the first people of our current age. This event in fact provides the hinge into the second part, insofar as these first people are also more narrowly defined as the first Quiché and the remotest ancestors of the dynasty reigning in that town when Alvarado arrived. The maize creation at the start of Part 2 is, then, the pivotal moment of the whole narrative, toward and away from which everything tends.

The difference between the two parts, thus understood, are multiple. The first moves between whole dimensions of time, has an intricate structure (Fig. 52), shifts between forms of address and verb tenses, and relies integrally on the complex numeracy of Mesoamerican ritual sign systems; the second moves progressively through one time dimension, has a simple structure, is grammatically uniform, and relies on ritual numeracy only at the calendrical level. Here there is more Nahuatl, no polite address form, and less dramatic dialogue. One commentator has gone so far as to posit two originally independent manuscripts, one from the Charchah region and

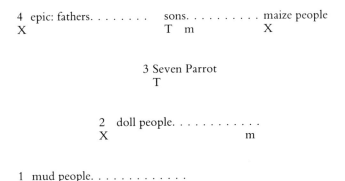

Figure 52. Structure of the *Popol vuh:* 1–4, creations; X, Xmucane; T, Twins; m, metamorphosis into monkey.

one from Quiché, that were put together by a Spanish cleric. In fact, as Tedlock has shown in his refutation of this view, precisely in the opposition between the two parts does the text display a strong integrity as a native artifact within its frame and turning on its maize-people hinge.[1]

As we saw earlier, the second part tells how the Quiché came to establish themselves in their mountain domain in mid Mesoamerica, visited the great lowland Tula, and strove for the political supremacy the text itself was designed to embody and defend. In other words, it is basically a historical statement, by no means devoid of its own literary elegance and strategy but engaged formally with a less elaborate narrative enterprise than is the case with the first part.

Not so straightforward in its procedure, the first part is far less easy to summarize. As the prologue tells us, it relates the four creations that inhere in the present. Identifying and numbering these creations has not proved simple. Discerning in them the phases of particular life-forms within an evolutionary story, Edmonson speaks of their beginnings and endings as "births and humiliations." Tedlock, on the other hand, follows the usual spatial preference and renders them as "fourfold siding, fourfold cornering, measuring, fourfold staking." Given the vast scope of the narrative, it seems likely that the key Maya terms in question (*tzuq, xukut*) encompasses both possibilities: American configuration of space and the evolutionary drive of the text itself preclude a spatial model from which time is absent.

What, then, are these four creations? In some measure the answer is quite clear, thanks to explicit pointers in the text. There can be no doubt in these terms about the creation centered on Seven Parrot and his family, or about the subsequent epic of underworld Xibalba, succeeded in turn by the creation of the maize people, the hinge moment with which Quiché history and Part 2 begin. At the start, however, where the text deals with the creation of the mud people and then the doll people, the key to its proper division is more cryptic. For their part, both Edmonson and Tedlock offer the following scheme:

[Part 1]
   1. Mud people; doll people
   2. Seven Parrot
   3. Xibalba

[Part 2]
   4. Maize people; history of Quiché (4 and 5 in Tedlock)

The reasons for wishing to revise this scheme are twofold. Externally the four creations in the *Popol vuh* in fact relate to the fourfold pattern of Mesoamerican cosmogony examined in the following chapters; internally the text itself, intricate in structure, gives precise if unobtrusive instruction on how the unit episodes in Part 1 are meant to fit together as four. For the four creations "of sky and earth" definitely belong to cosmogony rather than history, that is, to the first part rather than to both parts of the text. (Tedlock's uneasiness on this point led him to subdivide Part 2.) Then the mud people and the doll people (1 above) are cleanly denominated as not a continuum, by their respective agencies of creation and above all by the fact that the Seven Parrot creation is said to have occurred during the doll people's time, making of it a separate concept. (Mercedes de la Garza succinctly corrects the running together of the first creation with the second "when other people are formed.")[2] Then when the first maize people are created (4 above) and their eyes and intelligence have not yet been blinded by the gods, they are said specifically to remember the four creations out of which they have effectively emerged as the hinge into Era history. In other words, they themselves cannot reasonably constitute one of those four creations, which must rather be deemed to have their place within the scope and span of the first part. On these counts a preferable scheme would be:

[Part 1]
Prologue
   1. Mud people
   2. Doll people
   3. Seven Parrot
   4. Xibalba

Hinge. Maize people / first Quiché

[Part 2]
History of Quiché

This arrangement is further corroborated by the proportional lengths of creations in question as lines on the page, a factor brought out in Edmonson's verse translation. Hence, the first and second creations together are the same length as the third, and the first three creations are together half the length of the fourth.

THE MUD PEOPLE AND THE DOLL PEOPLE

At the very threshold of its time, the world lies expectant, knowable only insofar as it ripples, murmurs, sighs, and hums, "empty under the sky." On its unclear face the phenomena that will populate it are defined through absence: "Not yet one person, one animal, bird, fish, crab, tree, rock, hollow, canyon, meadow, forest." The first connection alternates atmosphere with sphere, a name flashed like lightning or thought between One Leg Sky Heart and Quetzal Snake, iridescent in the night water below.

Manifest as a trinity of lightnings named thunderbolt, newborn, and green, One Leg is *huracan* in Quiché, the Caribbean hurricane, a storm god whose whirlwind physically joins sea and sky.[3] Besides indicating shape, actually carved in single-leg, whirling-arm effigies from Jamaica and the Guianas, the term "One Leg" also relates to the *tonalamatl* via the lowland Maya Hun Oc (leg or foot), the counterpart of the normal Quiché and Nahuatl names for Sign X (Dog: *tzi, itzcuintli*). As for Quetzal Snake, Gucumatz or Quetzalcoatl, we encounter it here in its primeval form, glistening bird-reptile charged with upward evolutionary force to come. Like One Leg, it too belongs to the *tonalamatl,* since as one of the Quecholli Quetzal corresponds to number 12, and Snake is Sign V. By virtue of this fact, as the two think and converse they set up a *tonalamatl* rhythm of gestation deep in time whose phases and intervals may in principle be gauged.

The intense cogitation of One Leg and Quetzal Snake has the physical consequence of causing the earth's crust to form. Mountains thrust up to divide the draining rivers and offer slopes for forests of cedar and pine that then become the lairs of the wild creatures. These, however, prove incapable of articulating the hymn of worship required of them by their makers, and so there follows the first attempt specifically to shape and form a human being.

The substance chosen for this exercise is the proverbial clay of Adam. But the resulting image here emerges as altogether unsatisfactory. Its head couldn't nod, its face was lopsided, and it couldn't look around, talk, breed, or walk. As a creation it is abandoned by the gods and left to the water. The characteristics of this early antecedent of humankind – a head that turns only sideways and a face only one of whose sides can move – are curiously echoed in the asymmetrical masks of the Iroquois "mud people." In the history of the vertebrate species they correspond to fish, whose watery element these creatures were returned to.

After this failure, One Leg and Quetzal Snake decide to call upon the grandparent pair Xpiyacoc and Xmucane, known in Nahuatl as Cipactonal and Oxomoco, engenderers and bearers capable of switching their sex. With the power delegated to them, and as midwife counters of the *tonalamatl's* nights and days, these two appeal to the language of gender and genetics. They divine with maize kernels and *tzite* beans, saying, "Join now and be coupled"; this is an act widely celebrated in iconic script, for example *Borbonicus* (p. 21), where Oxomoco's maize kernels total nine, and the Yauhtepec Inscription[4] (Fig. 53), which emphasizes Cipactonal's role as carver and marker of days.

The creatures produced by Xpiyacoc and Xmucane, carved of wood, look and talk like people and multiply readily. Yet, just as their predecessors were too wet, these were too dry. Doll-like, they move jerkily, and since they forget their creators they too are done away with and dismissed as "a preliminary effort, a demonstration person."

Whereas the mud people were lone losers, the doll people become great exploiters of other life and of objects. Indeed, because they are so hard, stiff, wooden, and machinelike, having no reverence or respect for what they dominate and control, they have to be ground down by all they once exploited as well as by monsters that plunge earthward from the sky like the *tzitzimine* of solar eclipse, gouging and slashing with the flint knife of the bloodletter. "The face of the earth was darkened and there began a rain of darkness, night and day." For they have flouted the Fourth World notion of domestic contract, mistreating their dogs, the oldest friend of humans and widely associated with eclipse in the Fourth World, and their turkeys, the only other main domesticated creature of Mesoamerica. As a result, these creatures recover the savage state and assault their masters with violent recrimination. Even the doll people's grindstones (*metates*) and cooking pots complain of being used with complete insensitivity, in a passage of vivid phonetic effects:

> Every day, / every day
> in the dark, in the dawn, / all the time,/
> r-r-rip, / r-r-rip,
> r-r-rub, / r-r-rub,
> right in our faces / you went.
> – lines 737–46

The few who survive this revolution flee to the forests, where they become "the monkeys who live there today."

Figure 53. Cipactonal and Oxomoco. (Yauhtepec inscription.)

The first and the second creations, with which the narrative opens, have in common the fact that, in one as in the other, celestial agencies in need of recognition, or anagnorisis, produce antecedents of humankind and, failing to get it, destroy them through catastrophe. The break between the two efforts of the gods is clearly signaled, however; and in the second creation the narrative focus is altogether closer, and we are given details of agency and process that are absent in principle from the first. This tendency becomes more marked in the next phase of the narrative, which focuses on the family of Seven Parrot, his wife, Chimalmat, and his two sons, Cipacna and Two Leg.

SEVEN PARROT AND FAMILY

On approaching the third creation, the reader is given precise instructions about how to locate it in relation to the two already narrated. For the story of how Seven Parrot and his family were defeated by the boy Twins – a perfectly constructed quartet in itself – is said to have its place "during the time of the doll creatures," that is, after the end of the first creation and before the end of the second, which, as was noted, surely speaks against rather than for Edmonson and Tedlock's running together of the first two creations. In any case, by this stage the overall narrative cannot be thought to be proceeding in a simple chronological or even linear sequence. Generated *ex abrupto* by Parrot's sheer bravura rather than by the decision of the gods, this episode ends with the note that it belongs to the countless deeds performed by the Twins when they lived on the face of the earth.

As long a narrative as the first two creations put together, this third creation is best thought of as a four-act play whose dramatis personae fall into two antagonistic parties. On the one side there are Seven Parrot and his family; on the other, the Twins Hunter and Jaguar Deer, their protectors and allies. The play and struggle that engage them leave no room now for controlling deities or their delegates. With close attention to the appearance and behavior of individual types, the narrative analyzes what had been the undifferentiated qualities and predicament of the doll people; and whereas neither mud nor doll people ever uttered a word, these characters converse incessantly, with each other and in soliloquy.

Noting its clear self-definition as an episode, its dramatic mode, and its strong Nahuatl lexis, Munro Edmonson went so far as to refer to this third creation as a "tenth-century insert,"[5] a passage stuck, as it were, into an existing Maya text. Whatever the grounds for this claim may be, in literary terms the episode is brilliantly integrated into the larger story. It constantly alludes to the two previous creations, especially that of the doll people in whose time it is set, drawing out etymologies and evolutionary logic and completing the program of grand metamorphoses into fish, monkeys, stars, and mountains. At the same time, through the persons of the Twins, it looks forward to the fourth creation, which constitutes their epic. Moreover, in terms of argument, a common Mesoamerican substrate to both Maya and Nahuatl versions of the world ages and Twins epic exists in Otomonguan texts like *Nai tzult, nai tza,* which concerns the Mazatec solar–lunar Twins.

The play opens with Seven Parrot asserting his preeminence as the inheritor of creation so far. His great size, brilliant feathers, and features bright as jewels and precious metal equip him to be considered nothing less than sun and moon. His hubris extends to his two sons, Cipacna and Two Leg, who, possessed of massive strength, amuse themselves making and shaking down mountains. Observing the family and intuiting the preference of One Leg for another order of greatness, the Twins determine to cut them down to size, starting with the father, Parrot.

As Parrot devours fruit in his great tree, raucously announcing his dawn, the Twins Hunter and Jaguar Deer shoot him with their blow gun. In the ensuing fray, Hunter loses his arm, which Parrot carries off back home to his wife, Chimalmat, complaining of the unbearable toothache caused by Hunter's poison dart. Meanwhile the Twins, fatherless and now more forlorn than ever, are adopted by the ancient white-haired pair Peccary and Coati, who, protecting them as their own offspring, enable them to become Parrot's dentists: "What poisons can you make, what poisons can you cure?" he asks them. The Twins seize the opportunity to remove the teeth and the precious insignia that had made Parrot a lord, using anesthetics, replacing them with a false set. He then dies, followed by his wife, Chimalmat. Having recovered his arm, Hunter has it satisfactorily grafted back.

The second act of the play concerns the Four Hundred Suns, apparently orphans like the Twins who are first glimpsed hacking down trees with their axes in order to make themselves a home. Unable to raise the roof beam, they accept Cipacna's offer of help, but, unnerved by his terrible caiman strength, decide to kill him, digging a huge pit for him to fall into. Satisfied that he is dead on the evidence of hair and nails carried up by ants, they celebrate by drinking vast quantities of *pulque* home brew. Just when they are at their merriest, Cipacna, who has been lying doggo all the time, has his revenge by pulling the house down on top of them, killing them all. Their fate is then to rise to become the Pleiades, the least mistakable of the constellations along the zodiac road.

Learning of this, in the third act the Twins avenge the Four Hundred by killing Cipacna. They achieve this by luring him to a cave with a decoy crab whose pink flesh makes his mouth water. The entrance is so narrow that he has to go in on his back to get at the bait, and once he is wedged in, the mountain, named Meavan, crushed him. Tedlock remarks on the sexual innuendo this sequence continues to have for the Quiché today and on the position of Meavan in their local geography.

Finally, completing the foursome, the Twins bring Two Leg, Parrot's other son, into line. A monstrous travesty of One Leg and a giant saurian like his brother, this creature stamps down mountains to let light in from the east. He is brought down because he cannot resist the dish prepared by the Twins, a bird roasted in clay. Ingesting the clay, the substance he is closest to, causes Two Leg to curl up so that the Twins can bind and bury him.

With this, the play is complete, its fourfold logic, which admits of no subtraction or addition, perfected. Twins defeat Parrot; Parrot's first son defeats the Four Hundred; Twins defeat Parrot's first son; Twins defeat Parrot's second son. Satisfying in its own right, this creation develops the *Popol vuh*'s evolutionary argument by paying the closest attention to the anatomy, skin, and behavior of its main characters. Indeed, the agon of the piece is corroborated at the level of skin covering insofar as the Seven Parrot party dress in scale and feather, whereas their opponents have only hair, these three possibilities being the only ones available to American vertebrates. Called Chimalmat, from the Nahuatl for "shield," the woman of the Parrot family "covers" her brood, initially a nest of eggs, be they cold- or warm-blooded. Though born from the same amniotic sac, the mammals are, by contrast, defenseless, the Twins and the Four Hundred alike being cast as "lost boys" with no known parents. For just this reason do the ancient and "humble" Peccary–Coati pair, whose great age shows in their white hair and beard, offer to protect the Twins as their adoptive descendants. They do so out of the same order of solidarity that impels the Twins to avenge the Four Hundred, and ethologically this contrasts with the merely formal kinship of the oviparous bird-reptiles.

Although he is called Parrot (the Cakchiquel say Macaw), the character of this name must clearly have enjoyed vast stature and strength, for he was able to tear Hunter's arm right out by its roots: *Borgia* and other screenfolds carry the image of just such a monster parrot, severed arm in its beak. With the teeth that made him lord, and that he lost, he asks to be read as a primeval flier, one who lifts *quetzal* sheen from sea to sky: an archaeopteryx perhaps, or the more modest American hoatzin, whose brood in the first weeks of life still betray atavistic signs of the reptilian tooth and claw. Ritually, Parrot stands at the head of the Thirteen Quecholli, and his number-name through addition suggests the vigesimal base, i.e., 7 + 13 = 20. Through multiplication the name produces the sigma of the Quecholli; that is, all of them added together produce 7 × 13, or 91, a mathematical expression of combined potential, as we have seen (Chapter 2: "*Tlacuilolli*"). This numerical decoding is supported by the Ah Muzen Cab episode in the *Chilam Balam Books* (e.g., *Chumayel,* p. 42), where the figure whose pride and insignia are despoiled is named Oxlahun-ti-ku "god-13." At any event, the trouble with Parrot is that he takes too far and in the wrong direction the impulse announced at the start of the narrative in the feathers of Quetzal Snake.

Parrot's two saurian sons represent the other half of Quetzal Snake, the cold-blooded vertebrates that grew to such enormous proportions in the Cretaceous. The name of the first son, Cipacna, means caiman (Cipactli in Nahuatl, a root also visible in Oxomoco's consort Cipac-tonal/Xpiayacoc), whose habits he displays, lying doggo and faking death, and whose anatomy he shares in snatching at the crab upside down. For caimans and their ancestors are distinguished by the fact that their jaws hinge inversely, upward rather than downward, effectively limiting the size and shape of the brainpan. Once trapped under Meavan, Cipacna reverts to being earth itself, a mark of his antiquity celebrated for example in the Fourth World images of the caiman as the literal foundation for buildings, like the first house built by the Four Hundred, and as a soil base for crops. On Stela 25 at nearby Izapa, as in distant Chavin, the caiman serves as the root and foundation of vegetal growth in this way, at the same time as it displays the nails invoked in the *Popol vuh,* on well-manicured hands.

As the first of the Twenty Signs, Cipactli is also literally the basis of that *tonalamatl* sign set. Moreover, though he constitutes a hazard, with his telluric strength and his capacity to raise skyward whole strata of earth as they were raised by the gods at the start of creation, he is credited with forming the very volcanoes that much later in history stand as Quiché landmarks and guardians of their watershed: a deed that mitigates his aspect as sheer monster.

The other son, Two Leg, who knocks down what Cipacna sets up, also ends up earthbound, fatally weakened by eating what he is most like in a cooked form unwelcome to his gastric system. Anatomically his name suggests a tyrannosaurus shape, a maximal use of the hip-and-knee articulation detailed as such on the *Féjérváry* title page (see Fig. 62a). Through it, he is posed as a travesty of Sky Heart One Leg, to the extent that this last actually comments on the fact to the Twins when urging them to allow the world breathing space by taming and reducing all three males of Parrot's family.

On their side, the Twins, the Four Hundred they closely resemble as effective orphans, and the white-haired couple who adopt them have in common vulnerability plus a propensity to attack first, deceit, and subterfuge. Peccary and Coati lie (successfully) to Parrot, the Four Hundred lie (unsuccessfully) to Cipacna, and the Twins hoodwink the whole family as well as excelling in the art of decoy (the crab) and ersatz (Parrot's false teeth). The Twins and the Four Hundred are further distinguished as users of tools, notably the blow pipe and the manufactured poisons celebrated by Lévi-Strauss, the axe, and the *pulque* brewing pot. As pioneers in a savage landscape who fell trees to raise the roof beam of their house, the Four Hundred establish the paradigms of the *teoamoxtli* Mores chapter, the Roofbeams chapter (associated with omens in *Chumayel*), and above all the axe-wielding *pulque* drinkers who, following the prime example of the Pleiades (i.e., the Four Hundred in their celestial form) mark the stations of the zodiac road. A close reading of this *Popol vuh* passage brings to a common focus, deep in protohuman history, the apparently discrete features of the zodiac Eleven in such sources as the manuscript of Tepoztlan, the "Place of the Axe" close to the mountain centers of the *pulque* cult, and *Cospi, Laud,* and *Borbonicus,* where planetary periods are counted in dots of alcoholic effervescence. Most important, in the larger *Popol vuh* story, by rising to become the Pleiades they prepare the celestial route the Twins will later follow.

In the screenfold corpus, numerous images in the style of the human arm held by Parrot and the axed tree underpin the evolutionary dialectic of this four-part play, one that permeates the very logic of the *tonalamatl*. While Parrot heads the Thirteen Quecholli and his son Caiman provides the basis of the Twenty Signs, Two Leg, like One Leg, invokes an archaic version of Sign X. On the Twins' side, Hunter is the Quiché form of Sign XX (Flower in Nahuatl, Lord in Yucatec), and as Jaguar Deer, Signs XIV and VII, his brother conjoins carnivore and herbivore, hunter and prey, between whom the human stands on Powhatan's robe and who similarly combine in the name and attribute of the Mixtec hero Eight Deer Jaguar Claw. In numerical terms, this semiotic charge in the text refines the *tonalamatl* phases and rhythms set up initially by One Leg (1 X) and Quetzal Snake (12 V).

As proof of the Mesoamerican antiquity of the logic developed in these three creations, we find at Chalcatzingo a sequence of rock inscriptions from the early Olmec horizon. There, portraying the same agon, though with more savage a resolution, the image is of a naked, hapless mammal-human devoured by a dragon beast whose huge head and teeth are both saurian and birdlike and whose body, undulating and serpentine and equipped with a fin, is clad in a mixture of scales and feathers.[6]

DOWN TO XIBALBA

About the form and general significance of the fourth creation there can be little question. True to their lineage calling as cupbearers, the authors open proceedings by proposing a toast to the name of the Twins' father, One Hunter, and to the engendering of the Twins. And the sequence ends when the Twins are seen for the last time walking into the sky to join the Pleiades as sun and moon.

If the third creation was a four-act play of metamorphosis with epic overtones, the fourth entirely fulfills the requirements of the epic. It sees the Twins confirmed in their role as avengers, this time making good the murder of their father by the Lords of Xibalba, skeletal creatures of the netherworld. The plot in this respect can be summarized in a few sentences. Summoned to Xibalba to play the ballgame with its rulers, the Twins' father, One Hunter, and his brother Seven Hunter are humiliated and killed. Miraculously conceived from spittle issuing from the father's decapitated head, the Twins follow his footsteps, only to succeed where he failed. Having displaced their elder brothers as One Hunter's heirs, the Twins overcome the Lords of Xibalba and triumphantly reveal their names and motives. They then piously reassemble their father's head and body and walk on up into the sky.

On linguistic grounds, this Xibalba sequence has been highlighted by Edmonson as especially Maya; and Mayanists have repeatedly turned to it in their search for parallels between the *Popol vuh* and what has been dubbed its codex,[7] that is, scenes depicted on vases and other lowland Maya artifacts, particularly from the Carchah–Chamá area traditionally linked with the road to Xibalba. At the same time, the narrative follows the solar-walk paradigm characteristic of American epic heroes generally, that is, the astronomical route that passes between the western and eastern horizons through the netherworld (inferior conjunction) and the zenith (superior conjunction). The particular motif of the ballgame the Twins play against the Lords of Xibalba is common to Otomanguan texts in Mesoamerica and is known among the Sioux and Algonkin of Turtle Island.

Twice as long as the first, second, and third creations put together, the fourth weaves a whole web of significance about this paradigm and excels in counterpointing pairs and sets of characters. The chief pair, the Twins, relate logically first to their forebears, father One Hunter and uncle Seven Hunter (Sign XX); then to their older Monkey brothers One Spider and One Howler (Sign XI), the children of their father's first marriage; and finally to their archetypal foes, One Death and Seven Death (Sign VI) and the other Lords of Hell. In turn, this all-male cast ingeniously relates to the women Xmucane, the father's mother; Cipacyalo, the Monkeys' mother; and Blood Woman, the Twins' mother. Though only three in number, these women provide the thread of continuity without which the male adventure would belong or go nowhere.

The Lords of Xibalba decide to summon first the Fathers and then the Twins because they are irritated by the noise of the ballgames they play on the family court above their heads in the upper world; from their subterranean point of view, the problem is the people upstairs. On each occasion the summons is delivered by emissaries who are carnivorous birds and who fly right onto the court, perching there ominously. The Fathers are playing, just as they play dice, to pass the time; and the summons, carried direct by four high-ranking owls, leaves them no choice in their code of honor. By contrast, the Twins are playing with enthusiasm, having just recovered the Fathers' gaming gear; and they receive the summons indirectly, from Hawk, a day bird. The message had been taken first to their grandmother Xmucane in the family house, and she communicated it to them on the court by means of a flea that is caught in the drool of a toad that is swallowed by a snake that is devoured by Hawk. In recapitulating a food chain that alternates types of locomotion (hop, flow), this sequence also indicates that ultimately the Twins themselves feel the itch (hence the flea) to challenge their Fathers' assassins.

In saying goodbye to Xmucane, the Fathers can leave only their firstborn Monkey sons to keep the house and her heart warm; then on the way down to Xibalba, faced with roads colored red and black, white and yellow, they choose the fateful black. For their part, having no offspring to leave with Xmucane, the Twins entrust to her a maize plant to tend, which, rooted right inside the house, will thrive as they fare, intimating their eventual triumph and the new race of maize people that will result from it. Correspondingly, the colors of their roads pair black and white, red and green, the variable green denoting new growth in the maize register.

On actually arriving at Xibalba, the Fathers had been subjected to ignominy and the Lords' line in slapstick humor. Mistaking them for the Lords themselves, they courteously saluted a row of twelve wooden effigies put there as a joke and in fact the cause of huge hilarity; and when asked to sit down, it was on a hot stone that propelled them sharply upward, to more laughter. Very much on a losing wicket, they then had to deal with the gift of tobacco, traditionally the token of hospitality. Here, however, overnight in the House of Dark they were made to face the impossible choice of either not consuming the tobacco and seeming rude or of consuming it and seeming greedy. In other words, they had no chance from the start, and the Lords, rather than going through the formality of actually playing a series of ballgames with them, decided to sacrifice them and decapitated One Hunter right away. The other fearful guestrooms they would have occupied on intervening nights – the Ice, Jaguar, Killer Bat, and Knife houses – are merely listed.

On all these points the Twins do much better. Anticipating their foes, they enlist a mosquito to sting the Lords one by one and so learn which are wooden and the names of all who are not:

> "Ouch!" each one said as he was bitten.
> "What?" each one replied.
> "Ouch!" said One Death.
> "What is it, One Death?"
> "I am being bitten"
> > – lines 3497–503

They decline the hot seat and in the series of guestrooms find ways of outwitting their homicidal hosts. Accepting the cigar, they simulate its glow in the dark through the pulse of a firefly placed on a parrot feather. To the enraged denizens of the Jaguar House, Jaguar Deer says, "If you eat me you eat yourselves," and so on.

The first to set out on the epic trail through earth and sky, One and Seven Hunter are outdone at every turn; and they fail the tests that characterize the Native American shaman journey. Following in their footsteps and with the Pleiades sons now as their marker, the Twins fare much better, possessed of instinctual or genetic memory: The narrative insinuates this by closely paralleling event with event, as Edmonson has detailed. Their different fortunes are matched by their names: Arithmetically One and Seven Hunter imply the whole *tonalamatl* construed according to Sign XX, which in the terminal counting convention of the lowland Maya names *tun*s and *katun*s. Unnumbered, the Signs of the Twins continue this lordly precedent but enhance it with the dual animal name Jaguar Deer (XIV and VII), which points to the capacity to intuit and communicate with the natural world that saves their lives on many occasions, notably in the Jaguar House.

The Twins' relationship with their elder Monkey brothers, the firstborn of One Hunter, is largely one of animosity, a consequence above all of the Twins' unusual birth. For Blood Woman conceived them miraculously from spittle falling into her right hand from One Hunter's skull. Having traveled from Xibalba back up to Xmucane's house, she presented them as true offspring, much to the displeasure of their Monkey brothers. Perceived from the start as a threat and potential usurpers, the Twins are treated miserably by the Monkeys, being bossed about, kept outside the house, and deprived of food. In the process the Monkeys betray a cluster of imperfections – sloth, "red-faced" anger (the exact image of a Howler monkey), envy, and boastful pride – that lead to their downfall. With guile the

Twins contrive to displace them and turn them into monkeys proper; they go off to the forest to join the survivors of the doll people who had undergone the same metamorphosis, an event that, like the reappearance of Xmucane, ties this fourth creation into the second. Swaying extravagantly to the Twins' music, their loincloths let down to look like a simian penistail, they are effectively disowned by their grandmother Xmucane, who cannot help laughing at them, though she knows that to do so means losing them to the wild. This whole episode belongs under the rubric parthenogenesis,[8] the miraculous conception that typifies the Twins and other Fourth World epic heroes. The particular Quiché resolution of the formal anomalies in kinship it entails is notable for its ingenuity and shows how music and laughter may confound human rationality and control.

In taking over the Monkeys' inheritance, the Twins do not neglect, however, to honor their talents as craftsmen, dancers, and painters. In the *tonalamatl* their name figures as the Sign (XI) for these crafts and has the distinction of inaugurating its second decade, or second half.

Before actually setting off for Xibalba, the Twins further distinguish themselves from their Monkey brothers in terms of calling. Among the Monkeys' many jobs as scions of the house of One Hunter was keeping the *milpa* and supplying the family with food. Upon their demotion to the wild, the Twins automatically inherited this duty, though with bad grace. Again using guile, they pretend before their grandmother to be acting as farmers when in fact they are out hunting, true to the name Hunter and to its equivalent hieroglyphic Sign Ahau, whose mouth is rounded ready for the blowpipe. In this they were helped by their tools, axe and hoe, which were so efficient that they worked as if of their own accord and left them time to go off with their blowpipes.

As such, this opposition between sedentary farmer and mobile hunter corresponds to the one consecrated in *Totecuyoane* and the *Palenque Foundation Trilogy* examined earlier. Here the Twins' hunting preference and relegation of the farmer to mere tool bring retribution from the wild and its "guardians": by night, led by Jaguar (who has just this role in the *teoamoxtli* Mores chapter, defending his forest), the animals undo the fieldwork of the day. Stealthily observed by the Twins, the last and lowest of them is caught: Rat, who in exchange for his life offers to tell where their father's gaming gear had been hidden in the roof of the house. Recovering and reusing this heirloom takes the Twins to the ball court, where, summoned by Xibalba, they embark on their great epic adventure as hunter-travelers.

Rat's ratting leaves this particular farmer–hunter conflict unresolved for the moment and incidentally deprives Xmucane and Blood Woman of their fieldworkers; and indeed, things are put right only later, through the dialectic of Xmucane's care for the maize plant the Twins leave with her as a token of their farmer selves. Their implicit arrogance here toward both their brothers and their women anticipates their heroism in Xibalba and yet undercuts that heroism, placing it domestically in a fashion that would be inconceivable in the "noble" epic mode preferred by, say, Matthew Arnold. After all, the whole question of the Twins' responsibility is flavored by the fact that the voicing of their grand destiny was entrusted to Rat.

Within this fourth creation, the Twins' engagement with the Monkeys is notable in providing the clues and means by which their epic may be fitted into the overall narrative of the *Popol vuh*. For, following the narrative closely, we see that there is only one moment in their lives when they could possibly have engaged with Parrot, the subject of the third creation: after their birth, obviously, and before their descent to Xibalba, whence they reemerge only as zodiac creatures. More particularly it must have come before they displaced their Monkey brothers, when they and their mother were still being badly treated as intruders and were not allowed into Xmucane's house. For it is precisely then that we are told that they "flourished in the mountains," which is in fact the setting actually created by Seven Parrot's earth-heaving second son, Two Leg. In other words, while the third creation may be related back to the second as happening during it, it relates forward to the fourth as a fragment of the Twins' particular experience, a lost childhood world of monsters and enormous new days. This last conjunction of outer with inner memory, of cosmogony with psychology, testifies to the *Popol vuh*'s high literary sophistication.

On descending to Xibalba, the Twins have a private motive: to avenge their father. At the same time, they are acting on behalf of Sky Heart, as they were when suppressing Parrot. They now take the story into a social reality that extends beyond the family, to the council of the twelve Lords of Xibalba.

Lucifer-like and known as Tzontemoc in Nahuatl – the "fallen headlong" – these twelve show all the compassion of their individual sets of twelve skeletal ribs in their tasks of bringing people down with bloody vomit, stroke, and other kinds of sudden death, according to the ethic emblazoned in their leaders' names, One and Seven Death. Within their netherworld they exert rigorous power by means of their complots and armies of secret police: Puffing on their cigars, they want it all and brook no rivalry at home or abroad. As they showed in their treatment of One and Seven Hunter, they flout the basic rules of human intercourse and hospitality and play games only to humiliate the other team. Today, in their native-paper books, the Otomi of Pahuatlan continue to depict the "presidente del infierno" and his cronies as a power-obsessed council of twelve who likewise "cause sudden death on the road."[9]

Having eluded the pitfalls that finished off their fathers, the Twins finally come face to face with the Lords in their ball court. They play a set of games, actually allowing the Lords to win one of them without the fact being noticed. The report on play points up the significance of the game as such, its rules, the line that divides in from out of court, whose ball is used, and the scoring that attends its rubbery movement. In practice as much as ninety yards in length at Chichen, the ball court figures as a prime emblem of urban masonry and of human behavior within it: Through its halves and quarters it typically sets the terms of opposing political parties, of trimestral tribute, and of fortune. As for the ball, rubber, or *hule* in Mexican Spanish, the Sign Ollin (XVII) also means shift, change, and the earthquake that will end this Era (Four Ollin), and it denominates the Olmec "rubber people": Its elastic precision was nothing less than indispensable to the game. Without rubber, a product once exclusive to the Fourth World, the Mesoamerican type of ballgame could never have been, any more than the philosophy that evolved from it. At a deeper level, from carvings on surviving courts like those at Chichen and Tajin, we deduce an underpinning of the game in acts of decapitation that make of the head a surrogate ball and of the body's blood food for plant growth. Just these motifs appear in the *Popol vuh* epic, only with a twist that again advantages the Twins. Having lost his head the night before in the Killer Bat guest room, Hunter goes on court with a false head fashioned from a pumpkin. In the course of the game he manages to recover his original head; the pumpkin, believed by the Lords still to be what it had just been, rolls back on court. The Lords eagerly attack it, only to receive the splash of its seed in their faces.

All this recalls the story of the Twins' conception, when their mother, Blood Woman, disobeying the paternal command of the Lords of Xibalba, approached the tree where One Hunter's decapitated head hung like a gourd so that its seed or spittle could impregnate her. And just as Sky Heart had intervened at that critical moment to ensure the genetic worth of her offspring the Twins, so again Sky Heart intervenes to ensure the success of Hunter's ersatz head. These head analogues that grace One Hunter and his son, gourd and pumpkin, are early products of American plant science and feature exquisitely in the Olmec Chalcatzingo carvings.[10] Here they, as it were, fly back in the face of lower-earth Xibalba, to the benefit of future humankind. More immediately, both events represent sexual humiliation for the Lords.

Their victory now assured at the highest political level, the Twins plan further to ruin Xibalba by deciding the course of their own death and its consequence; and to that end they collude with characters called Rich and Poor. They leap into a furnace and, ground to powder, are thrown into the river; on the fifth day, running back down through evolution to the time of the mud people, they reappear as humanoid fish and then again as the pair of poorest beggars, the lowest of the low. In this guise they take Xibalba by storm through their skills as dancers and conjurors: They simulate arson and heart sacrifice to the extent that the Lords themselves want to see these phenomena and order a royal performance. Unsettled by "despair and desire" at the sight of the Twins' brilliance, they then want to join in and themselves demand to be sacrificed:

> "Do it to us!
> Sacrifice us!" they said then.
> "Sacrifice us the same way."
>   – lines 4471–3

With this psychic victory, to which all Xibalba is witness, the Twins at last reveal who they are and why they have come. Denouncing the narrowness of the Lords as binary creatures of the black and the white, they kill them for real, institute habeas corpus, and prescribe the future limits of Xibalba with its "low sun."[11] In this they reach back to the shamanist source of the epic as therapy; they make the world healthier to live in by containing the corrosive but necessary power of Xibalba. With piety the Twins then give their father a proper burial, establishing rites still recognized by the Quiché today. The whole sequence closes as they walk up into the earth's horizon of light and then on into the sky to join the Pleiades, male sun and male moon:

> Then they walked back up
> here amid the light,
> and at once
> they walked into the sky.
> the one is the sun
> the other the moon.
> Then it grew light in the sky
> and on the earth.
>
> They are still in the sky.
> In fact there climbed also
> the four hundred sons
> who had been killed by Alligator,
> so now they became their companions;
> they became the stars of the sky.
>   – lines 4695–708

So far, only the all-male side of this epic has been considered: that is, the Twins, their Fathers, the Monkeys, and the Lords. Matching them is the trio of females who, though few and rarely prominent, hold the story together. As three they equal the stones of the hearth they defend, this being an emblem of Mesoamerican women.[12]

Prime among them is Xmucane, mother of the fathers and a uniquely continuous presence both within and beyond this third creation. Initially encountered with Xpiacoc as the shaper of the doll people in the second creation, she survives, a widow, to form the ancestors of the Quiché after the end of the fourth. She brings to life and decides who shall inherit. When Blood Woman arrives at her house pregnant with the Twins, Xmucane sets her the task of showing that she can provide, by demanding she fill a net with maize from an empty field. Only when she passes this test is Blood Woman allowed into the house. Once the Twins are born, they remain unacknowledged until the moment when Xmucane, albeit despite herself, sells out their elder brothers, the Monkeys, by repeatedly laughing at them. She also keeps the house, in the sense of preparing food and drink with a care and literal economy such that it allows the Twins to deceive her when Rat tells them about their father's gaming things hidden well out of sight in the roof. In a cameo of sharp domestic focus, we see first Rat "in" the bowl of chili, that is, mirrored vertically from the roof, and second a microscopic leak in the water jar that has been made on the Twins' instructions by their ally Mosquito. Kept from Xmucane and Blood Woman's eyes, the rat image in wholesome food bodes no good: Brought to their attention, the water leak causes the women to fuss about the waste and therefore not notice the removal of the gaming things. In these respects, Xmucane's care earns her the role of guardian and effective arbiter within the home that the Twins will leave.

Above all, Xmucane expresses the pathos of One Hunter's house, crying silently and alone when first her sons and then her grandsons set out on the road all suspect will be of no return. In the absence of the Twins she bestows all her care on the maize plant they leave with her, rooted now not out in the fields but in the middle of the house. By tending the maize in the world above, she helps her grandsons below, for it thrives as they fare. For the same reason, she can gauge their fortune. At the critical moment of their final victory over Xibalba, the narrative intercuts to her weeping, this time with joy, because the maize tassels for a second time, having withered before as if blasted by the furnace the Twins had leapt into. As the corollary of the hunter Twins' epic, Xmucane's plant emerges as the effective and indispensable means by which maize, already indicated in her divining kernels in the second creation, comes to be the fit substance of which to create the human race she brings into being at the end of the fourth.

Xmucane's daughters-in-law Cipacyalo and Blood Woman, the other two women of the piece, represent an antithesis. In her Nahuatl name, Caiman Macaw, the former, One Hunter's first wife, conjoins the reptile and bird elements of Seven Parrot's family – his caiman son, Cipacna, and himself – and thus weaves in this genetic message from the third creation. Silent during her brief time at the start of the fourth creation, she harks back to a prior level of time constrained as if by genes that allow her sons no higher form than that of monkeys. By contrast, as the offspring of Blood Chief, the fourth Lord of Xibalba, Blood Woman heralds new possibilities. Precisely because of the perceived connection between blood and bone marrow, the rites and prayers of midwives invoke not just the grandmother Oxomoco/Xmucane but the skeletal Lord of the Underworld, as does the *teoamoxtli* Birth chapter, which actually shows good red blood being generated from marrow-yellow bone (Plate 7). So that this world may become habitable and the Era may begin, the Lords have to be tamed, a task allotted to the Twins; yet more critical is the need to export their strength. After One Hunter's death, the Lords attempt to keep things as they were by forbidding all Xibalba to approach the tree in which his head had become a gourd. Only Blood Woman defies the ban and becomes pregnant as a result, injecting strong Xibalba genes into the race heralded by the Twins. Rather than function as some abhorrent negative, the Lords One and Seven Death are integrated in this way into the very definition of life.

Indicted as traitor by the Lords, Blood Woman flees the netherworld to save herself and her sons, aided by turncoat Owl police who deliver to the Lords not her heart but a substitute made of cochineal and sap, thus precipitating their first "defeat." Her travels to the upper world pose a counterpart to the male epic, one relived in midwifery and one that logically offers the same chance of foreknowledge to the Twins, especially since they, after all, are themselves born via her from Xibalba.[13] She "comes up" waxing like the moon after six months, respecting a trimestral division of pregnancy characteristic of the *teoamoxtli* and matched by implication with the quarters of the year that start with the September equinox and culminate in the June solstice. Again, on being accepted by Xmucane in the upper world, she sets another precedent: The full net of maize she manages to gather serves as an emblem of inheritance generally in Mesoamerica. Blood Woman's story of curiosity and disobedience and of courage before both the paternal Lords of Xibalba and her mother-in-law, Xmucane, who greets her as a whore, furnishes the slender thread on which for nine moons the whole continuity of the epic depends. There is no miscarriage. "Only a maiden," she inflicts the first defeat on the Lords. She "enters the word" of One Leg in both the genetic and the narrative sense.

THE MAIZE PEOPLE

With the ascent of the Twins into the sky, the *Popol vuh* completes its account of the four creations and humiliations announced at the start. Having established the fates of the mud people, the doll people, Seven Parrot's family, and the Lords of Xibalba, it brings us now to the crux of things, the creation of the maize people, specifically the Quiché, who inhabit this Era. Over the four creations we have moved from the grandest to the subtlest metamorphosis, from ocean and volcano to a leaking water jar on the table, passing through strata and orders of time, outer and inner. From here on, the streams converge into history.

The maize creation requires the efforts of several parties. First, the animals have to fetch the yellow and white maize ears from the "cleft" mountain Paxil to the north of Quiché, where they are hidden, along with cacao, chocolate, and an abundance of other good foods. Returning to the narrative for the first time since the days of the mud and the doll people, Quetzal Snake and his companions supervise the grinding and molding of the maize; then Xmucane makes her final appearance in order to give it her midwife's ninefold blessing. This, her definitive act, recalls the moons of her own grandsons' gestation and establishes her as goddess of midwives and the nine Night Powers that enclose the male epic of days. This time the operation is so successful that the people who emerge, the Quiché forefathers, have godlike vision. "Far seers," they enjoy heightened sense perception and can see and know all the earth and sky in an instant. They understand the great fourfold scheme of which they are the final result, and they remark on the fact when giving due thanks to the gods. Perturbed by their very success, the gods decide to chip at the eyes and intelligence of these creatures so that they see "as in a darkened mirror." They impose mortal limits upon them, constraining them to sexual ontology as the progenitors of the Quiché.

As the culmination of cosmogony and the isthmus of the whole text, the maize creation draws together many threads of the narrative so far. The supreme achievement of American agriculture, developed as highland staple by the third millennium B.C. maize itself affirms the philosophy that you are what you eat. It concludes the development of cereal grasses, recounted in *Ríos* (pp. 4–8), and crowns the wider story hinted at in prior *Popol vuh* references to *tzite* beans, gourds and pumpkins, tomatoes, and the chilis set on the Twins' table. As the joint product of Xmucane's care and the Twins' daring, maize in this enhanced form resolves the antagonism between planter and hunter, giving a rationale for their social reciprocity. Moreover, since the emergence of the earth's crust, through intricate shifts of focus and time level the text affirms the domestic contract and sensitivity to all life that were flouted by the dolls, assures a place for mammals in the world of bird-reptiles, and sets out the rules of hospitality and the social game – all this providing the preconditions for the success of maize.

Finally, in proposing a way of life defended today by the Quiché (for example, in the lucid words of Rigoberta Menchú), the *Popol vuh* serves as a charter for that nation and human society more generally. Even more, and much to the point at this stage of planetary history, it does this thinking not out of narrow human advantage but by invoking and honoring the species and life forces that have filled its cosmogony. Tying the last thread, by participating in the maize event at Paxil the animals modify their unilateral defense of the wild, anticipating a place for themselves in a cultured world.[14]

10

World ages and metamorphosis

SUNS OF MESOAMERICA

In setting out the scheme of world ages and in telling the intricate story of cataclysm, metamorphosis, and epic quest, the *Popol vuh* stands unrivaled as a reference point for cosmogonies throughout the Fourth World. To start with, in Mesoamerica it corroborates the story of the cosmic "Suns," or world ages, characteristic of that area and preserves episodes that are absent or obscure in comparable sixteenth-century alphabetic texts in the Maya and Nahua languages. Like these, it draws on the rich iconography of ancient inscriptions and screenfold books prefiguring the charters that today defend survivors from pre-Cortesian times.

In the first instance, the *Popol vuh* parallels texts that stem from the same highland source as itself – closely in the case of other Quiché titles, like that of Totonicapan – and texts of the neighboring Kekchi and Cakchiquel. Las Casas's references to the doll people's catastrophe and the Twins' epic anticipate fuller versions of Kekchi cosmogony written out by them in this century, which follow and illuminate the *Popol vuh* story.[1] Though in much abbreviated form, the *Cakchiquel Annals* allude to the same foundation narrative, beginning with the unsuccessful molding of the first people "just from mud"; and in so doing they confirm how cosmic precedent validates territorial claims, according to the argument that in the *Popol vuh* pinpoints the guardian volcanoes of the Quiché raised by Cipacna. The primal flood inhabited by Quetzal Snake at the very start of the story is more narrowly defined as Lake Atitlan; at the same time, as a primeval life force, Quetzal Snake acquires the more threatening aspect of the reptilian monsters said elsewhere to inhabit such other highland lakes as Guatavita and Lacar. Similarly, the lower world of Xibalba, whose tokens here are the precious metals, stones, and obsidian of the nether earth, is set by the Cakchiquel into a four-part directional scheme that places it not just below but also down on the Pacific piedmont, where indeed there is plentiful archaeological evidence, at sites like Cozumalhuapa[2] and Izapa, of the ballgame that obsessed Lords One and Seven Death. (Historically, the Cakchiquel have always been more involved than the Quiché in this southern part of Guatemala.) Paxil, in Cuchumatanes, recurs as the place from which maize is bought.

Highland Maya who live in Chiapas across the modern border with Mexico, the Tzotzil and Tzeltal preserve a cosmogony that has recently become a focus of great political and cultural interest and that offers another angle on the *Popol vuh* scheme of world ages and attendant cataclysms. Sensitive to changing conditions over the four centuries that distance the *Popol vuh* from today, texts from both groups acknowledge the impact of the European invasion and the Mexican Revolution of 1910. At the same time, they still insist on Flood and Eclipse as the primary pair of disasters, affirming the *Popol vuh* distinction between the races of mud and doll people. And they adhere with remarkable tenacity to the moral lesson drawn by the *Popol vuh* from the disaster of Eclipse: Here, in the domestic revolt that marks the end of the doll people, household utensils, tired of exploitation, bite back with teeth of their own.[3] Similarly, they confirm the link between the Four Hundred house builders and the Twins as clearers of the *milpa,* by highlighting the tool they wield in common, the axe that destroys the wild and its denizens. Likewise causing these felled trees to grow back overnight, these creatures plead that the forests be saved, a message of immediate relevance in Chiapas today. From the west, these Chiapas texts also point to Paxil as the source of maize.

As for the lowland Maya of Yucatan, their tradition, though distinct in its loyalty to the *tun* rather than to the year calendar, offers a further counterpart to the *Popol vuh* in another story of four ages that end in cataclysm and continue to inhere in and shape the present. The Ah Muzen Cab episode of the *Chilam Balam Books* offers a tight numerical correspondence with the story of Seven Parrot, and the epic of the solar walk and descent to Xibalba (Metnal) told in the ceramic codex of the Classic and recast in the *Chumayel* (see Chapter 11: "How human time begins") still mediates between cosmos and history. Going deeper into time, the *Ritual of the Bacabs* relates *Popol vuh* cosmogony to the formation and health of the human body, underpinning the rhetoric of the shaman curer in the fight against, say, contagion from the underworld, or aphasic sexual urge. Forces to be appeased or invoked in aid are tracked back to the first age of creation and include first races of stone and wood, the great Itzam and other giant-boned saurians, the axe bearers (*batab*) and the Pleiades, Macaw the firebird, and Chuen the monkey.[4] Like the *Popol vuh*'s account of the Twins' childhood dream and the *Mu ikala* of the Cuna, the *bacab* ritual constructs a reality that is both outer and inner, a cosmic process concentrated in the body of the patient: his or her vertebrae, innards, and senses.

Structurally, the *Popol vuh* meets its most significant match not so much in Maya-speaking Mesoamerica as in inscriptions, screenfolds, and alphabetic texts from Mexico to the west. A major analogue can be found in the *Sunstone* of Tenochtitlan, that huge stone disk whose quincunx commemorates the four Suns, or ages, of the world that inhere in the present fifth age (Fig. 54). Although the product of a Nahuatl rather than a Quiché-speaking community, this text observes the same *tonalamatl* conventions as the *Popol vuh* and constructs cosmogony by the same means. Rarely noticed, the parallels between these two texts allow us to establish a firm term of reference for Mesoamerica against which local variation may be more finely assessed.

Once a prime cult object at the main temple of Tenochtitlan, the vast *Sunstone* brings together in one statement well-defined sets of data found separately on lesser examples of Aztec stonework. Its wealth of signs, complex numeracy, and ingenious structure of concentric rings and superimposed levels make it hard to render in descriptive prose, and in any case several elements remain enigmatic.

That cosmogony provides its literal focus is evident. From the very center of the disk there emerges the face of the earth, the god Tlaltecutli, whose eye-and-claw hands to either side recall the implacable telluric power[5] likewise displayed in the daunting statue of his female counterpart Coatlicue, with her twin-reptile head. Physically, this emergent earth is framed by the quincunx that constructs the name of the present Era, Four Ollin, which is framed in turn by a ring comprising the Twenty Signs; its first year, 13 Reed, appears directly above, on the outer rim, which consists of two cloud-snakes from whose maws emerge the heads of Xiuhtecutli and Tonatiuh, Fire and Sun, the same pair that in the same cosmic context face each other in the Huichol *Womb of the World* painting. Inset into the Sign Ollin, so as actually to constitute its four arms, are four further Signs, Water (IX), Jaguar (XIV), Rain (XIX), and Wind (II). Each of these, likewise qualified by the numeral 4, has an accompanying symbol, of which the most prominent are the Flint knife beside Four Jaguar and the blast of wind that issues from the imperial crown beside Four Wind (the other two Signs are accompanied by the *tonalamatl* days 7 Monkey and 1 Rain).

Embedded as they are in current time and the very Sign Ollin, this fourfold set of Numbers and Signs plots a cosmic story that can also be read in the discursive Nahuatl of the *Cuauhtitlan Annals,* the Nahuatl source quoted earlier in order to establish the name of the Era as Four Ollin and its first year as 13 Reed. Prompted by the founding of Mexquital Tula in the eighth century A.D., the Cuauhtitlan narrative flashes back to the start of the Era itself, setting it in the larger story of four Suns defined respectively by

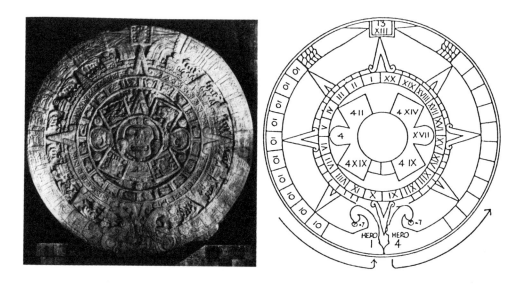

Figure 54. Sunstone: structure and detail.

their Signs, which point-for-point match those of the *Sunstone,* and their terminal catastrophes. From the same Highland Basin as the *Sunstone,* it details the same stark sense of this earth's past and predicament (fol. 2):

> The first Sun to be founded
> has the Sign Four Water,
> it is called Water Sun.
> Then it happened
> that water carried everything away
> everything vanished
> the people were changed into fish.

> The second Sun to be founded
> has the Sign Four Jaguar,
> it is called Jaguar Sun.
> Then it happened
> that the sky collapsed
> the Sun did not follow its course at midday
> immediately it was night
> and when it grew dark
> the people were torn to pieces.
> In this Sun giants lived.
> The old ones said
> the giants greeted each other thus:
> "Don't fall over," for whoever fell,
> fell forever.

The third Sun to be founded
has the Sign Four Rain,
it is called Rain Sun.
It happened then that fire rained down,
those who lived there were burned.
And they say that then tiny stones rained down and spread
the fine stones that we can see
the *tezontli* boiled into stone
and the reddish rocks were twisted up.

The fourth Sun,
Sign Four Wind,
is called Wind Sun.
Then the wind carried everything away.
The people all turned into monkeys
and went to live in the forests.

The fifth Sun,
Sign Four Ollin,
is called Earthquake Sun
because it started into motion.
The old ones said
in this Sun there will be earthquakes and general hunger
from which we shall perish.

In transcribing the *Sunstone,* this Nahuatl passage, brief as it is, points up the significance and interconnection of the four Signs that inhere in the present fifth Sun, tying in thereby the accompanying symbols of eclipse and wind. Hence, out of the first and third Suns, with their flood (water) and volcanic eruptions (rain of fire), a geological message may be read that leads into the earthquake of Ollin. Interwoven with this is the biological concern with species and metamorphosis into fish and monkeys in the first and fourth Suns; and the Jaguar of the second Sun, with its Flint knife alongside, evokes the bestial tearing apart of people (*tecualoya*) that happened during the solar eclipse and reign of darkness.

On this basis, the whole Mexican doctrine of Suns may be systematically compared with that set out in the *Popol vuh.* First of all, we find the pattern of four Suns, or ages, as such, which intricately forms part of the present Era and whose endings match the humiliations remembered by the maize ancestors of Quiché. The celestially induced destructions of the mud people and then the doll people are succinctly coded as Flood and Eclipse. The metamorphosis of the former into fish under the Sign Water is here quite explicit; in the latter there is the identical detail of the flesh-tearing Jaguars that descend from the blackened sky. And the rigidity of the doll people echoes that which prevents the "giants" of this time from getting up again once they have fallen over.

Under the Sign Rain, the rain of fire that fell on the earth is clearly volcanic and terrestrial in origin and hence appeals to the same seismic logic that pervades the Seven Parrot episode of the *Popol vuh* in the persons of his two sons Cipacna and Two Leg who overnight create mountains and shake them down again. Finally, in the fourth Sun that ends through the power of Wind we encounter the Nahuatl analogue of the Twins who triumphed over the underworld and whose Nahuatl counterpart is the Quetzalcoatl named Nine Wind and whose persona or mask is the Sign Wind. The political role of this Wind deity as patron and kingmaker, testified to in the *Tepexic Annals* and the *Relación de Cholula,* is alluded to in the symbol that accompanies the Wind Sun on the *Sunstone,* namely the imperial crown from which a blast of wind emerges. Those who metamorphosed into Monkeys during this Sun of course directly recall the Twins' elder brothers, who in turn went to the forests to join the survivors of the doll people.

Setting up these parallels between the *Sunstone* and the *Popol vuh* corroborates the reading made of the latter in the matter of the four creations remembered by the maize people at the start of this Era. Transcribed in the *Cuauhtitlan Annals,* this Mexican story of the four Suns amounts to a schematic summary[6] of the *Popol vuh*'s extended story of how, following the promptings of the deities, the Twins prepared the way for modern humankind. Emphasizing the catastrophes that terminally identify the Suns, the Nahuatl account takes no space to trace out the *Popol vuh*'s tale of human wit and intelligence or to pose humanity's emergence as an achievement. Nor do we find the intricate structuring of the *Popol vuh* beyond the basic principle of stating this fifth age as the consummation of the other four. Yet a similar evolutionary perspective is implied, if only through the mention of geology and species metamorphosis.

As a succinct visual statement glossed by the Cuauhtitlan text, the *Sunstone* offers in turn to resolve discrepancies that exist between it and other Nahuatl and Spanish transcriptions of the sixteenth century, where the sequence of Suns varies, though their individual identities remain recognizably the same. Sources like *Inomaca tonatiuh,* the *Pinturas Manuscript,* and the *Histoyre du Mechique* may in these terms be understood as variant readings of a cosmic map or design similar to the *Sunstone* (*Inomaca tonatiuh,* for example, reads, counterclockwise from the right: Four Jaguar, Four Wind, Four Rain, Four Water, and Four Ollin, with Four Rain confirming the link between volcano and birds). In any case, as we saw in the *Popol vuh,* the four ages do not simply follow each other in linear succession. On the basis of the information given, for example about the life of the Twins, it would be quite possible to rearrange the sequence if a different thematic emphasis was desired. Hence, the recurrence of the pattern of four Suns depicted on the *Sunstone* massively supports the notion of it as a paradigm; the detail proper to each age remains highly consistent. *Histoyre* focuses on the giant dolls and jaguar killers of the second age, the rain of fire of the third, and the epic of the fourth that involves Queztalcoatl, the Twins' Nahuatl counterpart.

Visually this consistency is reflected in the quincunx design itself, shared by such classic *teoamoxtli* maps as that of Coixtlahuaca, whose toponyms, position for position, may at the deeper level be read as images of the world ages: Mictlantongo with its flood and heart-fish, Teotlillan with its eclipse and *tzitzimine* knives, Nexapa with its volcanic rain and defeated saurian, Tepexic and its howling wind, and the central earth of Coixtlahuaca (Fig. 55). On this basis, a similar reading may be made of the same and cognate toponyms as they appear in the other Papaloapan *teoamoxtli, Cuicatlan* and *Laud,* especially the two final pages of the latter. These show an icon of Tlaloc bringing together the waters above and below, and the divine darkness of Teotlillan emerging in the struggle between the Sun and Death, which eminently correspond to the pair of sky-inspired catastrophes Flood and Eclipse (see Plate 4a, Table 3g). These *teoamoxtli* examples of toponyms that can be read on both the cosmic and political level follow the logic established in the *Popol vuh* when Cipacna raises the landmarks of Quiché.

Within the same iconic tradition, yet other pages and chapters demand comparison with the *Sunstone–Popol vuh* scheme, the most accessible of which is the opening chapter of *Ríos,* with its profuse Italian glosses. A late copy on European paper, the *Ríos* chapter has undergone a certain formal dislocation; it is evident, for example, that the left-to-right reading order demanded by the alphabetic glosses runs counter to that of the text in native script. Moreover, its account of the Suns is inset in an argument whose prime topic is the development of the cereals that culminated in maize, so that the problem of reading order is compounded by there being more than one level of reading, as in the *teoamoxtli.* Nonetheless, we may still actually see successive images of the Flood and those who changed into fish (*tlacamichin*), the fallen giants (along with a highly suggestive note on native interest in the fossil evidence for such creatures)[7] (Plate 17a), the volcanic rain of fire falling between reptile bodies through which fly birds brilliant like Seven Parrot, and those who changed into Monkeys driven forth by the gales of the Wind Sun (the order of the last two has been inverted). Finally, this concordance encourages us to note the comparable sequence of four or five Suns inset into the tribute-grid chapter that opens the *Borgia* group of *teoamoxtli,* especially since *Borgia* itself also includes the image of Parrot carrying a human arm, severed like that of Jaguar Deer in the third Sun. *Borgia* also devotes a magnificent page (p. 71) to the "sun of suns" Tonatiuh, enthroned as master of the present age of Era Four Ollin.

In all this, the *Sunstone* of Tenochtitlan and the *Popol vuh* of Quiché complement each other in affirming the shape of Mesoamerican cosmogony, one that has its literary roots in the pre-Cortesian books, encompasses the main languages of the region – Nahuatl, Maya, Otomanguan[8] – and

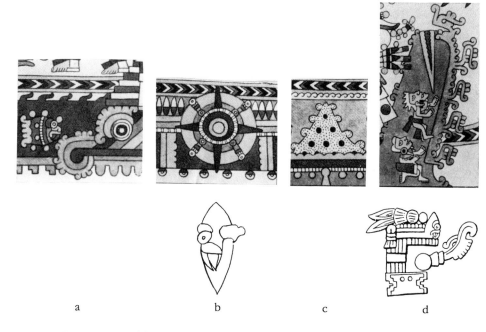

a   b   c   d

Figure 55. World-age emblems: (a) fish in rising flood; (b) flint knife with sun; (c) volcanic ash; (d) wind. (Upper emblems, *Coixtlahuaca Map* [see Plate 11]; lower emblems, *Sunstone* [see Fig. 54].)

remains an important political element in the lives of native peoples today. Availing itself of the resources of native script to produce an ingenious visual statement of five Suns in one, the *Sunstone* actually shows how deeper levels of time may inhere in the present (the four humiliations remembered by the maize people) and employs *tonalamatl* Numbers and Signs to suggest not just their story but their rhythms and phases in time, again like the *Popol vuh*.

SIPAPUNI

"Place of emergence" in Hopi, Sipapuni provides a focal point for the heirs to Anasazi, that is, the Hopi themselves, the Zuni, and the other Pueblos as well as the Athapaskan Navajo and Apache.[9] Prior to their acts of foundation, the ancestors of these peoples climbed up through Sipapuni (or its linguistic equivalent), leaving below them a set of netherworlds. Characteristically these worlds are matched with sets of strata and minerals, storeys of a building numbered from the top down (a trait of Anasazi domestic architecture), trees, birds, and colors. They are also assigned to different races who struggle against rival life-forms and who are overcome by cataclysms of flood, fire, and wind. Again we find earthquake as the geological factor in the particular struggle with giant monsters who, once dispatched, leave their blood as lava and their limbs as volcanic rock formations.[10] The gods who oversee and the heroes who participate in this story include the sun, thunderbirds and the lightning that leaves the air sharp with ozone, the grandmother, and the trickster twins.

The different local versions of this story echo each other constantly, yet no single scheme can be elaborated to accommodate the finer detail of them all, even in the arithmetical matter of how many worlds precede or inhere in the present. The very title of Courlander's account is *The Fourth World of the Hopis,* and Waters's *Book of the Hopi* speaks too of the present world as the fourth, taking advantage of its resonance with the notion of the Fourth World of geography; in the murals painted on Hopi *kivas,* Sipapuni, adorned with cloud terraces, is four-sided. On the other hand, in Tedlock's careful transcription of the Zuni "Beginning," which in all respects closely adheres to the genesis of their near neighbors and allies the Hopi, we read that after the great emergence "some of the people were still living in the fourth room beneath,"[11] that is, somewhere arithmetically prior to the present fifth world. Five is also the total of the Navajo worlds.

Insofar as emergence is an explicit analogue for human birth, one that inverts descent from the womb, Sipapuni readily recalls the female epic of the *Popol vuh* and Blood Woman's coming up from Xibalba, "downstairs." In turn, her offspring the Twins are exactly matched by counterparts who, also compulsive game players, blaze the trail to the upper world, where necessary providing a ladder. Indeed, on the subject of twins the parallels are so compelling as to demand discussion in their own right within the enabling paradigm of their epic or trance-journey.

In the strange webbed and furry creatures who existed during Tokpa, the Hopi "dark midnight," or second age, and who surface in the Moss Lake of the Zuni, we detect a familiar argument that, as the Zuni author Joseph Peynetsa put it, "sounds like evolution"; the same applies to the waterbound feather-snake depicted in Zuni painting. Again, for the people of this age to be properly constituted, the right kind of maize has to be found to make their flesh heavy and good.[12] The source of this vital ingredient is, however, not a local food mountain like Paxil; instead, obtaining it involves a long journey south to the Coral Sea. In the Hopi version, the southward journey, to the red city Palatkwapi,[13] acquires many traits of the Xibalba epic, for example sacrifice and burial in the main plaza and the subsequent appearance of hero twins. Also, the gift of maize is here effectively made in exchange for a child's life, the victim of a shaman foreign to the Hopi–Zuni band, all of which further underpins the long-standing link between Anasazi and Mesoamerica.

Complementing these Pueblo accounts, that of the Navajo likewise deals with sets of minerals, plants, and colors pertinent to previous worlds and strongly elaborates the epic of the Twins: Poqangwhoyas in Hopi, Nayenezgani in Navajo. Emergence as such is a central concern of the Blessing Way, just as the Twins' epic gives focus to the Shooting Chant, first in the Holy Way series. In *Dine bahane* a set of four worlds ends in flood and other disasters before the people emerge through the equivalent of Sipapuni; Klah, Gray Eyes, and other great scribes who conveyed the master narratives that accompany their Emergence dry paintings generally distinguish four prior worlds, not least since the present age comes after the fourth, the time of the "ancient" Pueblos, or Anasazi.[14]

Place of Emergence, the seventh and last great pollen painting used in the Blessing Chant, sets the matter out comprehensively in the quincunx pattern of the *Sunstone* and the *Coixtlahuaca Map* (Plate 12b). At the center lies the Navajo equivalent of Sipapuni, a round black disk of emergence from which four oval arenas extend diagonally, colored in memory of the four ages, white and black above, turquoise and yellow below. Almost touching their respective minerals, to east and west stand Sun in turquoise mask and Moon in white; pairing them are Badger and Coyote, who issued from the contact between earth and sky in the fourth age. Around these inner designs spreads the flood that sums up past cataclysms, and stretching across it is the ladder cane by which people arrived at the present, represented now on the outer edge by four matching mountains, two of shell and two of stone.

A mountain of abalone, Dokoslid, the home of the Twins' mother, Changing Woman, lies opposite the white-shell mountain home of her sister, shown here literally as the "black-banded one" (Tsisnadjini). On the other diagonal the turquoise mountain of the sun, Tsodzil, is paired with the Jet, or Black, Mountain Dibentsah, named after the "mountain sheep" that was first killed there by one of the Twins (the other having gone to Tsodzil), an act that caused outrage among the black thunder and sky gods. In the grand opening of the nine-night Night Chant, the properties of these four guardian mountains are celebrated in a space delineated by a smaller and simpler version of this quincunx map painting, and for the cure sand is actually brought from each in turn and applied to the patient, whose body here occupies the center.

As a set that matches the arenas of four past ages, and with redstone as a variant for jet, these mountains have a similar function in other related chants and paintings. They reappear, for example, in the notable fourfold set of paintings whose theme is the road of Emergence. Based architecturally on the Pueblo *kiva* design (rather than the round Navajo hogan), the first of the set ranges the four age mountains concentrically around Sipapuni; the second and third display their original colors in four steps, or degrees, along the pollen exit road, and in the fourth these are incorporated in the four-colored tassel of the maize plant that the road has now become.

At the same time, at the political level the four mountains in this quincunx design stand literally as the four great landmarks of Navajo territory, as we have seen. Hence, as a center, itself a quincunx that has four corresponding outer guardian mountains, it succinctly defines a historical as well as a cosmic structure for Navajo Anasazi. In so doing it of course rehearses, half a millennium later and at a thousand miles' distance, exactly the procedure of the *Coixtlahuaca Map* and the Tenochtitlan *Sunstone*. For this reason, it is yet more chastening to discover that in the Blessing Way painting, the central quincunx corresponds to Dzilinaxodili, Huerfano peak on the watershed and at the center of the world, "the mountain of motion or which customarily turns"[15] – exactly the meaning of the Ollin Sign at the center of the *Sunstone* that identifies this fifth world as one of earthquake or movement.

The geological continuum of Anasazi and Mesoamerican Suns is negatively defined by its attenuation or absence everywhere farther to the north. In Turtle Island, it is true, former worlds typically number four, and they may be imaged as strata, like the sky levels of Menomini or Osage charts, or as stages in the burrowing through the earth depicted in Mide origin scrolls.[16] Moreover, there are certain echoes of the emergence doctrine in, for example, Appalachian texts, and the ubiquitous story of the Flood is sometimes matched with other cataclysms. Yet generally it is this Flood that of itself provides the hinge into present time, the formation of this earth island resulting from the single motif of the diver or plunger who from a great depth brings up or provides out of the water the irreducible atom of matter from which terra firma can grow. The geographical concept of Turtle Island itself arises from the particular role played by the turtle in this basically sedimentarian process, according to Algonkin, Iroquoian, and Siouan sources.[17]

Farther up the same cordillera that links Mesoamerica with Anasazi, the narratives of the Northwest correlate with vertically aligned totem-pole images, presenting a special case. Despite a "confusion" in this cosmogony attributed by scholars to local clans bending larger stories to their particular interests, in the Tsimshian Raven Cycle and other texts there are clear echoes of the world-age scheme. Combining the fish metamorphosis of the first age with the flouted domestic contract of the second, these texts feature the salmon as heroes or people who voluntarily turned into fish, strengthening the capacity of these vertebrates to serve precisely as the all-important food source of the region; failure on the part of humans continuously to respect this transaction results in catastrophe. In addition, old Haida accounts represent the creation of the Queen Charlotte Islands and the mainland as the result of two pebbles being put into the floodwater, an etiology that conforms to the general sedimentarianism of northern America. In the first place, however, the pebbles are said to have been taken from the innermost of five nested boxes, each of which corresponds to an age or "village below us";[18] though faint, the echo here is from Anasazi and Mexico.

In the published English version of *Dine bahane,* the succession of the four world ages, a section in itself, is followed by two longer cycles about Coyote and the Twins, which mediate between those cosmic beginnings and this world age with its culmination in the annals of the Navajo "clans." As "monster slayers" and celestial travelers, Nayenezgani and his twin are clearly epic, like the Twins of *Popol vuh.* Coyote too has been seen as epic in his way, yet his animal condition implicates him more thoroughly in the genetic story of emergence epitomized by Seven Parrot. This is also true about Coyote in relation to such Turtle Island counterparts as the Great Hare of the Algonkin. In the *Place of Emergence* painting, Coyote's pedigree entitles him to appear in its quincunx, his birth having been brought about by the very contact of the upper and lower regions, Sky and Earth, in the succession of ages.

Elsewhere depicted tracking through the fields of stars he himself threw out at random around their eleven constants, Coyote follows the farthest scent, gambles, and loves passionately. His partner is Bear Woman. Also a dry-painting subject, the bear is a cosmic creature in its own right throughout North America, that is, above the habitat line of the large bears: grizzly and black. Omnipresent in Athapaskan and former Navajo territory in the Northwest, Bear Mother features on totem poles, with her odd-numbered teeth; councils of bears live and dance under the four guardian mountains of the Cherokee, and they push through the earth walls of the four former worlds in the Mide scrolls. In the Navajo story, Coyote and Bear, furry mammals, utterly destroy each other four times and yet survive because they want each other so badly. Their experience corrects the gender conflict of a previous age,[19] which, relegating female and male to lonely masturbation, had engendered the primeval monsters slain by Nayenezgani; and it relates thematically to a domestic contract broken not by a species, as in *Popol vuh,* but by a gender. It also corresponds to the human emergence from coyote skin depicted in the *Red Mountain* painting, through the four hoops of senses and sensibility.

ANDEAN ASCENT

From the creation of the world up till this time there have passed four suns, not counting the one that at present gives us light. The first was lost through water, the second by the sky falling on to the earth which killed the giants that there were and the bones which the Spaniards have found hidden in various places are theirs. . . . The third sun they say ended through fire, the fourth, through wind; of this fifth sun they had a great account. . . .[20]

In the absence of other information, there is no reason at all why "they" here should not be Mesoamerican. In fact they are Inca, the Quechua-speaking inhabitants of Tahuantinsuyu. Given the supposed dearth of communication between pre-Hispanic Mexico and Peru, the coincidence of imperial cosmogonies is startling. The number, sequence, and detail of the Suns recorded in iconic script and epitomized in the *Sunstone* of Tenochtitlan's main temple recur, identically according to this 1613 account by Murúa, in the *quipu* script and the huge gold disk that adorned the Coricancha in Cuzco (" . . . and they had it painted and encoded in the temple of Coricancha and placed in their quipus up till the year 1554,"). The Quechua terms that correspond to the suns listed by Murúa (in Spanish) surface in several sources and are neatly listed, albeit with one slight variation, in González Holguín's 1608 dictionary. There the sun as such is rendered as *pachacuti,* a turning or shift in time–space. The cataclysms that provoke these shifts are qualified successively as *lloqlla unu,* water avalanche, or flood; *quilla unqo,* sick moon, or eclipse; *nina,* fire; and *auca,* warlike spirit, here the counterpart of wind.

A detailed Quechua account of these Suns is given in the *Runa yndio niscap Machoncuna* manuscript of Huarochiri, a work that indeed was prompted by Spanish colonial attempts to extirpate "idolatrous" cults founded on Andean cosmogony.[21] Tracing the origins of these cults, the Huarochiri text pays particular attention to Pariacaca and Pachacamac, between whose shrines that town lies, the one a snow-capped mountain upstream on the river Lurin, and the other a pyramid downstream on the coast. Listed by Guaman Poma as the major shrines of Chinchasuyu, these local forces are contrasted specifically with Viracocha and other features of the religion imposed on the area by Cuzco and the Inca. Because of its sheer scope and choice of detail, the Huarochiri text has been called the *Popol vuh* of the Andes by José María Arguedas and others, a fair comparison that reminds us nonetheless that it lacks the extreme narrative finesse of the Quiché text, consisting rather of chapters devoted to particular *huaca*s and the offerings and prayers made to them. Indeed, it is this expository mode that has tended to occlude the scheme of four ages reported in the text.

At the very outset, in chapter 1, we are taken back to first beginnings, the times of Yanamca Tutañamca, or "black night and eldest darkness," and Huallallo Carhuincho, whose cannibal tendencies made of him a main opponent of the hero who emerges as a focal point for the whole text: the lightning god Pariacaca. The claims of the Inca founder god Viracocha are then in turn matched against those of Pariacaca, to the advantage of the latter (chap. 2). With this, leaving aside creator heroes, the narrative adopts the mode of cosmic event whose scale exceeds kinship and rather concords with the pattern of the Suns. Instead of the set of four Suns, we are first told, however, about just two, each of which lasts five days. These are the celestially induced pair Flood and Eclipse (chaps. 3 and 4). This initial pair of American disasters here includes the decidedly Andean motifs of the towering mountain Huillcacoto – which serves as a flood refuge for a human family and a handful of domestic and other animals – and the sea that subsides back into the Pacific; more particularly, each invokes the pastoral llama that transformed the Andean economy.

Before the Flood, a llama with sixth sense warns its human masters of impending disaster, a gesture of solidarity in tune with Tahuantinsuyu pastoralism. Before the Eclipse we again see the heartless exploitation of domestic objects, a theme visible on Moche ceramics,[22] and disregard of the contract that binds humans to creatures who have left the wild to fall under their control. Whereas in the *Popol vuh* the upheaval is led by the mortars and kitchen utensils tired of unfeeling use, and by the enraged dog and turkey, the two creatures whose long-standing alliance with American peoples is likewise celebrated in Anasazi ritual, in Tahuantinsuyu the revolt of the utensils is accompanied by that of the llamas. As *Runa yndio* (chap. 4) reports, these flock animals turn on their masters in savage herds:

> How the sun died.
>
> Long ago the sun is said to have died.
> For five days after its death it was night.
> The stones began to jostle each other;
> the mortars, large and small, began to eat people,
> the pestles too.
> The mountain llamas attacked people.
> As Christians we account for this today
> by saying that it was the eclipse at Jesus Christ's
> death. And possibly it was.

As for the third and fourth cataclysms, of fire and wind, they may be discerned as events that belong to the subsequent cycle of Pariacaca's deeds: Both explicitly develop the mountain motif announced with the Flood, and both occur precisely after five-day warnings. Pursuing Huallallo and his companion, Manañamca, Pariacaca attempts to annihilate them with lightning, flood, and an immense torrent of red and yellow fire sent from five directions that reaches high up into the sky; as they retreat, one to the rainforest and the other to the ocean, Pariacaca sets up guardians in the form of sons who petrify into the mountains Sulluyallap and Chuquihuampo, who have allotted to them their dues as *huaca*s (chap. 8). Huallallo is last seen as a giant reptile that comes to form a stratum of Andean rock – another third-age analogue of the crushed Cipacna; and it is after Pariacaca's definitive victory over him that the notion of Tahuantinsuyu is first established in the text. The final catastrophe of the four concerns the people of Colli, who, like the Lords of Xibalba, flout the laws of hospitality. Punishing them for their meanness, Pariacaca sweeps them all away in a violent wind, except for one of their number whom he also transforms into a stone *huaca,* again allotting him his economic due (chap. 25).

Although spread awkwardly over the text, these four cataclysms clearly form a pattern equivalent to that reported by Murúa, and hence to that of the *Popol vuh* and the *Sunstone*. Each main event is identified with a five-day period, and the first two, the celestially induced Flood and Eclipse, form a pair, as do the second two, the rain of fire and wind associated with Pariacaca (who in this respect acts as an epic hero comparable to the Twins); and the argument of the whole is underpinned by such clear-cut parallels as the domestic contract of the second world age and the hospitality motif of the fourth. Moreover, through the assigning of the four cataclysms to features of the landscape surrounding Pariacaca, notably other *huaca* mountains, the scheme acquires the quality of the territorial quincunx epitomized in the *Coixtlahuaca Map*. In other words, in filling out the bare Inca scheme reported by Murúa and other Spanish colonial authors, *Runa yndio* intimately confirms its American nature.

With its concentration on *huaca*s that result from petrification of bygone deities and monsters, the Huarochirí text sharpens our focus on the implicit link made in the *Popol vuh* and the Mesoamerican texts between geology and biology, the common point of reference being rock fossils. The Huallallo reptile of stone is such a case, as is the heaving reptilian beast reported by Bertonio that, like Cipacna, threatens the stability of the earth's crust.[23] (In architecture, this Andean ideology of stone informs the serpentine courses of masonry that have over centuries resisted *pachacuti,* or earthquake.) A further Andean trait relative to the *huaca*s of the Fourth World scheme is their hierarchy and the dues paid to them. Being the direct agent of what elsewhere are cataclysms beyond individual control, Pariacaca recalls such other Andean superheroes as Viracocha, who personally destroyed his opponents with volcanic fire, and Bachue of the Chibcha to the north, who could both cause and stem flood. Under the supreme auspices of these almighty figures, cosmogony sanctions the duties of daily life, like the clearing of irrigation canals – artifacts of stone themselves thought of as *huaca*s.

In Guaman Poma's *Nueva corónica,* this political reading of the world ages, in which a contrast is established between an almightly ruler and his human subjects, is taken much farther, reflecting Inca ideology more specifically. His chapter on cosmogony structurally reproduces the scheme of Suns, yet at every turn humanizes it, adducing a political message proper to the Inca. Rationalized by the *quipu,* the *tahuantinsuyu* governed by Cuzco is here not just stable as stone but exemplary of the work ethic. In the *Nueva corónica,* this world-age pattern informs the whole account of Tahuantinsuyu and its fourfold spatial division into *suyu*s; and what is more, it retroactively gives shape to biblical accounts of creation.

Guaman Poma's cosmogony chapter (pp. 48–78; Fig. 56) reproduces a scheme of four world ages defined not so much by catastrophic endings as

Figure 56. Inca world ages. (Guaman Poma, *Nueva corónica*, pp. 47–63.)

by the habits of the people who lived during them, who are qualified successively as Uariviracocha, Uari, Purun, and Auca. The fourth, identical with Murúa's description, invokes conflict, and the third means something like "crude" or "unfinished"; *uari,* the element common to the first two, means "original," and first of these having a deity affix. In the corresponding images, the first two ages are distinguished from the succeeding ones as an initial pair on several counts. Like the Flood and Eclipse, they are shown to be directly subject to celestial forces, emblemized by the sun (first to the right, then to the left), while from below simple prayers are offered up to the sky. Further, these docile humans have yet to learn to weave and are clothed only in leaves and skins; the cotton distaff first appears with the Purun (structurally, these three skin coverings find their more radical presocial analogues in the scale, feather, and hair of the *Popol vuh* third world age). Nevertheless, even then the human capacity and, indeed, duty to work are signaled by the Andean footplough that appears as early as the first age, and by the appearance in the landscape of a *pucullo,* a small house and fixed abode, in the second. The theme of work and effort continues to be strongly developed in the large thatched buildings of the Purun and in the massive stone-built fortifications of the Auca, which physically exclude the sky. Visually, this set of images affirms the Inca ideology of labor and progress, in which Andean humankind is offered a chance of ascent, at the price of obedience to the system. In succeeding chapters Guaman Poma explains how this humanist imperative was translated into the Inca state religion. Placed at the center of the Coricancha disk described by Murúa, Viracocha is exalted as supreme deity, personifying Inca power; by the same logic, the cataclysmic Pachacuti is appropriated as an Inca name or title.

Supplemented by Spanish chronicles, the cosmogony reported in *Runa yndio* and Guaman Poma's *Nueva corónica* announce priorities of their own, yet it conforms to the same scheme of Suns that informs Mesoamerican texts. As an Andean scheme with its particular emphasis on rock formation and its moral imperatives, it survives in Quechua ideology today and is echoed in cultures along the former borders of Tahuantinsuyu: Chibcha, Amazonian, Gran Chaco, and Mapuche. A much-cited example taken from Quechua speakers in the town of Tacana concerns the revolt of the utensils during the Eclipse,[24] versions of which are recounted by groups close to the old Antisuyu frontier. The story can also be heard among the Desana in Colombia, the Chiriguano in Paraguay, and even in Ge in the eastern highlands of Brazil, together with the concept of automatic tools of the kind used by the Twins in the *Popol vuh.* In texts gathered this century in the Gran Chaco, to the southeast, a series of catastrophes recognizable as those of the Suns continues to punctuate cosmogony: a flood, caused here by subsidence; a prolonged darkness or sunless year in which people eat dogs, rather than the inverse; a rain of fire linked with the story of the Pleiades; and a further disaster most often identified as the cold of altitude. As such, the motif of fallen giants, and the fossil evidence they left of themselves, reaches down from Mesoamerica and Darien through the whole length of the Andean chain.[25]

Until the loss of autonomy a century ago, the same scheme of ages throve in the Mapuche polity, in its way a *tahuantinsuyu,* not least in the education of children. From the lips of people born before that date, notably the anonymous Huinkulche interviewed by Kössler-Ilg,[26] a remarkable story has emerged that adapts the Fourth World Suns to the landscape of the southern cordillera, Pire Mahuida. The first and least mistakable of the Mapuche cataclysms is the Flood. Threshing the waters of the ocean or, in the highland version, Lake Lacar, the serpent Cai Cai forces the land creatures to seek refuge on the mountain Threng threng, the domain of another reptile known by that name who causes its strata to bend upward so as to stay above the floodwaters. The traces of those who experienced this disaster are found in fossil-rich strata at Trompul near Lacar in the sacred-lakes region, chiefly the fish to which many of the proto-humans of the time reverted. Literally "bone-stone" in Mapuche (*fora-lil*), these fossils also correspond to other vertebrates who at night come out to haunt as snake, bird, or vampire, possessed of the same beady eyes and fin-wings that monstrously prefigure the eventual human image. The skulls of primeval horses with their gendered sets of teeth (four more for males), some of which bear marks of human design, are likewise given their interpretation.

Rather than a straightforward blotting out of the sun, the Mapuche texts interpret the cataclysm of Eclipse as a prolonged darkness that lasts "not ten days, nor ten months, nor yet ten years," a time shift via the decimal that leads in turn to estimates of the great cycles of cold and snowline meticulously observed throughout the Andes in the same cosmic frame. At the same time, instead of a domestic revolt involving utensils and animals, men and women vie for power, a motif widespread in South America that features amazons and lost wives sought in remorse in the land of the dead.[27] It even reaches into North America, as *Dine bahane* and certain Turtle Island texts testify. Yet thematically the connection is clear, for the male–female strife in question is provoked by the breach of just the order of domestic contract featured in Tahuantinsuyu and Mesoamerican texts.

About the volcanic origin of the rain of fire that corresponds to the third Sun, there can be no possible doubt in the Huinkulche text, where it provides a sequel to the Flood. Indeed, striving for refuge on Threng threng, survivors of the former people were next rained upon from above by ashes and hot stones. For protection they made themselves hats – tiles made from clay – a precedent still respected in the Chilean countryside when the cordillera erupts. As for the wind of the fourth Sun, it too threatened those striving for safety in the mountains, notably a couple and their child who were transformed by its blast into stones, said still to be visible near Quillen and the sacred lakes. Published in several versions, the Mapuche tradition extends to the farthest south, to the Yama and Alacalufe, especially on the subjects of the great tidal flood, human metamorphosis, and the male–female strife proper to the age of darkness.

Appearing four centuries later than the classic Mesoamerican and Tahuantinsuyu version of the Suns, these Mapuche texts strongly evidence its continuity and extension in the Fourth World. Through the model of the Melihuinkul, the four mountains that center precisely on the place of survival Threng threng, the quincunx of ages is translated this time into Mapuche territory, at the southernmost end of America's Andean chain. Particularly striking is the detail of the biogeological message read from the *fora-lil* embedded in those mountains.

FLOOD AND FOOD TREE

The Soto-Carib text *Watunna* superbly represents the cosmogony of the territory it itself brings down from the sky. To the west, to slake thirst, came the Casiaquare canal, the water that physically links the two great drainage systems of the Orinoco and the Amazon; to the east, to satisfy hunger, came Roraima, the great food tree later transformed into the towering sentinel of the Guyana highlands that separate the lower courses of those rivers. In the middle lies the Soto heartland, Marahuaka, also once a tree and plant cutting from Roraima, now the mountains from which the headwaters of the Orinoco spring. Among published rainforest cosmogonies, it is distinguished as a narrative that consciously asserts its shape and integrity, allowing us to deduce from it an overall argument. Part of this argument is glossed in a shorter companion piece known as *Medatia,* which includes a rare diagram of the Soto shaman's cosmos (see Chapter 11, esp. Fig. 58).

From its center, Marahuaka, *Watunna* finds immediate resonance in the cosmogonies of other Caribs and of the Arawak, who together settled much of the northern rainforest, Guyana, and the islands of the Carib sea. It lies particularly close to the Guyana narratives that feature the hero Makunaima, as well as the Pemon stories and cures (*panton, taren*), which, moreover, explicitly defer to Soto authority. As a text characteristic of the rainforest, which in these matters stretches effectively from Panama to Paraguay, it likewise finds echoes, for example, in the narratives of the Tucano and Witoto in the upper Amazon and the many Brazilian groups who now recognize a common focus in Xingu.[28]

From the start, it will be clear that *Watunna* does not simply offer another version of geological quincunx detected in Mesoamerica, Anasazi, and Tahuantinsuyu texts. Nor does it allow us, over the narrative as a whole, so readily to separate out from metamorphosis a specifically epic story of the kind typified by the Twins: Like the Guarani account, it involves its twins and heroes in the deeper processes of creation. At the same time, by virtue of presenting a carefully constructed, large-scale argument, divisible into episodes and cycles that are overtly concerned with the major questions of earth formation and life-forms, it not only offers a yardstick for the rainforest tradition but fully bears comparison with the *Popol vuh* itself.

As it stands in Guss's English translation, *Watunna* takes us from the very beginnings of time, when earth and sky were one, to the invasion of the rainforest that continues today. In the process we experience two types of narrative, cosmogonical and historical, which hinge on the creation of Wahnatu, the forebear of the Soto nation. The historical part runs through a recognizably linear account of settlement and later encounter with Spanish, Dutch, and other invaders; the cosmogony obeys more complex schemata and threads genealogy and kinship into repeated and large-scale metamorphosis.

The story begins in the sky with Wanadi, light source and owner of the electricity that strikes as lightning, tokens of which are the shaman's quartz crystals; from his privileged position, Wanadi enjoys the overview of earth aspired to by the shaman in his trance, dramatically envisioned later in the narrative. From above, Wanadi starts things off, making two initial attempts to people the earth, in the person first of Seruhe Ianade and then of Nadeiumadi. In neither guise is he successful, and the surrogates concerned return to the sky. From Seruhe Ianade's placenta rises the satanic Odosha, who enslaves the first people, urging them to gain a surfeit of fish by killing their owner. Having learned to kill, they grow ill and turn into animals. Then in the second attempt Odosha ensures that the remaining people learn to die; general death results from his bettering Nadeiumade, whose nephew, moreover, causes a reign of darkness during which the first corpse shifts under the earth and he himself changes into a monkey. After this, Wanadi descends to earth in a third aspect, the "house-builder" Attawanadi, who eventually, after four intervening cycles of events, creates the ancestral Soto. The first of these cycles concerns Attawanadi himself; the second, his offspring by proxy, the twins Iureke and his brother. The third and fourth cycles deals with further pairs of heroes, both antagonistic to Mado the Jaguar and none naturally born.

From the start, Attawanadi lives exemplarily, bringing manioc from the sky and helping people to settle. He confirms the monkey's diminished status, assigning it, as it were, the tail that in *timehri* designs and rainforest discourse generally distinguishes it from humans (Fig. 57), and he anticipates the status of humans through his vision, his capacity to imagine. Ever aided by Wade, the grandfather of sloths and hairy mammals and capable of adopting the humblest aspect as an untidy old man, he confronts Odosha in a power dialogue like that held between Paï and Charia, the Tupi lords of life

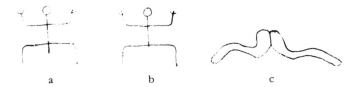

Figure 57. Timehri: (a) monkey with tail; (b) human without tail; (c) first human birth. (Inscription at Wainambi.)

and death. In his power to dream he particularly resembles heroes of the Witoto, the Tucano and other groups to the west, and of the Guyanese Arawak to the east. Indeed, the Witoto creator Rafuema has been taken as exemplary of this faculty, one that involves the psychotropic and hallucinogenic substances like *ayahuasca* named in *Watunna* and that presupposes them to be a means of recovering contact with the deities and forces of life.[29]

In practice, Attawanadi outdoes the deathly Odosha through his love for his fish bride, Kaweshawa. A blowpipe hunter who secretly farms, he earns the right to marry Kaweshawa by building a house and field (*conuco*) for his future father-in-law, the fish master. When she is stolen away he puts all into getting her back, passing through a dizzying series of transformations. He also attempts to find a substitute for her: Rehearsing Wanadi's two initial failures and following Nadeiumade, who dreamed his own mother into existence, he dreams two women into life, the one from white clay, which dissolves in the water, the other from black tree resin, which burns in the sun. Eventually, having disguised himself by swapping heads with Wade, he finds his wife in the sky and rescues her. Immersing her in the intensely blue waters of Lake Akuena, he makes a new wife out of her charred body and out of her arm a second woman for his friend the lizard. Finally he settles down.

From this pause the story moves forward into the next cycle, when Attawanadi decides to go back to the sky to ask Wanadi for the egg from which his people are to be born and from which in fact Iureke and his twin emerge. Called Huehanna, this life source buzzes with the dancing and singing of future generations. Attawanadi is frustrated in his purpose because Huehanna has been stolen, first by Nuna the cannibal moon and then by Nuna's sister, to whom he makes incestuous advances in an episode that accounts for the dark blemishes on Nuna's face and that is reproduced all but identically throughout the rainforest. Bringing the egg down to earth and guarding it as her own, the sister becomes the feathered anaconda Huiio, the mistress of Orinoco and all the rivers. Drying her feathers in the sun, Huiio is pursued and shot by the team of prototype hunters who in the Urubu-Tupi version number the zodiac eleven. She releases the egg Huehanna into the air, where the birds are waiting to catch it, but it smashes on a rock, and the people in it fall into the water, turning into eggs; from these eggs in turn emerge fish, caimans, and other cold-blooded denizens of Huiio's rivers. Huiio's Great Snake body is then eaten in a carnivorous orgy initiated by the jaguar Manuwa and the nocturnal Owls. A huge flood covers the entire earth, leaving only two fish eggs dry and unopened; these become the twins Shikiemona and Iureke.[30]

At first the Twins are fostered by the fire-breathing toad Wawao and her jaguar husband, Manuwa, whose evil intentions toward them they repeatedly frustrate as tricksters who match brute force with cunning and the shaman/*huhai*'s capacity to turn into cricket, cockroach, fish, turtle, or bird. So as to discover Wawao's secret fire, Iureke hides in the roof; and although she spots him reflected in her cooking pot, he succeeds in taking the fire. As for Manuwa, they lure him undignifiedly into a cave with a meat bait, steal his eyes, and finally send him off swinging into space on a liana. Again, this whole episode has close parallels throughout the rainforest in stories of twins torn literally out of their mother's belly by what become adoptive jaguar parents, toad cooks with secret fire, and the swinging jaguar whose Tupi cousin, colored a hypnotic blue, later waits in the sky to plunge and kill during the Eclipse.

In subsequent adventures the Twins continue to live exemplarily, setting precedent. The Wanwanna celebration is established, for example, when Iureke forgives his brother, a bachelor, for seducing his wife. They complete their cycle upon avenging their mother, Huiio, in fire and another flood, caused by spilling the *caruto* oil from her gourd. They save themselves by taking refuge in twin Mariche palms[31] that turn into the mountain Ekuadi hidi, northeast of Marahuaka. But when the water ebbs specifically to the limit of the Caribbean Sea, they discover that they have not eliminated all those they blame for Huiio's murder, notably four birds who in fact elsewhere prove helpful to humans. They also find that the Piaroa, the Soto's downstream Carib neighbors, have appropriated the quartz crystals that they themselves had thrown away on the rock Madan tahu, not realizing at first their value as stones of lightning power. These Twins too then travel back up to the sky.

Relative to the jaguar Mado, one sacred to Wanadi and born from the blood of a certain Sahatuma, the remaining two cycles have as heroes the pioneer Wachamadi and the evening star Kuamachi. Like his twin brother, Wachamadi is the second-born of a woman impregnated by snake poison and has elder brothers, also twins, the ferocious harpy eagles Dinoshi. One of his uncles, Mominaru, is responsible for spilling the blood of Sahatuma that produced Mado; but it is with the other uncle, Kasenadu, that he has most dealings, as nephew and potential son-in-law.

Wachamadi's pioneer arms have "the strength of four hundred" (thanks to the Mariche potion he takes [p. 56]), and his axe cuts as if of its own accord. Thus equipped, in the impossibly short time allotted to him he makes house and *conuco* for Kasenadu, master of lightning and thunder. According to Attawanadi's precedent, now general rainforest custom, he thus earns the right to Kasenadu's daughter in marriage but is thwarted because this uncle hates him as he did his sister (Wachamadi's mother); and in any case, as the Pemon commentary explains, his wooing one so high is effrontery.[32] In the newly completed house, Kasenadu tries to get Wachamadi drunk on *iarake* and destroy him, only to be badly damaged himself by his own lightning. After this, Kasenadu exchanges his fire for an axe he is now too weak to wield. Shown to have superior methods and tools in the all-important art of the *conuco,* Wachamadi becomes the new master of field clearing, beside whom old Kasenadu appears poor and ineffectual.

With Kuamachi, the link with Mado is much more direct, since this creature, leading other animals and the star people, butchers his mother. Kuamachi avenges this act first by killing Mado and his daughter. He then attacks the star people under their leader, Wlaha, as they gorge themselves on fruit they said they would help to harvest from a giant tree. He causes a flood, which again issues from a gourd – caiman-infested water that cuts off the star people's escape and that he and his grandfather negotiate in a canoe dreamt into existence. Next he sets the tree afire and shoots arrows at them, provoking a carnage that leaves entrails floating on blood-red water. In a dazzling and final set of metamorphoses, this Götterdämmerung is translated into the sky and astronomy, into relations between the fixed stars and the planets. As seven elements of himself, Wlaha ascends to become the Pleiades, the group that marks the zodiac path followed by the planets and the planting seasons; a one-legged companion becomes the adjacent Orion. The orange troupial turns into the planet Mars, and Kuamachi assumes his true identity as Vesper, or western Venus. Joining Wlaha in the sky, Kuamachi also makes up his quarrel with him and offers him the "peace plant" *akuaniye.* Also part of this astronomical register is the supplementary story of Makusani, the blowgun hunter who travels between the houses of moon and sun.

With all this, the way has been cleared for the climactic events that follow: the founding of communal agriculture at Marahuaka and the creation of the first Soto. But first we backtrack so as to be told how these events had been prefigured by Wanadi's spirit people, the creatures of the plot so far, when a manioc-tree cutting was brought from the sky to Roraima, that "botanical eldorado"[33] and the first of the tree mountains, and another cutting was brought to what becomes the heart of Soto territory, the tree mountain Marahuaka. Stretching between earth and sky, with roots feeding on both, Marahuaka's branches bore all known fruits in such profusion that they fell on those who surrounded its base. To ease this situation, Attawanadi reappears, ever the sloth Wade's companion, and provides Semenia's bird people as gatherers and then instructors in *conuco* agriculture. In fact, all the birds and animals collaborate – all, that is, except Mado the jaguar and Wachedi the tapir, who think only of themselves and refuse to work or share. Champions of the wild, they are removed from the scene as the moment comes to fell the great free Marahuaka.

Crashing down, the food tree Marahuaka turns into the Soto mountain of that name while the rains that fall from its severed upper roots fill the upper Orinoco waterfalls and rivers. Widespread in the rainforest, this felled-tree event typically provokes major flood, and here it is said utterly to transform the face of the earth, confounding archaic pathways; among the Tupi it accounts for the first gushing forth of the Amazon. With the riverine earth soon soft and ready for planting, the switch to agriculture occurs: "Now there were buds everywhere, the Earth became green. The forest bloomed, our *conuco*s blossomed. The forest filled with trees, our *conuco*s filled with manioc" (Civrieux 1980:135).

At harvesttime, all gather to sing and dance, led by Semenia and the bird people, Attawanadi and Wade; and they recall all that had happened in the text itself: "Watunna, what we call the memory of our beginning." The account of the departure has an especial brilliance (pp. 136–7):

> As they were dancing and singing, they turned into birds of every colour. They flew off. The air was filled with feathers, all red and green and yellow and blue. It was beautiful. Now the Water Mother, Huiio, the Great Snake, came leaping out of the water and shot into the air.
> "I want my crown," she said, looking for birds and feathers for her crown. Huiio threw her great body into the sky. Many birds came. She covered herself with feathers. (Civrieux 1980:136–7)

After these first harvesters had all gone up to the sky, leaving only signs or forms of themselves here on earth, Wanadi is faced with a fundamental problem: Who will keep the food from getting lost, the dearly won knowledge of how to plant and prepare the crops? Out of this dilemma comes the decision to create the Soto, the true earth people, shaped from clay, whose first acts are indeed to rehearse Marahuaka: that is, to fell the tree, clear the *conuco*, harvest the food, and celebrate. At this human dance the ancient ones return and join in, invisible to all but shaman eyes.

In the narrative, the original Marahuaka event concludes the two paired cycles initiated by Attawanadi and Kaweshawa. Yet it is said actually to have occurred much earlier, as first rather than last in the series of flood events that punctuate the hero cycles: Huiio's, Iureke's, and Kuamachi's. Bringing Huehanna to earth at the beginning, Huiio found that Marahuaka "had just been cut down" and that the Orinoco "had just been born"; so her ascent after being butchered technically overlaps with the one at the harvest dance.

Again, provoking Kuamachi's flood, Wlaha is said to have eaten greedily "like the Jaguar and the Tapir at Marahuaka." In the 1970 Spanish translation, Marahuaka is in fact placed in this earlier slot in the narrative. But the Soto themselves are said to prefer the arrangement we have followed, that is, that of the 1980 English translation, which as a literary construct[34] draws out key features of the cosmogony as a whole.

First of all, delaying Marahuaka achieves through juxtaposition a categorical contrast between the world of invisible spirits that, like *yvy tenonde* or Tupi first-earth paradise, prefigures our human experience and the linear history that begins with the Soto. Hence, in turn it adds significance to the moment of transition, or hinge in the text, when we emerge from the whole web of complex processes that eventually made human agriculture and society possible. It asks us too to consider the respective levels and qualities of time that characterize these two parts of the text, especially in respect of Marahuaka, both first (in principle) and last (in narrative practice) in the set of four flood events and in the dance whose rhythm expands the normal boundaries of the present.

Issuing from a tree that turns to stone, the Marahuaka flood anticipates the one in which Iureke and his twin, avenging their mother, Huiio, are saved from drowning by twin palm trees that also turn to stone; in turn, Iureke's flood complements Kuamachi's, since it was designed to avenge a butchered mother, is accompanied by fire, and issues from a gourd. Indeed, in other rainforest texts these separate flood events are run together or transposed; here in *Watunna* they are set into a pattern that invites scrutiny and whose logic is commensurable with that of the *Popol vuh*.

First and last of the floods and the most complex, Marahuaka may be read in several registers. Cutting its stem and then its upward-reaching aerophyte roots ended the umbilical flow between sky and earth – a cosmic change that still resonates throughout the rainforest.[35] A definitive severing, it highlights the modes of Wanadi's involvement in earthly affairs: From the direct intervention and failure in his first two aspects, we pass into hero cycles initiated by his third, Attawanadi, who, coming to earth before the severing, is still found there when it comes to creating the Soto. Defined in this way, the pair of initial failures find a readier echo in the twin disasters of Flood and Eclipse that feature in Tupi, Desana, Witoto, and yet other lowland cosmogonies.

Then as the suckling tree, Marahuaka nourishes the gatherer-hunter like its Nahuatl namesake Chichiualcuauhtli (*Ríos,* p. 4), being assigned actual teats and rubber flowing as milk in the Piaroa version; and when felled, it provokes the need for agriculture. Identified with the prime crop manioc, it bears a multitude of other foods, yet those actually specified – manioc, two types of palm nuts, and gourds plus the plantains and rubber-tree fruit mentioned in other texts – strongly represent vegetative as opposed to seed reproduction. The corresponding idiom of tubers, cuttings, and grafts, quite explicit in itself, is echoed, moreover, in anatomy, in Attawanadi's exchanged head and divided wife and in Wlaha's seven outgrowths of himself. Similarly Attawanadi's Carib cousin Makunaima also becomes two or five of himself. In all this the priority of the "bone" crop manioc is reflected in the Island Carib story of Louquou, the Attawanadi-like bringer of manioc who made humans by cutting open his leg; the Waiwai account of the charred foster parent whose bones turn into manioc tubers; the Barasana version, where the charred body is that of the great anaconda and the manioc is explicitly the first crop of the *conuco;* and the Witoto tree of abundance Moniya Amena that was both a man and the first manioc crop.[36]

As a tree that turns to stone, Marahuaka exemplifies the process of rock formation attributed likewise to Roraima and to the Ekuadi hidi, at the east and west ends of the Pacaraima ridge. Consistent with the notion of carbonized flora, the process is set in an overall sedimentary frame. Indeed, in one varient of Iureke's flood, as in the Shuar story of Tsunki, the hero is saved by a growing pile of nut-stones thrown from the tree, basically the silt or terra firma motif; even igneous quartz crystals found on Madan tahu are not expelled in eruption but just wash up there. Again, insofar as they have a geological message, the repeated metamorphoses into fish fit this same sedimentarian scheme.

Finally, as the venue for truly communal agriculture, in which all the birds and animals except the last defenders of the wild are ready to partake, Marahuaka confirms the intricate mesh of contracts and relationships that holds *Watunna*'s people in nature, like Attawanadi with his monkey nephew, his fish bride, and his sloth ally. The subsequent flood of Huiio's opens up further this whole question of vertebrate life-forms and the particular definition of the three skin coverings. Trailblazers for the hairy mammals, Iureke and his twin are born from eggs that emerge from an egg; are physically disputed by the egg layers both cold-blooded and warm, the scaly fish, snake, and caimans below and the feathered birds above; and are then fostered and menaced by a toad and a jaguar. At the rainforest's other edge, in *Ayvu rapyta* the same logic weaves the thread of survival for Kuaray after he is cut as an embryo from his mother's womb. The great principle of all this argument of course remains the anaconda who can encompass the world, the great feather-snake Huiio herself, from whom springs all vertebrate life below. Brilliantly hued, Huiio is most often identified with the rainbow, an ambiguous or even dangerous upper manifestation of herself; at the same time she represents the notion of vertebrate evolution as surely as Quetzalcoatl.

At this level of analysis, which the very structure of the text invites, it becomes easier to perceive how *Watunna* may relate to the scheme of world ages represented in the *Popol vuh*[37] and other texts examined earlier. The Carib and Maya texts alike hinge on the turn into history signaled by agriculture proper to humans (in each case named as the total of their digits: "Soto" means twenty, like the Maya root *uinaq/uinic* "man"). Both begin by recounting a pair of failures to create humans through direct intervention from above, which logically match each other, appeal more or less directly to the notion of Flood and Eclipse, and result in metamorphoses into fish (possibly) and tailed monkey (certainly; see Fig. 57); and through all this they establish a vertical duality between the powers of lightning above and the feather-snake below. In between, in all that concerns the deeds of the Quiché Twins on earth, the parallels in detail and argument are persistent: the skin coverings of the egg layers and the hairy-mammal solidarity that extends to the exchange of heads; the blowpipe hunter skilled in poisons who pretends to be a farmer, and vice versa; the food bowl that reflects one hiding in the roof; the pioneer axe of the Four Hundred and the drunken housewarming with alcohol brewed for three days; the axe that cuts as if of its own accord and the jaguar who defends the wild against it; the star people threatened by the caiman who become the Pleiades and establish a bond with the planetary travelers.

In some of these cases it is in fact possible to map actual lines of connection between the two texts, which hitherto have not been at all associated with each other. For example, the tree-felling episode that typically leads to flood in South American but not Mesoamerican texts occurs in the Cuna *Tatkan ikala*, where, thanks to Ipelele's solar axe, the water issues from Paluhuala as the salt ocean of Panama's Caribbean coast; at the same time the Cuna jaguar, ever the defender of the wild, protects the tree against the axe by at night licking better the wounds made in the bark by day, just as in the *teoamoxtli* image. Then for the Desana the construction of the first *maloca*, at Wainambi, is likewise matched with the first human drunkenness. Again, the vivid domestic detail of the food bowl that reflects the roof above leads us to detect in the South American toad cook and rejected foster mother a remote antecedent for Oxomoco, toward whom at this point her foster sons express impatience and the desire to discover their lost parent-father.

Indeed, the myriad rainforest narrative represented by *Watunna* echoes over the continent: a substratum in the Andes and a counterpart for North America. The incestuous male moon, the quest for the stolen wife and her repeated destruction, the felling of the food tree also known as Tamoanchan, the hummingbird's gift of tobacco, the fish bride who lives below the rapids, the potential father-in-law who owns thunder, the scavenger twins fostered by eagles: Though absent in *Popol vuh,* these and many other rainforest motifs recur in Maya and Nahuatl texts and in Anasazi, as they do in southern Appalachia, their precision in Cherokee cosmogony[38] suggesting a parallel passage northward across the Caribbean. Indeed, just this extension led Lévi-Strauss to make the rainforest into the American base of his "mythic" syntheses, as it has led others to identify it as the source of "all the stories."

For this very reason, in the story of world ages and metamorphosis it is worth noting certain key absences in *Watunna* and the tradition it represents. Geologically there is no more place for a volcanic idiom[39] – the Cipacna mountain maker – than there is biologically for giant prehistoric saurians; nor does a stratified underworld provide Odosha with a home. Similarly, in the language of plant reproduction the emphasis falls more on the vegetative than on the gendered and genetic involvement in seed that *Popol vuh* ascribes above all to Oxomoco, midwife and blesser of the maize people.

11

The epic

HEROES AND THE VISION QUEST

In the *Popol vuh*'s account of genesis, the story of the Twins achieves an epic identity of its own. Miraculously conceived, these heroes fight to survive and embark on a journey of ultimate danger, penetrating hell itself. Preternaturally aware of the natural world, interpreters of the wild and its languages, they establish social norms and an ethos for the future nation. In short, they mediate between the cosmic forces of creation and everyday history. Since they have this special place in the world-age scheme, their quest requires separate attention as a Fourth World epic. For, as both kin and seekers, the Twins have counterparts throughout the continent who in their various ways have the same mediatory role. True, the autonomy of the epic varies from one genesis to another; even in the *Popol vuh* itself, before their exemplary journey to Xibalba, the Twins engage in the third-age story of metamorphosis. In the rainforest, this engagement is far more thoroughgoing and involves successions of heroes who embody the process of creation. Pioneers who fell the first tree, the Carib and Cuna heroes then sever the umbilicus between sky and earth, creating, as it were, the need for themselves as mediators between the two. In the Guarani case, together with the father-principle Maira, Kuaray and his twin come to constitute a creative trinity. Conversely, throughout Greater Mexico, Anasazi, and Turtle Island, the epic journey is always highly defined as a narrative in its own right.[1]

Just as the American epic hero is never conceived naturally, drawing seed from spittle, sun ray, feather, jade, a snake phallus, so his birth will be premature or require excision from the belly. Full of trials, early life will carry the blot and conundrum of parthenogenesis. Resolved in the *Popol vuh* through

Oxomoco's involuntary laughter (which gives the Twins their birthright), the anomaly of miraculous conception is both unavoidable in social logic and interpreted according to local priorities. Hearing his mother insulted by her brothers, the imperial Huitzilopochtli leaps right out of the womb to slay them there and then for touching on his illegitimacy, in an act of violent self-assertion. Literally *éventrés,* the heroes of the Sioux and the Tupi themselves narrowly escape death and continue to be not just badly treated by stepkin, like the Quiché Twins, but actively threatened by foster parents. Similar in both North and South American traditions, this deprivation encourages scavenger skill and the capacity to survive by sharing the nests of the wild, a theme found alike in *Watunna,* the *teoamoxtli,* and the Bead Chant dry paintings.[2] Survival also depends typically on their very plurality, not just as twins but other multiples, like the Makunaina, who are five as well as two, and the seven Wlada of *Watunna,* where, moreover, seven sets of twins succeed each other. One translation of "Quetzalcoatl" is precious twin," *coatl* having survived in everyday Mexican as *cuate,* "partner."[3]

Neither of the Quiché Twins marries or indeed is ever mentioned as a suitor: Like that of Quetzalcoatl, their mission exceeds sexuality from the start. Not so in the typical rainforest case, where encounter with or recovery of a woman loved provides a constant spur – hence, in turn, the fact that these South American heroes attain or deserve the woman by performing tasks for her father, clearing the *conuco* magically, the way the Quiché Twins clear the *milpa* for their grandmother. This service rendered by the prospective son-in-law allows a new order to replace the paternal status quo without shattering social bonds entirely. Despite his domicile in the Andes, the hero son of Pariacaca in *Runa yndio* (chaps. 10–11) adheres to this model. Huatyacuri, whose distinction it was to witness his own father Pariacaca's birth from five eggs, belongs, as others have already shown, to an argument altogether identifiable with the rainforest. As his name indicates, he lived poorly on tubers roasted in the earth itself (*huatya*). Socially he is contrasted with the great Tamtañamca, owner of a large house in upland Anchicocha and father of daughters who include Urpayhuachi and Chaupiñamca, Huatyacuri's future partner. Though powerful, Tamtañamca suffers from a secret illness, the result of his wife's infidelity with a snake that gnaws away the roof ties and a two-headed toad that lives under the grindstone. Having overheard two foxes, one from above and the other from below, who comment upon and diagnose the case, Huatyacuri offers to cure Tamtañamca in return for being adopted as a son and gaining Chaupiñamca in marriage. This agreement and his success outrage Chaupiñamca's brother-in-law, who challenges Huatyacuri to a series of tests; these lead in practice to yet further success, for, unlike his rich opponent, Huatyacuri can draw on the strength of the wild. For music he plays the panpipes of the rainforest, for hospitality he serves the more potent drink, and as house builder he relies not on armies of tame workers but on snakes and birds and employs mountain lions to stampede his opponent's train of pack llamas.

Following the same logic and still echoing the rainforest tradition, this Quechua narrative also brings out the quality of the true epic hero as one without received privilege, devoid of the a priori authority and power attributed to the deity figures in the state religions of the Inca and the Chibcha, namely Viracocha and Bochica.[4] The resourceful Huatyacuri is shown to be deserving, but the Inca Viracocha is exposed as less so despite his own undoubted origins in the same heroic tradition of magicians and tricksters. On the one hand, celebrated as magically conceived in the Zithuwa liturgy, he simply imposes civilization on the landscape in imperial fashion; on the other, he acts like a shoddy opportunist who specializes in seducing women who have only their mothers to protect them. First it is Cavillaca, whom he impregnates by subterfuge in yet another miraculous conception that combines the fruit-gathering motif of the rainforest with the tree gourd and semen–spittle of the *Popol vuh*. So averse is she to Viracocha's person that Cavillaca resists attempts to marry her off when later her son is deemed to need a father's parental care (the Andean solution to the social dilemma of parthenogenesis): With her child she flees to the ocean, where they both turn to stone. He then makes love to one of two daughters whose mother is away at the time visiting Cavillaca in the sea (*Runa yndio* chap. 2).[5]

In the quest that lies beyond kin and sexuality, the epic hero brings skill and knowledge as compensation for the loss of the cosmic womb and the divorce between sky and earth: tobacco, maize, songs and their images, medicines, and secrets of life. The "far-seer" of the *Popol vuh,* he becomes the exemplar of the shaman who travels afar in mind and space, foreseeing every eventuality and anticipating every disease and as psychopomp safely conveying his patient's soul beyond death. In *Medatia,* the narrative that is a sequel to *Watunna,* the Soto shaman powerfully records this apprenticeship in rainforest terms: the rush on the senses heightened by hallucinogenic or other means, the blasting wind and other trials that precede the ascent through four levels of consciousness – hearing all creatures' languages, sight, the rattle (*maraca*) and the quartz crystal (lightning semen) that belongs in it – finally to attain the water of life, the *tinamou* egg, and the all-encompassing view of the world that can be resurrected. Then, stepping down, he returns to teach, free, and restore memory to the men enslaved in Odosha's dark cave and to the women dragged down under the rapids by Huiio's water monsters[6] (Fig. 58).

Unquestionably a key to Fourth World shamanism, Medatia's experience illuminates that of the Quiché Twins on several counts. In particular, the trials and hazards that beset him as he searches for the right path directly recall theirs, among them the hanging bat–scissors, jaguars, rivers to cross,

Figure 58. Levels of the Carib shaman's ascent. (Drawing by Dawasehuwa, after Guss 1985:57.)

and crossroads that oppose black and white, these being test motifs that are further echoed in the Cuna Islands, Anasazi, and Turtle Island. Then Jaguar Deer's power of interspecies communication is prefigured in Medatia's changing first his ears and voice so that he can talk with other creatures, and then his eyes so that he sees the world as they do, intuiting root equivalences of image and energy. Medatia is able to receive the gifts they bring as if in response to unspoken requests in Zuyua language (see p. 322): manioc fish, hammock web, falcon mosquito, and star-eye tear.

Spatially, the Soto route to knowledge here extends between lower and upper terms, between Odosha's dark cave and Huiio's subaquatic domain below and the moment of all-knowing above. These moments technically relate to the Inca opposition between zenith (*ushnu*) and antizenith; the astronomical analogy is further strengthened through the fact that epic figures akin to Medatia rise as sun and moon or the twin star Venus, as in the Tupi and Inca cases. The same journey is implicit in the Orpheus motifs in rainforest, Mapuche, and Patagonian epics, a journey to an underworld likewise just perceptible in Ge cosmogony.[7] Throughout North America, from Quiché to the Midwiwin, the planetary mode is absolutely unmistakable in the "solar walk" of the shaman's trance journey, followed by the Quiché Twins as they descend to Xibalba and then walk up into the sky – sun and moon at the eastern horizon[8] (Fig. 59).

Identified with the searcher-hunter in Mide texts, this mobility in turn complements the sedentary mode of the planter, exactly as in the case of the maize plant left with Oxomoco by the Twins that thrives as they fare. Conjoining astronomy with agronomy, these matching ways are well represented in the Anasazi painting of Sky and Earth: Sky's body displays sun, moon, and Venus passing through the mesh of stars that themselves turn with the year; Earth's, the umbilical lake from which the four plants grow. It is according to this doctrine, which reached agricultural societies as distant as the Iroquois, that the epic hero, traveling along the solar walk, prepares the way for maize to become the substance and sustenance of humans in the culminating event that succeeds the two experiments with mud and wood.

QUETZALCOATL

His name the honorific of priests and kings, Quetzalcoatl was revered as Mesoamerica's greatest deity. In the syllables of it, he carries the evolutionary charge of the feather-snake, or plumed serpent, intimated by Huiio in *Watunna*: A hybrid of bird and reptile, he, like Gucumatz (his namesake) or Caiman Macaw in the *Popol vuh*, epitomizes the story of the egg-laying vertebrates who preceded the mammals and could like them assume monstrous shape or attitude. At the same time, in the alternative translation of his name, as the precious twin, or *cuate*, he figures as the prime epic hero, a true counterpart to the Quiché Twins, who avenges his father, travels to hell, makes the first people of this Era, and introduces the culture of maize and the painted page. The two are clearly distinguished, as "snake" (*culebra*) and deity-priest, respectively, in the *tonalamatl* Trecenas chapters.[9]

The epic Quetzalcoatl predominates in surviving *teoamoxtli* and in *Inomaca tonatiuh* and other major Nahuatl narratives of genesis. In turn, he serves as a prototype in the story of Tula and its bringers of culture and political prestige, accounts that have the advantage of establishing beyond all doubt his planetary nature. Just as the *Tepexic Annals* show the patron deity Quetzalcoatl Nine Wind being born from the sky, so the *Cuauhtitlan Annals,* in a passage of astounding beauty (fol. 7), tell how Quetzalcoatl One Reed became Venus. At the culminating moment, having attired himself in the plumes and mask also depicted in the Tepexic text, Quetzalcoatl of his own accord burned himself; glowing to incandescence, his heart appears as the planet:

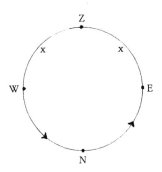

Figure 59. Solar walk: tetradic structure, heliacal rising. E, east; W, west; Z, zenith; N, nadir; X, halfway moments. Time units – *Quarter-day:* In travel- ing from E to W, the sun rests halfway at Z, pausing at X halfway to and from Z; the overall four-part movement is complemented by the night half of the journey, from W to E, below. *Day:* Venus, in moving from W to E – changing from the evening star to the morning star that rises heliacally (i.e., just before the sun) – apparently travels through N over a period ritually estimated as 4 + 4 days throughout North America (cf. Plate 17). *20 days:* The Maya *uinal* (20 days) makes its primordial journey from E to Z; its prior "step" was technically of 40 days (i.e., W to E). *Year:* After eight years the sun and heliacal Venus coincide again at E, having gone through eight and five cycles, respectively; known as the *octaeteris* (approxi- mated as 2,920 days), this period also synchronizes with ninety-nine moons.

When they reached the place they were searching for, now again there he wept and suffered. In this year 1 Reed (so it is told, so it is said), when he had reached the ocean shore, the edge of the sky-water, he stood up, wept, took his attire, and put on his plumes, his precious mask. When he was dressed, of his own accord he burnt himself, he gave himself to the fire. So that where Quetzalcoatl burnt himself is called the place of Incineration.

And it is said that when he burned, his ashes rose up and every kind of precious bird appeared and could be seen rising up to the sky: roseate spoonbill, cotinga, trogon, blue heron, yellow-headed parrot, macaw, white-fronted parrot, and all other precious birds. And after he had be- come ash the quetzal bird's heart rose up; it could be seen and was known to enter the sky. The old men would say he had become Venus; and it is told that when the star appeared Quetzalcoatl died. From now on he was called the Lord of the Dawn.

Only for four days he did not appear, so it is told, and dwelt in Dead Land. And for another four days he sharpened himself. After eight days the great star appeared called Quetzalcoatl on his ruler's throne. And they knew, on his rising, which people, according to Sign, he penetrates, shoots into and loathes.

There follows a catalog of the five particular targets wounded by the planet, according to the day Sign of its heliacal appearance as morning star in the east over eight years (the *octaeteris;* see Fig. 59). These match the set of five targets shown in the Venus chapter of the *teoamoxtli* and the hieroglyphic *Dresden* screenfold, where astronomical tables are supplied and where the eight years of the cycle are matched with the eight days of inferior conjunction, that is, the time when the planet, traveling between earth and sun, disappears from view and moves in fact from the western horizon as evening star in order to rise again in the east heliacally, or ahead of the morning sun. Specifying precisely the same period of eight days, the *Cuauhtitlan Annals* describe this phenomenon as the passage through Mictlan, the Nahuatl underworld, or place of the dead, equivalent of Xibalba. In other words, Quetzalcoatl's journey to Mictlan is to be unambiguously identified with Venus's inferior conjunction.

For its part, the creation chapter in *Ríos,* noted above for its representation of the Suns within a sequence devoted to the story of maize, prefaces its depiction of Mictlan/Xibalba with a scheme of eight passages, four characterized by black-tipped flints as especially dangerous and four less so (p. 2). Structurally these correspond to the two halves of Venus's inferior conjunction as these are distinguished in the *Cuauhtitlan Annals;* that is, facing danger, Quetzalcoatl journeyed for four days and for the subsequent four he sharpened himself in self-defense.

In *Inomaca tonatiuh* (fol. 2), Quetzalcoatl mediates between the scheme of the four Suns and the present world, Four Ollin, identified there with Tamoanchan and Teotihuacan. In the council of gods he is the traveler who solves the dilemma of successive cataclysms: "Who now shall be alive" and its corollary "What shall they eat?" – questions answered with the single fact of maize in the *Popol vuh* epic. He begins by making the great descent to Mictlan to face its overlords, owners of the bones from which future humans will be made.

> And then Quetzalcoatl goes to Mictlan, the Dead Land.
> He approached the Lord and Lady of Mictlan and said:
> "What I have come for is the precious bones which you possess;
> I have come to fetch them."
> And he was asked:
> "What do you want to do with them, Quetzalcoatl!"
> And he answered:
> "What worries the gods is who shall live on earth."
> And the Lord of Mictlan then said:
> "All right. Blow this conch and carry the bones four times round my jade
>   circle."
> But the conch is totally blocked up.
> Quetzalcoatl summons the worms, they hollow it out.

The large and the small bees force their way through.
He blows it; the sound reaches the Lord of Mictlan.

In order to obtain the bones he has to perform an impossible task, of the kind demanded of the Quiché Twins by the Lords of Xibalba; and like them, he is aided by an insect, here the bee rather than the mosquito. Announced in a trumpet salvo, his success means the victory of his persona, the second of the Twenty Signs that identifies him as the god of wind (hence Quetzalcoatl Nine Wind) and breath who opposes and struggles to free himself from the grip of Mictlantecutli in the latter's dark and windless underworld. In the *teoamoxtli* he is represented as just this life-giving force, ever threatened by the stasis and suffocation of death and locked in mortal combat with his skeletal opponent. Indeed, in *Borgia* (p. 73) and *Laud* (p. 19) the two antagonists symbolize nothing less than the antithesis between life and death.

After a further test in which his *nahual,* or companion self, helps him to lie, Quetzalcoatl makes his way back to the upper world. Clutching the bones, male to one side and female to the other, he faces further obstacles: a pit dug for him and an attack by Quails. Defended in fact by no more than its startling buzz on takeoff, the inoffensive edible Quail, fourth of the Quecholli, became the standard Mesoamerican bird of sacrifice in memory of this occasion, as the Four Ollin Era page in *Borgia* (p. 71) shows. *Inomaca tonatiuh* (fol. 2) continues:

And the Lord of Mictlan next said to him:
"All right, take them."
But to his vassals, the Micteca, he said:
"Tell him, o gods, he should leave them here."
But Quetzalcoatl answered:
"No; I'm taking them with me."
And then his nahual said to him:
"Just tell them: 'I've left them here.' "
And so he said, he shouted to them:
"I have left them here."
But then he really went back up, clutching the precious bones,
male bones on one side, female on the other.
He took them and wrapped them up, and took them with him.
And the Lord of Mictlan again spoke to his vassals:
"O gods, is Quetzalcoatl really taking the bones? Dig him a pit."
They dug him one; he stumbled and fell in.
And Quails menaced him and he fainted.
He dropped the precious bones and the Quails tore and pecked at them.
And then Quetzalcoatl came to and weeps and says to his nahual:
"O my nahual, what now?"
And the reply came:
"What now? Things went badly; let it be."

> And then he gathered the bits, took them and wrapped them in a bundle
> which he took to Tamoanchan.

When Quetzalcoatl finally manages to deliver the bones at Tamoanchan,
they are ground up by Snake Woman Cihuacoatl, who places the meal in a
jade bowl; piercing his penis, he then drops his blood on them. These
penitential acts by the gods – grinding meal and bloodletting – belong to
female and male like the two sets of bones; they are then set up as the
premise on which this present race is born: These people are to be servants
of the gods (*macehualli*), since the gods did penance in order to create them.
In *Ríos* (p. 9) this theme is powerfully developed through the figure of a
Quetzalcoatl whose lordly prerogative it is to bring the people under control
like so many unwilling deer (*maza-me*).

> When he had brought it there it was ground up by the
> woman named Quilaztli, that is, Cihuacoatl.
> Then she placed the meal in a jade bowl and Quetzalcoatl dropped blood
>   on it by piercing his member.
> Then all the gods named here did penance like
> the Bridger, the Tiller,
> the Emerger, the Earth-firmer,
> the Plunger, the Shooter:
> Quetzalcoatl.
> And they said:
> "The servants of the gods are born." For indeed they did penance for us.
> – Inomaca tonatiuh, fol. 2

Much turns on the name of the place where this happens, Tamoanchan,
which is represented visually as a tree whose upper part has been axed and is
falling (Plate 17b). Used to confirm decisive moments in history, for example the start of migration in the *Aztlan Annals,* it has its prototype in the
trecena of the *tonalamatl* that commemorates Quetzalcoatl's deed; in one
source it is glossed as "the bloodied broken tree . . . where they descended"
(cf. *temoa* "to descend"). The prime location of Tamoanchan is appropriately
the Tepoztlan ridge, the mountains of the *pulque* drinkers who axe trees
(*tepuztli* = axe) and prepare a way in the sky for Quetzalcoatl,[10] just as they
do for the Quiché Twins in the *Popol vuh.* This much conforms to the zodiac
complex of Mesoamerica, echoed in turn in the Huichol creation paintings
that depict the axe-wielding clearer of the *milpa* Watacame.

Yet through Tamoanchan's "bloodied broken tree" itself, absent from the
Popol vuh, there is a yet more suggestive parallel with *Watunna* and the
rainforest. For in the Trecenas chapter of the Mesoamerican ritual books
(Table 2) it is depicted as the bearer of many different kinds of fruits, which
grow upon it as if grafted; and the felling of it changes the world. On both
these counts the link with Marahuaka is direct; indeed, it forms a part of a

larger set of connections between Carib and Nahuatl narrative otherwise visible in texts collected in this century from West Mexico.[11] According to the rainforest reading of the Fourth World doctrine of your being what you eat, manioc, the staple crop that is reproduced vegetatively rather than fertilized, is the "bone" of human substance, as in the Arawak and Tupi examples quoted above. Moreover, though far less significant in Mesoamerica, tubers emerge with a similar role there, as in the Maya riddle that equates manioc with the buried bones of the father, or the Nahuatl variant that conversely derives *camote* from Quetzalcoatl's fingers.[12] Taken together, this would indicate a possible rainforest origin for the bones ground into human substance by Quetzalcoatl in the *Inomaca tonatiuh* and therewith, in Tamoanchan, a distant memory of Marahuaka's grafted fruits.

Now alive, Quetzalcoatl's humans need to be fed; and to this end, with Red Ant as a helper, he makes a subsidiary journey to "the mountain of our flesh" Tonacatepetl, a food mountain like Roraima and Paxil.

> Then they said: "What shall they eat? The gods must find food";
> and the ant fetched the maize kernels
> from the heart of the Food Mountain.
> Quetzalcoatl met the ant and said:
> "Tell me where you went to find them?"
> He asked repeatedly but it didn't answer.
> Then it said: "Over there, pointing."
> And he accompanied it,
> becoming a black ant himself.
> They both went in
> and carried off the maize to Tamoanchan.
> The gods chewed it
> and put it in our mouths to strengthen us.
> – *Inomaca tonatiuh*, fol. 3

Completing the episode, the gods then wonder what to do with the Food Mountain, and, again the lone hero, Quetzalcoatl tries unsuccessfully to carry it off on his back. Finally, through the divination of Oxomoco, here male and accompanied by a now female Cipactonal, Nanahuatl and the four-colored rain gods release the four-colored maize – white, black, yellow, and red – along with beans, amaranth (*huauhtli*), sage, and all the other foods.

This Nahuatl account clearly parallels the *Popol vuh* in such details as the Food Mountain, animal helpers, the strengthening quality and coloring of maize, and Oxomoco's divination. And in tamale ceremonies held to "revive maize from death" every eight years, over precisely eight days (Quetzalcoatl's Venusian *utas–octaeteris*), Nahuatl ritual reinforces the Quiché doctrine of maize as human substance.[13] Yet there remains the instructive difference. For *Inomaca tonatiuh*'s Nahuatl accounts of the bone and then maize substance correspond to types and indeed phases of American experiments in plant genetics, vegetal grafting, and seed fertilization: These the *Popol vuh* integrates into the discourse of the latter. Making a predominantly genetic argument, it insists that the first Quiché were made only from maize, as if to distinguish them from Quetzalcoatl's creatures and even from the neighboring Cakchiquel, who are made from maize but need the (penis) blood additive of tapir and snake. And it converts the bones into the prior inherited source of Blood Woman's superior breeding capacity. The tuber–cereal sequence as such is made quite explicit in the Tuzantan and Kekchi versions of the same food-mountain story: The one states a preference for the newly found maize on the ground that, unlike older root crops, it could be kept from one annual harvest to the next; the other notes the novel effects that maize first had on the gastric system of coati and the helper mammals who, five-toed and "like us," anticipated the switch in human diet.[14] The Kekchi text furthermore vividly compounds Oxomoco's dual role as midwife and blesser of maize by identifying the release of maize from the Food Mountain with its emergence from the body of a pregnant woman.

In his astronomical guise, Quetzalcoatl has further fellow travelers in Mesoamerica, two of whom correspond to precisely the celestial bodies that the Quiché Twins became, sun and moon, and that with Venus are easily the brightest bodies in the sky. Stated in the very concept of Venus's heliacal risings and the 5:8 Venus:sun arithmetic in the *teoamoxtli* chapter that records them, the sun is given an epic role near identical to that of Quetzalcoatl through Xolotl, the aged canine figure of Chichimec history whose prototype carries the sun through the underworld at night from west to east. (Nine marks drawn on Xolotl's ruff commemorate the Nine Night Powers that contain the eight days of Venus's inferior conjunction.) In the *tonalamatl trecenas*, Xolotl embodies all three levels – the earth, the above of the rain god, and the below of the death god – and his mediatory role between cosmos and history is indicated by the accompanying Era date Four Ollin. Rather than at Tamoanchan, Xolotl creates humankind at Chicomoztoc, the Seven Caves of the Chichimec womb. There the institution of service is a harsher affair and produces fourfold male and female groups reminiscent of the days of the Venus passage through Mictlan.[15]

As for the moon, whose ninety-nine nights also form part of the *octaeteris*, new in the west and a waxing threat to Venus's brilliance, it has been identified with the mirror-smoke Tezcatlipoca, Quetzalcoatl's conscience and tormenter. Sharing male gender with the second Quiché Twin and with Nuna of *Watunna*, Tezcatlipoca does not commit incest as the rainforest figure does; but he does provoke his great rival Quetzalcoatl to commit it and thereafter to embark on his cosmic journey to the east. They are shown together in *Borbonicus* (p. 22), in the chapter whose other half features Oxomoco and Cipactonal.[16]

With its numerous analogues, only a few of which are examined here, the Quetzalcoatl story corroborates that of the Quiché Twins as an epic intermediary between cosmic metamorphosis and history. It also confirms their common reliance on the astronomical paradigm of the heroic journey through hell to the eastern horizon, followed likewise by Xolotl and yet other planetary travelers. Decidedly more marked in North than in South America, the primacy of the path as such is registered visually in the deeper reading of the quatrefoil map, where by north and south double as zenith and nadir, either side of the east–west axis.[17] Indeed, in the *Féjérváry* example the set of anatomical emblems placed as sources of the diagonal blood streams ranges female versus male like the bones carried up by Quetzalcoatl; it simultaneously appeals to the *Popol vuh* story, literally crossing One Hunter, here a severed head and traveler's foot, with Blood Woman, here the right hand that caught One Hunter's spittle and the blood-producing ribcage from paternal Xibalba.

MAIZE THRIVES, TRAVELER FARES

Engendered by the Sun, the Twins who dominate Navajo epic first live with their mother, Changing Woman, at the Place of Emergence. Their gestation had lasted nine nights rather than nine moons, and once they are born, each four days of their life equal four years. As "Slayers of Foreign Beasts" (Nayenezghane) or in the guise of Holy Man and Holy Boy, they go on a series of four expeditions, the first being the search for their father, the Sun. On their journey to the Sun's house on Turquoise Mountain in the east, they elude a series of hazards and upon arrival are subjected by their father and his wife to a further series of tests. Having proved themselves worthy heirs, they have bestowed upon them the chapters of traditional wisdom, in the form of chants and paintings. They also receive insignia and weapons with which to rid the earth of its primeval monsters, a task they embark on with their father's help, having brought him down from the sky at noon through the power of one of his paintings. As they are dispatched, the monsters turn into the mountains and rocks of Anasazi, their blood petrifying like lava.

Thus initiated and equipped, the Twins then engage in three further quests, among people known as Earth, Sky and Water, and Buffalo, each of which quests results in their learning and acquiring further sets of paintings. Evocative of the people who occupied Anasazi before the Navajo did, the Earth People quest takes them to the Arrows and the Snakes, with whom they have to use guile as ever-potential sons-in-law; at the same time they acquire knowledge that protects and then cures them, restoring the full range of human senses. The third quest, Sky and Water, opposes the two male boundary mountains: From Black Mountain (northwest) Holy Man is tugged upward as the captive of Black Thunder; from Turquoise Mountain (southeast) Holy Boy is swallowed by a transparent fish that takes him to Whirling Waters below. Finally, in the Buffalo quest they traverse Navajo territory along the other diagonal; starting in the southwest, they pass the central Chinlee area before trespassing beyond to alien territory in an encounter with the buffalo and *tipi* dwellers of the Plains. With all the knowledge they gain from these experiences, the Twins instruct people generally on how to live as humans; taking their original deerskin paintings with them, they finally rise into the sky.

Together these four quests, to Sun and to Earth, Sky–Water, and Buffalo people, constitute the enabling narrative of the Shooting Chant (male), acknowledged to be the first and foremost in the Holy Way group. It boasts spectacular sequences of paintings and serves as a common point of reference for subsidiary chants like the Hail, Water, Wind, Bigstar, and Red Ant (an echo here of Quetzalcoatl). Moreover, extensive as it is, it provides a yardstick for other epic adventures commemorated in chants like Bead and Eagle Trapping, where as Scavenger the Twins learn the arts of basic survival, and Feather or Plume, where as Self-Teacher they travel downstream in a log canoe and trade agricultural knowledge with another menacing father-in-law figure, the shaman Deer Raiser in his underworld abode.

Central as it is to Holy Way, the Shooting Chant cannot, however, easily serve as a term of reference for all the exploits of the Twins. Their guises and names are very various, and in any case some chants and paintings have now become extinct. Moreover, in the deployment of the known paintings there operates a highly intricate logic of inversion, compensation, and gender and of cross-reference that defeats any brief analysis. Yet there can be no doubt that overall, in the larger cosmic scheme of ages, the Twins operate as mediators who bring the present world into being; and that in so doing they tread the shamanic path of sun and planets, the "solar walk." The stations to east and west, above and below, are clearly signaled. They may reach a living father at the zenith rather than a dead one at the nadir, inverting the Mesoamerican arrangement; but the paradigm as such remains. Again, though they are not said to travel 4 + 4 days through the underworld, their gestation lasts nine nights and their growth is by lots of four day–years.

The paradigm becomes clearer through comparison with the epic of the Pima midway between Anasazi and Mesoamerica. There the hero travels through the underworld to find his ancestor and emerges again stepping up into the sky in the east, at the same time as displaying such Anasazi traits as winning the eagle feather that denotes bravery. But the strongest proof of all comes in the remarkable parallels that in this context Anneliese Mönnich has shown to exist between, on the one hand, Anasazi (Navajo, Apache, Hopi, Zuni, and other Pueblo) and, on the other, Mesoamerica (Nahuatl, Quiché Maya, Purepecha, Popoloca).[18] Nothing short of "amazing" (Mönnich), these parallels should be understood within the Mesoamerica–Anasazi continuum evidenced by the *teoamoxtli* and the dry paintings.

On their way to see their father, the Twins first encounter the hazards of landscape, which are listed in two sets. Fourfold, the first includes a stream that widens treacherously; *symplegades,* or mountains that crash together; a field of cutting reeds and a sliding-sand dune. Less dangerous, the sequel includes four mountains whose materials and colors correspond to those of the four guardians made of redstone, abalone, whiteshell, and turquoise. Strongly reminiscent of the landscape traversed by One Hunter and then the Twins (i.e., the rapids, the spikes, and the four colored roads), this list fits most tightly with the eight passages shown in the *Ríos* creation chapter: river, symplegades, cutting blades, and cold wind plus four more shown to be less dangerous through the absence of black-flint markers.

Approaching their father's house, the Twins then outwit hostile doormen through having previously learned their names; ushered inside rather than being asked to sit, they are hidden by Sun's wife. Upon the Sun's return, they are subjected to tests, four designed by the father and two by his wife. The paternal four consist of smoking a proffered pipe without being poisoned and then passing the night first entirely exposed without freezing, then in an overheated sauna without suffocating, and finally in a room of knives without being ground to death. The echoes here of One Hunter's and the Twins' experience in the guest rooms of Xibalba are so close as to require no comment.

The Quiché and Navajo Twins are similar not just by virtue of their journeying and its shamanic tests but in their kin network, that is, their relationship with their father's two wives and with their older half-brothers. They coincide above all in their role as hunter-travelers whose exploits are reciprocated in the sedentary mode of the farmer and who prepare for the creation of humans from maize, the crux of the narrative in *Dine bahane,* as in the *Popol vuh.* Counterpointing the birth of the gods at the start of the world ages, this event requires that white and yellow maize cobs be placed between two deerskins in a ceremonial intercourse that again invokes the genetic language of cereals. The people who then are born recall their origin in the chants and paintings of Blessing Way that endlessly cross-reference human and maize forms.

As heroes of the epic, the Navajo Twins have a notable array of analogues in other chants and ways. In the Bead Chant they appear as Scavenger, who, desperately poor and exploited, earns the status and rights of the hunter. Forced by hostile Pueblo people to trap eagle twins, he defends them using feathers that, like those of Dinoshi, turn into weapons and ends up living with them in their nest as part of the family.[19] The hero is in fact succored by these ace predators of the wild. This food supply is then supplemented by another: packs of maize that the pumas and wild felines agree to carry in on their backs, again contrary to their apparent hunter calling. Both acts of succor are the subject of a vivid painting.[20] In Mesoamerica exactly this experience is credited to the Chichimecs when, still "scavengers" in the northern deserts, they were fed by eagles and jaguars, the pair of predators denoting the orders of Aztec knights – the *Cuauhtinchan Annals* show them perched in the aerie, like Scavenger. Moreover, as Nowotny has shown, the same pattern of initiation and the same images of succoring eagle and jaguar occur in the heart of the *teoamoxtli,* in the maize-offering feast Tozoztli, part of the *Borgia* Feasts chapter.

Implicit in much of their activity, the Twins' responsibility for agriculture is brought out at length through the person of Self-Teacher, hero of the Feather Chant. When almost starved, this character is saved by his pet turkey, who drops seeds of domesticated plants from under her wings. The Feather Chant paintings celebrate the turkey for this deed, along with the plants she bestowed, which are typically ranged as sets of four – white, yellow, blue, and black maize, for instance, or beans, squash, tobacco, and maize – in quartered and diagonal patterns found in many other paintings, like *Earth and Sky,* where they radiate from the Place of Emergence. Displaying the same images, the *teoamoxtli* likewise celebrate the role of the turkey, the creature that, initially domesticated in Mexico, figures as such among the Quecholli; the Feasts chapter in *Laud* (p. 21) shows it bestowing its gift of seeds – maize, beans, squashes – to one journeying beyond this life.

Specifying his own hunter nature, the hero of the Feather Chant then trades this agricultural knowledge for game kept on underground farms by Deer Raiser, an event whose logic is commemorated in turn in the dry-painting frame that matches deer with the maize plant. Developing this reciprocity, the Blessing Way paintings of the Road of Emergence actually establish a visual pun between the hunter travel's path and the stem of the maize plant, along or up which trails of footprints mesh. In one reading of the highly wrought language of the Night Chant, the same pun is expressed verbally in the soundplay between walking far in time (*saa nagai*) and thriving as a plant (*sa'aa nagai*) on the path of or according to the ideal (*bike hozhon, bigke hozhon*). In the Pima epic, the hero himself is said actually to "green" on coming up from the underworld.[21]

THE NORTHERN TRANCE JOURNEY

The epic paradigm traced so far from Mesoamerica up through Anasazi recurs yet farther north, in Turtle Island cultures once focused on Cahokia. Indeed, leading out from a generally less intricate scheme of world ages, it is defined there with yet greater clarity. In the Midewiwin, at the frontier with the Arctic, it is clearest of all: The birchbark scrolls explicitly identify the Algonkin hunter-seeker – Michabo, Manabozho, Nanabush[22] –

with the astronomical road and arithmetic that integrate Venus with moon and sun. Indeed, in these texts the phases and rhythms of the solar walk establish the degrees of shamanic initiation, the sets of tests undergone by the candidate in quest of enlightenment and knowledge, and the very structure of the script that records all this, the gift of the epic hero, as in the case of Anasazi and Nahuatl epics. So firmly felt are these norms that in turn they come to prompt and shape accounts of trance experience that are both highly individual, a progress of pilgrims, and readily translatable into the language of politics and ideology.

An authoritative introduction to all that concerns the northern trance journey is provided by the Ottawa-Algonkin shaman Chusco's narrative "Iosco, or a Visit to the Sun and Moon: A tale of Indian cosmogony, from the Ottawa."[23] The opening incorporates tales told by Indians who by one means or another had visited the Old World: Traveling east, Iosco and five companions first cross the sea and end up in a gilded European capital. Still determined to encounter the sun and the true source of life, the six press on with their journey; only from this point does the cosmogony proper begin. Changing entirely, the landscape becomes subterranean, and after three days that "were really three years" the six meet the rattle-wielding Manabozho. In conversation he offers them guidance and notes that on arrival they had already passed over three-fourths of their way and were to spend the remaining time with him, a day that also is really a year, making four day-years in all. Before setting off again, in twos, each of the three pairs makes a wish about how long he should live, with the result that only the humblest pair, Iosco and his companion, succeed in crossing a chasm that opens before them.

On the other side, these two meet the moon, here a woman in white "approaching as from behind a hill." She tells them that they are now halfway to her brother's (the sun), that from the earth to her abode was half the distance; and she promises in due time to lead them to her brother, then absent on his "daily course." In this halfway position they stay with her until the "proper time" arrives to meet the sun. The story goes on:

> When the proper time arrived, she said to them, "My brother is now rising from below, and we shall see his light as he comes over the distant edge: come," said she; "I will lead you up." They went forward, but in some mysterious way, they hardly knew how, they rose almost directly up, as if they had ascended steps. (Schoolcraft 1839, 2:55)

At a point "halfway" between the edge of the earth and "midday," Iosco converses directly with the sun, being in effect blessed by him. Then, having reached the point of plenitude, the "Heart of Heaven," or midday, they set off down again, making the last half of the descent "as if they had been let down by ropes."

With its references to Europe and the Old World, Iosco's solar quest is no doubt Chusco's own and reflects the struggle he felt in himself between Mide and Christian teaching.[24] Technically the tale lives up to its cosmogonical epithet; overcoming the obstacle of the chasm, as in a shamanic test, the hero leads us from the lower to the upper paths of the solar walk. For in time and space Iosco follows the apparent course of the sun and moon; and the 4 + 4 day-years, *utas* and *octaeteris,* that he spends between west and east evoke the four-year leap-day span of the sun, each year acquiring the quarter-day later defined between east and west. As for Manabozho, the third figure in the story encountered prior to the moon in the underworld, he has to be equated with Venus, the third factor in the *octaeteris* formula. His long-nosed rabbit or hare image at Chillicothe actively recalls the Maya hieroglyph for Venus, which as Sign VIII numerically equates with the Rabbit of iconic script.[25]

The moral concerns implicit in Iosco's quest were anticipated in a famous story recounted by Pontiac,[26] likewise an Ottawa and a Mide shaman as well as a great military opponent of the English. Faced with the task of closely uniting his diverse forces, he described a pilgrimage similar to Iosco's undertaken by a member of the "grandfather" tribe of the Algonkin nations and the Huron alike, a Lenape of the Wolf clan. The day chosen by Pontiac to relate his narrative, 27 April 1763, was reported as the fifteenth of the moon, that is, the full moon. Anxious to know the "Master of Life," the Lenape sets out on his journey, making much the same preparations as Iosco. Overall the journey again lasts eight "days," and it leads to a choice of three paths that grow strangely luminous in the twilight of the eighth day. This motif conjoins the two lots of three paths evoked in Iosco: those of the bright trio on the solar walk (sun, moon, Venus) and those chosen respectively by the three pairs of travelers, only one of which led to midday in the sky (the path of the sun). This reading is strengthened by the fact that again only one path, the third, takes the Lenape hero the whole way through the day; the other two go only "halfway" and issue into a large fire "coming from underground," which is where Iosco encounters Venus and the moon and where the unsuccessful pairs of companions go no farther. Having traveled the right path, the Lenape is shown the way to his goal by the moon, who likewise appears on a mountain as a white woman.

In their particularity and emphasis, Chusco's and Pontiac's narratives are best understood in relation to the Midewiwin. For both invoke doctrines basic to that body, notably those relating to the hunt and to the initiation of novices by degrees, which feature Manabozho as guide, intermediary, and instructor of the Mide, the moon and its phases, and the quest for life's sources in the noon sun. Actually mapping the right and wrong roads, Mide charts on birchbark, including one notable example from the Menomini, record the novice's attainment of degrees that, like the "days" of the solar walk, conform to an ideal total of 4 (+ 4), while certain chronological symbols specify fast and feast periods, each of four actual days. More graphi-

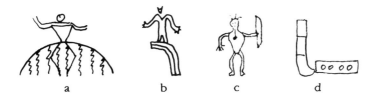

Figure 60. Trance symbols: (a) vision atop the celestial arch; (b) traveler going up the half-arch from east to zenith; (c) Venus/Manabozho as hunter; (d) the path back to the Mide lodge with its set of four markers. (*Sikassige Song Scroll.*)

cally still, symbols recording antiphonal verses intoned during initiation, which also normally fall into stanzas of four, depict both the physical course of the solar walk the candidate aspires to make and the celestial travelers along it: sun, moon, and Venus.[27]

Hence, pictographic texts copied and interpreted by Sikassige, Little Frenchman, Kweweziashish, and other Mide shamans[28] begin with the entry into the Mide lodge, the collecting of fees, and preparatory activities like taking a sweat bath and digging down into the earth for "medicine" with which to enhance perception for the journey itself. This may start "below" and follow the course, for example, of the otter sacred to Manabozho, or the beaver, renowned for its capacity to travel great distances before resurfacing. Or it can be celestial: The candidate rises up on and into the arch of the sky by steps or like a bird and there encounters the Great Spirit (Gitche Manito) depicted as the sun. To a figure mounting the celestial arch from the east like "the sun pursuing his diurnal course till noon" and like Iosco and the Lenape traveler correspond the words "I walk upon half the sky"[29] (Fig. 60); similarly the moment of plenitude at noon, or midday, is registered by a figure atop the arch, to which Sikassige puts the words "The spirit has given me power to see."

The lower and upper courses of the solar walk are epitomized as such at their "halfway" moments, in paired or double-headed symbols: arms "taking life from down in the earth or up in the sky; trees with root and foliaged crown that walk; upright and inverted heads that rotate through the walk and to which attach the words "I come up from below, I come down from above – I see the spirit, I see beavers." In a single-stanza song "for beaver hunting and the Metai-Mide" collected by Tanner, the down–up opposition occurs in the first and last symbols: a subterranean lodge and a flying eagle. This text is also notable for the chronology encoded in its second symbol, which depicts the four day-years familiar from Chusco and Pontiac. Referring to marks drawn on a fasting figure, on chest (two) and legs (four), come the words "Two days must you sit fast, my friend; four days must you sit fast." A binding around the legs, the four lines mean actually sitting fast for four days; but as far as the candidate's inner devotion goes, they are understood simultaneously to mean four years.

A definite link between these Mide texts and the extended alphabetic narratives of Chusco and Pontiac is provided by Catherine Wabose, an apostate like Chusco, who described her first solar walk both verbally and in a pictographic Mide chart.[30] Prepared by a ritual fast of four days, she sets off on a mysterious path stretching down between the setting sun and the new moon at the western horizon; having passed figures equivalent to the full moon and Venus, she rises to the heart of the sky, the climax of the vision, before again descending on a snake. The importance of the moon's phases is clear from Wabose's and one of Little Frenchman's symbols; moon and Venus in the posture of the guide Manabozho are similarly conjoined in a single stanza of hunter pictographs also recorded by Schoolcraft. The accompanying words read:

> I am rising (like the sun)
> I take the sky, I take the earth (at the horizon)
> I walk through the sky (like the moon)
> Venus guides me.
>   – Schoolcraft 1851–7, 1:402

As Siouan-speakers living on the southern border of the Mide heartland, the Winnebago offer insights of their own into the meaning and function of the solar walk as the route of not just the shaman-hero but also the soul after death. Instructed by a great-grandmother figure, the Winnebago soul sets off on a path that takes him or her past the underworld fire of the Lucifer-like Herecgunina, leads step by step over the eastern horizon, and brings him or her up to the circle of relatives in the heart of the sky. He or she is told:

> My grandchild, Earthmaker is waiting for you in great expectation. There is the door to the setting sun. On your way stands the lodge of Herecgunina, and his fire. Those who have come [the souls of brave men] from the land of the souls to take you back will touch you. There the road will branch off towards your right and you will see the footprints of the day on the blue sky before you. These footprints represent the footprints of those who have passed into life again. Step into the places where they have stepped and plant your feet into their footprints, but be careful you do not miss any. Before you have gone very far, you will come into a forest broken by open prairies here and there. Here, in this beautiful country, these souls whose duty it is to gather other souls will come to meet you. Walking on each side of you they will take you safely home. As you enter the lodge of the Earthmaker you must hand to him the sacrificial offerings. Here the inquiry that took place in the first lodge will be repeated and answered in the same manner. Then he will say to you, "All that your grandmother had told you is true. Your relatives are waiting for you in great expectation. Your home is waiting for you. Its door will be facing the mid-day sun. Here you will find your relatives gathered."[31]

The number of days in the Winnebago wake is four, during which period the mourners concentrate on helping the soul on its way beyond death, until it has passed the critical halfway encounter with Herecgunina. Indeed, what the mourners say and do, whether or not they exaggerate or lie about their own capacity to help, directly affects the soul's passage. For his or her part, the traveler enters another type of time, the ancient time of the spirits and shamanism in which the mourning period lasts both four days and four years. The particular motif of having to get into step in order to pass the test or boundary line recalls the steps by which Iosco ascended into the sky; in addition, it suggests a link with the less and more synchronized left and right footprints measured along the Road of Emergence in the Navajo dry paintings.

In the epic cycles of Winnebago cosmogony proper,[32] the trance journey again marks the route for several heroes, notably the Twins, who alternate between Earthmaker above and Herecgunina below. In turn, the Twins are intimates of Red Horn, whose epic experiences include losing a ballgame contest against a community of menacing giants. He is defeated and his head is hung in a tree; his two sons avenge him by defeating his killers and reassembling his body. These parallels with the *Popol vuh* are the more remarkable for being set at the same epic juncture in the story of the world and for having a similar astronomical subtext.

HOW HUMAN TIME BEGINS

Bay tzolci yax ah miatz Merchise yax ah bovat Napuctun sacerdote yax ah kin	It was set out this way by the first sage Melchisedek, the first prophet Napuctun, sacerdote, the first priest.
lay kay uchci u zihil uinal ti ma to ahac cab cuchie	This is the song of how the uinal was realized, before the world was.
ca hoppi u ximbla tuba tu hunal	He started up from his inherent motion alone.
ca yalah u chich ca yalah u dzenaa ca yalah u min ca yalah u muu	His mother's mother and her mother, his mother's sister and his sister-in-law, they all said:
5 bal bin c'alab ca bin c'ilab uninc ti be	How shall we say, how shall we see, that man is on the road?
ca thanob tamuk u ximbalob cuchie minan uinic cuchi	These are the words they spoke as they moved along, where there was no man.
catun kuchiob te ti likine ca hoppi yalicob	When they arrived in the east they began to say:
mac ti mani uay le yocob lae Ppiz ta uoci	Who has been here? These are footprints. Get the rhythm of his step.
ci bin u than u colel cab	So said the Lady of the world,

10	cabin u ppizah yoc ca yumil ti Ds citbil
	lay u chun yalci xoc lah cab oc lae lahca Oc
	lay tzolan zihci tumen oxlahun Oc
	uchci u nup tanba yoc likciob te ti likine
	ca yalah u kaba ti minan u kaba kin cuchie
15	ximbalnahci y u chiich y u dzenaa y u min y u muu
	zi uinal zihci kin u kaba zihci caan y luum
	eb haa luum tunich y che zihci u bal kabnab y luum
	Hun Chuen u hokzici uba tu kuil u mentci caan y luum
	Ca Eb u mentci yax eb. Emci likul tan yol caan
20	tan yol haa, minan luum y tunich y che
	Ox Ben u mentci tulacal bal, hibahun bal
	u bal caanob y u bal kaknab y u bal luum
	Can Ix uchci u nixpahal caan y luum
	Ho Men uchci u meyah tulacal
25	Uac Cib uchci u mentici yax cib
	uchci u zazilhal ti minan kin y u.
	Uuc Caban yax zihci cab ti minan toon cuchi
	Uaxac Etznab etzlahci u kab y yoc ca u chichaah yokol luum
	Bolon Cauac yax tumtabci metnal
30	Lahun Ahau uchci u binob u lobil

and our Father, Dios, measured his step.

This is why the count by footstep of the whole world, *xoc lah cab oc,* was called *lahca oc* "12 Oc."

This was the order born through 13 Oc,

when the one foot joined its counter print to make the moment of the eastern horizon.

Then he spoke its name when the day had no name

as he moved along with his mother's mother and her mother, his mother's sister and his sister-in-law.

The *uinal* born, the day so named, the sky and earth,

the stairway of water, earth, stone, and wood, the things of sea and earth realized.

1 Chuen, the day he rose to be a day-ity and made the sky and earth.

2 Eb, he made the first stairway. It ebbs from heaven's heart, the heart of water, before there was earth, stone, and wood.

3 Ben, the day for making everything, all there is, the things of the air, of the sea, of the earth.

4 Ix, he fixed the tilt of the sky and earth.

5 Men, he made everything.

6 Cib, he made the number one candle and there was light in the absence of sun and moon.

7 Caban, honey was conceived when we had not a caban.

8 Etznab, his hands and feet were set, he sorted minutiae on the ground.

9 Cauac, the first deliberation of hell.

10 Ahau, evil men were assigned to

uinicob ti metnal tumen Ds Citbil	hell out of respect for Ds.
ma chicanac cuchie	that they need not be noticed.
Buluc Imix uchci u patic tuni y che	11 Imix, he construed stone and wood;
lay u mentah ichil kin	he did this within the face of the day.
Lahcabil Ik uchci u zihzic ik	12 Ik, occurred the first breath;
35 Lay u chun u kabatic Ik tumen minan cimil ichil lae	it was named Ik because there was no death in it.
Oxlahun Akbal uchci u cħaic haa, ca yakzah luum	13 Akbal, he poured water on the ground;
Ca u patah ca uinic-hi	this he worked into man.
Hunnil Kan u vax mentci u leppel yol tumenal u lobil zihzah	1 Kan, he "canned" the first anger because of the evil he had created.
Ca Chicchan uchci u chictahal u lobil hibal yilah ichil u uich cahe	2 Chicchan, he uncovered the evil he saw within the town.
40 Ox Cimil u tuzci cimil	3 Cimi, he invented death;
uchci u tuzci yax cimil ca yumil ti Ds	as it happened the father Ds. invented the first death.
[. . .]	[4 Manik missing]
Ho Lamat lay u tuzci uuclam chac haal kaknab	5 Lamat, he invented the seven great seas.
Uac Muluc uchci u mucchahal kopob tulacal	6 Muluc, came the deluge and the submersion of everything
ti mato ahac cabe. Lay uchci yocol u tuz thanil ca yumil ti Ds	before the dawning. Then the father Ds. invented the word
45 tulacal ti minan tun than ti caan ti minan tunich y che cuchi	when there was no word in heaven, when there was neither stone nor wood.
Catun binob u tum tubaob ca yalah tun bayla	Then the twenty deities came to consider themselves in summation and said:
Oxlahun tuc: uuc tuc, hun	Thirteen units plus seven units equals one.
Lay yalah ca hok u than ti minan than ti	So said the *uinal* when the word came in, when there had been no word,
Ca katab u chun tumen yax Ahau kin	and this led to the question by the day Ahau, ruler,
50 ma ix hepahac u nucul than tiob	Why was the meaning of the word not opened to them
uchebal u thanic ubaobe	so that they could declare themselves?
Ca binob tan yol caan ca u machaah u kab tuba tanbaobe	Then they went to heaven's heart and joined hands.

From the *Chilam Balam Book of Chumayel,* this passage sums up a long and complex section of text (pp. 42–63) whose overall concern is cosmogony (in Roys's edition, the chapters entitled "The Creation of the World," "Ritual of the Angels," "Song of the Itza," and "The Creation of the Uinal"). The story begins with the formation of the world itself, told through allusions to the Nine Generations (Bolon Dzacab, a primeval lunar and earth force like the midwife's nine Night Lords) and the augur's upper-world deity Thirteen, Oxlahun-ti-ku, whose insignia are stolen, like Parrot's in the *Popol vuh* (the Ah Muzen Cab episode). There are also references to catastrophes of water, falling sky, and flaming fire and to the release of the precious long-haired maize. All this is told in highly esoteric terms and engages furthermore with versions of genesis imported by the Roman church and the language of Latin ritual. Then in conclusion we have this narrative about the *uinal,* the twenty-day character upon which or whom all operations of lowland Maya ritual and calendar converge. Completing the argument of creation by numbers, Nine, Thirteen, and Twenty, the steps of the *uinal* here recapitulate its great moments of metamorphosis and emergence. With this passage we are brought forward into the present world, the time and space presided over by the four "Burners," who include the Era day-name 4 Ahau.

In registering the birth and trajectory of the *uinal,* the text appeals to the same solar-walk paradigm that we have seen characterize the epic phase of cosmogony in other North American traditions. For underlying the ingenious Maya wordplay and apparent denial of simple narrative sequence, there is the course followed by the *uinal* as the male traveler, the man on the road; just as in the Navajo and other "visits to the sun," his steps, twenty in number and hence definitive of his self, lead him and us precisely from the eastern horizon to the zenith, Sky Heart (*yol caan*), the half-arc of the Mide pictograph. Moreover, exemplifying the epic hero, he is defined by movement, issuing from feminine kin; and at the eastern horizon he undergoes exactly the shamanic test of getting into step that is so clearly stated in epic journeys from farther north. Again it is through his efforts that the present order of things comes about, translated down through him from the sky.

As a beginning, the *uinal* stirs in the absence of all else. The first proof of his existence is a movement that is inherent and axiomatic and that sets in motion the human time of this world. Vertically and laterally he is held by a mesh of feminine beings who anticipate his separate existence; yet his birth, once consummated (line 16), is not just from a "mater-ial" womb but from a place that could as well be external as internal, the outer as much as the inner cosmos. At first he amounts to no more than the footprints on the road foreseen and then seen by the women. But these tracks reveal a good deal about him: his direction along the solar walk, his posture and articulation as a biped, and that he indeed is human, *Homo erectus.* A common etymology links *uinal* with *uinic* "human";[33] and in hieroglyphic writing, besides denoting the calendrical period of twenty days, the *uinal* sign could also indicate humankind and hence a Maya notion of rationality.

When the *uinal*'s steps come to be measured in the east, their intervals and positions are registered as specifically human, like the footprints in the final Navajo Road of Emergence painting. At the same time, through the resource of the Thirteen Numbers and the Twenty Signs used to name Mesoamerican days, the way is prepared for an enumeration of the world that correlates the *uinal*'s journey with deeper levels of time. In fact the series starts off (line 11) with a pun made available by this resource, in the phrase "xoc lah cab oc lae lahca Oc." *Xoc* means "count"; *lahcab* means "whole world," and *lahca* is the number twelve; *oc* is "foot" or "footprint"[34] and, like the archaic Quiché term for leg, names the tenth of the Twenty Signs. In other words, the half-repetition of *lahca*[*b*] *oc* hints at a Number plus Sign and therefore a position in the lowland Maya 260-day equivalent of the *tonalamatl*. This verbal agility engages us unawares in the potent internal logic of the *uinal* and brilliantly overcomes those "paralogistic" problems (as Kant called them) of explaining the start of serially named time. For from here we move immediately to 13 Oc, now unequivocal as a Number plus Sign, as the other foot moves forward. The ploy is further enhanced by the fact that such a "step" is anatomically impossible: Signs qualified by consecutive numbers, like 12 Oc and 13 Oc here, fall forty days, or two *uinal*s, apart. Yet precisely because of this, the narrative movement or step aptly corresponds to that moment of stasis, shown to be undefinable in the Eleatic paradoxes, when the one foot is exactly even with the other moving past it. This is the moment of the eastern horizon, the space–time edge of the day unit so highly defined as an arithmetical unit in Maya cosmogony. It is the start position of right with left, of even with odd (12, 13) not *ex nihilo* (0 to 1). Characteristic of the Maya and Mesoamerican dualism exemplified earlier in the earth–sky figure of lines 9–10, this parity at the horizon coincides in turn with that which balances the two halves of the Twenty Signs and of the 260-day count as we step from 13 Oc (Sign X) to 1 Chuen (Sign XI). Thus defined, this parity starts the sequence that enumerates the world day by day.

Beginning in 13 Oc and running through to 6 Muluc, the journeying *uinal* through his twenty day-events repeatedly invokes the larger processes of creation. Yet he does so very much in his own terms, according to the paradigm that is strongly reasserted in the first upward steps: 1 Chuen, when he rises; and 2 Eb, which represents the tooth-steps of the pyramid stairway that now not so much rises as descends toward him from the zenith, in anticipation. Just because the course of the narrative is so firmly preset by this paradigm and the sequence of day names itself is there room for play with concepts and words and the patterning of cosmic events, and for glancing irreverence toward biblical genesis.

Overall we learn or are reminded of the levels of creation that separate the waters below from the sky above (2 Eb), the tilting of earth (4 Ix) that produces the swaying or drunken path of the zodiac in the sky, the forming of Adam or the mudpeople (13 Akbal), the great Flood (6 Muluc), the epic struggle between Wind and Death (12 Ik), the authority that sentences people to the lower world Metnal or Xibalba (9 Cauac, 10 Ahau), and the twenty articulated digits that came to distinguish humankind (8 Etznab). Yet the sequence respects above all the particularities of the Numbers and Signs in question, like the breath of Ik, the candle of Cib, and the honey of Caban – respective meanings of those Signs themselves. The Monkey of 1 Chuen, the name of the Monkey brothers in the *Popol vuh*, is honored as in that text for an artistry that could rival and even substitute glyphically for that of humans; hence the images of monkey scribes on classical pottery. With its watery associations, the final day, 6 Muluc, plays on the verb *mucchahal* "to drown"; at the same time, as a hieroglyph it may also mean to count and hence neatly echoes the other verb glyph with that meaning, *xoc,* which introduced the passage.

Through all this, the text warrants attention for its specifically literary qualities; like the riddles in the *Chilam Balam Books,* it offers multiple levels of reading that derive directly from hieroglyphic practice and precedent, where a main Sign customarily has more than one meaning. For instance, the event for 11 Imix could be read as "rocks and trees were created on this day." However, the verb *patic* basically means to mold, as Gates pointed out when censuring Roys for his monotonous use of "create" for no fewer than seven distinct Maya verbs in this passage; and Motul dictionary adds the notions *inventar* and *fingir.*[35] At the same time, the materials that are being invented in this sense, stone and wood, may conventionally evoke the art of painting and carving and hence of writing; "within the day" has the inherent meaning of "in the face of the day," and thus the whole phrase could refer to the day unit of lowland Maya calendrics and hieroglyphic script. Traveling from the east to the zenith, the *uinal* not only defines himself in calendrical time but writes himself into existence.

Finally, upon reaching the zenith the constituent Numbers and Signs of the *uinal* remind us of their nature in the formula "thirteen plus seven equals one"; and the twentieth Sign, Ahau, is entrusted with proposing the *uinal*'s ascent as alternative to the "word" claimed exclusively by imported Christianity. Implying remarkable faith in the idea of universal human intelligence, this gesture also reminds us that the purpose of the Mide trance journey to the zenith is to gain knowledge and enlightenment. Their work done, the Twenty Signs then join hands in the heart of the sky, forming a ring like that found around the five Suns on the Aztec *Sunstone* and reminiscent in turn of the hoop in the sky seen in Sioux and Algonkin visions.

In sheer mathematical terms, this pause at the zenith, midway between east and west, further appeals to the solar-walk logic found in other epic journeys, in the sense that in order to complete the whole circuit four *uinals* would be needed, a further one to take us back to the western horizon, and then two more to return us to the starting point at the eastern horizon. A hint of this last calculation was given in the distance that separated 12 Oc and 13 Oc at the start, that is, forty days, or two *uinals*; moreover, the eighty-day total, which governs the *teoamoxtli* Birth chapter and is shown as actual footprints on the Boban Calendar Wheel,[36] fits admirably with Tichy's demonstration that the principal divisions of the Mesoamerican orbit are eighty. Hence, in addition to the time shifts already detailed as a feature of the solar walk, in the 4 + 4 days of Venus's inferior conjunction, the matching 4 + 4 years of the *octaeteris,* and the internal divisions of the day itself between sunrise, midday, sunset, and midnight we have yet another time shift, whereby the double 4 + 4 formula is referred to halves of the *uinal,* that is, two full *uinals* below and two above (see Fig. 59).

This technical detail helps us better appreciate the formulation that follows, when the four Ah Toc, named 4 Chicchan, 4 Oc, 4 Men, and 4 Ahau, are installed as rulers over the land below. In the day count so far established by the *uinal,* the last of these, the Era date 4 Ahau, occupies the position exactly halfway between the zenith and the western horizon, intimating diagonal or intermediary positions for the set as a whole. This model accords excellently with accounts that have generally been given of the otherwise enigmatic Ah Toc, who also appear or are alluded to in other *Chilam Balam Books* and the hieroglyphic screenfolds. On this basis we may identify them as somehow equivalent to the set of year bearers found at the diagonals in the *Féjérváry* map, to the four kindlers disposed in the same diagonal pattern in *Borbonicus* (p. 34), and to fourfold sets of rains and winds. Most important, the *Chilam Balam Book of Tizimin*[37] unequivocally describes the process whereby the *uinal* literally brings the fourfold set of Ah Toc down to earth as such, translating them from the up–down dimensions of the solar walk onto the four "flattened" fields of the earth's surface. Exactly this shift occurs in the classic case of *Féjérváry,* where the zenith and nadir of the solar walk, either side of the east–west axis, translate into the north and south of the quatrefoil tribute map.

Intricately bound up with the complex mechanisms of lowland Maya calendrics, the *Chumayel* story of the *uinal* appeals basically to the model of the solar walk that characterizes the epic all over northern America. He is born approaching the east, defines himself walking from east to zenith in search of knowledge, and sums himself as a ring in the sky that is then translated to earth, installing fourfold political order. Recognizing this fact, we perceive more readily how his life and in particular the events assigned to each of his steps resonate within a greater cosmogonical frame, and understand how the corresponding pattern of "days" invokes the time shifts typical of this shamanic journey.

12

American cosmos

CONVERGENCE AT QUICHÉ

Through the episodes and stages of its cosmogony, the *Popol vuh* weaves several epistemological threads, each identifiable in terms of literary tradition and even geography and biosphere. Behind the successive arguments, or demonstrations, of the Quiché text we may detect conventions and schools of thought distinguished by particular ranges of evidence and observable phenomena as well as inherited learning and scholarship. In this perspective, as an American Bible transcribed from native script, the *Popol vuh* can be read as the product of a privileged multilayered geography, the synthesis of several ways of American knowledge.

Literally the most basic of these is geology. According to the *Popol vuh*, affirming the earth's surface and wrenching order from chaos are matters of cataclysm, on the grand scale so dramatically celebrated in the Aztec story of the Suns and their dire endings. After the initial pair of celestially governed disasters, Quiché landmarks are physically thrust into prominence by the tectonic action that has raised the western rim of the whole continent, the Andean vertebrae profiled in texts from Ftah Mapu to Anasazi. For the mountain home of the *Popol vuh* came into being not just through the sedimentarian layers of flood but also through violent upheavals of the earth's crust and volcanic eruption. So powerful is this geological factor that the *Sunstone* frames the face of the earth itself in the Sign Ollin, the mark of radical instability likewise caught in the Quechua term *pachacuti*.

In this geology, shifts in the shape of the landscape can be as rapid and dramatic as those caused by Cipacna and Two Leg in the *Popol vuh* when they play at raising mountains and knocking them down again. As a result, whole buried strata are thrown into relief, propelling the fish of ancient seas to the highest peaks, exposing the bones of obsolete monsters and lost species, and intimating frontiers between blank and fossil rock and then between pre- and post-vertebrate life. In the *Popol vuh* these two discourses of what we recognize as geology and biology are thoroughly conjoined in the figures of Cipacna and Two Leg, at once giant saurians and the rock that bears evidence of them. This same connection is made in the *Ríos* world-age chapter, which explicitly mentions the fossilized bones of vanished giants, duly brought and shown to uncomprehending Spaniards in the sixteenth century as evidence for the cosmogony depicted therein. The same story can be heard down the South American Andes, among the Chibcha, the Quechua, and the Mapuche: Sharing a general curiosity about seashells promoted to 14,000 feet, these last also focus on the *fora lil,* or "bone rocks," in their language, whose eyes stare fixedly through time, predicating those of later vertebrates and of humans themselves.

Encoded in stone, this dimension of American cosmogony appears to be a prerequisite for the scheme of world ages typified by the Mesoamerican and Inca set of Suns, the quincunx that bears in itself the memory of the earth's four cataclysms. It provides the large single framework for what otherwise remain separate stories of geological strata, like the nested boxes of the Tsimshian world or the multiple floods and petrifications of just the plant forms of the rainforest example. Thus tied to specifically Andean geology, the scheme of cataclysms in turn more narrowly frames the doctrine of domestic contract identified with the Eclipse of the second Sun, which in itself bears the marks of urban and economically complex provenance and which receives so strong an onomatopoeic emphasis in the *Popol vuh*. What Mapuche, Amazonian, and Anasazi texts report in this situation as strife between gender and within marriage, a family affair of the neglected spouse, is translated by Aztec, Inca, and Maya into relations of use and labor and the lexis of utensils. In the Inca case, the contractual notion is extended to include the mass exploitation signified by pastoralism; the revolution here is led by whole herds of llamas no longer ready to accept the system of control imposed upon them.

In elaborating its narrative of the world ages, into which the social catas- trophe of Eclipse is ingeniously set, the *Popol vuh* appeals not just to the Andean geology of the continent's western edge; it also draws heavily on the zoological teachings of the Amazonian cosmos on whose northern rim Quiché territory lies. From the literary evidence available, this continuum with the rainforest habitat appears to have been decisive for the larger evolutionary message of the Quiché text. It is true that the rainforest envi- ronment impinges on literature produced outside its geographical extent, as we have seen in the case of the *Runa yndio* with its Amazonian substratum, the Iroquois Cusick's astounding reference to the monkey as predecessor of humankind (1823), and certain Nahuatl traditions that survive today in western Mexico. Indeed, several of the Twenty Signs of Mesoamerica are to be precisely identified with this source, like Caiman (I), Monkey (XI), and Jaguar (XIV). Yet the *Popol vuh* exudes a palpably greater intimacy with this tropical lowland world, being in this sense far more readily intelligible in the terms proposed by the Carib classic *Watunna*.

The domain of an unrivaled range of biota – flora and fauna – the rainforest has even now not been fully reduced to latinate taxonomy. This is the hot, moist territory of unending snakes whose bodies issue into water and rivers and whose scales aspire to the condition of feather; eels that capture the sky's electricity; caimans that can bite off a leg; the most variegated parliament of birds; the great feline hunter and aristocrat whose Guarani name is Jaguar; and our simian half-brothers, notably the red-faced howler monkeys with their unkempt hair and expression of perpetual discontent who lose their tails to become human.

Only in the rainforest do these creatures have concourse, and only there is it possible to observe the curious intimacies between their life-forms: the hoatzin bird, for example, whose offspring with their tiny claws uncannily resemble those of the cold-blooded reptilian egg layers. Indeed, in *Watunna* this myriad potential of life is contained in the great egg *huehanna,* an Amazonian and South American motif, as Krickeberg noted, that logically underlies the construction of Seven Parrot's reptile-bird family in the *Popol vuh.*

As for the forest itself, its vegetative wealth outdoes received axioms of single upward growth. In *Watunna,* the primary case is stated by the great tree Marahuaka; through it, earth and sky flow into each other, and fruits of all kinds grow from its branches as if in a community of grafted sap. Aerophyte, its roots reach up as well as down; and its versatile power to sustain attendant life and limb anticipates the mode of transplantation by which human limbs are interchanged and whole bodies are resurrected, in *Watunna* and the *Popol vuh* alike. Beyond this, particular plants in this environment reflexively open human senses to its inner workings, clearing ears and eyes and teaching the languages of the forest. In native texts emanating from the South American rainforest this environmental system is read as renewable metamorphosis, dazzling and actual. It embodies the exuberance of "the great procreative circuit of the biosphere," as Reichel-Dolmatoff puts it in his *Amazonian Cosmos,*[1] and suggests a theory of energy and form that endlessly conjoins man and animal, society and nature. In the *Popol vuh* this rainforest philosophy gives immediacy of character and form to the age-old evolutionary story of the Suns.

Drawing in this way on both Andean and southern rainforest traditions when first establishing its cosmogony, the *Popol vuh,* plurivalent, goes on to recount its epic Xibalba sequence in terms identifiable rather with Turtle Island and the northern half of the continent. For in assigning a lunar–solar identity to the Twins as they walk into the sky at the eastern horizon and follow the zodiac road marked out by the Four Hundred, the text appeals to the astronomical solar-walk paradigm repeatedly developed in North American texts in relation to the *octaeteris* that correlates the cycles of sun, moon, and Venus. The Fathers' and the Twins' journey follows that of the shaman and the soul after death, particularly in the passage to and through the underworld; and this fact encourages us to search for hints of the *octaeteris* model.

Taking the *tonalamatl* names of the Twins and other characters as the means for calculating day units, several scholars have offered complex arithmetical readings, particularly in relation to the synodic period of Venus,[2] a comparison that certainly respects the principle of the *octaeteris*. Yet this should not lead us to overlook the fact that in the first place the *octaeteris* correlates the sun and moon actually cited in the Quiché text, and that it has characteristic halves of just the kind alluded to in the respective journeys of the Fathers and the Twins, the first ending in failure in Xibalba and the second in ascent over the eastern horizon. Indeed, in linking these halves and "coming up" from below after six months, Blood Woman intercalates the moons of her pregnancy into the solar year, from the autumn equinox to the following summer solstice. Strong structural parallels for this reading can be found everywhere in the Mesoamerican epic, notably in the 4 + 4 passages or landscape hazards recorded in *Ríos,* which, grim and less grim and with their matching set of 4 + 4 skeletal underworld gods, formally correspond to the experiences of the Fathers and the Twins in Xibalba.

Correlating human days with spirit years, the octaeteris typically mediates between dimensions of time; and this possibility is intimated here: a shift into cosmic time of "Great Years" detailed below, through the cryptic citing not so much of *tonalamatl* names as Maya names for the annual Feasts, legible in the hazards faced by the fathers and Twins on their journey (four-colored roads) and at their resting places (guest houses of Xibalba) and in the *pop* of the title itself, identified by Landa with the start of the year. In sheer narrative terms, the time shift formally corresponds to the epic transition from grand cosmogony to history proper, according to the model set out in *Ríos* and other iconic texts. Not generally perceived as a factor in South American texts, yet fundamental in those of the North, the astronomical paradigm appealed to in the Xibalba epic of the *Popol vuh* has important consequences when it comes to decoding the time scale implicit in the story as a whole.

Finally, in celebrating maize as the substance from which the people of this Era were formed, the Quiché text announces its commitment to a doctrine diagnostic of precisely those parts of the Fourth World where that cereal achieved greatest economic and dietary significance. As we saw above, the equation of vegetal and human flesh as such accompanies plant domestication in America and widely instances manioc and the rainforest tubers (Fig. 61). In that perspective, the maize creation marks a further culminating moment, a supplanting and shift in diet explicitly acknowledged in other highland Maya versions of the story. Moreover, it appeals to the distinct genetic idiom epitomized in the Kekchi image of the impregnated woman giving birth to maize inside the Food Mountain: The mode of production is now not vegetal grafting or transplanting but seed and cross-fertilization. By the same token, the stages of human growth even from the embryo correspond to those of the maize plant, as both do to the moon (maize in fact grows at night). Hence Oxomoco's role as both midwife and supervisor of the growing maize, the one who divines with nine kernels and pours nine libations on the newly formed flesh of maize.

Central to Mesoamerican ritual, as we saw, for example, when analyzing the Foliated Cross panel at Palenque, this maize doctrine continues to inform the lives of the Chibcha, who share the same Western Caribbean arena, like the Talamanca of Costa Rica or the Kogi of Colombia, who go so far as to make the nine stages of human gestation into the model for their whole cosmogony.[3] The supreme achievement of Fourth World botanical intelligence, maize in this way sets up another isomorph at the very culmination of Quiché cosmogony. The text itself makes this point by emphasizing that maize and maize only became the flesh of the first humans, as if in contradistinction to the more mixed ingredients of the Cakchiquel and Nahuatl versions.

Following this genetic argument, which in the *Popol vuh* binds humans so closely to maize, we may even interpret it as symptomatic of a larger theory of mutation or transformation (Fig. 62). Key evidence here is provided by the screenfold pages and dry paintings relevant to the epic of human emergence. The *Féjérváry* quatrefoil details a set of four growth emblems at its diagonals, a remarkably sophisticated statement that persistently correlates plant and other life forms and moves from the less to the more complex. The first pair contrasts binary with spiral growth, and the third actually exemplifies transformation through the insect language of the cocoon, directly echoing here the quatrefoil cocoons that denote metamorphosis in Turtle Island texts.[4] Epitomizing the paths of vegetal growth and animal movement traced in the set of Navajo Road of Emergence paintings, the fourth emblem integrates flowering maize with the articulated hip of the mammal. However these further examples are understood, there can be no doubt about the *Popol vuh* doctrine that quite explicitly defines the invention of humans as genetically analogous to that of maize, or about the significance of this doctrine in Fourth World philosophy.

In all, the *Popol vuh* overwhelmingly vindicates its status as the American Bible by incorporating intellectual traditions identifiable respectively with the Andean chain, the rainforest, Turtle Island and North America, and the

Figure 61. Gifts of the caiman. Culti-vated plants growing from the caiman body include manioc and gourds (mid-dle), chilis (lower left), and peanuts (lower right). (Caiman Stela, Chavin; after Willey 1974: fig. 60.)

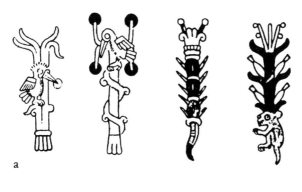

a

b

Figure 62. Symbols of growth and trans-formation: (a) four roots and body stems (*Féjérváry,* p. 1; see Plate 13a); (b) human emerging as butterfly (shield de-sign, *Tepetlaoztoc Codex*).

maize lands of Mesoamerica and the Caribbean, all of which converge on Quiché as nowhere else. By virtue of the *Popol vuh*'s provenance in time and space as well as its own ingenuity as a text, it offers a synthesis of American cosmogony that has not been rivaled anywhere.

TIMING

The Fourth World cosmogony narrated in the *Popol vuh* falls into recognizable phases that, encompassing eons of geology and evolution, begin with the time of this world itself. For their part, certain other native sources offer to measure the phases of this cosmogony, actually quantifying their duration (*durée*). Hence, the "millennium" ascribed to themselves by the Mapuche (in the *Shaihueke Narrative*) echoes in the high peaks of the Pire Mahuida and their 60,000-year glacier cycle; observing the same evidence at the northern end of the Andes, the Kogi perceive through it the death of the world as we know it. "Millions of years" are said to have elapsed since the Flood in the *Canimani Narrative* of the Witoto; approximated in the 73,000 years of Chimalpahin's Seventh Relation, spans of 80,000 years are still counted out by the Tzotzil in Maya vigesimal arithmetic and matched with the succession of the four world ages.[5] From the Classic period, the hieroglyphic inscriptions spell out spans of hundreds of millions of *tun* years. In other cases, chronological depth is achieved through the shamanic ciphers, especially the 4 + 4 of the *octaeteris,* which permits shifts between dimensions of time.

In all this, an indispensable concept is that of the Great Year unit of 26,000 solar years. Neglected by those Europeans who first reported on Fourth World cosmogony, this Great Year corresponds to the precession of the equinoxes, which, detectable only over centuries, confounds the Renaissance trope of a fixed pole star and has the effect of gradually moving the equinoctial sun "back" through the zodiac. The idea that Fourth World astronomers might have calculated and made use of this cycle is most often dismissed out of hand. In principle, it should rather seem surprising had they not done so, given the length of urban and agricultural history in the continent and the fact of an unbroken calendrical record for at least two and a half millennia before Columbus.

The main evidence for Fourth World knowledge of precession comes from Mesoamerica, where year dates are inscribed in stone from 600 B.C. or earlier, and where the standardized year of exactly 365 days was finely measured against both the synodic year of the seasons (365.24 days) and the sidereal year of the stars (365.56 days). With the seasonal year, the 0.24-day difference itself builds up to a year over just the 1,508 years, or twenty-nine Rounds, depicted in the *Mexicanus Codex* (see Fig. 36); with the sidereal year, the 0.56-day difference does the same over 1,427 years, the span marked in the *Tepexic Annals* by a specific date (2 Reed 1681 B.C.) plus star device (Fig. 63). The 0.14-day difference between the two, which phenomenologically corresponds to precession, amounts cumulatively to a year in just under 26,000 years, and this span in turn is registered as such in several texts, among them the *Sunstone* and the *Ríos Codex* from Tenochtitlan. Turning to the Maya hieroglyphic texts, scholars have found similar evidence, like base dates that relate to the Era in terms of Great Years, as well as calculations of a more astronomical order in the *Paris* screenfold (pp. 23–4).[6]

How this Great Year functioned in cosmogony is well illustrated by the pair of iconic texts, the *Sunstone* ("Montezuma's watch," as it has been popularly called) and *Ríos,* that most clearly define this Era, the fifth in the story of the world ages, as a fifth of the Great Year, that is, 5,200 years, 100 Rounds (100 × 52), or 13 *tzontli* (13 × 400). In neither text can there be doubt that cosmogony is the subject and the frame into which the Era is set: The *Sunstone* tells how the time named Four Ollin emerged from the world-age catastrophes of flood, eclipse, volcanic rain, and hurricane; *Ríos* insets these same catastrophes into the story of cereals that culminates in maize.

Just as the Era Four Ollin visually frames the preceding four world-ages at the center of the *Sunstone,* so its length is recorded on the rim, as we saw, in ten lots of 10 Rounds imaged as cloud-snakes that issue from the squared scales of the sky dragons to right and left. Now, as we noted above, the heads peering from the dragons' maws below belong respectively to Fire Lord (left) and the Sun (right), who are One and Four in the set of Thirteen Heroes. Hence, each endows its dragon and the Rounds on its back with number value, a capacity they and others among them display, for example, in the *Pinturas* transcription of the world-age story.[7] As One, Fire Lord simply confirms the 5,200-year total; as Four, Sun multiples it to 20,800, the remaining four-fifths of the Great Year. Hence:

$$
\begin{aligned}
1 \times 10 \times 10 \times 52 &= 5,200 \\
4 \times 10 \times 10 \times 52 &= 20,800 \\
\hline
&26,000
\end{aligned}
$$

In the *Cuauhtitlan Annals* transcription of the *Sunstone* cosmogony, the four-fifths of the Great Year is noted as "CCCC mixcoa," that is, four hundred cloud-snake Rounds.

Taking as its basic unit the 400-year *tzontli* rather than the Round, and incorporating the catastrophes of the Suns, the *Ríos* chapter subdivides its story of cereals into four principal moments, which form two pairs. The first pair is each ten *tzontli* in length (4,000 + 4,000 years); the second, twelve and thirteen (4,800 + 5,200 years), this last being the Era that begins with maize and the history of Tula. Inaugurating this whole sequence stands the suckling tree from which humans, sitting around it as yet innocent of

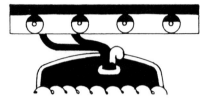

Figure 63. Star toponym. (*Tepexic Annals,* p. 10 [accompanies the 2 Reed 2 Reed date that occurs at Round 27 and then at 9-Round intervals].)

agriculture, received their food like drops from nature's breast. These are shown as liquid circles that gather on gourdlike fruit and fall into their mouths, their downward flight being marked by feathery lines. In *tlacuilolli* terms (the *Vaticanus* screenfold shows time units as round fruit on a tree [Figs. 10, 64a]), this design – a circle with a feather extending upward – prefigures just the 400-year multiple used in the calculations that follow. Indeed, the very term *tzontli* means "feather," so that as the first event in this food chapter as a whole, the suckling tree incipiently provides an install- ment of years. Numerically, falling to either side of the tree, this initial installment anticipates the first pair of 4,000 + 4,000 years, though it stops short of complete measurement (some drops are just forming; others have just been consumed), an apt indication of both the fact that the cycle is a little less than 26,000 years and that it is very hard to estimate exactly. (Even in the last hundred years Western astronomers have found themselves obliged to revise their calculations.) The overall statement is then:

$$
\begin{array}{rcr}
<20 \times 400 = & & <8,000 \\
10 \times 400 = & & 4,000 \\
10 \times 400 = & & 4,000 \\
12 \times 400 = & & 4,800 \\
13 \times 400 = & & 5,200 \\
\hline
& & <26,000
\end{array}
$$

The clarity of these two examples encourages similar readings for others embedded in the corpus of iconic texts, the "valentine" image in the open- ing chapter of *Borgia,* for example, which also includes a set of four Suns plus an image of the human arm severed and held by a giant Parrot. To- gether with the hieroglyphic evidence deciphered by others, this Mesoamer- ican affirmation of the Great Year in turn provides a reference point for cosmogonical statements from farther afield that involve time periods that otherwise must seem opaque or fortuitous, like the five-age 5,000-year model of Tahuantinsuyu or the Oglala history of High Hawk (Plate 18a).[8]

a

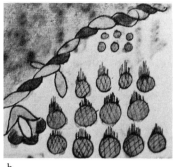

b

Figure 64. Details from the *Ríos* world-age chapter: (a) suckling tree (p. 4); (b) this Era's 5,200 years (i.e., 13 × 400; p. 8).

Detailing the Siouan vision in which Buffalo Woman's body incorporates four previous world ages as legs whose hairs are their years, High Hawk actually spells out an initial year sequence in arabic numerals. True to a duodecimal base, this produces just under 24,000 years:

$$
\begin{array}{r}
6,000 \\
11,900 \\
3,000 \\
1,100 \\
1,900 \\
\hline
23,900
\end{array}
$$

Identified as buffalo units, these periods correspond to the very beginnings of human culture – dog-drawn travois, hide kettles, fire drills – like the equivalent chapter in *Ríos;* and, again as in *Ríos,* the text prepares the way for the annals of history proper.

The frame for the Era, the Great Year for that very reason involves us in the story of the Suns and in time periods that run into hundreds of millions of years on stelae at Quirigua and in other hieroglyphic texts. Salient among these is the opening chapter of the *Madrid* screenfold[9] where, prior to the quatrefoil map, a series of dates appears, precisely stated in the bar-and-dot numbers and vigesimal place value of the *tun* calendar (Fig. 65). Embedded like strata in mountains, the first two dates appeal to the geological discourse of the earliest Suns and cast back many million years. The third is inscribed on a scroll that issues from the mouth of a man, denizen of a cave whose walls he is about to paint (cave paintings characterize the Maya lowlands). It amounts to 78,066,983 days, just over the 208,000 years of eight Great Years; this total of eight is actually inset as disks in the cave walls in the form of the 4 + 4 cipher. That this order of time belongs to the epic of human emergence, mediating between geological eons and Era history, is indicated both here and in *Ríos,* where, in just this context, human emergence is enumerated in the eight "passages," four grim and flinty, four less so. According to the ciphered shaman shift between time dimensions,[10] each passage would correspond to that of the Great Year explicitly defined in the subsequent agriculture sequence. A similar statement appears to be made on the *Sunstone,* where 4 + 4 greatly enlarged solar year markers mediate between the quincunx of ages at the center and the Great Year and Era at the rim; and it could provide the chronological key to the *Popol vuh* epic, divided as it is into more and less grim halves each of which is punctuated with Feast names of the year.

In the ages of metamorphosis that precede the epic, timing enters the phases of rock formation, posited by *Madrid* as 7,800,000 years, and about thirty times that period. In this oldest date the bars and dots that convey the numbered time periods are bent over as strata in an ancient mountain, equivalent to the image of Colhuacan (Fig. 65a; Plate 14a). Over their range, other hieroglyphic dates respect these orders of millions and hundreds of millions of years, as well as the tens of millions represented by the *Ritual of the Bacabs* (64 million) and Quirigua Stela A (90 million). In so doing, they intimate a possible three-level model consistent with the three world-ages that underlie the fourth-age epic and octaeteris of Great Years.

Incontrovertible in the cases of the rock strata and the caveman utterance in *Madrid* and the periodization of cereals and maize in *Ríos,* this Fourth World timing of cosmogony urgently asks to be further explored. However it may have been arrived at, in its sheer imaginative scope it shows us our place. Counting the moment of our species as minutes on the planetary clock, it fosters awareness of the eons that issue into the body and society of humankind.

GARDEN OF THE PLANET

That the cosmogony of the New World has clear echoes in that of the Old has been noted from at least the time of Columbus. The shaping of a man from clay; the woman who takes and eats the fruit of the forbidden

Figure 65. Strata and scroll dates. (*Madrid Codex,* pp. 57, 69, 72.)

tree; the flood; heroes who reemerge from a flaming furnace: These and many other motifs were read by the first Christian missionaries as faint or distorted memories of the only creation story they recognized as valid, that of the Semitic books, where they have a very different configuration. Yet on this basis Native Americans could at least be deemed indeed to belong to the humanity created by Jehovah and the derisory five or so millennia of biblical world history.

Over time, this scriptural orthodoxy was challenged and inexorably modified, to the extent that it has become the scientific orthodoxy of today.[11] Involving the rediscovery of Semitic culture (through the Muslims of Spain) and of the classics of Greece and Rome, this change was also undeniably prompted by America. In the pubs of Deptford, talking to sailors who had visited the Algonkin coast, Christopher Marlowe proclaimed his great heresy that "holy communion would have been much better administered in a Tobacco pipe" and that Native Americans were above all wiser in affirming the earth to be far more ancient than the Bible said. First prompted to his vision of America by the Tupi guests at Charles IX's court at Rouen, Montaigne went on to reproduce the whole scheme of world ages in a passage ultimately based on the Suns and catastrophes of Mesoamerican texts, which intimated the "cosmological unity" of the New World and implicitly contravened the single masterful act of Jehovah and the single subsidiary disaster of the Flood.[12] Marlowe's and Montaigne's insights eventually issued into the science of the secular Enlightenment: the geology that came to detect volcanic activity in purely sedimentarian rocks of the Bible, and the history of Vico, Boturini's teacher, which began to construct the "ages" of human experience.

Fueling debates about the primate origins of man, America continued its subversion in the nineteenth century. Drawing on their experience of the Andes and the rainforest, Darwin and Wallace built their theories from "factual observation," yet, according to their admission, they also listened to the testimony of "affable savages" and other long-standing inhabitants of that environment. Rewriting Genesis, they eventually produced the evolutionary story of the human species that respects the vertebrate sequence of fish, saurian, bird, and monkey, that is, what had already been written down three centuries previously in Maya Quiché. In this way, the term "dinosaur" at last entered the English language, in 1841.

More recently, thanks to techniques of stratigraphy and the apparent truth of carbon-14, the spans over which all this is supposed to have happened have acquired vast dimensions for which there is no recorded precedent in the Western tradition.[13] Yet, remarkably, such a precedent does exist in the cosmogonies and calendars of the Fourth World, as we have seen. The rock strata in the *Madrid* screenfold and associated dates fall overall into the time range now proposed for geology and evolution after the basic forms of modern animals appeared around 600 million years ago; and there are even hints (mathematical in the case of the two hieroglyphic strata dates) of the 26-million-year pattern of cataclysms now discerned by some researchers, plus the astounding detail that the disappearance of Cipacna and the dinosaurs may indeed have been connected with volcanic activity.[14] Again, according to current estimates, the two hundred or so millennia of the Great Year octaeteris fit the order of time that it took humans to emerge, defining their culture in the Paleolithic and the last Great Year and their agriculture from the 3000 B.C. Neolithic Era date.

As the official story of humankind was successively revised in these terms, our species could no longer be scientifically sanctioned as dominant in time or in hierarchy over animal and other life that had lived far longer on earth, a lesson that is still being learned. Made in God's image on the sixth day, Adam was given dominion over the beasts and told to make what use he liked of "soulless" creatures. By contrast, the doll people of the *Popol vuh* were punished because they exploited animals and even because they behaved insensitively toward their cooking pots and grinding stones. The power of the American lesson was noted by Las Casas (in its Kekchi version) and recurs in Borges's story "The Handwriting of the God," where, reading in the glyphs of the jaguar's skin the "intimate designs of the universe," the Maya priest imprisoned by Alvarado recalls the fate of the doll people – "I saw the cooking pots turning against them, I saw the dogs destroying their faces" – as the one appropriate for the mindlessly exploitative Spaniards. In this century it has been related to unthinking human reliance on technology: The Cuban Alejo Carpentier has celebrated the *Popol vuh* as "the only cosmogony ever to have intuited the threat of the machine and the tragedy of the sorcerer's apprentice."[15]

Doctrinally guaranteed, American solidarity with other life-forms comes through with remarkable vivacity in all the major cosmogonies. This is especially the case in luminous vignettes that register conversations with and between animals; suffused with a characteristic humor and poignancy, these moments in the text preach the world-age doctrine in the opposite of a didactic manner. In *Watunna,* much turns on the ability to handle jaguars, the great carnivores that terrify but do not always think quickly. When Kuamachi is first introduced to Mado the jaguar, Mado says to his daughter, who had brought Kuamachi home with her, "Good, you brought my dinner." "Not your dinner," she answers, "my husband." Earlier, turned helpless on his back, his feet sticking up in the air, Waiamo the turtle is obliged to watch Manuwa, the other jaguar, devour the tapir he, Waiamo, had hunted; he succeeds in diverting Manuwa by promising better fare and manages to wave vaguely toward it with one of his feet:

> "Delicious tapir," said Manuwa as he went on eating.
> Waiamo just lay there thinking with his feet sticking up. Then he said: "I'd eat it with chili peppers."
> "What'd you say?"
> "It's a shame to eat it that way. It's much better with chili peppers. Meat without chili peppers is terrible."

"Shut up. I don't have any peppers," said Jaguar. He went on eating.

"I have a beautiful *conuco* just filled with peppers," said Turtle.

"Really? Where is it?"

"Over there," he answered, moving his feet.

"Go get some," Jaguar said.

"I can't. I'm upside down."

Jaguar stopped eating. Then he said: "Tapir without chili peppers is terrible."

Now he gave Turtle his kick. He set him right.

In the *Popol vuh,* the bird–reptile family join this conversation, notably in a domestic exchange in the language of birds that takes place when Seven Parrot returns home with One Hunter's severed arm in his still toothy beak; his wife, who otherwise never opens hers, says, "Where did you get *that?*" – that being the prototype of the human arm that can in fact be severed and sewn on again. Again, in *Dine bahane,* her passionate love affair with Coyote now over, the bear is banished back to the wild by her human brother; pausing, she turns with a sudden doubt:

> At once the creature got up on its feet and started to walk away. But after taking several steps it stopped, shaded its eyes with one paw, looked back at the youth, and asked this question:
>
> "But what if someone should attack me first?" it asked.
>
> "What if someone should threaten me?"
>
> "Then you may defend yourself in whatever way you can," replied the youngest brother. "And you may likewise defend your kin. Otherwise do not start a quarrel or a fight."[16]

In the rainforest texts, the major focus for this dialogue is the first harvest festival. When Marahuaka is cut down, the birds and animals have the opportunity of participating in the great cultural enterprise of growing food, and indeed teach the people how to do it, except for the two who "didn't want to work" and "didn't want to share," the jaguar and tapir. By the same logic, in Mesoamerica animals help to bring the food from the Food Mountain: The coati, who in the *Popol vuh* had first befriended the Twins and protected them from Seven Parrot, helps to prepare the first *milpa* in the Kekchi story and typifies a solidarity humans are told never to forget. Defying that hateful binary that separates even humans in *Natur-* and *Kulturvölker,* this arrangement does not exclude animals from culture on this earth or from the notion of community.

Since it is inextricable from the actual story of American agriculture, this ethic may be traced back to the Eve of the *Popol vuh:* the woman who takes the forbidden fruit from the tree of knowledge, conceives, and is forced into exile. Just because Blood Woman's story so resembles that of Eve in Eden, its difference is the more instructive. In the Garden of Eden, the fruit is owned and forbidden by God; Eve's disobedience and pregnancy lead to human misery in the world outside. In the *Popol vuh,* the tree stands in the underworld, its fruit is intelligence from the upper world, and it is forbidden by the Lord of Hell; Blood Woman's disobedience and conception lead eventually, through the Twins, to the great achievement of agriculture and the creation of the *milpa* garden, the living shrine. Precisely this human capacity to grow food is the one that comes most to be demeaned in the story of Eve's son Cain, the agriculturalist whose offerings are spurned by the Old Testament god who at the same time favors and blesses the flocks of his brother Abel. This divine preference superbly exemplifies that pastoralist ideology that, all-pervasive in the West, blinds even Rousseau and Marx and that in the Fourth World is intimated solely in the llama discourse of Tahuantinsuyu.

Inscribed in cosmogony, the skill and dedication of the American Cain, his understanding of the nature that bore him and its languages, made of the continent the garden of the planet.[17] From across the Pacific, its brilliance was historically glimpsed, to the east.

IV

Into the language of America

mac to ah bovat   mac to ah kin
bin tohol cantic u than uuoh lae

who the sage   who the sun-priest
that shall read the word of this book?

— Book of Chumayel

13

The translation process

SOURCE AND PERSPECTIVE

Variously construed according to geography and over time, the Fourth World account of origins rests on commonly held beliefs. These are the very ones that support political alliance in the Quito Declaration and argue against uncritical acceptance of all that has been imported into America in the wake of Columbus. A natural philosophy, the New World account has stood and stands as the greater reason, in custom, defense of land and landscape, and therapy. Relived every day in native language and gesture, the story of creation continues to inform worldviews, giving shape to interpretations of the alien and intrusive. This is explicitly so in the case of the creation texts published by the Shuar, which in the course of the telling repeatedly draw out the significance for their federation of this event or that action. Throwbacks from the earlier phases of the same Amazonian creation story, with their four-toed, twisted back feet, dangling penises, and whitish skin – as their name, *boraro*, suggests – the deadly forest spirits of the Barasana have also absorbed traits of later white invaders, like glowing red eyes and hairy chests (Plate 18b). For his part, retelling stories he heard as a child in Yucatan, Dzul Poot appeals to the presence of ancient Maya settlements known to all, so that Uxmal and Tihoo (Mérida), for example, are the terms for the account of Hapai Kan, the monster snake that will appear at the day of judgment. Keeping in mind the shape of their Appalachian landscape and towns even far to the west in Oklahoma, the Cherokee continue to construe the saga of Tsulkulla; and in the curing chants of Ayunini and Gatigwanasti, with their scheme of cosmic colors, they diagnose the blue of the north, the direction from which the worst invaders came, as the source of trouble – what became (via Cherokee-speaking Africans) Mississippi blues.[1]

More urgently, these native accounts of the world may serve actively to defend the societies they represent, vindicating where necessary a course of direct or military action. In *Watunna,* Spanish-speaking invaders of more recent years are expressly read as emissaries of Odosha who "want to own it all" and enslave people, depriving them of memory, and are resisted on just those grounds. Odosha's counterparts in the *Popol vuh,* the Lords of Xibalba, have been equated with the U.S.-backed dictatorships of Guatemala and the forces of genocide that have ravaged the Maya highlands; and again, instating here reverence for land and maize, cosmogony supports native resistance in the long-standing guerrilla war led by Gaspar Ilom, as well as through such testimonies as the paintings of Juan Sisay or Juan Gallo, Rigoberta Menchú's autobiography, and the letters sent by Maya exiles to the Mexican press. Updating *Runa yndio,* tellers of Quechua tales recount the need to expel the presocial cannibal ogre (*achkay*) and reembody Inkarri, so sustaining faith in the proper reconstitution of Tahuantinsuyu.[2]

In these and many other cases, the experience of the past five centuries is read in terms that have evolved over perhaps as many millennia. In the reading in question, a major factor has been that of American language itself, verbal and visual. In affirming his identity as an Acoma and the space between that language and English, Simon Ortiz put it like this: "At times, in the past, it was outright armed struggle, like that of present-day Indians in Central and South America with whom we must identify; currently, it is often in the legal arena, and it is in the field of literature." This coincides with the literary engagement that Marcio Souza in Brazil has termed the countermassacre: Here native language and history themselves serve as a resource in the struggle against the physical and intellectual violence of neocolonialism.[3] In his laconic poem "Keski nauamaseualme tiitstoke?" the bilingual teacher Joel Martínez Hernández puts the same argument, referring to official census figures for Nahuatl-speakers and the not-so-secret desire of the coyotes (whites) to see them dwindle:

Se tsontlixiuitl in techmachte	Four hundred years have taught us
tlen kineki koyotl	what coyote wants

Aymara newspapers like *Jiwasan Arusawa* and *Yatina Sawa,* published in La Paz in recent years, make the same point again, as does the school of Mapuche poets initiated by Sebastián Queupul (1966), whose more recent representative Leonel Lienlaf writes pieces of great literary power that draw equally on the brutal "pacification" of a century ago and the Andean cosmogony of Cai-Cai.[4]

In the literary medium, this process of native interpretation can be traced very exactly and calibrated through studying translation, that is, the reshaping of Old World texts in native languages. One sign that a language or literature is alive is that things get translated into it; this is as true of the

Fourth World as it is of anywhere else. In this sense, what an anthropologist might dismiss as "acculturation" (as if the only culture were Western) can present quite another face in literary discourse. After all, some of the major literatures of Europe have their beginnings in just such instances of "acculturation," translations of the Bible into German and English being cases in point. Exposing the racism inherent in some anthropologists' insistence that American languages are conceptually poor or inadequate, Neville Stiles has shown how an academic thesis can be written not just on but in Nahuatl, and he has participated in the key task of translating the Guatemalan constitution into the four closely related languages of the Maya highlands (Quiché, Kekchi, Mam, Cakchiquel).[5]

Translation was evidently practiced in pre-Columbian times at the courts of Mesoamerica and Tahuantinsuyu, and it produced many of the songs sung and exchanged at the Ghost Dance. With the Christian mission, a further dialectic was introduced, one between Old World and New. The first (or at least oldest surviving) American book (Mexico, 1539) was bilingual, a catechism in Nahuatl and Spanish, and it was followed by many other religious translations stimulated and in part effected by friars and clerics sent over from Europe to New Spain and Peru. In sixteenth-century Brazil, José de Anchieta designed dance dramas in the lingua geral, Tupi, to supplant those of local pagan cults, whose terminology and rhetoric he recast; in Turtle Island, John Eliot turned the Bible into "the language of America" (Algonkin or Mohican) in 1661.[6]

Just because of the complexity of Fourth World languages and their literary traditions, efforts to penetrate the Fourth World in this way have sometimes proved counterproductive. The liveliest pages of Guaman Poma's *Nueva corónica* ridicule solecisms typical of Christian sermons delivered in Quechua (pp. 610–12); indeed, that language came to be suspected of possessing a pagan logic of its own, and translation of the scriptures into it was actually forbidden. Even when the Christian original was somehow gotten across, it still ran the risk of ending up in a context or frame unconducive to its message. Though apparently deferential, in citing the biblical stories of flood and (possible) eclipse the Quechua narrative of Huarochirí effectively incorporates them into the American scheme of world ages. The same is true of the version of Matthew 25 incorporated in the *Chilam Balam Book of Chumayel* (p. 102) and of the direct translations from Genesis now included in highland Maya texts in the *Popol vuh* tradition. Certain poems in the *Cantares mexicanos* manuscript traduce the Epiphany, elsewhere piously translated and performed in Nahuatl under the supervision of Spanish friars, by making Aztec warriors out of the Three Kings,[7] and by the simple fact of its forming part of the collection as a whole, with all its wealth of pagan imagery.

Dramatized texts proved especially hazardous in this sense, as a result of the need, in performance, to adapt their sources to local characters and settings. For example, the lesson of Adam and Eve's Fall seems to have been quite modified in a Nahuatl play lavishly staged in Tlaxcala in 1538: Every skill went into highlighting Eden as the place American agriculture had actually made possible, into a testimony in maize and other plants to native achievement in the world-age, so that the mere verbal message, about human misery and helplessness, could only acquire a certain irony – and a political one, at that. Similar shifts are perceptible in the numerous Nahuatl and Quechua adaptations of the Golden Age doctrinal plays known as *autos,* which as a result become that much less persuasive as Counter-Reformation propaganda; an example of Calderón's *El gran teatro del mundo* (1641), whose doctrinal content is distinctly reformulated in the Nahuatl of Bartolomé de Alva Ixtlilxochitl, a descendant of the house of Texcoco. This is in line with what has happened to other types of drama: calls to conversion like *Tepozteco's Challenge,* which today is listened to by Nahuatl-speakers more for its roll call of old pagan names and ancient rock shrines; or the Dances of Conquest, which from Tlaxcala to Nicaragua sooner mock than celebrate the "victor," thanks to the older model of the *huehuentzin* plays with their satirical dialogues and gestures.[8]

From the first days of contact, texts devoid of a Christian message have equally engaged translators into American languages. Sharing a universe of animal dialogue, Aesop's fables and the corpus of European fairy tales (*Märchen*) have been a constant resource. Virgil and Racine were rendered into Quechua, an academically respectable language in colonial Peru, and a number of writers imitated Renaissance models and verse forms in Tupi–Guarani. Over the centuries, the lowland Maya have translated and incorporated a wide variety of items into their *Chilam Balam Books,* from philosophical treatises and almanacs to short fiction. Recent decades have seen Zapotec versions of Brecht's poetry and a Quechua version of Saint-Exupéry's *Le Petit Prince.* These exercises have effectively much enriched the languages in question; the case of the Saint-Exupéry novel in fact forms part of a program to enhance the status of Quechua in Ecuador and its range of readable texts.[9] Neville Stiles (1987) has written with great sensitivity about the "native-speakers' dream . . . of translating all types of literature into their first language."

What follows is a set of case studies of Fourth World versions of Old World secular texts. Greek, Arabic, and Germanic in origin, three have passed via Spanish into languages that have been written alphabetically since the sixteenth century (Nahuatl, Maya, and Quechua); the fourth, "Cinderella," one of the most widely told stories in the world, exists in America in both native and imported versions, the latter extending from Ftah Mapu to Anasazi.[10] As case studies they can of course no more than gesture toward what has been a highly complex process of adaptation over the last five centuries. Yet each offers us the chance of registering, from evidence on the page, a clear statement of Fourth World priority and preference.

AESOP IN AZTEC

Under the title *In sasanilli in Esopo,* forty-seven of Aesop's fables were translated into Nahuatl in the sixteenth century by hands unknown.[11] Though the Franciscan friar Sahagún is often asserted to have been the translator, the internal evidence makes this unlikely.

First, the animals in the fables are naturalized – fox into coyote, bear into *cuitlachtli,* jackdaw into parrot – not schematically, but according to whether and how they become familiar in Mexican eyes. In one case, the European cock (vividly rendered as "the male one with head flesh," *oquichuanaca*) turns into an indigenous Mexican turkey (*huexolotl*) actually in the course of the narrative (no. 24, "The Dog, the Fox, and the Cock"). Then at moments a phrase is inserted by the translator to explain something unusual; one of these phrases clearly represents a Mexican and not a Spanish viewpoint. In the fable "The Master and His Dog" (no. 14), a farmer is snowbound and left stranded for weeks out in his fields. This notion seemed so strange to the translator that he reported the man stranded and added, in the first person, "I don't know for what reason" ("amo nicmati tle ipampa"). A Spaniard might have said, if anything at all, "You would not understand the reason."

The translator's source text belongs, we can be sure, to the Accursiana group of Aesop's fables,[12] notable for its laconic style and reported speech. Quite transforming it and immersing us in the conversation of American creatures, the Nahuatl seizes every pretext for direct speech and dialogue, even at moments where there is none in any of the Aesop variants. This highlights the great rhetorical resources of the Mexican language, which are used with a finesse available only to a native speaker, like the *ecamecoyotl,* or "long speech," with its vocatives, reverentials, and binarism. In a veritable arena of performed rhetoric, Nahuatl is shown to be immensely rich in its formal capacity to distinguish subtle gradations of feeling and attitude in address, a classic example of this being *Totecuyoane,* where from self-abasement and apparent humility the Aztecs slowly and inexorably work up to a passionate defense of their past beliefs in the face of the first Franciscan missionaries. (In the Spanish translation, the speech comes out at about half the length, its whole persuasion gone.) In all, in periods of classical finesse these Nahuatl speakers locate themselves through a term favored in their rhetoric: *nican,* that is, very much here in their own Mexican environment.[13]

While vindicating the native identity of the translator or translators, these and yet other factors detail their worldview. The more we explore these versions, the worthier they seem of the literary interest denied them by the great Nahuatl scholar Angel María Garibay.[14] Whether or not the friars sent to Mexico first suggested, or even helped in the task of, carrying over Aesop's text, there can be little doubt about who the new author substantially was. For in fable after fable modifications are made, on a greater or lesser scale, that can be ascribed only to the demands and conventions of the native literary tradition. The fables come to occupy a place in a literature already rich in conversation between and with animals and are infused with that radiant natural language that informs Fourth World cosmogony and its survival in Nahuatl today. In this respect, *In sasanilli in Esopo* bears less resemblance to the Nahuatl catechisms and Bible stories produced by the friars and their local helpers than it does to a manuscript like the *Cantares mexicanos,* with which it was at one point bound.

Consider these two accounts of false alarm:

> A lion once heard a frog croaking; he turned towards the noise thinking it was some great beast; when he saw the frog by the pond he went up and squashed it. (No. 25, "The Lion and the Frog")

> A jaguar once heard a frog, screaming and croaking a great deal. The jaguar was frightened by it. He thought it was a large four-footed animal that was screaming so loud.
>
> To quieten his heart, he looked around him in all directions. He prepared himself to encounter the one who croaked in such a manner.
>
> But when the frog saw him at the waterside, he quickly fled.
>
> Arriving at the water's edge, the jaguar was very cross and ashamed for he thought nothing of the one by whom he had been so frightened. He squashed him and killed him.

In the original text, when the lion realizes that the noisy animal he has heard is only a frog, he steps on it without comment from the narrator, who then moves straight on to the moral: It is imprudent to be frightened by what cannot be seen. In the Nahuatl, the lion has become the big carnivore cat (*tecuani miztli*) epitomized by the jaguar; and the narrator here takes time to explain, with a certain wry amusement, that the jaguar trod on the frog because he was angry and ashamed at having been in the least put out by such a tiny creature. There is here an interest in the jaguar's motives and sensitivity, a feeling one's way into the animal's skin (literally rehearsed by the Aztec jaguar knights when they put on their uniforms), evident elsewhere in the many details supplied of the way animals hunt, kill, devour, and digest that are absent and would be out of place in the originals.

This intimacy or involvement with animal feeling comes through strongly in the fable about the hares and the frogs (no. 37), where, determined on suicide, the former hold back, drawing comfort from the fact that the latter are even more vulnerable and timorous than they. The hares' long lament as creatures threatened, hunted, and vulnerable on all sides reaches the heights of Nahuatl rhetoric exemplified in the *Totochtin icuic* (Rabbits' lament)[15] (Fig. 66)

Figure 66. Totochtin icuic (Rabbits' lament). (*Florentine Codex,* book 1, fol. 197v.)

and strongly recalls similar laments in the Aztecs' own poetry, notably songs in the "orphan" mode of the *Cantares mexicanos* performed for the emperors of Tenochtitlan. The boundary between the world of men and animals so firmly assured by Aesop's urbanity is here elided, partly thanks to the reluctance of Nahuatl necessarily to distinguish sharply between the two groups, both being included in the phrase used to describe the hares' pursuers: "tlalticpac tlaca" – "beings living on earth." In the story of locomotion told in the *Popol vuh* and encoded in the Twenty Signs, the cold- and warm-blooded pair Frog and Hare in fact corresponds to the "hoppers" (Signs IV and VIII) in human ancestry. Moreover, at the start of their lament, the identity of the "we/us" the hares use is continuously attenuated by being drawn into the verb as a passive subject and a constricted object; paradoxically and dramatically, they escape from their helpless dependence only on deciding to commit suicide, the emphatic and free-standing pronoun *totech* then being used.

In "The Dog and the Wolf" (no. 23), the latter becomes the wolflike *cuitlachtli,* who stands open-jawed over the dog, ready to devour. This encourages the dog to prepare the way most carefully for what he has to say, in an effort to save himself. He begins a speech classified as flattering by establishing his identity merely as a subject of the *cuitlachtli*'s majesty (he opens with "Notecuioe" – "O my lordship") and a possible item in his digestive tract. Only after he has hinted at how poor and ill he has been – this being entirely absent from all extant versions of the Greek – and how fat he soon will become does he dare come out with the strong independent form *nixcoian* ("I most personally") to assure the *cuitlachtli* that all he has said is true. The translator so relishes this speech play that when a short answer is given our attention is drawn to the fact; this happens at the end when the dog, now secure in his own house, addresses the *cuitlachtli* for a second time, telling it to get lost: "As for me [*Nehuatl* – an opening far more abrupt than in his earlier pleading speech], I'll give you but one word from my speech . . ."

As a sample of the resources, at once rhetorical and grammatical, with which Nahuatl allows interplay between person and situation, all this is paralleled in the speech of the coyote as he stands alone before the irritable jaguar, who has just devoured their third companion, the luckless, unthinking ass (*asno*). In the original fable (no. 26, "The Lion, the Ass, and the Fox"), there is not one word of speech, direct or indirect, at this point. Reapportioning the food the ass had failed to share out satisfactorily (he gave each an equal part), the coyote begins his speech by making the jaguar the dominant owning presence; he uses two reverential forms, -*tzin* and -*tzinco*, and says that the food all belongs to him twice in two short lines (*maxca, motech pohui*). Referring then to the tiny portion he would reserve for himself, he uses the belittling -*ton* intensified through the form *ixquich-*, and straightway reassures the jaguar again of his status as the one – *tlaquah tehuatzin* (a further reverential) – who found the food. A powerful oratorical effect is also obtained in the balanced contrast between the diminishing *ca çan* (which refers to the speaker) and the magnifying *ca nel* (directed at the jaguar):

ca mochi maxcatzin	All that is yours
motechtzinco pohui	to you belongs
in nican catqui	what is here
auh in nehuatl	as for me
ca çan ixquichton i noconnocuilia	I take only this tiny bit
ca nel tlaquauh tehuatzin	for you are truly the one
in otimotlamalli	who made the catch

In the case of the fable "The Peacock and the Jackdaw" (no. 36), not only are the characters made to look and talk like creatures of Mesoamerica, they are actually incorporated into the logic of the old rituals. For they enter the privileged company of the augur's Thirteen Quecholli, which epitomize knowledge gained from bird behavior and form part of the *tonalamatl* itself (Table 1). The peacock becomes Quetzal (Number 12); the jackdaw, Parrot (Number 13); and the eagle, Eagle (Number 5). Hence, in the exchanges among them there inhere not only the patterns of Nahuatl rhetoric but also those of *tlacuilolli* and the screenfold books.

In the original, when the birds discuss their future leader and decide against the peacock because he would be unable to defend them were an eagle to attack them, the eagle remains notional, essential to the lesson drawn ("fine feathers are not everything") only as a hypothetical possibility. In the parliament of the Quecholli, led by the speaker/Parrot, a dramatic speech by him literally displaces Quetzal by invoking Eagle, "our king" (*to-tlatocauh*), as another member of the present company of the Thirteen. Moreover, in addressing the company as a whole, "our lordships, you Quecholli," Parrot attaches the reverential epithet *ipalnemoani,* which means "the ones through whom we live." This could only signify as sacrilegious in Christian terms; the epithet was reserved for the highest life principles. Belonging to just the devilish forces that Sahagún swore to extirpate, these Quecholli are consecrated in the *teoamoxtli* and the *Popol vuh* and in names like Quetzalcoatl and Cuauhtemoc, the plunging Eagle who as the last Aztec emperor resisted Cortes.

The logic of the *tonalamatl,* together now with a clearer political subtext, may also be detected in the fable "The Old Man and Death" (no. 11). With Aesop, the movement of the tale is characteristically sprightly and goes quickly to the moral that everybody really loves life, however miserable he or she is. In Nahuatl the movement is slowed by the old man's dwelling on his misery and his earnest plea to death; crippled by the load he has to bear, he asks to be annihilated, seeking destruction like another of the hares:

Yio miquiztle	O death
cam mach yn tinemi	wherever you may be
macuele xinechpopolo	come now destroy me
xinechtlati	do away with me
ma xiccotona yn ixquich aqualli	take away all the evil
yn niquihioni	that I suffer.
	(Accursius runs: "He asked death to come.")

The rhetoric is powerful: The verb "destroy" is strengthened by a redoubled first syllable (*xinechpopolo*) and by the addition of the near synonym *xinechtlati* in a typically Nahuatl binary grouping. Finally, altering the fable almost beyond recognition, the moral insists further on the pain and ache of death, which "takes our dear life." The same thing happens in "The Cocks and the Partridge" (no. 5), where the original lesson drawn from the partridge's discovery that the cocks maltreat not just him but each other as well is a commonsense rule for living – the recommendation that we should observe how others treat their own kind before being hurt by their bad manners toward us. The Nahuatl replaces the notion of "kind" with status, insisting that pain and ache (*tecoco tetolini* – the same phrase as in the moral to "The Old Man and Death") afflict even the principal beings and emperors and that the whole world is encompassed by suffering and uncertainty (*in netoliniztli cemanahuac*).

The insistence on woe may be explained in part by the enduring majesty of the Mesoamerican Lord of the Underworld (Mictlan, Xibalba): the skeletal Death figure who as the central member of the *tonalamatl*'s Nine Night Powers controls life and death in our very bones, even from before birth. He is still everywhere to be seen on the Day of the Dead. At the same time, this is the complaint of a particular time and place: sixteenth-century Mexico, ravaged by invasion and the new world order. Complaints in the set funereal orphan mode of Nahuatl poetry, the lamentations of Nezahualcoyotl, the poet-king of Texcoco, were similarly referred by his descendants to the misery of their own time, the burden-carrying and labor tribute imposed on commoner and prince alike, and the ever-present threat of slaughter.

TAWADDUD AND MAYA WIT

From the time they first got hold of printed books from Spain in the mid sixteenth century, the Maya of Yucatan examined them with a certain literary and philosophical professionalism. They hardly had a large choice of imported texts, partly because of the restrictions imposed by the Spanish on printed matter in the New World, and partly because of the power of the Inquisition in Spain itself. But the devotional works, almanacs, *reportorios* (an early form of newspaper), and occasional works of fiction they did get hold of were scoured, appraised, and in some cases translated into Maya. The results of this curiosity are plain to see in the *Chilam Balam Books* of Yucatan. The books of Chumayel, Ixil, and Kaua, for example, are distinguished by the attention they pay to the biblical Genesis and to commentaries by such major Christian scholars as Saint John of Damascus and Alphonso X, which are integrated with Maya cosmogony to produce wholly ingenious accounts of the "beginning of time." In the *Book of Tusik,* with its selection of hagiographical and apocryphal tales, there is a more thoroughgoing involvement with narrative as such. As for the *Arabian Nights* of Tawaddud, described quite recently as "elegant" by a Yucatec Maya, it appears in no fewer than four of the dozen or so community books extant, those of Kaua, Chan Kan, Mani, and Ixil.[16]

Though hypothetical, the bibliographical source of these Maya translations of Tawaddud's story can be identified exactly;[17] further, the differences among them suggest that they were done and redone over two centuries or longer. They reveal a good deal about the linguistic development of Yucatecan Maya during this period. Their literary interest lies mainly in the way they excise and rearrange Tawaddud's story in order to incorporate it in its new context, the *Chilam Balam Books*. Looking at this process, and especially at the few small but significant changes of detail, tells us something about why the story was lit upon in the first place.

As a character in the *Arabian Nights* (nights 436–62), Tawaddud bears a certain resemblance to the narrator of that work, Shahrazad, who saves herself by her tongue, winning the challenge of filling successive nights with her wit and imagination. Tawaddud's predicament is that of the only slave girl remaining to Abu al-Husn, the self-impoverished son of a rich Baghdad merchant; she urges her master to sell her to Harun al-Rashid, the fifth caliph (and Charlemagne's contemporary) for as high a price as he can get, for she is not just beautiful but erudite in religion and philosophy and all the arts and sciences and is an expert musician and chess player to boot. The bulk of the narrative consists of her being tested at the caliph's court by a series of sages, not least by Ibrahin bin Siyyar, summoned from Basra for the purpose. Though omitted from Lane's English translation of the *Arabian Nights* because "extremely tiresome,"[18] Tawaddud's story was extremely popular on its first contact with Europe, in the Renaissance; it went through several editions in Spain, one of which was exported to the New World and furnished the Maya with their original.

In the Spanish versions of the story, Abu al-Husn becomes a Hungarian merchant, Tawaddud is christened Theodor/Teodora and made captive at Mansur's court in Tunis, and Ibrahin's name is recast in the more familiar form Abraham. These changes do nothing to alter the basic idea of the story, but they do introduce complication and a certain dramatic potential, exploited to the full by Lope de Vega in his comedy *La doncella Teodor* (ca. 1612),[19] in which how and why the heroine came to be interrogated, and not the interrogation itself, provides the main substance of the plot. The first and most obvious change made by the Maya to the Spanish translation was to counteract this tendency. In their version of the story, the Maya cut out the opening part of the narrative, before the heroine arrives at the royal court. No account is taken of prior personal motive here, nor indeed later on, when Teodora makes a bargain with the third and chief of Mansur's sages, Abraham: that whoever loses the contest of wits should strip before the assembled court. It is to save Abraham from this indignity that Mansur agrees both to pay Teodora's master and to let her leave with him. In the Maya texts this generosity goes unexplained. In other words, the emphasis is less on the motivation and behavior of individual characters than on the actual testing of Teodora as an intellectual experience in its own right.

In the Arabic original, the questions asked of Tawaddud before Caliph Harun al-Rashid are very much bound up with the Koran, directly so in the first two rounds, with the first two sages (nights 438–48), and indirectly in the examinations proper to medicine, astronomy, philosophy, poetry, and logic (nights 449–60). In all, the exchanges between Tawaddud and the sages amount to a compendium of the religion and science of the day as it was to influence medieval and Renaissance Europe. In the Spanish version of the story, this corpus of knowledge is Christianized, condensed, and set out according to the expertise of sage-examiners, whose number is reduced to three: specialists in cosmogony and divine law; astrological medicine and natural science; and last Abraham's subject, philosophy proper. In their turn, by further excision and reworking of certain small details, the Maya suggested a new taxonomy of their own to accord with the categories of knowledge found in the *Chilam Balam Books*.

In the Maya translations, in the first round of questions – about genesis and the creation of the world – matters of theological dogma are suppressed in favor of problems of temporal sequence of the kind tackled by Maya calendrics. In the second exchange, the timing of cures by bleeding, purging, and so on, according to the zodiac, becomes the main focus, "phlebotomist," incidentally, finding an exact equivalent in the old Maya term *Ah toc*. In the *Kaua,* though not in the *Mani,* Teodora's detailed month-by-month account of these practices, adopted in the Spanish from a *reportorio* compiled by Andres de Li (Zaragoza, 1495), is given a chapter to itself after the end of the story. This device concords with the general decharacterization of Teodora and her companions in the story and with the corresponding importance of knowledge itself as something formally transacted.

As for Teodora's third examiner, Abraham, he comes to be defined as supreme among the sages, a prophet because of his astronomical knowledge. Through the medium of the altered Spanish version of Tawaddud's story, the Maya thus contrive to recover something of its original emphasis. In answering a question about the planets and the zodiac and their place in computations of time, the Maya Teodora actually introduces into the narrative a technical term of Maya calendrics – a small detail that implies a great deal about the attitudes of the Maya translators and their involvement in their chosen story. The term in question, *pop,* is the Maya name of the first of the eighteen annual Feasts and denotes the mat of authority on which the ruler of a set time period is seated, which is alluded to in the *Popol vuh*'s title.

The climax of Tawaddud/Teodora's exchange with the wisest sage, Abraham, takes the form of riddles, the literary form traditional throughout Mesoamerica – in Nahuatl and Zapotec as well as Maya.[20] Known in the *Chilam Balam Books* as "Zuyuathan," Maya riddles were used in particular to test candidates for political power in the *katun* system.[21] Drawings among the few included in the *Chilam Balam Books* certainly bring out the connection. A woodcut copied by hand to embellish the *Book of Kaua* translation shows Abraham suffering the indignity, public nakedness, that would have been Teodora's had she failed to answer his riddles – exactly the same as what is suffered by the failed Maya candidate in the *katun* system, as a drawing in the *Book of Chumayel* confirms. With Zuyuathan in mind, the Maya asserted their priorities more in this than in any other part of their translation, trenchantly reducing the number of questions asked by Abraham and subtly reshaping those retained. What these priorities are can best be understood through considering the Maya riddles in their immediate context: American shamanism.

That riddles form part of the transfer of shamanic power in the Fourth World is brought out in such texts as *Dine bahane,* for example – the dialogues of the Twins with their Sun father – in the Algonkin cosmogonies, and above all in the account of Medatia's learning to hear and see the world. In the Arapaho case, the future chief symbolically redeems himself from the murder of his elders and predecessors by correctly answering a set of seven riddles.[22] Testing sense perception, these affirm basic needs like humility, shelter, and clothing. The initial pair of riddles invokes the innocent or unincriminated rabbit and the left-hand, proper "alternatives" to arrogance; another pair invokes the sense paths of the body, dual in the nose and distant in the brain (the latter traveling fast and far); the remaining three riddles deal with the *tipi* house with its flaps that wave "invitingly," its "sentinel" pegs, and the moccasin "essential for any purpose." In the *Chumayel,* the Zuyua-than chapter is inaugurated by a set of seven riddles (pp. 29–31) that shows a correspondence with the Algonkin model no less marked than in the case of the *uinal*'s shamanic journey: The Maya candidate also enters into power humbly, like "the second childhood at midday," on all fours, throwing the smallest shadow, with his wife like a faithful dog beside him, the honey candle of sweetness between his teeth. As for the sense paths, he recognizes the brains of the sky in copal incense; he acknowledges the need of *tipi* and moccasin by understanding that a hat can be a house and a *henequen* sandal can be "mountable" like a giant horse or Shanks' mare.[23] Further basic needs are emblemized by the tortilla, whose layers correspond to those of the Thirteen Numbers; the iguana, whose tail is a living liana; and the *xicama* gourd that plugs the *cenote* water well.

As a formula directly relevant to the Maya transformation of the Tawaddud riddles, and in its own right, the first of the *Chumayel* seven (p. 29) deserves to be quoted in full:

talez kin, mehene, cas a lathab tin plato;	Fetch the sun, childe, carry it to my plate;
ti chican lansa caanil cruz tan chumuc u pucsikal;	the lance of the heavenly cross is thrust right into its heart;
tiix culac yax balam yokol kin ukic u kikele	a green jaguar sitting above it drinks its blood.

The answer to this request is a fried egg blessed with the sign of the cross and garnished with a green pepper just turning red. Its lesson is manifold. The Christian hand gesture of blessing, associated with bloodthirstiness, is exposed as a threat to the integrity of the Maya calendar, based on the day/sun unit denoted by the round *kin* hieroglyph. Yet in this same hieroglyphic system the switch from green to red is also one from new to full, as in astronomy and agronomy, and thus suggests some benefit or "food" for that most Maya of sages, the jaguar-priest Chilam Balam. Moreover, in Zen fashion, the whole perception moves between the grand and the everyday kitchen, a reminder of the basic needs of any community that thinks to survive. And by its very nature, the equivalence here between the components of request and response works politically in favor of a shared consciousness (the "dream hieroglyph") and against the rigid hierarchy implied in some of the questions put to Tawaddud by Abraham, agent of the all-powerful caliph. Rather than affirm the authorized version of enigmatic speech or explain metaphor, Maya riddles identify qualities that may be perceived in either of two phenomena according to point of view; firefly = cigar in the dark = firefly, to quote one example that is also found in the *Popol vuh* (line 3650). Hence, whereas one riddle may request "a bunch of evenly spaced white flowers with tomorrow's sun on them," meaning maize roasted with honey (the "light born of earth"), in another these same flowers appear in the response, not the request, and signify a white rattle or asperger.

The sophistication of these Zuyua riddles explains both Maya interest in Tawaddud's story and the handling of the final exchange with Abraham the philosopher. For of the several dozen riddles put to her in the Spanish version, the Maya chose only six. Few as they are, these illustrate equally the two main types of riddle found in the Spanish: "What is *x?*" and "What is more or most *x?*" Of itself, this suggests a theoretical interest on the part of the Maya in Abraham's riddles, which is confirmed by the fact that each of the three riddles in the latter category involves a different kind of translation into the Maya world. The three riddles are:

Alten zuhuye macalmac hach chich xma azeroe	Tell me, maiden, what is stronger than steel?
lay u cantabal hahe xmanan yocoh tuzie ichile	– He who tells the truth, who never lies.
Ca u alten zuhuye macalmac chacuc xma cabe	Then tell me, maiden, what is sweeter than honey?
lay hunppel u yutzil mehentzil lay mac cu dzaic utz	– That one is a good child, who serves well
ti Cayumil ti Dioz yetel ti u yume	the father in heaven and on earth.
Alten zuhuye macalmac hach zeb u pec ichil tulacal balobe	Tell me, maiden, what is the swiftest of all things?
Yume lay u tucule uinice helae tac uayane	– Father, man's thought: now it is here,
helae tac ti yan Spana xane uaix tac tu xul yokol cabe.	now it is in Spain too, that is, at the end of the world.
	– *Book of Mani* (Solís Alcalá 1949:73)

In the Spanish text, these riddles are widely separated as the ninth, fifth, and twenty-seventh asked of Teodora by Abraham; however, when we compare them with their prototypes in the Arabic (there the teller of truth is the tongue, and thought is the envier's eye) we find that they originally did appear together, as they do in the Maya (the order of the first two being inverted), and indeed constitute the first three riddles asked of Tawaddud by Ibrahin. Since, as heightened language, riddles encapsulate so much, and since the selection made by the Maya is so precise here, the three are worth examining one by one.

The proposition in the second riddle that honey is like a good and loving child (compare the chapter "The Bee" in the Koran) proves completely translatable from the ancient Middle East to Yucatan and survives quite unaltered, except that the Maya specify the two parents not as mother and father, as the Spanish did, but as celestial and human. For their part, identifying honey as "the light born of earth, tomorrow's sun," the Zuyua riddles draw on a whole corpus of hieroglyphic texts about beekeeping and kinship; and in their Maya form, the very set of Twenty Signs honors the apiary, in beeswax (XVI) and honey (XVII); in the third of the twenty riddles that call for food, honey is the clarity that brightens the broad land of Peten.

The first riddle, about the truthful man, is slightly different, for it mentions something unknown to the Maya before the invasion from the Old World: smelted steel. This difficulty is, however, turned to double advantage. Rather than find a local substitute for "hardness," the Maya give prominence to the Spanish word for steel (*acero*); they thus intimate that the weapons used against them by the speakers of that language (cf. *lansa* in the preceding quotation) must ultimately prove weaker than their own truth (*hahe*). Other *Chilam Balam* chapters make a similar distanced or ironic use of imported vocabulary: *justicia,* for example.

The last of the three riddles, "What is the swiftest of all things?" (compare the Algonkin "brain" riddle above), is yet more pointed in its new Maya context, because of the intriguing insertion of the word "Spain" into Teodora's answer, which indeed would quite have confounded the sense in the original. Naming distant Spain as the "end of the world" (*cabo del mundo; xul yokol cabe*) gives, by contrast, a definitely local home to the riddle. It also plays on the notion that the Old World invasion begun in the sixteenth century could amount to the end of the world for the Maya in the system of world ages. This in turn involves us in a literary device much favored by the Maya in their writing. For just as the authors of the *Popol vuh* rue humankind's "loss of knowledge" of the world and its ages while in fact recording and preserving that very knowledge in that work, so the Zuyua riddles chapter in the community books notes that these texts are "copied down" in order to prevent just the catastrophe anticipated by "thought" in this last of the Maya Teodora's riddles: the violent end of the world age and of political continuity. In other words, as long as these riddle tokens of "humankind's thought" can be at all understood and interpreted, they of themselves keep alive the tradition they defend.

In preparing Teodora for her new home in these community books of

Yucatan, the Maya translators of her story neglected the daily circumstances of her narrative in favor of intellectual exchange; and by this they meant more than the supplying of facts that were correct according to the scientific orthodoxies of the day, or of answers that were right in terms of predefined authority. The process of thought itself was involved – the capacity to hear a question in more than one way. To this end they turned to American shamanism with its long-standing tradition of texts and initiation, which in Yucatan had been adapted to the particular needs of their *katun* system of federal government.

FAUSTIAN INCAS

During the Spanish colonial period, a Faust figure appeared in the Andes in the role of hero in two closely related Quechua plays. In the first, he is known as Yauri Titu and in the second, as Usca Paucar, names that for present purposes may serve as titles.[24] The plays belong to the considerable corpus of Quechua drama, which ranges from the overtly pagan to the Christian and which has roots deep in both local and imported traditions. Examining them raises important questions about drama translation and, in this case, about the exact cultural definition of the result.

Known in Spanish as *El pobre más rico, Yauri Titu* refers to the Virgin's miraculous appearance in Cuzco as Our Lady of Belen in the year 1618. Most likely a later text, in its published form *Usca Paucar* has the Spanish title *Auto sacramental: El patrocinio de Nuestra Señora Santícima en Copacabana,* which refers to the Copacabana Virgin and her shrine on the shores of Lake Titicaca, widely known in America and Europe from at least 1600. In both plays the appearance of the Virgin concludes a plot readily recognizable as that of the Faust legend made archetypal by Marlowe and Goethe. Discontented with the world surrounding him, the hero – Yauri, Usca – is seduced into signing a contract with the devil, "fiery" Nina, the letters of whose name are formed with his own blood. By selling his soul he gains the usual advantage in return, including wealth and the love of a well-born woman, the "golden" Cori. When the time comes for his soul to be collected and for him to go to the infernal fire, he is saved at the last moment by the feminine principle represented by the Blessed Virgin Mary and by the forces of Christianity in general. Structurally the works are also close, with the difference that *Yauri* has a long opening scene lacking in *Usca,* where, moreover, there is no counterpart to Achira, maid to Yauri's beloved; the beloved herself is respectively a widow, of one Inquil Tuta Inca, and a timorous daughter, of one Choque Apu.

In the Spanish Golden Age, Faust provided the theme of several plays, among them Mira de Amescua's *El esclavo del demonio* (1612),[25] the Spanish-Mexican Ruiz de Alarcón's *Quien mal anda en mal acaba,* also of 1612, and *El mágico prodigioso,* the *auto sacramental* composed by Calderón for Corpus week of 1637. Calderón also later authored *La aurora en Copacabana* (1651; his only New World piece), which focuses on the same episode of Mariolatry featured in *Usca Paucar.* Though not strictly speaking Faustian, the plot concerns an Inca ruler who is persuaded by the devilish arts of the character Idolatría to rebel, that is, refuse to submit unconditionally to Pizarro's armies and to the dogma of his priests, the Christian victory, or "dawn," being eventually assured by the miraculous intervention of the Virgin of Copacabana.

In itself, none of these Golden Age works is close enough to the Yauri–Usca plays to have served as a direct source; yet there can be no doubt about the Spanish influence. The three acts of each play are called *jornadas;* there is a *gracioso,* Quespillo; the love scenes are conducted on "high" and "low" levels, especially in *Yauri Titu; Usca Paucar* is actually designated an *auto sacramental.* Above all, there is no American precedent for such key features of the Quechua plays as the hero's highly individual blood pact with the devil or the mechanism by which he is saved: the Mariolatry typical of the *auto sacramental.*[26] Elements from different Spanish plays may even have been combined to produce a hero who is both the archetype of the Western malcontent and the imperial representative of the native Andean culture suppressed by the West.

At the same time, Yauri and Usca are by no means just characters transported from a foreign stage. By virtue of their title and position alone they belong to the Inca kingship cycle that includes *Apu Ollantay* and that runs from Manco Capac, founder of the Cuzco dynasty, to the thirteenth ruler, Atahuallpa, murdered by Pizarro in 1534. Moreover, these plays remained a major factor in post-Hispanic culture. Spanish chroniclers vividly record a 1555 performance in Potosi of four plays dedicated respectively to Manco Capac, Huayna Capac, Huascar, and Atahuallpa; and still in 1781, when condemning Tupac Amaru II to death, José Antonio Areche was banning "the staging of plays as well as other performances which the Indians celebrate in memory of their Incas."[27]

For its part, *Atahuallpa* provides us with a very different version of the encounter with Pizarro from that given by Calderón: Here the Inca hero dies purposefully to become the untainted emblem of the resistance, which historically was sustained from the redoubt of Vilcabamba until the execution of Tupac Amaru I in 1572 and which was then taken up by Tupac Amaru II; and he urges his son to remain loyal to the past, condemned as he will be to the same life of itinerant misery experienced by Yauri and particularly Usca. Indeed, unlike this European counterpart, who desires to taste power for the first time, Usca and Yauri, as Andean nobility, wish to *recover* it. Putting it another way, granted the local precedent, Usca and Yauri would appear not so much Inca Fausts – exotic heroes in a Golden Age theater – as they would Faustian Incas, heroes of the royal Quechua line grappling with new conditions.

Similarly, though of course an item of Christian theology, the devil who tempts Faust also has a counterpart in the *zupay,* mentioned in the Zithuwa liturgy of the Inca;[28] and even the Virgin bears certain local traits, just as the siting of her shrines in Cuzco, literally the navel of the Inca empire, and at Copacabana on Lake Titicaca, long worshiped as a water mother, attests the force of pagan devotion. On the Christian score generally, both plays even allow themselves at least some irreverence: Usca sums up Spanish charity as hypocrisy, and Yauri's Quespillo goes so far as to pun the Virgin's Kyrie with the Quechua *quiriy,* which means "to wound or harm" (line 423). In the same vein but with far heavier sarcasm, Pizarro in *Atahuallpa* begs Our Lady for strength when preparing to cut off the Inca's head.

Reinforcing these native angles on the main characters comes a series of songs that in both plays provide something of a chorus effect, one emphasized by their firmer and more elaborate metrics within the roughly octosyllabic norm of both plays. Although the pious invocations of the Virgin, along with the Góngoraesque rhetoric of precious courtship, can be readily detected as Spanish accretions, other such elements derive unquestionably from Quechua poetry. Like *Apu Ollantay,* both plays express the tenderest love in the song of the dove (*urpi*) and in that of the flower and the typically American hummingbird (as *huascar,* also an imperial name); both, too, introduce the lament of the bereaved woman, that of *Usca*'s Cori Tica being metrically intricate, as is the *yaravi,* or courtly lament, sung by Usca himself. As is made clear by the D'Harcourts' classic study *La musique des Incas et ses survivances* (1925) and more recent work by Yaranga and others, the tradition of Quechua verse to which these choruslike pieces belong has borne and continues to bear a powerful native sociology in its own right. Not least, the whole action is consigned to a palpably Andean landscape, with its high plains and valleys (*puna, yunca*) and its fauna of llamas and guinea pigs (*cuyes*), a fact that of itself weighs in the balance.[29] As a prospective candidate for hell, Usca is compared tellingly to a guinea pig roasted on a spit, a decidedly local image; Yauri's Quespillo announces that such roasting, like aborting with coca, is part of the skill of any true Andean bride.

In short, *Yauri Titu* and *Usca Paucar* embrace two traditions, Spanish and Quechua. Present in both plays, the tension between them is differently resolved in each.

Yauri Titu has generally been held to be superior to *Usca Paucar* in both structure and rhetoric. One thing is certain: It is far more Calderonian. The revelation of the resplendent Virgin, central to the very concept of the *auto sacramental,* is skillfully prepared for in *Yauri Titu* and is articulated as part of a detailed doctrinal message delivered by the angel at the start of Act 3. In

Usca Paucar it seems almost adventitious; indeed, the scene toward the end where Usca's beloved Cori Tica abruptly professes her devotion to the Virgin has been deemed by Meneses an interference from a later hand. Then, moving down from divine to secular love, we see that *Usca Paucar,* in having no equivalent to the maid Achira of *Yauri Titu* – the highly articulate *chola,* or mixed-blood – develops this theme neither in matching "low" and "high" dialogues (Achira–Quespillo, Cori Umina–Yauri) nor in dialogue between women (Achira–Cori Umina), these being characteristic of the Golden Age model. Above all, *Usca Paucar* diverges from the more Calderonian *Yauri Titu* in its presentation of the two major characters of the Faust story: the hero and his tempter. In the first instance, and within the framework set up so far, this divergence merits attention more for itself than as evidence of possible inferiority.

In *Yauri Titu,* the eponymous hero stands bereft of political memory. The putative heir to Inca glory fallen into penury, he is scarcely credited with a past of his own. Moreover, as the second husband of Cori Umina he is specifically revealed as an ersatz Inca, acknowledgment of ancestry and political status being made only in the case of her first husband, Inquil Tupa, who in the opening scene is referred to the line of Huayna Capac and Huascar, lords of Tahuantinsuyu; also, only Inquil (i.e., not Yauri) rates as the brother-in-law of Cori's protector Tupac Amaru, the name so highly resonant in the history of Quechua resistance. But of course it is the demeaned and surrogate Yauri who survives; the price for Inquil Tupa's remembered glory is death on his wedding day and complete eradication from the plot and the current history of his people. Whatever ideas Yauri himself may have had about the loss of Cuzco and Tahuantinsuyu, in his long opening speech he discourses only in the most general terms on the misery of life. In Cuzco he is dragged by hunger to the portals of the Virgin of Belen's church, and his subsequent journey is not the result of his initiative but of the devil's wishing to remove him from her sphere of influence. Beside his Quespillo he seems crass and lackluster, and he signs the demonic pact just as easily as Quespillo refuses it. Moreover, the material advantage he gains as a result, which he fecklessly says he doesn't know what to do with, is thoroughly exposed as no more than the vanity of man, born of vile clay and so on, in rhetoric wholly reminiscent of the Counter-Reformation and Calderón.

By contrast, the Faustian Inca of *Usca Paucar* establishes himself from the start in time and space as the heir of emperors whose seat is Cuzco, the heart of Tahuantinsuyu. He thus brings together the two strands of Inquil Tupa and Yauri Titu and hence more thoroughly patriates Faust as an Inca. Finding himself obliged to travel far in search of food and shelter, he unequivocally identifies the cause of his misery as the cruel and mean Spaniards, who have usurped power in his land.

Tahuantin suyu huyaichis	Towns of Tahuantinsuyu recognize
cai sonccoipa ccarasccanta	how my heart is split,
tucui pacha tanta tanta	all as one
ccasccoita cunan ccahuarei	look on my breast.
. . .	. . .
Noccan cani Husca Pauccar	I am Usca Paucar
hinantinpa hulpuicunan	once respected by all
ccapac cunac lirpucunan	a living example for the powerful
hatun Runa Auqui yahuar	a great man of royal blood.
. . .	. . .
maipachan hamun humaiman	When I chance to remember
machuicunac ccocha cusccan	the joy of my ancestors,
chaipachan sonccoiman llusccan	then into my heart
tucui mio chaiman caiman	all hatred pours.
. . .	. . .
hatun Ccoscoita ricuni	I see my great Cuzco
huc cunac maquin cunapi	in the hands of others
sondor huaseita ninapi	I witnessed my Sunturhuasi
ppuchu ccacta ccahuarini	vanish in flame.
chaipin ñocca minicuni.	

– lines 46–79

Because of this, the gold offered him by the devil has an immediate material and political relevance, although in practice it serves chiefly to win him the hand of Cori Tica and the paternal refuge of her home. Having the sensibility of his forebears, he is also successfully able to express his torment in the courtly form of the *yaravi*.

These striking differences in the construction of the heroes' social and political worlds, which link *Usca* far more strongly than *Yauri* with the tradition of Inca drama, find an echo at a deeper level of time and morality in the respective portrayals of the devil. For, like his victim, Yauri Titu's tempter, Nina Quiru, has very little of his own to offer, his two assistants remaining voiceless, whereas Usca's Nina Yunca is boosted by four supporting voices. What puny power Nina Quiru has derives almost entirely from Christian theology rather than from the native cosmogony that enables and entitles Nina Yunca to provide Usca with the wealth of Andean metals; and the allied concept of the infernal valley, or *yunca,* so central to *Usca*'s devil, is associated with Nina Quiru only once (line 2445). In the main, his characteristics continue to be more those of the Calderonian devil, who, as A. A. Parker reminds us,[30] is so constrained by the Counter-Reformation scenario of salvation that he cannot even imagine the success of his own schemes. True to this formula, Nina Quiru finds himself doubting his power to reclaim Yauri even before he tries to (line 2,230). He is no match for the Virgin even nominally, the saving utterance of her name having a much greater structural significance in this play than it has in *Usca Paucar.*

By contrast, from the start Usca's tempter Nina Yunca can be felt to inhabit his own world. Though, like Nina Quiru, he associates himself with Lucifer in telling of his defeat at the hands of San Miguel, more definitive is his intimacy with the very features of the Andean landscape that still serve to locate the devil there today. These are the "valley" of his name (*yunca*) that he would drag all down to, a false paradise that still symbolizes degeneration; and the cave-mine where he first approaches Usca. Bolivian miners continue to propitiate the devil, or *tío,* with old pagan rites in order to extract precious metals, which have included silver and gold.[31] Since Usca first meets Nina Yunca in such a cave, his subsequent "discovery" of these metals both concurs with the pagan pattern and need not be supernatural.

Besides being the lord of the valley and of native metals that gave the Inca and their predecessors wealth and power, the devil in Usca Paucar is celebrated as a major force in cosmogony. Holding still to an ancient wisdom, he is presented as a sage, or *amauta,* with expertise in the fourfold power manifest in whirlwind, solar and lunar eclipse, untamed beasts of decidedly South American origin, and the volcanic eruption that reveals the metals granted to Usca:

Chaipacmi callpaiqui can	for this you have your power
samai ñeique mana ateimi	your breath cannot be stopped
hucta phucu riptillaiquin	you hardly puff
chucucucum cai pachapas	and the whole earth shakes
millai hatun ccaccahuampas	the great rock-peak
ticsin mantan ticra camun	crashes to its base
. . .	. . .
Ccan ha mautta caiñeiquipe	with your knowledge
intitan tuta yachinquin	you make the sun darken
quillata ccosñerichispa	you make the moon smoky
ccoillorcunaat ttacanquin	you spread the stars everywhere
. . .	. . .
nina raurac pichucllaiqui	your jaws are of burning fire
uturuncu puma ranra	the jaguar the leaping puma
hashuan phiña macchachuaipas	the fiercest beast
quirun cama amarupas	the great-toothed boa
miyo ccallo Urucunapas	the most poisonous spider
caillai quipi ccumucachan.	yield before you
. . .	. . .
Ccomeryascca raurac ritti	the hard shining snow
ccan ccahuarinqui chaicca	when you look on it
mancharispan rittititin	melts away
poca lloccllan aiqqueripun	in a red flood flows.
ashuan chiri ccacca cuna	the coldest peaks
rittin huan ccataricuspa	that cover with snow
yana sacsanta quirpaspan	their black stains

soncconpi ccorita huihuan	in their heart keep gold
rurunpi ccollquita pacan	in their veins hoard silver
qquellaitapas antatapas	iron and copper
ccampacca masttariscanmi	and for you reveal all
manan pacanchu imatapas.	hide nothing.

– lines 455–94

Then when it comes to collecting Usca's soul, the scale of destruction threatened by Nina Yunca and his assistants recalls that of the earth-shaking *pachacuti,* the turn of the world age. For reasons like these, Rudolf Grossman spoke of *Usca Paucar* as an *auto sacramental* with a pagan core ("heidnisches Kern"). [32]

However inferior it may be thought, *Usca Paucar,* the later of the two texts, has certainly become far more integrated into the Andean world of Quechua-speakers; and to this extent it is appropriate that Sahuaraura Inca, himself of the Inca line, should in 1838 have chosen to copy and preserve it. One critic has positively praised the stronger indigenousness of *Usca Paucar.* Pointing to the tenser emotional charge in its protagonist, José Juan Arrom notes how it is far more likely than *Yauri Titu* to produce deep resonance in a public that, like the hero, "is vexed with no recourse but submission" and is gripped by a bitterness that "could have been avoided had the Christian ethic truly put a limit to human exploitation" in the Andes. [33] He points, too, to the advantage that the critic of drama, as opposed to other genres, has in being able thus to implicate society as a criterion. When refashioning the old fable of Faust in terms accessible to the conditions of life and feeling of its public, as Arrom puts it – and, no less important, being helped to do so by the prior existence of a strong tradition of drama in Quechua – *Usca Paucar* translates the more effectively the model and the disaster of Spanish.

CINDERELLA BETWEEN MAPUCHE AND ZUNI

The Old World Cinderella has traveled through Asia, Europe, and Africa, changing kinship, helpers, and fortune but not gender. In America, it is the fact of being female that distinguishes her as a post-Columbian import, since her indigenous counterpart there is usually male, the Ash Boy figure analyzed by Lévi-Strauss in just this connection in "The Structural Study of Myth," [34] or the ill-treated younger stepbrother, like the Sioux and Cherokee "Thrown-away" Boy or, for that matter, the Twins of the *Popol vuh.*

"Cinderella" traveled to America chiefly as the "Cendrillon" of Charles Perrault (1679) and the "Cenicienta" of his Spanish translators. [35] This is the source for many notable versions of the story, like those of the Nahua of western Mexico, where, as the youngest of Tonantzin's three daughters,

Cinderella wins in marriage a prince manifest now as Venus, the preparer of ground for planting; or the Carib, where the small *conuco* assigned to her flourishes magically, to the envy of her older sisters.[36] She is transformed yet again among the Mapuche and the Zuni, societies that lie equidistant from the equator, the one south of Tahuantinsuyu, the other north of Mesoamerica, both of which maintained political autonomy until only a century ago. The Mapuche story was first published in 1956; three versions of the Zuni story appeared between 1901 and 1972.[37] Unlike the Mapuche, the Zuni retain the midnight curfew; they also include the bird helper absent from Perrault but known in such other European sources as Giambattista Basile's "Cenerentola" and the Grimms' "Aschenbrödel."

We meet the Mapuche Cinderella living in her small house with her mother (Ñuke) and older sisters. It is winter, to be precise the season of the three "hunger months," Inan Tror, Weshá, and Pillel. To ease their hardship over these three months, the daughters go out in turn to find work in the house of a lord and his father (Chau). Each is distinguished by the posture she adopts when resting along the road and the type of work she does in the house. Cinderella lies face up but modestly covered and responds vivaciously when encountered by the lord as he rides by on his horse; and she cleans his house thoroughly. As earnings she accepts not the silver craved by her sisters but a wand that magically fulfills her wishes, in the first instance that her mother should have a silver *trarilonko* and the finest attire. These her mother puts to immediate use at the Nguillatun dance and festival, which her sisters also attend, leaving her behind. Thanks to the wand, she acquires the clothes she needs and a horse to ride to the Nguillatun, and she soon becomes the wife of the lord, who is the "sun," or ruler, of the district. Well equipped with servants, she invites her mother, but not her sisters, to her new home.

Devoted to her mother, Cinderella reconciles the matriarchal code of her old home with the patriarchy of her new one, Ñuke and Chau; and she bridges the gap between peasant walker and lordly rider. She owes her fortune to her modesty, which correlates with the fact that her turn of duty fell in the last of the three months, or moons, of hunger. In the first month the oldest sister lies supine by the road; in the second, the second sister lies on her side; in the third, Cinderella turns over to face the sun. In the traditional Mapuche calendar, these months correspond to the highly defined winter quarter of the year, feared for its cruelty and the fact that it annually brings back the memory of the great winters and glacier cycles of cosmogony, when spring never came and the whole land sank under snow.[38] The very names of the months point to food shortage and disease. Beginning at the southern hemisphere's winter solstice (June), they end at the spring equinox (September) with the Nguillatun feast of thanksgiving that changes this Cinderella's life.

As set periods of thirty days that mediate between solstice and equinox, these three hunger months have exact Inca counterparts in a twelve-month calendar year whose structure was doubtless influenced by Tahuantinsuyu; moreover, the three Inca months are likewise associated with scarcity and disease (*"falta de yuyos,"* *"pestilencia,"* as Guaman Poma puts it [p. 251]). The Inca comparison is especially instructive in the case of Cinderella's month, Pillel, which in Tahuantinsuyu is the time for spring cleaning – her activity – and the driving out of disease. Called Coya Raimi,[39] it celebrates the moon, and during it the *coya*s and principal ladies give hospitality, as she does. Indeed, it is the "pascua" of the queen of the sky and wife of the sun, the equinoctial lunar–solar union that epitomizes Easter: At her Nguillatun, as the last of the winter moons and true to her mediatory role,[40] Cinderella marries the sun, guaranteeing an upturn not just for herself and her family but for the whole community.

The Zuni Cinderella story was first published under that title in 1901 by Frank Cushing; recast, it reappeared in 1972 as "The Turkey Maiden," one of the Zuni "self-portrayals" edited by Robert Coles, and again as "The Girl Who Took Care of the Turkeys" in Dennis Tedlock's *Finding the Center* (1972). In each case the plot is basically the same. A Zuni girl lives humbly, looking after a flock of turkeys some way from the main town of Zuni, where a dance is to be held; she wants to go but lacks suitable clothes; her birds see this need and help her on the understanding that she will return by a certain hour; she attends and shines at the dance, forgets her bargain, and returns only to discover her turkeys gone. On regaining their freedom, the turkeys recover their own voice and sing their characteristic song. In Coles, Turkey Girl has elder and more privileged sisters who cannot believe she could so shine at the dance; in Tedlock the role of the prince is intimated in the keen interest shown in her by the "dance directors." The mode of telling also varies: Coles aims at little more than a précis; Tedlock goes the other way and in translating from Zuni to English attempts to capture finer qualities of the text by registering typographically the pitch and rhythms accorded to it in its 1967 performance by Walter Sánchez (who speaks no English).

The first thing that happens to Cinderella in Anasazi is that its landscape incorporates her, she, like the action, being drawn to the "Place of the Middle," the Zuni capital where the dance is held. An inhabitant of Matsaki ("Salt Place") in Cushing, in Tedlock she lives in Wind Place, one of the very first towns founded by the Zuni when, having just emerged from their Sipapuni yet farther downstream, they were traveling eastward up toward Zuni. At the end of the story, the turkeys go farther up the Zuni River chanting its place names, up toward the continental divide, where they leave their tracks imprinted in the rock.

As Turkey Girl living in the Zuni landscape, Cinderella mostly deals not

Figure 67. Turkey: (a) as helper (Plume Chant dry painting); (b) as warrior (Mississippian shell gorget).

with other humans but with the creatures she cares for, sharing with them a reciprocal need to talk, bargain, and love. The older male she has most to do with uncannily perceives her unspoken thoughts, and she may attend the dance only with his permission; and (in Cushing) when the whole company, against their better judgment, eventually provide her with clothes, they strut before her and brush her skin with what palpably amounts to sexual excitement:

> Before the maiden donned all these garments, the turkeys circled about her, singing and singing, and clucking and clucking, and brushing her with their wings, until her person was as clean and her skin as smooth and bright as that of the fairest maiden of the wealthiest home in Matsaki.[41]

Similarly, when she fails to return from the dance it is with great reluctance that the birds decide they have to leave, feeling sorry for both her and themselves.

Farmed as much for feathers as for food, the turkey was originally imported to Anasazi from Mexico; and, like the dog, it has a whole lore of companionship attached to it, as we have seen, within the broader world-age argument of the domestic contract. Turkey companions appear in both dry paintings (Fig. 67a) and *teoamoxtli,* providing from under their wings not just food for the journey after life but jewels and other precious objects. An act of provisioning occurs in the Zuni "Cinderella," when in addition to clothes the turkeys give the girl jewelry:

> Finally, one old Turkey came forward and said: "Only the rich ornaments worn by those who have many possessions are lacking to thee, O maiden mother. Wait a moment. We have keen eyes, and have gathered many valuable things, – as such things, being small, though precious, are apt to be lost from time to time by men and maidens."

> Spreading his wings, he trod round and round upon the ground, throwing his head back, and laying his wattled beard on his neck; and, presently beginning to cough, he produced in his beak a beautiful necklace; another Turkey brought forth earrings, and so on, until all the proper ornaments appeared, befitting a well-clad maiden of the olden days, and were laid at the feet of the poor Turkey-girl.

Hence, in promising to pay for her clothes and return to her turkeys before a certain hour, Cinderella engages in both an individual bargain and an ancient contract. The turkeys remind her, "Our lives depend on your thoughtfulness," and Andrew Peynetsa explains:

> Just because there's a dance doesn't relieve you of any responsibilities. If you've had your pleasure, it doesn't mean you have to stay out all day. It's like people who own sheep, maybe they like to see a lot of things that go on, but because they depend on them for their livelihood, they can't just let them stay in the corral and go hungry. (D. Tedlock 1972:73)

Once the contract is broken and the turkeys decide to leave their pen, they gather speed and strength as they recover their autonomy, and they sing their own song:

KYANA$_A$$_A$$_{AA}$$_A$ TOK TOK KYANA$_A$$_A$$_{AA}$$_A$ TOK TOK

YEE-E-E-E HU^{LI}HU^{LI}HU^{LI} TOK TOK TOK TOK

– Ibid., p. 72

They reinscribe themselves in the world by chanting the place names of the landscape and by making their prints on the rocks; said etiologically still to be visible at the place called Turkey Tracks six miles southeast of Zuni, these serve as a script or score for their song:

> Therefore, where you see the rocks leading up to the top of Cañon Mesa, there are the tracks of turkeys and other figures to be seen. The latter are the song that the Turkeys sang, graven in the rocks. . . . (S. Thompson 1966:231)

As here, the song is the self in North American iconography, that is, the voice or "heart" line desired by the hunter in his prey and depicted alike on Zuni ceramics, in dry paintings, and in Mide scrolls. And once emancipated, the turkeys acquire the ferocious qualities so admired by, among others, Benjamin Franklin and D. H. Lawrence:[42] They become the creatures who will "eat people back," as the *Popol vuh* puts it, the possibly satanic Quecholli of the *Ríos Codex,* a warrior on Mound Builder shell (Fig. 67b), or Atahuallpa.

As Turkey Girl, the Zuni Cinderella took to her new environment from the very start, and the motif of her bird helper could be richly elaborated, thanks to Fourth World notions of reciprocity highly developed in Zuni and Anasazi cosmogony. The process of adaptation as such may be further observed in the differences that separate Cushing's from Tedlock's text, especially in all that concerns the dance. Over time, Cinderella has further settled into a Zuni home, to the extent that in Tedlock's edition her story appears along with native cosmogonical texts, unidentified as a translation, and really detectable as such only through retrospective comparison with Cushing.

In European fashion, Cushing still includes something of a preamble on how Cinderella was very poor but "had a winning face and bright eyes," and he remarks on what kind of "character" she had; in the telling by Sánchez seventy years later, all this has gone. Here our idea of the protagonist derives rather from what is said and not said in the conversations she has with others; reports on her inner self are confined to the facts of the moment, like her initial indifference to the dance and then her eagerness to go and her forgetfulness during it. The narrative allows the characters, human and animal, to speak for themselves and in its verbal exchanges creates a keen sense of play:

> When she spoke to her turkeys about this, they said
> "If you went
> it wouldn't turn out well: who would take care of us?"
> that's what her turkeys told her.
> She listened to them and they slept through the night.
> Then it was the second day
> of the dance
> and night came.
> That night
> with the Yaaya Dance half over
> she spoke to her big tom turkey:
>
> "My father-child, if they're going to do it again tomorrow
> why can't I go?" she said. "Well
> if you went, it wouldn't turn out well."
> That's what he told her. "Well then
> I mustn't go."
>
> – D. Tedlock 1972:69

This dramatic emphasis corresponds in turn with the fact that in this later version the whole action centers on the dance. Whereas with Cushing we approach this event slowly, being told on first mention that it will begin "in four days," with Tedlock it is already going on when we first hear of it, right at the start, and Cinderella's shift from indifference to eagerness takes place over what are now the four days of the dance itself. As the days go by, her growing excitement finds a corollary in that of the dance nearby, with its insistent drum and crowds of people. Similarly, when Cinderella fails to return, the turkeys send their chief to the dance plaza to warn her instead of setting off for the hills straight from their pen, as they do in Cushing; the details given of this turkey's approach from the west and of his perching on a ladder to the north of the plaza further enhance our sense of its being the physical arena for the action. The dance becomes an explicit social and political focus to which Cinderella, living solitary on the other side of the river, nonetheless thoroughly belongs as one of the Zuni people.

The Zuni adoption of Cinderella may be considered the more intimate by the fact that the dance she attends becomes a major ritual, like the Mapuche Nguillatun. This much was hinted at already by Cushing when he reported his native storyteller's comment about "the Dance of the Sacred Bird . . . a very blessed and welcome festival to our people, especially to the youths and maidens who are permitted to join in the dance" (S. Thompson 1966:225). With Tedlock, the dance in question is the Yaaya, the first to be performed historically by the Zuni, according to their own cosmogony, and one that was being revived at just the time that Walter Sánchez and Andrew Peynetsa were recording the whole gamut of narratives that make up *Finding the Center.* As well as affirming the Zuni politically as a nation when they were still on their way to their capital, Middle Place, the Yaaya also anticipates the risk faced by Cinderella on attending the dance; for at the first performance of it a masked participant known as the White Shumeekuli so forgot himself that he ran from the plaza as she later had to, and his death followed four days later after he had been captured by none other than a herder of sheep – a perfect alter ego for Cinderella.[43]

The same cosmogonical context, provided at length in *Finding the Center,* explains not just the ritual origin but also the time and space of the Yaaya dance attended by Cinderella. The northern perch used to warn her corresponds to the first of the four directions visited by the Sun Priest in the underworld in "The Beginning," just as the western entrance gate denotes the sunset at which her forgetfulness is punished (in the layout of dry paintings, west commonly pairs with east as female to male). Above all, the four-day span of the dance involves a shamanic shift between dimensions of time of the kind known throughout North America and found in Zuni cosmogony. For during the first two days, that is, half of the dance, Cinderella only hears the drum and other sounds of the dance and actually sees it only on the third day, or the start of the second half; and whereas the days pass internally undifferentiated during the first half, during the second half they are each divided into four parts, with great emphasis being placed, for example, on the timing of the girl's renewed request to the turkeys on the third day: "When it was the middle of the day, she asked again, right at noon." Underpinning this quickening diurnal pace is the beat of the drum and the dance and of the story line itself, which as it were captures Cinderella, like another White Shumeekuli, and keeps her from her promise.[44]

The European Cinderella is generally a poor, misunderstood girl, pretty of face and dainty of foot, who gets to marry the prince. Existing in the undifferentiated time and space of the fairy tale, she is defined chiefly through private wish fulfillment; Perrault adds snobbery and a certain bourgeois individualism. Transported to the Fourth World, she fully enters her body, her species in nature, and her community. She inhabits a historical landscape and knows the rhythms of time according to which a moon or a morning may recapitulate the world.

Epilogue:
The American palimpsest

Diverse in provenance, language, and script, the literatures of the Fourth World ask to be perceived as chapters of a single book, one that contains not just patterns of timeless myth but physical maps of history and world age. In turn, this book acquires a functional unity as the palimpsest of Anglo and Latin American literatures. Cosmogony, history, poem, or manifesto – prior inscription on pages often assumed to have been blank – it has widely informed American works that in engaging with Indians draw on their own testimony.

A long and intricate process that reveals greater and lesser loyalties, this engagement with Native American texts characterizes a range of Western literature, particularly from the Romantics onward, and it played a key part in such twentieth-century movements as Expressionism and Surrealism. It may even be identified as a factor that led to the Western notion of world literature, specifically Goethe's "Welt-literatur" (1827). Matching critical appreciation of this whole process has been scant,[1] especially outside America, as Angel Rama intimates in his indispensable *Transculturación narrativa en América Latina* (1982).

Involvement with this Fourth World subtext has intensified, notably in Latin American prose and poetry of the last half-century. A turning point has generally been acknowledged in the publication of *Men of Maize* (*Hombres de maíz*) in 1949, the Nobel Prize–winning novel by Miguel Angel Asturias.[2] It draws profoundly on the *Popol vuh,* a work from the earlier stages of Guatemala's literature that Asturias had himself previously translated. The cases of José María Arguedas in Peru and of Augusto Roa Bastos in Paraguay are similar. In poetry, a special place is occupied by *Homage to the American Indians,* which the Nicaraguan Ernesto Cardenal has steadily elaborated on over the last twenty-five years. The first two editions of the

Homage appeared under that title (*Homenaje a los indios americanos* [1969; expanded in 1971]). A more recent collection of these "Indian poems" has the title *Los ovnis de oro* (*Golden Flying Saucers*);[3] though based on the Cuna *Olopatte ikala,* the flying-saucer allusion here is inept, since, going against the argument of the poems themselves, it seems to suggest that American culture originated somewhere other than in its own earth, the extraterrestrial being the most recent and most bizarre in the line of colonialist fantasies about the Fourth World.[4]

Taking further collage techniques initially learned from Ezra Pound and used previously in updated versions of the Psalms, Cardenal's acts of recognition rework and interweave native originals, so that through his Spanish we can appreciate the cadences and etymologies, script forms, and even material substance of the prior texts as well as the literary and cultural traditions to which they belong. On the map, these construct the Fourth World through its grammatology, radiating out from the isthmus north to Mesoamerica and Turtle Island, south to Tahuantinsuyu and the rainforest. Relying in this way on literal subtexts of native origin, the *Homage* strives for a continental voice that speaks, as it were, from beneath and despite the Latin and Anglo imposition. Rhetorically this is part of its immediate message: resistance to the U.S.-backed oppression typified by Somoza; social justice of the kind practiced in the Solentiname community (founded by Cardenal) and later advanced by the Nicaraguan revolution (in which Cardenal served as minister of culture). In this way, Cardenal underpins his general philosophy, a Marxism that grows from rather than murders America's "Indian soul" (as D. H. Lawrence and Antonin Artaud put it)[5] and a Christian theology that liberates rather than binds. (Pope John Paul II rebuked him on just this score.)

In large doses, the prosaic conversational lines of these poems, ingenious as they are, can tire, and the earlier ones especially suffer from a certain hagiography and that tell-tale dichotomy between good and bad Indians. Yet Cardenal's is a devout exploration, and the overall conviction of the homages is well summed up by José Miguel Oviedo when he says they "contain a utopia that is fulfilled between the time of indigenous myth and the apocalyptic time of the West, between origins and disaster: those worlds that we consider dead and distant are here, and History can, once again, begin."[6] On all these counts, the *Homage* may guide us when it comes to considering the larger palimpsest and the manifold instances of its power to shape within the America politically independent of Europe. Not least, it proposes a widening series of American perspectives within and beyond the domain of the Spanish language it uses. Indeed, the various poems of Cardenal's *Homage* collectively re-create nothing less than a literary geography of the Fourth World, as this has been discussed above; hence, they provide us with a common point of reference for many other key works of American literature written in Western languages that draw on native texts.

First of all, an isthmian base is defined for us by the poems that relate to the Cuna of Panama, like "Nele Kantule," "Los ovnis de oro," and "Entrevista con el cacique Yabiliguiña." Citing the *ikala* – chant and written character – the first two of these construct the Cuna version of history, the brilliant "amniotic waters" of their sea (Mu) and its islands, and the lives of their Neles. Among these exemplary shaman-heroes stand the ancient culture bringer of the golden plate (whence the unfortunate "ovnis de oro"), the plant spirits who cure the sick, and the political leader named in the first title, who presided over the indigenous republic of 1925. Part of the Chibcha legacy further shared by the Kogi (the object of homage in the poem "Sierra Nevada"), this experience belongs to the Caribbean and South American side of the poet's home, Nicaragua, just as its other side belongs to Mesoamerica. This particular understanding of Nicaragua as the crossroads of the continent was similarly won from native texts by Cardenal's compatriot and predecessor Pablo Antonio Cuadra, whose work sets up an interface between Chibcha gold and "double-ego" statues on the one hand and brilliant *teoamoxtli* images on the other.

Like Cuadra, and before him Rubén Darío, the *huehuence* who founded American poetry in Spanish,[7] Cardenal inclines more to the Mesoamerican side, to the annals that tell of Quetzalcoatl, Tula, and the ancient migrations and the opulent collection *Cantares mexicanos,* the ground text of no fewer than three long pieces in the *Homage.* Whole lines and stanzas of the *Cantares* are taken from the translations done by Garibay (*Poesía náhuatl* [1965–8]). Profoundly influential in Mexican poetry from Paz to Pacheco, Garibay's versions enhanced understanding of Nahuatl poetry ("flower song," *in xochitl in cuicatl*) and the acute joy in life variously expressed in its planting, orphan, and other modes. In particular, they raised the question, also asked by Cardenal, of how far earlier interpreters, among them the nineteenth-century U.S. historian W. H. Prescott, had given an ideological twist to the "laments" of the poet-king Nezahualcoyotl (1402–72), seeing in them covert yearning for Cortes and his religion.[8] Historically, like the archaeology that discovered earthly paradise in the murals of Teotihuacan, Garibay's revised *Cantares* form part of the massive reappraisal of indigenous culture brought about by the Mexican Revolution.[9]

Through another closely knit subgroup of Mesoamerican poems likewise interwoven with current archaeology – "Oráculos de Tikal," "Mayapan," "Ardilla de los tunes de un katun," "Katun 11 Ahau," and "8 Ahau" – the *Homage* traces continuity in lowland Maya consciousness from the Classic inscriptions to the *Chilam Balam Books,* drawing moral lessons from calendar structure and rescuing for the scribe-poet the honor of intuiting the true cause of eclipse. As a result, attentive to the *katun* revolutions of the lowland Maya, the poems implicitly argue their political cause, as does Ermilo Abreu Gómez's Yucatecan novel *Canek* (1940), which is similarly couched in *katun* logic and the Zuyua language of the *Chilam Balam Books.* Moreover, transcribing the hieroglyphs of Quirigua and Copan, these poems make the decisive link between their millions of years and the beginnings of earthly time recounted in the highland *Popol vuh,* plotting the vast scope of its evolutionary story. In this way, the *Homage* reveals further dimensions in Maya and Mesoamerican culture and a deeper reason for defending and learning from it. Having recourse to the same corpus of Maya classics – the *Chilam Balam Books,* the *Cakchiquel Annals,* and above all the *Popol vuh* – the Guatemalan Miguel Angel Asturias puts forward a similar argument in his novel *Men of Maize:* This work construes the reality of its hero, the *guerrillero* Gaspar Ilom, in *Popol vuh* terms as he leads an uprising in Cuchumatanes, the heartland and source of the first maize in highland Maya cosmogony. The whole episode is based on an actual Maya uprising of 1900. Politically this corresponds to the fact that engaging as a translator with the *Popol vuh* and other Maya classics actually transformed Asturias's view of his own country and of those who constitute its majority, curing him of an inherited white racism.[10] "Gaspar Ilom" is the name assumed today by his son, a *guerrillero* commander fighting for Maya rights in Guatemala's necessary revolution.

   Heirs to the civilization upon which Spain based its northern viceroyalty, the Mesoamericans in Cardenal's *Homage* have their southern counterparts in the heirs to Tahuantinsuyu. Dismembered now and shared by the Andean states of Ecuador, Bolivia, and Peru, Tahuantinsuyu is reconstituted in the first instance through that anatomy, still alive in Quechua, that places brow in Quito, uterus in Titicaca, and navel in Cuzco. Politically a similar anatomical logic makes the Inca head grow back into its body in the legend of Inkarri quoted here from José María Arguedas's 1956 publication. In the first *Homage* (1969), "Economía de Tahuantinsuyu" centers on Cuzco, node of South America's "broken roads," and the yearly round of the calendar detailed by Guaman Poma, where the emperor himself digs the first furrow. Occluded through invasion like the sun eclipsed at midday ("chuapi punchapi tutayaca," as the Quechua quotation puts it), this order or cosmos is held out in hope, like a *quipu* thread or maize kernels clutched in the mummy's hand. Twenty years later, following the defeat of Velasco's Peruvian revolution, "El secreto de Machu-Picchu" traces the voice of resistance more intimately through the long-secret "prayer in stone" of that city (whose revelation had earlier inspired Neruda to his very different all-American epic *Canto general* [1950]). A leitmotif in this poem, Quechua songs that tell of love also encode the summons to defend it militarily, invoking the "white mountains" of Antisuyu (i.e., the redoubts of Ollantaytambo, Vilcabamba, and Paititi) and hence the resistance that extends from Tupac Amaru I through Tupac Amaru II to today's "*tupamaros.*"

> After the great disaster
> the password was: Pusaj ("Let's go down"),
>   Let's go down to the rainforest.
> Down to the night, the dark, the forest.
> They said it too with songs:
>   "Go beyond the white peaks."
> (The Spanish didn't understand.)
> They were invoking the ancient realm,
>   These were love songs
>   with much-mentioned doves.
>   Beloved dove
>   come to your lover,
>   to your wilderness.
>   – Cardenal 1988:161–2

Among the Inca, similar songs had served to distinguish the leader and the sage, in the fashion of the riddles of the Maya *katun.* This discreet continuity also characterizes the living Quechua drama woven into the poem, like the tragedy of Atahuallpa's death.

Explicitly acknowledged in the *Homage,* the Peruvian José María Arguedas translated and edited several volumes of poetry and drama in this Quechua tradition as well as the Inkarri story; and he also wrote in Quechua himself, notably in correspondence with the *guerrillero* leader Hugo Blanco and in his homage to Tupac Amaru, the recurrent hero of revolution in Peru (*Tupac Amaru Kamaq taytanchisman: Haylli-taki* [1962]). As a Spanish-American novelist he is readily comparable with Asturias in structuring his written world on the native text. Grappling with the violent dichotomies of modern Peru, he turned to Huarochiri's *Runa yndio,* another of the texts he translated; it supplies the framework of his last work and its two principles of authority, *El zorro de arriba y el zorro de abajo* (1969; "The Fox from Above and the Fox from Below").[11] In turn, Arguedas's work directly impinged on that of the revolutionary Manuel Scorza, who likewise drew on *Runa yndio* and the Inkarri legend when honoring the Quechua who were massacred during the Andean uprising of 1962.

Within the Spanish-American novel, the indigenism of Asturias and Arguedas further compares with that of Augusto Roa Bastos, who has focused on his native Paraguay, the "República Guaraní" of Cardenal's *Homage.* Here, in "La Arcadia perdida," Cardenal detects echoes of the Tahuantinsuyu ideal prior to the Jesuit mission, and in "Los hijos del bosque de las palabras almas" he goes to the root concepts of *Ayvu rapyta* and rainforest cosmogony. In Roa Bastos's case, growing familiarity with the Guarani classics enabled him to set the endurance of that people, and the reason behind it, into the dialogues and dialectic of *Yo el supremo* (1974; "I the Supreme").

From here, ever reliant on its palimpsest, the *Homage* takes us on beyond the frontiers of Spanish to Turtle Island and to the rainforest, those great riverine theaters of North and South America whose official languages have become English and Portuguese. Within the larger idea of North America, whose birds fly from "Nicaragua to Ohio," Turtle Island is established through its charter statements, which cross-reference with those of Mexico. They include the wampum strings and book of rites that guaranteed the Pax Iroquoia ("Kayanerenhkowa"), the stately sung encounters, or "marches," of the Pawnee, and the speeches and songs of the Ghost Dance that united Sioux, Algonkin, Caddo, and Comanche in the call "We will live again." As he walks the shores of the Great Lakes in "Kayanerenhkow," Hiawatha recovers the original life message of the wampum "shell writing" (necessarily traduced, Cardenal says, in the typewritten poem); then, in "Marchas Pawnees," the symbol of the leader Tahirassawichi – the sky arch of the solar walk with power driving down from the zenith (identical in Mide script; see Fig. 60a) – is set into the alphabetic text to enliven it visually. Again, through quotation from speeches by the Shawnee Tecumseh (Shooting Star) and others, the Ghost Dance (1890) is placed in the longer perspective of Indian resistance to the United States:

> "These lands are ours
> no one has the right to remove us
>   we were the first owners"
> Shooting Star to Wells, 1807

> "And the President could stay easy in his big Village
>   drinking his wine in peace
>   while he and Harrison would have to fight"
> Shooting Star to Harrison, 1810

> The Great Spirit gave this great island to his red offspring . . .
>   – Cardenal 1978:178

By his own account, Cardenal was equipped to enter this territory above all through his long friendship with the U.S. poet Thomas Merton, one among few to have seriously pondered the expropriation carried out in the name of the American Revolution. Ironically, the Anglo-American poem that in practice has most diverted attention away from that catastrophe itself heavily exploited Indian originals: Longfellow's *Hiawatha* (1856). Reworking the Ojibwa source narrative published by Henry Rowe Schoolcraft in *Algic Researches* (1839), the twenty-two cantos of *The Song of Hiawatha* are put into the mouth of the bard Nawadaha, "from the land of the Ojibways, from the land of the Dacotahs," and concentrate on the epic of Manabozho, the Algonkin Venus figure who like Quetzalcoatl makes maize agriculture possible and gives his people their first writing lesson. (That he should have been given an Iroquois name reflects the vogue of Henry Morgan's *League of the Hodenosaunee or Iroquois* [1851]). Longfellow's poem is equipped with a glossary of more than a hundred native words, mostly Algonkin terms relative to the hero's kinship and "totems" and the "Meda" (Mide) animal spirits; and its finest effects occur in the cantos devoted to maize, whose song is sung in Algonkin syllables, and to Mide script, whose images are transcribed with great dexterity. Yet all this loving attention to native text has its categorical price: Manabozho/Hiawatha is celebrated only on condition that he disappear. Terminally epic, the hero follows the solar walk not through its circuit but just westward to annihilation in the "fiery sunset"; and upon leaving, he orders his people to concede all to the new representatives of the "Master of Life." Hence, they simply self-destruct, ensuring that all territory is vacated in principle even before the whites invade.[12] By definition, they belong to "prehistory," like the Mound Builders and all those who might otherwise have politically threatened the U.S. claim to being civilizers. In this arrangement, the few "historic" Indians who stay on, their memory hopelessly blurred, become last Mohican (Lenape) or evil Mohawk, doomed Pawnee or savage horse-borne Sioux, in Cooper's novels, for which read official white history, complete with its murderous silences.

Intrigued by the psychic effects of just this eradication, Jung produced a "landmark" (his term) in Western psychology, namely *Wandlungen und Symbole der Libido,* where he states that the animus of white Americans differs from that of Europeans in that it typically takes the form of a dark Indian. In the case of Miss Miller, to whose schizophrenic "fantasy" Jung devotes most of his analysis, the Indian appears explicitly as Hiawatha, a continental revenant from Longfellow's poem who simultaneously exudes Mexican and Inca presence.[13] Independently of Jung, it is this linkage that led Gary Snyder to wish to "kill the white American in me," quoting Ghost Dance songs in "A Curse on the Men in Washington" (quoted in Fiedler 1968:86–7); and which encouraged Ed Dorn to his radical reading of Shoshonean and Apache faith. According to Cardenal's "Coplas" in memoriam, it is also what Thomas Merton principally taught him "about the Indians" of Anglo America.

Still under siege today, the Amazonian rainforest continues to supply culture in its highest forms, like air, vegetal food, and vision. As his "Epístola a Monseñor Casaldáliga"[14] shows, Cardenal has increasingly entered this arena as well, to defend its cause in Xingu and its "cosmic song" of genesis and evolution. His statement here follows that dialectic of survival which can also be found in a whole constellation of Latin-American prose works, beginning with Mario de Andrade's *Macunaíma* (1928). The hero of Andrade's novel, said to be "without character," is in fact born and named in the domain of

Watunna and is formed by just that Carib belief system: Descending the Uraricoera and crossing the Amazon, he travels to São Paulo, traversing all the space and time of Brazil, only to return to a landscape of ghosts and stars, what he becomes. With agility and humor, the narrative makes clear that its life is that of its palimpsest, or life source, in this case the account of the Carib hero Makunaima published by Koch-Grünberg; and in so doing it anticipates the argument of the other novels that have emerged from the same biosphere.

Sharing with *Macunaima* its literal source in the Pacaraima ridge that extends from Roraima toward Marahuaka, the story of the Caroni River told in *Canaima* (1935), by the Venezuelan Rómulo Gallegos, likewise follows a native course. The Carib term that is this novel's title, defined in *Watunna* as the madness that white invaders induce, also identifies a short story by the Guyanese Wilson Harris,[15] whose novel *Palace of the Peacock* (1960) in turn traces an ascent to Roraima through the stages of the *Medatia* vision. In *El hablador* (1987), by the Peruvian Mario Vargas Llosa, Machiguenga texts are recounted by the titular "talker" and take over the plot, at key moments in their original Arawak language; texts of other Upper Amazon people are similarly treated in *Primitivos relatos contados otra vez* (1976), by the Colombian Hugo Niño. In the dialectic of *Yo el supremo* (1974), the Paraguayan Roa Bastos counterposes biblical and Western reason to the Guarani cosmogony he has translated, with its dual autogenesis and blue jaguars;[16] and this becomes the guideline threaded in turn through the bewildering forest of *Daimon* (1978), by the Argentinian Abel Posse. Resolving the literary dilemmas of the nineteenth-century Brazilian Americanists, who only succeeded in putting Western perceptions and thoughts into their Indians' heads, these same Guarani traditions appear yet again, in their Tupi version, to determine the structures of Darcy Ribeiro's *Maira* (1976); in the process, this work considers the fate of Brasilia, ominously sited as it is in the Tupi cosmic landscape.

Contemplating this wealth of imagination, of which the list above is the merest indication, Italo Calvino has suggested through his legendary old Indian, teller of all the stories, that the Amazonian cosmos could be the "primeval magma": an ultimate source for all the world's great narratives, among which he names the *Popol vuh*.[17] Perhaps it is, so adding to the growing list of gifts that have flowed from the munificent rainforest. In any case, wary of easy universalizing, we should not forget that the literary imagination at stake has not in fact been generated by some severed Cartesian head, abstract and out of time. It has drawn its sap and humor from people very much alive in and to their environment, whose resources and energy are quite specific; and through its very brilliance and magic it constantly warns against the exhaustion of that energy from within and from without.

With wit though inscrutable faith, the same warning is given in Posse's

**Indigenous Alliance of the Americas
on 500 Years of Resistance**

Declaration of Quito, Ecuador
July 1990

The Continental Gathering "500 Years of Indian Resistance," with representatives from 120 Indian Nations, International and Fraternal organizations, meeting in Quito, July 17-20, 1990, declare before the world the following:

Figure 68. Opening of the Quito Declaration.

Daimon,[18] the first of an American trilogy that, very much on its own terms, takes in the whole of Fourth World literature, from luminous *teoamoxtli* page and threaded *quipu* string to the legal depositions of today. In this novel, Native Americans from all over the continent gather at Chachapoyas, the astounding pre-Incaic city of rounded walls on the uppermost Amazon that Guaman Poma perceived as "rebellious"; there they take stock of their situation, analyzing their common history and planning future policy. In itself this uncannily anticipates the epochal Quito conference of July 1990, where representatives of 120 Indian nations did in fact meet to discuss precisely these issues (Fig. 68). In the novel, the Chachapoyas conference is also attended by the animals and the plants, who present their own reports, communicating as if in the shamanic language of *Medatia* or a *Popol vuh* dialogue, or like characters in a Cherokee or a Cuna cure. Embodying the natural philosophy in the Quito Declaration, they appeal to the human delegations of the Fourth World as the ones who have most cared to listen and have least "hidden their face" from the manifest text.

Abbreviations Used
in Notes and Bibliography

AA	*American Antiquity*
ADV	Akademische Druck und Verlagsanstalt, Graz
AGN	Archivo General de la Nación, México
APS	American Philosophical Society, Philadelphia
BAE	Bureau of American Ethnology, Washington
BM	British Museum, London
CCAMA	Corpus Codicum Americanorum Medii Aevi, ed. E. Menguin, Copenhagen: E. Munksgaard
Census	of Mesoamerican texts, pictographic (Glass 1975; nos. 1–) and alphabetic (Gibson and Glass 1975; nos. 1000–), in HMAI
Cham.	"A summary of possible astronomical information in Plains Indian calendars," V. D. Chamberlain 1984:4–11
Dewd.	"Inventory of Birchbark scrolls and charts," Dewdney 1975:183–91
ECM	*Estudios de cultura maya,* México: UNAM
ECN	*Estudios de cultura náhuatl,* México: UNAM
FCE	Fondo de Cultura Económica, México
HMAI	*Handbook of Middle American Indians,* general ed. R. Wauchope, Austin: University of Texas Press. 16 vols., 1964–76. Supplements, 1981–
HNAI	*Handbook of North American Indians,* general ed. W. C. Sturtevant, Washington, DC: Smithsonian Institution, 1978–
HSAI	*Handbook of South American Indians,* general ed. Julian H. Steward, Washington, DC. BAE Bull. 143, 7 vols., 1946–50 (reprinted 1963)
ICA	International Congress of Americanists / Congres International des Americanistes / Congreso internacional de americanistas
III	Instituto Indigenista Interamericano / Interamerican Indigenist Institute, México
ITC	Instituto tlaxcalteca de cultura
Kram.	"Systematic catalogue of selected works of Cuna literature," Kramer 1970:143–54

NG   *National Geographic Magazine* (Washington, DC)
QGA   Quellenwerke zur alten Geschichte Amerikas aufgezeichnet in den
            Sprachen der Eingeborenen. Berlin: Ibero-Amerikanisches Institut
UNAM   Universidad Nacional Autónoma de México, México

Notes

Prologue

1. At the opening of the XII Interamerican Congress of Philosophy in Buenos Aires in 1989, as if anticipating indigenist disbelief, the much-respected Leopoldo Zea asserted that "American philosophy began with its history under the sign of dependence, on 12th October 1492" (reported in *Excelsior,* México, 13 August 1989). This despite fundamental studies by Mariátegui (1926), M. León-Portilla (1956), and many others; on current signs of change, see the Epilogue. The three-world *mappamundi* is described in Bagrow 1964.
2. Statistics prepared by Utta von Gleich (Textual Authenticity Conference, Iberoamerkanisches Institut, Berlin, December 1988) reveal a close link in Latin America between indigenist policy and law on the one hand and broader ideology on the other. Socialism in Peru under Velasco led to the declaration of Quechua as a second official language in 1975, and in Nicaragua it has promoted Misquito and other native languages; by contrast, by Decree 4002 (1980) the dictator Pinochet prohibited all use of Mapuche in Chilean education from the primary level upward. Though in practice it is the main language of Paraguay, Guarani awaits official recognition. In the USA, Ward Churchill offers an excellent critique of New Right hostility to Indians and Indian studies in a review of James Clifton's obnoxious *The Invented Indian: Cultural fictions and government policies,* New York, 1990 ("The New Racism," *Wicazo Sa* [Eastern Washington University, Cheney] 7 [1991]: 51–9).
3. Signally so in the case of the Atacama mummies dated to 6000 B.C., according to press reports (e.g., *Guardian,* 22 June 1985). The Lévi-Strauss quotation is from "Race and History" (1978:338–9), originally "Race et histoire" in a UNESCO publication of 1952. A recent survey by Greenberg (1987), corroborated, it seems, by genetic evidence (*Scientific American,* November

1991, 72–9), reaffirms the coherence of American languages; Greenberg distinguishes eleven major subgroups in South, Middle, and North America and discusses separately the special case of Na-dene or Athapaskan.

4. Brody 1966:x; George Manuel, *The Fourth World: An Indian reality,* New York: Free Press, 1974. On Fourth World politics in Canada, see Noel Dyck, *Indigenous Peoples and the Nation-State,* St John's: Institute of Social and Economic Research, Memorial University of Newfoundland, 1985; the concept of the Fourth World of Renaissance cartography is referred to in my paper on grammatology (1986a; originally published in Colchester in 1984). Among the continental collections and accounts of Fourth World literature we may note Brinton's Library of Aboriginal American Literature (1882–90 (7 vols. by, among others, him, Hale [1883], and Gatschet [1884]), Borsari 1888, Alcina Franch 1957, Péret 1960, Montoya and Cardenal 1966, Arias Larreta 1968, Bierhorst 1974, Brotherston 1979, and Muñoz 1983.

5. The cumulative result of decades of patient work in regional groups like Americans Before Columbus and the Parlamento Indoamericano del Cono Sur and within world bodies like UNESCO and the International Labor Organization. I owe my copy of the Declaration to Peter Hulme, who received his copy from Gesa Mackentun.

6. Native leaders fomented the will to rebel by placing mutilated effigies of Spaniards in irrigation canals and by concealing reserves of maize, which had become scarce because of disease that afflicted the grain in the wake of the eclipse: Sigüenza y Góngora, *Alboroto y motín* . . . (1984:95–144). Zapata's Nahuatl manifestos have been edited by M. León-Portilla (1978) and are drawn in graffiti on walls in Tepoztlan (*tocepan tiaquiz ihuan temoc*). Jacinto Canek, the subject of Abreu Gómez's celebrated novel, took the names of both Moctezuma and Uc Canek, the last Itza ruler at Peten (Bricker 1981; Schele and Freidel 1990); on his significance in the nineteenth-century Caste War of Yucatan, see Reed 1964; Roldán Peniche Barrera, *La sublevación del brujo Jacinto Canek,* Mérida: Maldonado, 1986; and Paul R. Sullivan, *Unfinished Conversations: Maya and foreigners between two wars,* New York: Knopf, 1989. On the Andes, see Rappaport 1990; J. L. Phelan, *The People and the King: The Comunero rebellion in Colombia in 1761,* Madison: University of Wisconsin Press, and Valcárcel 1971 (Tupac Amaru). The last includes the range of the Andean leader's speeches and proclamations, from the early call to *desamparar,* or withdraw services from the Spanish, to the coronation edict (which caught the attention of the Foreign Office in London). Tecun Uman features in the sixteenth-century Quiché titles of Huitzitzil Tzunun and Ixcuin Nehaib (HMAI Census 1175, 1176); cf. Carmack 1973.

7. When already or not otherwise specified, details of native works may be found in the first section of the Bibliography.

8. A precise review of the changing situation is given in *América Indígena* (the III journal) 50 (1991), especially in "Indigenismo: Recuento y perspectiva" (pp. 63–91) and "La nueva política y estrategia de acción: Lengua, educación y cultura" (pp. 93–116). Modifying Decree 107 (1957) with Decree

169 (1989), the International Labor Organization speaks now of the peoples rather than the populations of America and recognize their "territories" as well as their lands (p. 82). For further details of new educational plans and practice, see Rodríguez 1983 and Zúñiga 1987.

Part I: Text

Epigraphs: Sherzer & Urban 1986:188 (line 285); K. T. Preuss 1921:166; Bierhorst 1985:220; Arzápalo 1987:292; Stuart 1989:153. Throughout, the sources given are for the native text; the English translations are the author's, based in most cases on the secondary sources listed.

Chapter 1: Provenance

1. Quoted by E. Carrasco (1983:5); an excellent map of this latent America is provided in Coe, Snow, and Benson 1986.
2. See the report on the "Primer encuentro del Caribe amerindio" in September 1988 in *Pueblos y políticas en el Caribe amerindio* (1990), edited by the III. Haiti's modern border with the Dominican Republic coincides with an ancient division between Arawak and Carib on Haiti, once the name for all of the island of Hispaniola; on this and language distribution generally, see the excellent survey *América Latina en sus lenguas indígenas* edited by Bernard Pottier (1983; map, p. 197). Focusing chiefly on the Taino and Arawak, José Juan Arrom pieces together the story of the islands from surviving artifacts and rereadings of Columbus, Las Casas, Anglería, and Pané (*Mitología y artes prehispánicas de las Antillas,* 1989); see also Fouchard 1972 and Antonio Benítez Rojo's homage to the Arawak goddess Atabey in Pérez Firmat 1990:85–106. The traducing of the Carib story is keenly analyzed by Peter Hulme in his *Colonial Encounters: Europe and the native Caribbean 1492–1797* (1986). Texts from the corpus of mainland Carib narratives have been edited by Koch-Grünberg (1924), Armellada (1972), Civrieux (1980), and Guss (1985).
3. In the annals of the highland Cakchiquel, whose former capital Chichicastenango lies at the head of the Motagua, the start of modern times coincides with the European entry into the Caribbean in 1493, "One Ah" in their calendar of 400-day years (Recinos, Goetz, and Chonay 1953:107). The *Popol vuh* manuscript of their Quiché neighbors was found at Chichicastenango. The *Chilam Balam* view of the east was affected by the unsuccessful exhortations to the Maya to convert to Christianity made at Cozumel by Cortes in 1519, before he landed at Veracruz (Roys 1967:119).
4. The main sources here are Nordenskiöld (1928, 1930, 1938) and Wassén (1937, 1938, etc.), which include texts authored by the Cuna president Nele Kantule (notably the *Tatkan ikala* [Nordenskiöld 1938:125–244]) and his secretary Rubén Pérez Kantule, who was brought to Sweden by Nordenskiöld. Also Kramer 1970:93–100; Howe 1986:51–6; Leander 1970; and C. Severi's analysis of "deux représentations du Blanc dans la tradition

chamanique cuna," *L'Homme* 28 (1968): 174–83. The question of the Cuna, their Cueva antecedents, and Panama is discussed by C. O. Sauer in his monumental *The Early Spanish Main,* which also cites Trimborn on the subject of their "forgotten kingdoms" (1966:226–9, 255). Montoya Sánchez includes stories by present-day Cuna in Colombia and a Carib–Catio view of them (1973:35–40, 70–1). For the Kogi, see K. T. Preuss 1919–27 and Reichel-Dolmatoff 1950–1. On Panamanian artifacts found in the Great Cenote, see M. D. Coe 1966:127–8.

5. Alexander von Humboldt (1810) was among the first to map the vigesimal number base in America. On the thirteen birds, or Quecholli, of Mesoamerica, see Table 1; for the Carib and Chibcha birds, see Koch-Grünberg 1907 and Brotherston 1979a. The Maya–Carib etymology of "hurricane" has only recently been assured; on this and the one-legged Bird Man figure, cf. Chapter 9, n. 3. Elsewhere "one leg" is Orion or Ursa Major, and its plurality of reference becomes the subject of a joke, at the expense of German pedantry, in Mario de Andrade's "Carib" novel *Macunaima.* Double-ego or "alter ego" stelae are published in Squier 1852 (Nicaragua); Hay, Linton, Lothrop, Shapiro, and Vaillant 1977 (1940): 213; Cuadra 1971; and K. T. Preuss 1929. The quartz crystals of the Carib appear in *Medatia* (Guss 1985), of the Maya in the *Popol vuh,* line 8147, and of the Kogi in Reichel-Dolmatoff 1971:48. As for manioc, the eastern boundary of the Chibcha coincides roughly with the western limit of bitter manioc; on this and on the ballgame in Haiti, see Sauer 1966:53–4, 241; 1975:197.

6. See Tables 2 and 5. An intelligent discussion of Mesoamerica and its continuities can be found in Monjarás Ruiz (1987), which gathers ancient and modern texts from the area, and in López Austin 1990:24–41.

7. Brinton 1883; Cid Pérez and Martí 1964; González Casanova 1977.

8. The significance of this text (Census 350) has recently been enhanced by the recovery of the Glasgow MS (1580; edited by Acuña 1984), which extends the geographical range of previously known versions; see Brotherston and Gallegos 1990.

9. See Chapter 10, n. 4. Schele and Freidel 1990 takes account of recent decipherments of Classic texts, of which Ian Graham has been making a complete photographic record since the mid-1970s for the Peabody Museum of Harvard University (*Corpus of Maya Hieroglyphic Inscriptions,* 1978–). The hieroglyphic books are customarily named after the European cities that now house them: Dresden, Paris, and Madrid; a fourth book now in Mexico has been dubbed the *Grolier Codex.* All are collected in Lee 1985; Barrera Vásquez and Rendón 1963 provides the standard Spanish text of the *Chilam Balam Books.*

10. Cid Pérez and Martí 1964; Acuña 1975; Edmonson 1985; Padial Guerchoux and Vásquez-Bigi 1991. Following Las Casas, Edmonson notes a Kekchi parallel to the *Popol vuh* (1971:142). The Maximon cult referred to above is examined by E. M. Mendelsohn, *Los escándalos de Maximón* (Guatemala City, 1965).

11. On Mesoamerica's eastern frontier, see Hay et al. 1977, Newson 1987:25,

and John W. Fox, "The Late Post-Classic Eastern Frontier of Mesoamerica," *Current Anthropology* 22 (1981): 321–46.

12. Barlow (1949) pioneered the geography of these texts, whose ritual structure of quarters is discussed in Chapter 3 below (see n. 15).

13. In the edition by Aguilera and León-Portilla (1986), the Tlatelolco map is identified with Tenochtitlan itself, rather than Tlatelolco, and is dated to 1550; for *Xolotl Maps,* Dibble 1980.

14. Screenfold texts include *Borbonicus* and the *Aztlan Annals;* transcriptions into Nahuatl include the celebrated *Inomaca tonatiuh* and *Inin cuic. Inomaca tonatiuh* ("the sun itself") is how the *Legend* names itself; *Inin cuic* ("the hymns") is taken from the introductory phrase in the manuscript that comes after the formula *nican mitoa* ("here is told"), which Garibay translated as "the hymns with which they honored their gods"; yet mysteriously this phrase is omitted from the standard editions in German (Seler), Spanish (Garibay), and English (Brinton), though Garibay does include it, untranslated, in his edition of the *Florentine* text (México: Porrúa, 1956).

15. Galarza 1972; M. Oettinger and F. Horcasitas, *The Lienzo of Petlacala,* APS *Transactions* 72, pt. 7, Philadelphia, 1982; C. Vega, "Los códices de Tlachinollan," in Martínez Marín 1989:130–48.

16. M. León-Portilla 1985; further reasons for favoring this provenance are given in Chapter 3 ("Quatrefoil").

17. A gesture of enormous political significance, as Jaecklein has pointed out (1978:33–5; see also Brotherston 1985). Dupaix's engravings of Tepexic, omitted from Humboldt's selection in *Vues des cordillères,* were reproduced in H. Baradère's *Antiquités méxicaines: Relation des trois expeditions de Dupaix* (Paris, 1834), where the town is accounted "au nombre des plus grands ouvrages qui soient au sol méxicain," and in vol. 4 of Kingsborough's *Antiquities,* grossly redrawn. Now Alcina Franch's claim (Guillermo Dupaix: *Expedición acerca de los antiguos monumentos de la Nueva España 1805–8,* Madrid, 1969, vol. 2, pl. 1) for the primacy of the Seville copy of Dupaix's engravings wrongly dates the Baradère edition 1844 and disregards the clearly superior quality of its prints. Initiated by Gorenstein, Merlo, Castillo, and others, archaeology at the site in 1991 yielded ceramic dates from well back into the Classic (Alfredo Dumaine, reported by Druzo Maldonado, pers. commun.). On the occurrence of Tepexic's place sign in native books, not least its own annals (*Vindobonensis* obverse), see Table 3. Candles burned at the site today are clues to native devotion. The Popolocan language area, which underlies the definition of Papaloapan, is mapped in Veeerman-Leichsenring 1984:15.

18. Coatlan annals, inscribed in stone, and a copy of the map are on display in the Cuernavaca Museum; the map, whose borders interface with those in *Mendoza* (Cuauhnahuac, Malinalco, Tlachco), is reproduced in Kenneth G. Hirth and Ann Cyphers Guillén, *Tiempo y asentamiento en Xochicalco,* UNAM, 1988.

19. Tlaxcala hence offered Cortes his bridgehead. For varying native accounts of the "peacefulness" of his entry in the *Tlaxcala Lienzo* (whose longer

version is, where appropriate, called the *Tlaxcala Codex*) and in the *Huamantla Codex* (pieced together and edited for the first time by Aguilera [1984]), see Brotherston and Gallegos 1990.

20. Remote antecedents in Monte Alban for Tenochtitlan's empire, down to continuity of toponymical detail, are noted by Marcus 1980 and Flannery and Marcus 1983. On Mixtec place signs, see Smith 1973; "Shonda vee," a modern Mazatec story told by Evaristo Venegas (Inchaustegui 1977:100–4), names over sixty features of Mazatec territory in Zongolica and the mid Papaloapan.

21. The title of Lumholtz's classic account of the area (1902). On the Nahua name of the Red Temple Chichitlicalli, north of Pima on the road from Culiacan to Cibola, see Sauer 1971:134; towns settled by the Tlaxcalans in Chimalhuacan (New Galicia) and noted in the *Lienzo* include Colotla (1591) and Mezquitic (1592). A useful collection of twentieth-century texts from this area is included in Benítez 1967–70 and in turn in Zaid 1973, along with unpublished texts. Of the Purepecha maps, the best known is that of Jucutacato (Census 177); starting out from Veracruz, it shows the introduction of metalworking. On this area in general, see Seler 1902–23, 3:33–156. Attested in the *Plancarte* manuscript of Pablo Cuiru (Census 1107) and other sources, Purepecha interest in Cibola is noted in Monjarás Ruiz 1987:209, 217.

22. The vast hill site at La Quemada dominates the broad valley of Zacatecas and is known to include seven caves; first mapped by Karl Nebel in the late nineteenth century, it is now dated to between the second and sixth centuries A.D. (It stands at the effective northern limit of Nahua town names today.) On the historical geography of the Chichimeca, see Powell 1975, and on the Huichol, A. Shelton, "Huichol Natural Philosophy," in McCaskill 1989:339–54. Juan Negrín (1975, 1985) has given excellent accounts of materials used in Huichol paintings, like colored yarn, as well as their structure and significance as cosmic maps. (He notes that Huichol was identical with Nahuatl in 1000 B.C.) Traditional disk designs that form a clear antecedent of the yarn paintings are noted by P. Furst (1968) and are published in Lumholtz 1986:51–93.

23. T. R. McGuire notes how the divine map of Rahem was copied back from Edward Spicer's publication of it and used for political defense in the singing of the boundary (*Politics and Ethnicity on the Rio Yaqui: Potam revisited,* Tucson, 1986, p. 54). Tarahumara sermons are read as means of social cohesion by W. L. Merrill, *Rarámuri: Souls, knowledge and social process in northern Mexico,* Washington, DC: Smithsonian Institution, 1986. Pima-Papago records are published in Underhill 1938 and Russell 1975; Margolin 1981 gathers Californian texts.

24. The term is used here to refer to the cultures of the U.S. Southwest generally, including those on the southern rim, like Mogollon and Hohokam (which boasts a ball court from Mexico of 300 B.C.: HNAI 9:89); map in NG 162 (1982): 566–7. On Zuni as Cibola, see HNAI 9:178, 189 (map); and on its water skater, see D. Tedlock 1972:297. Its seven cities are shown in the *Tlaxcala Lienzo* in a design that recalls the seven caves, or Púpsövi, of

the Hopi (Waters 1963:76, 90) and the 4 + 3 Navajo mountains arranged in a similar *kiva* shape (Reichard 1963:21). In the sixteenth century, the area coincided with "Le gran Teguaio" (from Tewa) of the *Delisle Map* (Sauer 1971:203). The very early dates for the cultivation of squash (3500 B.C. Bat Cave) and beans and maize (1500 B.C.), plus irrigation methods, establish a sharp frontier eastward to Texas (HNAI 9:47). Archaeologically the area centers on the 5,000-km^2 settlement at Gran Chaco.

25. Valdez and Steiner 1972; on the Tewa, Spinden 1933; on Moctezuma among them and nineteenth-century eastern Pueblos, Bierhorst 1985:106. The "vanished" Hohokam of the Pima ancestors is discussed by Russell (1975), who also reproduces their Year Counts; he further shows how Phoenix was sited near where the Pima epic hero was burned to ashes before the birth of his son.

26. Knowledge imparted by Gray Eyes, Miguelito, Klah, and other painter-scribes is drawn on in fundamental studies by Klah (1942), Reichard (1963, 1977), Newcomb and Reichard (1975); on antecedents among Hopi and on wider practice, see Wyman 1970, 1983, 1983a; Parezo 1983. The east and west oceans and the four guardian mountains are illustrated in Wyman 1983:100, 174; on pp. 112–13 there is a map of former and present-day Navajo territory.

27. Franz Boas, quoted in Bierhorst 1985:8; on the imagery of totem poles and their mask faces, see Barbeau 1950, 1951; Gunn 1965; Lévi-Strauss 1975–9; HNAI 15 (*The Northwest*). Dorn 1966 gives a highly perceptive account of the Shoshoneans, the Sun Dance ceremony and songs, the Basin and Plateau, and the modern predicament of Indians in the USA.

28. Peter Matthiesen dedicated to these parts of the USA his *Indian Country* (1987) and *Killing Mr. Watson* (1990). Chekilli's Muskogee narrative is reconstructed in Gatschet 1884; Cherokee texts are in Mooney 1891, 1898, reissued in one volume in 1982 (Cherokee, NC: Museum of the Cherokee Indian). See also Swanton 1979; Hudson 1984; and G. E. Lankford, *Southeastern Legends,* Little Rock, AR: August House, 1987.

29. Morgan 1851; Wilson 1959; Wallace 1969. The texts of the main rite of the League, that of Condolence, constitute one of the "masterworks" edited by Bierhorst (1974).

30. Barbeau 1960:225–6; C. Taylor 1990:pl. 10. I am grateful to Colin Taylor for sharing his expertise on this matter with me. The "Cahokia" gloss is discussed in Chapter 7, n. 13. On Oneota and Winnebago, Radin 1970, and on the Illinois skins, E.-T. Hamy, "Note sur d'anciennes peintures sur peaux des indiens illinois," *Journal de la Société des Américanistes* (Paris) 2 (1897–8): 183–93.

31. Principal censuses of Winter Counts appear in Howard 1979, McCoy 1983, V. D. Chamberlain 1984; see also C. Taylor 1990 and Wildhage 1990. On the Sun Dance as effective history, Mooney 1979:153.

32. The title of Roger Williams's famous guide of 1643; see Brotherston, "A Controversial Guide to the Language of America," in *1642: Literature and power in the seventeenth century,* ed. F. Barker and P. Hulme, vol. 2, Colchester: University of Essex, 1981, pp. 84–101.

33. Skinner and Satterlee 1915:240 (also S. Thompson 1966 [1929]: 12; School-craft 1851–7, 4:379). Siksika: Grinnell 1962. Algonkin names are promi-nent among those discussed in John P. Harrington, "The Origin of Our State-Names," *Journal of the Washington Academy of Sciences* 34, 8 (1944): 255–9.

34. Drawing centrally on the scrolls of Eshkwaykeezhik (James Red Sky), Dewdney demonstrates how the geographical focus of the scrolls provides the clue to the very identity of the Ojibway as Ashinaubeg (1975:167). As Nishnawbe-Aski, the same concept today also defines the Ojibway–Cree territory defended by the Grand Council Treaty Nine in northern Ontario. For Everwind's reference to Mexico, Dewdney 1975:57. The Mide water-shed emerges also in Lévi-Strauss 1964–71, 3: fig. 25. A version of this same Algonkin script, locally known as *babebibo,* has been kept up by the Kickapoo, who fled to Mexico (R. E. Ritzenthaler and Fred A. Peterson, *The Mexican Kickapoo Indians,* Milwaukee: Public Museum, 1956; Green-wood reprint, 1970).

35. Mooney 1896; on the preceding massacres, Brown 1971. For a native view, see Deloria's Custer manifesto (1969) and his *God Is Red* (1973). The musi-cal scores of Dakota, Pawnee, Arapaho, and other ghost songs are pub-lished in N. Curtis 1923:45–50.

36. A facsimile edition of Guaman Poma's work was published in Paris in 1936 and is the source of page citations throughout; a scholarly edition is pro-vided by Murra and Adorno (1980). Editions of the Huarochiri manuscript include those of Trimborn (1939–41), who suggested the first-line title *Runa yndio;* Arguedas (1966); and G. Taylor 1987; cf. Hartmann 1990.

37. Clearly reproduced and described in Willey 1974:316–17; cf. Benson 1971.

38. For assessments of the recently discovered Moche burials at Sipan, see "New Royal Tomb Unearthed," NG 177, 6 (1990): 2–17 and 17–33; on Chimu/Chimor, Michael Moseley et al., *The Northern Dynasties: Kingship and statecraft in Chimor,* Washington, DC: Dumbarton Oaks, 1990. Ceramic and other designs are reproduced in Kutscher 1954 and Larco Hoyle 1965. On the roads, see John Hyslop, *The Inka Road System,* New York, 1984. Mural painting throughout the area is surveyed in Bonavia 1985.

39. Guaman Poma, p. 112, one of Huayna Capac's campaigns; Wright 1984:37. Maritime communication with Mexico has now been yet more firmly proven in Dorothy Hosler et al., *Axe Monies and Their Relatives,* Studies in Pre-Columbian Art and Archaeology 30, Washington, DC: Dumbarton Oaks, 1990. The vigor of the Inca tradition as far north as the Sibundoy valley in Colombia, where the Cuzco variety of Quechua continues to be spoken, is brought out in McDowell's *Sayings of the Ancestors* (1989).

40. Originally told by the priests of Mama Ocllo, Murúa's version of this story is found in Markham 1873 and Krickeberg 1928:262–6.

41. Zuidema 1989:349–51.

42. Powerful examples of *tahuantinsuyu* ideology that survives today, including the notable geoanatomical cult of Inkarri, are noted by Arguedas 1975, Rama 1982, and Howard-Malverde 1986.

43. Told by an anonymous old man from the high mountains (*huin kul*) and published in Kössler-Ilg's remarkably rich collection of narratives (1956: 117–29), which also includes Antülwen's *Cristo Colón* (pp. 237–42) and the Shaihueke's account of Mapuche origins (pp. 159–67). A version of the Shumpall story has been studied by Hugo Carrasco (1989); cf. Iván Carrasco 1988, a useful account of the literature of the Chilean Mapuche. On place names, see Julio Figueroa, *Vocabulario etimológico de nombres chilenos,* Santiago, 1903, and E. W. Moesbach, *Voz de Arauco,* Santiago: ISF, 1960, a work prepared together with the Mapuche "maestro" Pascual Coña that suggests Coquimbo as the absolute northern limit of that language and, in addition to the highest peak, Threng-threng, lists others nearer the Pacific coast, at Maullín, Angol, Arauco, etc. (p. 250).

44. Kössler-Ilg 1956:167–73; E. S. Zeballos, *La dinastía de los Piedra,* Buenos Aires, 1884. Pascual Coña's *Testimonio de un cacique mapuche* (dictated to Moesbach and edited by Rodolfo Lenz in 1930 [Santiago: Imprenta Cervantes]) has been reissued (Santiago: Pehuén 1984).

45. See Kössler-Ilg 1956 for the references to ferrying whales (p. 224) and to trees, as grandfather (p. 48), of vision (p. 75), with heart (p. 81). For Patagonia, see Gusinde 1977 and Pueñ's dream of the pampa, in Kössler-Ilg 1956:29–38.

46. In Tupi-Guarani, the title means "fine speech" (Tupi itself is known as Nheen Gheta; the book's subtitle deliberately alludes to the Black Decameron of Leo Frobenius); Hemming 1987 details the invasion. Good surveys of published rainforest texts are provided by Vázquez 1978 and Bierhorst 1988; for those of Pacaraima and the Orinoco, see Civrieux 1970, 1980; Armellada 1972, 1973; Overing 1975; Guss 1985, 1989; Albert 1988.

47. *Bukura keti,* ancient stories, as transmitted by Reichel-Dolmatoff (1971) (from Antonio Guzmán); Montoya Sánchez 1973:104–8 (Wainambi narrative of José Arango, descendant of Diakala Baraku); Hugh-Jones 1979:263– 308; Juan Gallo, *Diccionario Tucano–Castellano,* Mitú, Vaupes: Prefectura Apostólica, 1972. The astronomical significance of the Pira-parana boulder is analyzed in Reichel-Dolmatoff, "Astronomical Models of Social Behaviour among Some Indians of Colombia," in Aveni and Urton 1982:168. Umusin Panlon's narrative was translated into Portuguese by his son and Bertha Ribeiro.

48. César Bardales, *Quimisha incabo ini yoia: Leyendas de los Shipibo–Conibo sobre los tres Incas,* Comunidades y Culturas indígenas, no. 12, Yarinacocha, Pucallpa, 1979; Roe 1982; "Cumancaya myth" (native text), E. Weisshaar and B. Illius, in Illius and Laubscher 1990, 1:578–85 (esp. p. 582, n. 22). Reichel-Dolmatoff (1971:253) records the Desana account of how Andean goldworking techniques were brought to them. Campa: Varese 1968; Weiss 1975. Napo: Santos, Ortiz 1976. Formerly known as Jivaro, the Shuar have begun to publish their own mythology in bilingual editions (Pellizaro 1979), as have the Aguaruna (Chumap 1979). Upper-Amazon ceramics are analyzed in Lathrap 1970.

49. Huxley 1956:10; see also Métraux 1928; Wagley and Galvão 1949; Pereira

1951; Cadogan 1959, 1965; D. Ribeiro 1971, 1974; Roa Bastos 1978; Riester 1984; F. G. Sturm, "The Concepts of History and Destiny Implicit in the Apapokuva–Guarani myth of the Creation and Destruction of the Earth," in M. Preuss 1989:61–6. Nimuendajú's translations are included in Bareiro Saguier's magnificent survey of Guarani literature (1980).

50. Villas Boas 1972; Agostinho 1974; Carmichael 1983; Basso 1985, 1987. Photographs of Quarup flute players are in Hopper 1967: pls. 9–12 (cf. the Brazilian film *Quarup,* based on the novel of the same name by Antonio Callado, Rio: Civilizaçao Brasileira; 1967). The publication of rainforest literature begins with Montaigne's 1580 essay "Of the Cannibatles" and was an avowed aim of the nineteenth-century Americanists in Brazil (see Brotherston 1972), yet texts became accessible only with the Carib, Witoto, and Guarani narratives mediated by Koch-Grünberg (1924), K.T. Preuss (1921), and Cadogan 1969 (which draws on Onkel/Nimuendajú's rare edition of 1944). They are meticulously surveyed by J. A. Vázquez (1978) and synthesized by Roe (1982).

Chapter 2: Language and its instances

1. Lévi-Strauss 1972:186–205; first as "L'efficacité symbolique," in *Revue de l'Histoire de Religions* 135 (1949): 5–27, which cites N. M. Holmer and S. H. Wassén, *Mu-Igala, or The Way of Muu* (Göteborg: Etnografiska Museum, 1947) as its source text; for the "complete" *Mu ikala,* see Holmer and Wassén 1953. An earlier version of this argument appears in my "Towards a Grammatology of America" (1986).

2. Zuidema 1982. Other critiques include Kramer 1970:12, Weiss 1975 (quoted by Vázquez 1978:259); Derrida 1976 (the edition used here for quotations); W. Rowe 1984. In the articles on "historical legends" that Lévi-Strauss contributed to HSAI 3 (1948): 321–48, no link is made with what he defines as myth; he analyzes his substitution of "sans-écriture" for "primitive" in "Comparative Religions and Nonliterate Peoples" (1978:60–9).

3. Sherzer argues that the "basic unit of Kuna narration is the line" ("Poetic Structuring of Kuna Discourse," in Sherzer and Woodbury 1987:103–39); Harriet Klein makes similar findings with Toba texts (Sherzer and Urban 1986:213–36), and Laura Graham notes that Shavante oratory involves "parallelistic repetition of lines" (ibid., pp. 83–118). See also D. Tedlock 1972; Bahr 1975; Hymes 1977, 1981, and "Tonkawa Poetics," in Sherzer and Woodbury 1987:17–61; Sherzer 1983.

4. Examples from the Soto and Guajiro traditions are quoted in P. Mason 1990:164.

5. Helbig 1984; *timehri* and other graphic designs are illustrated in the works of Reichel-Dolmatoff (1971) and Hugh-Jones (1979). Among the Wayapi, Campbell records how the Tupi term *ekosiware* denotes such designs, applied to ceramics or body skin or legible in the markings of jaguar and anaconda (1989:59).

6. Mallery 1893:328, where it is the final glyph; Negrín 1975:38. HSAI 4:262–3 illustrates Cuna balsa boards (*molas* and house); see also Chapter 1, n. 4.

7. For Stela J from Copan and the tongue as pen at Tikal, see Figures 51, 23; the Illinois deerskin, call no. 7832131, is in Hamy 1897–8:183 (Chapter 1, n. 30). An early study of the Powhatan mantle, in the Ashmolean Museum, Oxford, is that of the "father of English anthropology," E. B. Tyler (in *Internationales Archiv für Ethnologie* 1 [1888]: 215). On the "woven" verbal text, see Guss 1989.

8. Such is the opinion of McCoy (1983) and DeMallie (pers. commun.); Chamberlain (1984) provides a clear and updated list, subsuming J. Howard (1979). Umusin Panlon's work provides Angel Rama with the core of his argument in chap. 2 of his *Transculturación narrativa en América Latina* (1982:71–93). Referring to the cosmogonical chant of the Shawnee, Brinton noted that they "say that to repeat it to a white man would bring disaster on their nation" and added, with sublime scientific insensitivity: "I mention it as a piece of aboriginal composition most desirable to secure" (1884:145). Zolbrod (*Dine bahane,* 1984) found similar admonishment among the Navajo when restoring parts of their creation story that had been suppressed by Washington Matthews in his *Navaho Legends* (1897), and in making versions of their paintings Anasazi and Huichol scribes usually change or withhold given details (Matthews also noted that permanent icons would cause "quarrels": cited in Wyman 1983:42); politically, dry paintings served to cleanse Anasazi during the rising against the Spanish in 1680–92. In the rainforest there is a current notion that the telling and selling of the last story will bring the end of the world. Shamanist in origin, this valuing of the text is the Mesoamerican and Tahuantinsuyu practice of counting songs among items of tribute rendered by a defeated nation; and it ultimately relates to the hunter's capture not so much of a body prey as its imagination and voice – hence the "song lines" drawn from heart to mouth in Turtle Island and Anasazi texts (Brotherston 1979:263). The phenomenon as a whole is discussed by Eliade (1964) and is touched on in a recent article by Santos Granero (1986).

9. A concept used, for example, by H. Carrasco (1989: Mapuche); similar approaches are taken by T. Abler, "Dendrogram and Celestial Tree: Numerical taxonomy and variants of the Iroquian creation myth," in McCaskill 1989:195–222; Bareiro Saguier (1980: Guarani); R. Howard (1990: Quechua). For the Siksika, see Grinnell 1892, 1962.

10. René Acuña deserves recognition for having attempted to demolish these three works single-handed; see respectively his publications of 1984, objected to by, among others, Martínez Marín, "La fuente original del Lienzo de Tlaxcala" (in Martínez Marín 1989:147–58), and Brotherston and Gallegos (1990); 1975, *Introducción al estudio del Rabinal Achi,* deemed "absurd" by Edmonson (1985); and 1983, "El Popol vuh, Vico y la theologia indorum" (in Carmack and Morales 1983:1–16), found implausible by D. Tedlock (1988) and Himmelblau 1989:66.

11. Dewdney, "Inventory of Birchbark Scrolls and Charts" (1975:183–92);

Kramer, "Systematic Catalogue of Selected Works of Cuna Literature" (1970:128–41), which includes unpublished manuscripts in the Göteborg Museum of Ethnology and sound recordings.

12. Radin 1954–6, an early study that was important in preparing the way for comparisons between epic texts, above all within North America; see Chapter 11 ("The northern trance journey"). Hymns: J. H. Rowe 1953; Garibay 1958 (cf. n 31 below). Cures: Maya: See the epigraph to Part I (Arzápalo 1987); Nahuatl: Andrews and Hassig 1984:154 (i.e. speaker's reference as Cipactonal to *inamox innotezcauh* 'my book my mirror', Fifth Tratado, chap. 3, and to the *tonalamatl* apparatus found in Otomí native-paper books today); Carib: Armellada 1972:46 (on Makunaima's invention and tracing out of the road of the *taren* formulas); Cherokee: Mooney 1898 (Kanaheta Ani-Tsalagi – ancient Cherokee formulas – written by shamans in the Cherokee syllabary). Riddles: true to a Europeanist bias, Franz Boas fostered the widespread and erroneous notion that in America riddle literature (like epic poetry) was a late (post-Columbian) import: "Literature, Music, and Dance," *General Anthropology*, Boston: Heath, 1938, pp. 598–9; in the chapter of Mapuche riddles recorded by Kössler-Ilg (1956:293–300), the European type and procedure are in fact explicitly contrasted with native ones (Gisela Beutler has written perceptively on riddles in America: *Adivinanzas españolas de la tradición popular actual de México*, Wiesbaden: Steiner, 1979; see also Chapter 13, nn. 20–2). Literary critics who, like Ivor Winters's pupil A. G. Day (1951), have wished simply to impose a Western taxonomy of genre on native texts have for that reason been less successful; see Garibay's incisive comments in the introduction to his *Historia de la literatura náhuatl* (1953–4).

13. Brotherston 1979:63–9: *Totecuyoane,* my translation from the Nahuatl, Lehmann's German (1949), and M. León-Portilla's Spanish (1986). *Quipu* burning: Duviols 1977. Guaraní: N. González 1958:23–32. Mide "pagan libraries": Dewdney 1975:72; Brotherston 1981 (chap. 1, n. 32). The term "charter" is used here not in Malinowski's ungenerous sense of self-justification but of cosmic exegesis and historical validation. In making this point in respect of rainforest texts, Weiss (1975) also strongly takes issue with Lévi-Strauss and his ahistoricism.

14. M. León-Portilla 1956 gives a thorough account of the philosophy of the Nahuatl scribe and iconic script; the term was adopted by Nowotny as the title of his study of 1961, which in most essentials has not been surpassed. When introducing his wood-block plates of *Mendoza* (1625:1065–1107), the first extensive example of a *tlacuilolli* text to be printed, Purchas enthused about the capacities of this writing, which "so fully express[es] so much without letters."

15. Alfonso Caso, "Zapotec writing and calendar" and "Mixtec writing and calendar." HMAI 3 (1965); G. Whittaker, in Aveni and Brotherston 1983: 101–34. On Izapa, Norman 1976; on Chalcatzingo, Grove 1984.

16. Loo 1987 (see my comment in 1988:283); Ursula Dyckerhoff, "La historia de curación antigua de San Pablito Pahuatlan," *Indiana* 9 (1984): 69–86.

17. Gourd: The so-called Birger figurine is discussed as a Mississippian artifact in Galloway 1989. The Chimu runner is in Kutscher 1954: pl. 29. Faced joints, a feature of the *Sunstone,* Coatlicue (Fernández 1954) and the Chavin Caiman Stela (Tello 1952), occur alike in Alaskan house fronts and Tiahuanaco weavings. Anthropomorphic maize is seen in the *teoamoxtli* Planting chapter, the Cacaxtla murals (ca. 550 A.D.: *México Desconocido,* November 1989), Huichol yarn paintings ("Squash-boy," Negrín 1975: pl. 15), Anasazi dry paintings (Wyman 1970), and Chimu pottery (Kutscher 1954). Lévi-Strauss 1972:245–68 ("Split Representation in the Art of Asia and America") discusses facing profiles.

18. Subclassified by 90° angle as well as toe total, the remarkable trail of footprints that runs through the opening chapter of the *Cospi* and *Borgia* screenfolds establishes the formula $2(7^2 + 9^2) = 260$, i.e., the nights of the *tonalamatl;* see Table 1.

19. López Austin 1984; as a source of arithmetical number bases, Closs 1985. Odd teeth: See Plate 3; the Bear Mother also features in Bierhorst 1985:51; the Quitocara/Inca Tolitas face is acknowledged as Ecuador's national emblem. Napo urn: Santos Ortiz 1981. Maya vase: Robiscek and Hales 1981:220. Huichol paintings: Negrín 1975:27. This is one of many native conventions taken up in the murals of Diego Rivera, for example the jaguar knight in the Palacio de Cortés, Cuernavaca.

20. For example, in years 1858 and 1859 of the Kiowa calendars, set into the medicine-lodge design that indicates the Sun Dance, we find qualifiers that denote "Timber Circle" (on a creek that joins the Salt Fork of the Arkansas) and "Cedar Bluff" (near Fort Hays, Kansas): Mooney 1979:305–6. The conventions of Plains picture writing are highly developed in the Winter Counts (see Chapter 4 ("Year counts")) as well as other genres, like the rosters composed by Big Road (1883) and Red Cloud (1892), Bad Bull Heart's history of the Oglala (1967), the biographies of Black Elk (1932), Running Antelope (1873), and the Fort Marion prisoners (see Petersen 1971, which includes a pictographic dictionary), and battles like Red Horse's version of Little Bighorn (see in general Mallery 1893, Ewers 1939).

21. Negrín 1975:17, 71: "Here he is collecting 'memory,' or ideas, about the world of Watetuapa (the ideas symbolized by the heart pierced by an arrow)."

22. Wyman 1970:65, 1983:52; as Nowotny remarked, with reference to *Féjérváry,* p. 1, "Die Aehnlichkeit mit den Sandgemälden des Pueblo-Gebietes ist keine zufällige" (1961:43). Reciprocally, dry painting is known in Mesoamerica and is still practiced there. Pre-Cortesian examples, alluded to in the *Tilantongo Annals* and the *Cantares mexicanos,* are discussed in my "Sacred Sand in Mexican Picture-Writing and Later Literature," ECN 9 (1975): 303–9; at Tonantzintla, near Cholula, a large dry painting of sand, flour, and other materials is made in the church at Ascension.

23. The post-Cortesian documents are defined as an economic subgroup by Glass (1975), whose excellent survey is, however, not related back to clas-

sic precedent; though still poorly edited, it serves as an invaluable source of historical information about New Spain and the sixteenth-century interface between two quite distinct systems of finance, law, and literacy, the one native and the other imported and imposed. Some idea of the capacities of these texts can be gleaned from Galarza 1988 and the essays edited by Martínez Marín (1989). The *Tepotzotlan Codex* is analyzed in detail in Brotherston and Gallegos 1988. It is remarkable in evidencing so much literary sophistication at the local level, a point developed by Gruzinski 1989, and is relevant to the genre of Techialoyan, or Land Books of Mexico (Census in HMAI, vol. 14).

24. Studies by Harvey and Williams (1986) and Williams (1980) focus on the designation of field area and soil type in the *Tepetlaoztoc* ("Kingsborough") and related codices, which use a mathematics more sophisticated than anything the Spaniards were then capable of, based on "conventions and principles known throughout the Mesoamerican area for two millennia or more" (Harvey and Williams 1986:256). The particular arithmetical play with 5 is anticipated, for example, in the *Féjérváry* Feasts chapter, where 5 is not just squared but taken to the power of four ($5 \times 5 \times 5 \times 5$: p. 15). Inset information of this kind may even indicate year dates (Brotherston 1991); unlike the other *tlaxilacalli* names, Coamilco is not transcribed from the Archivo file.

25. Comparing copy with original, we may gauge the catastrophic loss in transcription into the separate imported modes of story (alphabetic glosses, or script) and arithmetical ledger entries now simply read from left to right, the geographical point of view being totally eliminated. Only the three "main" toponyms are retained, and these, abstracted entirely from their landscape (Xoloc loses its mountain pedestal), are simply inserted in the arithmetical table. The court copyist had neither interest in nor capacity for furthering the impression of a united tenfold front banded along the eastern horizon or the claims to precedence embedded in Xolotl's inaugural glyph.

26. Ixtlilxochitl 1985, 1:270; the *Huehuetlatolli* refer to these books as the highest object of literary study (ECN 18:174). The term was subsequently used for the Christian scriptures. Maybe *teoamoxtli* and *xiuhtlapoualli* were not the only genres known in pre-Cortesian times, and terms for what appear to be other genres exist in Nahuatl; yet the fact remains that as far as the classics go, only these two exist. Later, in the sixteenth century, there was certainly a greater diversity: legal and financial papers based on the Christian calendar, for example; or the large sheets known as *lienzos*, where the reading order follows footstep trails through landscapes of mountains and centuries; or again genealogies, with their purely genetic logic, produced to justify title in the courts of New Spain. Yet in many cases these may be considered variants of one or other of the classic genres.

27. Nowotny 1961; this was chiefly because of his only moderate interest in the yearly seasons and astronomy, which in his opinion had led his predecessor Eduard Seler (1902–23) to "excess." His account of the *tonalamatl* chapters is formally impeccable; not so, that of the seasonal-year chapters. Though

he detected elements of the 18 yearly Feasts in the 18-page *Borgia* chapter on that topic (pp. 29–46), he failed to clinch the connection ("Das Verhältnis dieser Rituale zu denen der achtzehn Jahresabschnitte ist jedoch nicht feststellbar" [1961:246]), as he did in the more esoteric cases of *Féjérváry* (pp. 15–22) and *Laud* (pp. 21–2, which he reads in inverse order, overapplying the *Florentine Codex* account of funeral ceremonies to the Feasts Miccailhuitl and Atemoztli). Nor did he see that without exception the other yearly cipher, 11, governs all the remaining *teoamoxtli* chapters (*Cospi,* verso pp. 1–11; *Féjérváry,* pp. 5–14; *Laud,* pp. 39–44), which are lumped by him under such miscellaneous headings as "Tempelkult" and "Rituale mit Bündeln abgezählter Gegenstände." His use of Schultze Jena's fieldwork to show their significance as "Jagdsühneriten" is, however, brilliant; and in general, *Tlacuilolli* has been absolutely essential for the readings made here – indeed, most of them were actually stimulated by its very thoroughness and repeated cross-reference.

28. A. Cyphers, "Thematic and Contextual Analyses of Chalcatzingo Figurines," *Mexikon* 5 (1988): 98–101. Though Mayanists like Eric Thompson have spoken against the link between the *tonalamatl* nights and the moons of gestation, it is fundamental in native ritual and the *teoamoxtli* Night Lord chapters (*Cospi,* pp. 1–8 – see n. 18 above; *Borbonicus,* pp. 21–2), which likewise show how the 260 total is achieved arithmetically by the deducting of one night ($29 \times 9 = 261$ – see Brotherston 1982:11). It was clearly established in scholarship by Schultze Jena in 1934 (P. Furst 1986); see also Tibón 1981 and Earle and Snow (1985), who report on the "nine bloods" taken by the moon from a pregnant woman to feed her child. The first of the Nine, Xiuhtecutli, appears as a baby at the Izcalli Feast of the year cycle. In Mexico the idea of comforting the child that is about to be born, part of the ancient midwifery that is still alive in the *arrullar al niño* custom, resulted in special permission being given for a set of nine masses to be celebrated over the nine nights before Christmas to commemorate the nine moons of gestation that were then near completion.

29. The pyrite mosaic from Las Bocas, Puebla, dates to 1000 B.C.; see Marshack's footnote in Hammond 1974:270. Seminal in the ancient calendars of the Zapotec (Caso 1965) and the Mixe (Lipp 1991 and pers. commun.), the Night Count as such also features in the Quiché play *Rabinal Achi.* In Anasazi, the count of nine nights corresponds to the full dry-painting ceremony; among the Mapuche it measures the wake and journey to the world of the dead (Kössler-Ilg 1956:224).

30. Dewdney 1975:112 (*Red Sky Scroll*); Hocquenghem 1987; Reichel-Dolmatoff 1971:275; Hunt 1977. On Amazonian taxonomy and logic based on bird behavior, see Roe 1962; and on the succession of sidereal moons among the Tukano, $8 + 5$, see Montoya Sánchez 1973:192–3. An archetypal augur, referred to more than once in the *Florentine Codex* and the subject of an entire native-paper manuscript (no. 12 in the Boturini collection), predicted Cortes's arrival to Moctezuma in 1507: a coot with a mirror on its beak (*cua-tezcatl*). On the foretelling of the fates of male and

female pairs through the sum of their respective birth Numbers, from twice One to twice Thirteen, see Nowotny 1961:218; this Number Pairs chapter appears to be the prototype for the principles of partnerhood and marriage, elaborated elsewhere for their own sake in other *teoamoxtli* chapters. In *Histoyre du Mechique* the Heroes are read as skies; in the living arrangements of the principals at Cholula, they matched sets of numbered rooms (Rojas 1985).

31. Seler 1902–23: vol. 2; Garibay 1958, Hymn III; Brotherston 1979:102–5. The *Inin cuic* appeared in the *Tepepulco MS* (Census 1098), an antecedent of the *Florentine Codex*, where they are reproduced in the appendix to Book 2, untranslated out of fear of their demonic power. Brinton translated them as the American *Rig Veda* (1890); K. T. Preuss drew analogies with Greek as well as Sanskrit texts in his "Dialoglieder des Rigveda im Lichte der religiösen Gesänge mexikanischer Indianer," *Globus* 95 (1909): no. 3. The Twenty Signs are also the subject of ingenious play in stucco at Palenque (site museum): a dog (Sign X) has a footprint (hieroglyphic Sign X) superimposed on its eye, perhaps signifying its oldest function, that of guide and companion on the journey beyond death.

32. The Eleven also bear axes in *Magliabechiano*, which as a result could reasonably be attributed to Tepoztlan, the "place of the axe," named in the text. Tamoanchan is in 1538 named as an Indian town on the Humilladero arch in neighboring Cuernavaca; it and the Olmec drinkers at Chichinauhtzin are discussed in the *Florentine Codex* (book 10:193) and inspired Francisco Plancarte y Navarrete's remarkable study *Tamoanchan: El Estado de Morelos y el principio de la civilización en México*, México, 1911; several of the names are preserved in those of towns along the ridge, and others are specified as cliff dwellers. As a set with astronomical significance, the Eleven were initially identified in my articles of 1982 ("Astronomical Norms in Mesoamerican Ritual and Time-Reckoning," in Aveni 1982:109–42) and 1988; Thomas Barthel kindly alerted me to his earlier thoughts along the same lines in his 1969 review of the facsimile edition of *Cospi* (*Tribus* 18:207–9). The Cempoala murals are in the eastern and east-facing "Pimiento" temple (see Fig. 28b). Subsequent references include Zolbrod 1984:93 (coyote and 1 + 7 + 3 Navajo stars: Plate 5a); Radin 1970:382–90, 477 (Winnebago); Negrín 1975:52 and pl. 11 (Huichol); Kössler-Ilg 1956:18 (Kolü Pan's notes on the Mapuche rain or sunspot cycle); S. M. Fabian, "Ethnoastronomy of the Eastern Bororo Indians of Mato Grosso, Brazil," in Aveni and Urton 1982:293–4 (eleven creatures that "set" at the western horizon). S. Hugh-Jones ("The Pleiades and Scorpius in Barasana Cosmology," in Aveni and Urton 1982:183–201) suggestively distinguishes between poisonous and nonpoisonous paths of constellations in the rainforest (of just the kind proposed for Mesoamerica in my article of 1988) on the basis of imagery in the *Cospi* and *Féjérváry* Zodiac chapter. In turn this division of the year helps to explain the switch from night-sky to twenty-day Feasts at Miccailhuitl in *Féjérváry* (p. 15; compare also *Laud*, p. 21). The eleven towns conquered by Tizoc are listed on a giant *cuauhxicalli* recovered in

1988 from under the archbishop's residence in Mexico City and now in the Museo Nacional de Antropología; Tenochtitlan's 11 + 11 garrisons are in *Matrícula de tributos* and *Mendoza* (pp. 17–18); Texcoco's conquests are listed in 11 columns and total 121 in Ixtlilxochitl (1975: 1, 383–4; said to be transcribed from a "pintura de México"). Kelley (1976:35–8) details the enigmatic Maya lunar series.

33. Marcus 1980 identifies such topics as marriage and the travel that is indicated by footprints. It has long been customary to deny *Mendoza* unity on the grounds of difference in style in its last section. Yet formally it testifies to just the distinction between commodity and labor tribute characteristic of the *teoamoxtli,* which under Spanish colonial rule proved so powerful as to achieve recognition in the royal legislation of 1549, in the face of *encomendero* opposition and abuse (Gibson 1966:60). For further details of the topic chapters, see Table 2. Ceremonies proper to the *pochteca* Travel chapters in *Féjérváry* were identified by Nowotny (1961:208) and M. León-Portilla (1985). The harlequin clothes of those in the four houses of the Judges chapter in the same screenfold recall those in the "god houses" in the Huichol paintings (Negrín 1975: pl. 41). An astoundingly precise transcription of the Hazards chapter is found in the poem "El mundo es un redondo plato de barro," by Pablo Antonio Cuadra:

La suspicaz adversidad rodea nuestro manjar.
En cada extremo un animal devora:
El Murciélago en el Oriente desea extraer tu sombra.
El Caimán en el Poniente acecha tu secreto.
En el Sur las Aguilas aniquilan tu historia
y en el Norte el Jaguar persigue tu estrella futura.
¡Ah! Decidme!
¿Quién podrá defender mi intimidad?

34. Ann Fink ("Shadow and Substance: A Mopan Maya view of human experience," in McCaskill 1989:399–414) discusses how customs depicted in the *Laud* Birth chapter are still observed in Belize, with regard to wicker seats to keep the woman from the ground and the hot or cold food she eats. This study also neatly disposes of the imperialist notion, put forward for example in G. M. Foster's *Culture and Conquest: America's Spanish heritage,* Viking Fund Publication no. 27, New York, 1960, that these practices are in part European in origin. Though not depicted, the placenta is referred to in the *Mendoza* commentary; on the gray bird of ill omen in Anasazi, see Reichard 1963:423. In general, see Launay on the *Florentine* account of "grossesse" (1979), and above all Tibón (1981), who, though he does not identify the Birth chapter as such, makes pertinent comparisons between it and birth imagery from many parts of the Fourth World.

35. On the umbilicus of the ruler's birth that descends from the zenith, or *xaman,* see Coggins 1980 and "The Manikin Scepter: Emblem of lineage," ECM 17 (1988): 123–58. The "diving gods" at Tulum descend from an umbilicus (Tibón 1981:22), as does Nine Wind in the *Tepexic Annals* (p. 4); in Nahuatl, *temo* means both to descend and to be born.

36. *Florentine Codex,* book 8 (esp. chaps. 10, 14, 17); M. León-Portilla 1988; Burkhart 1989. For the Purchas quotation, see Purchas 1625:1066.

37. "A ver a las milpas, a leñar"; from the Nahuatl biography by Librado Silva Galeana, in ECN 18:18. The cutting tool and planting stick are shown as paired emblems of Watacame in the Huichol creation (Negrín 1975:40). Depicted in the *Laud* Amazons chapter, the "casket" is invoked in *Totecuyoane;* the snake-penis clearly identifies the adulterer in the *Borgia* Number Pairs chapter (Fig. 19).

38. This is likewise a motif in the well-known Inca "hymn" to the powers of thunder and lightning quoted below in "The case of the *quipu.*"

39. Knorosov 1967; Houston 1989; Schele and Freidel 1990; cf. Chapter 1, n. 9. On what appear to be ideological grounds, Thompson resisted Knorosov's phoneticism (1960, 1962, 1967). Prehieroglyphic writing set out in columns, though not registers, is found at Kaminaljuyu and El Baúl in Guatemala, Huitzo in Mexico, and in Belize and is generally described as "heavy on pictorial, light on linguistic features" (Houston 1989:21).

40. Stuart 1989.

41. For several spellings of the same phrase or word – in this case, *yilah* "to see or witness" – see Houston 1989:39.

42. On this point, showing well-worn Western bias, Houston clearly misunderstands: "One sometimes hears that such counts were 'more accurate' than other systems. Nonsense: the calendar reckoned by whole days and as such could not deal easily with fractional sums" (1989:50). Accuracy is simply defined and achieved by other means, that is, by accumulating multiples of a given period until the fraction becomes a unit, as in the *Dresden* Venus and Eclipse tables (which are certainly more accurate than anything Europe could then boast of), or the *Mexicanus* Calendar Wheel discussed below.

43. Ceren: "Land of the Maya" map, NG 176 (1989), no. 4. Lee (1985) gathers the surviving screenfolds and appends an excellent bibliography; on the most recently discovered of the four, see also J. Carlson, "The Grolier Codex: A preliminary report on the content and authenticity of a 13th century Maya Venus almanac," in Aveni and Brotherston 1983:27–58.

44. Some hieroglyphic texts, like the celebrated Stela D at Copan, appear to want to recuperate the holistic possibilities of iconic script, for example in the splendid baroque figures, composites of Quecholli and Heroes, used with number value in the inscriptions (Brotherston 1979:90–1). Yet the attempt can never be fully realized, precisely because of the phonetic catch.

45. Goody 1968:6. The much-cited categorizations of Ong (1982) leave just as little room for America.

46. Ascher and Ascher 1981:158; Murra 1980. References to Tahuantinsuyu as a "schriftfern" society are quoted approvingly by Hartmann (1990), in apparent ignorance (to judge by her discriminating bibliography) of the Aschers' indispensable research on the matter. Examples of *quipus* dating back to ca. A.D. 700 are discussed in W. J. Conklin, "The Information System of Middle Horizon Quipus," in Aveni and Urton 1982:261–82. Val Fraser very kindly supplied me with several references confirming the multiple

use of the *quipu* under Spanish rule, including Garci Diez de San Miguel, *Visita hecha por la provincia de Chucuito* (1567), ed. Waldemar Espinosa Soriano, Lima, 1964, p. 232; Juan de Matienzo, *Gobierno del Perú* (1567), ed. G. Lohmann Villena, Paris and Lima, 1967, p. 51; Murúa (1590) 1962–4, 2:12, 58–60. Continuing the Huarochiri equation of "sin" with absence from work and therefore the *quipu* tally, women priests contrived to undermine the confession system instituted as a means of social control by the Spanish: Correlating a great range of information, their *quipu*s defended the old social order; see Silverblatt 1987:156. The minute detail of subjects listed by Guaman Poma in relation to the scribe (*Nueva corónica*, p. 814) further strengthens his claim to having used *quipu* sources and modifies the structuralist view of the "orality" of his text: R. Adorno, "On the Pictorial Language and the Typology of Culture in a New World Chronicle," *Semiotica* 36 (1981): 51–106, and "Visual Mediation in the Transition from Oral to Written Expression," in Brotherston 1986:181–95. Garcilaso copied out a pagan hymn to Viracocha said to have been transcribed from a *quipu* by Blas Valera (1966:88).

47. On the use of *quipu*s beyond Tahuantinsuyu, see the cases of the Carib (Armellada 1972:139; C. D. Dance, *Chapters from a Guianese Log Book,* Georgetown, 1881, p. 302; J. Rodway, "Timehri or Pictured Rocks," *Timehri* 6 [1919]: 1–11) and the Mapuche (Kössler-Ilg 1956:66; Medina 1952:411, where colors red, blue, and white are mentioned, as is the fact that data given in the knots include place of origin).

48. Nordenskiöld 1925.

49. Recorded and analyzed by Wiener (1880); reproduced in Mallery 1893:706–7 and Brotherston 1979:78.

50. Duviols 1977:305–6; the burning followed the Third Council of Lima, August – October 1583. Continuing use is evidenced by the chroniclers quoted in n. 46 above. Valera's hymn, quoted in Garcilaso 1966:88, is analyzed in my 1973 article.

51. Pietschmann notes the *schéma fixe* of Guaman Poma's page designs and "portraits en pied" and their importance relative to the matching alphabetic texts (preface to the facsimile edition: 1936:xix); see also Mendizábal Losack 1961 and Kaufmann Doig 1978. The old model proved so strong that it influenced the Christian prologue, where biblical history is made to conform to the Andean world-age scheme and where the total of frames dedicated to it and papal history add up to the calendrical twelve.

Chapter 3: Configurations of space

1. Bagrow 1964.

2. The term *tlatoyotl* is adopted from Maldonado 1990.

3. One of the great contributions of Nowotny's *Tlacuilolli* was to establish the link between these texts, and in so doing to indicate that the geopolitics they hold in common ideologically supported a ruling class. As in Cholula, he says, "die Aemter dieser Priesterschaft mögen in universistischer Weise

auf ein Weltbild bezogen gewesen sein" (1961:263–5). He also helps to show in detail how in the Cuicatlan screenfold an earlier map inset into the Night Lords chapter (pp. 1–2) closely relates to the Night Lords chapter in *Laud* (pp. 33–8), possibly from nearby Teotlillan (the same figures sit under the same sorts of trees and awnings). On this, and on the Cuicatlan Papaloapan link, see n. 9 below.

4. The taking over by sugar capitalists of land shown to be communal on these maps was a main spur to Zapata's crusade (Miguel Sedano, *Zapata, México*, 1974, quoted in Gallo 1988).

5. Negrín 1985: pl. 1; it is encrusted with eyes and flowers of ancestors.

6. This reading accords with the fact that in the *Chiautla Annals* the years of the Round are spatialized into this shape as four arms of 13 reaching to four horizons. These texts also remind us of the importance of choreography as a means of recreating the cosmos within a framed space, the microcosm on the page.

7. This argument was first set out in Brotherston and Ades 1975 and Brotherston 1976 and led to the conclusion that, whatever the correct reading for Mesoamerican signs and words for north and south may eventually prove to be, "they cannot always or exclusively be identified with our north and south while, as moments between, they sometimes must mean above and below" (1976:59). These thoughts coincided with those of several scholars at that time and have been further developed by Franz Tichy ("Ordnung und Zuordnung von Raum und Zeit im Weltbild Altamerikas," *Ibero-Amerikanisches Archiv* 2 [1976]: 113–54), Clemency Coggins (1980, 1988 [see Chapter 2, n. 35]), Tony Aveni (1980), Susan Milbrath ("Astronomical Imagery in the Serpent Sequence of the Madrid Codex," in Ray Williamson [ed.], *Archaeoastronomy in the Americas,* Los Altos: Ballena Press, 1981), Victoria Bricker ("Directional Glyphs in Maya Inscriptions and Codices," AA 48 [1983]: 352), John M. Watanabe ("In the World of the Sun: A Cognitive Model of Mayan Cosmology," *Man* 18 [1983]: 713), John Sosa ("Astronomía sin telescopios: Conceptos mayas del orden astronómico," ECM 15 [1984]: 117–42, and 1986), Michael Closs ("A Phonetic Version of the Maya Glyph for North," AA 53 [1988]: 386–93), and Evon Z. Vogt ("Cardinal Directions and Ceremonial Circuits in Mayan and Southwestern Cosmology," *National Geographic Society Research Reports,* no. 21 [1985]: 487, and "On the Application of the Phylogenetic Model to the Maya," in Ray DeMallie and Alfonso Ortiz [eds.], *Essays for F. Eggan* [in preparation]); the overall scholarly position is excellently summarized by M. Léon-Portilla 1987:185–205 (which also supplies bibliographical references). At the same time, the argument has been sadly misread by others as a claim that north and south did not signify at all in Mesoamerican space, even in the mapping of tribute provinces, which is obviously absurd. The whole point is that, with their characteristic ingenuity, native texts like the *Féjérváry* map may promote both possibilities, so that neither excludes the other, and in general terms the astronomical movement through zenith and nadir in early creation opens out onto the tribute map of terrestrial geogra-

phy. Affine ideas about the animate landscape of Navajo dry paintings with its east–west body tract were developed by Ray Pinxten (Ghent) at the St. Andrews Amerindian Cosmology Conference (September 1987); Bozzoli 1983 reports a similar model among the Talamancan Chibcha-speakers; Tyler (1964:169–79) discusses the clear-cut Pueblo model of six directions.

8. Modern testimony on Kinich Kakmo, the "zenith" pyramid at Izamal under which the sun sleeps at night on its way back east is given in María Montoliu Villar, "Utilidad de la tradición oral maya contemporánea en la reconstrucción de las historias sagradas del sol y la luna según los sistemas de ideas religiosas y míticas de este pueblo," in Serra Puche 1988:177–88; confirming the reading noted above, zenith is explicitly equated with *xaman* "north," as nadir is with *nohol* "south" (p. 183). Note also the *Ríos* image of the "night sun" Xolotl, which has earth and Tlaloc above. On Copan, see Schele and Miller 1986:122–3; the Palenque case is discussed below.

9. The close interrelation and even physical combination of toponyms in the Coixtlahuaca Valley group of texts have been discussed by Nowotny (1961:264), Caso (1961, 1979:118–35), Parmenter (1982 – critically aided by the discovery of *Tequiztepec Map 1,* which shows its own version of the Upper Papaloapan set of toponyms found in the *Tepexic Annals,* the *Cuicatlan* screenfold, the *Coixtlahuaca Map,* and the *Selden Roll*), König (1984), and Brotherston (1985). These analyses leave no doubt about the common focus and the fact that they point more toward the Papaloapan River, on whose drainage Cuicatlan and Coixtlahuaca lie, than toward the Mixteca to the south, over the continental divide. They also display a strong Chichimec involvement, for example in the story of Two Dog common to the *Selden Roll* and the *Tepexic Annals,* which is quite atypical of Mixtec histories. A meticulous reading of *Coixtlahuaca Lienzo 2* (also known as *Seler 2*) and its many glosses is given in König 1984. According to the nineteenth-century copy of the *Coixtlahuaca Map* and to details that are still just legible in the central area, the snake creature displayed there has the same star-eye and earth features as the toponym for "Coixtlahuaca" in *Mendoza* (pp. 7, 43), while its feathered body and saurian jaws are repeated in the Coixtlahuaca *lienzos.* Prominent to the northwest, the split mountain and checkerboard of Tepexic also feature in the *lienzos* of Tequiztepec, Coixtlahuaca (no. 2) and Tlapiltepec, the *Selden Roll,* and the Gómez de Orozco fragment; the split mountain further features on the southern limits of Cuauhtinchan and other Cholula Plain texts. Overall this argues strongly for an identification with that town rather than the "Yucunaa" of the Nochistlan fragment (*Becker II*) preferred by Anders and Jansen (1988:146). This source agrees, however, with the placing of Nexapa to the southwest in the *Coixtlahuaca Map;* to the southeast, Chalcatongo is read for Mictlantongo, the difference between the two being immaterial here, for both lie in that direction. The toponym to the northeast, read here as Teotlillan and identified with the title-page design in *Laud,* likewise appears in the *Tequiztepec Lienzo,* again paired with *Tepexic* (Parmenter 1982:60).

10. M. Closs, "Cognitive Aspects of Ancient Maya Eclipse Theory," in Aveni 1989:389–414 (Gabriel Espinosa drew my attention to this link). The Venus glyph is unmistakably present, with deathly aspect, in the *Dresden* Eclipse tables. The blood-red frame in which the sun is placed recurs in the arrangement of the same toponyms found in the Cuicatlan screenfold (p. 10).

11. This Nahuatl reading was suggested by William Fellowes shortly before his death in March 1991.

12. Night Chant and Blessing Way: Dunn 1968:116–19 and fig. 43; a version of the smaller quincunx, made on buckskin during the Night Chant, appears in Wyman 1983:174 (it dates from around 1901; see also p. 140). For Tutukila's painting "Before the Flood," see Negrín 1975:38–40; Hunt (1977:97–8) clearly details the geography and cosmic significance of the Cuicatec–Papaloapan quincunx. On "inner forms," Wyman 1970:98. Matos Mocte-zuma 1979 includes standard accounts of the *Sunstone,* discussed with the world ages in Chapter 10 below. Yet other suggestions of the model occur among the Cherokee (Chapter 7, n. 5) and in South America in Tupi ac-counts of the First World before the Flood, which found its supports in a quincunx of *pindo* palms (Bareiro Saguier 1990:166).

13. C. Taylor 1990:86; the perception of the diagonals as solstitial moments on the east and west horizons (which further enhances the argument referred to in n. 7 above), subscribed to by Franz Tichy, Villa Rojas, and others, is well set out in Aveni 1980:156–7. A very early example of the design as such occurs on Monument 46 at the Olmec site of San Lorenzo (M. D. Coe and Diehl 1980, 1:355).

14. Reichard 1977:56 and pl. XVI.

15. See Chapter 1, n. 13. The shift from metropolis to the quarters is marked on the map by the unique repetition of a *cabecera* name, Atotonilco (el Grande) on p. 30, after Atotonilco (de Pedraza) on p. 28; the shift between the quarters is marked by format, that is, the placing of more than one *cabecera* on a single page (otherwise the norm). Hence, Malinalco and Xocotitlan double up at the end of west on p. 35 before the start of south in Tlachco (Tasco) and the move from the state of Mexico to that of Guerrero; Tlacozauhtitlan, Quiauhteopan, and Yoaltepec are combined at the end of south on p. 40 before the start of east in Chalco. The end of east in far-flung Xoconochco is marked by unique calendar signs that indicate the equi-noxes as payment dates (p. 47). Maldonado (1990) notes how the Morelos towns Cuauhnahuac and Huaxtepec, included in the metropolitan area, formed part of Chichimec ceremonies centered on the Basin.

16. These dimensions of the text are skillfully brought out in Enrique Esca-lona's film version of this title page, *Tlacuilo;* see his book of that title (UNAM, 1989).

17. *Tudela* belongs to the *Magliabechiano* group of texts, meticulously discussed in Boone's edition (1983).

18. Brotherston 1990:321.

19. The four senses marked on Nayenezgani's cheek can be seen in Newcomb

and Reichard 1975:47 and pl. xv; on the four hoops that restore human senses, cf. Wyman 1983:32.

Chapter 4: Configurations of time

1. On the practical workings of the 400-day *huna,* see Brotherston 1979:43–4. In South America it is notable that no count of years at all accompanies the historical settling of territory and the naming of rivers, mountains, roads, and towns in such texts as the "Wahnatu" section of *Watunna* or the narratives of Wainambi (Tukano), Canimani (Witoto), and Shaihueke (Mapuche).

2. A comprehensive account of the many versions of Mesoamerica's year calendar is offered by Edmonson in *The Book of the Year* (1988), which in this respect has great value independent of the bold and highly schematic thesis the author proposes. This source respects the Tepexic correlation argued for in Brotherston 1982 on the basis of internal correlations and other evidence found in the *Tlapiltepec Map,* the *Baranda* scroll, the *Nepopoalco Maps* (HMAI Census 46), the *Ríos Codex,* and, not least, the *Tepexic Annals* themselves. It offers a unique means of interlocking the firmest of the calendrical correlations so far made by others in Mesoamerican studies: that of Tenochtitlan, fixed by Cortes's arrival; that of Tilantongo, deduced by Caso (1965a); and that of the *tun* calendar of the lowland Maya, which starts in 3113 B.C., according to J. E. S. Thompson (1960) and his predecessors.

3. Adrian Digby, "Crossed Trapezes: A pre-Columbian astronomical instrument," in Hammond 1974:271–84. In one case (*Texupan Codex;* HMAI Census 289), the solar-ray sign (Fig. 31h) is matched with a seasonal falling leaf, and the corresponding native years are correlated with Christian years. Antecedents for the annual-rains sign (Fig. 31i) are found in rain-deity markers used in conjunction with the quartered circle at Monte Albán (Fig. 31a).

4. Brotherston 1979:197–200. Places identifying those to the left of the dividing line of footprints, Huexotzinco, Chalco, Xochimilco, and Acolhuacan, all have planting emblems and lie east of Tenochtitlan; those to the right, Malinalco, Tlahuica, Tepanec, and Matlazinco, all have hunter emblems and lie to the west. In his painstaking edition of the *Aubin Annals,* Vollmer (1981) reviews these various Aztec histories. The biography of Eight Deer is also related in the *Colombino* screenfold, along with that of Four Wind, and appears more briefly in *Bodley* and the *Vienna* reverse: See Clark 1912 and Caso 1977–9.

5. Generally ignored by early travelers, or unrecognized for what they were, Winter Counts were first published by Mallery in the late nineteenth century; and significantly it was this work on chronology that first led him to the idea of a whole pictographic system shared by Indians on the Plains and elsewhere in North America. For recent censuses, see Chapter 1, n. 31.

6. C. Feest, "Another French Account of Virginia Indians by John Lederer," *Virginia Magazine of History and Biography* 83 (1975): 150–9. In early-

eighteenth-century Carolina, Lawson attests the use of notched sticks or reeds to record years or winters, as among the Pima and the Sioux; the records of several nations pinpointed a hard winter 105 years prior to his visit (Swanton 1979 [1946]: 257, 611).

7. Mooney [1898] 1979; Brotherston 1990:316–17.

8. Underhill 1938; Russell 1975:34–66 (the terms "Pima" and "Papago" are taken as equivalent here). The Wapoctanxi quotation is in Mallery 1893: 291; on the Santee stick, see Mooney 1898:142.

9. Charles Bareis and James Porter, *American Bottom Archaeology,* Champaign, IL, 1984; Warren Wittry, "The American Woodhenge," in M. L. Fowler (ed.), *Explorations into Cahokian Archaeology,* Urbana, IL, 1969, pp. 43–8; Sofaer, R. M. Sinclair, and L. E. Doggett, "Lunar Markings on Fajada Butte, Chaco Canyon, New Mexico," in Aveni 1982:169–81. Some still dismiss out of hand the notion of a calendrical year of the seasons in Mesoamerica (e.g., Bartl, Gobel, and Prem 1989), but J. Stewart reviews a wide range of evidence in "Structural Evidence of a Luni-solar Calendar in Ancient Mesoamerica," ECN 17 (1984):171–91.

10. J. E. Teeple, *Maya Astronomy,* Pub. 403, Washington, DC: Carnegie Institute, 1930, vol. 1, pp. 29–115. These dates have recently been connected with historical events and therefore for some have ceased to have astronomical significance: The whole point about dating in the Maya calendar is that it combines both possibilities.

11. Garibay 1958: Hymn 3; Brotherston 1979:105; Chapter 2, n. 31.

12. Mallery 1893:265; according to the *Xolotl Maps,* seventy years was also the span of poet-king Nezahualcoyotl's exemplary life (1402–72). For the Chibcha cycle, see Krickeberg 1928:192, 199.

13. The gloss on the *Tlapiltepec Map* proposed by the Mixtec A. Castellanos (1912) is referred to in Corona Núñez 1964–7, 3:114; Round symbols are read in Gemelli, "De los caracteres y modo de escritura de que usaban estos indios . . ." (1700), p. 38; Fuentes y Guzmán 1932–3, 2:107–12; and Martínez Gracida 1897–8:448 ("el año camaa del siglo xuxiyiquinuu"). The Coetzala and Tlacotepec texts are both in *Códices indígenas* 1933; see also Barlow 1949b on the former. The latter counts years as posts around a field, an indisputable fact that in turn makes less unlikely the reading of the stones that form the boundary of the *Nepopoalco Map* as four-year periods (Brotherston 1983, 1992).

14. Cuauhquechollan: 12 Reed 1259 and 13 Reed 1299; the eagles among the Quecholli are nos. 5 and 8, hence 5 × 8 = 40; Chalco, *chalcatl,* 11 Flint 1256 and 13 Flint 1336; the Nahuatl expression here for defeat, "inic yn poliuhque," could also mean termination, as of a time period. The 80-year Jade also appears in the *Aztlan Annals* (p. 13) and determined the reigns of Zacatlan (Brotherston 1983; see n. 19 below).

15. Lafitau 1983:56. See also Squier 1877:39 (Lenape); Skinner and Satterlee 1915, 3:482 (the Menomini Rip van Winkle); Schoolcraft 1839, 2:142 (Chusco's story "Wassamo"); Lévi-Strauss 1964–71, 3:183.

16. See Chapter 1, n. 28.

17. Edmonson 1982:197. Although pointing out the Maya interest in reconciling the *tun* with the seasonal year of other Mesoamericans and the Christians, this source does not explicitly note that A.D. 2088, likewise a "4 Ahau" date, marks the completion of 5,200 seasonal years from the first year of the first Round of the Era, 1 Flint 3112 B.C.

18. Chimalpahin's dates are discussed in Kelley 1980:15; days in the year 3113 B.C. in Brotherston 1982:31–3.

19. Itztli is the second of the Nine Figures; Papalotl, the seventh of the Quecholli. Absolutely explicit in the *Cuauhtitlan Annals,* this base is observed in the annals of Aztlan, Azcatitlan, Tlatelolco, and Cuauhtinchan, the maps of Quinatzin and Nepopoalco, and several stone inscriptions from Tula, Tenochtitlan, Tenayuca: see Brotherston 1983:196 (which also discusses such other cases as the Zacatlan history recorded by Torquemada and analyzed in the indispensable survey by H. B. Nicholson [1978]). In the hieroglyphic tradition, it coincides with the secondary base used in the *Dresden* Venus chapter. In the Mixtec area it is matched by a possible secondary base dating to the time of Christ; see n. 24 below. The Era date in the late fourth millennium B.C., in combination with these secondary bases early in the Christian era, forms a pattern also found in the Hindu calendar.

20. Prem 1978:275. I am grateful to Hanns Prem for correcting my earlier reading of this detail.

21. Brotherston 1983:184. Larger Christian cycles are discussed in J. D. North, "Chronology and the Age of the World," in Yourgrau and Breck 1977:307–34.

22. From this same year, which lies in Round 89 of the Era and which, as *Borbonicus* shows (p. 38), marks the end of the last Aztec Round begun before Cortes, *Inomaca tonatiuh* casts back to the Era base over 40 Rounds plus "2513 years" (49 Rounds), in sum the span recorded in *Mexicanus.* Though distorted by transcription and translation into Spanish, the *Pinturas MS* follows the same pattern over 39 Rounds plus "2618 years," that is, a "half-sun" (*medio sol*) of 50 Rounds (quoted in Monjarás Ruiz 1987:142–3). Chimalpahin's *Relaciones* calculate back to dates that cluster near 3000 B.C. (Kelley 1980); his *Memorial breve* uses the Chichimec Round 72 base.

23. On the 80-year Jade, see n. 14; the eight encircling subdivisions of the 52-year Round are basically four lots of six plus $5 + 7 + 7 + 9$. In the Boban Calendar Wheel, which within a ritual frame narrates Texcoco history from the time of Xolotl, Eight Deer's Chichimec contemporary, the 52-year Round is similarly encircled by quadrants of twenty footsteps that are designated as years: Charles Dibble, "The Boban Calendar Wheel," ECN 20 (1990): 173–82. "Nauh ollin" is one of several glosses in the Tilantongo text, apparently the work of a Spanish-speaker guided by a Nahuatl expert: Reading backward from left to right, we have accurate and suggestive examples of "tlacaxipehualiztli" for frame shooting and "tlan tepuztli amatl" for an ill-fated year. Tichy (1991:109–111) discusses the eightyfold division of the circle, into units of 4.5 degrees, which he finds present in the *Mendoza* title page.

24. P. 1; six star-eyes (52-year Rounds) are set above a bar-and-dot total of 66 made up of the sigma numbers 21 and 45, and itself a sigma number, i.e., $\Sigma6 + \Sigma9 = \Sigma11$ (Brotherston 1982:27; 1988; Fig. 34d). Totals of star-eye Rounds in other Mixtec screenfolds, like *Nuttall* and *Bodley,* which are likewise calculated from this Round 60 base, are specified in Brotherston 1983:196.

25. Nowotny 1961:47, 256; Melgarejo 1980; J. L. Furst 1978; Jansen 1982. Dates at the start of the *Tepexic Annals* have now even been read phonetically in Mixtec, for example to produce verbs of action; and they are deemed "dates in nondurational time" that are somehow scattered "among the chronological dates," there being absolutely no formal or visible difference between the two supposed categories: M. Jansen, "Rereading Mixtec Codices," (*Ancient Mesoamerica* 1 [1990]: 108). Whatever the justification for this procedure, if it dispenses with chronology it would be perverse in terms of genre.

26. This distinction accorded to the Tepexic toponym block (p. 32) clearly privileges it in relation to the four succeeding toponym blocks (pp. 35, 39, 43, 48); the individual place names of these latter surely yield the lunar total of 29 shown to characterize the *cabeceras* of the four quarters that surround the metropolitan area in *Mendoza* and other texts. Together with the geographical considerations touched on in Chapter 3, n. 9, these facts strongly argue for Tepexic as the provenance of the text.

27. Surrendering books: Núñez de la Vega, quoted in Krickeberg 1928:176–7; the event took place in Huehuetlan, a place named after the "ancient" artifacts in the "casa lóbrega" there (these and other details, omitted in Krickeberg, are taken from Walter Lehmann's handwritten copy of the Núñez MS in the Iberoamerikanisches Institut, Berlin). This Tzental tradition is the same as that invoked in the *Probanza de Uotan* (Census 1187). On the eclipse, see Sigüenza y Góngora 1984 ("no sólo total sino uno de los mayores que ha visto el mundo" [p. 108]). The end date in the *Dehesa* screenfold (Census 112; Chavero 1892) and the *Tlaxcala Annals* (Census 1125; unpub.) is 1692. Curiously, the last date in one of the *Chumayel* chapters, which catalogs famine, hurricane, drought, and disease, is also 1692 (p. 64). On the other calculations made from the Era base by year multiples, see Brotherston 1983:196. A gloss on the Tlapiltepec text by the Mixtec scholar Abraham Castellanos, which specifies the millennial tree span, is deemed unreliable in HMAI 15:578; on the descent to Chicomoztoc, explicitly at the start of the Era and part of the Chichimec Xolotl tradition, see Mendieta, quoted in Monjarás Ruiz 1987.

28. The eight centuries that elapse between the tree birth at Apoala and the second kindling in A.D. 805 is just the span recorded in the *Tilantongo Annals* when they too are read in orthodox fashion. Though usually assigned to a later period, as the inaugural event in many Mixtec annals this tree birth formally coincides with the Round 60 secondary base within the Era. In detail and structure the two narratives leave little doubt that they must be referring to the same events: the tree birth itself with its aristocratic

issue; the political union that culminated in the first kindling (A.D. 338); the privileges of and then the uprising against Nine Wind's bald-headed elite; and the restoration marked by twin "split-sun" emblems in Round 72.

29. In his *Probanza,* Moctezuma Mazatzin claims ancestors "desde la muy antigua, que memoria de hombre no era bastante para lo recordar y dar razón" (Jaecklein 1978:7). In the *Tepexic Annals,* the Chichimec secondary base in Round 72 of the Era is indicated on p. 50 on the lips of Tencaueyan, at a date fourteen Rounds from that base and from the end of the Era. Strong confirmation of the Round 72 calendar base has been provided by recently deciphered texts from Metlatoyuca and Itzcuintepec, which between them explicitly place the emergence from Chicomoztoc as many as twenty-eight generations and "860" years prior to the sixteenth century (Brotherston 1992b).

30. *Xolotl Map 1:* Dibble 1980:27.

31. Peter Mason, "Lévi-Strauss in Tenochtitlan," *Boletín de estudios latino-americanos y del Caribe* (Amsterdam) 45 (December 1988): 101–11 (which reviews, inter alia, Graulich 1987 and Gossen 1986). Significantly, Graulich excludes hieroglyphic texts from his generalizations about the nature of Mesoamerican time, perhaps because they show so clearly how a given moment may belong to both cyclic and linear time, an irrefutable case being the cyclic Venus risings in *Dresden,* which simultaneously are fixed in the Era by the Initial Series count. Using A. López Austin's *Religión y política en el mundo náhuatl* (UNAM, 1973), C. Noguez ("Códices históricos coloniales," in Serra Puche 1988:65–73) has taken further the key philosophical notion of nonrepeatability, which undoubtedly becomes more apparent in post-Hispanic texts. To suggest that it begins to appear only then and there, however, sells short the complexity of pre-Hispanic texts. W. Rowe (1984) offers a critique of the depoliticizing effects of Lévi-Strauss's structuralism.

32. As a rule, the *teoamoxtli* texts have been regarded as ritual and mantic literature, the means for predicting fates and deciding propitious moments in the endlessly recurring cycles of time identified above with the *tonalamatl* and the seasons of the year; and this was undoubtedly one of their functions. As a consequence, however, these books do not divorce or separate themselves from material history and geography. On the contrary, they embed in their archetypal discourse references to specific events and places of just the kind found in the annals genre, as the *Coixtlahuaca Map* confirms. Today the days and nights of Otomi curing rituals in Pahuatlan cast back to invasions made in the past by Moctezuma II and his Christian successors (*Historia de la curación*). A logical counterpart to the ritualizing tendency of annals like those of Tepexic and Tilantongo, the latent historicism of the *teoamoxtli* genre is most pronounced in the Feasts chapters in *Borbonicus, Borgia* (see Chapter 6, n. 11), *Laud* (the notorious name Eight Deer appears on p. 21, at Miccailhuitl), and *Féjérváry* (see Plate 13). As part of the seasonal experience of a particular year in a given tradition, the Feasts readily lend themselves to a definition or memory of it, as, for example,

Quecholli 1 Reed (1519), the month and year of Cortes's arrival in Tenochtitlan that were seared into Mexica memory. Completing the symmetry of the forty-page text as a whole, the *Borbonicus* Feasts chapter has inset into it an actual count of years, framed in Mexica style. Starting in 1 Rabbit, it runs through what can only be read as Moctezuma II's new-fire ceremony in the solstice Feast Panquetzaliztli, in 2 Reed (1507) at Huizachtepec (the place name and Huitzilopochtli's temple there are clearly shown), and culminates in the arrival of the Spanish in 1 Reed 1519 (now torn from the text, this last event is deducible from surviving Spanish glosses). So unambiguous is the historicity of this "cyclic" *teoamoxtli* chapter that it recalls straightforward *xiuhtlapoualli* versions of the same events, the Huitzilopochtli annals, for example, where, moreover, the years are reciprocally accompanied by a sequence of Feast dates of the kind the *Borbonicus* chapter is based upon. In these annals, Cortes's arrival is highlighted as Quecholli 1 Reed, just as the final surrender of Tenochtitlan in 3 House 1521 coincides with the feast of the dead Miccailhuitl. Because of its clarity, this *Borbonicus* chapter is critical for establishing possible historicity in the *teoamoxtli* genre, suggesting that the *teoamoxtli* indeed demand a more comprehensive literary reading that goes beyond the insistent Western binary opposition between diachronic and synchronic time.

33. Engels was influenced by Lewis Henry Morgan, who assumed a tiny time depth in his "Indian Migrations" (in Beach 1877:158–257) as well as in his better-known studies of Native American society (1901, 1909, 1967). For an assessment of these and related political issues, see the excellent essays by Vine Deloria and others in Ward Churchill, *Marxism and Native Americans,* Boston: South End, 1962.

Part II: Political memory

Epigraphs: Mooney 1891:375; M. León-Portilla 1986:152; Pietschmann 1936:451 (*uanacauri* is the name or title of the *huaca* of the Inca House of Dawn: ibid., pp. 261, 263).

Chapter 5: Peten

1. Stuart 1989. Decipherments of royal and place names by Proskouriakoff, Berlin, and Kelley, which prepared the ground for the recent spate of readings by Stuart, Mathews, Houston, Schele, and others, are summarized in Kelley 1976; cf. also George Stuart, "City of Kings and Commoners: Copan," NG 176 (1989): 496–7. The first of the Yaxchilan lintels was reproduced and analyzed in NG 168 (1985): 541 just two years after its discovery.

2. Hammond led the way in preparing a material–historical record that would correspond with early Initial Series dates, noting, for example, that Cuello, Belize, was probably in "continuous use . . . from about 2500 B.C." (1982:114). The megapolis El Mirador flourished from 150 B.C. to

A.D. 150: NG 172 (1987): 317–39; Schele and Freidel (1990) detect a critical moment of transition ca. 50 B.C. at nearby Cerros when the principle of royalty and hereditary succession is established.

3. Maudslay 1889–1902, 4: pls. 75, 81, 88 (cf. Kelley 1976:261–8).

4. Mathews and Schele, "Lords of Palenque – The glyphic evidence," in M. G. Robertson 1974:41–62.

5. See Chapter 2, n. 13.

6. Tenochtitlan pyramid: Broda, Carrasco, and Matos Moctezuma 1987. *Aztlan Annals:* Chapter 4, n. 4. Xochicalco stelae: see Pasztory, cited by M. Cahodas, "The Iconography of the Panels of the Sun, Cross and Foliated Cross," in M. G. Robertson 1974:95–108.

7. F. Lounsbury, "A Palenque King and the Planet Jupiter," in Aveni 1989: 246–59.

8. The paradigm as such, for which there is early South American and Olmec evidence (see Chapter 9, n. 10), must appear the more important in that Schele and Freidel now attribute the whole "cosmogram" not just to the lowland Maya but to its royalty, starting in Cerros in 50 B.C. (a sinister-sounding "new world order" dependent on "charismatic leadership"). The matter was previously discussed in my "Sacerdotes, agricultores, guerreros: Un modelo tripartita de historia mesoamericana," ECN 19 (1989): 95–106.

9. Clemency Coggins, "A New Order and the Role of the Calendar: Some characteristics of the middle Classic period at Tikal," in Hammond and Willey 1979:38–50, which even hints at "bourgeois" practice.

10. Thomas Gann, *Mounds in Northern Honduras,* BAE Report No. 19, Washington, DC, 1900, pp. 655–92; Miller 1982.

11. On the shift in post-Classic economy, which in reseparating commodity from labor tribute also fragmented the elaborate mechanism of the Initial Series, see Peniche Rivera 1990. A stela was erected to the dynast Kak u Pacal (Fiery Shield) at Chichen Itza in A.D. 880, according to Kelley; see Houston 1989:17.

12. Quoted by Roys 1933:184.

13. On *Ritual of the Bacabs* references to the Zuyua language of the *katun,* see Arzápalo 1987:413; cf. also Chapter 13 below. Edmonson (1982: map, p. x) places Zuyua near Motul, the home of the celebrated Maya dictionary (ca. 1600; Martínez Hernández 1930).

14. Alvarez 1974; Garza 1975; Brotherston 1977; Luxton 1977.

15. Meticulously detailed in Barrera Vásquez and Rendón 1963. For full details of the *Chilam Balam Books,* see this source and the HMAI Census.

16. But Roys's translation does little to bring out the wit: "Three times it was, they say, that the foreigners arrived. It was because of this that we were relieved from paying tribute at the age of sixty." It is notable that Maya who chose to collaborate with the Spaniards in renouncing the community of 'Maya men' likewise adopted the Christian calendar; see *U belil . . . ,* by Nakuk Pech.

17. These are qualities of cultural longevity and resilience that Médiz Bolio's

version does not bring out. He suppresses the Toltec name Nacxit Xuchit (line 28), for example; and he reads an obviously Spanish word like *oraob* ("hora-*ob*," line 14) as an unlikely native form *oxaob* "the Three." (For *oraob*, Roys has "their prayers.")

18. Arzápalo 1987; the Era date 4 Ahau is invoked, for example, on pp. 269 and 329, and the Maya glyph or book (*uoh*) that "gives the answer" in cures nos. 5, 7, 9, 11, 14, 39, and 58.

19. This reading order corresponds to that of hieroglyphic, i.e., verb–subject (–object), the introduction of a new subject being highlighted by special markers. Threefold patterns of lineage emblems are found at Uaxactun, Palenque, and other cities. On Olmec Monument 13, the bird and the flat stone are unmistakable; the third element is the trefoil sign that characteristically emerges from the mouths of jaguars, possibly as roar, at Teotihuacan; at Atetelco, it has inset jaguar claws.

20. On this whole question in later lowland Maya history, see Clendinnen 1987 and Wright 1989.

Chapter 6: Tollan

1. Rojas 1985:128.
2. MS by Hernando Ruiz de Alarcón (1629), ed. Andrews and Hassig (1984:96); the language of this charm recalls the "deer-trap" *nierika* that denotes power and control among the Huichol. The quotation is from the *Florentine Codex*, book 3, chap. 3 (my translation).
3. See Walter Lehmann's classic study "Ein Tolteken Klagegesang," in *Festschrift E. Seler*, ed. W. Lehmann, Stuttgart: Stecker und Schröder 1922, pp. 281–319.
4. Recorded on fols. 26v–27v of the *Cantares* manuscript, this poem was included among other texts relevant to Tula and Quetzalcoatl in Bierhorst 1974:17–97; he also argues cogently for its overall coherence. On the question of different modes and genres, see my "Nezahualcoyotl's Laments and Their Nahuatl Origins: The Westernization of ephemerality," ECN 10 (1974): 383–408. Commentaries on this poem are reviewed in Bierhorst's superb transcription and edition of the manuscript (1985).
5. Davies 1980:160.
6. Located just south of the state capital, this site has now been dated to A.D. 200–600; its massive architecture fits well with the account of its importance given in the *Histoyre du Mechique* (Garibay 1979).
7. These claims are urged by Jean Dubenard Chauveau, "¿Quetzalcoatl en Amatlan (Morelos)?" ECN 15 (1982): 209–17.
8. Maldonado 1990.
9. Vollmer 1981.
10. The *Cuauhtitlan Annals* also mention Atonal as Toltec (fol. 51).
11. For *Relación*, see Rojas 1985. Among others, Piña Chan has remarked on the fact that in the *Cuauhtinchan Annals* the distances covered by the Chichimecs during these "days" mean that they must represent longer time

periods; see Brotherston 1983:192. The parallels noted by Nowotny (1961:34–5) between the middle section of this text, i.e., the Chichimec migration, and the middle section of *Borgia,* i.e., the Feasts chapter (pp. 29–46), could suggest a latent historicism in the latter of the kind noted in *Borbonicus* (see Chapter 4, n. 32), yet referred here to the threefold perspective of the Cholula Plain (Bittmann 1968; the strong similarities between the style and detail of *Borgia* and murals at Cholula and at nearby Ocotelulco and Tizatlan suggest this provenance for this *teoamoxtli*). On the Pipil, see M. León-Portilla 1972:29.

12. What Graulich (1987) calls the "espejismo de Tollan."

13. Paul Kirchhoff, "La ruta de los tolteca – chichimeca entre Tula y Cholula," in *Miscellanea Paul Rivet,* vol. 1, UNAM, 1958, pp. 485–94 (this corrects his reading of 1940); idem (ed.), *Historia tolteca – chichimeca,* México, 1947 (revised by Lina Odena Güemes and Luis Reyes García, FCE, 1989). There is complete agreement about the placement of the towns in the westernmost group (Kirchhoff's easternmost), and thanks to recent decipherment of the Metalayuca and Itzcuintepec texts, Tlemaco and Itzcuintepec itself may be added to the list of recognizable places (Brotherston 1992b). An overall Gulf Coast location is preferred in W. Krickeberg, *Los totonaca,* México: Secretaría de Educación Pública, 1933. On the transferring of these lowland names to the highlands out of nostalgia for warmer climes, Melgarejo Vivanco is highly informative (1970:34).

14. Davies 1980:7. The *Pinturas MS* (Garibay 1979) mentions Honduras. References by Ixtlilxochitl and others to early migrations from Nonoualco are reported but chronologically disbelieved by Davies (1977:140ff.) in a study especially valuable for its analyses of Nahuatl texts (pp. 305ff.). On sources, see also my "Tula: Touchstone of the Mesoamerican Era," in Brotherston 1986:19–40.

15. For Muñoz Camargo, see Acuña 1984; for *Ríos,* see Figure 64b. Piña Chan (1977, 1989) has persistently urged that as a founder city Mezquital Tula comes too late in the Mesoamerican day.

16. Cited in my "Huitzilopochtli and What Was Made of Him," in Hammond 1974:155–66.

17. On Tepexic and Toltec kings in general, see Caso 1960:58; 1977–9, 1:118–36; Robert Chadwick, "Native Pre-Aztec History of Central Mexico," in HMAI 11 (1971): 477; Davies 1977:167–70. On the question of more local Tulas in the Coixtlahuaca area, see Caso 1977–9, 1:132.

18. W. Robertson 1778, 2:474–8, where he makes highly pertinent comparisons between the Tepexic history and that of Tenochtitlan recorded in *Mendoza* (which he knew through the woodblock prints published by Samuel Purchas in *His Pilgrimes* [1625]) and correctly detects in both a metropolitan interest in commodity tribute.

19. Archaeologically this record would correspond to developments in and around the Tehuacan valley at Chilac and the Cozcatlan cave (ca. 3000 B.C.); settlement in more complex buildings in the same central area from about 2500 B.C. would then indicate the towns and ceramics of the old

Chocho-Popolocans (2500 B.C.; Piña Chan 1969). Similarly, the striking intrusion into the narrative of a warrior at 1500 B.C. along with new emblems of tribute and political alliance, could reflect the big archaeological shift at that date in Cholula and elsewhere that corresponds to the appearance of radically new pottery types, probably from South America around 1700 B.C.). On hydrography in the upper Papaloapan and its representation in native texts of the area, see Eva Hunt, "Irrigation and the Socio-political Organization of the Cuicatec Cacicazgos" (1972, in the volume *Chronology and Irrigation* of the Tehuacan Valley project).

20. Dahlgren 1966:45; Nine Wind, who also appears at Palenque (initial glyph in the Temple XIV inscription; Tree-Cross panel; etc.), in the Cacaxtla murals, and elsewhere, has been discussed by Kelley (1976), H. B. Nicholson (1978), and others. Veerman-Leichsenring (1984:6) notes how the glottochronology of Otomanguan and of Popoloca in particular, correlates with archaeology, suggesting continuous occupation of Papaloapan for six millennia or more.

Chapter 7: Turtle Island

1. R. Clark Mallam, *Site of the Serpent: A pre-historic life-metaphor in South Central Kansas,* Occasional Publication of the Coronado–Quivira Museum (Lyons, KS), no. 1, n.d. (a reference kindly given me by Raymond DeMallie); R. T. Coe 1977:53.

2. Cameo gorgets: Hudson (1984) offers readings of these shell texts and keenly relates them to the narratives of the Cherokee and other inheritors of Misissippian culture. The Piasa painting is discussed in Mallery 1893:78–9.

3. Mooney 1898:330. the Nunnehi are also in peaks and the rivers Tugaloo, Cheowa, Blood, pp. 336–7; as defenders, p. 447; as Mound Builders, p. 396. The edition of Ayunini's manuscript was completed after Mooney's death by Frans Olbrechts in 1932 (BAE Bulletin 99).

4. Haywood 1823:293, where the Emergence Mound is noted also to be the ancestral origin of the Chickasaw; on the Muskogee, see V. J. Knight, *Tukabatchee: Archaeological investigations at an historic Creek town. Elmore County, Alabama,* Tuscaloosa: University of Alabama Press, 1984, and "The Institutional Organization of Mississippian Religion," AA 51 (1986): 675–87; on the Yuchi, see Speck 1909. On Natchez narratives gathered by Dupratz and a source of inspiration for Chateaubriand, and in general, see Swanton 1979 (1946) and Lankford (Chapter 1, n. 28).

5. Mooney 1891, who supplies the Cherokee syllabic text; this is a precise example of how health may ultimately depend on the logic of landscape and the shaping of the world. Oklahoma versions of these traditions are edited and discussed by the Kilpatricks, themselves Cherokee, in *Friends of Thunder* (1984); on the syllabary, see their *Shadow of Sequoya* (1965). Though the exact identity of one of the four guardian mountains (Uyaye) is now uncertain, the set, centering on the Cherokee heartland, appears to conform to the quincunx model discussed in Chapter 3; Kuwahi (Cling-

man's Dome) and Tsistuyi (Gregory Bald) lie to north and northwest; Gatekwa (Fodderstack) to the southeast (cf. Map 5).

6. Haywood 1823:226; Schoolcraft 1845:27; Brinton 1884:17. In a late-eighteenth-century version, the migration story was published by Haywood (1823:336), who supplies many other local details of southern cosmogony concerning Judkulla, the Natchez Teshyan, and the astronomical register of the ballgame (p. 285); he also refers to the Cherokee on Hiwassee Island in 1580 (pp. 235–7).

7. A highly informed and on the whole skeptical view of their deeper historical links is taken by William Fenton, "Cherokee–Iroquois Connections Revisited," *Journal of Cherokee Studies* 3 (1978): 239–49.

8. *Cherokee Phoenix,* 1 April 1829, in Kilpatrick (1968:44), who edits the issues of 1828–34. Feest 1986 includes the painting *Three Sisters* by Cornplanter (the Seneca-Iroquois artist and author who was involved in the revivalist movement inspired by the dream of Handsome Lake, Ganyadayu, in 1799; see Wallace 1969).

9. Reminiscent of Mississippian iconography in clay (Cahokia: Galloway 1989:197; Shepherd Mound: W. Wedel, *Archaeological Investigations in Missouri,* U.S. National Museum Bulletin 183 [1943], p. 140), the name glyphs of former chiefs are analyzed by Fenton (1950); a comparable list is given in Kahkewaquonaby Jones's *History* (1861) (see Donald B. Smith 1987:90). On the structure of the ceremony itself, see Bierhorst (1974), who reviews previous accounts of the League (starting with Morgan 1851) and publications of the Condolence Ritual (Hale 1883, etc.); Thomas Abler (Chapter 2, n. 9) correlates the nations with textual variants. A version of this ceremony caught the attention of Rabelais in the sixteenth century; see M. Barbeau, *Pantegruel in Canada,* Ottawa: National Museum of Canada, 1981.

10. An expert on Cusick, W. C. Sturtevant prefers to assign a far later date to this westward journey, identifying it rather with Iroquois involvement in the European fur trade from 1680 on (DeMallie, pers. commun.). This later period certainly fits Dooyentate's account (1870) of the Huron/Wyandot journey to "the father of waters" and the "backbone" of the Rockies.

11. Speck 1942:80–1.

12. J. Howard 1965:16–22.

13. In the Musée de l'Homme, Paris, nos. 34.33.4 (Buffalo Society), 34.33.6 (red moons), 34.33.7 (Quapaw Embassy). The "Cahokia" gloss was just discernible on the last when I examined the original in Paris in 1982; it is mentioned by neither Barbeau (1960) nor C. Taylor (1990). A clear idea of the Quapaw and their territory between the Mississippi and Arkansas rivers is given in *Rélation ou Journal du voyage du Père Gravier* (1700), *Les Rélations des Jésuites* 65:101–62. Copies of Catawba (Siouan) and Chickasaw deerskin maps, ca. 1725, are in London (BM Sloane Ms 4723; PRO CO. 700 no. 6 [2]).

14. The Wahpeton: J. Howard 1984:18, 36; ideas about the eastern origins of the Mandan are offered in Catlin 1841, 2:260 and J. O. Dorsey, "Migrations of the Siouan Tribes," *American Naturalist* 20 (1886): 210–22. DeMallie

(1985) revises the seven divisions claimed by Howard (who proposes a further Yankton unit at the expense of the Teton [1976]). Resistance to Red Cloud's "sale" of the Black Hills in 1876 led to the remarkable census on seven sheets illustrated by Mallery 1893:445.

15. Ray DeMallie passed to me a copy of McKiel's typewritten notes and a copy of Left Heron's unpublished history. Visions: Black Elk: Neihardt 1961 (1932): chap. 3; Thick-Headed Horse: in Hallam 1877.

16. Josephy 1975:111, 119. The "great water" of the Mississippi – Missouri confluence (*mini tanka*, a term that may also mean ocean) is depicted in year 1817 of the *Blue Thunder Count*, when strange red and blue birds were seen there.

17. Quoted by Carr (1991:173). Osage: Mallery 1893:252–3 (a chart taken from Dorsey).

18. Years 1684 and 1720: *John K. Bear* (J. Howard 1976); year 1833: *Settan* (Mooney 1979:255); the remaining years: *Wapoctanxi* ([Brown Hat/Battiste Good]: Mallery 1893:290–328). On the 1833 meteors and Winter Count astronomy, see V. D. Chamberlain 1984; on the historical tradition in general, see J. Howard 1960.

19. For references to maize and the pipe ceremony in the Ghost Dance, see Mooney 1896.

20. Throughout, "Algonkin" is used to designate those who belong to the Algonquian language family. "Not us": J. Howard 1965.

21. A broad survey of East Coast narratives is provided by Brinton (1884:137–47), who also reviews Heckewelder's account. A Shawnee tradition is published by Schoolcraft 1851–7, 4:255.

22. Aupumut's narrative has a patchy publication history: ed. A. Skinner, "A Note on the Mahikan Indians," *Public Museum of Milwaukee Bulletin* 2 (1925): 103–5; "Extract from an Indian History," *Collections of the Massachusetts Historical Society,* 1st ser., 9 (1857): 99–102; Jedidiah Morse, *A Report to the Secretary of War of the United States,* New Haven, 1822, pp. 108–16; and "The Oneida, Stockbridge and Brotherton Indians," *Heye Museum of the American Indian, New York* 54 (1955): 8–9. Another version of the Lenape divisions is given in Weslager 1972:473–99, from Trowbridge, whose ultimate source was Captain Pipe, sachem in Indiana in 1823.

23. See Chapter 11 ("The northern trance journey").

24. Heckewelder, in Brinton 1884:141.

25. Mallery 1893:77–9; R. L. Hall, "Cultural Background of Mississippian Symbolism," in Galloway 1989:241; the term "Chillicothe" is used for the Hopewell and Adena sites.

26. D. B. Smith 1987:10; the map on p. 2 precisely indicates the frontier between the Anishinabe and the Miami, Menomini, Shawnee, and other groups.

27. Mooney 1896:225.

28. Ojibwa migrations are clearly mapped in Dewdney's fundamental account of the scrolls (1975); this source (p. 57) also quotes Warren on the subject of Tugwauganay's copper-plate history.

29. Everwind's account is in Dewdney 1975:57–8; Roden Mound in Alabama, p. 71. On the Siksika, see Chapter 1, n. 33.
30. A. Marshack, "A Lunar–Solar Calendar Stick from North America," AA 50 (1985): 27–51; W. B. Murray, "A Re-examination of the Winnebago Calendar Stick," in Aveni 1989:325–30; on the effigy mounds, see Radin 1970.
31. In favor of the *Walum Olum*'s authenticity are its stated provenance, the settlement on White River in 1820 where, like Aupumut, Lenape chiefs were then promoting their own history as a means of legal defense; and its structure of four-unit stanzas reflexively confirmed by the Olumapi glyph and by the fact that the total number of glyphs, 184, equals the days between spring and autumn equinoxes, so that the end and the arrival of the whites implicitly signify the downturn into winter (a native trope adopted by Longfellow in *The Song of Hiawatha*). Against it are the fact that Rafinesque pays almost no attention to the original, supposedly painted and incised on wooden boards (how many? what wood? etc.); that he first mentions the text only in 1836, when he published it in *The American Nations* (vol. 1, chap. 5) in an effort to pay debts, although claiming to have obtained the original in 1820 and the gloss of Algonkin songs in 1822 (he fails to mention it in several intervening publications on American antiquity and even when writing to the *Cherokee Phoenix* in quest of native traditions like "that of Cusick" [letters of 30 July 1828 and 30 April 1831, in Kilpatrick 1968]); and that in his "copy" the pictographs are subordinated to the alphabetic text. See Brinton 1884; Glenn A. Black and Eli Lilly, *Walam Olum, or Red Score,* Indianapolis: Indiana Historical Society, 1954; and my "The Time Remembered in the Winter Counts and the Walam Olum," in *Circumpacifica: Festschrift für Thomas S. Barthel,* ed. Bruno Illius and Matthias Laubscher, Frankfurt: Peter Lang, 1990, pp. 307–37.

Chapter 8: Tahuantinsuyu

1. Drawing widely on these sources, several of them published only in this century, John Hemming (1970) rewrites the "conquest of the Incas" and offers a good bibliographical review.
2. Ably discussed in Zuidema 1964 and J. M. Ossio, "Intento de aproximación a las categorías del pensamiento del mundo andino," in Ossio 1973:199–200.
3. An earlier version of this argument, with fuller specialist references, appeared in my "Andean Pastoralism and Inca Ideology," in Clutton-Brock 1989:240–55; it draws heavily on Murra 1980 while appealing to the native authority of Guaman Poma's *Nueva corónica* (facsimile ed., 1936; Murra and Adorno 1980) and the *Runa yndio* of Huarochiri (see Chapter 1, n. 36).
4. It was formerly thought that the cargo–wool use spread north from Titicaca as late as A.D. 500 along with Tiahuanaco culture generally; Moche ceramics from Sipan (A.D. 0–250) illustrated in NG 177, no. 6 (June 1990) show a llama transporting jars and hence correct the late dating offered by

M. Shimadu and I. Shimadu, "Prehistoric Llama Breeding and Herding on the North Coast of Peru," AA 50 (1985): 3–26.

5. Matienzo 1567, quoted in Murra 1980:52. A striking indication of how powerful the Colla, with their massive llama herds, had become as the Inca's predecessors comes from the fact that of the four *suyu* theirs was the one that retained the most rights of local herd ownership under Inca rule; after the European conquest and the collapse of Cuzco, the Colla even recovered some of the llama wealth that had been alienated by the Inca.

6. These include the Kon Tiki figure made famous by Heyerdahl (who also added a beard); see Gisbert 1980.

7. Murra 1980:94, 69.

8. Murra 1980:55, 156, 52, 174, 178 (on the *mitima*).

9. Zuidema 1983; *Runa yndio,* chap. 29.

10. Kössler-Ilg 1956:75, 45 (tribute), 124 (dream of wealth), 64 (llamas are like women). On the Chibcha, see Krickeberg 1928:194.

11. J. H. Rowe 1953; Lara 1969:179–86. How the European Enlightenment interpreted these hymns and their presence in the rhetoric of Andean independence are discussed in my article of 1973.

12. Lara 1969:192. The vicuña was in fact never domesticated.

13. See Chapter 1, n. 40. On the survival of this literary pastoralism into the twentieth century, see Harcourt and Harcourt 1925, Kelm 1968, and Yaranga 1986.

14. Basadre 1938:31–8; Arguedas 1949.

15. See my "The Royal Drama *Apu Ollantay,*" *Comparative Criticism* 8 (1986): 189–212. The Quechua text was first published by J. J. von Tschudi (1853: vol. 1); translations followed into Spanish (J. Barranca, Lima, 1868), English (Markham 1871), German (Tschudi 1876), and French (G. Pacheco Zegarra, Paris, 1878). In a negative commentary of 1914 (*Romanic Review* 5:127–76), the Hispanist E. C. Hills shared his ignorance of Native American literature in asserting on the one hand that *Ollantay* was "the most important literary work that has been composed in any language indigenous to America" and on the other that to call it " 'an ancient Inca drama' is as absurd as to call Shakespeare's *Julius Caesar* and Corneille's *Horace* ancient Roman drama." (If nothing else, these last are, after all, not in Latin.) An excellent introduction to the play, and to Andean and Native American dramas in general, is provided by Cid Pérez and Martí 1964.

16. Meneses 1983; Arguedas 1975; Abraham Valencia Espinoza, "Inkari Qollari dramatizado," in Ossio 1973:261–300, and other studies in that volume. Atahuallpa play: Lara 1969:56–62; Cid Pérez and Martí 1964:81, 105–8; Edmonson 1971:184–5. Basadre (1938:135–262) notes another kingship play, *Utqha Paucar* – not to be confused with the *Usca Paucar* discussed in Chapter 13.

17. *Nueva corónica,* p. 159; cf. Wright 1984:156.

18. Also adapted in Peter Shaffer's "Inca" drama *The Royal Hunt of the Sun* (first staged in Chichester in 1964).

19. A point missed by Bramlage (1952) and pondered by Higgins (1987:13).

20. Cid Pérez and Martí 1964; Cardoza y Aragón 1975; HMAI supp. (1985): 115–16; Padial Guerchoux and Vásquez-Bigi 1991. English translation by Nathaniel Tarn in Rothenberg 1972:236–59.

21. A Tupi carbet by Cettvy-ci is in Brotherston 1979:49–50; those who inherit the name Anti today in the uppermost Amazon are Arawak-speakers.

22. See the recent perceptive surveys, both of 1987, by M. Burga and A. Flores Galindo. A highly informed account of native "memory" and native popular culture in the Andes today is given in Rowe and Schelling 1991.

Part III: Genesis

Epigraph: Popol vuh, lines 4939–42; Edmonson 1971:151. Subsequent quotations are from this source, modified in some cases by reference to D. Tedlock 1985.

Chapter 9: Popol vuh

1. D. Tedlock 1988:6; see Chapter 2, n. 10. The proceedings of the first international conference on the *Popol vuh* (Guatemala, 1979) are published in Carmack and Morales 1983. See also M. Preuss (1988), who notes the importance for a better understanding of the text of the Burgess and Xec transcription and Spanish translation published locally in Quetzaltenango in 1955; a facsimile edition has been published by Agustín Estrada Monroy, Guatemala City, 1973. On the *título,* see Munro Edmonson, "Historia de las tierras altas mayas, según los documentos indígenas," in Vogt and Ruz 1971:273–302; Carmack 1973; Carmack and Mondloch 1989. On continuity in Quiché life, see Robert M. Carmack, *The Quiché Mayas of Utatlan: The evolution of a highland Guatemalan kingdom,* Norman: University of Oklahoma Press, 1981. Tedlock shares his experience of translating the *Popol vuh* in R. Warren, *The Art of Translation: Voices from the field,* Hanover, NH: New England University Press, 1979, pp. 73–82.

2. "donde se crean otros hombres," in Monjarás Ruiz 1987:26. As a thread that runs through this cosmic scheme and culminates in the creation of the maize people, that of the two successive creations of protohumans (as here from mud and then from wood) has clear echoes throughout Mesoamerica and the Fourth World; among the Iroquois it is ritually established in the two distinct types of false-face mask (F. Speck, "Masking in Eastern North America," *University Museum Bulletin* [Philadelphia] 15 [1950]: 1–57; W. Fenton, "Masked Medicine Societies of the Iroquois," in *Annual Report to the Smithsonian Institution,* Washington, DC: The Institution, 1941, pp. 297–429; Fenton 1987).

3. Jerome Handler, "The Bird Man: A Jamaican Arawak wooden idol," *Jamaica Journal* 11 (1978): 25–9. Long disputed, this etymology of the hurricane that passed to Europe via the Caribs is now more accepted (D. Tedlock 1985:343).

4. Reproduced in Nowotny 1961:53; recent archaeological work on the fair-sized pyramid at Yauhtepec suggests that the inscription (known as "Los

reyes"), which lies to the west of it at Coatlantzinco or Las Tetillas, forms part of a larger landscape statement.

5. Edmonson 1985:111–12. With its undoubted time depth in Mesoamerican cosmogony, the Otomanguan version of this story argues strongly against such fragmentation: The Mazatec Twins, identical with those of the Quiché as prototypes of sun and moon (Nai Tzult, Nai tza), both go blowgun hunting for birds in the mountains and, having deceived their grandmother, engage in the epic ballgame (Incháustegui 1977:27–34); hence, they reaffirm the connection between the third and fourth creations in the *Popol vuh,* which in any case is implicit in their both having the Twins as main actors.

6. Of this "mythical composite saurian," Monument 5 at Chalcatzingo, Grove blandly says that although some archaeologists have wanted to see in it a prototype of the Mesoamerican Feathered Serpent, there is no visual evidence for this and that in any case "it is highly doubtful that correlations between concepts held during the 16th century and those of the Formative period 2000 years earlier can be demonstrated" (1984:112–13). Even a cursory inspection of the original reveals that those whom Grove dismisses are right, for the "scales" are most featherlike, and the head has definite bird features; as for the point about the continuity of Mesoamerican culture, it is fully assured by if nothing else the uninterrupted use over this period of the *tonalamatl,* whose first Sign is, after all, the caiman *cipactli.* More widely, as a bird-saurian that embodies Seven Parrot's family, this powerful early Olmec figure in turn recalls the monsters discussed by Lévi-Strauss in "The Serpent with Fish inside Its Body" (1972:269–76, especially the swallower on a Nazca vase). In situ at Chalcatzingo it begins the "hunter" sequence of Monuments 5, 4, 3, and 2, which includes predatory felines and issues into the human rendering of homage by warriors armed with spears (Grove calls them paddles despite their clear military definition at Palenque and Loltun).

7. M. D. Coe 1978; Robiscek and Hales 1981; Kerr 1989. The last includes Coe's essay "The Hero Twins: Myth and image," where again Xibalba is tied directly back into the hieroglyphic corpus without apparent awareness of the larger epic matrix (cf. n. 5); also, Coe here changes his mind about whether Twins or Fathers are the subjects in question.

8. This side of their nature becomes much clearer through comparisons with the trickster heroes of Mesoamerica, like the sun and moon Twins of the Mazatec (Incháustegui 1977) and the rainforest (Basso 1987). Matthew Arnold set out his preferences in "On Translating Homer," *Literary and Critical Essays,* London: Everyman, 1906, pp. 210–75.

9. Alfonso García Téllez, *Historia de la curación de antigua,* San Pablito, Pahuatlan, 1978, a screenfold book of *amate* paper of the kind discussed by Dyckerhoff (1984); the *presidente del infierno*'s team of twelve (pp. 9–16) includes whirlwind, rainbow, Moctezuma, Jews, and animals of European origin. On the cigars of hell, see Francis Robicsek, *The Smoking Gods: Tobacco in Maya art, history and religion,* Norman: University of Oklahoma Press, 1978.

10. Monuments 14 and 6 in the planting sequence that culminates in the celebrated image of the rainmaker in his cave (Monument 1) and that complements the hunter–warrior sequence mentioned in n. 6.

11. In the early political panorama of Tilantongo, which matches the *Popol
vuh*'s threefold division of Mesoamerica and identifies west with Mexico's
snow volcanoes, One and Seven Death appear in the east with just such a
sun, low and bleeding; between them are the Signs equivalent to their
victors, Hunter (Flower) and Jaguar Deer (*Tilantongo Annals,* pp. 11–13).
In Eight Deer's biography (on the verso of the same screenfold), the hero's
future inheritance is shown as a "maize net" (p. 3), which stands as the
fourth of the Twenty Signs in Quiché (*q'at*).

12. Commonplace in toponyms, the grouping of the three hearthstones is
shown as part of female equipment in, for example, *Mendoza* (p. 60).

13. This genetic link is alluded to in the foreknowledge that the Twins have of
Xibalba (line 3470) and in their ironic remark to the Lords "You are the
rulers of your born child, your engendered child" (line 4482); the equivalent in Virgil's *Aeneid* is the magnificent line "omnia praecepi atque animo
mecum ante peregi" (book VI, line 106). On the female epic, see *Florentine
Codex,* book 6, chaps. 27–9, which trace the journey of women who,
dying in the west, return to Mictlan.

14. This reading is borne out by modern Kekchi Maya narratives collected in
Purula by Otto Schumann; their version of the maize creation story involves as helpers the carpenter bird, the coati, and other mammals (who,
being five-toed, are "like us"): "Y dijo [Dios] a los animales que habían
ayudado por eso cuando fueran a las milpas no los iban a molestar, pues
ellos habían ayudado a encontrar el maíz" (in Serra Puche 1988:215).

Chapter 10: World ages and metamorphosis

1. The Kekchi account, written down by Tiburtius Kaal, is in R. Burkitt, *The
Hills and the Corn: A legend of the Kekchi Indians of Guatemala,* University of
Pennsylvania Anthropological Publications 8, no. 2, Philadelphia: Univer-
sity of Pennsylvania Press, 1920. For cognate narratives, see C. Guiteras
Holmes 1961; articles on Tzotzil (Gossen), Quiché (Edmonson), and
Chorti (Fought), in Edmonson 1985; and Mercedes de la Garza, "Los
mayas: Antiguas y nuevas palabras sobre el origen," in Monjarás Ruiz
1987:15–86.

2. A gruesome set of stelae removed from this ancient "rainbow" town (see
Chapter 1: "Mesoamerica") in the nineteenth century that insistently links
the ballgame with human sacrifice is now housed in the Museum für
Völkerkunde, Dahlem (Berlin).

3. Impact of modern history: Gossen, in Edmonson 1985:83–4; Garza, in
Monjarás Ruiz 1987:49–52, 57–9; Schumann, in Serra Puche 1988:215. How
the Chamula artist Juan Gallo paints explicitly to recover and defend Tzotzil
cosmogony (utensils with teeth, eclipse, flood) is reported in *La Jornada*
(México), 1 April 1990; Juan Sisay, a fellow Maya painter and friend of
Miguel Angel Asturias, similarly updated this highland tradition. (Shortly

before his assassination in 1988, he featured in the BBC-2 film *Made in Latin America.*)

4. Arzápalo 1987, glossary; the outer "first great world" is identified with inner human organs in the cure for amoebas (*Ritual of the Bacabs*, p. 360), and through *hyam cab* the Flood is implicitly associated with the amniotic waters. The Yucatecan Flood has been seen by many in *Dresden*, p. 74; on the Ah Muzen Cab account, see Barrera Vásquez and Rendón 1963:90–2. On the *Popol vuh* and the Lacandon *Book of Chan Kin*, cf. Bruce 1977, and the relevance of both to today's destruction of the rainforest is brought out in Victor Perera and Robert D. Bruce, *The Last Lords of Palenque,* Boston and Toronto: Little, Brown, 1982.

5. Aztec representations of Tlaltecutli, the terrible monster with myriad eyes and mouths, hungry for hearts, is discussed by Elizabeth Baquedano ("Aztec Death Sculpture," unpublished MS based on her Ph.D. dissertation, University of London, 1988); on sixteenth-century Nahuatl and Spanish accounts, see Castellón Huerta, in Monjarás Ruiz 1987:125–76. In providing an overall view of the Mesoamerican scheme, Monjarás Ruiz's volume is invaluable. It selects key passages from the classics (in the Nahuatl case, *Cuauhtitlan Annals, Inomaca tonatiuh, Histoyre du Mechique, Pinturas MS*) as well as strongly affirming the continuity of these beliefs in recently gathered narratives.

6. As a set and "immutable" paradigm, these ages are discussed by, inter alia, Caso (1954), Imbelloni (1956), Krickeberg (1968), Lahourcade (1970), Ossio (1973:188), Brotherston (1979:148–86), and Brundage (1979). Seler helps us further to link the fourth age with the Xibalba epic by referring to the *Sunstone*'s wind-breath sign as indicative of the dead warrior (1902–23, 2:799).

7. The Dominican Pedro de los Ríos is reported to have been shown a giant fossil molar (*tzocuilicxeque*) in Amecameca in 1566 (*Ríos*, fol. 5). *Histoyre* notes that the bone brought up from hell by Quetzalcoatl (see Chapter 11: "Quetzalcoatl") was of an enormous size (referred to by L. Burkhart, "Sahagún's Tlacuculcuicatl: A Nahuatl lament," ECN 18 (1986): 87. Impressed by the scale and range of fossil bones in Mexico, Tylor (1861:236) recalls how the Tlaxcalans, making the explicit link with past generations of "giants," had shown examples of them to Cortes (who straightaway sent them on to Europe).

8. Martínez Gracida (1897–8:424–9) and Vázquez (1981) report on Mixtec and allied versions (Zapotec, Trique, Mazatec, and Mixe); these display *Popol vuh* motifs, e.g., the birth of sun and moon from male twins who in turn are actually referred to by the Chatino as "cuates" (i.e., the snake twin in Quetzalcoatl – Vázquez 1981:149), as well as an interest in egg birth more characteristic of South America (as Krickeberg noted in 1928:278). All this is made quite explicit in the story of the solar–lunar Twins Nai tzult and Nai tza (see Chapter 9, n. 5), who are born from eggs; this tradition also acknowledges four types of monsters left over from previous creations, which include giants too stiff to bend (like the doll people and the

giants in *Inomaca tonatiuh*) and which have their feet turned backward (like those in rainforest texts): Incháustegui 1977:27–34, 119–21.

9. *Dine bahane* apart (Zolbrod 1984), the most accessible accounts of Anasazi genesis are those found in the dry-painter narratives collected in Haile 1938, Klah 1942, Reichard 1963, 1977, Wyman 1970, 1983, Newcomb and Reichard 1975; the Hopi texts in Waters 1963 and Courlander 1971; and the Zuni creation story performed for and recorded by D. Tedlock (1972).

10. Reichard 1963:22.

11. D. Tedlock 1972:285; on the murals, see HNAI 9 (1979) and 10 (1983); Waters 1963:76; W. Smith, *Kiva Mural Decorations at Awatowi and Kawaika,* Papers of the Peabody Museum of American Archaeology and Ethnology 37, Cambridge: Harvard University Press, 1952.

12. D. Tedlock 1972:271 (on the heavy flesh, p. 260). On the Zuni feather-snake, see Wyman 1983:164.

13. Waters 1963:72; for the return from south to the "flower mound" "Sichtil-kwi" (cf. the Nahuatl *xochitl* "flower"), see Courlander 1971:237.

14. Matthews 1897; used by Zolbrod as his matrix in *Dine bahane*.

15. Reichard 1963:240; in *Dine bahane* it is called "Traveler's Circle Mountain" (Zolbrod 1984:195). On this and other Blessing Way paintings, see Wyman 1970, and on the set of mountains, Wyman 1983:140, 174. On the quincunx map, see Chapter 3, n. 12.

16. Dewdney 1975:39–44 (Red Sky's master scrolls); for the Osage, see Chapter 7, n. 17.

17. An early Dutch report on the Lenape story (1679) is cited in Brinton 1884:132–3 (the turtle became their cattle brand in Oklahoma); the turtle symbol used by the Mide shaman Chusco (see Chapter 11: "The northern trance journey") is illustrated in Schoolcraft 1851–7, 1:390; on the symbol displayed on Arapaho shirts, see Mooney 1896:149; as a possible effigy among the Winnebago as creator of the third earth: Radin 1970. The Cherokee turtle has mud on its back (Kilpatrick 1968:44) and lives in the middle of the earth, causing earthquakes when it shifts position (Mooney 1898:475); the Iroquois account of the woman riding on the turtle is in Cusick 1825.

18. Bierhorst 1985a:32. On the totem-pole depiction of these events, see Barbeau 1950, Gunn 1965.

19. This point is sensitively made by Zolbrod in his introduction to *Dine bahane;* an excellent discussion of the northern bear cult is offered in Murray 1991 ("Grizzly Woman").

20. Murúa, quoted in Ossio 1973:188.

21. See Duviols 1977 and his postscript to the Arguedas edition of this text: "Francisco de Avila, extirpador de la idolatría: Estudio biobibliográfico." On the geography of the area, see Spalding 1984.

22. Gerdt Kutscher's drawings and thoughts on the matter are reproduced by Bierhorst (1988:222–4), who notes the distribution of the theme in South America, notably among the Pano-speaking Tacana in eastern Bolivia (from Karin Hissink and Albert Hahn, *Die Tacana,* vol. 1: *Erzählungsgut,* Stuttgart: W. Kohlhammer, 1961). Fernando Silva Santiesteban gives his

own reading of the five-day period in the Huarochiri text: "El tiempo de cinco días en los mitos de Huarochirí," in F. Miró Quesada, F. Pease, and D. Sobrevilla (eds.), *Historia, problema, promesa: Homenaje a Jorge Basadre,* vol. 1, Lima, 1978, pp. 571–81 (cited in Hartmann 1990:560).

23. Bertonio, discussed by W. Sullivan, *Precessional Time-Reckoning in Andean Myth,* unpublished Ph.D. diss., University of St. Andrews, 1987, chap. 4.

24. See n. 22; Bierhorst's volume compiles many South American echoes of the story of the Suns, notably in the Chaco area, and, like all his work, is impeccably documented.

25. This theme, and the fossil evidence for it, drew the attention of Alexander von Humboldt; Krickeberg suggests the beginnings here of a Western intellectual tradition (1928:328, 337).

26. Kössler-Ilg 1956:117–29; cf. Chapter 1, n. 43. Later published in Spanish translation in Buenos Aires, this collection of Mapuche narratives is easily the richest to have appeared to date and well complements the work in this area of the Carrasco brothers Hugo and Iván and of other Chilean scholars. In their own language, the Kogi spoke their warning about the snow line in Alan Ereira's film *From the Heart of the World* (1990; also published in the book of that title, London: BBC, 1990). Toward the far south and Tierra del Fuego, among the Selknam and Yamana, the domestic conflict resulted in separate bodies of narrative for men and women, as Gusinde and Chapman report (Bierhorst 1988:168).

27. Amazons from the Amazon are reported in *Makunaima* (episode 40).

28. Particularly significant here is the parallel drawn by Basso (1985:41) between *Watunna* and the cosmogony of the Carib-speaking Kalapalo of Xingu. For further references to these rainforest texts, see Chapter 1, nn. 46–8.

29. Monkey's tail: Brotherston 1979a; according to the Witoto, the tail was eaten off the human embryo by wasps, who got tired by the time it was the monkey's turn (K. T. Preuss 1921:169; the story is still told today: Montoya Sánchez 1973:145). Rafuema: K. T. Preuss 1921:165. Païand Charia are discussed in León Cadogan, "Takwa-Kama," in Roa Bastos 1978:53–5; the Tupi parallel further includes the hairy opossum who aids Maíra, the Twins' father (Wagley and Galvao 1949:137–40).

30. Huiio: "Wi" in the Pemon Carib story, where likewise Odosha is Orodan, Mawadi is Maware, Enneku is Enek (Armellada 1972). The Tsunki Flood story published by the Shuar includes a blood-chilling account of how this name, also "heard" in their language, results from the noise made by anacondas about to devour (Pellizaro 1979:79). The anaconda is imbued with shame by a team of eleven young men in Ribeiro's Tupi novel *Maíra* (1976: "Sucuridjureda").

31. A very widespread motif: Like the Twins in this refuge, the Shuar Tsunki and his daughter throw down palm nuts that, in sedimentarian discourse, presage the reappearance of terra firma (Pellizaro 1979:50–1). The palm saves the equivalent Guarani pair in chap. 7 of *Ayvu rapyta* (Bareiro Saguier 1980:27).

32. "Who would dare to marry the daughter of Lightning?" asks the father in the *taren* of the Pemon Carib (Armellada 1972:293); on son-in-law practice, see Rivière 1984.

33. This evocative term is Schomburgk's (*Travels* . . . , Leipzig, 1841), quoted by Meneses (1977:17) in her edition of Goodall's *Sketches of Amerindian Tribes*.

34. This point is critical because it impinges on the larger question of the world ages; the comparisons Civrieux himself draws between *Watunna* and Maya cosmogony are based on the 1970 edition and go in a different direction.

35. In relating the Arawak cosmogony published in part in Brotherston 1979:202–3, Cuthbert Simon placed singular emphasis on this event and its liminal nature. In the Cuna *Tatkan ikala,* the tree in question, the primordial Paluhuala (or Palewalla), is in some sources actually shown with an umbilical cord complete with fetal membranes entwined through its root branches (Keeler 1969:63, whose source is Chief Ikwaniktipippi of Ailigandi). This is the same tree that when attacked with the axe is licked better by the jaguar (Nordenskiöld 1938:158–60), as in the *teoamoxtli* model (see below). The Cuna designs also show Paluhuala with the fish that will occupy the floodwaters, a motif visually echoed in the enigmatic cosmogonical prologue of the *Dehesa* screenfold (HMAI Census 112). Yet another parallel: In Cuna *mola* designs, Paluhuala ("turning in the water of life") is shown in just the swastika shape that characterizes the "whirling logs" dry painting of the Navajo (Keeler 1969:35).

36. Louquou: HSAI 14:561, reminiscent of the Yanomamo man with a "pregnant" leg (Jacques Lizot, *El hombre de la pantorilla preñada y otros mitos yanomami,* Caracas, 1975); Barasana: Hugh-Jones 1979:293–4 (the subsequent list of plants directly evokes the caiman stela at Chavin: Lathrap 1973).

37. The continuities between the cosmogony of the two areas were first described at the beginning of the century by scholars in the German tradition of K. T. Preuss, Koch-Grünberg, and Krickeberg.

38. Far in advance of anything published in English in his day, Mooney explored a whole set of parallels between Appalachia and the rainforest (male-moon incest, woodpecker helper, hummingbird who fetches the consoling tobacco, the wooing of Lightning's daughter, etc.), the historical implications of which have still not been fully drawn out (1898:256 and notes section generally). Ballard (1978:54) proposes the Bahamas as a prior home of the Yuchi in their struggle with the monster caiman; in Taino sculpture and the story of Deminan, Arrom finds parallels for the emphasis on the primordial turtle of Turtle Island (1989:86–7 and pl. 57). The brilliant blue Carib lake whose waters heal finds an exact counterpart in the sacred Cherokee lake Atagahi near the guardian mountain Kuwahi.

39. It is significant that echoes of the volcanic episode can be heard in precisely the cosmogonies of those peoples who live closest to the Andes. For example, in the Canimani narrative of the Witoto, the bird that goes off in search of fire swallows and then spews glowing coals onto the earth (Montoya

Sánchez 1973:117); the violent appearance and destruction of the rock and town Canchahuaya on the Ucayali River are a major feature of Shipibo cosmogony (E. Weisshaar and B. Illius, in Illius and Laubscher 1990, 1:578–81).

Chapter 11: The epic

1. The fundamental account of this journey and its origins in the shamanic trance remains that of Eliade (1964 [1951]), which directly affected accounts of the North American epic journey elaborated by Radin (1954–6), Hultkranz (1957), and others. On the underlying similarity of the implied astronomical course of the epic journey in South America, see the "models" of earth and sky published by Hugh-Jones (in Aveni 1982:195) and Reichel-Dolmatoff (1971:44) as well as M. S. Cipolletti, "El motivo de Orfeo y el viaje al reino de los muertos en América del Sur," *Indiana* 9 (1984): 421–32, and T. Zuidema, "A Visit to God," in Gross 1973:358–76. In the Guarani *Ayvu rapyta*, the shift into the epic mode in chap. 8 is formally marked by a more discursive prose, which replaces the chantlike invocation of the previous disasters of Flood and Eclipse (Bareiro Saguier 1980:30–9).
2. Reichard 1977:pl. 1; Nowotny 1961:34; Civrieux 1980:85–8. The Bororo version of the scavenger story appears as the inaugural item ("M1") in Lévi-Strauss's *Mythologiques*.
3. See Chapter 10, n. 8. As we saw above, according to Molina's dictionary the *coatl* part of his name may mean, besides "snake," "twin" (*mellizo* in Spanish), as in the modern Mexican term *cuate* – a linguistic fact that further helps to identify him with the Hero Twins of the Quiché and other American cosmogonies.
4. Krickeberg 1928:193–7.
5. Called Urpayhuachac, the mother is identified as Pachacamac's wife and the daughter of the highland Tamtañamca who was later honored as a *huaca* at Pachacamac's temple – none of which does much for the notion of Viracocha's priority. In his analysis of this story Tom Zuidema (1982) illustrates the complex in-law relationships evident alike here and in numerous rainforest texts, not least the very Bororo myth on which Lévi-Strauss based the first volume of his *Mythologiques*. On son-in-law practice, see Chapter 10, n. 32.
6. Guss 1985:55–75; this source includes an actual diagram of the ascent, drawn by an apostate shaman. The corresponding Cuna experience is given in Nele Kantule's "A Journey through the Next World" and in accompanying graphic designs (Nordenskiöld 1930:36–47); again, passing through a series of tests that includes river crossings, scissors that behave like the hanging bats, a house of angry jaguars, and so on, the pilgrim reaches a point so high that the world appears as small as a coconut. Like Medatia's, this quest leads to the discovery of the beautiful blue egg in which the voices of future generations can be heard.
7. J. Wilbert and K. Simoneau 1978:30, 104; Kössler-Ilg 1956:315 (on the

nine-night period that follows death); vol. 5, Zuidema 1989; Yaranga 1986 (on the Quechua Venus); Cipolletti and Zuidema in n. 1 above.

8. See my " 'Far as the Solar Walk': The path of the North American sha-man," *Indiana* 9 (1984): 15–29, and Fig. 59.

9. Nowotny 1961:224. The Cuauhtitlan account of his heliacal appearance as morning star on the eastern horizon has been alluded to and paraphrased by many writers, including D. H. Lawrence in *The Plumed Serpent*.

10. Such is the arrangement in *Magliabechiano,* where the zodiac (pp. 37–47) precedes the double appearance of Quetzalcoatl (pp. 49–50); in *Telleriano* the bloodied-tree gloss refers to the "árbol ensangrado y quebrado" in the "huerto donde bajaron" (day 1 House, fifteenth *trecena* of the *tonalamatl*); the verb *bajar* could conceivably be transitive and therefore the passage could mean "where they felled the tree." Watacame: Negrín 1975: pl. 2 (*After the Flood*).

11. K. T. Preuss 1912, 1968.

12. *Histoyre du Mechique,* p. 110, in Monjarás Ruiz 1987:153. The Zuyua riddle of the Maya, third in the set of twenty that refer to the bringing of food: "Childe, bring me the bones of your fathers, those that you buried three years ago; I wish to look at them." "So it shall be." What is asked for is manioc cooked under the earth (Barrera Vásquez and Rendón 1963:140). Places named after this crop are found in the Otomanguan and Nahuatl languages, e.g., Son-daye (in the Mazatec "Shona-vee": Incháustegui 1977:103) and Camotlan, on the southern edge of Papaloapan (*Mendoza,* p. 44; *Coixtlahuaca Lienzo*).

13. *Florentine Codex,* book 2, appendix (after the Eighteen Feasts of the year).

14. "Se presenta la necesidad del maíz como un elemento que les permitiera sustituir el cultivo de los tubérculos y raíces como la yuca, ya que no podían guardarlos todo el año" (Schumann 1988:217). See also Chapter 12, n. 3.

15. Mendieta, in Monjarás Ruiz 1987:149–50; as regent of the sixteenth of the *trecenas*, Xolotl is further glossed in *Ríos* and *Telleriano*.

16. Stanislav Iwaniszewski, "Mitología y arqueoastronomía," in Marco Antonio Moreno Corral (ed.), *Historia de la astronomía en México*, FCE, 1986, pp. 112–21; Martínez Gracida (1897–8:424) notes that the male moon Tezcatlipoca is the same as "el dios luna llamado Yyacaahuiyu o nuhu yooera" of Mixtec cosmogony. Though identified by another name, the Nahuatl moon is definitely male in the *Florentine Codex,* book 7. In general on lunar gender in America, see Lévi-Strauss 1978:211–21 ("The Sex of the Sun and Moon").

17. The Tzotzil circuit has been compared with a fairground Ferris wheel (Monjarás Ruiz 1987:69).

18. Mönnich 1971; pioneering in its day, this source cites previous notes on Anasazi links with Mesoamerica (by Parsons, Fewkes, Nowotny, and others). Mönnich speaks in particular of contact at the "Chichimec" horizon, which must seem late in the day given evidence for the Venus trance paradigm in the Classic inscriptions and the deeper shamanic links with the South American *Medatia.* On Anasazi sources, see Chapter 10, nn. 9–11.

19. In *Watunna* the twin eagle brothers Dinoshi shed feathers that grow into

cane, the material used by the Soto to make the blowguns they trade: in the Bead Chant, the twin eagle brothers who shelter the Navajo hero shed feathers that turn into weapons on reaching the ground. Further parallels include the fish that swallows the hero and the visit to water people under rapids, subjects of sand paintings.

20. Reichard 1977: pls. v and vii; Reichard 1963:23. Reichard 1977 includes Miguelito's account of the Bead Chant (p. 26) and the Male Shooting Chant (Visit to the Sun, p. 37; Earth, Sky, and Buffalo people, pp. 50, 57, 68).

21. Turkey: Newcomb and Reichard 1975:37; maize path: Wyman 1970:92–3; "greening": Bahr 1975:47, 106.

22. For sundry references to this epic Algonkin figure, see Brinton 1884:167 (Nanabush); Spence 1914:119 (Michabo); Skinner and Satterlee 1915:255 (Manabus); S. Thompson 1966 8–13, (1929):53–7. Bierhorst 1985:223 reproduces a painting of him (1975) by the Ottawa artist Blake Debassige. Gerald Vizenor's portrait of him (Naanabozho, in the novel *Griever* [1987]) is touched on in the Epilogue, n. 13.

23. Schoolcraft 1839, 2:40–60.

24. Dewdney 1975:159; Schoolcraft 1851–7, 2:163. In this respect it is worth noting that in the Lenape tradition the moon is not female but male, brother of the sun, according to the sachem Captain Pipe (reported by Trowbridge in Weslager 1972:491; this source also clearly details how the sun going along his path passes under the Turtle at night).

25. R. B. Hall, "The Cultural Background of Mississippian Symbolism," in Galloway 1989:241; Brotherston 1979:150.

26. Navarre 1913:22–4.

27. Hoffman 1891; Densmore 1910; Landes 1968; Dewdney 1975. Skinner 1915:103 and Dewdney 1975:168–9 reproduce similar scrolls of the Menomini; the former shows levels of the sky, the latter the "three roads" referred to by Chusco. The Mide standardization of shamanic practice is discussed in Eliade 1964:314.

28. "The Ghost Lodge and Sky Degree Scrolls": Dewdney 1975:103–14.

29. For matching symbols and song texts by Kweweziashish and others quoted here, see Tanner 1830:341–4; Schoolcraft 1851–7, 1:332–411; Mallery 1893:231–55; Brotherston 1979: 256, 268 (a previously unpublished song board in the British Museum).

30. Schoolcraft 1851–7, 1:390–7, 402. Yet further examples of the Algonkin trance journey occur in Siksika texts: These propose a solar walk that involves not just the correlated passages of the big three – sun, moon, and Venus – but a test faced by the traveler upon emergence from the underworld that directly echoes that faced by Quetzalcoatl; i.e., as the Morning Star he is set upon and attacked by birds (Spence 1914:199–200, 204).

31. Radin 1970:104–5.

32. The Winnebago epic cycles of Trickster were written down by Sam Blowsnake in the Winnebago syllabary: Radin 1956:111; on the links with Hare, and especially the closely linked Red Horn and Twins, see ibid. pp. 118ff.; the cycle is discussed by Robert L. Hall in making similar links with

Mesoamerican epics, notably the heroes Red Horn and Hun Hunahpu ("The Cultural Background of Mississippian Symbolism," in Galloway 1989:240–5). Other Siouan examples of Venus and sun as hunters are quoted in Spence 1914:304.

33. There is, however, a possible further play, noted by Médiz Bolio (1973 [1930]:), with the word for moon; cf. the expression "uil uinal" in a Tizimin passage reminiscent of this one from Chumayel (Edmonson 1982:180; the *uinal* glyph typically indicates moon age, i.e., plus 9 or 10, in the hieroglyphic texts). Though fragmented into separate chapters by Roys and other editors, the *uinal* passage completes the *Book of Chumayel*'s lowland Maya story of creation (pp. 42–63), told here in highly allusive fashion. Indeed, with details like the rush of water, falling sky, and flaming fire, the weak ones who relapsed into the sea and the yellow ones destroyed by the four Bacabs (p. 43, ?mud people and doll people), the robbing of the insignia of the Thirteen Oxlahun-ti-ku (p. 43, Seven Parrot's emblems of power), and the "grace" with its long locks of hair and the rock that is broken open by the rain god (pp. 48, 51, maize and its release from the food mountain), the Chumayel text is comprehensible only by reference to other Mesoamerican accounts (cf. Garza, in Monjarás Ruiz 1987:40–8).

34. Anticipating this order of word–number pun, a stucco dog at Palenque (site museum) shows the footprint as the eye: See Chapter 2, n. 31. In general, this pronounced emphasis on the epic as script – arithmetical and verbal play typical of the hieroglyphic texts – is matched in the earlier phases of lowland Maya cosmogony by the absence of unforeseen eclipse, a phenomenon accurately calculated and predicted in *Dresden*.

35. Martínez Hernández 1930; William E. Gates, review of J. E. S. Thompson, *Archaeology of the Cayo District,* in *Maya Society Quarterly* (Baltimore) 1 (1931): 37–44.

36. In the Boban Wheel (see Chapter 4, n. 23), the footsteps are marked out as here, odd and even, in sets of twenty per quadrant of the circle. On germane hieroglyphic examples of the eighty-day period, see n. 37.

37. Edmonson 1982:48–9, 180, where the earthly geography of east, south, west, and north is clearly stated; in the *Book of Mani* (Solís Alcalá 1949:144) the eighteen Feasts of the year are also involved. The eighty-day period, stated glyphically as four *uinals*, occurs with the 4 Ahau date in *Dresden,* pp. 42–5 (and again with chapters that feature rain gods with axe, canoe, and seine and mounted). In this connection, the Ah Toc are considered as burners (J. E. S. Thompson 1972:106) and "explorers" (Solís Alcalá 1949:110); see also Sosa 1986.

Chapter 12: American cosmos

1. Reichel-Dolmatoff 1971:218, 50.
2. E.g., D. Tedlock 1988.
3. Reichel-Dolmatoff 1950–1; Enrique Margery Peña, "Algunos alcances en torno a la configuración de motifemas y temas en la narrative oral talamanqueña," in M. Preuss 1989:53–8.

4. A superbly lucid account of "the two divergent traditions" of plant domestication, through vegetative cuttings or through seed, is given in Wolf
1959:51–2. On notations of transformation expressed in Turtle Island imagery of the cocoon, see C. Taylor 1990. The intricate role that tubers and
root vegetables have in Turtle Island cosmogony comes through, for example, in the turnip stories of the Siksika and in the potato-man hero of the
Chippewa (Ojibwa) Pochiku, whose inventive life has recently been retold
by Louise Erdrich in *Granta*, 1989.

5. Gossen, in Edmonson 1985:83–4; Kelley 1980; Kössler-Ilg, 1956:296, Part
of the riddle series (see Chapter 2, n. 12), pp. 41–3, "Ueber Schnee,
Eisberge, Trockenheit, Weltende"; Schele and Miller 1986:272–3; Arzápalo
1987:380, 396.

6. Severin 1981; as he says, "The movement of the vernal equinox through
the zodiacal constellations was the basis of a series of world ages" (p. 69);
he calculates 101 *katun* counts, approximately 25,900 years. Brotherston
1982:42–4: The 29-Round, or 1,508-year, "solar span" in *Mexicanus* (see
Fig. 36) is touched on in Edmonson 1988; in the *Tepexic Annals*, the $27\frac{1}{2}$-
Round, or 1,427-year, "sidereal span" is distinguished by a star device (Fig.
63) and a specific date (2 Reed, day 2 Reed). Precession has been related to
Greek cosmogony by Giorgio de Santillana and Hertha von Dechend in
Hamlet's Mill: An essay on myth and the frame of time (New York: Macmillan,
1969), a contentious work that nonetheless exposes the limits of the linear
philosophical approach of, for example, S. Toulmin and J. Goodfield's *The
Discovery of Time* (London: Hutchinson, 1965).

7. Though as a result of transcription the number values have been distorted,
a total of 13 Rounds (676 years) accompanies, for example, the joint
"walk" of Quetzalcoatl (Hero 9) and the Sun (Hero 4).

8. Brotherston 1990:326; High Hawk: E. Curtis 1908.

9. *Madrid*, pp. 57, 69, 72; this last has been transcribed and discussed by David
H. Kelley (1980) in a world-age context, along with Chimalpahin's millennial dates.

10. The possibility of a time shift between the pulse of blood and larger time
units, of an order basic in Buddhism, is suggested by the numeracy of
blood flow in the time maps of the *teoamoxtli* (*Borgia*, p. 72; *Féjérváry*, p. 1)
and by the occurrence of the word "pulse" in alphabetic texts (e.g., the
Book of Chumayel, p. 153 above, and the *matsuara* read in Huichol paintings:
Negrín 1975:30; the 26,000 years of the Great Year in fact occur as pulses, at
seventy-two per minute, over half the night, so that four such years correspond to the night–day unit).

11. H. Butterfield, *The Origins of Modern Science*, London: G. Bell & Sons,
1957 (especially informative on the geological debates between vulcanists
and sedimentarians in the late eighteenth century); Bieder 1986.

12. On Montaigne and his sources, see E. Núñez 1972:94–5; whereas in the
1580 edition of the *Essais* Montaigne's interest in America stemmed mainly
from these direct encounters with the Tupi at Rouen, in the 1588 edition,
notably in "On Coaches," where the world ages appear, Las Casas,
Gómara, Benzoni, and other historians become important. The charges of

heresy against Marlowe were drawn up in what is known as the Baines Note, which shows him to have been influenced by Raleigh and by Heriot's *A Briefe and True Report of the Newfoundland of Virginia* (1558), and party to the opinion – deplored in Thomas Nashe's *Christs Teares over Ierusalem* – that "the late discovered Indians are able to shew antiquities thousands before Adam" (Paul Kocher, *Christopher Marlowe*, Chapel Hill: University of North Carolina Press, 1960, p. 45; I thank Helen Carr for giving me this reference). Before the Christians, pagan Rome had ridiculed the notion of the world's antiquity, Cicero pouring scorn on the 400,000 years posited by the Babylonians (ibid., p. 44).

13. Yourgrau and Breck 1977. There is certainly no precedent in the Roman–Christian case.

14. A 2–3-cm layer of quartz suggests that volcanic activity coincided with the end of the giant saurians at the end of the Cretaceous. The *Madrid* strata dates relate to the 26-million-year cycle in terms of x0.3. For recent summaries and charts, see Colin Trudge, "The Evolution of Evolution," *Listener* 19 (June 1986): 11–12; *Scientific American*, September 1989, pp. 63–4.

15. "En este texto sagrado de los antiguos quichés se inscribe ya, con trágica adivinación, el mito del robot; más aún: creo que es la única cosmogonía que haya presentido la amenaza de la máquina y la tragediá del Aprendiz de Brujo" (*Los pasos perdidos* (1953), chap. 27); Jorge Luis Borges, "La escritura del dios," *Ficciones*, 1944.

16. Zolbrod 1984:166. Quotations from *Watunna* and *Popol vuh* are from, respectively, Civrieux 1980:64–5, 106 and Edmonson 1971:38–9. The Navajo parting from the bear "at the edge of the forest" is very closely paralleled in the Cherokee story told by Ayunini (Mooney 1891:310–11).

17. On America as the garden of the planet, a dominent theme in Diego Rivera's murals, see Lathrap 1970, 1973; Sauer 1975; Ramón Cruces Carvajal, *Lo que México aportó al mundo*, México, 1986; Weatherford 1988. Some of the early evidence was supplied in Thor Heyerdahl's *Kon-Tiki* (Oslo, 1948), though rather in the name of Viking interest. This is not the place to explore the ultimate origins of traditions held in common by the New and Old World, like the world-age echoes in the Book of Daniel, Hesiod, and Ovid, the trance journey of Asiatic shamanism and Gilgamesh, and, in Virgil, Aeneas's "pious" reassembling of the father in the underworld, or the predyed threads for weaving in the fourth Eclogue.

Part IV: Into the language of America

Epigraph: Roys 1933:62.

Chapter 13: The translation process

1. Cherokee: Mooney 1891:342, 377–8; Kilpatrick and Gritts 1964; Hudson 1984 (he also notes the Cherokee antecedents of Tar-baby and other Uncle Remus stories). Maya: Dzul Poot 1985–6; Shuar: Pellizaro 1979.

2. See Epilogue, n. 10, for the literary origin of Gaspar Ilóm's name, taken

from *Hombres de maíz,* the novel Miguel Angel Asturias based on the *Popol vuh,* and the case of a Maya *guerrillero.* See Cardoza y Aragón 1955 and the note on the equation of the USA with Xibalba in S. Clissold, *Latin America: A cultural outline,* London: Hutchinson, 1965, p. 50. On Gallo and Sisay, see Chapter 10, n. 3. (Recognized in Noam Chomsky, *Turning the Tide,* the Maya cause characteristically escapes mention in F. Chalk and K. Jonassohn, *The History and Sociology of Genocide,* New Haven: Yale University Press, 1990, which, though moving in the right direction, still fails to do full justice to America as a whole.) On the *achkay,* see Howard-Malverde 1986, 1989.

3. Ortiz: in Swann and Krupat 1987:193, which also quotes the noted Lenape scholar Jack Forbes. Souza (*A expressão amazonense* [1978]) is quoted in Rama 1982:80; Rama also notes the Quechua poetry of Kilkawaraka (Taki Parwa) and the reaction to it of José María Arguedas, who in 1955 compared Kilkawaraka's mastery of language to that of the author of *Apu Ollantay,* saying he had believed it beyond the reach of a present-day speaker. See also Bendezú 1986 and Cornejo Polar 1989. Montoya and Montoya 1987 includes powerful examples of modern political poetry and song in Quechua.

4.

mutrungreke trekan	I walked through the tree trunk
chew ñi rupamum füchake antikuyem	a hundred generations,
ngümanmew ayenmew	suffering, laughing
dakinmew ñi pewma	within my soul
ina pen kine cruz katrünmaetew ñi lonko	and saw a cross that cut off my head
ka kiñe espada bendecipeetew petu ñi lanon	and a sword that blessed me before my death
	– "Rupamum" [Footsteps], in Lienlaf 1989:54

On Queupul, see I. Carrasco 1988. On modern Aymara texts, see Albó 1985. Martínez Hernández's poem is in ECN 20:358–63, part of a remarkable anthology of modern Nahuatl texts, *Yancuic tlahtolli,* published in nos. 18–20 of ECN. In the political arena, native languages played a role in what became Latin America's struggle for independence: e.g., Quechua (Tupac Amaru II's speeches), Guarani (Manuel Belgrano's proclamations to Paraguay, in Roberto Romero, *Antecedentes de la independencia paraguaya,* Asunción, 1988), Maya (acts of the Spanish Cortes in Tzotzil couplets, in Bricker 1981), and Nahuatl (a whole set of printed declarations and counterdeclarations, in Ascensión de León-Portilla 1988).

5. Stiles 1987.

6. Information on Bible translation into American languages is available in E. M. North, *The Book of a Thousand Tongues* (New York: Harper Bros., 1938), and Pottier 1983:338, notable examples being Algonkin (Mohican, 1661), Iroquois (Mohawk, 1715), Arawak (1799), Otomi (1826), Ojibwa (1828), Cherokee (1829), Aymara (1829; cf. Yapita 1976), Nahuatl (1833), Muskogee (1835), Sioux (Santee, 1839), Carib (1847), Maya (1862), Quechua (1880), Guarani (1888), Quiché (1898), Mapuche (1901), Cakchiquel (1902), Navajo (1910), Cuna (1916). Reference to translation between Fourth World languages can be found in Guaman Poma's *Nueva corónica*

(Quechua, Aymara), in the *Cantares mexicanos* (Nahuatl, Otomi, Huaxtec), and in the Ghost Dance songs (Mooney 1896).

7. Bierhorst 1985:87; Burkhart 1986:189 (on nuance in Nahuatl versions of Genesis). Guaman Poma is clearly amused by the high-flown Quechua of Molina, the dictionary compiler, and by Murúa's emphatic outrage at being misunderstood by his flock.

8. Tlaxcala performance: Arrom 1967:27. See also Paso y Trancoso 1902; Hunter 1960; Frances Kartunnen and Gilka Wara, "The Dialogue of El Tepozteco and his rivals," *Tlalocan* 9 (1982): 115–41. On the Huehuentzin, see references in Chapter 1, n. 7.

9. Brecht, in *Guchachireza* (Juchitan), December 1982; Saint-Exupéry, *Auquicu,* version Quichua by Teodoro Gallegos and León Coloma, Quito: Centro de Documentación e Información de los Movimientos Sociales del Ecuador, 1989; I am grateful to Michael Dürr and Ruth Moya for these references. (See also Ruth Moya in Zúñiga 1987 and Rodríguez 1983 on the standardization of Quechua orthography. On this point, educational texts in Cree are notable for using the syllabary of that language, a recent example being *Waskahikaniwiyiniw acimowina: Stories of the House People,* ed. Peter Vandall, Winnipeg: Manitoba University Press, 1987.)

10. Earlier versions of my four studies are "How Aesop Fared in Nahuatl," *Arcadia* 7 (1972): 37–42; "Tawaddud and Maya Wit: A story from the *Arabian Nights* adapted to the Community Books of Yucatan," *Indiana* 7 (1982): 131–41; "Faustian Incas and Inca Fausts," *Comparative Criticism* 9 (1987): 97–110; and "The Zuni Cinderella," *Latin American Indian Literatures Journal* 2 (1986): 110–26.

11. Two main MS copies of the forty-seven translated fables exist, in the Biblioteca Nacional of Mexico and the Bancroft Library; they are critically compared in the edition of the text prepared by the late Gerdt Kutscher, Günter Vollmer, and myself (1987).

12. The bibliography of the six hundred or so original fables is myriad. The first Spanish edition (1489) cannot have been the source text for the Nahuatl, as many of the forty-seven in question are absent from that collection, large as it is. On the other hand, there is a high degree of correspondence with the Accursiana, the last of the three main groups of fables listed by August Hausrath in his monumental edition of 1940 (*Fabulae aesopicae soluta oratione conscriptae,* Munich): While about a quarter of the forty-seven fables are entirely absent from one or other or both of the first two of these groups (*Augustana* and *Vindobonesis*), Accursius's *Aesopi fabulae graece et latine* (1479) contains all forty-seven (no. 26, "Leo et asinus et vulpes," is, for example, present in Accursius only). Accursius lies behind the Latin texts included in the Paris copy of the Mexican manuscript (Bibliothèque National), and certain narrative traits peculiar only to these late concise versions often reappear word for word in the Nahuatl. All this was pointed out in my article of 1972 (see n. 10).

13. *Ecamecoyotl:* Zimmerman 1955. *Totecuyoane:* See Chapter 2, n. 13.

14. Garibay 1953–4, 2:183. Sixteenth-century animal stories in Nahuatl are included in the *Florentine Codex* (book 11; cf. Garibay 1961:172); their

modern counterparts are published in González Casanova 1965; W. Jiménez Moreno, *Los cuentos de Doña Luz Jiménez*, UNAM, 1979; and "Yancuic tlahtolli," ECN 18–20 (1986–90).

15. *Florentine Codex*, book 2, p. 213; Garibay 1958: Hymn 17.

16. *Kaua* (unpublished), nos. 50–9 of T. Maler's photographs in the Ibero-Amerikanisches Institut, Berlin, and pp. 99–117 of Roys's transcription, Tulane University; *Chan Kan* (unpublished), pp. 74–99 seen briefly in a copy held at Mérida, by courtesy of Alfredo Barrera Vásquez; *Mani*, in Solís Alcalá 1949:62–74 and Craine and Reindorp 1979:59–62 (who report a further version in the *Book of Ixil*, which I have not examined). Current Maya use of the epithet "elegant" to describe the story was reported to me by the late Günter Zimmermann.

17. In his "Zuhuy Teodora–Doncella Teodor–Tawaddud: Eine Geschichte aus 1001 Nacht in einer yukatekischen Mayahandschrift des 18. Jahrhunderts," Cologne, 1969 (unpublished Habilitationsvortrag), Peter Tschohl identifies their source as an edition of the group denominated "PT" by Walter Mettmann in his fundamental treatment of the story: *La historia de la Donzella Teodor: Ein spanisches Volksbuch arabischen Ursprungs: Untersuchung und kritische Ausgabe des ältesten bekannten Fassungen*, Wiesbaden, 1962 (Mettmann also details how knowledge transmitted in the story relates to the *repartorio*s of fifteenth-century Europe). I am grateful to Tschohl for his ready response when I was preparing my study of 1972.

18. Richard Burton, *The Book of the Thousand Nights and a Night*, vol. 5 London, 1885, p. 189; on this and Lane's translation, see Jorge Luis Borges, "Los traductores de las 1001 noches" (1935), in *Historia de la eternidad*, Buenos Aires, 1953, pp. 99–133.

19. Melveena McKendrick, *Woman and Society in the Spanish Drama of the Golden Age*, Cambridge: Cambridge University Press, 1974, pp. 222–3.

20. *Florentine Codex*, book 6, chap. 43 (Johannson in ECN 20:297–300); Parsons 1936 (Zapotec).

21. Barrera Vásquez and Rendón 1963:131–43, based on the sequences in the books of *Chumayel* (pp. 28–42, 67–71) and *Tusik* (unpublished, pp. 32–54). Günter Lanczkowski detects Toltec elements in these riddles, though he perhaps underestimates their politically protective function against Toltec and Christian: "Die Sprache von Zuyua als Initiationsmittel," *Studies in the History of Religions*, supp. to *Numen* 10 (1965): 27–39; R. S. Boggs simply describes their "folkloric" nature: "Las adivinanzas en el Libro de Chilam Balam de Chumayel," *Actas y memorias del 35 Congreso Internacional de Americanistas*, vol. 3, UNAM, 1962, pp. 365–8.

22. Bierhorst 1976:141; told by River Woman and first published by Dorsey and Kroeber in 1903. The dazzling dialogues of *Medatia* are noted in Chapter 11; for Mapuche riddles, see Chapter 2, n. 12.

23. The image of lords mounted on thrones that are jaguars or other beasts is commonplace in Mesoamerican iconography and occurs in the murals at Tulum; royalty at Tequiztepec (*Tequixtepec Map*) rode on jaguars. Cf. Plate 2b.

24. Found in Cuzco in 1922, the manuscript of *Yauri Titu* was published by Suárez and Farfán (Lima, 1938) under the Spanish title *El pobre más rico*, a

rough version of the Quechua one; the author is identified as a certain Gabriel Centeno de Osma, otherwise unknown in Quechua literature. What is clearly a separate manuscript of *Yauri Titu* with variant character names had been reported earlier by Clements Markham in *The Incas of Peru* (1911). Of *Usca Paucar*, which is anonymous, no fewer than seven manuscript copies are known; the one made in 1838 by Dr. Sahuaraura Inca served as the basis for the critical edition by Teodoro Meneses (1951). Meneses includes both plays plus *Apu Ollantay*, the tragedy of Atahuallpa, and two more Europeanized pieces (about the Prodigal Son and Proserpina) in his extremely useful and well-prepared anthology of 1983.

25. This play has the distinction of being the first to present the devil on the Spanish stage: A. Valbuena Prat, *Mira de Amescua: Teatro*, vol. 1, Madrid, 1943, p. 63; subsequently it served as a model for plays by Lope de Vega and Calderón's *El mágico prodigioso* (which much later caught Shelley's attention as a translator). As E. B. Tylor noted (1871, 2:230), "even the Aztec war god Huitzilopochtli may be found figuring as the demon Vitzliputzli in the popular drama of Dr Faustus."

26. Other plays in the Quechua corpus to which *Yauri Titu* and *Usca Paucar* belong are explicitly related to the Spanish Golden Age. For example, Yauri's devil, Nina Quiru (Fire Tooth; Usca's is Nina Yunca), also appears under that name in *The Prodigal Son*, an *auto sacramental* by Juan de Espinosa Medrano (?1629–88), the cleric from Cuzco famous equally as a Quechua playwright and for his deep involvement with such Spanish Golden Age figures as Góngora and Calderón; and whole lines from the devil's speeches in both Faust plays find echoes in another of Espinosa Medrano's plays, *The Rape of Proserpine*, and refer in particular to the devil-killer San Miguel, who actually appears on stage in the same play, anachronistically in the style of the Counter-Reformation *auto sacramental*. At the same time it should be noted that certain key features of the Spanish Faust are striking by their absence, for example the macabre and melodramatic switch of the beloved into a skeleton that precipitates the hero's remorse in the plays of both Mira and Calderón.

27. Lara 1969:61; Arrom 1967:20.

28. Lara 1969:189; the larger resonance of the Quechua "devil" *zupay* is well explored by Harrison (1989).

29. These songs have an important function even in the more Europeanized plays: In *The Rape of Proserpine*, songs of the dove and of the flower (T. Meneses 1983:1145, 1250); in *The Prodigal Son*, songs of the painted mask (an eerie and brilliant piece) and of the erotic hummingbird (ibid., pp. 506, 678) as well as a final *haylli* to express the father's jubilation. Then again, by being set physically in the Andes, the Quechua version of *Proserpine* draws out a moral contrast between *puna* and *yunca* (the devil is Nina Yunca in *Usca Paucar*) and equips Pluto with an owl messenger, Taparaco, who stems directly from local shamanism, as does the baleful Owl messenger in *Apu Ollantay*.

30. A. A. Parker, "The Devil in the Drama of Calderón," in Bruce Wardopper (ed.), *Critical Essays on the Theatre of Calderón*, New York University Press,

New York: 1965, pp. 3–23; see also Parker's partisan account of the Counter-Reformation in Spain: *The Allegorical Drama of Calderón,* Oxford: Oxford University Press, 1943. It should be noted in passing that Parker's view of the American versions of these Golden Age plays was no less distorted by Hispanist ignorance than was E. C. Hill's view of *Apu Ollantay* (see Chapter 8, 15): "In general, of course, the interest of the translations lies in the evidence they offer for the quite remarkable cultural quality of Spanish colonization and for the conception the Spaniards had of their duties as bearers of civilization. One cannot imagine the English at any time translating into a North American language a play of Shakespeare or of anybody else!" (quoted in Hunter 1960:151). He did not realize that these translations were made not by Spaniards but by Native Americans and that they were adapted to existing literary languages and traditions of drama.

31. On the *tío* concept in Bolivian mining today, see Tristan Platt, "Conciencia andina y conciencia proletaria: Qhuyaruna y ayllu en el norte de Potosí," *Revista latinoamericana de historia económica y social* (Lima) 2 (1983): 47–73. The *entumillahue,* or metal mines, of the Mapuche are guarded by devils thirsty for blood (Kössler-Ilg 1956:147).

32. In *Geschichte und Probleme der lateinamerikanischen Literatur,* Munich: Hueber, 1969, p. 181.

33. Arrom 1967:128–9.

34. Lévi-Strauss 1972:206–31, which is based on the "Zuni origin and emergence myth" as well as comparable narratives of the Hopi and Pueblos (p. 219). Referring to Cinderella and her male counterpart Ash Boy, Lévi-Strauss sums up his inquiry as follows: "They are impossible to interpret through recent diffusion, as had been contended, since Ash-Boy and Cinderella are symmetrical but inverted in every detail (while the borrowed Cinderella tale in America – Zuni Turkey-Girl – is parallel to the prototype)" (p. 226).

35. A. B. Rooth, *The Cinderella Cycle,* Lund, 1951; M. R. Cox, *Cinderella: Three Hundred and Forty-five Variants,* London, 1893. E. Carilla, *El romanticismo en la América hispánica,* vol. 2, Madrid: Gredos, 1967, p. 77, confirms that "Cenicienta," the Spanish version of Perrault's "Cendrillon" (1697), was widely read in the Americas under Spanish colonial rule. At the same time, the American versions include elements absent from Perrault but present in such other European sources as the "Cenerentola" of Giambattista Basile's *Pentamerone* (the earliest published text), the "Aschenbrödel" of Grimm, and such Slav variants as do not derive from Perrault. Most notable is that arcane contract between her and the family of birds that epitomizes the Zuni story: Cenerentola is favored by "the dove of the fairies of Sardinia," Aschenbrödel works secretly together with a whole range of birds, and her Czech sister is particularly indebted to the owl. In the Perrault text, with its bourgeois concern for social display and its Louis XIV snobbery, the reason for and agency of Cinderella's transformation into a well-clothed beauty is most removed from that magic empathy with the natural world that may be traced back ultimately to augury and other archaic shamanist codes.

36. K. T. Preuss 1968:173; Armellada 1973:235–8 ("de algún libro de los españoles").

37. Mapuche: "Die arme Ñuke mit ihren drei Töchtern": Kössler-Ilg 1956:266–70. The Zuni versions are published by F. V. Cushing, *Zuni Folk Tales,* New York and London, 1901, pp. 54–9 (reprinted in S. Thompson 1966 [1929]: 225–31 along with other "Tales Borrowed from Europeans"); Robert Coles, *The Zuni: Self-Portrayals,* New York, 1972; and D. Tedlock 1972:65–73.

38. "Ueber Schnee, Eisberge, Trockenheit, Weltende," in Kössler-Ilg 1956; also "Vom Urwald Ñulnu," pp. 50–2.

39. There is also an intriguing Inca echo in the "Origin of Maize" story (Kössler-Ilg 1956:52–4), which features a hero who arrives from the north (i.e., Tahuantinsuyu): Over the same three "hunger months" the field of his youngest wife provides a rich crop, to the envy of the older wives. In turn this story echoes the Chaco account of the Venus bride who brings maize, again to the envy of other women (Bierhorst 1988:131).

40. For Lévi-Strauss, this is the key trait of the Ash Boy–Cinderella character, as he explains, referring back to the essay quoted in n. 34: "We thus established the pre-Columbian character of a mediator, which had generally been held to be a recent importation. . . . It presents, even in detail (in spite of a systematic inversion of all the terms, which excludes borrowing), a regular correspondence with a character reduced to a minor role on the European and Asiatic scene: Cinderella" (1978:64).

41. S. Thompson 1966:228. A similar provision in the *Laud teoamoxtli* is shown in Plate 6b. Cushing's translation is included in S. Thompson's collection of tales, the source used here for all quotations (1966: 225–31).

42. S. Thompson 1966:231. Perceiving these qualities in the turkey, Benjamin Franklin proposed it as the emblem of the independent United States, and D. H. Lawrence celebrated its revolutionary drive in his poem "The Turkey Cock":

Your aboriginality
Deep, unexplained,
Like a Red Indian darkly unfinished and aloof,
Seems like the black and glossy seeds of countless centuries.
    . . .
Turkey cock, turkey cock
Are you the bird of the next dawn?

Together with the dogs, in the *Popol vuh* they cry:

"Pain you have caused us.
  You have eaten us,
And now we are going to eat you back,"
  Said their dogs
And their chickens to them.
           – Edmonson 1971:28

In the same cosmogonical context, the *Ríos Codex* (p. 3) reveals that logic of compensation by which the mild and helpful turkey may revert to a positively satanic rebel and hazard.

43. In ancient Anasazi, bighorn sheep (who appear in the dry paintings) provided wool but were not strictly speaking herded (Sauer 1975:245). The
analogy between imported herd animals and turkey flocks is brought out
at the start of Cushing's tale: "Long, long ago, our ancients had neither
sheep nor horses nor cattle; yet they had domestic animals of various
kinds – amongst them Turkeys."
44. D. Tedlock 1972:223–97.

Epilogue: The American palimpsest

1. A pioneer was G. Chinard, *L'Exotisme américain dans la littérature française au
XVIe siècle,* Paris, 1911, and *L'Amérique et le rêve exotique dans la littérature
française au XVIIe et XVIIIe siècle,* Paris, 1913 (the latter, along with his
edition of 1932, includes a thorough analysis of René Chateaubriand's
sources in *Les Natchez,* a theme later taken up by Michel Butor). Goethe was
much influenced by Alexander von Humboldt, the first to give wide circula-
tion to Mesoamerican books and the story of ages; see Núñez 1972, who also
refers to German Expressionists like Gerhard Hauptmann, Alfred Döblin,
and Eduard Stücken. Artaud, Breton, and Péret (who translated the *Book of
Chumayel* into French) stand out among the Surrealists who turned to Fourth
World literature (see n. 5); LeClézio, who also translated the *Book of
Chumayel,* surveys these links (1988), noting in particular the 1909 Veracruz
exhibition of Mexican art and sculpture and the influence that this native
tradition had on such figures as the Dadaists and Henry Moore (today, Keith
Hering's paintings openly rework Huichol imagery). Bareiro Saguier 1990
and Castro-Klaren 1989 also take an overall view of this process.
2. See Ariel Dorfman, *Imaginación y violencia en América,* Santiago: Editorial
Universidad, 1970, pp. 65–92, and my "The Latin American Novel and Its
Indigenous Sources," in John King (ed.), *Modern Latin American Fiction: A
Survey,* London: Faber, 1987, pp. 60–77.
3. Seventeen of those "Indian poems" appear in a first edition (León, Nicaragua, 1969), and two more in a second (Santiago de Chile, 1971); a later
edition (*Los ovnis de oro: Poemas indios,* México: Siglo XXI, 1988) omits ten
poems that had been included in *Nueva antología poética* (México: Siglo
XXI, 1978) and adds twelve new ones (thereby the two *Cantares mexicanos*
poems become one, making thirty in all). On the *Homage,* see my *Latin
American Poetry: Origins and presence,* Cambridge: Cambridge University
Press, 1975, pp. 193–7; Vicente Cicchitti, "Homenaje a los indios americanos," in Elisa Calabrese (ed.), *Ernesto Cardenal: Poeta de la liberación latinoamericana,* Buenos Aires: Tamesis, 1975, pp. 133–58; Paul W. Borgeson,
Hacia el hombre nuevo: Poesía y pensamiento de Ernesto Cardenal, London,
1984. Like Asturias (1960), Montoya Toro and Cardenal (1966) have also
added to the continental surveys and anthologies listed in the Prologue, n.
4. Robert Pring-Mill has been extremely generous in sharing knowledge
derived from his close acquaintance with Cardenal over the years and in
forwarding copies of manuscript material.

4. E. von Dänicken's best-seller *Chariot of the Gods* (1968) flagrantly misreads native texts, detecting spacecraft on Pacal's sarcophagus and saying that upon burning himself Quetzalcoatl went back to rather than became Venus. It was preceded by the fantasies of Mu (Churchward) and Atlantis (Le Plongéon): See Robert Wauchope's caustic *Lost Tribes and Sunken Continents: Myth and method in the study of American Indians,* Chicago: University of Chicago Press, 1962.

5. See my "Revolution and the Ancient Literature of Mexico, for D. H. Lawrence and Antonin Artaud," *Twentieth Century Literature* 18 (1972): 393–408.

6. Quoted by Pablo Antonio Cuadra in his introduction to the second edition of the *Homenaje.*

7. He appears as that in Cuadra's "Mayo" and in Octavio Paz's fundamental study of Darío, "El caracol y la sirena," *Cuadrivio,* México: Joaquín Mortiz, 1967; see also J. J. Arrom, "El oro, la pluma y la piedra preciosa; Indagaciones sobre el trasfondo indígena de la poesía de Darío," *Hispania* 51 (1967): 971–81, which focuses on "Tutecotzimi," a version of the Nahua migration from Mexico to Nicaragua. With Cuadra, in poems like "El dolor es una águila sobre tu nombre" ("Pain is an eagle upon your name"), we feel ancestral weight like the huge bird and feline creatures superimposed on humans in the "double-ego" statues characteristic of Nicaragua and northern South America (*El jaguar y la luna;* 1973); his brilliant compositions integrate Sandino and the self-immolating Quetzalcoatl into the "codex" of the year or precisely transcribe the all-encompassing logic of a *teoamoxtli* chapter (see Chapter 2, n. 33). See Gloria Guardia de Alfaro, *Estudio sobre el pensamiento poético de Pablo Antonio Cuadra,* Madrid: Gredos, 1971.

8. These royal laments are a whole subject in themselves that stretches back through the historian Ixtlilxochitl, a descendant of the royal house, to the *Cantares* manuscript of Tenochtitlan and the *Xolotl Maps* of Texcoco; Ixtlilxochitl relates them to misery caused not by "bloodthirsty" Aztecs (as Prescott did) but by tribute imposed by Christians. The first complete version of the *Cantares* manuscript to have appeared in translation, Garibay's translations fight shy of Christian terms embedded in certain poems, as if out of a fear of travesty and sacrilege, which Cardenal as a Christian to a certain extent shares. These more subversive possibilities in the text are well brought out in John Bierhorst's excellent transcription, *Cantares mexicanos: Songs of the Aztecs.* On the Nezahualcoyotl poems and the long history of the translations and readings made of them, see V. M. Castillo 1972; my "Nezahualcoyotl's Laments and Their Nahuatl Origins: The Westernization of ephemerality," ECN 10 (1972): 393–408, and "An Indian Farewell in Prescott's *The Conquest of Mexico,*" *American Literature* 45 (1973): 348–56; and Castro-Klaren 1989.

9. The key figure in interpreting the Revolution in its earliest years was Manuel Gamio, archaeologist author of *La población del valle de Teotihuacan* (1922) who stimulated Garibay's *Llave del Náhuatl* (Otumba, 1940). The

Teotihuacan murals are the subject of "El paraíso terrenal en Teotihuacan," *Cuadernos americanos* 2, no. 6 (November–December 1942): 127–36, by Alfonso Caso, who later transformed Mexico's knowledge of its past through his work on Monte Albán, the Mixteca, and Coixtlahuaca. On this "reconstruction of the past" in general, see Florescano 1987.

10. A reading of his youthful *El problema social del indio* (Guatemala, 1923) leaves no doubt on this score; see Brotherston 1979:25–44; Gerry Martin, *Journeys through the Labyrinth*, London: Verso, 1989, pp. 296–7.

11. Brotherston 1975:98–109; W. Rowe 1979; Rama 1982; Lienhard 1990. See also Laura Lee Crumley, "El intertexto de Huarochirí en Manuel Scorza: Una visión múltiple de la muerte en *Historia de Garabombo, el invisible*," AI 44 (1984): 747–55 (Scorza incorporates part of chap. 27 of *Runa yndio* into his novel, the second in his fivefold series on the violent "guerra callada" waged against the Quechua in 1962). On the impact of Quechua literature on Enlightenment Europe and the champions of Spanish-American Independence, see my "Inca Hymns and the Epic-Makers," *Indiana* 1 (1973): 199–212. Paititi was claimed as part of his domain by Tupac Amaru II: See Prologue, n. 6; Carpentier, *Tientos y diferencias*, UNAM, 1964; Nicole Cartagena, *Paititi: dernier réfuge des Incas* (1981). Sendero Luminoso is discussed by Gorriti Ellenbogen 1990.

12. Schoolcraft gained access to the source texts through his Ojibwa wife, an episode detailed in Lewis 1964 (1932). Leslie Fiedler described *Hiawatha* as a native text "revised and sentimentalized for a bourgeois reading public, who needed desperately to be reassured that if not all Indians, certain better Indians, at least, had welcomed the end of their, alas, pagan, though idyllic world" (1968:77). The impact of Longfellow's poem was also considerable in Latin America, notably in Brazil and in Uruguay (Zorrilla's epic based on the doomed Guarani hero Tabaré); see Brotherston 1972. On nineteenth-century U.S. rhetoric and its roots, see my "*The Prairie* and Cooper's Invention of the West," in *James Fenimore Cooper: New critical essays*, ed. R. Clark, London: Vision Press, 1985, pp. 162–86, and "A Controversial Guide to the Language of America," in *1642: Literature and power in the seventeenth century*, ed. F. Barker and P. Hulme, Colchester: University of Essex, 1981, pp. 84–100.

13. *Wandlungen und Symbole der Libido*, published in Leipzig and Vienna, 1912; translated as *Psychology of the Unconscious*, New York, 1916; expanded as *Symbole der Wandlungen*, 4th rev. ed., 1952; translated as *Symbols of Transformation: An analysis of the prelude to a case of schizophrenia*, London, 1956 (*Collected Works*, vol. 5). This edition (pp. 447–62) includes the full text of Miss Frank Miller's "Some Instances of Subconscious Creative Imagination," which had first been published in French in 1905 and which forms the whole basis of Jung's analysis, especially sect. IV, "Chiwantopel, a Hypnagogic Drama" (pp. 457–62), the prompt for the long discourse on Hiawatha (pp. 312–57). With respect to his break from Freud and Adler, Jung refers to this study as "landmark" (p. xxiv). A key term in psychology, *totem*, is Algonkin in origin (Dewdney 1975:30). Jung also comments

on the American epic in Radin 1956; he was anticipated in his sounding of the Anglo-American consciousness by William James, who profoundly affected Willa Cather's understanding of native culture (Lois Parkinson Zamora, in Pérez Firmat 1990:20–5). These preoccupations surface in early-twentieth-century anthologies like those of Cronyn (1918), Austin (1923), N. Curtis (1923), and Spinden (1933) and are discussed in Rexroth (1960), Zolla (1973), and Castro (1983) and in Cardenal's "Poesía de los indios de Norteamérica," AI 21 (1961): 355–62. They are given a "postmodern" formulation in the novel *Griever*, by Gerald Vizenor (part Ojibwa and publisher of Ojibwa texts), where Manabozho (Naanabozho)'s epic quest for Mide scrolls takes him to China.

14. In *Nueva antología poética*, México: Siglo XXI, 1978 pp. 286–96, which inter alia reports on readings of the *Homage* by such defenders of the rainforest as Chico Mendez; the beginnings of this involvement of Cardenal's are marked by his article "El retrato de la Creación, de los indios uitotos de Colombia," *Revista de la UNAM* 18, 3 (1963): 28–9.

15. Included in Walmsley and Caistor 1986 (which also includes a Maya poem by Belize's former prime minister George Price). In his prologue to the recent reissue of *Palace of the Peacock* (London: Faber, 1988), Wilson Harris invokes the Carib mysticism discussed by Michael Swan in *The Marches of El Dorado* (1958), which was earlier drawn on by William Henry Hudson in *Green Mansions* (1904).

16. *Yo el supremo*, p. 144. Having inspired the title of an earlier Expressionist novel by Döblin (*Der blaue Tiger*), this creature also appears in Ribeiro's *Maíra* (p. 167), a novel developed from the author's earlier essay report on the Urubu (*Uirá vai ao encontro de Maira*, in Ribeiro 1974). On *Macunaima* and the "Carib" revolution of the *modernistas*, see Franco 1937 and Randal Johnson, "Tupy or Not Tupy: Cannibalism and nationalism in contemporary Brazilian literature and culture," in J. King (ed.), *Modern Latin American Fiction*, Faber, London: 1987, pp. 1–59. Despite its Americanist intent, José de Alencar's novel *O guaraní* (1857) reads the rainforest flood as that of the Old World Genesis. The profound and various influence of the Makunaima of the Taulipang and Arekuna on Andrade's *Macunaima* is detailed in Telê Porto Ancona López's superb edition of the novel (São Paulo, 1988).

17. *If on a Winter's Night a Traveller*, p. 94, quoted by Gerald Martin in *Journeys through the Labyrinth*, London: Verso, 1989, p. 306. The *Popol vuh* is among the major classics uninterruptedly told by this "old Indian," who is, "according to some, the universal source of narrative material."

18. In *Daimón* (1978) and *Los perros del paraíso* ("The Dogs of Paradise," 1987), novels from his "trilogy of discovery," Abel Posse urbanely juxtaposes life with native palimpsest: scenes framed by the pages of *Codex Vaticanus C* ("that pantheon of light . . . forever lost in the burning of Aztec documents ordered by the brutal archbishop Zumárraga" [trans. Margaret Sayers Pedden, London: Macmillan, 1989, p. 34]; *A* and *B* do exist); Huaman Collo, the ambassador from Tahuantinsuyu who alludes in Mex-

ico to Guaman Poma's organization of the Inca state; or the Taino inscription of a calendrical date. In his approach to Native American fortune, Posse on the one hand works the camp vein of Gary Jennings's *Aztec* (1980); on the other, his radicalism at moments touches that of the superb pioneer study by his compatriot David Viñas *Indios, ejército y frontera* (1982). Viñas engages in particular with the rewriting of Argentinian frontier history and policies toward the Mapuche, whose heroes had been celebrated in literature from Ercilla's *La araucana* (1569–89) to Darío's "Caupolicán"; in this connection he quotes the liberal president Domingo Sarmiento, a great admirer of Cooper and of the United States generally: "For us, Colocolo, Lautaro, and Caupolicán, despite the noble and civilized trappings with which Ercilla invested them, are just a bunch of disgusting Indians whom we'd have hanged today" (Viñas 1982:267). Sarmiento's irritation returns us to our starting point, since he complains that the Araucanian–Mapuche state, which as late as 1883 impeded Buenos Aires's imperialist advance southwestward, had initially been fostered by *literary* recognition on the part of Ercilla and others.

Glossary

Algonkin: composite term used by analogy with, say, Maya or Carib to denote people who speak an Algonkian language and what pertains to them

amauta: "sage, scholar" (Quechua), especially one whose knowledge is drawn from *quipu* archives

carbet: in South America, the speech of defiance delivered by a captive facing death

ceque: a line of political division that radiated from Cuzco in the *tahuantinsuyu* system

chunkey: Siouan (Catawba) *chenco;* game played with stone disk and curved sticks by the Mississipians and their descendants

codex: term widely applied to native Mesoamerican texts; used here just for post-Cortesian nonscreenfold texts

Era: the current epoch or world age, which in the Olmec inscriptions starts in the year 3113 BC; a concept also adopted by the lowland Maya and others in Mesoamerica, and possibly beyond

Feast: *ilhuitl* in Nahuatl; 20-day period of the Mesoamerican calendar, of which eighteen make up the seasonal year; the lowland Maya equivalent is *uinal*

haravek: "court poet" (Quechua)

huaca: "sacred object" (Quechua); applied to mountains, springs, and other features of the Andean landscape as well as to idols and man-made structures

huehuence: from *huehuentzin,* "grand or old man" (Nahuatl); a type of drama or play, pre-Hispanic in origin, in which the hero is indigent yet claims to know and to have seen much of the world

iconic script: term of convenience for what is often referred to as the Mixtec–Aztec or pictographic writing system of Mesoamerica, especially as distinct from Maya hieroglyphic writing (cf. *tlacuilolli*)

ikala (igala, ikar), "chant, way, work of literature" (Cuna); typically attached to names of cosmogonic and epic texts, e.g., *Tatkan ikala, Mu ikala*

413

katun: Maya period of twenty tuns (360 days); calendrically the unit of the *katun* count (*u kahlay katunob*) that consists of thirteen *katuns*

lienzo: "linen or canvas" (Spanish); post-Cortesian map that typically includes dated conquests, genealogies, and other historical information

mesquite: Nahuatl *mexquitl,* leguminous thorny shrub, long-lived and native to arid regions; fruit pods have edible pulp

Mide (Meeday, Metai): relative to the Midewiwin, a shamanic society organized according to degrees of knowledge and centered on Ojibwa Algonkin territory at the watershed between Mississippi, Great Lakes, and Arctic Ocean

nahual: "familiar" (Nahuatl); the double or twin soul of the shaman that exists beyond the human species

napa: a llama that was decorated in Inca ceremonies

octaeteris: 8-year period that conjoins the synodic cycles of sun (8), moon (99), and Venus (5), commonly standardized as 2,920 days

pochteca (Nahuatl): a long-distance trader and official agent in Mesoamerican tribute systems

Quecholli: "fliers, birds" (Nahuatl), notably the set of Thirteen that forms part of the *tonalamatl*

quipu: (Quechua) knotted-string device used throughout Tahuantinsuyu to communicate all kinds of information and to record literary texts like annals and hymns

Round: see *xiuhmolpilli*

screenfold: Mesoamerican book of native paper or skin, folded like an expandable screen and similar to the Japanese *emaki*

suyu: "district" (Quechua); see *tahuantinsuyu*

tahuantinsuyu: "four districts" (Quechua); a political model especially developed in the Andes, at Huamanga and Tiahuanaco, and above all by the Incas in the empire they centered on Cuzco

tameme: "carrier" (from a Nahuatl term)

teoamoxtli: "divine book" (Nahuatl); genre of pre-Cortesian texts in iconic script, made up of topic chapters whose reading order is determined by the *tonalamatl* (Table 2)

timehri: "sign" (Carib); petroglyph, used here for rainforest glyphs and designs generally

tlacuilolli: "something painted or written" (Nahuatl); iconic script especially as it is exemplified in pre-Cortesian texts

tonalamatl: "allotted signs" (Nahuatl); Mesoamerican time period and arithmogram relevant to the 260 nights and days of human gestation, from the first missed menses to birth (Table 1)

trarilonko: "headdress" (Mapuche); a head adornment, especially one worked in silver

trecena: "group of thirteen" (Spanish); one of the twenty periods of thirteen days that constitute the *tonalamatl;* counting out these periods, with their respective regents, the Trecenas chapter is basic to the *teoamoxtli* books

uinal: cognate of "human" and "moon" in Maya; twenty days in lowland Maya calendrics, a thirteenth part of the *tonalamatl,* and the numerical equivalent of the Feast

waniyetu yawapi: "Winter Count" (Sioux); a yearly calendar record

Weaving Woman: the principal goddess of Mesoamerican midwives, who wears a spindle in her hair; seventh of the Night Lords and also known as Lust Goddess (Tlazoteotl)

xiuhmolpilli: "year binding" (Nahuatl); the Round or cycle of 52 years in the Mesoamerican calendar, produced arithmetically by the combination of the Thirteen Numbers with four of the Twenty Signs

xiuhtlapoualli: "Year Count" (Nahuatl); genre of pre-Cortesian texts in iconic script whose reading order follows a sequence of years

yaravi: from *haravek* (Quechua, q.v.); a poignant song or poem

Bibliography

Native texts

This list is meant for ready reference to works mentioned in the text and notes, though not every such work is included. Each entry respects the title of a text, or the author when that is the main distinguishing feature, and notes:

medium or *language,* with English equivalent of title where appropriate;
genre or *type,* with the term *teoamoxtli* reserved for pre-Cortesian texts (cf. Glossary and Table 2);
author or *transmitter,* only when especially significant and not already given;
provenance and *date,* in the case of manuscripts, and where known;
relevant *census number* (Census, Cham., Dewd., Kram.; see Abbreviations);
alternative titles;
publication, with priority given to quality of reproduction or transcription, and further references usually of historic or other interest.

Commentaries and translations are generally specified in the notes.
   The following symbols and additional abbreviations are used:
★   native visual language or script; otherwise alphabetic
†   native verbal language; otherwise translation only
f   facsimile reproduction
pt   partial reproduction only

Anko Winter Count. Pictographs, Kiowa annals and lunar count, 1892, Cham. 60–1; Mooney 1979★.
Apu Ollantay. Quechua ["Lord Ollantay"], drama, Cuzco; Tschudi 1853†; Markham 1871; Cid Pérez and Martí 1964.
Atahuallpa. Quechua, drama, *Tragedia del fin de Atawallpa;* Lara 1957.
Aupaumut. See *Mahikan Indians, Note on.*
Ayunini Manuscript. Cherokee syllabary, formulaic cures; Olbrechts and Mooney 1932★† (*The Swimmer Manuscript*); Mooney 1891†.

417

Ayvu rapyta. Guarani ["Origin of human speech"], cosmogony; Cadogan 1959†.

Aztlan Annals. Iconic script screenfold, *xiuhtlapoualli,* Tenochtitlan, Census 34, *Boturini;* Corona Núñez 1964–7, vol. 2.

Baranda. Iconic script scroll, *xiuhtlapoualli,* Census 24; Acuña 1989*f.

Bead Chant. Dry paintings and Navajo, epic; Reichard 1977: pls. i–ix*f.

Blessing Way. Dry paintings and Navajo, cosmogony; Wyman 1970*; Dunn 1968: 116–19*.

Blue Thunder Winter Count. Pictographs, Yanktonai annals, 1922, Cham. 45; Howard 1960.

Borbonicus. Iconic script screenfold, *teoamoxtli,* Tenochtitlan/Colhuacan, Census 32; Nowotny 1974.

Borgia. Iconic script screenfold, *teoamoxtli,* ?Cholula, Census 33; Nowotny 1976.

Brown Hat. See *Wapoctanxi.*

Bull Plume Winter Count. Pictographs, Piegan Siksika annals, 1924, Cham. 56; Raczka 1979*.

Butterfly Winter Count. English (from pictographs), Mandan Hidatsa annals, 1876, Cham. 51; Howard 1960a.

Cakchiquel Annals. Cakchiquel Maya, annals (of years of 400 days), Solola ca. 1605, Census 1172; Menguin 1952†f (*Memorial de Tecpan-Atitlan – Solola,* CCAMA 4); Recinos, Goetz, and Chonay 1953 pt.

Canimani Narrative. Witoto, cosmogony, Cacique J. O. García, Putumayo (Puerto Leguizamo); Montoya Sánchez 1973:115–29.

Cantares mexicanos. Nahuatl, poetry, Tenochtitlan, Census 1019; Bierhorst 1985a†; Garibay 1964–8†; Brinton 1887†pt.

Castillo, Cristóbal, q.v. 1966 (1908).

Chan Kan, Book of. Maya, Chilam Balam book, Chan Kan, Census 1145; unpublished 132-page MS in Instituto Nacional de Antropología e Historia.

Chiautla Annals. Iconic script screenfold, *xiuhtlapoualli,* Chiautla–Texcoco–Tepetlaoztoc ca. 1569, Census 84, *Códice en Cruz;* Boban 1891, vol. 1*.

Chilam Balam [Maya "jaguar priest"], *Books of.* See *Chan Kan; Chumayel; Ixil; Kaua; Mani; Nah; Oxcutzcab; Tizimin; Tusik.*

Chimalpahin Cuauhtlehuanitzin (Census 1023–7), q.v. 1889, 1958, 1963–5, 1965.

Cholula Maps. Iconic script and Nahuatl, history, Cholula 1586, Census 57; Glass 1964: pls. 12, 59–60*; Bittmann 1968*.

Chumayel, Book of. Maya, Chilam Balam book, Chumayel 1782, Census 1146; Gordon 1913†f; Roys 1933†; Edmonson 1986†.

Cloud Shield Winter Count. Pictographs, Oglala Teton annals, 1879, Cham. 23; Mallery 1893*.

Coetzala Codex. Iconic script and Nahuatl, map, Coetzala, Census 69; *Códices indígenas* 1933*.

Coixtlahuaca Lienzo. Iconic script, lienzo, Census 71, *Seler 2;* Koenig 1984.

Coixtlahuaca Map. Iconic script map, *teoamoxtli,* Coixtlahuaca, Census 14, *Aubin MS. 20;* Nowotny 1961: pl. 51*.

Cospi. Iconic script screenfold, *teoamoxtli,* Census 79; Nowotny 1968*f.

Cuauhtinchan Annals. Iconic script and Nahuatl, *xiuhtlapoualli,* Cuauhtinchan after 1544, Census 359; *Historia tolteca – chichimeca;* Kirchhoff, Güemes, and Reyes García 1989*†f; Menguin 1942*†f (CCAMA 1).

Cuauhtinchan Map 2. Iconic script, map, Cuauhtinchan, Census 95, *Mapa de la ruta Chicomoztoc–Cuauhtinchan;* Yoneda 1981★.

Cuauhtitlan Annals. Nahuatl, *xiuhtlapoualli,* Cuauhtitlan 1570, Census 1033, *Historia de los reynos de Culhuacan y México;* Velázquez 1945†f; Lehmann 1974†.

Cuicatlan (*teoamoxtli* and annals). Iconic script screenfold, *teoamoxtli* (pp. 1–10 obverse) and *xiuhtlapoualli* (remaining pages), Cuicatlan, Census 255, *Porfirio Díaz;* Chavero 1892:plates★.

Cusick, q.v. 1825.

Dine bahane. Navajo ["Origin of the people"], cosmogony; Zolbrod 1984; Matthews 1897.

Dooyentate, q.v. 1870.

Dresden. Hieroglyphic script screenfold, Maya *teoamoxtli,* Census 113; ed. F. Anders and H. Deckert, ADV 1975★f; J.E.S. Thompson 1972★f; Lee 1985★f.

Dzul Poot, q.v. 1985–6.

Eight Deer. Iconic script screenfold, *xiuhtlapoualli,* Tilantongo, Census 240, *Codex Zouche–Nuttall* (reverse of *Tilantongo Annals,* q.v.).

Eight Deer and Four Wind. Iconic script screenfold, *xiuhtlapoualli,* Census 72 and 27, *Codex Colombino–Becker;* Caso and Smith 1966★; Nowotny 1961a★f.

Eshkwaykeezhik Master Scroll. Mide writing, initiation, Shoal Lake, Dewd. GAI-7; Dewdney 1975:95★.

Eshkwaykeezhik Migration Scroll. Mide writing, Ojibway migration, Shoal Lake, Dewd. GAI-4; Dewdney 1975:62–3★.

Eshkwaykeezhik Origin Scroll. Mide writing, cosmogony, Shoal Lake, Dewd. GAI-2; Dewdney 1975:24–5★.

Féjérváry. Iconic script screenfold, *teoamoxtli,* Census 118; Burland 1971★f.

The Flame Winter Count. Pictographs, Itazipco and Oohenupa Teton annals, Cham. 12; Mallery 1893★.

Florentine Codex. Nahuatl with iconic script insets, history, Tlatelolco ca. 1580, Census 274 (Sahagún); *Historia general de las cosas de Nueva España,* 3 vols. México: Secretaría de Gobernación, 1987★†f; Dibble and Anderson 1950–69†.

Gatigwanasti Manuscript. Cherokee syllabary, formulaic cures; Olbrechts and Mooney 1932★†; Mooney 1891†.

Guaman Poma de Ayala, Felipe. See *Nueva corónica.*

Hehaka Sapa. See Black Elk 1932, 1953.

High Dog Winter Count. Pictographs, Hunkpapa-Teton annals, 1912, Cham. 2; Howard 1960★.

High Hawk Winter Count. Pictographs, Sicangu-Teton annals, 1907, Cham. 41; E. Curtis 1908★.

Historia de la curación de antigua. Iconic script figures and Spanish in screenfold, cure, A. García Téllez, Pahuatlan 1978; unpublished MS, Pahuatlan, Hidalgo.

Histoyre du Mechique. (French from Spanish from) Nahuatl, cosmogony, ca. 1543, Census 1049; Garibay 1979.

Huamantla Codex. Iconic script, Otomi migration map, Huamantla Tlaxcala, Census 135; Aguilera 1986f★.

Huarochiri MS. See *Runa yndio.*

Huehuetlatolli. Nahuatl ["Word of the elders"], homilies, Juan Baptista 1600 (Tlatelolco, Ocharte), Census 1080; León-Portilla 1988†f.

Huichol Creation. See Tutukila; Yucauye Cucame.

Huinkulche Narrative. Mapuche, cosmogony; Kössler-Ilg 1956:117–29.

Ikala (Cuna "chant" or "way"). See Mu; Olopatte; Pap; Serkan; Tatkan.

Inin cuic catca intlatlacuteculo inic quin mauiztiliaia inin teupa. Nahuatl ["Hymns with which they honored the gods"], liturgy, Tepepulco 1547, Census 1098 (Sahagún Primeros Memoriales), 1104 (Sahagún Florentine Codex), *Veinte himnos sagrados;* Garibay 1958†; Seler 1902–23, vol. 2†; Brinton 1890†.

Inomaca tonatiuh. Nahuatl ["The sun itself"], cosmogony, Tenochtitlan, 1558, Census 1111, *Leyenda de los soles;* Velázquez 1945†f; Lehmann 1974†.

Iosco. Ottawa Algonkin, trance journey, Chusco (cf. *Wassamo*); Schoolcraft 1839, 2:40–60.

Ixil, Book of. Maya, Chilam Balam book, Ixil, Census 1147; Roys 1946.

Ixtlilxochitl, q.v. 1975–7.

John K. Bear Winter Count. Sioux, Yanktonai annals, 1883, Cham. 48; Howard 1976†.

Kaema A (Snake Head) Year Count. Pictographs, Pima annals, Kamatuk Wutca (Gila Crossing) 1902; Russell 1975:38–66★.

Kahkewaquonaby, q.v. 1861.

Kaua, Book of. Maya, Chilam Balam book, Kaua ca. 1789, Census 1148; Barrera Vásquez and Rendón 1963:33–4pt.

Kuifike mapuche yem chumnechi ni admonefel enn. Mapuche, autobiography, Budi 1927, *Vida y costumbres de los antiguos araucanos,* by Pascual Coña; Moesbach 1984†.

Kweweziashish Migration Chart. Mide writing, Ojibway migration, Dewd. BM-1; Dewdney 1975:75★.

Kweweziashish Song Scroll. Mide writing, initiation songs; Brotherston 1979:268★ (BM 2252).

Laud. Iconic script screenfold, *teoamoxtli,* ?Teotlillan, Census 185; Burland 1966★f.

Legend of the Suns. See *Inomaca tonatiuh.*

Libellus de medicinalibus indorum herbis. Iconic script and (Nahuatl trans. into) Latin, herbal, Cruz and Badiano, Tlatelolco 1552, Census 85; various eds., México: Instituto mexicano de Seguro Social, 1964★f.

Lone Dog Winter Count. Pictographs, Miniconjou Teton annals, 1871, Cham. 14; Mallery 1893★.

Madrid Codex. Hieroglyphic script screenfold, Maya *teoamoxtli,* Census 187; Anders 1967★f; Lee 1985.

Magliabechiano Codex. Iconic script and Spanish commentary, ritual, ca. 1566, Census 188; Boone 1983.

Mahikan Indians, Note on. Lenape-Algonkin, history, Aupaumut (Hendrick); see Chapter 7, n. 22, esp. Morse 1822.

Makunaima. Carib (Taulipang and Arekuna), cosmogony, Mayuluaipu and Moseuaipu; Koch-Grünberg 1924†pt.

Mani, Book of. Maya, Chilam Balam book, Mani, Census 1149; Solís Alcalá 1949†; Craine and Reindorp 1979 (from Solís's Spanish only).

Matrícula de tributos. Iconic script pages, account of commodity tribute of Mexica empire, Tenochtitlan, Census 368, *Tribute Roll of Montezuma:* Berdan and Durand-Forest 1980★f.

Medatia. Soto Carib, account of shamanic apprenticeship; Guss 1985.

Mendoza Codex. Iconic script with Spanish glosses and commentary, tribute history of the Mexica empire, Tenochtitlan ca. 1542, Census 196; Clark 1938★f; Purchas 1625★pt (wood-block).

Menomini Scroll. Mide writing, initiation, Leech Lake, Dewd. SC-4; Dewdney 1975:168★.

Mexicanus Codex. Iconic script, *teoamoxtli* data and *xiuhtlapoualli,* ca. 1590, Census 207; Menguin 1952★f.

Mide Birchbark Scroll. See Eshkwaykeezhik; Kweweziashish; Menomini; Sikassige; Skwekomik.

Mu ikala. Pictographs and Cuna ["Childbirth ikala"], therapeutic epic, G. Hayans, Ustupo 1949, Kram. 1.1.5; Holmer and Wassén 1953★†.

Nah, Book of. Maya, Chilam Balam book, Teabo, Census 1150; unpub. 36-folio MS in Princeton University Library.

Nai tzult, nai tza. Mazatec ["Sun, moon"], cosmogony, Pablo Quintana; Incháustegui 1977:27–34.

Night Chant. Dry paintings and Navajo, cosmogony; Bierhorst 1974: 281–352★pt; Wyman 1983:174★pt.

Nueva corónica y buen gobierno. Spanish ["New chronicle and good government"] and Quechua plus page illustrations, history, Felipe Guaman Poma de Ayala, Cuzco ca. 1613; Pietschmann 1936†★f; Murra and Adorno 1980†★.

Okayondonghsera Yondennase. Iroquois ["Ancient rites of the Condoling Council"], charter chant; Hale 1883†; Bierhorst 1974:109–86.

Ollantay. See *Apu Ollantay.*

Olopatte ikala. Cuna ["Gold-disk ikala"], epic for the dead, Kramer 1970: 1.3.3. See also *Olopatte,* Kram. 2.1.3.5; Holmer and Wassén 1951† (*Tatkan ikala*).

Olowitinappi's Report. Cuna, account of shamanic apprenticeship, Mulatupo 1970; Sherzer and Urban 1986:180–212†.

Osuna Codex. Iconic script, tribute statements, Tenochtitlan, Texcoco, etc. 1565, Census 243, *Pintura del Gobernador;* ed. Luis Chávez Orozco, *Pintura del Gobernador,* III 1947†f.

Oxcutzcab, Book of. Maya, Chilam Balam book, Oxcutzcab ?1689, Census 1151; Solís Alcalá 1949:298–329†; Barrera Vásquez and Rendón 1963:49–67.

Palenque Foundation Trilogy. Maya hieroglyphic, history, Palenque ca. 692; Maudslay 1889–1902, vol. 4★ (pls. 75, Temple of the Cross; 81, Temple of the Foliated Cross; and 88, Temple of the Sun).

Pap ikala. Cuna ["God ikala"], political poetry, Kram. 2.2.1–2; Wassén 1938; Leander 1970.

Paris Codex. Hieroglyphic script screenfold, Maya *teoamoxtli,* Census 247; ed. F. Anders, ADV 1968★f; Lee 1985★.

Pemonton taremuru. Pemon–Carib ["Taren cures of the Pemon"]; Armellada 1972†.

Pinturas Manuscript. (Spanish from) iconic script and Nahuatl, cosmogony, ca. 1535, Census 1060, *Historia de los mexicanos por sus pinturas;* Garibay 1979.

Plume Chant. Dry paintings and Navajo, epic, Wyman 1983:180–8, pls. 16–21★.

Poolaw Year Count. ?, Kiowa annals, 1901, Cham. 64; Marriott 1945.

Popol vuh. Quiché Maya ["Book of counsel"], cosmogony, Quiché ca. 1550, Census 1179; Burgess and Xec 1955†; Edmonson 1971†; Nelson 1976; Tedlock 1985; Saenz de Santa María 1989.

Porfirio Díaz. See Cuicatlan

Quapaw Embassy. Pictographs on skin, history; unpublished MS in Musée de l'Homme, Paris (34.33.7).

Quiotepec Annals. Iconic script scroll, *xiuhtlapoualli,* Santiago Quiotepec (Oaxaca), Census 119, *Fernández Leal;* J. B. Tomkins 1942 (*Pacific Art Review* [M. H. de Young Memorial Museum, San Francisco] 2:39–59).

Rabinal Achi. Quiché Maya ["The knight of Rabinal"], drama, Rabinal, *Quiché Vinak;* Brasseur 1862†; Padial and Vázquez-Bigi 1991.

Ríos Codex. Iconic script and Italian, cosmogony and annals, Tenochtitlan late 16th c., Census 270, *Vaticanus A;* Anders 1979★f.

Ritual of the Bacabs. Maya, formulaic cures, Census 1142; Arzápalo 1987†f.

Runa yndio niscap Machoncuna. Quechua ["Ancestors of the people called Indians"], cosmogony, Huarochiri ca. 1608; G. Taylor 1987†; Trimborn 1939; Arguedas 1966; Urioste 1983.

Santos Year Count. Pictographs, Pima–Papago annals, San Xavier del Bac 1932; Underhill 1938★.

Selden Roll. Iconic script scroll, *xiuhtlapoualli,* Coixtlahuaca region, Census 284; Burland 1955.

Selden Screenfold. See *Xaltepec Annals.*

Serkan ikala. Pictographs and Cuna. ["Ikala for the ancients, or dead"], therapeutic epic, Kram. 1.1.3; Holmer and Wassén 1963★†.

Settan Year Count. Pictographs and Kiowa, annals, 1892, Cham. 69; Mooney 1979★†.

Shaihueke Narrative. Mapuche, history; Kössler-Ilg 1956:159–67.

Shooting Chant (Male). Dry paintings and Navajo, epic; Reichard 1977: pls. x–xxiv★.

Sigüenza Map. Iconic script, *xiuhtlapoualli,* map, Census 290, *Mapa de la peregrinación de los aztecas;* Glass 1964: pl. 16.

Sikassige Migration Scroll. Mide writing, Ojibway migration, Mille Lacs, Dewd. Ho-1; Hoffman 1891★.

Sikassige Song Scroll. Mide writing and Ojibway, initiation songs, Mille Lacs; Mallery 1893: pl. 18★†.

Skwekomik Master Scroll. Mide writing, initiation, La Pointe, Dewd. SI-2; Dewdney 1975:89★.

Sunstone. Iconic script, cosmogonic *cuauhxicalli,* Tenochtitlan 1479, *Piedra del Sol / Stone of Axayacatl;* Zantwijk 1985:231★.

Tatkan ikala. Cuna ["Forefather ikala"], cosmogony, Kram. 2.1.0–4; Holmer and Wassén 1951:130–57†pt; Wassén 1937:14–24†pt; Nordenskiöld 1938:125–44; Wassén 1938.

Tauron panton. Pemon–Carib ["So the story goes"], stories; Armellada 1973†.

Tcokut Nak (Owl Ear) Year Count. Pictographs, Pima annals, Amu Akimult (Salt River) 1901; Russell 1975:38–66★.

Telleriano Codex. Iconic script and Spanish, cosmogony and annals, Tenochtitlan 1563, Census 308; Corona Núñez 1964–7, vol. 1.

Tepexic Annals. Iconic script screenfold, *xiuhtlapoualli,* Tepexic (Puebla) ?1273, Census 395, *Codex Vindobonensis obverse;* Adelhofer 1963*f.

Tepotzotlan Codex. Iconic script page, tribute statement, Tepotzotlan 1556, Census 322 (AGN copy only); Brotherston and Gallegos 1988*.

Tepoztlan MS. See *Magliabechiano.*

Tequixtepec Map (1). Iconic script, *lienzo,* Tequixtepec, Census 433; Parmenter 1982:55*.

Tezozomoc, q.v. 1949.

Tilantongo Annals. Iconic script screenfold, *xiuhtlapoualli,* Tilantongo region, Census 240, *Codex Zouche–Nuttall;* ed. Miller 1975*f; ed. F. Anders and N. Troike, ADV 1987*f.

Tizimin, Book of. Maya, Chilam Balam book, Tizimin, Census 1157; Edmonson 1982†; Makemson 1951.

Tlapa Annals. Iconic script screenfolds, *xiuhtlapoualli,* Tlapa and Azoyu (Guerrero) 1565, Census 21 (years grouped in sevens with genealogy on reverse) & 22 (years grouped in eights with tribute on reverse), *Azoyu Codices 1 & 2;* Glass 1964:115–9*; Constanza Vega in press (FCE)*f.

Tlapiltepec Map. Iconic script, *lienzo,* Tlapiltepec (Oaxaca), Census 8, *Lienzo Antonio de León;* Caso 1961*; Parmenter 1982*.

Tlatelolco Annals. Nahuatl and iconic script, *xiuhtlapoualli,* Tlatelolco 1528, Census 344 & 1073, *Unos Annales [sic] Históricos de la Nación Mexicana;* Menguin 1945*f (CCAMA 2); ed. R. Barlow, *Anales de Tlatelolco,* México: Porrúa, 1948.

Tlaxcala Lienzo and Codex. Iconic script, history, Tlaxcala 1550 & 1580, Census 350; Chavero 1892: plates*; Acuña 1984*.

Tonalamatl Aubin. Iconic script screenfold, *teoamoxtli,* Tlaxcala, Census 15; Aguilera 1981*f.

Totecuyoane. Nahuatl ["O our lords"], address to Franciscan missionaries 1524, Tenochtitlan; León-Portilla 1986:50–55†f; Lehmann 1949†.

Totonicapan Title. Quiché, history, Totonicapan ca. 1554, Census 1186; Recinos, Goetz, and Chonay 1953.

Tsunki. Shuar, cosmogony; Pellizaro 1979†.

Tula Annals. Iconic script scroll, *xiuhtlapoualli,* Tula (Hidalgo), Census 368; Zantwijk 1979*f.

Tusik, Book of. Maya, Chilam Balam book, Tusik, Census 1158; Barrera Vásquez and Rendón 1963:204–19pt.

Tutukila (Tiburcio Carrillo Sandoval) Creation. Huichol yarn *tablas,* cosmogony; Negrín 1975: pls. 1–12*.

U belil u kahlil Chac-Xulub-Chen. Maya, chronicle, Chicxulub (Yucatan), Ah Nakuk Pech, Census 1166, *Crónica de Chac-Xulub-Chen;* Brinton 1882†; Yáñez 1939.

Umusin Panlon, q.v. 1980.

Vaticanus Codex A. See *Ríos.*

Vaticanus Codex B. Iconic script screenfold, *teoamoxtli,* Census 384; Anders 1972*f.

Wainambi Narrative. [Timehri and] Desana–Tucano, cosmogony, Daikala Baraku family, Wainambi; Montoya Sánchez 1973:104–8; Reichel-Dolmatoff 1971:56.
Wapoctanxi Winter Count. Pictographs, Sicangu Teton annals, 1880, Cham. 36; Mallery 1893★ (extended to 1910 in V. D. Chamberlain 1984:25★).
Wassamo. Ottawa Algonkin [subtitle: *or The Fire Plume*], trance journey, Chusco; Schoolcraft 1839, :132–51.
Watunna. Soto Carib ["Celebration"], cosmogony; Civrieux 1980, 1970.
Winter and *Year Counts.* See Table 5 and *Anko; Blue Thunder; Bull Plume; Butterfly; Cloud Shield; The Flame; High Dog; High Hawk; John K. Bear; Kaema A; Lone Dog; Poolaw; Santos; Settan; Tcokut Nak; Wapoctanxi.*
Witoto Genesis. Witoto, cosmogony, Rigasedyue; K. T. Preuss 1921†.
Xaltepec Annual. Iconic script screenfold, *xiuhtlapoualli*, ?Xaltepec (Oaxaca) ca. 1560, Census 283, *Selden Codex;* Corona Núñez 1964–7, vol. 3:77–99★.
Xolotl Maps. Iconic script maps, historical sequence of ten, Texcoco, Census 412; Dibble 1980★f.
Yucauye Cucame (José Benítez Sánchez) Creation. Huichol yarn tablas, cosmogony; Negrín 1975: pls. 13–47★.
Zithuwa Hymns. Quechua ["Cleansing"], liturgy, Cuzco; J. H. Rowe 1953†.

Secondary sources

Abreu Gómez, Ermilo. 1975. *Canek: Historia y leyenda de un héroe maya.* 29th ed. México: Oasis.
Acuña, René. 1975. *Introducción al estudio del Rabinal Achi.* UNAM.
   1984 (ed.). Diego Muñoz Camargo, *Descripción de la ciudad y provincia de Tlaxcala.* UNAM.
   1985. *Relaciones geográficas del siglo XVI: Tlaxcala.* UNAM.
   1989 (ed.). *Códice Baranda.* México: Toledo.
Adelhofer, Otto (ed.). 1963. *Codex Vindobonensis Mexicanus I.* ADV. Facsimile repr. of the 1929 edition by W. Lehmann and O. Smital, Vienna.
Adorno, Rolena. 1982. *From Oral to Written Expression: Native Andean chronicles of the early colonial period.* Syracuse, NY: Syracuse University Press.
   1986. "Visual Mediation in the Transition from Oral to Written Expression." In Brotherston 1986:181–96.
Agostinho, Pedro. 1974. *Kwaryp: Mito e ritual no Alto Xingu.* São Paulo.
Aguilera, Carmen (ed.). 1981. *Tonalamatl Aubin.* Tlaxcala: ITC.
   1986. *El códice de Huamantla.* Tlaxcala: ITC.
Aguilera, Carmen, and Miguel León-Portilla (eds.). 1986. *Mapa de México y sus contornos hacia 1550.* México: Celanese.
Albert, B. 1988. "La fumée du metal: Histoire et représentations du contact chez les Yanomami," *L'Homme* 28:87–119.
Albó, Xavier. 1985. *Desafíos de la solidaridad aymara.* La Paz: CIPLA.
Alcina Franch, José. 1957. *Floresta literaria de la América indígena: Antología de los Pueblos indígenas de América.* Madrid: Aguilar.
Alvarez, M. Cristina. 1974. *Textos coloniales del Libro de Chilam Balam de Chumayel y textos glíficos del Códice de Dresde.* UNAM.

Anders, Ferdinand (ed.). 1967. *Codex Tro-Cortesians* (Codex Madrid). ADV.
  1972. *Codex Vaticanus 3773*. ADV.
  1979. *Codex Vaticanus 3738, or Ríos*. ADV.
Anders, Ferdinand, and Maarten Jansen. 1988. *Schrift und Buch im alten Mexiko*. ADV.
Andrews, J. Richard, and Ross Hassig (eds.). 1984. *Treatise of Ruiz de Alarcón* (1629). Norman: University of Oklahoma Press.
Antigüedades mexicanas. See Chavero 1892.
Arguedas, José María. 1938. *Canto Quechwa*. Lima: Club del Libro Peruano.
  1949. *Canciones y cuentos quechuas*. Lima: Huascaran.
  1956. "Puquio, una cultura en proceso de cambio." In Arguedas 1975:34–79.
  1957. *The Singing Mountaineers: Song and tales of the Quechua*. Austin: University of Texas Press. Includes English translation of Arguedas 1938 by R. W. Stephen.
  1962. *Tupac Amaru Kamaq taytanchisman: Haylli-taki*. Lima: Salqantay.
  1964. *Todas las sangres*. Buenos Aires: Losada.
  1966 (ed.). *Dioses y hombres de Huarochiri: Narración quechua*. Lima: Museo Nacional de Historia e Instituto de Estudios Peruanos.
  1975. *Formación de una cultura nacional indoamericana*. México: Siglo XXI.
Arias-Larreta, Abraham. 1968. *Literaturas aborígenes de América*. 2 vols. Buenos Aires: Editorial Indoamérica.
Armellada, Cesáreo de. 1972. *Pemonton taremuru*. Caracas: Universidad Católica de Andrés Bello.
  1973. *Tauron panton*. Caracas: Universidad Católica de Andrés Bello.
Armellada, Cesáreo de, and C. Bentivenga de Napolitano. 1974. *Literaturas indígenas venezolanas*. Caracas: Monte Avila.
Arrom, José Juan. 1967. *Historia del teatro hispanoamericano (época colonial)*. México: Ediciones de Andrea.
  1971. "Mitos tainos en las letras de Cuba, Santo Domingo y México," *Cuadernos americanos* 29, no. 1.
  1989. *Mitología y artes prehispánicas de las Antillas*. México: Siglo XXI.
Artaud, Antonin. 1971. *Oeuvres complètes*. Vol. 8, *Les Tarahumaras*. Paris: Gallimard.
  1971a. *Oeuvres complètes*. Vol. 9, *Lettres du Méxique*. Paris: Gallimard.
Arzápalo Marín, Ramón. 1987. *El ritual de los bacabes*. UNAM.
Ascher, Marcia, and Robert Ascher. 1981. *Code of the Quipu: A study in media, mathematics, and culture*. Ann Arbor: University of Michigan Press.
Astrov, Margot. 1962. *American Indian Prose and Poetry*. New York: Capricorn, 2d ed. of *The Winged Serpent*, New York, 1946.
Asturias, Miguel Angel. 1949. *Hombres de maíz*. Buenos Aires: Losada. See 1975.
  1957. *Leyendas de Guatemala* (1930). Buenos Aires: Losada.
  1960. *Poesía precolombina*. Buenos Aires: Fabril.
  1971. *Trois des quatre soleils*. Geneva: Editions d'Art Albert Skira.
  1975. *Men of Maize* (Hombres de maíz), trans. Gerald Martin. New York: Delacorte.
  1977 (ed.). *Popol vuh, o libro del consejo*. Buenos Aires: Losada.
Austin, Mary. 1923. *The American Rhythm*. New York: Harcourt Brace.

Aveni, Anthony F. 1975 (ed.). *Archaeoastronomy in Precolumbian America.* Austin: University of Texas Press.
   1980. *Skywatchers of Ancient Mexico.* Austin: University of Texas Press.
   1982 (ed.). *Archaeoastronomy in the New World.* Cambridge: Cambridge University Press.
   1989 (ed.). *World Archaeoastronomy.* Cambridge: Cambridge University Press.
Aveni, Anthony F., and Gordon Brotherston (eds.). 1983. *Calendars in Mesoamerica and Peru.* Oxford: BAR.
Aveni, Anthony F., and Gary Urton (eds.). 1982. *Ethnoastronomy and Archaeoastronomy in the American Tropics.* New York: New York Academy of Sciences.
Bagrow, Leo, and R. H. Skelton, 1964. *History of Cartography.* Cambridge: Harvard University Press.
Bahr, Donald M. 1975. *Pima and Papago Ritual Oratory.* San Francisco: Indian Historian Press.
Ballard, W. L. 1978. *The Yuchi Green Corn Ceremonial: Form and Meaning.* Los Angeles.
Bancroft, H. H. (ed.). 1883. *The Native Races of the Pacific States of North America.* 5 vols. San Francisco: A. L. Bancroft.
Bankes, George. 1977. *Peru before Pizarro.* Oxford: Phaidon.
Barbeau, Marius. 1950. *Totem Poles: According to crests and topics.* Anthropological Series, no. 30. Toronto: Department of Resources and Development.
   1951. *Totem Poles.* National Museum of Canada Bulletin no. 119. Ottawa: The Museum.
   1960. *Indian Days on the Western Prairies.* National Museum of Canada Bulletin no. 163. Ottawa: The Museum.
Bareiro Saguier, Rubén. 1980. *Literatura guaraní del Paraguay.* Caracas: Monte Avila.
   1990. *De nuestras lenguas y otros discursos.* Asunción: Universidad Católica.
Barlow, Robert. 1949. *The Extent of the Empire of the Culhua Mexica.* Berkeley and Los Angeles: University of California Press.
   1949a. "El Códice Azcatitlan," *Journal de la Société des Américanistes* 38:101–35.
   1949b. "El códice de Coetzala, Puebla," *Tlalocan* 3:91–2.
Barlow, Robert, and H. Berlin (eds.). 1948. *Anales de Tlatelolco y El códice de Tlatelolco.* México: Porrúa.
Barreiro, Joel (ed.). 1990. "View from the Shore: American Indian perspectives on the quincentenary," *Northeastern Indian Quarterly* (Ithaca) 7, no. 3:4–21.
Barrera Vásquez, Alfredo (ed.). 1965. *El libro de los cantares de Dzitbalche.* México: INAH.
Barrera Vásquez, Alfredo, and Silvia Rendón. 1963. *El libro de los Libros de Chilam Balam.* FCE.
Bartl, Renate, Barbara Gobel, and Hanns J. Prem. 1989. "Los calendarios aztecas de Sahagún," *ECN* 19:13–82.
Basadre, Jorge. 1938. *Literatura Inca.* Paris: Biblioteca de Cultura Peruana.
Basso, Ellen. 1985. *A Musical View of the Universe: Kalapalo myth and ritual performances.* Philadelphia: University of Pennsylvania Press.
   1987. *In Favor of Deceit: A study of tricksters in Amazonian society.* Tucson: University of Arizona Press. Kalapalo texts.
Baudin, Louis. 1961. *A Socialist Empire: The Incas of Peru,* trans. Katherine Woods. New York: Van Nostrand.

Baudot, Georges. 1976. *Les Lettres précolumbiennes.* Toulouse: Privat.
Baudot, Georges, and T. Todorov. 1983. *Récits aztèques de la conquête.* Paris.
Beach, W. W. (ed.). 1877. *The Indian Miscellany.* Albany, NY: J. Munsell.
Bendezú, Edmundo. 1986. *La otra literatura peruana.* FCE.
Benedict, Ruth. 1935. *Zuni Mythology.* 2 vols. New York: Columbia University Press.
Benítez, Fernando. 1967–80. *Los indios de México.* 5 vols. México: Biblioteca Era.
Benson, Elizabeth. 1968 (ed.). *The Dumbarton Oaks Conference on the Olmec 1967.* Washington, DC: Dumbarton Oaks.
  1971 (ed.). *The Dumbarton Oaks Conference on Chavin.* Washington, DC: Dumbarton Oaks.
  1972. *The Mochica: A culture of Peru.* London: Thames and Hudson.
  1973 (ed.). *Mesoamerican Writing Systems: A conference at Dumbarton Oaks, Oct. 30th and 31st, 1971.* Washington, DC: Dumbarton Oaks.
Berdan, Frances, and J. Durand-Forest (eds.). 1980. *Matrícula de tributos.* ADV.
Bieder, Robert E. 1986. *Science Encounters the Indian 1820–1880.* Norman: University of Oklahoma Press.
Biedermann, H. 1971. *Altmexikos heilige Bücher.* ADV.
Bierhorst, John. 1971. *In the Trail of the Wind: American Indian poems and ritual orations.* New York: Noonday.
  1974. *Four Masterworks of American Indian Literature: Quetzalcoatl, The Ritual of Condolence, Cuceb, The Night Chant.* New York: Farrar, Straus and Giroux.
  1976. *The Red Swan: Myths and tales of the American Indians.* New York: Farrar, Straus and Giroux.
  1985. *Cantares mexicanos: Songs of the Aztecs.* 2 vols. Stanford, CA: Stanford University Press.
  1985a. *The Mythology of North America.* New York: Morrow.
  1988. *The Mythology of South America.* New York: Morrow.
Bird, Junius (ed.). 1981. *Museums of the Andes.* New York: Newsweek.
Bittmann Simons, Bente. 1968. *Los mapas de Cuauhtinchan y la Historia tolteca–chichimeca.* UNAM.
Black Elk (Hehaka Sapa). 1932. *Black Elk Speaks: Being the life story of a holy man of the Oglala Sioux as told to John Neihardt.* Illustrations by Standing Bear. New York: Morrow. 2d ed., 1961, "As Told through John Neihardt." Lincoln: University of Nebraska Press.
  1953. *The Sacred Pipe: Black Elk's account of the seven rites of the Oglala Sioux recorded and edited by J. E. Brown.* Norman: University of Oklahoma Press.
Boas, Franz. 1925. "Romance Folk-lore among American Indians," *Romance Review* 16:199–207.
  1928. *Primitive Art.* Cambridge: Harvard University Press.
  1938 (ed.). *General Anthropolgy.* Boston: Heath.
Boban, Eugène. 1891. *Documents pour servir à l'histoire du México.* 2 vols. and atlas. Paris: Ernest Leroux.
Bocabulario. 1972. *Bocabulario de Mayathan, or Vienna Dictionary,* ed. E. Menguin. ADV.
Bonavia, Duccio. 1985. *Mural Painting in Ancient Peru.* Bloomington: Indiana University Press.

Boone, Elizabeth Hill. 1983. *The Codex Magliabechiano*. Berkeley and Los Angeles: University of California Press.

Borsari, Ferdinando. 1888. *La letteratura degl'indigeni americani*. Naples.

Borunda, Ignacio. 1898. *Clave general de jeroglíficos americanos*. Rome.

Boturini Benaducci, Lorenzo. 1746. *Idea de una nueva historia general de la América septentrional*. Madrid.

Bowra, C. M. 1962. *Primitive Song*. London: Weidenfeld and Nicholson.

Bozzoli de Willie, María E. 1983. "De dónde nace el sol a dónde el sol se pone: Mitología talamanqueña," *América Indígena* (México) 43:125–45.

Bramlage, Julia. 1952. *Lo incaico del Apu Ollantay*. Lima: Universidad Nacional Mayor de San Marcos.

Brasseur de Bourbourg, Charles Etienne. 1861. *Popol vuh: Le livre sacré et les mythes de l'antiquité américaine*. Paris: Arthus Bertrand.

  1862. *Grammaire de la langue Quiché*. Paris: Arthus Bertrand.

  1871. *Bibliothèque México–Guatemalienne*. Paris: Maisonneuve.

Bray, Warwick, Ian Farrington, and Earl H. Swanson. 1975. *The New World*. London: Elsevier Phaidon.

Bricker, Victoria Reifler. 1981. *The Indian Christ, the Indian King: The historical substrate of Maya myth and ritual*. Austin: University of Texas Press.

Brinckmann, Barbel. 1970. *Quellenkritische Untersuchungen zum mexikanischen Missionsschauspiel 1533–1732*. Beiträge zur mittelamerikanischen Völkerkunde. Hamburg: Museum für Völkerkunde.

Brinton, Daniel Garrison. 1882. *The Maya Chronicles*. Library of Aboriginal American Literature, vol. 1. Philadelphia: The Library.

  1883. *The Güegüence: A comedy ballet in the Nahuatl–Spanish dialect of Nicaragua*. Library of Aboriginal American Literature, vol. 3. Philadelphia: The Library.

  1884. *The Lenape and Their Legends*. Library of Aboriginal American Literature, vol. 5. Philadelphia: The Library.

  1887. *Ancient Nahuatl Poetry*. Library of Aboriginal American Literature, vol. 7. Philadelphia: The Library.

  1890. *Rig Veda Americanus: Sacred songs of the ancient Mexicans*. Library of Aboriginal American Literature, vol. 8. Philadelphia: The Library.

Broda, Johanna. 1991. "The Sacred Landscape of Aztec Calendar Festivals: Myth, nature and society." In *To Change Place,* ed. D. Carrasco. Niwot: University Press of Colorado, pp. 74–120.

Broda, Johanna, David Carrasco, and Eduardo Matos Moctezuma. 1987. *The Great Temple of Tenochtitlan–Center and periphery in the Aztec world*. Berkeley and Los Angeles: University of California Press.

Brody, Hugh. 1986. *Maps and Dreams*. 2d ed. London: Faber.

Bronowsky, Jacob. 1973. *The Ascent of Man*. London: BBC.

Brotherston, Gordon. 1972. "Ubirijara, Hiawatha, Cumanda: National virtue from Indian literature," *Comparative Literature Studies* 9:243–52.

  1973. "Inca Hymns and the Epic Makers." *Indiana* 1:199–212.

  1974. "Huitzilopochtli and What Was Made of Him." In Hammond 1974:155–66.

1975. *Latin American Poetry: Origins and presence.* Cambridge: Cambridge University Press.

1976. "Mesoamerican Description of Space: Signs for direction," *Ibero-Amerikanisches Archiv* (Berlin) 2, 1:39–62.

1977. "Continuity in Maya Writing." In Hammond and Willey 1979:241–58.

1979. *Image of the New World: The American continent portrayed in native texts.* London: Thames and Hudson.

1979a. "What Is written in Timehri?" *Journal of Archaeology and Anthropology* (Georgetown) 2:5–9.

1982. *A Key to the Mesoamerican Reckoning of Time.* Occasional Paper 38. London: British Museum.

1983. "The Year 3113 B.C. and the Fifth Sun of Mesoamerica." in Aveni and Brotherston 1983:167–221.

1984. " 'Far As the Solar Walk': The path of the North American shaman," *Indiana* 9:15–30.

1985. "The Sign Tepexic in Its Textual Landscape," *Ibero-Amerikanisches Archiv* 11:209–51.

1986 (ed.). *Voices of the First America: Text and context in the New World.* New Scholar (Santa Barbara), vol. 10.

1986a. "Towards a Grammatology of America: Lévi-Strauss, Derrida and the native New World." In *Literature, Politics and Theory,* ed. F. Barker, P. Hulme, M. Iversen, and D. Loxley. London: Methuen, pp. 190–209.

1988. "Zodiac Signs, Number Sets, and Astronomical Cycles in Mesoamerica." In Aveni 1989:276–88.

1990. "The Time Remembered in the Winter Counts and the Walam Olum." In Illius and Laubscher 1990:307–37.

1992. "The Tepotzotlan Codices and Tribute Literature in Mesoamerica." In *Iconography in Highland Mexican Texts,* ed. J. Durand-Forest. Oxford: BAR.

1992a. "Lenguaje verbal y lenguaje visual: El caso de los códices mesoamericanos." In *Vitalidad e influencia de las lenguas indígenas en América Latina,* ed. R. Arzápalo and Y. Lastra. UNAM.

1992b. *Mexican Painted Books: Originals in the United Kingdom and the world they represent.* Colchester: University of Essex in association with the British Museum.

Brotherston, Gordon, and Dawn Ades. 1975. "Mesoamerican Description of Space, I," *Ibero-Amerikanisches Archiv* 1:279–305.

Brotherston, Gordon, and Ana Gallegos. 1988. "The Newly-Discovered Tepotzotlan Codex: A first account." In *Recent Studies in Pre-Columbian Archaeology,* ed. N. Saunders and O. de Montmollin. Oxford: BAR, pp. 205–27.

1990. "El Lienzo de Tlaxcala y el manuscrito de Glasgow," ECN 20:117–40.

Brown, Dee. 1971. *Bury My Heart at Wounded Knee: A history of the Sioux uprising of 1870.* London: Barrie and Jenkins.

Bruce, Robert D. 1977. "The Popol vuh and the Book of Chan Kin," ECM 10:90–8.

Brundage, B. C. 1979. *The Fifth Sun: Aztec gods, Aztec world.* Austin: University of Texas Press.

Burga, Manuel. 1987. *Nacimiento de una utopía. Muerte y resurrección de los Incas.* Lima: Instituto de Apoyo Agrario.

Burga Freitas, Arturo. 1980. *Ayahuasca: Mitos, leyendas y relatos de la Amazonia peruana.* 3d ed. Lima: Ediciones Tipo Offset.

Burgess, Dora, and Patricio Xec. 1955. *El Popol Wuj.* Quetzaltenango: Talleres gráficos "El Noticiero Evangélico."

Burgos-Debray, Elisabeth. 1984 (ed.). *I, Rigoberta Menchú–An Indian woman in Guatemala.* London: Verso.

Burkhart, Louise M. 1986. "Sahagún's *Tlauculcuicatl:* A Nahuatl lament," ECN 18:181–229.

    1989. *The Slippery Earth: Nahua–Christian moral dialogue in sixteenth-century Mexico.* Tucson: University of Arizona Press.

Burkitt, R. 1920. *The Hills and Corn: A legend of the Kekchi Indians of Guatemala, put in writing by the late Tiburtius Kaal.* Philadelphia: University of Pennsylvania Museum.

Burland, Cottie. 1950. *The Four Directions of Time.* Santa Fe: Wheelwright Museum.

    1953. *Magic Books from Mexico.* Harmondsworth: Penguin.

    1955 (ed.). *The Selden Roll.* Berlin: Mann.

    1960. "The Map as a Vehicle for Mexican History," *Imago Mundi* 15:11–18.

    1965. *North American Indian Mythology.* London: Hamlyn.

    1966 (ed.). *Codex Laud.* ADV.

    1967. *The Gods of Mexico.* London: Eyre and Spottiswoode.

    1971 (ed.). *Codex Féjérváry–Mayer.* ADV.

Bushnell, G. H. S. 1968. *The First Americans.* London: Thames and Hudson.

Bustios Gálvez, L. 1956–66 (ed.). Guaman Poma, *Nueva corónica y buen gobierno.* 3 vols. Lima.

Cadogan, León (ed.). 1959. *Ayvu rapyta.* Boletim 227, Antropologia 5. São Paulo: Faculdade de Filosofia, Ciências e Letras, Universidade de São Paulo.

    1965. *La literatura de los Guaraníes.* México: Joaquín Mortiz.

Campbell, Alan Tormaid. 1989. *To Square with Genesis: Causal statements and shamanic ideas in Wayapi.* Edinburgh: Edinburgh University Press.

Campos, Rubén M. 1936. *La producción literaria de los Aztecas.* México: Museo Nacional.

Cardenal, Ernesto. 1967. "In xochitl in cuicatl," *La palabra y el hombre* (Xalapa) 44:665–95.

    1970. *Homenaje a los indios americanos.* Santiago de Chile: Colección Cormorán. Prologue by José María Oviedo.

    1973. *Homage to the American Indians,* trans. Monique and Carlos Altschul. Baltimore: Johns Hopkins University Press.

    1978. *Nueva antología poética.* México: Siglo XXI.

    1988. *Los ovnis de oro: Poemas indios.* México: Siglo XXI.

Cardoza y Aragón, Luis. 1985. *Guatemala: Las líneas de su mano.* Managua: Companic.

    1975 (ed.). *Rabinal Achi.* México: Porrúa.

Carkeek Cheney, Roberta. 1979. *The Big Missouri Winter Count.* Happy Camp, CA: Naturegraph.

Carmack, Robert. 1973. *Quichean Civilization: The ethnohistorical, ethnographic and archaeological sources.* Berkeley and Los Angeles: University of California Press.

1988. *Harvest of Violence.* Norman: University of Oklahoma Press.

Carmack, Robert, and James Mondloch. 1989. *El título de Yax y otros documentos de Totonicapan.* UNAM.

Carmack, Robert, and Francisco Morales (eds.). 1983. *Nuevas perspectivas sobre el Popol vuh.* Guatemala City: Piedra Santa.

Carmichael, Elizabeth. 1983. *The Hidden People of the Amazon.* London: British Museum.

Carr, Helen. 1991. *The Poetics and Politics of Primitivism.* Unpublished Ph.D. diss., University of Essex.

Carrasco, David. 1982. *Quetzalcoatl and the Irony of Empire.* Chicago: University of Chicago Press.

Carrasco, Eulalia. 1983. *El pueblo Chachi: El jeengume avanza.* Quito: Colección Ethnos.

Carrasco, Hugo. 1989. "La matriz funcional del mito mapuche." In M. Preuss 1989:67–75.

Carrasco, Iván. 1988. "Literatura mapuche," *América Indígena* (México) 48:695–730.

Carrasco, Pedro, and Johanna Broda. 1978. *Economía política e ideología en el México prehispánico.* México: Editorial Nueva Imagen.

Carrasco Pizaña, P. 1950. *Los Otomíes.* UNAM.

Caso, Alfonso. 1958. *The Aztecs: People of the Sun.* Norman: University of Oklahoma University Press.

1960. *Interpretation of the Codex Bodley 2858.* México: Sociedad Mexicana de Antropología.

1961. "Los lienzos mixtecos de Ihuitlan y Antonio de León." In *Homenaje a P. Martínez del Río.* México, pp. 237–74.

1965. "Zapotec Writing and Calendar," HMAI 3:931–47.

1965a. "Mixtec Writing and Calendar," HMAI 3:948–61.

1968. *Los calendarios prehispánicos.* UNAM.

1977–9. *Reyes y reinos de la Mixteca.* 2 vols. FCE.

Caso, Alfonso, and Mary Elizabeth Smith. 1966. *Interpretación del Códice Colombino.* México: Sociedad Mexicana de Antropología.

Castañeda, Carlos. 1968. *The Teachings of Don Juan.* New York: Simon and Schuster.

1971. *A Separate Reality – Further conversations with Don Juan.* New York: Simon and Schuster.

Castillo, Cristóbal de. 1966. *Fragmentos de la obra general sobre historia de los mexicanos . . . escrita en lengua Náhuatl* (ca. 1600), ed. F. del Paso y Troncoso. New ed. México: Erandi. 1st ed., Florence, 1908.

Castillo, Víctor M. 1972. *Nezahualcoyotl: Crónica y pinturas de su tiempo.* Texcoco.

Castro, Michael. 1983. *Interpreting the Indian: Twentieth-century poets and the Native American.* Albuquerque: University of New Mexico Press.

Castro-Klaren, Sara. 1989. *Escritura, transgresión y sujeto en la literatura latinoamericana.* Puebla: Premia.

Catlin, George. 1973. *Letters and Notes on the Manners, Customs and Condition of the*

North American Indians. 2 vols. New York: Dover. Repr. of the 1844 London ed.

Chamberlain, R. S. 1955. *The Conquest and Colonization of Yucatan 1517–1550.* Washington, DC: Smithsonian Institution.

Chamberlain, V. D. 1984. "Astronomical Content of North American Plains Indian Calendars," *Archaeoastronomy* 6:S1–S54.

Chavero, Alfredo (ed.). 1892. *Antigüedades mexicanas publicadas por la Junta Colombina de México.* 2 vols. and atlas of plates. México: Secretaría de Fomento.

Chevigny, Bell Gale, and Gari Laguardia. 1986. *Reinventing the Americas.* Cambridge: Cambridge University Press.

Chimalpahin Cuauhtlehuanitzin, Domingo Francisco de San Antón Muñón. 1869. *Annales: 6e et 7e Rélations,* ed. R. Siméon. Paris: Maisonneuve.

    1958. *Das Memorial Breve,* ed. W. Lehmann and G. Kutscher. QGA 7. Stuttgart and Berlin: Mann.

    1963–5. *Die Relationen C.'s zur Geschichte Mexikos,* ed. G. Zimmermann. 2 vols. Hamburg: Museum für Völkerkunde,

    1965. *Relaciones originales de Chalco Amaquemecan,* ed. S. Rendón. FCE.

Chinard, Gilbert. 1913. *L'Amérique et le rêve éxotique dans la littérature française au xvii et au xviii siècle.* Paris.

Christensen, B., and S. Martí. 1971. *Witchcraft and Pre-Columbian Paper.* México: Ediciones Euroamericanas.

Chronicles of American Indian Protest. 1971. *Chronicles of American Indian Protest.* New York: Fawcett.

Chumap Lucía, Aurelio, and Manuel García Rendueles (eds.). 1979. *Duik Muun; Universo mítico de los aguaruna.* 2 vols. Lima: Centro Amazónico de Antropología.

Churchill, Ward (ed.). 1982. *Marxism and Native Americans.* Boston: South End Press.

Churchward, J. 1931. *The Lost Continent of Mu.* New York: Ives Washburn.

Cid Pérez, José, and Dolores Martí del Cid. 1964. *Teatro indio precolombino.* Madrid: Aguilar.

Cipoletti, María Susana. 1984. "El motivo de Orfeo y el viaje al reino de los muertos en América del Sur," *Indiana* 9:421–32.

Civrieux, Marc de. 1970. *Watunna: Mitología makiritare.* Caracas: Monte Avila.

    1980. *Watunna: An Orinoco creation cycle,* trans. David Guss. San Francisco: North Point Press.

Clark, J. Cooper. 1912. *The Story of Eight Deer.* London: Taylor and Francis.

    1938 (ed.). *Codex Mendoza.* 3 vols. London: Waterlow and Sons.

Clendinnen, Inga. 1987. *Ambivalent Conquests: Maya and Spaniard in Yucatan, 1517–70.* Cambridge: Cambridge University Press.

    1991. *Aztecs: An interpretation.* Cambridge: Cambridge University Press.

Closs, Michael P. (ed.). 1985. *Native American Mathematics.* Austin: University of Texas Press.

Clutton-Brock, Juliet (ed.). 1989. *The Walking Larder: Patterns of domestication, pastoralism and predation.* London: Unwin Hyman.

Códices indígenas. 1933. *Códices indígenas de algunos pueblos del Marquesado del Valle.* AGN.

Coe, Michael D. 1966. *The Maya*. London: Thames and Hudson.

1973. *The Maya Scribe and His World*. New York: Grolier.

1978. *Lords of the Underworld: Masterpieces of classic Maya ceramics*. Princeton, NJ: University Art Museum.

Coe, Michael D., and Richard Diehl. 1980. *In the Land of the Olmec*. 2 vols. Austin: University of Texas Press.

Coe, Michael D., Dean Snow, and Elizabeth Benson. 1986. *Atlas of Ancient America*. New York: Facts on File.

Coe, R. T. 1977. *Sacred Circles: Two thousand years of North American Indian art*. London: Arts Council.

Coggins, Clemency. 1980. "The Shape of Time: Some implications of a four-part figure," AA 45:727–9.

Copway, George (Kah-gegagah-bowh). 1847. *The Life, History and Travels of Kah-gegagah-bowh*. Albany, NY.

Cordy Collins, Alana. 1982. *Pre-Columbian Art History: Selected readings*. Palo Alto.

Cornejo Polar, Antonio. 1989. *La formación de la tradición literaria en el Perú*. Lima: CEP.

Cornyn, J. H. 1930. *The Song of Quetzalcoatl*. Yellow Springs, OH.

Corona Núñez, José. 1964–7. *Antigüedades de México, basadas en la recopilación de Lord Kingsborough*. 4 vols. México: Secretaría de Hacienda y Crédito Público.

Cortés, Hernán. *Cartas de relación de la conquista de México*. México: Austral.

Coulthard, G. R. 1971. "Dos casos de literatura no-enajenada en la época colonial," *Revista de la Universidad de Yucatán* 78:15–25.

Courlander, H. 1971. *The Fourth World of the Hopis*. New York: Crown.

Covarrubias, Miguel, and R. Piña Chan. 1964. *El pueblo del jaguar*. México: Museo Nacional de Antropología.

Craine, Eugene, and Reginald Reindorp (eds.). 1979. *The Codex Pérez and the Book of Chilam Balam of Maní*. Norman: University of Oklahoma Press.

Cranfill, T. M. 1959. *The Muse in Mexico: A mid-century miscellany*. Austin: University of Texas Press.

Cronyn, G. W. 1918. *The Path on the Rainbow: An anthology of songs and chants from the Indians of North America*. New York: Norton.

Cruikshank, Julie. 1990. *Life Lived like a Story*. Lincoln: University of Nebraska Press.

Cruz, Martín de la. 1939. *The de la Cruz–Badiano Aztec Herbal of 1552*, ed. W. Gates. 2 vols. Baltimore: Maya Society.

1964. *Libellus de medicinalibus indorum herbis* (1552). México: Instituto Mexicano de Seguro Social.

Cuadra, Pablo Antonio. 1971. *El nicaragüense*. Managua.

1984–8. *Obra poética completa*. 8 vols. San José, Costa Rica: Libro Libre.

Curtis, Edward. 1908. *The American Indian,* vol. 3. Cambridge, Mass.: University Press.

Curtis, Natalie. 1923. *The Indian's Book*. New York: Harper.

Cushing, Frank Hamilton. 1901. *Zuni Folk-Tales*. New York: Putnam.

Cusick, David. 1825. *Sketches of Ancient History of the Six Nations*. Tuscarora Village, NY.

Dahlgren de Jordan, Barbra. 1966. *La Mixteca: Su cultura e historia prehispánicas.* UNAM.

Däniken, E. von. 1968. *Erinnerung an die Zukunft.* Düsseldorf: Econ Verlag.

Dark, Philip. 1958. *Mixtec Ethnohistory: A method of analysis of the codical art.* Oxford: Oxford University Press.

Davies, Nigel. 1977. *The Toltecs until the Fall of Tula.* Norman: University of Oklahoma Press.

1980. *The Toltec Heritage.* Norman: University of Oklahoma Press.

Day, A. Grove. 1951. *The Sky Clears: Poetry of the American Indians.* New York: Macmillan.

Delanoë, Nelcya. 1982. *L'entaille rouge: Terres indiennes et démocratie américaine 1776–1980.* Paris: Maspero.

Deloria, Vine. 1969. *Custer Died for Your Sins: An Indian manifesto.* New York: Macmillan.

1973. *God Is Red.* New York: Grosset and Dunlap.

DeMallie, Raymond. 1985. *The Sixth Grandfather: Black Elk's teachings given to John G. Neihardt.* Lincoln: University of Nebraska Press.

Densmore, Frances. 1910. *Chippewa Music.* BAE Bulletin no. 45. Washington, DC: Smithsonian Institution.

1926. *The American Indians and Their Music.* New York.

Derrida, Jacques. 1967. *De la grammatologie.* Paris: Minuit.

1976. *Of Grammatology,* trans. Gayatri Spivak. Baltimore: Johns Hopkins University Press.

Dewdney, Selwyn. 1975. *The Sacred Scrolls of the Southern Ojibway.* Toronto: Toronto University Press.

Diamond, Stanley (ed.). 1960. *Culture and History: Essays in honor of Paul Radin.* New York: Columbia University Press.

Díaz, Bernal. 1963. *The Conquest of New Spain,* trans. J. M. Cohen. Harmondsworth: Penguin.

Dibble, Charles E. 1963. *Historia de la nación mexicana: Reproducción a todo color del Códice de 1576 (Códice Aubin).* Madrid: Ediciones José Porrúa Turanzas.

1980 (ed.). *Códice Xolotl.* UNAM.

Dibble, Charles E., and A. J. O. Anderson. 1950–69. *Florentine Codex* (Bernardino de Sahagún): *General history of the things of New Spain,* trans. from the Aztec. 11 vols. Santa Fe: School of American Research; Salt Lake City: University of Utah Press.

Diringer, D. 1968. *The Alphabet.* 2 vols. London: Hutchinson.

Dockstader, Frederick J. 1967. *Indian Art in South America.* Greenwich, CT.

Dooyentate Clarke, Peter. 1870. *Origin and Traditional History of the Wyandotts.* Toronto.

Dorn, Edward. 1966. *The Shoshoneans.* New York: Morrow.

1974. *Recollections of Gran Apacheria.* San Francisco: Turtle Island Foundation.

Driver, H. E. 1961. *Indians of North America.* Chicago: University of Chicago Press.

Dundee, N. 1964. *Morphology of the North American Indian Folk-Tale.* FF Communications, no. 195. Helsinki.

Dunn, Dorothy. 1968. *American Indian Painting of the Southwest and Plains Areas.* Albuquerque: University of New Mexico Press.

Dupaix, Guillermo. 1969. *Expedición,* ed. J. Alcina Franch. 2 vols. Madrid: Porrúa.
Durán, Fray Diego. 1967. *Historia de las Indias de Nueva España,* ed. Angel María
   Garibay. 2 vols. México: Porrúa.
Duviols, Pierre. 1977. *La destrucción de las religiones andinas.* UNAM.
Dyckerhoff, Ursula. 1984. "La historia de curación antigua de San Pablito, Pahua-
   tlan," *Indiana* 9:69–86.
Dzul Poot, Domingo. 1985–6. *Cuentos mayas.* 2 vols. Mérida: Maldonado. Bilingual
   ed.
Earle, Duncan, and D. Snow. 1985. "The Origin of the 260-Day Calendar: The
   gestation hypothesis reconsidered in the light of its use among the Quiché
   Maya." In *Fifth Palenque Round Table,* ed. V.M. Fields. San Francisco: Pre-
   Columbian Art Research Institute, pp. 241–4.
Edmonson, Munro. 1971. *The Book of Counsel: The Popol vuh of the Quiché Maya of
   Guatemala.* New Orleans: Tulane University Press.
   1974 (ed.). *Sixteenth-Century Mexico: The Work of Sahagún.* Albuquerque: Uni-
   versity of New Mexico Press.
   1982. *The Ancient Future of the Itza.* Austin: University of Texas Press.
   1985 (ed.). *Literatures.* Supp. to HMAI, vol 3. Austin: University of Texas
   Press.
   1986. *Heaven Born Merida and Its Destiny.* Austin: University of Texas Press.
   1988. *The Book of the Year.* Salt Lake City: University of Utah Press.
Edwards, Emily. 1966. *The Painted Walls of Mexico from Prehistoric Times until Today.*
   Austin: University of Texas Press.
Eggan, Fred. 1967. "From History to Myth: A Hopi example." In Hymes 1967:
   33–53.
Eliade, Mircea. 1964. *Shamanism: Archaic techniques of ecstasy,* trans. W. R. Trask.
   Princeton, NJ: Princeton University Press.
Emmerich, André. 1977. *Sweat of the Sun, Tears of the Moon.* Seattle: University of
   Washington Press.
Escalona, Enrique. 1989. *Tlacuilo.* México: CIESAS/UNAM.
Ewers, J. C. 1939. *Plains Indians Painting.* Stanford, CA: Stanford University Press.
Fagan, Brian M. 1987. *The Great Journey: The peopling of ancient America.* London:
   Thames and Hudson.
Feder, N. 1971. *American Indian Art.* New York: Abrams.
Feest, Christian. 1986. *Indians of North East North America.* Iconography of Religions
   10, 7. Leiden.
Fenton, William N. 1950. *The Roll-call of the Iroquois Chiefs: A study of a mnemonic
   cane from the Six Nations Reserve.* Smithsonian Miscellaneous Collections 3,
   15. Washington, DC: Smithsonian Institution.
   1978. "Cherokee–Iroquois Connections Revisited," *Journal of Cherokee Studies*
   (Chattanooga) 3:239–49.
   1987. *The False Faces of the Iroquois.* Norman: University of Oklahoma Press.
Fernández, Justino. 1954. *Coatlicue: Estética del arte indígena antiguo.* México: Centro
   de Estudios Filosóficos.
Fernández de Piedrahita, L. 1973. *Noticia historial de las conquistas del Nuevo Reino de
   Granada.* Bogotá: Kelley.
Fiedler, Leslie A. 1968. *The Return of the Vanishing American.* London: Cape.

Fink, Ann E. 1989. "A Mopan Maya View of Human Existence." In McCaskill 1989:399–414.

Flannery, Kent, and Joyce Marcus. 1983. *The Cloud People: Divergent evolution of the Mixtec and Zapotec civilizations.* New York: Academic Press.

Fletcher, Alice C. 1900. *Indian Story and Song from North America.* Boston: Small Maynard.

Flor y Canto. 1964. *Flor y canto del arte prehispánico de México.* México: Fondo Editorial de la Plástica Mexicana.

Flores Galindo, Alberto. 1987. *Buscando al Inca: Identidad y utopía en los Andes.* Lima: Instituto de Apoyo Agrario.

Florescano, Enrique. 1987. *Memoria mexicana: Ensayo sobre la reconstrucción del pasado: época prehispánica–1821.* México: Contrapuntos.

Forbes, Jack D. 1988. *Black Africans and Native Americans.* Oxford and New York: Blackwell Publisher.

Förstemann, Ernst (ed.). 1892. *Die Maya Handschrift der Königlichen Öffentlichen Bibliothek zu Dresden.* Leipzig: Verlag der A. Naummann'schen Lichtdrückerei.

Fouchard, Jean. 1972. *Langue et littérature des aborigènes d'Ayti.* Paris: Editions de l'Ecole.

Franco, Alfonso Arinos de Melo. 1937. *O indio brasileiro e a revolução francesa, as origens brasileiras da theoria da bondade natural.* Coleção Documentos Brasileiros, no. 7. Rio de Janeiro.

Fraser, Valerie. 1990. *The Architecture of Conquest: Building in the viceroyalty of Peru, 1535–1635.* Cambridge: Cambridge University Press.

Fraser, Valerie, and Gordon Brotherston (eds.). 1982. *The Other America.* London: Museum of Mankind.

Fuentes y Guzmán, F. A. de 1932–3. *Recordación Florida . . . del reyno de Guatemala.* 3 vols. Guatemala City: Biblioteca "Goathemala."

Furst, Jill Leslie. 1978. *Vindobonensis mexicanus I: A commentary.* Albany: Institute for Mesoamerican Studies, State University of New York.

Furst, Peter. 1968. *Myth in Art: A Huichol depicts his reality.* Los Angeles.

1986. "Human Biology and the Origin of the 260-Day Sacred Almanac: The contribution of Leonard Schultze Jena (1874–1955)." In Gossen 1986:69–76.

Galarza, Joaquín. 1972. *Lienzos de Chiepetlan (Guerrero).* México: Mission Archéologique et Ethnologique Française au Méxique.

1988. *Estudios de escritura indígena tradicional Azteca–Náhuatl.* AGN.

Galeano, Eduardo. 1982. *Memoria del fuego, I: Los nacimientos.* Madrid: Siglo XXI.

1987. *Genesis: Memory of fire,* trans. Cedric Belfrage. London: Methuen.

Galloway, Patricia (ed.). 1989. *The South-Eastern Ceremonial Complex: Artifacts and analysis.* Lincoln: University of Nebraska Press. Cottonlandia Conference, 1984.

Gamio, Manuel. 1972. *Arqueología e indigenismo.* México.

García Granados, Rafael. 1952. *Diccionario de historia antigua de Méjico.* 3 vols. México: Instituto de Historia.

Garcilaso de la Vega, "El Inca." 1966. *The Royal Commentaries of the Incas,* trans. H. V. Livermore, Austin: University of Texas Press.

1967. *Los comentarios reales de los Incas.* Lima: Editores de Cultura Popular.

Garibay, Angel María. 1940. *Poesía indígena de la Altiplanicie.* UNAM.

  1953–4. *Historia de la literatura náhuatl.* 2 vols. México: Porrúa.

  1958. *Veinte himnos sacros de los náhuas.* UNAM.

  1961. *Llave del Náhuatl* (1940). 2d enlarged ed. UNAM.

  1964–8. *Poesía náhuatl.* 3 vols. UNAM.

  1979. *Teogonía e historia de los mexicanos: Tres opúsculos del siglo XVI.* México: Porrúa.

Garza, Mercedes de la. 1975. *La conciencia histórica de los antiguos mayas.* UNAM.

Gatschet, A. S. 1884. *A Migration Legend of the Creek Indians.* Library of Aboriginal American Literature, vol. 4. Philadelphia: The Library.

Gelb, Ignace Joy. 1952. *A Study of Writing: The Foundations of grammatology.* London: Routledge and Kegan Paul.

Gemelli Careri, Gio Francesco. 1700. *Giro del mondo,* vol. 6. Naples.

Genet, Jean, and P. Chelbatz. 1927. *Histoire des peuples Mayas-Quichés (Méxique, Guatemala, Honduras).* Paris: Les Editions Genet.

Gerhard, Peter. 1972. *A Guide to the Historical Geography of New Spain.* Cambridge: Cambridge University Press.

Gibson, Charles. 1964. *Aztecs under Spanish Rule.* Stanford, CA: Stanford University Press.

  1966. *Spain in America.* New York: Harper and Row.

  1967. *Tlaxcala in the Sixteenth Century.* Stanford, CA: Stanford University Press.

Gibson, Charles, and John B. Glass. 1975. "A Census of Middle American Prose Manuscripts in the Native Historical Tradition," HMAI 15:322–400.

Gilmor, Frances. 1949. *Flute of the Smoking Mirror (A Portrait of Nezahualcoyotl).* Albuquerque: University of New Mexico Press.

  1964. *The King Danced in the Market-place.* Tucson: University of Arizona Press.

Gisbert, Teresa. 1980. *Iconografía y mitos indígenas en el arte.* La Paz: Ediciones Gisbert.

Glass, John B. 1964. *Catálogo de la colección de códices.* México: Museo Nacional de Antropología.

  1975. "A Census of Native Middle American Pictorial Manuscripts," HMAI 14:81–250.

Gonçalves Dias, A. 1858. *Dicionário da lingua tupi.* Leipzig: Brockhaus.

González, Nicolás. 1958. *Ideología guarani.* III.

González Casanova, Pablo. 1965. *Cuentos indígenas.* UNAM.

  1977. *Estudios de lingüística y filología náhuas.* UNAM.

González Holguín, Diego. 1901. *Arte y diccionario quechua–español.* Lima.

Goody, Jack. 1968. *Literacy in Traditional Societies.* Cambridge: Cambridge University Press.

  1977. *The Domestication of the Savage Mind.* Cambridge: Cambridge University Press.

Gordon, G. B. (ed.). 1913. *The Book of Chilam Balam of Chumayel.* Philadelphia: University of Pennsylvania Press. Facsimile.

Gorriti Ellenbogen, Gustavo. 1990. *Sendero: Historia de la guerra milenaria en el Perú.* Lima: Apoyo.

Gossen, Gary H. (ed.). 1986. *Symbol and Meaning beyond the Closed Community.*

Albany: Institute for Mesoamerican Studies, State University of New York.

Graham, Ian. 1978–. *Corpus of Maya Hieroglyphic Inscriptions*. Cambridge, MA: Peabody Museum, Harvard University.

Granados y Gálvez, J. de. 1778. *Tardes americanas*. México: Zúñiga y Ontiveros.

Grant, Campbell. 1967. *Rock Art of the American Indian*. New York: Promontory Press.

Graulich, Michel. 1987. *Mythes et rites du México ancien préhispanique*. Brussels: Académie Royale de Bélgique.

Greenberg, Joseph H. 1987. *Language in the Americas*. Stanford, CA: Stanford University Press.

Grinnell, George Bird. 1892. "Early Blackfoot History." *American Anthropologist* 5:153–64.

    1962. *Blackfoot Lodge Tales: The Story of a prairie people* (1923). Lincoln: University of Nebraska Press.

Gross, Daniel R. 1973. *Peoples and Cultures of Native South America*. New York: Doubleday.

Grove, David C. 1984. *Chalcatzingo: Excavations on the Olmec Frontier*. London: Thames and Hudson.

Gruzinski, Serge. 1989. *Man-Gods in the Mexican Highlands*. Stanford: Stanford University Press.

Guardia Mayorga, C. 1961. *Diccionario Kechwa–Castellano*. Lima.

Guiteras Holmes, Calixta. 1961. *Perils of the Soul: The World-view of a Tzotzil* [Maya] *Indian*. New York: Free Press.

Gunn, S. W. A. (Kwe-Kwala-Gila). 1965. *Totem Poles of British Columbia*. Vancouver: Whiterocks Publications.

Gusinde, Martin. 1977. *Folk Literature of the Yamana Indians*. Vol. 4 of Wilbert and Simoneau 1970–86.

Guss, David. 1985. *The Language of Birds: Tales, texts and poems of interspecies communication*. San Francisco: North Point Press.

    1989. *To Weave and to Sing: Art, symbol and narrative in the Upper Orinoco*. Berkeley and Los Angeles: University of California Press.

Hagen, Victor Wolfgang von. 1944. *The Aztec and Maya Papermakers*. New York: J. J. Augustin.

Haile, Bernard. 1938. *Origin Legend of the Navajo Enemy Way*. New Haven, CT: Yale University Press.

Hale, Horatio. 1883. *The Iroquois Book of Rites*. Library of Aboriginal American Literature, vol. 2. Philadelphia: The Library. 2d enlarged ed., Toronto, 1963.

Hallam, John. 1877. "Thick-headed Horse's Dream." In Beach 1877:127–44.

Hammond, Norman (ed.). 1974. *Mesoamerican Archaeology – New approaches*. Austin: University of Texas Press.

    1982. *Ancient Maya Civilization*. London: Duckworth.

Hammond, Norman, and Gordon Willey (eds.). 1979. *Maya Archaeology and Ethnohistory*. Austin: University of Texas Press.

Harcourt, Raoul, and Marie d'Harcourt. 1925. *La musique des Incas et ses survivances*. 2 vols. Paris: P. Guenther.

Hariot, T. 1590. *A Briefe and True Report of the New Found Land of Virginia.* Frankfurt.

Harrison, Regina. 1989. *Signs, Songs and Memory in the Andes: Translating Quechua language and culture.* Austin: University of Texas Press.

Hartmann, Roswith. 1990. "Zur Ueberlieferung indianischer Oraltradition aus dem kolonialzeitlichen Peru: Das Huarochiri Manuscript." In Illius and Laubscher 1990, 1:543–61.

Harvey, Herbert R. 1986. "Household and Family Structure in Early Colonial Tepetlaoztoc," ECN 18:275–94.

Harvey, Herbert R., and Hanns Prem. 1984. *Explorations in Ethnohistory: Indians of central Mexico in the 16th century.* Albuquerque: University of New Mexico Press.

Harvey, Herbert R., and Barbara J. Williams. 1986. "Decipherment and Some Implications of Aztec Numerical Glyphs." In Closs 1986:237–60.

Hay, Clarence L., Ralph L. Linton, Samuel K. Lothrop, Harry L. Shapiro, and George C. Vaillant. 1977. *The Maya and Their Neighbors* (1940). New York: Dover.

Haywood, John. 1823. *The Natural and Aboriginal History of Tennessee up to the Settlements Therein by White People in 1768.* Nashville.

Helbig, J. W. 1984. "Einige Bemerkungen zum *muu ikala,* einem Medizingesang der Cuna Panamas," *Indiana* 10:71–88.

Hemming, John. 1970. *The Conquest of the Incas.* London: Macmillan.

1978. *The Search for El Dorado.* London: Michael Joseph.

1987. *Amazon Frontier: The defeat of the Brazilian Indians.* London: Macmillan.

Heyerdahl, Thor. 1950. *The Kon-Tiki Expedition,* trans. F. H. Lyon. London: Allen and Unwin.

Higgins, James. 1987. *A History of Peruvian Literature.* Liverpool: Francis Cairns.

Himmelblau, Jack J. 1989. *Quiché Worlds in Creation: The Popol vuh as a narrative work of art.* Culver City, CA: Labyrinthos.

Hinz, Eike. 1970. *Die Magischen Texte im Tratado Ruiz de Alarcóns 1629: Antropologische Analyse altaztekischer Texte.* Beiträge zur mittelamerikanischen Völkerkunde. Hamburg: Museum für Völkerkunde.

Hocquenghem, Anne Marie. 1987. *Iconografía mochica.* Lima: Pontificia Universidad Católica del Perú.

Hodge, F. W. (ed.). 1907. *Handbook of the American Indians North of Mexico.* Washington, DC: Smithsonian Institution.

Hoffman, Walter James. 1891. *The Midewiwin of the Grand Medicine Society of the Ojibway.* BAE Report no. 7. Washington, DC: Smithsonian Institution.

1894. *The Beginnings of Writing.* New York: Appleton.

Holmer, Nils M., and S. Henry Wassén. 1951. *Cuna Chrestomathy.* Böteborg: Etnografiska Museum.

1953. *The Complete Mu-Igala in Picture-Writing: A native record of a Cuna Indian medicine song.* Göteborg: Etnografiska Museum.

1963. *Dos cantos shamanísticos de los indios cunas.* Göteborg: Etnografiska Museum.

Hopper, Janice H. 1967. *Indians of Brazil in the 20th Century.* Washington, DC: Institute for Cross-Cultural Research.

Horcasitas, Fernando. 1968. *De Porfirio Díaz a Zapata.* UNAM.

1974. *El teatro náhuatl.* UNAM.

Houston, S. D. 1989. *Maya Glyphs*. London: British Museum.

Howard, James. 1960. "Dakota Winter Counts as a Source of Plains History," *Smithsonian Institution Bulletin* 173:335–416. BAE Anthropological Papers.

1960a. "Butterfly's Mandan Winter Count," *Ethnohistory* 7:28–43.

1965. *The Ponca Tribe*. BAE Bulletin no. 195. Washington, DC: Smithsonian Institution.

1976. *Yanktonai Ethnohistory and the John K. Bear Winter Count*. Memoir 11. Lincoln, NE: Plains Anthropologist.

1979. *The British Museum Winter Count*. Occasional Paper 4. London: British Museum.

1984. *The Canadian Sioux*. Lincoln: University of Nebraska Press.

Howard-Malverde, Rosaleen. 1986. "The Achkay, the Cacique and the Neighbour," *Bulletin de l'Institut Français des Etudes Andines* (Lima) 15, 3–4:1–34.

1989. "Story-telling Strategies in Quechua Narrative Performance," *Journal of Latin American Lore* 15:3–71.

1990. *The Speaking of History: Willapaakushay, or Quechua ways of telling the past*. London: Institute of Latin American Studies.

Howe, J. 1986. *The Kuna Gathering: Village politics in contemporary Panama*. Austin: University of Texas Press.

Hudson, Charles M. 1984. *Elements of Southeastern Indian Religion*. Leiden: Brill.

Hugh-Jones, Stephen. 1979. *The Palm and the Pleiades: Initiation and cosmology in Northwest Amazonia*. Cambridge: Cambridge University Press.

Hulme, Peter. 1986. *Colonial Encounters: Europe and the native Caribbean 1492–1797*. London: Methuen.

Hultkranz, Åke. 1957. *The North American Indian Orpheus Tradition*. Stockholm: Statens Etnografiska Museum.

Humboldt, Alexander von. 1810. *Vues des cordillères et monumens des peuples indigènes de l'Amérique*. Paris: F. Schoell.

Hunt, Eva. 1972. "Irrigation and the Socio-Political Organization of the Cuicatec Cacicazgos." In *The Prehistory of the Tehuacan Valley,* ed. F. Johnson and R. Macneish. Austin: University of Texas Press, vol. 4 (*Irrigation and Chronology*), pp. 162–261.

1977. *The Transformation of the Hummingbird: Cultural roots of a Zinacantecan mythical poem*. Ithaca, NY: Cornell University Press.

Hunter, William A. 1960. *The Calderonian Auto Sacramental: El gran teatro del mundo. An edition and translation of a Nahuatl version*. New Orleans: Middle American Research Institute, Tulane University.

Huxley, Francis. 1956. *Affable Savages: An anthropologist among the Urubu Indians of Brazil*. London: Travel Book Club.

Hyde, George E. 1951. *The Pawnee Indians*. Norman: University of Oklahoma Press.

1956. *A Sioux Chronicle*. Norman: University of Oklahoma Press.

1962. *Indians of the Woodlands from Prehistoric Times to 1725*. Norman: University of Oklahoma Press.

Hymes, Dell H. 1967 (ed.). *Studies in Southwestern Ethnolinguistics*. The Hague: Mouton.

1977. "Discovering Oral Performance and Measured Verse in American Indian Narrative," *New Literary History* 8:431–57.

1981. *"In Vain I Tried to Tell"*: *Essays in Native American ethnopoetics.* Philadelphia: University of Pennsylvania Press.

Ibarra Grasso, Dick Edgar. 1953. *La escritura indígena andina.* La Paz: Biblioteca Pacena, Alcaldía Municipal.

Illius, Bruno, and Matthias Laubscher (eds.). 1990. *Circumpacifica: Festschrift für Thomas S. Barthel.* 2 vols. Frankfurt: Lang.

Imbelloni, J. 1956. *La segunda esfinge indiana: Antiguos y nuevos aspectos del problema de los orígenes americanos.* Buenos Aires: Librería Hachette.

Incháustegui, Carlos. 1977. *Relatos del mundo mágico mazateco.* México: Secretaría de Educación Pública.

Ixtlilxochitl, Fernando de Alva. 1975–7. *Obras históricas,* ed. Edmundo O'Gorman, 2 vols. UNAM.

Jacklein, Klaus. 1978. *Los popolocas de Tepexi.* Wiesbaden.

Jansen, Maarten E. R. G. N. 1982. *Huisi Tacu: Estudio interpretativo de un libro mixteco antiguo Codex Vindobonensis Mexicanus I.* 2 vols. Amsterdam: Centro de Estudios Latinoamericanos y del Caribe.

Jennings, Francis. 1976. *The Invasion of America: Indians, colonialism, and the cant of conquest.* Chapel Hill: University of North Carolina Press.

Johansson, Patrick. 1990. "La devinette: Parole-jeu des Azteques," ECN 20:297–310.

Jones, Julie. 1985. *Art of Pre-Columbian Gold.* London.

Joralemon, P. D. 1971. *A Study of Olmec Iconography.* Washington, DC: Dumbarton Oaks.

Josephy, Alvin M., Jr. 1961. *The American Heritage Book of Indians.* New York: American Heritage.

1975. *The Indian Heritage of America.* Harmondsworth: Penguin.

Kahkewaquonaby Jones, Peter. 1861. *History of the Ojebway Indians.* London.

Kantule, Nele, and Rubén Pérez Kantule. See Nordenskiöld 1928, 1930, 1938; Wassén 1938.

Kartunnen, Frances, and James Lockhart. 1986. "The Huehuetlahtolli Bancroft MS: The missing pages," ECN 18:171–80.

Katz, Friedrich. 1972. *Ancient American Civilizations.* New York: Praeger.

Kauffmann Doig, Federico. 1978. "Los retratos de la capaccuna de Guaman Poma y el problema de los tocapo." In *Amerikanistische Studien: Festschrift für Hermann Trimborn,* ed. R. Hartmann and U. Oberem. St. Augustin, pp. 298–308.

Keeler, Clyde. 1969. *Cuna Indian Art.* New York: Exposition Press.

Keen, Benjamin. 1971. *The Aztec Image in Western Thought.* New Brunswick, NJ: Rutgers University Press.

Keiser, Albert. 1933. *The Indian in American Literature.* New York: Oxford University Press.

Kelley, David H. 1976. *Deciphering the Maya Script.* Austin: University of Texas Press.

1980. *Astronomical Identities of Mesoamerican Gods.* Miami. Institute of Maya Studies, Inc.

Kelm, Antje. 1968. *Vom Kondor und vom Fuchs*. Berlin: Mann.

Kerr, Justin. 1989. *The Maya Vase Book: A corpus of rollout photographs of Maya vases*. New York: Kerr Publications.

Kidd, K. E., and S. Dewdney. 1967. *Indian Rock Painting of the Great Lakes*. Toronto: University of Toronto Press.

Kilpatrick, Jack Frederick, and Anna Gritts. 1964. *Friends of Thunder: Folktales of the Oklahoma Cherokees*. Dallas: Southern Methodist University Press.

　　1965. *The Shadow of Sequoya: Social documents of the Cherokees, 1862–1964*. Norman: University of Oklahoma Press.

　　1968 (eds.). *New Echota Letters ("Cherokee Phoenix" 1828–34)*. Dallas: Southern Methodist University Press.

Kingsborough, Lord (Edward King). 1831–48. *Antiquities of Mexico, Comprising Facsimiles of Ancient Mexican Paintings and Hieroglyphs*. 9 vols. London.

Kirchhoff, Paul, Lina Odena Güemes, and Luis Reyes García. 1989. *Historia tolteca–chichimeca*. Rev. ed. FCE.

Klah, Hasteen. 1942. *Navajo Creation Myth: The story of the emergence*, ed. M. Wheelwright. Santa Fe: Museum of Navajo Ceremonial Art.

Knorosov, Yuri V. 1967. *Selected Chapters from the Writing of the Maya Indians*. Cambridge, MA: Peabody Museum.

Koch-Grünberg, Theodor. 1924. *Vom Roroima zum Orinoco*. Vol. 2, *Mythen und Legenden der Taulipang und Arekuna-Indianer*. Stuttgart: Strecker und Schröder.

König, Viola. 1979. *Inhaltliche Analyse und Interpretation von Codex Egerton*. Beiträge zur mittelamerikanischen Völkerkunde. Hamburg: Museum für Völkerkunde.

　　1984. "Der Lienzo Seler II und seine Stellung innerhalb der Coixtlahuaca Gruppe," *Baessler Archiv* 32:229–320.

　　1989. "Zwei Lienzos aus Oaxaca, Mexiko," *Mitteilungen aus den Museum für Völkerkunde* (Hamburg) 19:75–205.

Kössler-Ilg, Bertha. 1956. *Indianermärchen aus den Kordilleren*. Düsseldorf: Eugen Diederich.

Kramer, Fritz W. 1970. *Literature among the Cuna Indians*. Göteborg: Etnografiska Museum.

Krickeberg, Walter. 1928. *Märchen der Azteken und Inkaperuaner, Maya und Muisca*. Düsseldorf: Eugen Diederich.

　　1968. *Pre-Columbian Mexican Religions*. London: Wiedenfeld and Nicholson.

Kubler, George. 1962. *The Art and Architecture of Ancient America: The Mexican, Maya and Andean peoples*. Baltimore: Penguin.

Kutscher, Gerdt. 1954. *Nordperuanische Keramik*. Berlin: Mann.

Kutscher, Gerdt, Günter Vollmer, and Gordon Brotherston. 1987. *Aesop in Mexico*. Berlin: Mann.

La Barre, Weston. 1964. *The Peyote Cult*. Hamden, CT: Shoestring Press.

Lafitau, Joseph-François. 1983. *Moeurs des sauvages américains comparées aux moeurs des premiers temps* (1724), ed. Edna Hindie Lemay. 2 vols. Paris: Maspero.

Lahourcade, Alicia N. 1970. *La creación del hombre en las grandes religiones de América precolombina*. Madrid.

Lambert, Jean-Clarence. 1961. *Les poésies méxicaines: Anthologie des origines à nos jours*. Paris.

Lanczkowski, Gunter. 1962. *Quetzalcoatl: Mythos und Geschichte. Numen* (Leiden) 9, fasc. 1.

Landa, Diego de. 1937. *Yucatan before and after the Conquest, by Friar Diego de Landa* [his *Relación de las cosas de Yucatán*], ed. and trans. William Gates. Baltimore: Maya Society.

Landes, Ruth. 1968. *Ojibwa Religion and the Midewiwin.* Madison: University of Wisconsin Press.

Lara, Jesús. 1947. *Poesía popular quechua.* La Paz: Editorial Canata.

— 1956. *Notas sobre el teatro de los Incas.* La Paz: La Razón.

— 1957 (ed.). *Tragedia del fin de Atawallpa.* Cochabamba: Imprenta Universitaria.

— 1969. *La literatura de los quechuas.* La Paz: Editora Juventud.

Larco Hoyle, Rafael. 1965. *Checan: Essay on erotic elements in Peruvian art.* Geneva: Nagel.

Las Casas, Bartolomé de. 1909. *Apologética historia de las Indias.* Madrid: Bailly, Baillière e Hijos.

Lathrap, Donald. 1970. *The Upper Amazon.* London: Thames and Hudson.

— 1973. "The Gifts of the Cayman: Some thoughts on the subsistence basis of Chavin." In *Variation in Anthropology,* ed. D. Lathrap and Jody Douglas. Urbana: University of Illinois Press, pp. 91–105.

Launey, Michel. 1979–80. *Introduction à la langue et à la littérature aztèques.* 2 vols. Paris: L'Harmattan.

Lawrence, David Herbert. 1983. *The Plumed Serpent* (1926), ed. Ronald G. Walker. Harmondsworth: Penguin.

Leander, Birgitta. 1967. *El Códice de Otlaxpan.* México: Instituto Nacional de Antropología e Historia.

— 1970. *Pab igala: Historias de la tradition Kuna.* Panamá: Centro de Investigaciones Antropológicas.

LeClézio, J. M. G. 1976. *Les prophéties du Chilam Balam.* Paris: Gallimard.

— 1988. *Le rêve méxicaine, ou la pensée interrompue.* Paris: Gallimard.

Lee, Thomas. 1985. *Los códices mayas.* Tuxtla Gutiérrez: Universidad Nacional Autónoma de Chiapas.

Lehmann, Walter. 1949. *Sterbende Götter und christliche Heilsbotschaft.* QGA 3. Stuttgart: Mann.

— 1974. *Die Geschichte der Königreiche von Colhuacan und Mexiko: Codex Chimalpopoca* (1938). QGA 1. Stuttgart and Berlin: Mann.

Lenz, Hans. 1961. *Mexican Indian Paper: Its history and survival.* México: Editorial Libros de México.

Lenz, Rodolfo. 1895–7. *Estudios araucanos.* Santiago

León-Portilla, Ascensión H. de. 1988. *Tepuztlahcuilolli: Impresos en náhuatl, historia y bibliografía.* UNAM.

León-Portilla, Miguel. 1956. *La filosofía náhuatl estudiada en sus fuentes.* III.

— 1959. *Visión de los vencidos: Relaciones indígenas de la conquista.* UNAM.

— 1963. *Aztec Thought and Culture,* trans. Jack Emory Davis. Norman: University of Oklahoma Press.

— 1964. *Las literaturas precolombinas de México.* México: Pormaca.

— 1964a. *El reverso de la conquista: Relaciones aztecas, mayas e incas.* México: Joaquín Mortiz.

1967. *Trece poetas del mundo azteca.* UNAM.

1969. *Pre-Columbian Literatures of Mexico.* Norman: University of Oklahoma Press.

1972. "Religión de los Nicaraos," ECN 10:11–112.

1978. *Los manifestos en náhuatl de Emiliano Zapata.* UNAM.

1985. *Tonalamatl de los pochteca (Códice Féjérváry).* México: Celanese.

1986. *Coloquios y doctrina cristiana: Los diálogos de 1524 según el texto de Fray Bernardino de Sahagún y sus colaboradores indígenas.* UNAM.

1987. *Time and Reality in the Thought of the Maya.* Norman: University of Oklahoma Press. 2d enlarged ed. of English trans. of *Tiempo y realidad en el pensamiento maya* (1968).

1988. *Huehuetlahtolli: Testimonios de la antigua palabra.* México: Comisión Nacional Conmemorativa del V Centenario del Encuentro de Dos Mundos.

Le Page du Pratz. 1758. *Louisiane.* 3 vols. Paris.

Le Plongeon, Augustus. 1886. *Sacred Mysteries among the Mayas and the Quichés.* New York: R. Macoy.

Léry, Jean de. 1957. *Journal de bord: Le Brésil en 1557.* Paris: Editions Mayeux.

Levine, Stuart, and Nancy O. Lurie. 1968. *The American Indian Today.* Baltimore: Penguin.

Lévi-Strauss, Claude. 1955. *Tristes tropiques.* Paris: Union Générale d'Editions.

1964–71. *Mythologiques.* 4 vols. Paris: Plon.

1969. *The Raw and the Cooked: Introduction to a science of mythology,* trans. J. and D. Weightman. London: Cape. Vol. 1 of *Mythologiques.*

1972. *Structural Anthropology,* (1958), trans. Claire Jacobson and Brooke Grundfest Schoepf. Harmondsworth: Penguin.

1975–9. *La Voie des masques.* 2 vols. Paris.

1978. *Structural Anthropology,* vol. 2, trans. Monique Layton. Harmondsworth: Penguin.

Lewis, Janet. 1964. *The Invasion* (1932). Denver: Alan Swallow.

Lienlaf, Leonel. 1989. *Se ha despertado el ave de mi corazón.* Santiago: Editorial Universitaria.

Lienhard, Martin. 1990. *Cultura andina y forma novelesca: Zorros y danzantes en la última novela de Arguedas.* Lima: Tarea.

Lipp, Frank. 1991. *The Mixe of Oaxcaca: Religion, ritual and healing.* Austin: University of Texas Press.

Lom d'Arce (Baron de Lahontan). 1703. *Voyages du baron de Lahontan dans l'Amérique septentrional.* Amsterdam.

Longfellow, Henry Wadsworth. 1855. *The Song of Hiawatha.* Boston and London.

Loo, Peter van der. 1987. *Códices, costumbres, continuidad: Un estudio de la religión mesoamericana.* Leiden: Centro de Estudios Latinoamericanos y del Caribe.

López Austin, Alfredo. 1984. *Cuerpo humano e ideología.* UNAM.

1990. *Los mitos del tlacuache: Caminos de la mitología mesoamericana.* México: Alianza.

Lumholtz, Carl. 1902. *Unknown Mexico: Explorations in the Sierra Madre and other regions.* 2 vols. New York.

1986. *El arte simbólico y decorativo de los huicholes.* III.

Luxton, Richard. 1977. *The Hidden Continent of the Maya and the Quechua.* Unpublished Ph.D. diss., Essex University.

McCaskill, Don (ed.). 1989. *Amerindian Cosmology.* Edinburgh: Cosmos; Brandon, Manitoba: Canadian Journal of Native Studies.

McCoy, Ron. 1983. *Winter Count: The Teton Chronicles to 1799.* Unpublished Ph.D. diss., University of Northern Arizona.

McDowell, John. 1989. *Sayings of the Ancestors: The spiritual life of the Sibundoy Indians.* Lexington: Kentucky University Press.

McGee, W. J. 1897. *The Sioux.* BAE Annual Report 1893–4. Washington, DC: Smithsonian Institution.

Makemson, Maud. 1951. *The Book of the Jaguar Priest.* New York: Henry Schumann.

Maldonado Jiménez, Druzo. 1990. *Cuauhnahuac y Huaxtepec: Tlahuicas y xochimilcas en el Morelos prehispánico.* Cuernavaca: UNAM.

Malinowski, Bronislaw. 1960. *A Scientific Theory of Culture and Other Essays.* New York: Oxford University Press.

Mallery, Garrick. 1893. *Picture-Writing of the American Indians.* 2 vols. BAE 10th Annual Report. Washington, DC: Smithsonian Institution.

Malotki, Ekkehart. 1978. *Hopitutuwutsi: Hopi tales.* Flagstaff: Museum of Northern Arizona Press.

Manuel, George. 1974. *The Fourth World: An Indian reality.* New York: Free Press. Foreword by Vine Deloria.

Marcus, Joyce. 1976. *Emblem and State in the Classic Maya Lowlands.* Washington, DC: Dumbarton Oaks.

1980. "Zapotec Writing," *Scientific American,* February.

Margolin, Malcolm. 1981. *The Way We Lived: California Indian reminiscences, stories and songs.* Berkeley, CA: Heyday.

Mariátegui, J. C. 1955. *Siete ensayos en torno a la realidad peruana* (1928). Santiago de Chile: Colección América Nuestra.

Markham, Clements Robert. 1856. *Cuzco: A journey to the ancient capital of Peru, with an account of the history, language, literature and antiquities of the Incas.* London: Chapman and Hall.

1871. *Ollantay, an Ancient Inca Drama.* London: Trubner.

1873. *Narratives of the Rites and Law of the Incas.* London: Hakluyt Society.

1910. *The Incas of Peru.* London: Smith, Elder.

Marriott, Alice. 1945. *The Ten Grandmothers.* Norman: University of Oklahoma Press.

Martínez, José Luis. 1972. *Nezahualcoyotl, vida y obra.* FCE.

Martínez Gracida, Manuel. 1897–8. "Mitología mixteca," *Memorias de la Sociedad Científica Antonio Alzate* 11:424–48.

Martínez Hernández, Juan. 1930. *Diccionario de Motul, Maya–Español.* Mérida, Yucatán.

Martínez Marín, M. (ed.). 1989. *Primer coloquio de documentos pictográficos de tradición náhuatl.* UNAM.

Mason, J. Alden. 1964. *The Ancient Civilisations of Peru.* Harmondsworth: Penguin.

Mason, Peter. 1986. "Lévi-Strauss in Tenochtitlan," *Boletín de Estudios Latinoamericanos y del Caribe* (Amsterdam) 45:101–11.

1990. *Deconstructing America: Representations of the Other.* London: Routledge.

Matos Moctezuma, Eduardo. 1979. *Trabajos arqueológicos en el centro de la ciudad de México.* México: Instituto Nacional de Antropología e Historia.

Matthews, Washington. 1897. *Navaho Legends.* Boston: American Folklore Society.

Matthiesson, Peter. 1987. *Indian Country.* New York: Fontana.

1990. *Killing Mr. Watson.* New York: Random House.

Maudslay, A. P. 1889–1902. *Archaeology: Biologia centrali-americana.* 5 vols. London: Dulau.

Means, Philip Ainsworth. 1931. *Ancient Civilizations of the Andes.* New York: Scribner.

Medina, José T. 1952. *Los aborígenes de Chile.* Santiago de Chile: Imprenta Universitaria.

Médiz Bolio, Antonio (ed.). 1973. *Libro de Chilam Balam de Chumayel* (1930). UNAM.

Melgarejo Vivanco, José Luis. 1970 (ed.). *Códices de tierras: Los lienzos de Tuxpan.* México: Petróleos Mexicanos.

1980. *El Códice Vindobonensis.* Xalapa: Instituto de Antropología, Universidad Veracruzana.

Menchú. See Burgos Debray.

Méndez Plancarte, Alfonso. 1944. *Poetas novohispanos: Primer siglo (1521–1621).* UNAM.

Mendieta, Fr. Gerónimo de. 1971. *Historia eclesiástica indiana,* ed. J. García Icazbalceta. México: Porrúa.

Mendizábal Losack, Emilio. 1961. "Don Felipe Guamán Poma de Ayala, señor y príncipe, último quellcakamayoc," *Journal of Latin American Lore* 5:83–116.

Meneses, M. N. (ed.). 1977. Edward A. Goodall, *Sketches of Amerindian Tribes (1841–3).* London: British Museum.

Meneses, Teodoro (ed.). 1951. *Usca Paucar.* Lima.

1983. *Teatro quechua colonial.* Lima: Edubanco.

Menguin, Ernst. 1952. "Commentaire du Codex Mexicanus," *Journal de la Société des Américanistes* 41:387–498 plus album.

Mera, Juan León. 1868. *Ojeada histórico-crítica sobre la poesía ecuatoriana desde su época más remota hasta nuestros días.* Quito.

Métraux, Alfred. 1928. *La religion des Tupinamba et ses rapports avec celle des autres tribus tupi–guarani.* Paris: Ernest Leroux.

1962. *Les Incas.* Paris: Seuil.

Meyer, William (Yonv'ut'sisla). 1971. *Native Americans: The new Indian resistance.* New York: International Publishers.

Miller, Arthur G. 1973. *The Mural Painting of Teotihuacan.* Washington, DC: Dumbarton Oaks.

1975 (ed.). *The Codex Nuttall.* New York: Dover.

1982. *On the Edge of the Sea: Mural paintings at Tancah-Tulum.* Washington, DC: Dumbarton Oaks.

Miranda, José. 1952. *El tributo indígena en la Nueva España.* México: Colegio de México.

Moesbach, E. W. (ed.). 1984. Pascual Coña *Testimonio de un cacique mapuche.* 4th ed. Santiago: Pehuén.

Mohar Betancourt, Luz María. 1990. *La escritura en el México antiguo.* 2 vols. México: Plaza y Valdés.

Molina, Fr. Alonso de. 1977. *Vocabulario en lengua castellana y mexicana* (1571). México: Porrúa.

Monjarás Ruiz, Jesús (ed.). 1987. *Mitos cosmogónicos del México indígena.* México: Instituto Nacional de Antropología e Historia.

Mönnich, Anneliese. 1971. "The Test Theme: A possible Southwestern trait in Mesoamerican mythology," *Berliner Gesellschaft für Anthropologie Festschrift* 3:310–19.

Montoya, Rodrigo, Edwin Montoya, and Luis Montoya. 1987. *La sangre de los cerros: Urqukunapa yawarnin.* Lima: Cepes.

Montoya Sánchez, Fr. Javier. 1973. *Antología de creencias, mitos, teogonías, leyendas y tradiciones colombianos.* Bogotá: Concejo de Medellín.

Montoya Toro, J., and Ernesto Cardenal. 1966. *Literatura indígena americana.* Antioquía: Publicaciones de la Revista de la Universidad.

Mooney, James. 1891. *Sacred Formulas of the Cherokees.* BAE 7th Report. Washington, DC: Smithsonian Institution.

    1896. *The Ghost-Dance Religion and the Sioux Outbreak of 1890.* BAE 14th Report, pt. 2. Washington, DC: Smithsonian Institution.

    1898. *Myths of the Cherokee.* BAE 19th Report. Washington, DC: Smithsonian Institution.

    1979. *Calendar History of the Kiowa Indians* (1898; BAE 17th Report). Washington, DC: Smithsonian Institution. Introduction by John C. Ewers.

Morgan, Lewis Henry. 1901. *League of the Ho-de-no-sau-nee, or Iroquois* (1851). 2 vols. New York: Dodd Mead.

    1909. *Ancient Society* (1877). 2d ed. Chicago.

    1959. *The Indian Journals 1859–62.* Ann Arbor: University of Michigan Press.

    1967. *Montezuma's Dinner: An essay on the tribal society of North American Indians* (1876). New York.

Morley, S. S. 1915. *An Introduction to the Study of the Maya Hieroglyphs.* Washington, DC: Smithsonian Institution.

    1956. *The Ancient Maya.* Stanford, CA: Stanford University Press.

Motolinía (Fray Toribio de Benaventel). 1971. *Memoriales o Libro de las cosas de la Nueva España,* ed. Edmundo O'Gorman. UNAM.

Muñoz, Braulio. 1983. *The Indian Literatures of Latin America.* New Brunswick, NJ: Rutgers University Press.

Murra, J. V. 1980. *The Economic Organization of the Inca State.* Greenwich, CT: JAI Press.

Murra, J. V., and R. Adorno (eds.). 1980. Guaman Poma, *El primer nueva corónica y buen gobierno.* 3 vols. México: Siglo XXI.

Murray, David. 1991. *Forked Tongues: Speech, writing and representation in North American Indian texts.* London: Pinter.

Murúa, Martín de. 1946. *Historia del origen y genealogía real de los incas* (1590), ed. Constantino Bayle. Madrid: Consejo Superior de Investigaciones Científicas.

Navarre, Robert. 1913. *Journal ou dictation d'une conspiration.* Detroit. French text with English trans. by R. Clyde Ford, *Journal of Pontiac's Conspiracy.*

Needham, Joseph. 1958–9. *Science and Civilisation in China,* vols. 2–3. Cambridge: Cambridge University Press.

Negrín, Juan. 1975. *The Huichol Creation of the World.* Sacramento, CA: Crocker Art Gallery.

　　1985. *Acercamiento histórico y subjetivo al huichol.* Guadalajara: Universidad de Guadalajara.

Neihardt, John G. See Black Elk.

Nelson, Ralph (ed.). 1976. *The Popol vuh: The great mythological book of the ancient Maya.* Boston: Houghton Mifflin.

Newcomb, Franc J., and Gladys A. Reichard. 1975. *Sandpaintings of the Navajo Shooting Chant.* New York: Dover.

Newson, Linda. 1987. *Indian Survival in Colonial Nicaragua.* Norman: University of Oklahoma Press.

Nicholson, Henry B. 1978. "Western Mesoamerica: A.D. 900–1520." In *Chronologies in New World Archaeology,* ed. Means and Taylor. New York, pp. 285–325.

Nicholson, Irene. 1959. *Firefly in the Night: A study of ancient Mexican poetry and symbolism.* London: Faber.

Nicolau d'Olwer, Luis. 1963. *Cronistas de las culturas precolombinas.* FCE.

Niño, Hugo. 1977. *Primitivos relatos contados otra vez: Héroes y mitos amazónicos.* Bogotá: Instituto Colombiano de Cultura.

　　1978. *Literatura de Colombia aborigen.* Bogotá: Instituto Colombiano de Cultura.

Nordenskiöld, Erland. 1925. *The Secret of the Peruvian Quipus.* 2 vols. Göteborg: Etnografiska Museum.

　　1928. *Picture-Writings and Other Documents by Nele, Paramount Chief of the Cuna Indians, and Rubén Pérez Kantule, His Secretary.* Göteborg: Etnografiska Museum.

　　1930. *Picture-Writings and other Documents by Nele, Charles Sister, Charlie Nelson and other Cuna Indians.* Göteborg: Etnografiska Museum.

　　1938. *An Historical and Ethnographical Survey of the Cuna Indians, in Collaboration with the Cuna Indian Rubén Pérez Kantule,* ed. Henry Wassén. Göteborg: Etnografiska Museum.

Noriega, R. (ed.). 1959. *Esplendor del México antiguo.* 2 vols. México: Centro de Investigaciones Antropológicas.

Norman, V. Garth. 1976. *Izapa Sculpture.* Papers of the New World Archeological Foundation, no. 30. Provo, UT: Brigham Young University.

Nowotny, Karl A. 1961. *Tlacuilolli: Die mexikanischen Bilderhandschriften, Stil und Inhalt.* Berlin: Mann.

　　1961a (ed.). *Códices Becker I/II.* ADV.

　　1968 (ed.). *Codex Cospi.* ADV.

　　1969. *Beiträge zur geschichte des Weltbildes.* Vienna.

　　1974 (ed.). *Codex Borbonicus.* ADV.

　　1976 (ed.). *Codex Borgia.* ADV.

Núñez, Estuardo. 1972. "Lo latinoamericano en otras literaturas." In *América latina en su literatura,* ed. C. Fernández Moreno. México: Siglo XXI, pp. 93–120.

Nuttall, Zelia (ed.). 1902. *Codex Nuttall.* Cambridge, MA: Peabody Museum.

O'Gorman, E. 1961. *The Invention of America: An enquiry into the historical nature of the New World and the meaning of its history.* Bloomington: Indiana University Press.

Olbrechts, F., and James Mooney. 1932. *The Swimmer Manuscript: Cherokee sacred formulas and medicinal prescriptions.* Washington, DC: Smithsonian Institution.

Olson, Charles. 1953. *Mayan Letters.* Mallorca: Divers Press.

Ong, Walter. 1977. *Interfaces of the Word.* Ithaca, NY: Cornell University Press.

    1982. *Orality and Literacy: The technologizing of the word.* New York: Methuen.

Ossio, J. M. (ed.). *Ideología mesiánica del mundo andino.* Lima: Colección Biblioteca de Antropología.

Overing, Joanna. 1975. *The Piaroa: A people of the Orinoco Basin.* Oxford: Clarendon Press.

Paddock, John. 1966. *Ancient Oaxaca.* Stanford, CA: Stanford University Press.

Padial Guerchoux, Anita, and Manuel Vázquez-Bigi (eds.). 1991. *Quiché Vinak: Tragedia.* FCE.

Padilla Bendezú, Abraham. 1979. *Huaman Poma, el indio cronista dibujante.* FCE.

Pagden, A. R. 1972. *Mexican Pictorial Manuscripts.* Oxford: Bodleian Library.

Parezo, Nancy J. 1983. *Navajo Sandpainting: From religious act to commercial art.* Tucson: University of Arizona Press.

Parkman, Francis. 1902. *The Struggle for a Continent,* ed. Pelham Edgar. London: Macmillan.

Parmenter, Ross. 1982. *Four Lienzos of the Coixtlahuaca Valley.* Washington, DC: Dumbarton Oaks.

Parsons, Elsie Clews. 1967. *American Indian Life* (1922). Lincoln, NE: Bison.

    1936. *Mitla: Town of the Souls and other Zapoteco-speaking Pueblos of Oaxaca.* Chicago: University of Chicago Press.

    1939. *Pueblo Indian Religion.* 2 vols. Chicago: University of Chicago Press.

Paso y Troncoso, Francisco del. 1902. "Comédies en langue nahuatl." In *12th International Congress of Americanists.* Paris, pp. 309–16.

    1908 (ed.). "Fragmento de la obra general sobre Historia de los mexicanos escrita en náuatl por Cristóbal del Castillo." *Biblioteca Nauatl* (Florence) 5, 2:41–107.

Pease, Franklin (ed.). 1980. Guaman Poma, *El primer nueva corónica y buen gobierno.* Caracas: Ayacucho.

Pellizaro, Siro (ed.). 1979. *Tsunki: El mundo del agua y de los poderes fecundantes.* Mitología shuar, vol. 2. Sucua, Ecuador: Mundo Shuar.

Peniche Rivera, Piedad. 1990. *Sacerdotes y comerciantes: El poder de los Mayas e Itzaes de Yucatán en los siglos VII a XII.* FCE.

Pereira, Nunes. 1951. *Historias e vocabulario Uitoto.* Belem.

    1967. *Moronguetá: Um decameron indigena.* 2 vols. Rio.

Péret, Benjamin. 1956 (ed.). *Livre de Chilam Balam de Chumayel.* Paris: Denoël.

    1960. *Anthologie des mythes, légendes et contes populaires d'Amérique.* Paris: Albin Michel.

Pérez Firmat, Gustavo (ed.). 1990. *Do the Americas Have a Common Literature?* Durham, NC: Duke University Press.

Perrin, Michel. 1980. *El camino de los indios muertos: Mitos y símbolos guajiros.* Caracas: Monte Avila.

Petersen, Karen Daniels. 1971. *Plains Indian Art from Fort Marion: With a pictographic dictionary.* Norman: University of Oklahoma Press.

Pferdekamp, Wilhelm. 1963. *Die Indianer-Story.* Munich.

Pietschmann, Richard (ed.). 1936. Felipe Guaman Poma de Ayala, *Nueva corónica y buen gobierno.* Paris: Musée de l'Homme. Facsimile ed.

Piña Chan, Román. 1977. *Quetzalcoatl, serpiente emplumada.* FCE.

1989. *The Olmec: Mother culture of Mesoamerica,* ed. Laura Laurencich Minelli. New York: Rizzoli.

Platt, Tristan. 1985. *Pensamiento político aymara.* México.

Pottier, Bernard. 1983. *América latina en sus lenguas indígenas.* Caracas: Monte Avila.

Powell, Philip W. 1975. *Soldiers, Indians and Silver.* Norman: University of Oklahoma Press.

Prem, Hanns J. 1978. "Comentario a las partes calendáricas del Codex Mexicanus 23–4," ECN 13:267–88.

Prescott, William Hickling. 1843. *History of the Conquest of Mexico, with a preliminary view of the ancient Mexican civilization.* 3 vols. London: Richard Bentley.

Preuss, Konrad Theodor. 1912. *Die Nayarit Expedition.* Leipzig.

1919–27. "Forschungsreise zu den Kagaba-Indianer: Beobachtungen, Textaufnahmen und linguistische Studien," *Anthropos,* nos. 14–22.

1921. *Die Religion und Mythologie der Uitoto.* Göttingen–Leipzig.

1929. *Monumentale vorgeschichtliche Kunst: Ausgrabungen in Quelle-gebiet des Magdalenas in Columbien 1913–14.* Göttingen.

1968. *Nahua Texte aus San Pedro Jícora in Durango.* QGA 9. Berlin: Mann.

Preuss, Mary. 1988. *Gods of the Popol vuh.* Culver City, CA: Labyrinthos.

1989 (ed.). *In Love and War, Hummingbird Lore.* Culver City, CA: Labyrinthos.

Pring-Mill, Robert. 1977. *Ernesto Cardenal: "Apocalypse" and Other Poems.* New York: New Directions.

Propp, V. 1968. *Morphology of the Folktale.* Austin: University of Texas Press.

Purchas, Samuel. 1625. *Purchas, His Pilgrimes,* vol. 3. London: William Stansby.

Raczka, Paul M. 1979. *Winter Count: A History of the Blackfoot people.* Brocket, Alberta: Oldman River Culture Center.

Radin, Paul. 1928. *The Story of the American Indian.* London.

1954–6. *The Evolution of an American Indian Prose Epic: A study in comparative literature.* Basel: Ethnographical Museum.

1956. *The Trickster: A study in American Indian mythology.* New York: Schocken.

1970. *The Winnebago Tribe* (1923; BAE 37th Report). Lincoln: University of Nebraska Press.

Rafinesque, Constantine Schmalz. 1836. *The American Nations.* 2 vols. Philadelphia.

Rama, Angel. 1982. *Transculturación narrativa en América Latina.* México: Siglo XXI.

Rappaport, Joanne. 1990. *The Politics of Memory: Native historical interpretation in the Colombian Andes.* Cambridge: Cambridge University Press.

Raynaud, Georges, M. A. Asturias, and J. M. González. 1927. *Los dioses, los héroes y los hombres de Guatemala antigua.* Paris: Editorial Paris–America.

Recinos, Adrián. 1950. *Popol vuh: The sacred book of the ancient Quiché Maya,* trans.

Delia Goetz and Sylvanus G. Morley. Norman: University of Oklahoma Press.

1957. *Crónicas indígenas de Guatemala.* Guatemala City: Editorial Universitaria.

Recinos, Adrián, Delia Goetz, and José Chonay. 1953. *The Annals of the Cakchiquels: Title of the lords of Totonicapan:* Norman: University of Oklahoma Press.

Reed, Nelson. 1964. *The Caste War of Yucatan.* Stanford, CA: Stanford University Press.

Reichard, Gladys. 1963. *Navajo Religion: A study of symbolism.* New York: Bollingen Foundation.

1977. *Navajo Medicine Men Sandpaintings.* New York: Dover.

Reichel-Dolmatoff, Gerardo. 1950–1. *Los Kogi: Una tribu de la Sierra Nevada de Santa Marta, Colombia.* 2 vols. Bogotá: Instituto Etnológico Nacional and Editorial Iqueima.

1971. *Amazonian Cosmos: The sexual and religious symbolism of the Tukano Indians.* Chicago: University of Chicago Press.

Rexroth, Kenneth. 1960. "American Indian Songs in the U.S. Bureau of Ethnology Collection." In Rexroth, *Assays.* New York: New Directions, pp. 52–68.

Reyes, Alfonso. 1956. *Visión de Anahuac* (1915). FCE.

1948. *Letras de la Nueva España.* FCE.

Reyes García, Luis (ed.). 1976. *Der Ring aus Tlalocan: Mythen und Gebete, Lieder und Erzählungen der heutigen Nahua in Veracruz und Puebla.* QGA 12. Berlin: Mann.

Ribeiro, Bertha G. 1983. *O indio na historia do Brasil.* São Paulo: Global.

Ribeiro, Darcy. 1971. *Fronteras indígenas de la civilización.* México: Siglo XXI.

1974. *Uirá sai à procura de Deus: Ensaios de etnologia e indigenismo.* Rio: Coleção Estudos Brasileiros.

1976. *Maíra, romance.* Rio: Editora Civilização Brasileira.

Ricard, Robert. 1933. *La "Conquête spirituelle" du Méxique.* Paris: Université de Paris.

Riester, Jürgen. 1984. *Textos sagrados de los Guaraníes en Bolivia.* La Paz: Los Amigos del Libro.

Rivière, Peter. 1984. *Individual and Society in Guiana.* Cambridge: Cambridge University Press.

Roa Bastos, Augusto. 1978. *Las culturas condenadas.* México: Siglo XXI.

Robertson, Donald. 1959. *Mexican Manuscript Painting of the Early Colonial Period.* New Haven, CT: Yale University Press.

1975. "Techialoyan Manuscripts and Paintings, with a Catalog," HMAI 14: 253–80.

Robertson, Merle Greene (ed.). 1974. *Primera mesa redonda de Palenque,* pt. 1. Pebble Beach, CA: Robert Louis Stevenson School.

Robertson, William. 1778. *A History of America.* Rev. ed. 2 vols. Edinburgh.

Robiscek, Francis, and Donald Hales. 1981. *The Maya Book of the Dead: The Ceramic Codex.* New Haven, CT: Yale University Press.

Rodríguez, Nemesio (ed.). 1983. *Educación, etnias y descolonización en América latina.* 2 vols. III.

Roe, Peter G. 1982. *The Cosmic Zygote: Cosmology in the Amazon Basin.* New Brunswick, NJ: Rutgers University Press.

Rojas, Gabriel de. 1985. *Relación geográfica de Cholula* (1581). In Acuña 1985:125–45.

Rojas, Ricardo. 1937. *Himnos quechuas.* Buenos Aires: Instituto de Literatura Argentina de la Universidad.

Rojas Garcidueñas, José. 1973. *El teatro de Nueva España en el siglo XVI.* México: Secretaría de Educación Pública.

Rothenberg, Jerome. 1972. *Shaking the Pumpkin: Traditional poetry of the Indian North Americas.* New York: Anchor.

    1985. *Technicians of the Sacred.* 2d enlarged ed. Berkeley and Los Angeles: University of California Press.

Rowe, John Howland. 1946. "Inca Culture at the Time of the Spanish Conquest," HSAI 2:183–330.

    1953. "Eleven Inca Prayers from the Zithuwa Ritual," *Kroeber Anthropological Society Papers,* nos. 8–9:82–99.

    1962. *Chavin.* New York: Museum of Primitive Art.

Rowe, William. 1979. *Mito e ideología en la obra de José María Arguedas.* Lima: Instituto Nacional de Cultura.

    1984. "Ethnocentric Orthodoxies versus Text as Cultural Action," *Romance Studies* 5:75–87.

Rowe, William, and Victoria Schelling. 1991. *Memory and Modernity: Popular culture in Latin America.* London: Verso.

Roys, Ralph L. 1933 (ed.). *The Book of Chilam Balam of Chumayel.* Washington, DC: Smithsonian Institution.

    1972. *The Indian Background of Colonial Yucatan.* Norman: University of Oklahoma Press.

    1946 (ed.). "The Book of Chilam Balam of Ixil." *Carnegie Institution of Washington Publication* 75:90–103.

Russell, Frank. 1975. *The Pima Indians* (1908; BAE 26th Report). Tucson: University of Arizona Press.

Saenz de Santa María, Carmelo (ed.). 1989. *Popol vuh.* Madrid.

Sahagún, Bernardino. 1956. *Historia general de las cosas de Nueva España.* 4 vols. México: Porrúa.

Sandstrom, Alan R., and Pamela Effrein. 1986. *Traditional Papermaking and Paper Cult Figures of Mexico.* Norman: University of Oklahoma Press.

Santillana, Giorgio, and Hertha von Dechend. 1970. *Hamlet's Mill: An essay on myth and the frame of time.* London: Macmillan.

Santos Granero, Fernando. 1986. "Power, Ideology and the Ritual of Production in Lowland South America," *Man* 21:657–79.

Santos Ortiz, Juan. 1976. *Sacha pacha: El mundo de la selva.* Quito: CICAME. Bilingual ed.

    1981. *Antiguas culturas amazónicas ecuatorianas.* Quito: CICAME.

Sauer, Carl Ortwin. 1966. *The Early Spanish Main.* Cambridge: Cambridge University Press.

    1971. *Sixteenth-Century North America.* Berkeley and Los Angeles: University of California Press.

    1975. *Man in Nature.* Berkeley, CA: Turtle Island Foundation.

Schele, Linda, and David Freidel. 1990. *A Forest of Kings: The untold story of the ancient Maya.* New York: Morrow.

Schele, Linda, and Mary Ellen Miller. 1986. *Blood of Kings: Dynasty and ritual in Maya art.* New York: Braziller in association with the Kimball Art Museum, Fort Worth.

Schoolcraft, Henry Rowe. 1839. *Algic Researches.* 2 vols. New York.

— 1845. *Oneota.* New York.

— 1851–7. *Historical and Statistical Information Respecting the History, Condition and Prospects of the Indian Tribes of the United States.* 5 vols. Philadelphia: Bureau of Indian Affairs.

Schultze Jena, Leonard (ed.). 1957. *Alt-aztekische Gesänge.* QGA 6. Stuttgart: Mann.

Schumann, Otto. 1988. "El origen del maíz, versión Kekchi." In Serra Puche 1988:213–18.

Seler, Eduard. 1902–23. *Gesammelte Abhandlungen zur amerikanischen Sprach- und Alterthumskunde.* 5 vols. Berlin. Repr. 1960, ADV.

Serra Puche, Mari Carmen (ed.). 1988. *Etnología: Temas y tendencias. I Coloquio Paul Kirchhoff.* UNAM.

Severin, Gregory M. 1981. *The Paris Codex: Decoding an astronomical ephemeris.* Transactions of the APS 71, pt. 5. Philadelphia: The Society.

Sherzer, Joel. 1983. *Kuna Ways of Speaking: An ethnographic perspective.* Austin: University of Texas Press.

Sherzer, Joel, and Greg Urban (eds.). 1986. *Native South American Discourse.* Berlin: Mouton de Gruyter.

Sherzer, Joel, and Anthony C. Woodbury (eds.). 1987. *Native American Discourse: Poetics and rhetoric.* Cambridge: Cambridge University Press.

Sigüenza y Góngora, Carlos de. 1984. *Seis obras,* ed. William G. Bryant. Caracas: Ayacucho.

Silva Galeana, Librado. 1986. "Inoc imoztlayoc in miccailhuitl," ECN 18:13–40.

Silverblatt, Irene. 1987. *Moon, Sun and Witches: Gender, ideology and class in Inca and colonial Peru.* Princeton, NJ: Princeton University Press.

Skinner, Alanson Buck, and John B. Satterlee. 1915. *Folklore of the Menomini Indians.* Anthropological Papers 13, pt. 3, New York: American Museum of Natural History.

Smailus, Ortwin. 1975. *El Maya-Chontal de Acallan.* UNAM.

Smith, Donald B. 1987. *Sacred Feathers: The Reverend Peter Jones (Kahkewaquonaby) and the Mississauga Indians.* Lincoln: University of Nebraska Press.

Smith, Mary Elizabeth. 1973. *Picture Writing from Ancient Southern Mexico: Mixtec place signs and maps.* Norman: University of Oklahoma Press.

Smith, V. G. 1988. *Izapa Relief Carving.* Washington, DC: Dumbarton Oaks.

Sodi Morales, Demetrio. 1964. *La literatura de los mayas.* México: Joaquín Mortiz.

Solís Alcalá, E. 1949. *Códice Pérez.* Mérida de Yucatán: Ediciones de la Liga de Acción Social.

Sosa, John R. 1986. "Maya Concepts of Astronomical Order." In Gossen 1986: 185–96.

Soustelle, Jacques. 1955. *La vie quotidienne des Aztèques à la veille de la conquête espagnole.* Paris: Hachette.

Spalding, Karen. 1984. *Huarochirí: An Andean society under Inca and Spanish rule.* Stanford, CA: Stanford University Press.

Speck, Frank. 1909. *Ethnology of the Yuchi Indians.* Philadelphia: University of Pennsylvania Museum.

1942. *The Tutelo Spirit Adoption Ceremony: Reclothing the living in the name of the dead.* Harrisburg, PA.

Spence, Lewis. 1914. *The Myths of the North American Indians.* London: Harrap.

Spinden, Herbert Joseph. 1933. *Songs of the Tewa: Preceded by an essay on American Indian poetry.* New York.

Squier, Ephraim George. 1877. "Historical and Mythological Traditions of the Algonquins." In Beach 1877:9–42.

1852. *Nicaragua: Its people, scenery, monuments and the proposed interoceanic canal.* New York: Appleton.

Stiles, Neville. 1987. "Purist Tendencies among Native Mayan Speakers of Guatemala," *Linguist* 26:187–91.

Stokes, Philip. 1987. *The Legitimation of Political Power: An interpretation of the first 22 pages of the Nuttall screenfold.* Unpublished Ph.D. diss., Essex University.

Stuart, David. 1989. "Hieroglyphs on Maya Vases." In Kerr 1989:149–60.

Suárez Alvarez, H., and J. M. B. Farfán (eds.). 1938. *El pobre más rico.* Lima: Editorial Lumen.

Swan, Michael. 1958. *The Marches of El Dorado.* London: Cape.

Swann, Brian, and Arnold Krupat. 1987. *I Tell You Now: Autobiographical essays by Native American writers.* Lincoln: University of Nebraska Press.

Swanton, John R. 1979. *The Indians of the Southeastern United States* (1946). Washington, DC: Smithsonian Institution.

Tanner, John. 1830. *Narrative of the Captivity and Adventures of John Tanner.* New York.

Taylor, Colin. 1990. *Reading Plains Indian Artefacts.* Unpublished Ph.D. diss., Essex University.

Taylor, Gerard. 1987. *Ritos y tradiciones de Huarochirí: Manuscrito quechua, versión paleográfica.* Lima: Instituto de Estudios Peruanos e Instituto Francés de Estudios Andinos.

Tedlock, Barbara. 1982. *Time and the Highland Maya.* Albuquerque: University of New Mexico Press.

Tedlock, Dennis. 1972. *Finding the Center: Narrative poetry of the Zuni Indians.* Lincoln: University of Nebraska Press.

1985. *Popol vuh: The definitive edition of the Mayan book of the dawn of life and the glories of gods and kings.* New York: Simon and Schuster.

1988. *The Sowing and the Dawning of All the Sky-Earth.* Philadelphia: University of Pennsylvania Museum.

Tello, Julio C. 1952. "Mitología del norte andino peruano," *América Indígena* (México) 12:235–51.

Tezozomoc, Hernando Alvarado. 1949. *Crónica Mexicayotl,* trans. from Nahuatl by Adrián León. UNAM.

Thompson, J. Eric S. 1960. *Maya Hieroglyphic Writing.* Norman: University of Oklahoma Press.

1962. *A Catalog of Maya Hieroglyphs.* Norman: University of Oklahoma Press.

1967. *The Rise and Fall of Maya Civilization*. Norman: University of Oklahoma Press.

1972. *A Commentary on the Dresden Codex*. Philadelphia: APS.

Thompson, Smith. 1966. *Tales of the North American Indians* (1929). Bloomington: Indiana University Press.

Tibón, Gutierre. 1981. *La Triade Prenatal: Cordón, placenta, amnios. Supervivencia de la magia paleolítica*. FCE.

1984. *Los ritos mágicos y trágicos de la pubertad femenina*. México: Diana.

Tichy, Franz. 1991. *Die geordnete Welt indianischer Völker*. Stuttgart: Steiner.

Titu Cusi Yupanqui, Diego de Castro. 1973. *Relación de la conquista del Perú*. (1570). Lima: Biblioteca Universitaria.

Todorov, Tzvetan. 1982. *La conquête de l'Amérique: La question de l'autre*. Paris: Seuil.

Tolstoy, Paul. 1974. "Utilitarian Artifacts of Central Mexico," HMAI 10:270–92.

Toulmin, Stephen, and June Goodfield. 1965. *The Discovery of Time*. London: Hutchinson.

Tovar, Juan de. 1972. *Relación del origen de los yndios que havitan en esta Nueva España según sus historias*, ed. J. Lafaye. ADV.

Tozzer, Alfred Marston. 1921. *A Maya Grammar*. Cambridge, MA: Peabody Museum.

Trimborn, Hermann (ed.). 1939. *Dämonen und Zauber in Inkareich: Fr. de Avila, Tratado de los errores*. Quellen und Forschungen zur Geschichte der Geographie und Volkerkunde, no. 4. Leipzig.

Tschudi, J. J. von. 1853. *Die Kechua Sprache*. Vienna.

1876. *Ollanta, ein altperuanisches Drama aus der Kechuasprache*. Vienna: Akademie der Wissenschaften.

Tyler, Hamilton A. 1964. *Pueblo Gods and Myths*. Norman: University of Oklahoma Press.

Tylor, Edward Burnett. 1861. *Anahuac; or, Mexico and the Mexicans, ancient and modern*. London: Longman Green Longman Roberts.

1873. *Primitive Culture*. 2d ed. 2 vols. London: John Murray.

Umusin Panlon Kumu. 1980. *Antes o mundo não existia*, trans. Tomalan Kenhiri and Berta Ribeiro. São Paulo.

Underhill, Ruth. 1938. *A Papago Calendar Record*. University of New Mexico Bulletin 322. Albuquerque.

Urioste, George L. 1983. *Hijos de Pariya Qaqa: La tradición oral de Wara Chiri*. 2 vols. Syracuse, NY: Maxwell School of Citizenship, University of Syracuse.

Vaillant, George C. 1937. "History and Stratigraphy in the Valley of Mexico," *Science Monthly* 44:307–24.

1965. *The Aztecs of Mexico*. Harmondsworth: Penguin.

Valcárcel, Carlos Daniel (ed.). 1971. *La rebelión de Tupac Amaru*. Colección Documentos de la Independencia del Perú, vol. 2. Lima.

Valdez, Luis, and Stan Steiner. 1972. *Aztlan: An anthology of Mexican American literature*. New York: Random House.

Valle, Perla. 1988. "Registro gráfico y contexto pictográfico." In Serra Puche 1988:27–34.

Varese, Stefano. 1968. *La sal de los Cerros: Una aproximación al mundo campa*. Lima.

Vázquez, Juan Adolfo. 1978. "The Present State of Research in South American Mythology," *Numen* 25:240–76.

    1981. "El origen del sol y de la luna: Ensayo de reconstrucción de un mito trique," *Scripta Etnológica* 6:141–53.

Veerman-Leichsenring, Annette. 1984. *El popoloca de Los Reyes Metzontla*. Paris: Amerindia.

Velázquez, Primo Feliciano (ed.). 1945. *Códice Chimalpopoca: Anales de Cuauhtitlan y Leyenda de los soles*. UNAM.

Villas Boas, Orlando, and Claudio Villas Boas. 1972. *Xingu: Os indios, seus mitos*. Rio: Zahar.

Villoro, Luis. 1950. *Los grandes momentos del indigenismo en México*. México: Colegio de México.

Viñas, David. 1982. *Indios, ejército y frontera*. México: Siglo XXI.

Vizenor, Gerald. 1981. *Summer in the Spring: Ojibwa lyric poems and tribal stories*. Minneapolis: Nodin Press.

Vogt, Evon. 1969. *Zinacantan: A Maya community in the highlands of Chiapas*. Cambridge: Harvard University Press.

    1976. *Tortillas for the Gods*. Cambridge: Harvard University Press.

Vogt, Evon Z., and A. Ruz Lluillier (eds.). 1971. *Desarrollo cultural de los mayas*. 2d ed. UNAM.

Vollmer, Günter. 1981. *Geschichte der Azteken: Der Codex Aubin*. QGA 13. Berlin: Mann.

Wachtel, Nathan. 1977. *The Vision of the Vanquished: The Spanish conquest of Peru through Indian eyes, 1530–70*. London: Harvester Press.

Wagley, Charles, and Eduardo Galvão. 1949. *The Tenetehara Indians of Brazil*. New York: Columbia University Press.

Wallace, Anthony F. C. 1969. *The Death and Rebirth of Seneca*. New York: Random House.

Walmsley, Anne, and Nick Caistor. 1986. *Facing the Sea: A new anthology for the Caribbean region*. London: Heinemann.

Warren, Rosanna. 1989. *The Art of Translation: Voices from the field*. Boston: Northeastern University Press.

Wassén, S. Henry. 1937. *Some Cuna Indian Animal Stories, with Original Texts*. Göteborg: Etnografiska Museum.

    1938. (with G. Haya and Rubén Pérez Kantule). *Original Documents from the Cuna Indians of San Blas*. Göteborg: Ethnografiska Museum.

Waters, Frank. 1963. *The Book of the Hopi*. New York: Viking.

Weatherford, Jack. 1988. *How the Indians of the Americas Transformed the World*. New York: Crown.

Weiss, G. 1975. *Campa Cosmology: The World of a forest tribe in South America*. American Museum of Natural History Anthropological Papers 52. New York: The Museum.

Weslager, C. A. 1972. *The Delaware Indians: A history*. New Brunswick, NJ: Rutgers University Press.

Whitecotton, Joseph W. 1977. *The Zapotecs: Princes, priests and peasants*. Norman: University of Oklahoma Press.

Whittaker, Gordon. 1983. "The Structure of the Zapotec Calendar." In Aveni and Brotherston 1983:101–34.

Wiener, Charles. 1880. *Pérou et Bolivie*. Paris.

Wilbert, Johannes, and Karin Simoneau (eds.). 1970–86. *The Folk Literature of South American Indians*. 12 vols. Los Angeles: Latin American Center, UCLA.

Wildhage, Wilhelm. 1990. "Material on Short Bull," *European Review of Native American Studies* 4, 1:35–42.

Willey, Gordon. 1974. *Das alte Amerika*. Munich: Propylaen.

Williams, Barbara J. 1980. "Pictorial Representation of Soils in the Valley of Mexico," *Geoscience and Man* 21:51–62.

Wilson, Edmund. 1959. *Apologies to the Iroquois*. New York: American Book – Stratford Press.

Wilson, Richard. 1991. "Machine Guns and Mountain Spirits," *Critique of Anthropology* (London) 11:33–61.

Wolf, Eric. 1959. *Sons of the Shaking Earth*. Chicago: University of Chicago Press.

Wright, Ronald. 1984. *Cut Stones and Crossroads: A Journey in Peru*. Harmondsworth: Penguin.

1989. *Time among the Maya*. London: Bodley Head.

Wyman, Leland C. 1970. *Blessingway*. Tucson: University of Arizona Press.

1983. *Southwest Indian Dry Painting*. Albuquerque: University of New Mexico Press.

1983a. "Dry Painting," HNAI 10:536–57.

Yáñez, Agustín. 1939. *Crónicas de la conquista de México*. UNAM.

Yapita, Juan de Dios. 1976. "Problemas de traducción de aymara al castellano." In *Actas del 3er Congreso de lenguas nacionales*, La Paz: INEL.

Yaranga Valderrama, A. 1986. "The Wayno in Andean Civilization." In Brotherston 1986:178–95.

Yoneda, Keiko. 1981. *Los mapas de Cuauhtinchan y la historia cartográfica prehispánica*. AGN.

Yourgrau, Wolfgang, and Allen O. Breck (eds.). 1977. *Cosmology, History and Theology*. London: Plenum.

Zaid, Gabriel (ed.). 1973. *Omnibus de poesía mexicana*. México: Siglo XXI.

Zantwijk, Rudolph van. 1979 (ed.). *Anales de Tula*. ADV.

1985. *The Aztec Arrangement*. Norman: University of Oklahoma Press.

Zavala, Silvio. 1982. *Libros de Asientos de la gobernación de la Nueva España*. AGN.

Zimmermann, Gunter. 1955. "Ueber einige stereotype Wendungen und Metaphern im Redestil des Aztekischen," *Baessler Archiv* 3:149–68.

Zolbrod, Paul G. 1984. *Diné bahané: The Navajo creation story*. Albuquerque: University of New Mexico Press.

Zolla, Elemire. 1973. *The Writer and the Shaman: A morphology of the American Indian*. New York.

Zuidema, R. T. 1964. *The Ceque System of Cuzco: The social organization of the capital of the Inca*. Leiden.

1982. "Myth and History in Ancient Peru." In *The Logic of Culture: Advances in structural theory and methods,* ed. Rossi. South Hadley, MA, pp. 150–75.

1983. "Towards a General Star Calendar in Ancient Peru." In Aveni and Brotherston 1983:235–61.

1989. "A Quipu Calendar from Ica, Peru, with a Comparison to the Ceque Calendar from Cuzco." In Aveni 1989:341–51.

Zúñiga, Madeleine (ed.). 1987. *Educación en poblaciones indígenas: Políticas y estrategias en América Latina*. Santiago: III.

Credits

Quotations: Cambridge University Press (pp. 330–1), from *Comparative Criticism* 9 ("Inca Fausts and Faustian Incas," by Gordon Brotherston) and (pp. 208–9) from *Comparative Criticism* 8 ("The Royal Drama *Apu Ollantay,*" by Gordon Brotherston); © Cambridge University Press 1987. Marc de Civrieux (pp. 43, 261, 305), from *Watunna: An Orinoco Creation Cycle,* trans. David Guss; © North Point Press 1980. Pablo Antonio Cuadra ("El mundo es un redondo plato de barro," p. 369), from *Obra poética completa;* © Libro Libre (San José, Costa Rica) 1984–8. Jacques Derrida (p. 42), from *De la grammatologie,* trans. Gayatri Spivak; © Johns Hopkins University Press 1976. Munro Edmonson (pp. 222, 230, 234, 407), from *The Book of Counsel: The Popol vuh of the Quiché Maya of Guatemala;* © Tulane University Press 1971. Gebr. Mann Verlag and Ibero-Amerikanisches Institut (pp. 316, 318–19), from *Aesop in Mexico,* ed. Gerdt Kutscher, Gordon Brotherston, and Günter Vollmer; © Gebr. Mann Verlag 1987. Indiana University Press (pp. 335–6), from Stith Thompson, *Tales of the North American Indians;* © Indiana University Press 1966. Alvin M. Josephy (p. 184), from *The Indian Heritage of America;* © Penguin Books 1975. Claude Lévi-Strauss (p. 406), from *Structural Anthropology,* vol. 2, trans. Monique Layton; © Penguin Books 1978. Leonel Lienlaf ("Rupamum," p. 402), from *Se ha despertado el ave de mi corazón;* © Editorial Universitaria S.A. 1989. Harold Livermore (p. 78), from Garcilaso de la Vega, "El Inca," *The Royal Commentaries of the Incas;* © University of Texas Press 1966. Abel Posse (p. 411), from *The Dogs of Paradise,* trans. Dorothy Sayers Pedden; © Macmillan (London) 1989. Dennis Tedlock (pp. 336–7), from *Finding the Center: Narrative Poetry of the Zuni Indians;* © University of Nebraska Press 1972. Thames and Hudson (pp. 49–50, 134, 139–40, 148–50, 157–60, 198), from Gordon Brotherston, *Image of the New World;* © Thames and Hudson 1979. University of Nebraska Press (p. 284), from Paul Radin, *The Winnebago Tribe;* © University of Nebraska Press 1970. Paul G. Zolbrod (p. 306), from *Diné bahané: The Navajo Creation Story;* © University of New Mexico Press 1984.

Color plates: Bear Mother, Tlingit totem pole (pl. 3a), courtesy of Alaskan Tourist Board. Big Star dry painting (pl. 5a), Hand Trembling Evil Way, MS33-2-3, Leland C. Wyman Collection, courtesy of Museum of Northern Arizona. Boraro Spirits, drawing by Paulino (pl. 18b), courtesy of Stephen Hugh-Jones and Museum of

Index